AMERICAN RCAF WARRIORS
US World War II Royal Canadian Air Force Volunteers

TOM WALSH

Published by Key Books
An imprint of Key Publishing Ltd
PO Box 100
Stamford
Lincs PE9 1XQ

www.keypublishing.com

The right of Thomas Walsh to be identified as the author of this book has been asserted in accordance with the Copyright, Designs and Patents Act 1988 Sections 77 and 78.

Copyright © Thomas Walsh, 2023

ISBN 978 1 80282 795 8

All rights reserved. Reproduction in whole or in part in any form whatsoever or by any means is strictly prohibited without the prior permission of the Publisher.

Typeset by SJmagic DESIGN SERVICES, India.

Cover design by Myriam Bell Designs
Flag image: © Lukas Gojda/123RF.com
Canadian Volunteer Service Medal: Hsq7278, CC BY-SA 4.0
https://creativecommons.org/licenses/by-sa/4.0/, via Wikimedia Commons

Getting these amazing untold stories to print would have been most difficult if it were not for the guidance and assistance of Nicholas A. "Nick" Veronico of San Carlos, California. Nick is a prolific author with some 50 book titles to his credit. He is also a specialist in communications and media relations and patiently steered me through the publishing maze to the goal line.
Thank you, sir.

Contents

Introduction..9
Abbreviations and Acronyms...12

HOME WAR ESTABLISHMENT

George Croil: First Chief of the Air Staff..19
David Langmack: Oregon Instructor Pilot.......................................24

CHINA-BURMA-INDIA THEATER OF OPERATIONS

John Barrick: Texas Hurricane Ace..31
Walter Duke: Maryland Lightning Ace..37
John Herbst: That Other Pappy..41
Owen Keech: New York Dive-Bomber Pilot.....................................49
Lloyd Thomas: Michigan Hurricane Pilot..55

EUROPEAN THEATER OF OPERATIONS

Ethan Allen: Deadly Encounter..63
Charles Anderson: No Longer Missing..69
Duane Beeson: Idaho Mustang Ace...75
Hipolitus Biel: Minnesota Mustang Ace..81
De Peyster Brown: Battle of Britain Pilot...86
Kendall Carlson: California Mustang Ace.......................................89
Robert Coffey: Illinois Typhoon Pilot..95
Russell Curtis: Pennsylvania Bomber Pilot....................................101
James Dalglish: Pioneer Mustang Group Ace................................107
Paul Davoud: Dean of the Night Fighter Squadrons......................113
Richard Dose: California Spitfire Pilot..122

George Dunaway: Arkansas Tactical Reconnaissance Pilot..........126
Clyde East: Virginia Mustang Ace 129
David Fairbanks: New York Tempest Ace..........................135
Frank Gallion: The Long Journey Home 144
Edward Gimbel: Illinois Spitfire Ace 148
Frederick Glover: North Carolina Mustang Ace...............155
John Godfrey: Rhode Island Mustang Ace........................161
Archibald Harrington: New Jersey Mosquito Ace............167
Ralph Hofer: 673 Days in the RCAF 176
Glen Holland: New York Mosquito Ace.............................183
David Howe: Pennsylvania Mustang Ace 189
Clarence Jasper: California Intruder Ace...........................193
Paul Johnson: Connecticut Spitfire Ace 200
George Keefer: New York Spitfire Ace................................207
John Magee: The Poet Pilot..214
Joe McCarthy: The American Dambuster 220
Charles McDonald: Louisiana Spitfire Pilot......................227
Bernard McGrattan: Two Sets of Wings 231
Pierce McKennon: Arkansas Mustang Ace 237
Evan McMinn: Pennsylvania Thunderbolt Ace 243
Michael McPharlin: Three Uniforms, One War...............248
Nicholas Megura: Connecticut Mustang Ace 255
George Mitchell: The Oldest Volunteer Pilot 261
Gerald Montgomery: An Above Average Pilot 265
Leslie Moore: Massachusetts Spitfire Ace 272
John Morgan: Texas MoH Awardee....................................279
Clifford Newton: Michigan Lancaster Pilot......................287
Leland Norton: California Havoc Pilot..............................292
Richard Patterson: Virginia Spitfire Pilot..........................295
Donald Pieri: Illinois Spitfire Ace 299
Clinton Pudney: New York Halifax Air Gunner..............304
Robert Reed: Ohio Reconnaissance Pilot..........................309
Albert Schlegel: Down Over France 313

Contents

William Smith: West Virginia Fighter Pilot 321
Michael Sobanski: The Bounced Around Ace 327
William Sprinkle: Instructor Pilot 333
Claybourne Waldrop: The Extended Three-Day Pass 337
Claude Weaver: The Youngest Allied Ace 344
Vasseure Wynn: Georgia Fighter Ace 356
Henry Zary: New York Spitfire Ace 361

MEDITERRANEAN THEATER OF OPERATIONS

John Avise: Iowa Hurricane Pilot 369
Leroy Clary: Wisconsin Beaufighter Pilot 374
Arthur Cleaveland: Ohio Warhawk Ace 379
John Curry: Texas Spitfire Ace 386
Richard De Bourke: The Almost Ace 391
James Gray: Third Time is the Charm 395
Herold Marting: Indiana Fighter Pilot 401
Reade Tilley: Florida Spitfire Ace 409
Frederick Vance: Virginia Fighter Pilot 417
Thomas White: Oregon Lightning Ace 422

PACIFIC THEATER OF OPERATIONS

Donald Aldrich: Illinois Corsair Ace 429
George Carr: Florida Hellcat Ace 435
Hollis Hills: California Hellcat Ace 441
Christopher Magee: Blackest of the "Black Sheep" 448
Donald Moore: Texas Corsair Pilot 460
William Senger: North Dakota B-29 Pilot 464
John Stickell: Illinois Bomber Pilot 470

Bibliography 478

Introduction

World War II began at 0440hrs on Friday, September 1, 1939, after German air and ground forces bombed and invaded Poland. This belligerent act of aggression against a sovereign nation galvanized Great Britain, France, Australia, and New Zealand into declaring war on the Nazi regime two days later. Just over a week later, on Sunday, September 10, the Canadian federal government, on behalf of its then 12 million citizens, issued a similar declaration.

Canada was far removed from the European battle areas, and it was quickly realized that one of the major roles the country could play in helping to win the war would be to use its vast land mass to safely train thousands of Commonwealth airmen. Representatives from Canada, Britain, Australia and New Zealand met in Ottawa, Ontario, on December 17, 1939, and signed into being a joint air training agreement entitled the British Commonwealth Air Training Plan (BCATP). The plan was to be wholly administered by the Royal Canadian Air Force (RCAF). It was a monumental task since Canada's air force had only been in existence for 15 years and its total complement of personnel stood at just 4,061, one quarter of which were reservists. The RCAF's paltry aircraft inventory numbered 270 with the majority being considered obsolete. The only modern fighter in Canada's small arsenal was the Hawker Hurricane Mk I, of which it had 19.

The RCAF quickly embarked on a massive building program, eventually administrating 107 flying schools and other training units at 231 sites from coast to coast and utilizing 10,840 aircraft in the process. By war's end, the RCAF was the fourth largest of the Allied air forces. Some 249,669 men and women proudly served in the RCAF over the course of the six-year war, but sadly, 17,100 would lose their lives.

The United States managed to stay out of the European conflict for the first two years by maintaining a position of neutrality. There were a number of Americans who believed the US should go to the aide of the besieged European nations and one such powerful voice in Washington who advocated intervention from the outset was President Franklin Delano Roosevelt. However, an isolationist-led US Congress kept the president from embroiling the nation in a war, which many Americans considered a European issue that they should stay out of. As well, the majority of Americans simply had no will or stomach to fight the same enemy it had helped to defeat in World War I some 21 years earlier.

Many of the young men who grew up in the late 1930s were keenly interested in aviation and many wanted to learn how to fly. However, the entry requirements for cadet training in any of the American military flying services in 1939 was, to say the least, daunting. Whether it was with the United States Army, Navy, or Marines, the applicants had to be single, they could not be any younger than 21 years of age, no older than 25 years of age and they had to have a minimum of two years of college.

The country was still emerging from the Great Depression and, with the unemployment figure hovering at just over the 10 million mark, there were very few families who could afford to send their children to university for a post-secondary education. Some enterprising air-minded applicants spent their hard-earned dollars obtaining a private pilot's license, reasonably figuring this would offset the strict military educational entry requirement. It did not.

The catalyst for so many young men who yearned to fly was the Battle of Britain. That monumental struggle for air supremacy raged over the English countryside beginning in the summer of 1940, from July 10 to October 31. The intrepid Spitfire and Hurricane pilots, who so valiantly defended England during that crucial period, came to be known as "The Brylcream Boys." Their heroic deeds were featured weekly in newsreel clips shown in every local movie theater across the North American continent. Also, widespread daily newspaper and weekly magazine coverage of those dashing young airmen flying high-performance fighters in combat had a tremendous impact on Canadian and American youth of the day.

To quickly build up its air force, the RCAF began taking applications from would-be pilots from all across North America. It made no difference whether one was single or married. All that was required of the applicants, educationally speaking, was a high school diploma. Some volunteers were as young as 17 and others were as old as 42. The RCAF quickly got its message out by putting up recruiting posters at every civilian flying club and airport in Canada and in all 48 states. The air force also opened recruiting offices in 17 large American cities to handle the flood of inquiries. The Americans flocked to Canada in droves in 1940–41 to enlist and, by the conclusion of the European war on May 8, 1945, no fewer than 8,864 US citizens had served part or all of their air force careers in the RCAF. The RCAF had even taken steps so as not to violate any American's citizenship by having them swear an oath of allegiance to Britain's King George VI. For every British Commonwealth citizen who put on a uniform, this oath was an obligatory part of the process. All the Americans had to swear was that they would obey their superiors and would serve for the duration of the war.

One month after America's entry into the war on Monday, December 8, 1941, negotiations began in earnest between the two neighboring countries to voluntarily repatriate those Americans who were serving in the RCAF. From May 1942 to

Introduction

May 1945, some 3,797 personnel transferred from the Canadian air force to an American military service of their choosing. The remaining 5,067 chose to stay where they were and serve out their time for the duration of the war.

Within the pages of this book are the selected biographies of 75 American warriors who took the extreme measure of donning the uniform of a foreign nation during wartime. In doing so, they realized their dream – to fly.

This work is dedicated to their memory.

Thomas Walsh
May 2023

Abbreviations and Acronyms

AC2	Aircraftman 2nd Class
ACG	Airfield Construction Group
ACGS	Army Chief of the General Staff
AFB	Air Force Base
AFC	Air Force Cross
ALG	Advanced Landing Ground
AM	Air Marshal
AOC	Air Officer Commanding
API	Armor Piercing Incendiary
AVG	American Volunteer Group
AWL/AWOL	Absent Without Leave (AWOL is the US designation)
BAFO	British Air Forces of Occupation
BCATP	British Commonwealth Air Training Plan
BG	Bombardment/Bomb Group
BS	Bomb Squadron
BSO	British Senior Officer
CAB	Canadian Aviation Board
CACW	Chinese-American Composite Wing
CAS	Chief of the Air Staff
CBI	China–Burma–India Theater of Operations
CCRC	Combat Crew Replacement Center
CFI	Chief Flying Instructor
CGI	Chief Ground Instructor
CI	Chief Instructor
CO	Commanding Officer
CWGC	Commonwealth War Graves Commission

Abbreviations and Acronyms

DFC	Distinguished Flying Cross
DFM	Distinguished Flying Medal
DND	Department of National Defence
DSC	Distinguished Service Cross
DSO	Distinguished Service Order
DVA	Department of Veteran Affairs
EAB	Engineer Aviation Battalion
EFTS	Elementary Flying Training School
ETO	European Theater of Operations
FBI	Federal Bureau of Investigation
FBW	Fighter Bomber Wing
FG	Fighter Group
FL	Flight Lieutenant
FO	Flying Officer/Flight Officer
FS	Flight Sergeant
FS	Fighter Squadron
FTG	Flying Training Group
GC	Group Captain
GI	Ground Instructor
GM	George Medal
GR	General Reconnaissance
HWE	Home War Establishment
IG	Inspector General
IJAAF	Imperial Japanese Army Air Force
IJN	Imperial Japanese Navy
IP	Initial Point
ITS	Initial Training School
JG	Jagdgeschwader
KG	Kampfgeschwader
KIA	Killed in Action
LAC	Leading Aircraftman
LG	Landing Ground

MCAS	Marine Corps Air Station
MD	Manning Depot
MEC	Middle East Command
MIA	Missing in Action
MiD	Mention in Despatches
MM	Military Medal
MoH	Medal of Honor
MP	Military Policeman
MTO	Mediterranean Theater of Operations
MU	Maintenance Unit
NAA	North American Aviation
NAS	Naval Air Station
NCO	Non-Commissioned Officer
NFS	Night Fighter Squadron
NJG	Nachtjagdgeschwader
OC	Officer Commanding
OTU	Operational Training Unit
PO	Pilot Officer
PoW	Prisoner of War
PPO	Provisional Pilot Officer
PTO	Pacific Theater of Operations
RAE	Royal Aircraft Establishment
RAF	Royal Air Force
RAAF	Royal Australian Air Force
RCAF	Royal Canadian Air Force
RD	Repatriation Depot
RFC	Royal Flying Corps
RNZAF	Royal New Zealand Air Force
ROTC	Reserve Officers' Training Corps
R&R	Rest and Recuperation (or Rest and Relaxation)
SAAF	South African Air Force
SAC	Strategic Air Command
SAO	Senior Air Officer
SCU	Servicing Commando Units
SFTS	Service Flying Training School

Abbreviations and Acronyms

Sgt	Sergeant
SL	Squadron Leader
SNCO	Senior Non-Commissioned Officer
SP	Sergeant Pilot
S/Sgt	Staff Sergeant
STOL	Short Take Off and Landing
TAF	Tactical Air Force
TR	Tactical Reconnaissance
TRS	Tactical Reconnaissance Squadron
T/Sgt	Technical Sergeant
USAAC	United States Army Air Corps
USAAF	United States Army Air Forces
USAF	United States Air Force
USMC	United States Marine Corps
USN	United States Navy
USNR	United States Navy Reserve
WC	Wing Commander
WDAF	Western Desert Air Force
WO1	Warrant Officer 1st Class
WO2	Warrant Officer 2nd Class

HOME WAR ESTABLISHMENT

George Croil
First Chief of the Air Staff

A ir Marshal (AM) George Mitchell Croil is considered by many to be the Father of the Royal Canadian Air Force (RCAF). The only offspring of Scottish immigrants, Thomas Croil and Christian C. Mitchell, George was born in Milwaukee, Wisconsin, on June 5, 1893.

He spent four years in the American public school system before moving, with his parents at the age of 11, to Montreal, Quebec. In that predominantly French-speaking community, he attended Westmount Academy from 1903 to 1907. For the next three years he was enrolled at Robert Gordon's College in Aberdeen, Scotland. George then studied civil engineering for two years, utilizing the services of a private tutor. He successfully passed a written examination and was granted a British engineering certificate.

In 1912, Croil was hired on as an assistant superintendent with the Mahawale Tea and Rubber Estate in Ratnapura, Ceylon. Employed there until September 1914, he kept the company's machinery running and supervised the daily work schedules of some 700 plantation workers.

When World War I broke out, Croil was commissioned as a lieutenant in the 5th Battalion of the Gordon Highlanders, where he served as a machine gun officer. This storied British Army Infantry Regiment recruited its personnel from in and around the city of Aberdeen and, to a lesser extent, from the northeast area of Scotland. On January 15, 1915, George was promoted to captain and assumed responsibilities as a company commander. He was seconded to the Royal Flying Corps (RFC) in May 1916, where, after only two months of flight training, he earned his pilot wings. On July 24, Captain Croil then transferred to the RFC as a flying officer. Croil carried out his duties as a flying instructor, training new pilots in the Middle East until March of 1919. He operated from bases at Abu Sueir, El Rimmal and Suez in Egypt with No. 57, No. 58, No. 169 and No. 19 Training Squadrons. At one point, he was station commander at a training depot and, for a short period, was acting commander of the 69th Training Wing. Captain Croil also flew operational sorties as a bomber pilot with the RFC No. 47 Squadron in Egypt and Macedonia.

Croil occasionally transported a British Army major named T. E. Lawrence to various desert camps. This individual was more commonly known as "Lawrence of Arabia."

George Croil received the French Croix de Guerre with Palm from France on February 8, 1919. It was granted for valuable services rendered in connection with the war. Four months later in June, he was Mentioned in Despatches (MiD):

> For consistent devotion to duty whilst a Flight Commander in a training squadron and for his determination on the following two occasions.
>
> December 6, 1917 – When on information being received that a pilot had got lost on the way to Akaba [Jordan] from Suez where he had been sent to retrieve Major T. E. Lawrence by air, Captain Croil set out in search of this officer making repeated searches for the missing pilot and machine along the way. Picking up Major Lawrence at Akaba, Captain Croil returned him to Suez all the while continuing to search and inquire about the missing pilot and aircraft.
>
> December 23, 1917 – When a party organized by Captain G. M. Croil set out to search for a machine which had been reported as missing on a flight between Suez and Akaba, one of the machines of the search party having had engine failure, landed in the desert half way between the two points. Captain Croil showed great resource by flying into high winds and a sandstorm while leading two other aircraft carrying mechanics, spare parts and fuel for the disabled machine. Reaching the downed aircraft, repairs were quickly carried out. The return flight against gale force winds was most difficult as blowing sand obscured the whole countryside. Also, two of the pilots were mere students. Keeping his flight on the right compass heading, Captain Croil showed great skill as he flew behind them, safely shepherding his charges home. The journey, which was normally one hour in duration, took three due to the adverse weather conditions.

Croil was promoted to the rank of major on April 20, 1919. At war's end, he had logged in excess of 1,100 hours of flying time on 18 aircraft types – land and floatplanes.

Major Croil was awarded the Air Force Cross (AFC) on June 3, 1919. It was for distinguished services in the Middle East during the war while he was serving at No. 32 Training Wing.

Returning to Canada, Croil was appointed to the Canadian Aviation Board (CAB) in June 1920. As one of six Canadian Air Station Superintendents, Croil was instrumental in establishing air bases at Morley and High River, Alberta. He left the CAB on February 28, 1923, and the next day joined the Canadian Air Force (CAF) as a squadron leader. While in western Canada, George met Ailsa Swabey Arnold and the two were married in High River on June 5, 1923, which just happened to be Croil's 30th birthday! Their union produced five children.

George Croil: First Chief of the Air Staff

George Croil was one of the original 62 officers whose members made up the core of the newly organized RCAF when that service came into being on April 1, 1924. Preparatory to being posted to England as a liaison officer, Croil undertook an officer's staff course at Royal Military College, Kingston, Ontario, from October 1924 to February 1925. While in Britain for the better part of three years (March 1925 to November 1927), Croil benefited from additional training undertaken at the Royal Air Force (RAF) Staff College at Andover, followed by a flying instructors' course at RAF Cranwell. Cranwell, established in 1919, was the world's first air academy. Returning to Canada in November 1927 as a wing commander (WC), Croil then served for five years as station commander at Camp Borden near Barrie, Ontario. From January 17 to December 31, 1933, Croil returned to England to study at the prestigious Imperial Defence College in London. He was appointed the RCAF's Senior Air Officer (SAO) in January 1934, with the rank of group captain (GC).

From this position, he tirelessly fought for autonomous status for the air force. A year later in January 1935, he was promoted to air commodore. Over the strong objections of the Army's Chief of the General Staff (ACGS), Croil won admission to a seat on the Defence Council. On August 4, 1938, Croil succeeded in removing supervision over the RCAF from the ACGS's office when he was promoted to the rank of air vice marshal. From then on, he reported only to the Minister of National Defence. On November 19 of that year, Croil's title changed from SAO to Chief of the Air Staff (CAS), and this was most fortunate for the RCAF as war clouds were beginning to form once again over Europe.

Canada's declaration of war against the Nazi regime was issued on September 10, 1939. As a nation, it had very little in the way of an effective air arm at the time, possessing only 270 aircraft, the majority of which were considered obsolete. Its manpower strength – all ranks – was a paltry 4,061 in total. A reserved man, strict and professional, Croil stood out as a conscientious, dedicated officer. When Charles Gavin "Chubby" Power became Canada's Minister of Defence for

Air Marshall George M. Croil, CBE, AFC, MiD, was the First Chief of the Air Staff. He is considered to be the "Father of the RCAF." (Canada Department of National Defence)

Air in May 1940, he asked for Croil's resignation as he did not believe they could effectively work together. While acknowledging Croil's qualities as an exceptional administrator, Power admitted to being somewhat put off by his "puritanical and regimental" disposition. Power said, "Rightly or wrongly, I got the impression that friendly sympathetic co-operation with him would, owing to our fundamental differences of temperament, be difficult if not impossible. I wanted friendship and co-operation; he, I imagine, expected me to give little more than routine supervision, leaving to him the unquestioned authority over members of the service and possibly over the purely civilian functions of the department." For the good of the service, Croil stepped down and accepted an appointment as Inspector General (IG) of the RCAF. Less than two months later, Power had been replaced as the Minister of Defence for Air.

By war's end, the RCAF's growth had reached its zenith when its personnel numbers peaked at 249,669. This figure included 15,153 females who served in the women's division. The RCAF capably fielded no less than 78 squadrons for home and overseas duty. Canada's air force rose to become the fourth largest in the Allied cause and it all happened because of the implementation and execution of the BCATP in Canada, coupled with the influence and guidance of George Mitchell Croil.

George Croil was made a Commander of the Most Excellent Order of the British Empire on January 1, 1943. The text of this award is as follows:

> This officer's extensive experience and devotion to duty over a considerable period of time has marked him as an officer of exceptional ability. Prior to the opening of hostilities he held the appointment of CAS and as such was largely instrumental in drawing up the BCATP and in laying plans for the future development of the plan. As IG, his worth was outstanding both in his efforts in the measures taken for the defence of Canada and in his suggestions for the improvement of morale and discipline of the service. His leadership and mature judgement has been invaluable in the direction of the RCAF.

Interestingly, Croil's first cousin, who also hailed from Milwaukee, was none other than Brigadier General William Lendrum "Billy" Mitchell. In 1920, Mitchell was appointed Deputy Director of the United States Army Air Service. A renowned pioneer of US air power, General Mitchell was generally regarded as one of the most far-sighted military leaders of his age. Immediately after World War I, he predicted that air bombardment would dominate warfare in the future. In 1924, he horrified and angered US Army and Naval strategists with his public claim that bombs could sink ships. That same year, he correctly predicted the Japanese attack on Pearl Harbor, which came to pass some 17 years later in 1941. When his superiors refused to believe him, he successfully bombed and sank captured German World War I warships to prove his point. Furious at his constant outspoken criticisms, the war department directed that his reappointment as assistant chief of the Army Air Service be denied. They further directed that he be demoted to the rank of colonel and that he stand for a general court martial on the charge of conduct prejudicial to good order and discipline. After a seven-week public trial, which ended in December 1925, Mitchell was found guilty. He was suspended from rank, command and duty and was required to forfeit all pay and allowances for a period of five years.

Afterward, President Calvin Coolidge reviewed Mitchell's sentence and judged it to be too severe. He changed the forfeiture from all to half pay and benefits for five years. Billy Mitchell chose to retire from the military and did so on February 1, 1926. He died a broken man in New York city at the age of 56 on February 19, 1936. In 1942, President Franklin D. Roosevelt petitioned congress to award Colonel Mitchell a special Medal of Honor, together with a promotion to the rank of major general. It was not until 1946 that both awards were posthumously bestowed. Mitchell's reputation as a national hero was completely restored through the release of the 1955 Otto Preminger movie *The Court Martial of Bill Mitchell*, starring Gary Cooper. Mitchell was the only US citizen who ever had a military aircraft named in his honor. He is rightly considered to be the "Father of the United States Air Force."

On October 5, 1946, RCAF AM Robert Leckie sent the following letter to George Croil, which said in part:

> It gives me great pleasure to inform you that you have been granted the award of the 1939–45 Star. This award, normally made in recognition of operational service against the enemy, is granted to you in view of the responsibilities you carried as CAS in the making of operational decisions. The wisdom of those decisions are today reflected by the magnificent record achieved by the RCAF. It is felt, therefore, the award of the 1939–45 Star will be in some small measure further recognition of your efforts in forming a striking force which was definitely instrumental in bringing about the successful conclusion of the war. The medal of this award has not yet been struck, but it will be forwarded to you as soon as it becomes available.

In March 1953, a 171,200sq ft technical training school, dedicated as Croil Hall, opened at RCAF Station Camp Borden, Ontario. Croil Hall continues to serve to this day as the home of air force technical training at what is now known as Canadian Forces Base Borden.

George Mitchell Croil was promoted to the rank of air marshal on July 2, 1944. He retired with a full pension that day.

Croil's early years of unwavering advocacy for a strong and independent national air force had come to fruition. His many hard-fought battles on that singular issue would be the greatest achievement of his 30-year military career.

He passed away in his 65th year on April 8, 1959, in Vancouver, British Columbia.

David Langmack
Oregon Instructor Pilot

David Francis Langmack's career in the RCAF began on Friday, August 9, 1940, at No. 12 Recruiting Centre in downtown Ottawa, Ontario. On that warm summer day, the 38-year-old native of Lebanon, Oregon, was appointed a flying officer (FO) in Canada's embryonic air force under Regimental Service No. C. 2492. Langmack, who had been flying since before he was 16, had accumulated in excess of 4,300 hours of flight time in aircraft types ranging from tiny home-built single-seaters all the way up to Boeing Model 80A and Ford tri-motor passenger airplanes. Over the years, he operated and owned several flying businesses. He served as a pilot for many companies, was an instructor, flew exhibition displays, did charter work, ferried aircraft across the country, barnstormed, and, for a short while, even tried his hand at aerial advertising (skywriting). He once said his flying experiences had touched nearly every phase of the aviation industry.

One of the letters of reference he presented to the RCAF was signed by Robert B. Porterfield, President of the Air Transport Broadcast Corporation:

> This corporation, organized for a special aviation enterprise during the summer of 1937, employed the services of David F. Langmack as transport pilot for its three-engined Boeing Model 80A and its single engine Arrow Model F. We recommend him both as a flyer and as a man. He came to us with an unusual record of theoretical and practical experience. As a pilot he proved to be efficient, diligent and careful. In addition, he was most helpful in his appreciation of business problems and active in advancing the interests of the corporation. He inspired the confidence of those he came in contact with and this ability together with his loyalty should be of additional importance and advantage to any concern needing the services of a competent aviator such as Mr. Langmack.

David was born to Robert Hening Langmack and Grace Helena Dyson on June 9, 1902, in Pipestone, Minnesota. The family, who were farmers, relocated from Minnesota to Oregon in the early 1900s. David learned to fly on his father's grain fields beginning in March 1918. He completed his high school education in 1920

A Westland Lysander Mk II was the aircraft type Flying Officer (FO) David Langmack tragically lost his life in on September 22, 1941. (UK Ministry of Defence)

at Lebanon High School. After working for a few years, he returned to school in 1923 and undertook a one-year mechanical engineering course at Oregon State College in Corvallis, Oregon. While there he was an officer cadet in the Reserve Officers' Training Corps (ROTC).

For the next 15 years, Langmack led a vagabond aviation lifestyle, flying and living in a multitude of cities in both North and South America.

On January 5, 1938, he married Margaret H. Shelley in Lebanon, Oregon. This union did not last, and the couple separated within a year.

From May 1939 to February 1940, David worked on the assembly line at the Lockheed Aircraft Manufacturing Company in Burbank, California. At the end of February, he and hundreds of others were temporarily laid off due to a parts shortage. Never one to be without work, Langmack accepted a position as an aircraft inspector at the Douglas Aircraft Company in Santa Monica. He resigned from Douglas in July to accept a commission in the RCAF.

FO H. E. Stewart, the recruiting center's interviewer, recorded the following comments in Langmack's file: "Good flying experience. Has a slight speech impediment. Should make a good officer and an excellent pilot. Above average in all categories."

Following his air force indoctrination at air stations at Ottawa, Trenton and Borden, Langmack was posted as a staff pilot to the newly opened No. 2 Bombing & Gunnery School (B&GS) at Mossbank, Saskatchewan. There he flew twin-engined Avro Ansons and Bristol Bolingbrokes. Single engine aircraft types flown included Westland Lysanders and Fairey Battles. In a memo to the Officer Commanding (OC) of No. 2 dated November 23, David respectfully requested a transfer to a ferrying or communication flight as he felt his flying credentials could be of more value to the RCAF.

A confidential report dated December 13, 1940, rated David's efficiency and professionalism at a three on a scale of one to seven. His superiors recommended that he could be better employed flying multi-engined aircraft.

On March 28, 1941, Langmack was posted to No. 10 Bomber Reconnaissance Squadron at Dartmouth, Nova Scotia. Nicknamed the "North Atlantic Squadron," No. 10 was the only Canadian unit to fly the Douglas Digby Mk 1. Only 20 aircraft of this type were acquired by the RCAF, and these were employed in the anti-submarine role with Eastern Air Command. Less than a month later, on April 22, David moved a short distance down the Dartmouth ramp after transferring to No. 11 Squadron. There he flew coastal and anti-submarine patrols in Lockheed Hudson Mk IVs until September 11.

Langmack moved back to western Canada on September 20, after he was posted to No. 34 Service Flying Training School (SFTS) at Medicine Hat, Alberta. Before he had the opportunity to begin his duties as a flying instructor on Airspeed Oxfords and North American Aviation (NAA) Harvards, he was tragically killed in an airplane crash.

Two days after arriving at the air station, David was taken on an area familiarization flight on Lysander Mk II, No. 417, piloted by RAF Squadron Leader (SL) Kenneth Lewis Ashfold. This aircraft was taken on strength by the RCAF on September 8, 1939, and was one of 225 of the type constructed under license by the National Steel Car Company at Malton, Ontario.

Herein are the reports and statements relating to the incident. The first was the accident report of the Royal Canadian Mounted Police by Corporal W. H. Debbin, the officer in charge of the Medicine Hat detachment:

> I would advise that a telephone call was received by this detachment from the Suffield Experimental Station at 1115 hours on September 22, 1941 advising that a plane had crashed in the near vicinity and two airmen in same had been killed. As both police cars were attending to other duties, these could not be used on this investigation. We contacted Coroner Patterson who indicated that he was busy with other matters and could not attend the accident scene until 1300 hours at the earliest. Thereafter, the Coroner, the writer and Constable Allen proceeded to Suffield in a private car shortly after 1 o'clock p.m. Upon

arrival, it was found the crash had occurred one quarter mile northeast of the main buildings at this station. The aircraft, a two seat Lysander coming from a westerly direction, first hit the edge of a road, bounced back into the air, snapped the wires of a fence seventy-five yards further on and struck the ground with such force that the aircraft was almost completely destroyed. Wreckage was scattered over a wide area and from blood stains on the ground it was apparent that one body came to rest near the wrecked cockpit while the other was found forty yards further on near part of the fuselage. Both victims had been removed before our arrival.

From Lieutenant E. M. Wilder, the Medical Officer of the Suffield station, Royal Canadian Army Medical Corps, the following:

On September 22, 1941 at 1045 hours I was summoned in haste to attend the scene of a flying accident which occurred near the toxic stores of this station. I arrived at the site within five minutes of the crash and found two deceased officers. Their bodies had been covered with their parachutes by other personnel of this station prior to my arrival, but otherwise the scene had not been disturbed. Body No. one, later identified as squadron leader Ashfold – found on the ground near the remains of the cockpit still strapped to the seat by the safety belt. Death was instantaneous – crushed cranium and numerous body fractures. Body No. two, later identified as flying officer Langmack – found on the ground forty yards east of body No. one near part of the planes undercarriage. The deceased was strapped in his seat which was thrown clear of the main wreckage. This officer died from shock, multiple body fractures and a crushed skull. Under supervision both bodies were removed to a temporary mortuary at the station. At 1215 hours, the deceased were removed from the Suffield station by an RCAF ambulance.

From witnesses Major J. S. Campbell and Lieutenant S. W. Gelfoy, Royal Canadian Army:

At the above mentioned time and date, we were testing gun sights two hundred and fifty yards east of the Suffield-Jenner Road and approximately three hundred yards south of where the accident occurred. We observed a Lysander aircraft approaching from a southwesterly direction just north of the camp at an altitude of two hundred feet. When nearing the road, it suddenly appeared to lose height. After crossing the road, the plane dove to the ground. Pieces from the aircraft flew in every direction. The wreckage was strewn one hundred and fifty yards from the point of impact. We immediately procured a fire extinguisher, ordered a guard to get a doctor and proceeded to the scene as quickly as possible. We were unable to identify the dead occupants and observed that the aircraft was a total wreck.

Leading Aircraftman (LAC) J. S. Currier, RCAF, stated: "This is to certify that I carried out a daily inspection on the engine of Lysander No. 417 on September 22, 1941 and found it to be in a serviceable condition."

From LAC C. F. W. Churcett RCAF: "This is to certify that I carried out a daily inspection on the airframe of Lysander No. 417 on September 22, 1941 and found everything to be in a serviceable condition."

Lysander No. 417 had taken off from No. 34 SFTS Medicine Hat on a routine flight to the Suffield Experimental Station. The purpose of the flight was to acquaint Langmack with the station's general operating territory. The plane was piloted by 23-year-old Ashfold, who was assigned to No. 34 by the United Kingdom Mission out of Ottawa. The plane's other occupant was 39-year-old Langmack, who had in excess of 4,900 hours of flying experience. Ashfold's flying experience amounted to 1,500 hours.

The coroner, Corporal Debbin and Constable Allen accompanied the bodies of the deceased airmen to the Pattinson Funeral Home in Medicine Hat. The coroner decided an inquest was unnecessary and issued the required burial permits. It was his understanding that the air force would convene an accident investigation. The cause of the accident was never officially determined.

CHINA–BURMA–INDIA THEATER OF OPERATIONS

John Barrick
Texas Hurricane Ace

Monday, May 22, 1944: It was early in the morning and Ottawa's Union Station was already jammed with people. The mayor was there along with an air vice marshal, an air force band and a crowd of excited relatives. Some 200 Canadian airmen, from humble ground crewmen to two of Canada's aces, were coming home to the nation's capital after long tours overseas. The airmen piled off the train, shuffled into line and impatiently waited for the twaddle of an official welcome. As the ceremony ended, the men quickly broke ranks and the real welcoming began. One airman appeared, brandishing an ice-cream cone. Another shouted, "Cones!" Some of them had not seen an ice cream cone in four years.

Two in the group were Texans. Flight Lieutenant John "Tex" Barrick had thumbed his way from Texas to Canada some three-and-a-half years earlier. As a member of RCAF, he had flown Hawker Hurricanes with the RAF, became an ace and had been awarded a Distinguished Flying Medal (DFM). He intended to stay with the Canadians for the duration of the war, instead of joining the United States Army Air Forces (USAAF). He said, "You guys in Canada gave me a chance to fight, you spent a lot of money making me a pilot."

The other Texan, air gunner Sergeant (Sgt) Raymond Carroll, a veteran of 40 operational bomber sorties, said, "I married an English girl and as soon as this is over, I'm going to settle in Vancouver." The crowd roared its approval.

John Frederick Barrick was born in Sweetwater, Texas, on May 12, 1918. He grew up in Odessa, and was a graduate of Decatur Baptist Junior College. At the age of 22, he decided he would rather fight World War II in the air than on the ground.

It was common knowledge that America would soon be swept up in the European conflict and, in preparation for that eventuality, the Congress of the United States had passed the Selective Training and Service Act on September 14, 1940. President Franklin D. Roosevelt signed it into law two days later. This became the first peacetime conscription in US history. The act required that men between the ages of 21 and 35 register with local draft boards. The US Army planned to induct more than a million men in the first 13 months beginning in October 1940.

Barrick and thousands of other Americans who wanted to fly were not going to wait around to be drafted into the Army. In 1940–41, they headed off to Canada in droves.

Barrick hitchhiked more than 1,300 miles from Odessa to Detroit, Michigan. He crossed the border into Windsor, Ontario, on September 28, 1940, and voluntarily enlisted at No. 8 Recruiting Centre located on Ouellette Avenue. Assigned Regimental Service No. R. 67788, Barrick's rank was as an aircraftman 2nd class (AC2). Guard duty at air stations Borden and Trenton was on Barrick's agenda for the next two months.

On November 30, Tex began his six-week air force indoctrination training at No. 2 Initial Training School (ITS) at Regina, Saskatchewan. The course concluded on January 3, 1941. Promoted to LAC, Barrick began flying yellow Fleet Finch biplane aircraft at No. 16 Elementary Flying Training School (EFTS) at Edmonton, Alberta. On February 12, Barrick was posted to No. 10 SFTS at Dauphin, Manitoba, where he flew Harvard Mk IIs until graduating as a sergeant pilot (SP) on June 14, 1941. Barrick's class was the first to graduate from this new facility, which had opened on March 5, 1941.

Four days later, he was at "Y" Depot Halifax, Nova Scotia, where he boarded a troop ship heading to England. For the next five weeks, Tex was at No. 3 Personnel Reception Centre in Bournemouth waiting to go on course. Posted to No. 55 Operational Training Unit (OTU) at RAF Usworth on July 29, 1941, Sergeant Barrick undertook fighter conversion training on Hurricane Mk Xs.

In September, Tex was assigned to RAF No. 17 Squadron, which was flying Hurricane Mk IIbs, from Tain, Scotland. In November, the squadron began moving to the Middle East. While en route, Japan's early morning sneak attack on Sunday, December 7, 1941, at Pearl Harbor, Hawaii, resulted in the squadron being redirected to Burma. During January 1942, No. 17 set up shop at Mingaladon airfield outside Rangoon where they were equipped with Hurricane Mk IIas.

On the morning of February 7, 1942, Tex downed two Imperial Japanese Army Air Force (IJAAF) Nakajima Ki-27 "Nates" and damaged another. Ten Hurricanes had scrambled to intercept the incoming threat, but only four made contact with the 20-plus Japanese fighters from the 50th and 77th Sentais. In addition to Barrick's claim, RCAF Pilot Officer (PO) Lloyd Duncan "Tommy" Thomas, an American from Detroit, Michigan, claimed one Ki-27 as destroyed. Two other Nates fell to the guns of RAF No. 136 Squadron pilots PO Eric Brown and SP Ting Bunting. No loss or serious damage was suffered by any of the British fighters on this occasion.

Constant patrols were maintained over Mingaladon all through the morning of February 25, but it was not until midday that a big Japanese fighter sweep approached the airfield. There were 21 Ki-27s from the 50th Sentai, 23 more from the 77th Sentai and three Nakajima Ki-43 Hayabusa "Oscars" from the 64th Sentai. Three P-40s

John Barrick: Texas Hurricane Ace

Flight Lieutenant John Barrick, DFM, became an ace flying Hawker Hurricanes in the China-Burma-India (CBI) Theater of Operations. A total of 14,533 Hurricanes were produced from 1937 through to 1944. (Parr Yonemoto)

from 1st Pursuit Squadron of the American Volunteer Group (AVG) were scrambled together with six Hurricanes from No. 17 Squadron. Sergeant Barrick first spotted the oncoming mass of hostile fighters, which he accurately assessed to be 50 strong. Excitedly he yelled, "Snapper! Snapper!" over the radio telephone, forgetting that this was the emergency code word used in the European Theater of Operations (ETO) to indicate that they were being jumped. His leader did not react and continued heading southwest, away from the enemy's position. "Snapper! Snapper!" was then repeated with even greater urgency. Meanwhile, Barrick, believing that the rest of the squadron were following him, sailed all alone into the Japanese fighters. "I attacked and shot down one Ki-27 army type and was then jumped from above by an Oscar. I went into a tight turn which caused one of my gun panels to fly open. This made the aircraft 'flick' and probably saved my life because the enemy aircraft was in an excellent position behind me. As it was my plane was not hit."

Defensive patrols were continuously flown until the Burma airfields were overrun. When the squadron was forced to evacuate Mingaladon, Tex flew a battered Hurricane to Magwe. It had no working instruments, and its engine oil leaks were plugged with pieces of wood! He landed with a sigh of relief only to have a careening truck smash into the side of his aircraft demolishing it.

There were four RCAF-trained American flyers in No. 17 Squadron – John Barrick, Jack Gibson, Clarence Wisrodt and Lloyd Thomas. These pilots helped break down the standoffish relations that initially existed between the AVG and RAF squadrons when they jointly shared airfields at Mingaladon and Magwe. Acting as go-between, the four would regularly visit their American cousins at the latter's Officers' Club to socialize and catch up on the latest news back in the US. It followed that, from the top down, each group then began working and supporting one another.

After Rangoon was lost to the Japanese, the AVG also relocated to Magwe, a small airfield more than 300 miles north of Rangoon. General Claire Lee Chennault started moving elements of the now reconstituted 3rd Pursuit Squadron to Magwe as reinforcement to his worn-down 1st and 2nd squadrons. Aircraft attrition became so high that, at this point, individual squadron distinctions became meaningless, and all three squadrons had elements based there along with a number of RAF aircraft. In total, the Allies had 38 aircraft, including eight P-40s and 15 Hawker Hurricanes. Opposing them were 271 Japanese aircraft, including 115 fighters. Although the AVG and RAF scored some successes against the Japanese, Magwe was continuously bombed, including a very heavy raid on March 21 by 151 bombers and fighters.

Another Nate fell before the guns of Barrick's Hurricane on March 21. On that same sortie, he strafed and destroyed two enemy aircraft on the ground, one being a bomber.

In early April, with only four aircraft serviceable between them, the RAF and AVG were forced to relocate to Loiwing, just across the Chinese border.

Over Loiwing on April 10, Barrick downed a Ki-43. As he circled to watch it crash, he was jumped by three other Oscars. He managed to damage one, but the other two shot him down. Suffering burns from hot oil on his face, chest and hands, he crash-landed striking his face hard on the gunsight. Leaping from the still moving Hurricane, Barrick ran for cover just before the Japanese pilots strafed his stricken aircraft. Meanwhile, some AVG P-40 Warhawks showed up and shot down the Oscar Barrick had damaged. The other two were then driven off. After walking for two hours, Tex was given first aid by missionary doctors who got him to Chennault's headquarters, where he remained for the next two weeks. Later, he was flown to Calcutta, India, on a C-47 transport and rejoined his squadron.

In August, Barrick was promoted to warrant officer 2nd class (WO2) and was awarded a DFM, the details of which stated:

BARRICK, Sergeant John Frederick (R. 67788) – Distinguished Flying Medal – No. 17 Squadron – Award effective 23 July 1942 as per London Gazette dated 24 July 1942 and AFRO 1243/42 dated 7 August 1942. Born Sweetwater, Texas, 1918. Home in Odessa, Texas. Enlisted in Windsor, Ontario, 28 September 1940. Trained at No. 2 ITS (30 November 1940 to 3 January 1941), No. 16 EFTS and No. 10 SFTS (21 February to 14 June 1941). Embarked from Halifax, 18 June 1941 for UK and on 29 July 1941 to No. 55 OTU. Served with No. 17 Squadron, India, January 1942 to 27 January 1944. Arrived in UK 19 March 1944, and Canada 1 May 1944. To No. 1 OTU, Bagotville, 16 June 1944 to No. 133 Squadron Western Air Command 14 October 1944. Released 2 October 1945.

During the campaign in Burma, this airman displayed exceptional keenness to engage the enemy. During a raid in March 1942, he destroyed an enemy fighter in the air and probably destroyed another fighter and damaged a bomber on the ground. During another engagement, he shot down an enemy aircraft which was closing in on one of his fellow pilots. Sergeant Barrick himself was attacked by two fighters during the combat, his engine failed and he was compelled to make a landing. Although almost blinded by oil he succeeded in his purpose with the assistance of flaps. The enemy continued to fire at him whilst he was on the ground. Although suffering from shrapnel splinters and the effects of hot oil on his face, chest and arms, Sergeant Barrick walked for some two hours until he reached some Chinese troops. Throughout he displayed great courage and fortitude. He has destroyed five enemy aircraft.

Promotions quickly followed: May 1, 1942, to PO; November 1, 1942, to flying officer (FO); December 22, 1943, to flight lieutenant (FL). As an officer, his Regimental No. was changed from R. 67788 to J. 16032.

During the two years Tex Barrick flew with No. 17 in Burma, India, Ceylon and China, the ebb and flow of the battle necessitated the squadron to be constantly on the move, serving from the following locations:

January 16 to February 1942 – Mingaladon
February to March 1942 – Magwe
March 1942 – Lashio
March to April 1942 – Pankham Fort
May to August 1942 – Jessore
August 4 to September 4, 1942 – Alipore
September 4, 1942, to March 6, 1943 – Red Road
March 6 to April 16, 1943 – Kalyanpur
April 16 to May 29, 1943 – Alipore
May 29 to August 17, 1943 – Agartala
August 17, 1943, to January 13, 1944 – China Bay
January 13 to June 30, 1944 – Minneriya

The Mk IIa Hurricane that Barrick victoriously flew in combat was powered by a Rolls-Royce Merlin XX engine, which produced 1,280 shaft horsepower. This motor gave the aircraft a maximum speed at altitude of 341 miles per hour. Wing armament consisted of eight Colt Browning .303 machine guns. A total of

14,533 Hawker Hurricanes were produced from 1937 through to 1944 by Hawker Aircraft, Gloster Aircraft Company, Canadian Car & Foundry and the Austin Motor Company. During the Battle of Britain, it was the workhorse Hurricane that scored the highest number of RAF victories, accounting for 1,593 of the 2,739 enemy aircraft destroyed.

Tex ended his second tour at the end of December 1943 and was returned to England on March 19, 1944. He was repatriated to Canada on May 1, 1944.

After a period of leave and a four-week flying instructor's course, Barrick began a new job on June 16, 1944, as a Hurricane instructor pilot at RCAF No. 1 OTU at Bagotville, Quebec. On October 14, he was posted to RCAF No. 133 Squadron at Patricia Bay, British Columbia, where he flew Curtiss-Wright Kittyhawk Mk 1s and Mk IVs with Western Air Command.

In July 1945, No. 133's Kittyhawks were replaced by de Havilland Mk XXVI Mosquito fighter-bombers. Barrick remained with the squadron until it stood down and was inactivated on October 2, 1945.

Tex finished the war with a record of five-and-a-half aircraft destroyed in the air, one claimed as damaged and two aircraft destroyed on the ground. His war had been a long one, serving more than five years on three continents.

The job done, Tex Barrick, like millions of other Allied personnel, was finally able to return home. He passed away in his 79th year on September 6, 1997, in Mobile, Alabama.

Walter Duke
Maryland Lightning Ace

USAAF Captain Walter Francis "Wally" Duke from Leonardtown, Maryland, was just one of the 8,864 Americans who enlisted in the RCAF in World War II. He flew Lockheed P-38H and J Lightnings with the 459th Fighter Squadron (FS), known as "The Twin Dragons." The squadron operated from southern India in the China-Burma-India (CBI) Theater of Operations. Walter Duke was the highest scoring member of the 459th, personally accounting for 13 IJAAF aircraft destroyed in the air and a further eight and one half destroyed on the ground.

Walter was born on August 6, 1921, at Leonardtown to Roland Duke and Lillian Drury. From 1928 until early 1941, he attended St. Mary's Academy, Leonard Hall School and the University of Maryland.

Unable to meet the high standards as set forth by the prewar US Army Air Corps for pilot training, the 5ft 6in tall 19-year-old traveled from his home on July 24, 1941, to No. 13 Recruiting Centre at Montreal, Quebec, where he voluntarily joined the RCAF. The interviewer, FO F. W. McCrea, made the following observations in his file, "Quiet and competent. Pleasant and respectful. Fair education. Likeable and intelligent."

Duke's assigned rank was that of an AC2 and his Regimental Service No. was R. 117665. He completed his basic training at No. 1 Manning Depot (MD) at Toronto, Ontario, on August 9. From there, he was sent to perform guard duty at No. 4 Bombing and Gunnery School at Fingal, Ontario, until October 10. During the month of September, he was charged with being Absent Without Leave (AWL) for a period of three days. He was fined and forfeited three days' pay for that infraction. Duke spent the next two months at No. 1 ITS back in Toronto. Graduating from course No. 38 on December 6, Walter scored an overall 81 percent in eight subjects, earning the following comments from the school's WC: "Bright and cheerful. Ambitious and aggressive. Has applied himself diligently to his studies. Reliable, dependable and has a keen sense of responsibility. Recommended for a commission."

Promoted to LAC, Duke commenced flight training on Fleet Finch Mk II biplanes course No. 44 at No. 9 EFTS at St Catharines, Ontario, on December 8.

A Lockheed P-38J Lightning flown by Captain Walter F. Duke and belonging to the 459th FS is serviced at Chittagong, India, in 1944. (US Department of Defense)

Passing out of this course on February 13, 1942, with 68.30 flying hours in his logbook (dual and solo), Walter was advanced to No. 6 SFTS course No. 50 at Dunnville, Ontario, where he flew the single-engine NAA Harvard Mk II. This course was set to conclude on June 19, but Walter decided to laterally switch air forces a scant few weeks before graduating and receiving his RCAF Wings. He had flown 102.55 hours (dual and solo) on the Harvard and was assured by the American Air Corps recruiters when they came calling that he could continue his advanced flying training stateside and become an officer. This guarantee was given due, in large part, to the glowing recommendation from the RCAF stating that he was above average in all aspects of his training and flying. They were sorry to lose him. After serving 302 days in the RCAF he was granted an Honourable Discharge on May 21, 1942. That same day he joined the USAAF as a flight cadet.

Within days, he arrived at Napier Field at Dothan, Alabama, where he continued his advanced flight training on the NAA AT-6C Texan. He graduated at the top of his class on August 5, 1942, receiving, in the process, a commission as a 2nd lieutenant under Service No. O-790505. He was assigned to the 89th FS, 80th Fighter Group (FG) at Mitchell Field at Long Island, New York, where he flew Curtiss-Wright P-40N Warhawks. In March, he was promoted to 1st lieutenant.

Home on leave for one week, Wally married Verja Graham, a girl he had known since childhood.

The 80th FG transited by sea to India in May 1943. Assigned to the US 10th Air Force, it began operations from Sadiya-Assam with its P-40s in September. That same month, a newly formed fighter squadron, the 459th, was activated at that location flying P-38H Lightnings. Although it was assigned and came under the control of the 80th, the unit for the most part operated independently of group headquarters. On November 30, 1943, 1st Lieutenant Walter Duke moved over from the 89th to the 459th. By the end of December, his total military flight time amounted to 719 hours and 45 minutes.

Walter did not see any action in the first few months as the squadron was tasked to provide escort for bomber missions to and from Burma. He began to rack up his aerial score in 1944. Between March 11 and May 23, he shot nine Nakajima Ki-43 Hayabusa Oscars and one Nakajima Ki-44 Shoki Tojo out of the sky. His eight-and-a-half ground kill tally resulted from strafing and bombing several Japanese airfields. He was the squadron's highest scoring pilot and received a promotion to captain.

At the end of April, he was assigned a newer model Lightning, a P-38J-10-L0, which he named *Miss-V* in honor of his wife.

Nearing the end of his first tour, Walter was set to return home for a well deserved rest in May–June 1944. A large local gathering and celebration was planned for his return, but it was not to be as he went Missing in Action (MIA) on June 6, 1944.

The squadron's history recounts Duke's last mission:

> The 459th was tasked to attack the Japanese air bases at Heho and Meiktila, Burma. Major V. D. Luehring led one group of eleven aircraft while Captain W. C. Broadfoot led the second group of seven aircraft. After a long transit flight both facilities were strafed and bombed. Heading home and low on fuel, the Americans were intercepted by many Oscar and Mitsubishi A6M Zero-Sen Zeke fighters. The 459th proceeded to shoot their way out of the enemy mass as they did not have enough gas to stay and fight. One of the Americans, 1st Lieutenant B. C. Goodrich, was shot down. Clearing the battle area, Captain Duke discovered his wing-man, 2nd Lieutenant W. G. Baumeister, was missing. The concerned Duke radioed that he had enough fuel and was going to circle back to look for Baumeister. Baumeister did manage to return to their operating base at Chittagong, India that day, Walter Duke did not.

After the war, Captain Hampton E. Boggs, a nine-kill ace with the 459th, traveled to the Japanese air bases with an interpreter in an effort to determine what happened to Captain Duke. After interviewing several Japanese pilots, Boggs learned the fate of his friend. Duke encountered several Zekes, which were waiting and hoping for just such an opportunity to bounce any stragglers. Instead of fleeing, the 22-year-old captain courageously turned into the numerical enemy force and the lopsided dogfight began. Walter Duke was eventually overwhelmed, but not before sending three of the "Sons of Nippon" to meet their ancestors.

Captain Walter Francis Duke was officially declared deceased by the USAAF on February 8, 1946. He is remembered on the Tablets of the Missing at the Manila American Cemetery and Memorial in the Philippines.

In 2012, Duke's family was notified that the crashed remains of his aircraft had been located. The US military visited the site and confirmed the aircraft's serial number matched that of his P-38. One of Walter's sisters, Eleanor Ann Fearns, was asked to provide a DNA sample to compare against the human remains found at the site.

As of January 2023, the family has not received official confirmation from the government that the remains discovered in 2012 are that of Captain Walter. F. Duke. No explanation has been forthcoming for this delayed notification.

When, and if, this ever comes to pass, the family wishes his remains to be returned stateside for burial in the family plot at the old St. Aloysius Cemetery in Leonardtown.

As a tribute to their local fallen son, the terminal building at the St. Mary's County Regional Airport bears Duke's name. One further honor was bestowed upon Maryland's leading ace when on August 19, 2015, the newly built Walter Francis Duke Elementary School was opened and dedicated to his memory.

John Herbst
That Other Pappy

The highest scoring fighter pilot in the USAAF's 14th Air Force in World War II was Major John Coleman "Pappy" Herbst. Initially flying Curtiss-Wright P-40N Warhawks, then later North American P-51B and C Mustangs, Herbst accounted for 18 confirmed aerial victories. Additionally, he claimed one enemy aircraft as probably destroyed and three as damaged. This occurred over a seven-month period from June 17, 1944, to January 17, 1945. Most of his kills were in a P-51B Mustang (Serial No. 43-7060 coded #40), which he named *Tommy's Dad*.

Known to his men as "Pappy" or "Guerrilla One," Major Herbst commanded the 74th FS, which formed part of the 23rd FG. The 23rd fought and lived in the backwaters of the CBI Theater of Operations and was the direct descendant of General Claire Chennault's famous all volunteer group, the "Flying Tigers."

John C. Herbst was born to Charles Lincoln Herbst and Margaret Louise Coleman in San Mateo, California, on September 25, 1909. He was the youngest of three children. His older brother, Charles Clarence Herbst, was born in 1903 and their older sister, Ardelle, died early in childhood at the age of three. John graduated in 1928 from Huntingdon Park High School in Los Angeles (LA). He attended the University of Southern California where he earned a degree in Petroleum Engineering.

In his senior year at college, he met and married Ida Dempsey, the daughter of a wealthy influential lawyer. Herbst wanted the marriage to work, but his wife, who was used to the finer things in life, was not prepared to lower nor amend her standard of living just because of the recent marriage. As a result of her continued high living, her parents had to routinely assist the young couple financially. Their union produced a son, Thomas Dempsey Herbst, who was born on November 13, 1933.

John's father-in-law convinced him to work at his law firm during the day and to take night school courses at Loyola University with the aim of becoming an income tax lawyer. Herbst completed his law studies but did not write the final bar examination. This did not overly upset him as he really did not enjoy laboring in the legal profession. Working days and studying most nights did, however, put a great strain on his marriage. Ida, never one to sit at home, took up with her sorority sisters and partied hard on the LA social scene. This led to many arguments and fights between the two, mostly relative to her scandalous behavior, particularly when she was in mixed company. The marriage ended in divorce in October 1940.

John, meanwhile, had taken up flying and would often fly clients on business trips in the law firm's aircraft. His passion for flying was so great he contacted the United States Army Air Corps (USAAC) and offered up his service as a pilot. They told him he was too old.

On May 16, 1941, Herbst, at the age of 31, enlisted in the RCAF at No. 1 Recruiting Centre in Vancouver, British Columbia, as an AC2. His assigned service number was R. 101469. In his enlistment documents, he listed his permanent home address as 10328 Wilkins Avenue in Westwood, California.

The first stop in his RCAF training was at No. 2 MD in Brandon, Manitoba, where he remained until July 14. The next day, he reported to No. 2 ITS in Regina, Saskatchewan. He graduated from this school, formerly a teachers' college, with a 79 percent average on August 30 along with the following written comments of an RCAF WC: "A happy-go-lucky type of American citizen who is aggressive and thinks for himself. Has plenty of initiative and leadership qualities that are well above average. He handles a flight well, should prove a credit to himself and to the service and is recommended for a commission."

Promoted from AC2 to LAC, Herbst commenced flight training on Fleet Finch II biplanes, flying from the grass runways of No. 12 EFTS at Goderich, Ontario. The airport, located on the eastern shore of Lake Huron, sits on a bluff overlooking the sandy beaches of this popular summer vacation community.

Pappy, as he was quickly nicknamed, was the oldest student in his class, Course No. 37, and developed "an attitude" when told he would have to start flight training at the beginning just like everyone else. His instructor recorded the following, "This student dislikes having to start over and has an elevated opinion of his own ability. General flying is average. Needs more practice on instrument flying and aerobatics. He views his primary training here with supercilious indifference and feels that it is completely unnecessary."

Herbst finally came around to the RCAF's way of doing things and graduated on October 25 with a 77.9 percent average after having accumulated a total of 58 flight hours on the yellow trainers.

He was posted on the 27th to the newly opened No. 13 SFTS at Saint-Hubert, Quebec, Course No. 41, where he completed his advanced training on Harvard Mk IIbs. On January 16, 1942, he graduated from No. 13 with a 76.13 percent grade average. He was awarded his wings and was promoted to SP. Later that day, he was one of several who were commissioned from the ranks as POs.

When promoted, the RCAF replaced his original service number with a new one, J. 10109. His squadron commander noted: "A pilot with plenty of ability who has the makings of a good instructor. Keeps improving with gratifying results. Keen on instruments, steady, accurate and smooth." His chief instructor wrote, "Has steadily improved. Has had previous flying experience. Good all around pilot. Pupil's preference – fighter pilot." From the chief ground instructor: "Mature type – Very good education – Intelligent – High marks in ground instruction subjects."

PO Herbst was on leave until March 1, 1942, whereupon he reported to the RCAF Central Flying School in Trenton, Ontario, to begin a flying instructor's course. When it concluded on April 24, Herbst had a total of 319.50 military flight hours in his logbook. He achieved a Category "C" level instructor's certificate flying Harvards, de Havilland Tiger Moths, Avro Ansons and Fleet Finchs. FO J. F. Reed, the Chief Flying Instructor (CFI), wrote in his file, "This student's manner is misleading. He appears quiet and disinterested, but actually is quite keen. He should develop into a very good instructor. Never has to be told anything twice."

By now the US was firmly in the war and it needed to quickly build up and expand its neglected prewar military flying services. Pilots like John Herbst were openly solicited in Canada to return to the States as their training and, in some cases, experiences were very much in demand.

Herbst dutifully answered the call, honorably resigning his RCAF commission on May 19, 1942. He joined the USAAF that same day as a 2nd lieutenant. His first posting was to Sarasota Army Airfield in Sarasota, Florida, where he served for eight months as a gunnery instructor on P-40K Warhawks at the Replacement Training Unit. He was promoted to 1st lieutenant in February 1943 and to captain two months later.

On a warm sunny Sunday afternoon in the summer of 1943, Lieutenant Colonel David Lee "Tex" Hill of "Flying Tiger" fame was relaxing on a Florida beach with his wife, Mazie, and some friends. Hill was surprised to see a lone Allison-powered P-51A Mustang winging its way over the water. He squinted, blocking the sun with his hand to get a better look. The Mustang had to be from Eglin – which meant it was one of his!

He had taken command the previous December of the army's proving ground group at Eglin Army Airfield. Suddenly the aircraft went into a dive, leveling out right on the water and doing a barrel roll just above the ocean swells. Then it climbed again, beginning a series of loops, turns and spins worthy of any air show performance in the country. Tex could not believe it. Whoever the guy was, he was an amazing pilot. He was also breaking every rule in the book. The P-51A was a new aircraft, still in testing, and it was only to be flown by designated test pilots. Solo stunts at wave top height were definitely taboo, but none of the test pilots in Tex's group could have put on a performance like that anyway. When he found the nearest telephone, Tex called base operations telling them to ground the unknown pilot immediately upon landing and to figure out what was going on.

USAAF high-scoring ace Major John C. Herbst sits in the cockpit of a North American Aviation (NAA) P-51D Mustang in 1944. (US Department of Defense)

The following morning Tex's curiosity was satisfied. The mystery pilot was Captain John C. "Pappy" Herbst, a hot shot aviator assigned to a specialized Arctic-Desert-Tropic Unit. He had been attached to the proving ground group to get his flying time. While Tex appreciated the man's skill in the cockpit, he could not simply let the incident pass. He approached Colonel Winslow "Winnie" Morse, General Gardner's deputy, and recommended that Herbst be grounded for 30 days – essentially a "slap on the wrist" for the pilot. Morse agreed and Tex thought no more about it until much later when he returned to China.

On May 30, 1944, days after evacuating Hengyang, Tex touched down in Liangshan on an errand. Shortly after he landed, a transport plane came in and

John Herbst: That Other Pappy

out of it stepped a fellow with a vaguely familiar face. It was Herbst. Remembering who he was, Tex greeted Herbst warmly. "What are you doing here?" asked Tex, after shaking hands. "I'm supposed to report to General Morse," replied Herbst. "I guess I'm to take over the 3rd Squadron of the Chinese-American Composite Wing [CACW]."

Herbst had been assigned to the 5th FG in the CBI since February 20, 1944, and had flown operationally with it until bumping into Tex that day at Liangshan. Winnie Morse, who had concurred with Tex's recommendation for grounding Herbst, was now in China commanding the CACW. It was a new outfit formed on the assumption that American pilots could train Chinese flyers more effectively if they were in the same unit. So far, it was working.

Tex recalled the amazing daredevil flying he had witnessed standing on the beach at Eglin. Hill immediately knew that, with Herbst's piloting skills, he could put him to better use flying in the 23rd rather than leaving him with General Morse's outfit. The 23rd had also lost numerous good squadron commanders in the brutal effort to stop the rampaging Japanese forces. "Wait a minute," he said to Herbst, thinking quickly. "I'm short as hell of squadron commanders right now. Don't report in yet. Let me see if I can get you over with me."

That was fine with Herbst, and he waited while Tex paid a call on his old boss.

Tex considered how to couch his request, deciding that a little "tactical deception" was in order. Once in Morse's office, he got right to the point. "General, do you remember that damned 'eight ball' we had down at Eglin that time – when we ended up having to ground him for running wild in that P-51?" asked Tex. Morse's face clouded over. "Yeah, I remember," he replied. "Why?" "Well, he's back," Tex continued, "and he's here to join your group." He watched as Morse's jaw set. If there was anything the general was allergic to it was an "eight ball." Tex could already see the wheels turning in Morse's mind as he tried to figure a way to get out of the situation. "You know," said Tex in as offhanded a manner as he could manage, "I'm real short of squadron commanders right now. At this point, I'd even take this guy off your hands if you'd rather do that." He watched the general out of the corner of his eye. "Hell, you can have him!" Morse exclaimed immediately, his face betraying his relief. The matter thus settled, Tex departed to make the arrangements and Pappy promptly reboarded the transport and winged his way back to Kweilin.

When Tex arrived, he gave Herbst command of the 74th FS. Pappy would soon prove to be the greatest combat leader that unit had ever seen.

Herbst's aerial victory list 1944–45:

Nakajima Ki-43 Hayabusa Oscar
Oscar and a Nakajima Ki-44 Shoki Tojo
Two Oscars

Two Aichi D3A Vals
Oscar, Mitsubshi A6M3 Hamp and a Tojo
Oscar
Oscar and an Aichi E13A Jake
Two Oscars
Mitsubishi G3M Nell and a license-built Douglas DC-2 Tess
Tojo

Promotions for John Herbst quickly followed, becoming a major in August 1944 and a lieutenant colonel on February 10, 1945. Six days after his last promotion, Pappy was forced to relinquish command of the 74th, as Tex grounded him after learning Herbst had flown 144 combat sorties, totaling more than 400 hours. Pappy had done his share of fighting and Tex rotated him home.

Also returning to the States around this same time was Colonel Hill who, in September 1945, took command of the 412th FG. The 412th was the Air Corps' prestige, all-jet unit that flew Bell P-59 A/B Airacomets from Santa Maria Army Airfield in California. In December 1945, the group transferred to March Army Airfield and, with this transfer, came a new jet, the Lockheed P-80A Shooting Star.

Many distinguished World War II aces from the CBI and the Mediterranean Theater of Operations (MTO) elected to remain in the downsized postwar USAAF. They gravitated to the 412th, perhaps looking to stay on the cutting edge of military flying.

It was at this point that Pappy went to work for Colonel Hill for the second time, taking command of the 445th FS, one of four squadrons that comprised the 412th.

On May 2, 1946, the leader of the fledgling Tactical Air Command, Major General Elwood R. "Pete" Quesada, issued a directive for Project Comet. The operation would entail the deployment of 25 P-80s from March on a nine-city, 13-day tour of the nation to principally demonstrate to the public the need for a strong separate air force.

As part of the tour, Lieutenant Colonel Herbst was directed to work up and lead a two ship P-80A aerobatic display that would be performed at each of the cities visited. Pappy chose as his wingman Major Robin Olds, another gifted fighter pilot at the 412th. Olds had 13 kills in the war flying P-38J Lightnings and P-51D/K Mustangs with the 479th FG in England. The two practiced incessantly for five days, perfecting their routine, which first premiered at March Field on May 7 for a group of visiting military dignitaries from Brazil.

At a press conference on the evening of Tuesday, May 14, 1946, Project Comet's nine-city itinerary was announced: Tucson, Arizona; Fort Worth, Texas; Memphis and Smyrna, Tennessee; Washington, District of Columbia; Rantoul, Illinois; Oklahoma City, Oklahoma; Midland, Texas; and Phoenix, Arizona.

John Herbst: That Other Pappy

The tour's aircraft were suitably dressed in appropriate squadron color trim, individual nose art and "scoreboards" on the vertical fin showing the pilot's World War II combat tallies.

Major Olds' P-80A, coded PN-155, was named *Scat X* and Pappy's, coded PN-083, was named *Jeanne*, in honor of his soon-to-be wife, Jeanne Eve Murphy, a graduate of the National Academy of Dramatics in New York and a Manhattan stage and radio actress.

On July 3, 1946, the engaged couple were wed in the Flyers' Chapel at California's Riverside Mission Inn with Herbst's close friend, Phil Loofbourrow, the 412th Deputy Commander, doing the honors as best man.

The following day, July 4, the groom was back in the cockpit as he and Major Olds were scheduled to perform their two-ship routine at San Diego's Del Mar fairgrounds. Herbst's bride was in the audience along with thousands of spectators as the duo started their show. One of their maneuvers was a formation loop. At the top of the loop, Herbst and Olds threw out landing gear, flaps and speed brakes keeping the second half of the loop tight enough to maintain an air speed of less than 200mph. At the finish of the loop, a gliding climb was initiated "trading airspeed for altitude" in those familiar air show announcer words. At 2,000ft, the pair rolled inverted to perform a split-s to finish the pattern at low altitude directly in front of the crowd. As the pair started through the split-s, Olds felt things going wrong. His leader was not pulling as hard as he usually did, and the numbers were rolling off the altimeter at an alarming rate. Shouting over the radio, "Pull, Pappy, pull!", Olds broke formation and continued the pull, recovering about 400ft above the field. As he looked over his shoulder, Olds saw Herbst's ship hit the ground at a shallow ten-degree angle. The P-80 broke apart, the wreckage scattering along a 120-yard path.

Lieutenant Colonel John Herbst was fatally injured in the crash and died en route to the San Diego military hospital The news of the popular commander's death devastated the personnel at the 412th. "In my opinion," Olds wrote in his account for the accident investigation board, "Throughout the entire demonstration, Colonel Herbst was obviously not in his best form. Normally smooth to perfection, his maneuvers were harder to follow as a wingman. I know that he was under an emotional strain."

The six-man accident investigation team, headed by Lieutenant Colonel Glenn E. Hubbard, seemed to concur with Olds' analysis. "It is believed that the emotional strain referred to," the report reads, "was a result of Colonel Herbst's wedding the evening prior to the accident which was given considerable publicity in that both parties were socially prominent."

According to Jeanne, Johnny (as she called him) was exhausted when he came to their room on the morning of the wedding. His pilots had thrown him an all-out bachelor party at a cabin in the hills the night before. Pappy had fallen into a bathtub and struck his head after indulging in several rounds of exuberant toasting. He complained to Jeanne his head hurt and that, overall, he was not feeling well. She pleaded with him not to fly the show the next day, as for weeks she and her mother had been experiencing horrible premonitions of his plane crashing! Pappy took a couple of aspirin for his headache and told her she just had a bad case of bridal jitters and that everything would be fine. The morning of the 4th, he awoke, and his head was still aching. Jeanne was convinced that he suffered a concussion in the fall and blacked out during the final sequence of the aerial display. The add-on display, which was not part of the original tour, had been scheduled by someone at the wing at the last minute. That person was fully aware of the impending nuptials of the high-profile busy couple but committed Herbst and Olds to the performance anyway.

Lieutenant Colonel J. C. Herbst was laid to rest in the Sawtelle Cemetery in Westwood, California. This historic military burial ground has since been renamed the Los Angeles National Cemetery. When he died, Pappy was in his 36th year.

In 1969, his 36-year-old son, Tommy, died by his own hand.

The two USAAF FSs that Herbst commanded have survived to this day. The 74th FS is part of the 23rd Wing, flying A-10C Thunderbolt II aircraft from Moody Air Force base at Valdosta, Georgia. The 445th FS is now the 445th Flight Test Squadron and operates as part of the 412th Test Wing, flying a variety of aircraft from Edwards Air Force Base at Rosamond, California.

Owen Keech
New York Dive-Bomber Pilot

On September 1, 1954, Mrs. Doris Dillenbeck, a resident of Parish, Oswego County, New York, received the following letter from RCAF WC W. R. Gunn in Ottawa, Ontario:

I am sorry indeed to have to refer again to the loss of your nephew, Pilot Officer Owen Andrew Keech, but you will wish to know that the graves of your nephew and that of his navigator, Warrant Officer E. R. Watkins, a member of the Royal Air Force, have at long last been located. Their remains have been moved to the Taukkyan Military War Cemetery which is located twenty-one miles outside the city of Rangoon, Burma. Most unfortunately individual identification could not be obtained, but their resting sites for the past ten years were positively identified. They have recently been interned at Taukkyan in Graves No. 17 and 18, Row F, Plot No. 16A. This war cemetery will be permanently maintained by the Imperial War Graves Commission. The Commission will erect permanent individual headstones at the graves of your nephew and WO Watkins.

Please disregard my letter of February 4, 1953, wherein I informed you that your nephew's name would appear on a memorial to be erected at Singapore for service members who have no known graves. It is my sincere hope that you will be comforted by the knowledge that the resting place of your nephew is now known and will be permanently maintained. May I take this opportunity of expressing to you and the members of your family my deepest sympathy in the loss of your gallant nephew.

Owen Andrew Keech was born on February 7, 1921, in Watertown, New York. His Canadian-born father, Louis Keech, was from Gananoque, Ontario, and his American-born mother, Gladys Wann, came from the Cavish, New York, area. Keech's parents divorced before he was born. His mother married a man named Darling, but Keech never formally took his stepfather's surname.

Owen attended Academy Street Public School in Watertown from 1926 to 1934, then Watertown High School and Parish High School from 1934 to 1938. For the next two years, he worked locally as a farm hand. From March 1940 until April 1941, Keech was enrolled in a one-year aviation mechanics course at the Lincoln Aeronautical Institute & Flying School in Lincoln, Nebraska. He successfully completed 520 hours of classroom instruction and 1,130 hours of practical shop work. It was there, after riding as a passenger on numerous occasions in the school's aircraft, that he was bitten by the flying bug. He had already begun working toward obtaining his private pilot's license and had accumulated 40 hours of civilian flight time by the time he enlisted in the RCAF on May 22, 1941, at Ottawa's No. 12 Recruiting Centre.

His air force paperwork indicates that his birth father, with whom he never had any contact, died in the 1930s in Jamesville, New York. At the time of his enlistment, Keech was living at 12 Market Street in Alexandria Bay, New York.

FL I. H. Christie swore him into Canada's air force as an AC2 under Service No. R. 96261. Owen's basic training was undertaken from May 23 until June 22 at No. 1 MD in Toronto, Ontario. This was followed by an obligatory stint of guard duty from June 23 to August 7 at No. 6 SFTS at Dunnville, Ontario. Keech was posted to Course No. 33 on August 8 at No. 5 ITS at Belleville, Ontario. He graduated from this facility on September 24 with an 82 percent average and was promoted to LAC. In the remarks section of his file, the school's WC made the following observations: "Pilot – ought to be a good one. Moderate flying experience. Average at sports. Does not want a post war career in the RCAF."

Just before he graduated from the Belleville school, Owen was found to be AWL for a period of three days from September 12 to September 15. His punishment was seven days confined to barracks and the forfeiture of three days' pay.

On September 25, Keech reported in to No. 1 EFTS at Malton, Ontario. Assigned to Course No. 39, he flew de Havilland Tiger Moth biplanes for 60½ hours until graduating on November 21, 1941. The CFI made the following remarks: "Above average pilot. Methodical and thinks for himself. Has no outstanding faults. Has had previous flying experience." The Chief Ground Instructor (CGI) said the following, "Appears to be a slow even tempered student. Easy going. Should prove a capable all round pilot under proper supervision. Conduct and discipline fair." Both instructors, however, said that he was unsuitable for a commission.

On November 2, Keech, again, was found to be AWL, this time for a period of one day, 20 hours and 35 minutes. His punishment – four days confined to barracks and the forfeiture of two days' pay.

Owen was posted on November 24 to No. 2 SFTS at Air Station Uplands located just outside Ottawa. He completed his flying training to wings standard on Course No. 43 after amassing 155 flight hours on Harvard Mk IIbs. He graduated on March 16, 1942, was awarded his pilot wings, and was promoted to the rank of SP. His squadron commander recorded the following: "Above average. Smooth and steady. Instrument flying average. Should watch altitude more closely. Navigation average. Link trainer progress and ability above average." From the CGI: "In the lower half of the class. Rather sloppy. Only interested in flying fighters." The CFI

Vultee Vengeance Mk II dive-bombers on the production line at the Vultee plant at Nashville, Tennessee, in 1941. (US Department of Defense)

added: "Willing and considerate. Character good. Leadership qualities are not outstanding. Pupil's preference – Fighters, Bombers or Reconnaissance Aircraft."

Keech was sent to No. 118 Fighter Squadron at RCAF Dartmouth, Nova Scotia, where, for a four-week period, he flew Curtiss-Wright P-40 Kittyhawk Mk Is until April 17.

While there, a third charge of being AWL was laid against him. This time he was absent for seven days, 20 hours and 50 minutes. His punishment this time was a severe reprimand and the forfeiture of eight days' pay.

Owen desperately wanted to get into combat, but he was going about it the wrong way. In a move to teach the rebellious young pilot that he had to abide by air force regulations, the RCAF posted him to western Canada for the next four months as a staff pilot. During his time spent in the prairie provinces, Keech flew Fleet Forts, NAA Harvards, Airspeed Oxfords and Avro Ansons at No. 2 Wireless School, Calgary, Alberta, No. 32 SFTS at Moose Jaw, Saskatchewan, and No. 19 SFTS at Vulcan, Alberta.

On August 21, 1942, Owen finally received his long-awaited orders for overseas deployment. He traveled by train to Pier 21, "Y" Depot, Halifax, Nova Scotia, where he waited for the next sea-going convoy to assemble.

At 0100hrs on September 1, he was found passed out in a drunken stupor on the corner of Sackville and Bedford Row streets in the city of Halifax. Two days later, a fine and reprimand were assessed and levied. Ironically, ten days after that incident he was promoted to the rank of flight sergeant (FS).

Owen departed Canada on October 27 and arrived at No. 3 Personnel Reception Centre in Bournemouth, England, on November 6. Assigned to No. 56 OTU at RAF Tealing, Scotland, he flew a combined 73 hours on Miles Masters and

Hawker Hurricanes on Course No. 53 from December 1, 1942, until February 16, 1943. The following comments in his file were attributed to the air station's WC: "Average pilot. Quite keen and reliable in the air, but is inclined to be slack on the ground. Not yet recommended for a commission."

Assigned to Far East Command in Southeast Asia, Keech left England from No. 5 Personnel Dispatch Centre at Padgate. He arrived at No. 152 Bomber OTU in Peshawar, Pakistan, in early April.

Days later, he received word that his 48-year-old mother had passed away on April 19 of natural causes. By the time he received the news half a world away, the funeral service had concluded.

Keech trained on Harvards and Vultee Vengeance dive-bombers at No. 152 until September 23, 1943. Days before the course concluded he was promoted to warrant officer (WO). He was posted directly to RAF No. 84 Squadron, which, at the time, was based at Ranchi, India.

The Vultee Vengeance single-engined dive-bomber had its beginnings in September 1940, after the British Purchasing Commission identified a requirement for an aircraft that could match the capabilities of the German Junkers Ju 87 Stuka. Vultee Aircraft Corporation at Downey, California, responded to the request and was awarded an initial contract by Britain to produce some 700 aircraft. With the Downey facility running flat out building intermediate BT-13/15 Valiant trainers for the USAAC and SNV-1/2 trainers for the US Navy, the company opened a manufacturing plant in Nashville, Tennessee, specifically to handle the British order. The Vengeance was designated by the Air Corps as the A-31, but that service never used the type in combat during World War II. Unable to keep pace with demand for aircraft, Vultee had to subcontract some of its production out to Northrop Aircraft Incorporated. The Northrop-built machines were designated by the RAF as Mk I and Mk Ias. The Vultee-built units were designated as Mk IIs, IIIs and IVs. In addition to the RAF, the Vengeance served with India's Air Force, the Royal Australian Air Force (RAAF) and later as target tow aircraft with the USAAF under the designation A-35A and A-35B. RAF No. 84 Squadron was one of four British units that operated the Vengeance in the close air support role. This is the type of aircraft Keech flew right up until the day of his death.

As he took off on Saturday, March 4, 1944, on what would be his last combat sortie, Keech was unaware that he had been promoted the day previously to the rank of PO. The RCAF had assigned him new Regimental Service No. J. 86313, replacing his enlisted No. R. 96261.

A flying accident report was completed on behalf of the squadron on March 5 by FL J. H. Ramsden, which said in part; "An 84 Squadron Vengeance Mk II, coded AN 706, crashed on an operational day mission one mile west of Yazagya in western Burma on March 4, 1944. Both crew members, O. A. Keech and E. R. Watkins, are missing in enemy territory and are believed to have been killed in action."

On March 7, SL A. M. Gill, the OC No. 84 Squadron, sent the following report to RAF No. 168 Wing Headquarters:

> Vengeance AN 706 was in the No. 5 position in a box of six aircraft detailed to dive bomb Kontha, Burma on the afternoon of March 4, 1944. On approaching the area, the six aircraft changed formation to echelon starboard and immediately peeled off to port to attack the target. The instructions were to dive from approximately 10,000' to 2,000' which meant that bombs had to be released and a pull-out commenced at between 4,000' and 5,000'. Vengeance AN 706 was seen to dive to earth in a ball of fire. The aircraft fell amongst the bomb bursts one mile west of Yazagya. Neither of the crew was seen to leave the aircraft by parachute. Attached are accounts of members of the formation who witnessed the crash.

The wireless operator/air gunner in aircraft No. 3 filed the following report:

> I was flying in Vengeance AN 713 in the No. 3 position in the formation. As we pulled out of our dive at 2,500 feet I was watching the path of the bombs coming down from the aircraft behind us. As the bombs burst, I looked up and saw AN 706 come screaming down completely engulfed in flames. I informed my pilot who immediately turned our aircraft to a position from which we could both see. Vengeance AN 706 was in an 80 degree dive and at one stage in the descent, we could faintly see its fin and rudder through the massive sheet of flame. No one was seen to get out. It hit the ground with a thunderous explosion! When I first noticed the aircraft on fire it was at 5,000 feet.

The pilot of aircraft No. 6 reported:

> I was the pilot of Vengeance AN 830 and was formatting on Vengeance AN 706 piloted by WO Keech who was flying in the No. 5 position. I saw that he had fully opened his bomb doors, turned onto his port wing and commenced his dive. I followed him down from a distance of between 1,000 to 1,500 feet. I kept my eye on him noticing his dive was a bit shallow but he suddenly steepened it with an aileron turn over the target. I then lost sight of him having to concentrate on the task at hand. My gunner called out our altitude at 6,000' which prepared me for his next shout when we reached 4,000' whereupon I released four general purpose 500 pound bombs. Before my bombs struck, I noticed a huge cloud of debris that had been blown upward into the air. Not wishing to damage my aircraft, I commenced an immediate pull out. My exit unavoidably took me through this debris field which consisted of aircraft panels and cowlings. My gunner thought for a moment that it was pieces coming off our aircraft. As I assumed the position of straight and level flight, I noticed a brilliant red fire burning in the centre of the target area. The flames were obviously from a burning aircraft and upon rejoining the formation I discovered AN 706 was missing.

On March 5, SL Gill sent the following letter to Mrs. Sarah Warn who resided at Parish, Oswego County, New York:

> You will have already been informed by the Air Ministry that your grandson has been reported 'Missing Believed Killed in Action' after carrying out an operation over enemy territory yesterday. I write, not only for myself, but on behalf of the whole squadron, to express our deepest sympathy with you in a great loss. I have already written a letter to you, but I am also sending this airgraph copy in case the original is lost. Your grandson was flying his aircraft on a dive bombing attack against a Japanese occupied village in Burma. Whilst his aircraft was in a vertical dive just prior to releasing its bomb load, it was seen to explode and crash in flames in the target area. In my opinion the aircraft was hit by machine gun or light anti-aircraft artillery fire from the ground and your grandson and his observer had little or no realization of what happened and were killed instantaneously. Your grandson had recently been promoted to the rank of WO. He was a first class pilot and was greatly admired by his colleagues, both officers and airmen alike. The fact that he has been reported missing believed killed has caused a feeling of great loss throughout the squadron. Your grandson's personal belongings are being sent to the Standing Committee of Adjustment from whom you will be hearing in due course. I know how inadequate a letter is to express the sympathy that is felt for you here or to soften your grief and I can only hope that the steady belief in the justice of the cause for which your grandson gave his life will do something to comfort you in your great loss.

On April 26, 1946, the RCAF asked the Vital Statistics Department of the Province of Ontario to officially register the date and place of death of Owen Andrew Keech of Alexandria Bay, New York.

Two years later, on May 19, 1947, RCAF WC W. A. Dicks sent the following letter to Mrs. Sarah Warn on behalf of the CAS:

> It is a privilege to have the opportunity of sending you the operational wings and certificate in recognition of the gallant services rendered by your grandson, PO O. A. Keech. I realize there is little which may be said or done to lessen your sorrow, but it is my hope that these "wings," indicative of operations against the enemy, will be a treasured memento of a young life offered on the altar of freedom in defence of his home and country.

On November 2, 1949, Mrs. Warn received her grandson's World War II Canadian Medals: 1939–45 Star, Burma Star, Defence Medal, General Service Medal and the Canadian Volunteer Service Medal with Clasp. She personally received, from the Canadian federal government, a Memorial Cross.

Lloyd Thomas
Michigan Hurricane Pilot

On Friday, September 6, 1940, four days before he celebrated his 25th birthday, Lloyd Duncan "Tommy" Thomas from Detroit, Michigan, voluntarily enlisted in the RCAF. He was processed into Canada's embryonic air arm at No. 11 Recruiting Centre in Toronto, Ontario, as an AC2 under service number R. 72018.

Thomas, an American, had been living and working in Toronto since 1935 and was employed as an audit clerk by the accounting firm J. P. Langley and Company. He resided at 60 King George Road and was within one month of becoming a chartered accountant. He had just completed a five-year correspondence course through Queen's University at Kingston, Ontario, in preparation for writing his final examination for his license from the Ontario Institute of Chartered Accountants.

Lloyd Thomas was born to Marjorie Duncan and Charles Sidney Thomas on September 10, 1915, in Marshall, Texas. There were three older children in the family – sisters Alexina and Jean and a brother, Robert. Lloyd's father was an American citizen, while his Canadian-born mother hailed from Stouffville, Ontario. The two were married in Hamilton, Ontario, on July 24, 1907. Charles Thomas was the chief traveling accountant with the Grand Trunk Railroad. The Grand Trunk operated in the Canadian provinces of Ontario and Quebec as well as the American states of Connecticut, Maine, Michigan, Massachusetts, New Hampshire, and Vermont.

Thomas spent the first several weeks of basic training at No. 1 MD in Toronto. On November 6, he was posted to RCAF No. 4 Bombing & Gunnery School at Fingal, Ontario, where he performed guard duty until November 27. The next day, he returned to Toronto to begin classes at No. 1 ITS. Lloyd stood fourth in his class when the course graduated on January 4, 1941.

Promoted from AC2 to LAC, Thomas began his primary flight training on de Havilland Tiger Moth biplanes at No. 9 EFTS at St. Catharines, Ontario. This seven-week course concluded on February 21, with Lloyd again scoring well and finishing in the top of his class. For the next nine days, he was based at No. 1A MD at Picton, Ontario.

Passed to No. 6 SFTS at Air Station Dunnville, Ontario, on March 6, Lloyd began an intensive ten-week course learning to fly the 200mph Harvard Mk IIb advanced trainer. LAC Thomas placed sixth overall in this phase of his service flying training.

On May 16, 1941, he was awarded his pilot wings in a graduation ceremony at Dunnville and was promoted to the rank of SP. The next day, he was commissioned from the ranks as a PO. Reflecting his officer status, his service number was changed from R. 72018 to J. 5473.

Granted the standard two-week pre-embarkation leave, PO Thomas departed from Canada on a troop ship for England from Pier 21, Halifax, Nova Scotia, on June 14, 1941. Arriving in the United Kingdom on June 27, he checked in at No. 3 Personnel Reception Centre in Bournemouth for assignment and processing.

On July 21, Lloyd was sent to RAF No. 57 OTU at Hawarden, Flintshire, Wales. There he flew Miles Master Mk I trainers and Supermarine Mk Ia Spitfires. Many of the Hawarden instructors were experienced combat pilots, having fought in the Battle of Britain during the summer of 1940. These veterans not only instructed the students on how to safely fly and operate a Spitfire, but they also taught them how to fight and survive in the unforgiving arena of aerial combat.

Successfully completing the OTU training in August, Lloyd was posted to RAF No. 132 "City of Bombay" Squadron. No. 132 formed at RAF Peterhead in Scotland on July 7, 1941, and became operational 12 days later flying Spitfire Mk IIs. Its primary function was to provide air defense coverage to the northern part of the country.

Having had little to no contact with the enemy, in November, Thomas requested that he be transferred to an active war zone.

On December 2, 1941, Tommy embarked from Britain with orders to report to the Middle East. He arrived at Freetown, Sierra Leone, West Africa, on December 29, then flew onward to join RAF No. 17 Squadron at Mingaladon Airfield outside of Rangoon, Burma.

No. 17 had left Scotland in November 1941 and its original destination was North Africa. However, after the Japanese declared war on December 7, 1941, the squadron was rerouted to Burma where it set up shop in January 1942, flying Hawker Hurricane Mk IIas. The Japanese, fresh from their success in Singapore, were hitting Rangoon hard and Lloyd and several other pilots arrived right in the middle of the raids.

On the morning of February 7, 1942, Tommy shot down an IJAAF Nakajima Ki-27 Nate. The squadron was fighting a desperate defensive battle alongside the famous AVG Flying Tigers, which was flying early model P-40 Warhawks. Constant patrols were maintained over Mingaladon all through the month of February. At midday on February 25, a big Japanese fighter sweep approached the airfield. It is believed that Tommy scored his second aerial victory on this date shooting down another Ki-27 Nate.

After Rangoon was lost to the Japanese, everyone relocated to Magwe. While the AVG and RAF had some success against the Japanese, Magwe was continuously bombed, including a very heavy raid on March 21 by 151 bombers and fighters. In early April, the RAF and AVG were forced to relocate to Loiwing, just across the Chinese border, as they only had four serviceable aircraft between them.

On May 17, 1942, Lloyd received a promotion from PO to FO.

On August 25, 1942, an exhausted and tour-expired Thomas was rested when he was posted from No. 17 Squadron to a staff officer's position at headquarters.

On October 12, he resumed flying and was assigned to No. 3 Anti-Aircraft Flight. On December 1, he returned to the role of a fighter pilot when he was posted to RAF No. 5 Squadron at Agartala, India. There, he flew Curtiss-Wright Mohawk Mk IVs (Hawk 75A-9 variants).

Britain came into possession of 229 Hawk model 75s by way of diverted shipments to occupied France and aircraft flown by escaping French pilots. This aircraft type equipped one other RAF squadron, No. 155, and it was mainly used in 1942–43 for bomber escort and ground attack.

Flight Lieutenant Lloyd Thomas, DFC, was shot down and killed in the CBI Theater of Operations in 1944 while flying a Hawker Hurricane similar to the one depicted. (Parr Yonemoto)

Powered by a 1,200shp Wright Cyclone GR-1820-G205A nine-cylinder, air-cooled, radial engine, the lightly loaded Mohawk had a top speed of 323mph. The bulk of these aircraft were discovered sitting on a dock, still in their shipping crates. They were transported to the maintenance unit at Drigh Road in Karachi where they were assembled and test flown.

On April 21, 1943, Thomas, now newly promoted to the rank of FL, was posted as a staff officer to RAF headquarters at Ramu, India.

He returned to No. 5 Squadron as a flight commander on January 1, 1944. In his absence, the squadron had traded in its Mohawks for Hurricane Mk IIc and IIds. Fitted with wing racks for carriage of 250lb or 500lb bombs, the pilots, who called their aircraft Hurri-Bombers, flew them from Sapam airfield in the Imphal Valley. The Allied squadrons in this area fought and operated under less-than-ideal operating conditions. Poor food, terrible living accommodations and airfields that always seemed to be covered in mud were the order of the day. In some instances, Japanese troops hiding in the jungle would harass the squadron's personnel with rifle and machine gun fire from less than 200 yards away.

On April 18, 1944, 28-year-old Lloyd Thomas took off at 0820hrs in Hurricane LD580 on a combat sortie from Lanka Airfield in India. One hour later, he led his flight in a dive-bombing attack against the Japanese-held airfield at Kawlin. Nosing over in a 40-degree dive to release his bombs, Tommy's Hurricane was repeatedly struck by large caliber antiaircraft rounds fired by the airfield gunners. His uncontrolled fighter dove vertically into the ground and exploded into a ball of fire.

Ten days later, Thomas was awarded a British Distinguished Flying Cross (DFC), the details of which are as follows:

> THOMAS, FL Lloyd Duncan J.5473 – Distinguished Flying Cross – No. 5 Squadron – Award effective 28 April 1944 as per London Gazette dated 5 May 1944 and AFRO 1296/44 dated 16 June 1944. Born 1915 in Marshall, Texas. Home in Detroit, Michigan. Enlisted in Toronto, 6 September 1940. Trained at No. 1 ITS (graduated 4 January 1941), No. 9 EFTS (graduated 21 February 1941) and No. 6 SFTS Dunnville (graduated 16 May 1941). Commissioned 1941. Killed in action serving with RAF No. 5 Squadron on 18 April 1944 in Burma. Flying a Hurricane Mk II he was shot down by ground fire over the Japanese airfield at Kawlin.
>
> FL Thomas has been engaged on operational flying since October, 1941 and has completed a large number of sorties in the European and Burma theatres of war. During the period of evacuation from Burma, he set a fine example of courage, leadership and skill. Since then he has flown on bombing and low level attacks in support of the army on the Arakan and Imphal fronts and has displayed outstanding

keenness and tenacity in air combat. This officer has destroyed at least two enemy aircraft and has destroyed many more on the ground.

On May 3, 1944, the RCAF casualty officer in Ottawa, Ontario, on behalf of the CAS, wrote the following letter of condolence to his parents in Detroit:

> It is my painful duty to confirm the telegram recently received by you which informed you that your son, FL Lloyd Duncan Thomas, is reported missing and believed killed on active service. Advice has been received from the RCAF Casualties Officer, Overseas that the aircraft of which your son was the sole occupant was seen to strike the ground as a result of enemy action at 0920 hours on April 18th, 1944 near Kawlin, Sagaing, Burma. You may be assured that any further information received will be communicated to you immediately. May I extend to you and the members of your family my deepest sympathy.

On April 26, 1946, a Memorial Cross bearing the cypher of King George VI was sent by the Canadian federal government to Mrs. Marjorie Duncan Thomas at 13973 Rosemont Road in Detroit, Michigan. This award, together with a Royal Message of Sympathy, was forwarded to her in recognition of the loss of her son, RCAF FL L. D. Thomas, on active service in the Far East on April 18, 1944. The Memorial Cross is often referred to as the Silver Cross for Mothers.

In RAF Search Report No. 21, dated July 31, 1946, No. 2 Search Party detailed the following information relative to the crash of RAF No. 5 Hurricane LD5809 on April 18, 1944:

> Only small pieces of wreckage found at the scene of the crash. No trace of the wings, engine or of any large pieces found, except for a wing-tip. A few pieces of no importance were removed by the Burmese natives to the local village. The crash site is located a half a mile west of the village of Kya-in-ashe. Latitude and longitude – 23 Degrees 48 Minutes North; 95 Degrees 38 Minutes East. A makeshift grave was located which consisted of a mound of earth with a five foot pole placed at the head and foot of the mound. This marked the burying place of the pilot believed to be RCAF FL L. D. Thomas J.5473. The Village Headman states that a single-engined aircraft crashed in April, 1944, but he could not say whether the Japanese or the Burmese buried the pilot. Oxygen pipes and small pieces of the aircraft were also buried with the pilot. As this single-engined aircraft crashed in April, 1944 and the location is within a few feet of the location reported for the loss of Hurricane LD580 of No. 5 Squadron, then the remains of the pilot, now reburied in the Mandalay Military Cemetery, must certainly be that of Canadian FL L. D. Thomas J.5473. Signed: Officer in Charge, No. 2 RAF Search Team, Mandalay, Burma.

In 1951, the Commonwealth War Graves Commission (CWGC) opened the Taukkyan War Cemetery in Burma. It was a complicated project that involved transferring the graves from four existing Battlefield Cemeteries, located at Akyab, Mandalay, Meiktila and Sahmaw, to Taukkyan. In their original locations, the four were difficult for the public to access and were impossible to maintain in accordance with CWGC standards. When moved, the graves were then grouped together to preserve the individuality of the former cemeteries. Today, Taukkyan meticulously maintains the graves of 6,374 commonwealth personnel killed in World War II. The remains of FL Lloyd Duncan "Tommy" Thomas, DFC, from Detroit, Michigan, are interned at this location in R. 19. G. 10.

EUROPEAN THEATER OF OPERATIONS

Ethan Allen
Deadly Encounter

Late in the day on Tuesday, June 6, 1944, the German naval submarine U-256 sailed from its base at Brest, France, out into the English Channel. Assigned to the 9th U-Boat Flotilla, the 857-tonne type VIIC submarine was embarking on its fourth war patrol. Its task was to engage and disrupt Allied naval forces that were landing massive amounts of men and equipment on to the five Normandy beachheads, codenamed Omaha, Utah, Gold, Sword, and Juno.

That same day at 2139hrs, a fully loaded RAF Coastal Command General Reconnaissance Consolidated Liberator Mk V lifted off the runway from Air Station St. Eval, Cornwall, England. The aircraft, coded BZ942 from "M" flight of 224 Squadron, was ordered to carry out an anti-submarine patrol in the western end of the Channel in support of D-Day operations.

The next morning, in the pre-dawn darkness, the two combatants converged into the same patrol area.

At the range of ten miles, U-256 showed up as an unidentified surface contact on BZ942's air-to-surface radar. The aircraft's captain, 25-year-old RCAF FO Ethan Allen II from Los Angeles, California, called his crew to action stations. In the early morning light, two miles from the target, Allen spotted the telltale wake of a U-boat running on the surface. Diving from 5,000ft, he leveled the heavy, four-engined, patrol aircraft out just 100ft off the water.

Switching on the aircraft's underwing 24in Leigh-light, U-256 was suddenly bathed in 22 million candle power of high intensity illumination. The sub's crew, however, had been forewarned of the approaching aircraft by their vessel's onboard detection system. The U-boat's antiaircraft conning tower and deck gun crews were ready and waiting. As the Liberator thundered in, the boat's captain, Oberleutnant Wilhelm Brauel, had his vessel swing broadside to the oncoming attack so that all his weapons could be brought to bear. Immediately a wall of 37mm and 20mm tracer, high-explosive and incendiary rounds from the sub's eight rapid-fire flak cannons arched upwards, instantly bracketing the B-24. Repeatedly hit, the crew of BZ942 valiantly struggled to keep their aircraft in the air. With one engine out of commission and another on fire, they had a most difficult time trying to hold their crippled Liberator steady on the bomb run. The aircraft's released stick of depth charges detonated just wide of its target. As the bomber passed low overhead, the sub's gunners stitched a final withering burst of cannon rounds all along and into the belly of the doomed warplane. The aircraft, reeling from the unrelenting pounding, flew on for 100 yards, stalled and fell into the sea, killing all aboard. The aircrew did not have time to send out a Mayday signal.

BZ942's crew had the terrible misfortune that day of not only meeting up with a German submarine that had been up-gunned with heavier caliber antiaircraft weaponry, but whose crew had received specialized surface-to-air gunnery training. U-256 had earlier undergone a conversion from that of a standard sub to a flak boot. It was one of four such Kriegsmarine submarines that were modified in the summer of 1943. The flak boat's mission was to escort and protect the large "Milk Cow" submarines from Allied air attack as they resupplied the U-boat fleet in the middle of the Atlantic Ocean with munitions, fuel, food and even, in some cases, personnel. Flak boats were so heavily armed that they were expected to remain on the surface and fight it out with any attacking aircraft. Overall, the concept was not considered that successful. Three of the subs were later re-configured and returned to the U-boat fleet as standard submarines. U-256, for whatever reason, did retain its upgraded antiaircraft armament and highly trained flak crews. As an example of its deadly firepower, U-256 destroyed an RCAF Wellington bomber from No. 407 Squadron on March 11, 1944, and, on the 19th, an RAF Liberator from No. 224 Squadron.

The circumstances surrounding the loss of the Liberator BZ942 and the fate of its crew were not immediately known. The details of the encounter finally came to light in 1949 after Allied officials examined postwar German military records.

FO Allen and his crew did damage U-256 to the extent that it caused the sub to abort its mission. The boat returned to Brest on June 8 for repairs.

Ethan Allen II was born to wealthy American parents, Horace Ransome Bigelow Allen and Alice "Kiki" Gwynne, in Biarritz, France, on June 4, 1919. A socialite and heiress, Allen's mother

FO Ethan Allen II, DFC, was killed in action on D-Day, June 6, 1944, along with his entire crew. (Canadian National Defence Image Library)

was a grandniece of Mrs. Cornelius Vanderbilt, Sr. After six years of marriage, Kiki divorced her World War I army veteran husband and married investment banker Jerome "Gerry" Preston in 1925.

Ethan's extensive, worldly education began in 1925 at Mr. Gibbs Private Boarding School near Sloane Square in London, England. Many of his classmates arrived at school each day in chauffeur-driven limousines. For the years 1927–29, Allen attended Pembroke House Boarding School at Gilgil in East Africa. Beginning in 1930 and for the next five years, he was educated at La Chataigneraie – the International School of Geneva, Switzerland. Arriving in the United States in 1936 at the age of 16, Ethan was considered an exemplary student during the time he spent at St. George's Private Boarding School at Newport, Rhode Island. He graduated from there with honors in 1938. Then, in 1939, the 6ft 1in tall, 185lb, athletically inclined Allen began studying at the University of California. After completing his second year of studies, Ethan married Martha Ester Cook in Las Vegas, Nevada, on September 29, 1940.

The newlyweds set up house in Los Angeles where Ethan went to work selling rare books and French art at Tone Price Galleries. In May 1941, Allen secured employment as a script reader/writer at Metro-Goldwyn-Mayer Studios in Culver City, California. He harbored a serious interest in aviation and began taking private flying lessons in the summer of 1941. He checked out the possibility of serving in the US military services as a pilot but was disappointed to learn that his marriage the previous year had automatically disqualified his entry. After America got into the war on December 8, 1941, the policy of accepting married applicants for combat duty was amended. One of Allen's old school chums, Charles S. Foreman, was a FO in the RCAF at the time and was serving at Air Station Dartmouth, Nova Scotia. Foreman encouraged his friend to head north and join the RCAF, as there were no such marital restrictions applicable in Canada's air force.

On December 4, 1941, the 22-year-old Allen walked into the RCAF's No. 13 Recruiting Centre in Montreal, Quebec, and voluntarily enlisted as an AC2 with Regimental No. R. 141721. Ethan, who was fluent in both French and English, had 16 hours of dual flight instruction to his credit. The interviewing officer noted the following in his report: "From a very good family, good personality, intelligent and co-operative. Recommended for pilot training and possibly a commission." Allen spent only 18 days at No. 1 MD in Toronto, Ontario, before he was posted to No. 1 Training Command Headquarters. He remained at this facility on guard duty until March 14, 1942. Remaining in Toronto, Ethan began classes the next day at No. 6 ITS. The course concluded on May 8 with Allen placing 18th in a class of 95. He was recorded as: "Excellent background. Educated largely abroad. Good appearance. Self possessed. Likeable and very much in earnest."

Promoted to LAC, Allen began his primary flight training on Fleet Finch biplanes on June 7 at No. 3 EFTS at Air Station Crumlin[1] at London, Ontario. Two weeks later, on June 21, the school's remaining students were shifted over to No. 9 EFTS at St. Catharines, Ontario. RCAF Crumlin had closed out its EFTS operation in order to make room for No. 4 Air Observation School, which was scheduled to start flying twin-engined Avro Ansons the next month.

Allen's elementary training continued at No. 9, but it was on a different aircraft – the de Havilland Tiger Moth. Ethan logged a total of 68 hours and 20 minutes dual and solo flight time at No. 9 and finished fifth in a class of 32 students. In his file were the following comments from his superiors: "Very good background. Did a good job at this unit. Keen, responsive, intelligent."

Flying solo in Tiger Moth No. 3951 on August 7, 1942, LAC Allen was involved in a flying mishap. The ceiling that warm summer day in the Niagara region was unlimited, visibility was three to eight miles in haze, with the winds light at 5–15mph. Allen's aircraft was seriously damaged after it collided in mid-air with another aircraft at 4,500ft. With his propeller smashed and his ailerons ineffective, Ethan managed to pull off a forced landing, resulting in his aircraft coming to rest upside down. He did not sustain any injuries. The other solo pilot, LAC James C. Cummings in Tiger Moth No. 8906, was slightly injured after his demolished aircraft came to rest in a farmer's field near Four Mile Creek Road. An investigation into the incident concluded that, in contravention of air regulations, the two aircraft were flying too close to one another. Blame was, therefore, allocated to both pilots for failure to observe each other – in other words, "careless airmanship."

Ethan was posted, on August 16, to No. 16 SFTS at Hagersville, Ontario. There he logged 138 hours on twin-engined Ansons. His work at No. 16 was described as follows: "Above average in ground school. Excellent type. Good worker and keenly interested. Commission material." Allen received his wings in a graduation ceremony on December 4, 1942, and was promoted to the rank of PO. His service number was changed from R. 141721 to J. 21435.

Earmarked to fly RAF Coastal Command aircraft, PO Allen was posted for advanced training to No. 1 General Reconnaissance (GR) School at Summerside, Prince Edward Island. The course ran from December 28, 1942, until February 26, 1943. Allen excelled in such subjects as ship recognition, meteorology, reconnaissance, compasses and instruments, signals, coding photography, visual

---

1 The author at one time lived within two miles of the former air station. In its civilian guise, it is known by the locals as Crumlin Airport. During World War II, the author's wife's grandmother worked as a cook at No. 3 in the Airmen's Canteen. Today, only two buildings from that era remain standing at the airport. One of the structures is used for storage and second, the former Airmen's Canteen, is now the home of No. 427 Wing RCAF Association. For the three weeks LAC Ethan Allen was stationed in London, he would have relaxed, had a bite to eat and socialized in that very building.

signals, and dead reckoning navigation. He flew an additional 42 hours and 35 minutes on Ansons at this facility. One of the course instructors, FL J. W. Woodley, noted the following in his file: "A very intelligent, keen and conscientious pupil. His work both in the air and on the ground has been consistently above average. He is a very steady dependable type, not inclined to lose control in a crisis." CFI WC Reynell added: "Keen, solid, reliable pupil. Should prove very useful in a GR squadron."

After taking his pre-embarkation leave, Allen reported to "Y" Depot, Pier 21, Halifax, Nova Scotia, on March 25 for onward deployment to the United Kingdom. The slow ocean passage took some 15 days, with the ship finally arriving in Scotland on April 10. He and the other air force personnel took an overnight troop train to No. 3 Personnel Reception Centre situated at Bournemouth on England's south coast. Ethan's stay at No. 3 was brief as he was posted on May 4 to RAF No. 224 Squadron at St. Eval.

PO Allen was promoted to FO on June 4, 1943.

In July 1943, Allen and his crew achieved a degree of notoriety at 224 when, on the third, they sank U-628 and, 25 days later, on the 28th, they sank U-404. In each attack, their aircraft was badly shot up.

On October 8 at 1620hrs, Allen damaged the tail skid of Liberator BZ790 while recovering the aircraft in bad weather at St. Eval. The lightly loaded aircraft, on a non-operational flight, floated too long over the runway in its landing phase. To arrest this action, Ethan pulled the control stick all the way back in the attempt to force the big bomber onto the runway. Landing nose high, a three-point landing was achieved scraping the tail skid in the process. At the time of the incident, Allen's total flying time amounted to 490 hours of which 230 were on Liberators. 224's OC, WC A. E. Clouston, made the following observation: "Under the circumstances, with a young captain at the controls, and while operating under a 600ft ceiling with hills behind the drome in cloud, I consider the pilot did well in landing at St. Eval. The fact that the tail skid touched is no fault of the captain but due to the lightly loaded aircraft and the aircraft's centre of gravity position."

FO Allen was awarded a British DFC on January 25, 1944. The citation read as follows: "Flying Officer Allen has completed many sorties and throughout has displayed great keenness and determination. One night as captain of aircraft he executed an attack on a large U-boat. Pressing home his attack with great determination, Flying Officer Allen straddled the vessel with a number of depth charges. On several occasions this officer has participated in successful attacks on the enemy's underwater craft. By his skill, courage and coolness he has set a very fine example".

Allen's friend, FL Charles Foreman, wrote a letter on July 21, 1944, to WC Clouston inquiring about Ethan's fate after he and his crew were posted as missing on operations. The response, dated August 14, came from WC A. B. Matthews, who was replying on behalf of the air officer commanding, RCAF Overseas Headquarters. It read:

> Your letter addressed to the Officer Commanding, RAF Air Station, St. Eval, concerning FO E. Allen, DFC, has been passed to this office for a reply. I regret to advise you that FO Allen was reported missing as a result of air operations on the night of 6/7 June 1944. He was a captain of an aircraft which took off on the night of the 6th of June, to carry out an anti-submarine patrol in the English Channel and failed to return. No news has since been received concerning him, or any other members of the crew, however, inquiries are being made through all available sources and it is hoped that better news may be forthcoming. Please accept my deepest sympathy with you in your great anxiety.

Allen and his crew were lost off the coast of Normandy, France. Ethan's young wife was notified a year later that her husband's classification had been changed from that of MIA to that of Killed In Action (KIA). At the time of the notification, she was living at 215 South Normandie Avenue in Los Angeles. Allen's death was then registered by the RCAF with the Province of Quebec's Vital Statistics Branch.

The 11 crew members of BZ942 have no known graves. Their names are commemorated on Panel 244 at the Runnymede Memorial in Surrey, England. They are listed as follows:

FO E. Allen, Captain, Pilot – RCAF
FO M. N. Hayward, 2nd Pilot – RCAF
FL W. J. Esler, Navigator –RAAF
PO H. E. Pugsley, Navigator – RAF
FL L. R. Aust, Wireless Operator/Air Gunner – RAF
WO H. McIlaney, Wireless Operator/Air Gunner – RAF
Sergeant D. E. Froggart, Wireless Operator/Air Gunner – RAF
Sergeant J. A. Mitchell, Wireless Operator/Air Gunner – RAF
Sergeant A. McLaughlin, Air Gunner – RAF
Sergeant J. B. C. Gray, Air Gunner – RAF
Sergeant A. R. Croft, Flight Engineer – RAF

Charles Anderson
No Longer Missing

Captain Charles Frederick "Andy" Anderson flew with many gregarious characters and personalities that made up the famous 4th FG, USAAF, in World War II. He was not, however, one of the 4th's "media darlings" that the war correspondents were always chasing after and interviewing for articles for the folks back home. No, Andy was a quiet unassuming fellow who, without any fanfare, just went to work each day and did his job.

When Anderson went missing on Wednesday, April 19, 1944, over central Germany, no one knew for sure what happened to him. Flying a P-51B Mustang with the 335th FS, it was believed that he had gone down somewhere over Belgium as he attempted to return alone to his army air force station located 40 miles north of London, England.

The day prior to Andy's disappearance, April 18, the 335th suffered a huge blow when its popular CO and leading ace, Major George "Carp" Carpenter from Oil City, Pennsylvania, was downed on a mission to Berlin. Carpenter was Anderson's friend and the pair had teamed up at the beginning of 1944 to destroy almost three dozen German aircraft between them. Carp was captured after bailing out, but his Prisoner of War (PoW) status was unknown to the other 4th pilots back at Debden and, in particular, to a very concerned Captain Anderson.

On the day Andy was lost, Captain Mike Sobanski led the group to Eschwege, Germany, on a target withdrawal support mission from 0815 to 1250hrs. At 1023hrs and northeast of Eschwege, it joined up with five combat wings of Boeing B-17 Flying Fortresses flying at 24,000ft. Two minutes later, more than 50 enemy fighters attacked the rear boxes of bombers, ripping through the formations in groups of six and eight. The 4th bounced and fought the Germans from 25,000ft to the deck, claiming six. When it formed up to go home, Captain Anderson was missing. No one had seen him go down and no one heard him call over the radio.

Charles F. Anderson was born to Hardy and Ottlie Anderson on March 31, 1919, at Crab Orchard, Kentucky. In 1923, Hardy Anderson moved his young family, which also included a daughter, Doris, to Gary, Indiana, where he found steady work as a carpenter.

Andy attended Lew Wallace Grade School and Lew Wallace High School from 1926 to 1937. In his last three years of high school, Anderson served in the ROTC working his way up the rank structure from private to 2nd lieutenant in "D" Company. After graduation, Andy went to work locally as an apprentice machinist at the Carnegie Steel Company from June 1937 to September 1940. Leaving Indiana for a better paying job in California, Andy accepted a position as a machinist with the Menasco Manufacturing Company in Burbank, remaining there until August 12, 1941. Building aircraft engines was challenging enough, but it did not satisfy his personal belief that he should be contributing to the European war effort in a more direct manner.

Packing his bags, he spent the next several days leisurely traveling north up the Pacific Coast Highway to No. 1 Recruiting Centre in Vancouver, British Columbia, where he voluntarily enlisted in the RCAF as an AC2. The date was August 21, 1941. Anderson, then aged 22, told the air force recruiter he wanted to be a fighter pilot. Before leaving for Canada, he registered his whereabouts with Selective Service Board No. 200, which was located on Whittier Boulevard in Los Angeles.

FO L. H. Eyres at the recruiting center conducted Anderson's interview and recorded the following: "An American candidate of good appearance. Manner courteous. Has mechanical experience. Keen on flying. Recommended for pilot or observer."

Sent to No. 2 MD in Brandon, Manitoba, on August 22, Andy remained there until being posted to No. 5 Bombing & Gunnery School in Dafoe, Saskatchewan, on October 11. There he performed guard duty until November 23. The next day, he began his pilot training on Course No. 41 at No. 2 ITS in Regina, Saskatchewan.

A notice from the Selective Service Board followed Anderson from Los Angeles to Dafoe, advising him that he was classified as 2-B and could be drafted for service anytime within the next 18 months. This prompted FO McBeth at No. 5 to reply to them on Andy's behalf with the following letter: "For your information, AC2 Charles Frederick Anderson, Service No. R. 122455, enlisted in the RCAF on August 21, 1941. It is understood that particulars were taken and forwarded to your branch at the time of his enlistment, but subsequent correspondence between the airman and his parents has brought about the request that you officially be advised to this effect directly from this Air Station."

On December 5, 1941, Andy was observed breaking out of the barracks at No. 2 after roll call at 2215hrs. He also was observed breaking back into the barracks at 0150hrs on the morning of December 6. He was absent three hours and 35 minutes. For punishment, he was confined to barracks for the next seven days. Seems Andy met a local girl and had a date that evening that could not be broken.

Anderson graduated from No. 2 on January 14, 1942, with a 73 percent average. The school's CO wrote the following in his file: "This man showed up well on course. Has worked hard and stands 96th in a class of 136 students. Has been a machinist in civilian life in the aircraft industry and has a good sense of responsibility. Posted to No. 19 EFTS at Virden, Manitoba. To report there by February 1, 1942."

Promoted to LAC, Anderson flew 69.5 hours on de Havilland Tiger Moths at Virden, graduating on March 26 with a passing mark of 72 percent. The CFI recommended that his training be continued, but only on single engine aircraft. His written comments were as follows: "Slow to learn but thorough, keen, tries hard. Conscientious, no bad flying faults. Instrument flying average. Deportment and punctuality good."

Andy was posted to No. 13 SFTS at Saint-Hubert, Quebec, on April 12. He had only a few hours of instruction on Harvard Mk IIs on Course No. 53 when a virulent case of pneumonia put him in the station hospital for the next four weeks.

Falling significantly behind his fellow classmates, the air force transferred him to upcoming Course No. 55.

On May 11, the joint Canadian–American transfer train, traveling across Canada from east to west, stopped in Montreal. The goal was to repatriate American-born RCAF-trained airmen into a US military service. Anderson, who had just been released from the hospital, traveled from No. 13 to Montreal where he was interviewed by representatives of the USAAF and the United States Navy (USN). Both services rejected his application for pilot training on the grounds that he was, by their standards, medically unfit. They encouraged Andy to continue his RCAF training and when he had fully regained his health, they would take a second look at his transfer application.

On May 22, Andy violated an RCAF regulation and, as punishment, was confined to barracks for the next three days. On his general conduct sheet it read: "Neglect to the prejudice of good order and air force discipline."

Then, on June 5, while flying a Harvard coded 2653 along with his

Captain Charles F. Anderson poses with his Republic P-47C Thunderbolt *Hell's Belle* in 1943. (US Department of Defense)

instructor, PO K. S. Sleep, they damaged the aircraft at Chambly Basin, Quebec, when they hit a tree while making a precautionary landing in a field.

Anderson's next misstep was to report late for parade at 0745hrs on June 29. For this infraction, he received five days confined to barracks and three hours of pack drill!

On August 28, with 188.4 hours on Harvards in his logbook, Andy passed out of the course with a 68.1 average. He was given a pay raise and promoted from LAC to SP.

Sailing from Pier 21, Halifax, Nova Scotia, on September 25, 1942, Anderson arrived in England on October 8 and immediately went to No. 3 Personnel Reception Centre in Bournemouth.

Assigned to No. 17 Pilot Advanced Flying Unit, RAF Station, Calveley, Andy flew Miles Masters and Hawker Hurricanes from October 20 to December 21. The next day he was sent to No. 56 OTU, RAF Tealing, Scotland. Enrolled in Course No. 54, Anderson continued his conversion training on Masters and Hurricanes, flying 55.45 additional hours until March 17, 1943. In air-to-air gunnery exercises, he fired 3,750 rounds and on air-to-ground training sorties he fired 1,505 rounds. In airmanship, armament, meteorology, navigation and signals, Anderson's passing grade was 72 percent. In general, applied, instrument and night flying he managed a score of 73 percent.

The Tealing WC recorded: "Good average. Keen and reliable. Has plenty of dash and initiative combined with a good sense of responsibility. Recommended for a commission."

When in England, Andy reapplied to join the USAAF, and this time was accepted. He formally requested that he be released from the RCAF and was honorably discharged from that service on March 24, after having served one year and 216 days.

With overseas flight allowances, SP Anderson was making CAN$157.50 monthly. Since April 1942, he had directed that $22.00 of his pay be sent every month to his mother and father, who resided at 3835 Pennsylvania Street in Gary, Indiana.

Joining the USAAF as an FO, Andy reported to Station No. 342 Atcham located in Shropshire. Known as the Combat Crew Replacement Centre, this unit flew Spitfires and P-39 Airacobras in the fighter training role. As an Air Corps officer, Andy's pay jumped almost US$150 a month over and above what he had previously been earning. He also had the protection of a $10,000 life insurance policy paid for by the US government, which was not available to RCAF or RAF aircrew.

Just as Andy was finishing the three-month course at Atcham, the 4th FG flew its last operational Spitfire mission and began converting to the Republic P-47 Thunderbolt. After completing the Spitfire/P-39 course, Anderson then had to tackle the P-47 conversion, which explains the five-month time lag between his resigning from the RCAF on March 24, 1943, and joining the 335th on August 11. During the eight months Andy served in the 4th, he received three promotions from FO to 2nd lieutenant to 1st lieutenant and, finally, to captain.

Anderson and Carpenter's combined destruction of 33.33 German aircraft (air and ground) was accomplished in only a few weeks beginning early in 1944. Between January 30 and April 12, 1944, Anderson's score was 10.5 aerial and 5.5 ground, for a total of 16. Carpenter, from February 22 to April 18, 1944, had 13.33 aerial and four ground, for a total of 17.33. These two were the second-best scoring duo at the 4th, surpassed only by Captains Don Gentile and John Godfrey.

The following is Anderson's personal combat report for April 12, 1944:

Time 1410 hours
Location 10 Miles Northwest of Brunswick, Germany
Two Bf 109s Destroyed in the Air, 1 Ju 88 Damaged on the Ground

I was flying Greenbelt White 3 when White section went down on a bounce northwest of Brunswick. White Leader (Carpenter) dropped his tanks and attacked the No. 4 aircraft in a section of 4 109's who were flying line astern at 8,000'. I attacked the No. 3 aircraft and as he started to turn left I fired. I saw only one strike which was right in his cockpit. He more or less fell off on his left wing and did a spiral dive into the ground. Upon hitting the deck he did not explode but the aircraft broke up into many small pieces and a large cloud of black smoke rose 300 to 400 feet into the air. I then went after their No. 2 man which had by this time split. While firing at him I saw his leader coming at me from my 9 o'clock position. I could see that he was not getting deflection so I did not break off from the attack. I believe the No. 1 aircraft was trying to ram me as he passed about 5 or 10 feet behind my tail. I saw many strikes on No. 2 and he started streaming glycol from his starboard radiator. At this time his No. 1 got behind me and started firing but was still pulling no deflection. As he began closing I tightened my turn for a few seconds until Major Carpenter attacked him and made him break off. I then went back to No. 2 and fired one more. He pulled up to about 5,000 feet and bailed out. His aircraft crashed and exploded. We reformed the section and rejoined the group. As the bombers did not show up we went down and strafed the airdrome at Volkenrode. I fired at a Junkers Ju 88 bomber on the ground and saw many strikes. Since I saw no flames I can only claim this aircraft damaged. The return fire from this drome was quite heavy so we only made one pass.

Aircraft P-51B 10NA 43-7181
Ammunition Used – 665 Rounds .50 Caliber API and T.
Charles F. Anderson
1st Lt US Air Corps.

In a letter dated April 26, 1946, Anderson's father was notified by USAAF headquarters in Washington that his son was indeed killed in combat on April 19, 1944, but not in Belgium as was recorded. The wreckage of his crashed Mustang (serial number 43-7181 coded WD-L) was found in the heavily forested area of Hoher Meissner near Kassel, Germany. The letter, signed by Brigadier General Leon W. Johnson, Chief of the Personnel Services Division, went on to say that Captain Charles F. Anderson was positively identified by German authorities by means of his identification tags.

Captain Anderson was the 4th's only casualty that day and was shot down east of Kassel at 1055hrs from a height of 300ft by Luftwaffe ace Leutnant Franz Schwaiger, Staffelkapitan of 1./JG 3.

Schwaiger, a veteran of the North African and Russian campaigns, had been recalled from the Eastern Front to help defend the German fatherland. Commissioned from the ranks, he had replaced the fallen previous Staffelkaptain, Hans Frese. Five days after bringing down Anderson, Schwaiger, who had run his score to 67 victories, was dead. In a fight with American P-51s from the 355th and 357th FGs, Schwaiger attempted to leave the battle area due to low fuel. Pursued by several Mustangs, he led them on a low-level rat race across the countryside until he ran out of gas. Witnesses state he safely belly-landed his Bf 109G-5 "White 5" (Werk No. 110 682) in a large field north of Augsburg. As he unstrapped and attempted to exit his relatively undamaged fighter, one of the trailing P-51s strafed and killed him.

Andy, unfortunately, never made it out of Germany that fateful day in April 1944 and fell where the fight began. Newly promoted, he had only worn his captain's bars for six days. The information relating to his final fate lay undisturbed in his file in Washington and Ottawa until the author uncovered the facts 79 years after his death.

Duane Beeson
Idaho Mustang Ace

I was flying Pectin White 1 and, as we made a starboard turn near Hanover, Germany, we sighted a box of bombers west of us. As we approached, we could see that they were under attack and I saw several bombers going down, one of them in flames, another minus a wing. P-38s could be seen circling above and around the bomber formation. There were many enemy aircraft around and then a Bf 109 made a head-on pass through our squadron, circling around behind as though to come in again, so I turned after him. He dove to 12,000 feet and as I started to close on him, he suddenly pulled up into a steep climb, so I opened up everything and went after him. I closed slightly at first then I fell back a little between 15,000 and 18,000 feet where I operated the second blower manually to get full boost and was able to close again. In range, I fired and got good strikes on him; he began to smoke and dove for the cloud at 6,000 feet. I got on his tail as he came out of cloud and clobbered him again, but he stuck to his airplane and crash-landed in a field. I strafed the aircraft on the ground but as I came around again, I saw the engine beginning to flame and the pilot getting out of the cockpit. He ran very fast across the field and hid behind a fence post as I came over again.

Climbed to cloud level and saw a Bf 109 flying with its wheels down so I turned after him but he went into the cloud. Saw tracers going past my port wing so I made a quick break to starboard and saw another 109 behind. He pulled up into cloud and as I came around in the turn, he dove down, allowing me to get on his tail. Fired short bursts and saw many flashes. He jettisoned his hood so I fired again, got more strikes and oil from his aircraft covered my windscreen. The pilot bailed out at about 1,000 feet but the chute did not open, his aircraft crashed nearby and burst into flames.

I then made a pass at a freight train and got good strikes on the locomotive. I claim two Bf 109s destroyed and 1 locomotive damaged.

Combat report of D. W. Beeson, USAAC
Ammunition used: 935 rounds
Date: March 23, 1944 – Position: East of Münster, Germany

Major Duane Willard "Bee" Beeson hailed from Boise, Idaho. Born there on July 16, 1921, to Carl and Zelda Beeson, he was the eldest of four siblings and their only son. He honored his birthplace by naming his Republic P-47D Thunderbolt fighter *Boise Bee*. The artwork on the aircraft's nose was that of a bumble bee dressed in flight gear, holding two six-shooters while standing on a cloud. He had the emblem of a bumble bee sewn on the front of his leather flying helmet just below the word "Bee." *Bee* was also the name of his last assigned aircraft, a P-51B Mustang, which he flew with the 334th FS, 4th FG, USAAF.

In World War II, the 4th produced a total of 81 aces and, in overall scoring within this group, Major Beeson ranks No. 6 with 24.08 victories (19.33 air and 4.75 ground). He was one of the deadliest fighter pilots in the ETO. His score, no doubt, would have been higher had he not been shot down by flak while strafing Gardelegen airdrome in Germany on April 5, 1944. The famed 4th commander, Colonel Donald J. M. "Horseback Leader" Blakeslee said, "Duane Beeson was the most determined pilot we had."

Growing up, Beeson took piano lessons and loved to listen to classical music. While attending Boise High School, he played the trumpet and was a platoon bugler in ROTC. He was on the debate team and took an active part in speech club functions. He was also a member of the boxing club and played football. After school, he liked

to hang out with his classmates at Tillotson's where they would eat burgers, drink malted milk shakes and listen to big band music on the juke box. When he graduated from Boise High School in June 1939, he told his buddies that he was headed to the west coast and hoped to attend the University of California's Law School. He had an aunt who lived in Oakland and the plan was to stay with her while he worked his way through school. To save money, he set out hitchhiking, and a few miles outside of Boise, he got a ride that took him all the way to San Francisco. Beeson found work

High-scoring 4th FG ace Captain Duane W. Beeson climbs into his Republic P-47C Thunderbolt at Debden, England, in 1943. (US Department of Defense)

in Oakland as a spring oiler with the National Motor Bearing Company, then as a salesman with the Cranwell Publishing Company, and, finally, as a desk clerk and a bell boy in two Oakland hotels – the San Pablo and the Piedmont. He worked nights at the hotels and the plan was to go to school during the day.

As the war broadened, he knew that it would not be long before the US was swept up in the fray. Beeson wanted to be a fighter pilot, but he was not prepared to stay in school just to meet the prewar USAAC requirement of having a minimum of two years of college.

The Battle of Britain had been fought in the summer and early fall of 1940 and the exploits of those dashing RAF flyers had been well chronicled in every newspaper, magazine and movie theater newsreel in the US. After making some inquiries, Beeson learned that he could join the RCAF as a pilot trainee, as he had the necessary qualifications to meet the entry requirements.

One month shy of his 20th birthday, he traveled up the Pacific Coast Highway to No. 1 Recruiting Centre in Vancouver, British Columbia, where he voluntarily enlisted. The date was June 23, 1941. His assigned service number was R. 110106 and his rank was that of an AC2.

Over the next several months, Beeson was at the following training establishments: No. 2 MD at Brandon, Manitoba, June 23 to July 26, 1941; and No. 4 ITS at Edmonton, Alberta, July 27 to September 12. On his last day at No. 4, he was promoted to LAC.

On September 12, he began his pilot training at No. 6 EFTS at Prince Albert, Saskatchewan, on de Havilland Tiger Moth biplane trainers. He successfully passed this course on November 7, after accumulating 73.55 flying hours on type.

Beeson reported to No. 11 SFTS at Yorkton, Saskatchewan, on November 8, where he would learn to fly the twin-engined Cessna Crane. On February 27, 1942, and after having flown 127.30 hours on type, he was promoted to SP and was awarded his pilot wings in a graduation ceremony. However, before he had a chance to sew on his sergeant stripes, he was commissioned later that day as a PO and was assigned new Service No. J. 10522.

Duane W. Beeson's three younger sisters were Esther, Louise, and Elizabeth. In a 1978 interview, Elizabeth said, "His first visit home after joining Canada's air force was one of the proudest times of my life. He looked so handsome in his officer's uniform. Nothing he did in the future could beat that."

Having enjoyed the standard two-week pre-embarkation leave, Beeson reported to Pier 21 "Y" Depot, Halifax, Nova Scotia, where he boarded a troop ship leaving for England on March 20, 1942. From March 30 to May 18, he was at No. 3 Personnel Reception Centre in Bournemouth.

On May 19, he reported to No. 5 Pilot Advanced Flying Unit, Ternhill, Shropshire, for training on Miles Masters and Hawker Hurricanes, remaining there until June 8. On June 9, he was sent to No. 55 OTU at Annan, Dumfrieshire, Scotland, where he also flew Masters and Hurricanes.

Completing the course, Beeson was posted to No. 71 RAF Eagle Squadron at Debden, Essex, on September 6.

His request for severance from the RCAF in order to join the USAAF was honorably granted on September 22 in London, England. Beeson joined the USAAF as a 2nd lieutenant one day after resigning his Canadian commission.

Seven days later, on September 29, 1942, the three American Eagle Squadrons of RAF Fighter Command were disbanded and transferred – lock, stock, and barrel – to the USAAF: 71 Squadron became the 334th FS; 121 became the 335th FS; and 133 became the 336th FS.

These three squadrons came together as the 4th FG under the umbrella of the mighty 8th Air Force, specifically 8th Air Force Fighter Command.

An earlier attempt by Beeson to join the "Debden Eagles" was not successful. Prior to becoming the 4th commander, Don Blakeslee was the 336th squadron commander. Beeson was finishing up his Spitfire conversion training and had come in for an interview. Blakeslee said, "Beeson didn't appear to me to be a fighter pilot. He didn't seem to be the type. So I said we didn't have any vacancies. But in the long run he ended up at the 4th and every time he got drunk, he'd come over to me and say, 'And you said I wasn't a fighter pilot'. He turned out to be a real tiger".

On November 6, 1942, Beeson was ordered to take an overhauled 334th Spitfire up for a flight and test fire its guns. Having not seen any action and being a little bored, he flew across the Channel and tested them on some German trucks parked near a coastal gun emplacement at Knocke, Belgium. He torched his targets but return antiaircraft artillery fire peppered his aircraft with shell fragments! When he returned to Debden, he sheepishly explained to his superiors that no precise order had been given as to exactly where he was supposed to test the guns!

When the 4th reluctantly converted from its much-loved Supermarine Spitfires to the Republic Thunderbolt, many pilots in the group did not like the 7-ton, coke bottle-shaped P-47. The Spitfires Vbs were lighter and far more maneuverable and the only benefit the Thunderbolt conversion offered was a little extra range. In fact, Colonel Blakeslee hated the P-47 to such an extent that he could not wait to get rid of it.

While his fellow pilots were operating in a "state of funk," Beeson used the P-47 to good effect, knocking down German aircraft with great regularity! As a result, he became the 334th's gunnery officer on September 25, 1943, and the group gunnery officer two months later. From early December 1943 to mid-January 1944, Beeson undertook a six-week course at the Pilot Gunnery Instructor Training Wing at the RAF's Central Gunnery School at Sutton Bridge, Lincolnshire.

Beeson was a diminutive fellow with big hands and wrists. He had the bodily architecture of a boy not quite grown. His manner was aggressive, and he was intense to the point of fretfulness. He was fastidious and painstaking in everything he did and not even one comma of his combat reports could be altered by his intelligence officer, Captain Ben Ezzell, unless Bee first gave his permission.

Bee shared the distinction of becoming the group's first ace with Major Roy William Evans, when both downed aircraft on a ramrod penetration support mission to Cloppenburg, Oldenburg, Bremen, Germany, on October 8, 1943. Beeson destroyed two Bf 109s that day, bringing his total to six and Evans downed an Fw 190, bringing his total to five. The 4th had its first two heroes and the ace race within the group was on!

Beeson would bore in very close to his aerial adversaries before he would open fire – on average it was 50–75 yards! Most of his victories were when he was flying the Thunderbolt and, at that close range, very few could escape the withering fire from his P-47's eight Colt-Browning M-2 .50 caliber machine guns. Beeson wanted to make certain that when his opponents went down, they stayed down. His aircraft's gun camera combat films were both a source of inspiration and entertainment for the other 4th pilots. Many would cringe when they viewed them for it appeared that Bee would actually collide with the enemy before he destroyed them.

As Beeson's personal score increased, promotions quickly followed: promoted to 1st lieutenant on April 23, 1943; promoted to captain, February 6, 1944; and promoted to major and CO of the 334th FS, March 15, 1944.

After flying in excess of 150 combat missions over an 18-month period, Major Beeson was brought down by airfield flak at 1600hrs on April 5, 1944, while flying his personal P-51B Mustang *Bee*, serial number 43-6819, coded QP-B. He describes that mission:

> Our group was strafing aerodromes near Berlin. We left one drome behind with many burning Ju 88s on the ground when we sighted another and went in to attack. There were five Ju 88s parked wing tip to wing tip along the perimeter track so I opened fire on them. The first one burst into flames and there were strikes all over the others. I picked out a big-assed Me 323 six-engined heavy transport to shoot at next. Just as I opened fire and began to see some results, some orange "Golf-Ball" sized tracers flashed past my cockpit and my kite was hit! The engine was running rough so I climbed to 1000 feet then it seized up tight. I tried to get it running again, but had no such luck so I decided to get out. My altitude was down to two hundred feet when I finally shoved the stick forward and bunted my way out of the aircraft. The chute opened just in time to carry me over a fence and deposit my carcass in a field surrounded by many members of the 'super race' including 1 blonde fräulein on a bicycle!

Major Beeson immediately became a PoW and was imprisoned in Stalag Luft 1 in Barth, Germany, along with 8,938 other Allied airmen.

Frustrated at having missed out on D-Day, he called a German guard a "Hun" and was placed in solitary confinement for several days. His internment lasted one year in room 24, south barrack five, which he shared with one French and three British officers. The advancing Russian army, on its way to Berlin, liberated this camp on May 1, 1945. A few days later, the PoWs were flown on B-17s to a tent rehabilitation camp in France for processing.

Major Beeson returned to Boise in June 1945. He was the hometown hero, and a big fuss was made over him everywhere he went. He attended social functions, dances, and spoke at practically every service club meeting in town. But through it all, he just wanted to get back into combat and made every effort to be reassigned, but the war in the Pacific ended before that could happen.

Beeson had thoughts of returning to college to study law but decided on a career in the air force at war's end. He was granted a permanent commission in the peacetime USAAF and was promoted to lieutenant colonel on November 12, 1945, at the young of 24.

While stationed in Sarasota, Florida, he met a secretary named Tracey Waters. They were married in her hometown of Baltimore, Maryland, on January 25, 1946.

Lieutenant Colonel Beeson took a jet conversion course at Williams Army Airfield in Chandler, Arizona, and was posted to 9th Air Force Headquarters in Greenville, South Carolina, where he flew Lockheed F-80C Shooting Stars.

It was there in early 1947 that he suddenly fell ill and was diagnosed as having a brain tumor. He was scheduled to have an operation at Walter Reed Army Hospital but died on February 13, 1947, just as the Douglas C-54 transport that was carrying him landed in Washington. He was buried on February 19 with full military honors in Section 11 Site 34 in Arlington National Cemetery. He was just 26 years of age.

Lieutenant Colonel Beeson's date of birth is incorrectly inscribed on his headstone. It reads 1922, whereas it should read 1921. In her grief, Beeson's young widow inadvertently gave the wrong information to officials and that error has never been corrected.

In November 1993, the city of Boise honored its native son when it named the new terminal building at the Boise airport the Duane W. Beeson Air Terminal.

Noted warbird restorer John Paul of Nampa, Idaho, restored an early P-51 bird cage model Mustang to flying condition, which is painted and dedicated to Duane Beeson's memory.

Hipolitus Biel
Minnesota Mustang Ace

The German Fw 190 pilot felt the concussion as half-inch armor-piercing, high-explosive and incendiary machine gun rounds slammed into his aircraft. He could not shake the persistent American, who was chasing him across rooftops and around the church steeple over this small town near Gifhorn, Germany, from his tail. It was Wednesday, March 29, 1944, and the time was 1330hrs.

The determined American was 28-year-old 1st Lieutenant Hipolitus Thomas "Tom" Biel. Biel had two aerial victories to his credit and his intent was to make sure this Luftwaffe fighter would be his third! Tom was flying a P-51B Mustang, coded QP-T, from the 334th FS, 4th FG, USAAF.

1st Lieutenant Biel closed to 200 yards, triggered a short burst that started a fire under the enemy fighter, his tracer rounds igniting the 190's center line on the external fuel tank. The German pilot then ducked into a snow squall, hoping to evade his American pursuer. Biel was not about to let him escape and plunged into the snowstorm in full pursuit. The two adversaries emerged into clear air on the other side of the squall, practically flying beside each other! For a few moments, they looked each other over, then Biel slid his Mustang in behind his quarry and opened up at point-blank range, inflicting heavy damage to his opponent's cockpit area. Thinking that he must be dead, Biel pulled alongside and was utterly amazed to see the other pilot staring at him. Tom dropped back a second time and poured a withering burst from his four Colt-Browning .50 caliber MG53-2 heavy machine guns into the severely damaged, but still flying, 190. Now the enemy fighter was on fire from nose to tail. The German popped off his canopy in an effort to leave but was too low to safely bail out. Biel again pulled up alongside and flew wingman to his victim right down to ground level as this skilled Luftwaffe pilot made a perfect, wheels up, belly landing in the snow-covered field. Tom could not stick around to see if this lucky German flyer exited his burning fighter, as his P-51 was attracting accurate ground fire, so he prudently decided to leave.

Hipolitus Thomas "Tom" Biel was born on July 28, 1916, in St. Paul, Minnesota. His parents, Edward and Agnes Biel, had immigrated to the United States from southern Poland. Tom was the second of five children and their only son.

His father worked as a marble polisher and his mother was a homemaker and a part-time butcher. Economically, they were considered a poor family. Poland is predominantly Catholic and Polish families often name their children after Polish saints. The feast day for Polish Saint Hipolit was August 13 and, as it was closest to Tom's birthday, it was decided to name him Hipolitus, which is the English translation of the name. Tom hated his given name, and for years children unmercifully teased him and called him "Hippo." He was a protective brother to his four sisters – Estelle, Eleanor, Elizabeth, and Theresa – but, being a very private person, he seldom disclosed details of his personal life with his family.

4th FG ace 1st Lieutenant Hipolitus T. Biel is pictured in his P-51B Mustang in the spring of 1944 at Debden, England. (US Department of Defense)

Hipolitus Biel: Minnesota Mustang Ace

His sisters say he was a bit of a rogue when he was young and, for a time, he was a member of a gang. That membership got him into many fights and, after his nose had been broken several times, it had to be surgically corrected. He graduated from Cretin High School, a Jesuit military academy, in 1935. Tom attended the College of St. Thomas (now the University of St. Thomas) from September 9, 1935, to June 4, 1936, studying in the liberal arts program. He worked for First National Bank and dabbled in local politics, campaigning for, but losing, an election to be a Justice of the Peace in the 6th Ward.

He had always loved airplanes and applied to the USAAC to become a cadet in its pilot training program. He was not accepted at that time because the prewar air corps had very strict entry guidelines.

Lesser restrictions applied in the RCAF. A massive recruiting program was underway to train and equip a large air force as Canada had been at war with Germany since September 10, 1939. Days after celebrating his 25th birthday, Biel traveled from the family home at 88 East Belvedere Street in St. Paul to No. 6 Recruiting Centre in Winnipeg, Manitoba, where, on August 5, 1941, he enlisted as an AC2. His assigned Regimental Service No. was R. 123557.

From August 5 to December 20, 1941, he was at the following RCAF training establishments: No. 2 MD at Penhold Alberta; No. 3 MD at Edmonton, Alberta; No. 3 SFTS at Calgary, Alberta; and No. 2 ITS at Regina, Saskatchewan.

On December 21, Biel began flight training on de Havilland Tiger Moth biplane trainers at No. 19 EFTS at Virden, Manitoba. The day prior he had been promoted to LAC. He graduated from Virden on March 14, 1942, after having flown 69 hours and 15 minutes on the 145shp Moths.

The next phase of his pilot training took him to No. 2 SFTS, Uplands Ottawa, Ontario, to fly the 5,300lb, 550shp Harvard.[1] One of Tom's instructors at No. 2 was a fellow American, who hailed from Littlefield, Texas. SP Gerald Emerson "Monty" Montgomery and LAC Tom Biel would later serve together in the 334th FS and would become very good friends – Montgomery as a major and Biel as a 1st lieutenant.

After having accumulated 179.2 flight hours on Harvards, LAC Biel became SP Biel and was awarded his RCAF pilot wings in a graduation ceremony on July 24, 1942. Tom took his two-week pre-embarkation leave from July 10–23. He reported to "Y" Depot, Pier 21, Halifax, Nova Scotia, on the 25th. His troop ship left Halifax

---

1 One of the Harvard Mk IIs (3039) that Tom Biel flew at No. 2 SFTS regularly flies today as a restored warbird with the Canadian Harvard Aircraft Association from the Tillsonburg airport in Ontario. Biel flew 3039 solo seven times in May–June 1942. This aircraft was manufactured under license by Noorduyn Aviation in Montreal, Quebec, and entered RCAF service on May 3, 1941. Besides serving at No. 2, it was also stationed at No. 6 SFTS Dunnville, Ontario; No. 16 SFTS Hagersville, Ontario; and with the Royal Canadian Navy at Shearwater, Nova Scotia, from June 1955 until the end of its military service career on November 25, 1960.

on August 6 and arrived in England on the 18th. For the next ten days, Biel was at No. 3 Personnel Reception Centre in Bournemouth. This is where the newly arrived Canadian-trained aircrews had a few days to acclimatize themselves to the British money system, travel procedures, and perhaps some local customs.

Tom's advanced flying and operational training took place from August 29, 1942, to March 7, 1943, at the following RAF stations: No. 5 Pilot Advanced Flying Unit, Ternhill and Calveley, August 29 to September 22, flying Miles Master Is, IIIs and early model Hawker Hurricanes; No. 57 OTU, Hawarden, Wales, September 23 to November 2, flying Miles Master Is and Supermarine Spitfires; No. 58 OTU, Grangemouth and Balado Bridge, Scotland, November 3, 1942, to March 7, 1943, flying Miles Master Is, IIIs and Supermarine Spitfires.

The assessment of his ability as a pilot and of his air gunnery skills were rated above average.

In order for Biel to join the USAAF, he first had to be released from the RCAF. On March 24, 1943, the Overseas Headquarters of the RCAF in London, England, honorably discharged SP Biel, citing that he had served one year and 234 days. His combined flying time stood at 343 hours and 45 minutes.

Between March 25 and April 16, he joined the USAAF as an FO. His logbook shows him at the Combat Crew Replacement Centre at Station 342, Atcham, Shropshire, on April 17. He remained there until September 3, converting to American flying procedures and aircraft. While at Atcham, he flew Piper Cubs, Spitfire Vbs, Master IIIs and Republic P-47C and D Thunderbolts.

On September 7, 1943, Biel joined the 334th FS, 4th FG, based at Station F-356 Debden, located two miles southeast of the village of Saffron Walden, Essex. He was promoted to 2nd lieutenant in January 1944 and to 1st lieutenant in February.

Tom flew combat with the 4th for just over seven months, destroying 11.333 German aircraft (5.333 aerial and six on the ground). His list of aerial victories was:

January 14, 1944 – Fw 190
February 10, 1944 – Bf 109
March 29, 1944 – Fw 190
April 5, 1944 – 1/3 of a Ju 88 shared with Beeson and Fieldler
April 11, 1944 – Me 110 and Me 410

On April 24, 1944, the 4th FG commander, Colonel Donald J. M. Blakeslee, led a freelance support mission to Munich, Germany, from 1055 to 1520hrs. The group arrived over Frankfurt at 1233hrs at 18,000ft, turned south and let down to 10,000ft. Just north of Worms, a combined force of 34 Fw 190s and Bf 109s was spotted heading down the Rhine river. Opposing the 4th were two Staffels from Jagdgeschwader (JG) 2. 1./JG 2 was flying Fw 190A-7s and 2./JG 2 was flying Bf 109G-6s.

All three squadrons of the 4th (334th, 335th and 336th) engaged the enemy at 1245hrs. When the battle was over, the 4th had lost three Mustangs, but in the exchange it had destroyed 16 German fighters. Two 335th pilots – 2nd Lieutenant Milton G. Scarbrough and 1st Lieutenant Paul Sidney "Rip" Riley – were shot down and became PoWs. 1st Lieutenant Hipolitus Thomas "Tom" Biel was killed in aerial combat at 1300hrs while flying a P-51B Mustang coded QP-I. Tom was shot down from a height of 6,000ft by Unteroffizier Krauss of 2./JG 2, who was flying a Bf 109G-6.

Months after Biel's death, Major Montgomery wrote a letter to the family after he had returned home to Texas. He described how, in Tom's last fight, they were separated and the last time he saw him, a Bf 109's cannon and machine gun rounds had set Biel's plane on fire, and it was falling out of control. Monty was unable to go to his aid as he was busy outmaneuvering some Germans who were trying to shoot him down! He went on to say that he was unable to give the family any ray of hope for Tom's survival. He said his very good friend died a brave fighting man.

Another letter found its way to the family in St. Paul, this one from England from a young lady claiming to be Tom's steady girlfriend. She said they planned to be married and they even had a joint bank account. The family, unaware of this relationship and still reeling from the news of his death, did not respond and her name and address were subsequently lost over time.

The wreckage of his aircraft was not discovered for several years. Biel's remains were returned to the US where, on February 17, 1949, he was interned in Calvary Cemetery in St. Paul, Minnesota.

De Peyster Brown
Battle of Britain Pilot

Britain's wartime Prime Minister, Sir Winston Spencer Churchill, proclaimed the following in a stirring speech on August 20, 1940, when he said: "The gratitude of every home in our island, in our empire, and indeed throughout the world, except in the abodes of the guilty, goes out to the British airmen who, undaunted by odds, unwearied in their constant challenge and mortal danger, are turning the tide of the world war by their prowess and by their devotion. Never in the field of human conflict was so much owed by so many to so few."

He was, of course, referring to the 2,945 Allied airmen who flew at least one operational sortie as a pilot, observer or air gunner with the RAF Fighter Command during the Battle of Britain. No less than 574 of this number came from other nations aligned to assist the United Kingdom in its darkest hour. Those countries represented were Canada, Poland, Australia, New Zealand, South Africa, France, Czechoslovakia, Belgium, Ireland, United States, Jamaica, Barbados, Rhodesia, British Palestine, and Newfoundland.

De Peyster Douw "Peter" Brown was one of only nine American citizens who fought in that epic aerial confrontation, which raged over the English countryside from July 10 to October 31, 1940.

Brown was born to Samuel Robbins Brown and Rachel Atkinson in Canton, China, on December 12, 1915. He was educated in that country from 1925 to 1933 at the Shanghai and Peking American schools. In 1929, he was a corporal in the junior division of the Shanghai Volunteer Infantry Corps.

Peter moved to the States in 1934 where he attended Trinity College in Hartford, Connecticut. Later, he furthered his education after enrolling at an engineering school in Pittsburgh, Pennsylvania. He graduated with a Bachelor of Science in 1938. In the summer of 1937, he worked as a junior officer for the Grace Steamship Line out of New York City. In 1938, he was employed as a design engineer at the Pittsburgh Forgings Company in Coraopolis, Pennsylvania. During his last two years of college, Brown was also a 2nd lieutenant in the United States Naval Air Service.

World War II was only eight days old when 24-year-old Brown showed up on Saturday, September 9, 1939, at the RCAF No. 12 Recruiting Centre in Ottawa,

Ontario. He brought a great deal to the enlistment process that day; he was a college graduate, had solid military training and had accumulated 249 hours and 31 minutes flying time on USN aircraft. Some of the types he flew were Great Lakes BG-1 Dive-Bombers, Vought SBU-1 Scouts, Curtiss SOC Seagulls and Douglas TBD Devastator Torpedo-Bombers. His ground officer duties while in the navy included security watches, officer of the day, inspections of quarters, mess halls, and other buildings. He was the prime type of candidate the Canadian air force was looking for and they wasted no time in processing him into their service as a Provisional Pilot Officer (PPO) under Regimental Service No. C. 1094.

Peter, who wanted to get in on the action right away, was not prepared to wait for America to join the war effort.

Brown's only brother, Lieutenant Samuel R. Brown, Jr., was serving at the time as a Navy pilot aboard the aircraft carrier USS *Yorktown*.

Peter was sent, on September 16, to the Regina, Saskatchewan Flying Club for refresher pilot training. His military records show that in late October and early November he was attached to RCAF Air Station Trenton, Ontario, for officer training. At the conclusion of that, he was promoted to the rank of FO. On December 10, he moved over to No. 1 SFTS at Camp Borden, Ontario, to fly Harvard and Yale advanced trainers. On March 2, 1940, he was posted to RCAF No. 112 "City of Winnipeg" Army Co-operation Squadron, which was flying Canadian-built Westland Lysanders from Rockcliffe, Ontario.

No. 112 went overseas on June 9, and began flying coastal patrols from RAF Old Sarum, Wiltshire. Brown then spent the month of August flying Hawker Hurricanes and Miles Masters at RAF No. 5 OTU located at Aston Down, Gloucestershire.

On September 2, 1940, he was posted to RCAF No. 1 "City of Westmount" FS, which was based at Northolt, Uxbridge. No. 1 FS was the first Canadian unit to engage the enemy, score victories, suffer casualties and win gallantry awards.

USAAF 1st Lieutenant De Peyster D. Brown is pictured somewhere stateside just after transferring from the RCAF. (US Department of Defense)

On September 27, Brown, piloting a Hurricane Mk I, downed a Luftwaffe Dornier Do 17Z-2 light bomber from Kampfgeschwader (KG) 76. On that same sortie, he shared in the destruction of a German Ju 88 medium bomber from KG 77. On October 5, Peter's aircraft was badly shot up during an encounter with Messerschmitt Bf 109s. Nevertheless, he pursued one of them into a cloud bank and was later given a credit for damage.

Returning to Northolt, he crash-landed his aircraft and luckily sustained no injuries as the plane proceeded to shed its various appendages.

RCAF No.1 FS was renumbered as No. 401 FS at Driffield, Yorkshire, on March 1, 1941.

Serving overseas for ten months, Brown returned to Canada on April 10 for a well-deserved rest.

From May 1941 until May 1942, he served as a staff pilot at the following facilities: RCAF Air Station Rockcliffe; No. 1 Air Navigation School, Rivers, Manitoba; RCAF Armstrong, Ontario; No. 10 SFTS, Dauphin, Manitoba; No. 12 SFTS, Brandon, Manitoba; and No. 8 Repair Depot Winnipeg, Manitoba.

On May 25, 1942, Peter voluntarily separated from the RCAF in order to join the USAAF.

He entered as a 1st lieutenant under Service No. A01699391. Brown remained in the USAF for the next 15 years, retiring as a major in 1957.

On May 28, 1963, Peter Brown was living at 4281 Admirable Drive in Portuguese Bend, California. He requested that RCAF Headquarters in Ottawa forward him his earned World War II service medals. These included the Battle of Britain Clasp attached to the 1939–45 Campaign Star, General Service Medal, Aircrew European Star, Operational Wings and the Canadian Volunteer Service Medal & Clasp.

De Peyster Douw "Peter" Brown passed away in his 75th year on August 3, 1991, in Santa Maria, California.

Kendall Carlson
California Mustang Ace

USAAF Station F-356 in Essex, England, was the home of the famous 4th FG in World War II. Known as the "Debden Eagles," the 4th became the USAAF's highest scoring fighter unit, accounting for 1,016 enemy aircraft destroyed in the air and on the ground. When the 4th was constituted on September 29, 1942, the group's initial cadre of personnel was comprised of RCAF and RAF trained pilots. Those adventure-seeking American volunteers had left the safety of their homes and country and traveled to Canada and England in 1940–41 to help fight Nazi tyranny and aggression.

Britain, Canada, Australia, and New Zealand had been in the war since September 1939. The United States, by maintaining a position of neutrality throughout the first two years of the conflict, did not effectively join the war effort until Monday, December 8, 1941.

The 4th's initial aerial mount was the Supermarine Spitfire Mk Vb. This aircraft was replaced on March 10, 1943, by the Republic Aviation P-47 Thunderbolt. On February 14, 1944, the Thunderbolt was replaced by the Rolls-Royce Merlin-engined NAA P-51B, C, D, and K Mustangs.

Eight of the top ten scorers at the 4th graduated and earned their wings through the RCAF in Canada. They were Colonel D. J. M. Blakeslee, Major J. T. Godfrey, Major J. S. Goodson, Major D. W. Beeson, Major F. W. Glover, Major P. W. McKennon, Major G. E. Montgomery and 1st Lieutenant R. Hofer. Together these eight pilots destroyed 194.66 German aircraft in the air and on the ground. This represented a phenomenal 19 percent of the group's overall total score. The first wholly US-trained pilots did not arrive at the 4th until January 26, 1944.

There were many other RCAF trained fighter pilots who served in the 4th and one of these was Captain Kendall Eugene "Swede" Carlson from Red Bluff, California. Swede was born to Mary Alva Sharp and Otto Ernest Carlson in Red Bluff on July 14, 1919. The family resided in that community at 427 Jefferson Street. Carlson attended the Red Bluff Grammar School from 1925 to 1932, then Red Bluff Union High School from 1932 to 1936. In 1937, he took a one-year commercial course at Heald's Business College in Sacramento, California. Most of the way through high school, Carlson worked part time as a mailing clerk at the *Red Bluff Daily News*. To raise money to go to business college, he worked as a soda fountain clerk at Frank's Creamery on the corner of Oak and Main. In 1937, he helped his parents operate their small family business. For the next three years, Carlson was employed as a bookkeeper and fountain clerk at the Peter Pan outlet in Red Bluff. Beginning in March 1938, Swede learned how to fly and, by the end of 1940, had accumulated a total of 223 hours of civilian flight time.

Unable to meet the educational requirements for military pilot training in any of the prewar US services, Swede packed his bags and traveled north to Toronto, Ontario. There, on January 18, 1941, he voluntarily enlisted in the RCAF at No. 11 Recruiting Centre. Entering the air force as an AC2 under Regimental Service No. R. 91047, Carlson completely bypassed the MD and ITS aspect of service life. Instead, he proceeded directly to RCAF Air Station Trenton, Ontario, where he underwent a one-week Link Trainer Course,[1] which concluded at the station's Central Flying School on February 24, 1941. A certificate signed by

---

[1] The Link Trainer was invented by Edwin Albert Link of Binghamton, New York. Edwin, as a young man, had moved with his family from Indiana to upstate New York, when his father established the Link Piano and Organ Company. Edwin dropped out of high school in 1927 and went to work in his father's factory. He learned how to fly, but often said that flight lessons were far too costly. Link came up with the idea of how to lessen those costs by designing and building a ground aviation trainer that would produce safer pilots in a shorter space of time. Drawing from his expertise in air driven pianos and pipe organs, Link used organ parts and compressed air to build the world's first rudimentary flight simulator. Organ bellows and a motor provided the means for his wooden invention, which, when mounted on a pedestal, enabled the device to pitch, roll, dive and climb as the student flew it. For 18 months, he worked on his idea in the basement of his father's factory, naming the trainer the Pilot Maker. In the beginning there was very little interest from the flying community for his product. His first sales were actually to amusement parks where they were used as novelty rides. Link's first military sale came about as a result of the air mail scandal after the USAAC took over carriage of US air mail.

Twelve pilots were killed in a 78-day period due to their lack of instrument training while trying to fly at night and in bad weather. This unnecessary loss of lives prompted the military to look at a number of solutions, including Link's pilot trainer. The Air Corps was given a stark demonstration of the potential for blind flying when, in 1934, Link flew to a meeting from Binghamton to Newark, New Jersey, in a fog so dense that it had grounded all army pilots and planes on the east coast. The evaluation team was duly impressed! As a result of this demonstration, they ordered the first of six pilot trainers for a total cost of $21,000. Before and during World War II Britain had placed restrictions on buying war goods from non-Commonwealth nations. Link realized that his business would dramatically increase if he had a manufacturing plant in Canada. He owned an island in the St. Lawrence River just east of Gananoque, Ontario, and frequently traveled back and forth to his cottage there by seaplane. Determining the concept was indeed feasible, he built a factory in 1938 on the edge of the Gananoque River at the point where the river empties into the St. Lawrence. This plant eventually employed 200 workers and produced just over 5,000 Link Trainers for the war effort. The Gananoque production, coupled with the Binghamton output, resulted in nearly 11,000 Link Trainers being constructed for the winning Allied cause.

USAAF 2nd Lieutenant Kendall E. Carlson (second from the right) is pictured at a social event at Station F-356 in Essex, England, in 1943. (US Department of Defense)

Wing Commander D. Edwards on the 26th certified that Carlson had achieved an 80 percent mark on his test and had graduated as a competent Link Trainer instructor in all elementary sequences. Promoted directly to the rank of sergeant on March 1, 1941, Carlson was posted to No. 8 EFTS at Vancouver, British Columbia, where he commenced his duties as an instructor. This facility, now the site of the Vancouver International Airport, opened on July 22, 1940, and operated de Havilland Tiger Moth biplane trainers.

Carlson married Miss Anne Myson in Vancouver on July 2, 1941. He was fined several days' pay as he had not obtained the RCAF's permission for the union in advance. He was also AWL for several days in order to attend the ceremony.

Swede was promoted to FS on October 1, 1941, then to WO1 on April 1, 1942. On June 19, he was posted from No. 8 EFTS to No. 15 EFTS at Regina, Saskatchewan, where he was scheduled to continue instructing.

Days after arriving in Regina, Carlson was informed that his previous requests to go overseas as a fighter pilot had finally been approved. He was posted, on July 19, to No. 6 SFTS at Dunnville, Ontario, for training on single-engined Harvard and Yale aircraft. To keep his pilot skills sharp along the way, Swede had flown, in his off-duty hours, Tiger Moths and Fairchild PT-26 Cornells at Vancouver and Regina, respectively. Carlson finished up at Dunnville on September 11, was awarded his pilot wings and was commissioned from the ranks as a PO. His service number was changed from R. 91047 to C. 23862, reflecting his change in status. He was posted the next day to No. 1 OTU at Bagotville, Quebec. There he learned how to tactically use the Hawker Hurricane fighter in combat. Swede graduated from the course on December 5, 1942, and, during this training period in Quebec, his wife resided nearby at the commercial hotel in the town of Bagotville.

After seven days' leave, PO Carlson shipped out to England from "Y" Depot, Pier 21, Halifax, Nova Scotia, on December 11. He arrived dockside at Liverpool on December 18 and, after an overnight train ride, checked in for his assignment at No. 3 Personnel Reception Centre in Bournemouth. On January 14, 1943, Swede was posted to No. 56 OTU at Tealing, Scotland. There he flew Miles Masters and early model Hurricanes until completing the course on March 14. Three days before the course ended, Carlson was promoted from PO to FO.

Prior to joining the USAAF, Swede first had to obtain a release from the RCAF. His honorable discharge papers in this regard were signed in London on April 23, 1943. The document stated that he had served two years and 63 days in Canada's air force. It also stated that his conduct and character had been assessed as very good and his qualifications as a pilot were satisfactory. Days later, Carlson was accepted into the USAAF under Service No. 0-2044438 with the rank of 2nd lieutenant.

For the next three months, Swede was at the US Combat Crew Replacement Centre (CCRC) at Station F-342 Atcham. Located in Shropshire, five miles southeast of Shrewsbury, Atcham trained both 8th and 9th Air Force fighter pilots from June 15, 1942, to March 31, 1945. Carlson converted to American aircraft and flying procedures, piloting Piper Cubs, Supermarine Spitfire Vbs, Miles Master IIIs and Republic P-47C and D Thunderbolts. Later in the war, the CCRC was renamed the 495th Fighter Training Group.

Swede joined the 336th FS, 4th FG at Debden on July 25, 1943.

On August 16, in a P-47C Thunderbolt (serial number 41-6192), Carlson damaged an Fw 190 near Paris, France.

2nd Lieutenant Carlson was promoted to 1st lieutenant on January 1, 1944.

On January 31 at 1500hrs, in a P-47C Thunderbolt (serial number 41-6574), Swede bested a Bf 109 in the region of Gilze-Rijen, Holland. Following is his combat report for the mission:

> I was flying Blue 4 when about 10 to 15 109s started swinging around behind and up sun from us. At the same time eight came directly over our Blue and Green sections, half rolled and came down and the ones up sun also came down. I called for Green section to break. I broke – in fact all of Blue section broke and I saw a 109 go after a P-47 and I started after him. He was extremely close to the 47 so I took about a 30 to 40 degree deflection shot using about three rings and there were about four or five strikes on the engine cowl and cockpit. He started

to smoke then rolled over very slowly and the pilot dropped out. His chute did not open until he was fairly close to the ground and was right above an inlet or river. The kite went straight in. I saw another 109 behind a 47 so I started down calling to the pilot to keep turning, but he thought I said to take him down so he went straight down. At the same time Lt. Ellington and another 47 were diving with me but as the pursued P-47 broke down it put me outside on the turn. Lt. Ellington cut inside of me and took the 109 off the 47's tail. This 109 hit in a ball of smoke and flame on a mud flat. These 109s were really raring to go but the pilots must have been very green because they had the advantage but buggered it all up. When they did see me behind them, they broke and turned inside of me and I broke off up sun. I claim one BF 109 destroyed and I confirm one 109 for Lt. Ellington.

Flying a P-51B Mustang (serial number 43-6507), Carlson destroyed three Me 110s during the month of March; the one on the 3rd was east of Hanover and the two on the 16th were at Kaufbeuren, Germany.

On April 22 at 1800hrs, southwest of Kassel, Germany, in P-51B 43-7059, Swede was credited with downing 1.5 Bf 109s and damaging two others.

1st Lieutenant Carlson was promoted to captain on April 23, 1944. By the end of July, his total flying time amounted to 1,397 hours.

His last aerial credit was north of Ingolstadt, Germany, at 1318hrs on February 20, 1945, when he was given a half credit for the destruction of an Fw 190.

On February 25, 1945, on flying orders 1662A, Major Pierce W. "Mac" McKennon led the wing on a freelance fighter sweep to Dessau, Germany, from 0800 to 1420hrs. Upon reaching the target area at 1010hrs, Röhrensee and Köthen airdromes were hit. Captain Carlson, as leader, led the 336th FS in the attack on Köthen.

As observed by 1st Lieutenant Paul M. Morgan and 2nd Lieutenant Beachem O. Brooker, Jr., Carlson strafed and immediately set fire to an unidentified four-engined aircraft. Blasting his way across the enemy base at more than 345mph and less than 35ft off the deck, Carlson's P-51K-1 Mustang (coded VF-Y, serial number 44-11356) suddenly mushed in, hit the ground and slid to a dusty stop in the middle of the Luftwaffe airfield. Swede got out, stood on the wing, and proceeded to direct his fellow pilots to targets on the field over his radio. He spotted an Fw 190 attempting to land and called out the aircraft's position to Morgan and Brooker, who promptly shot it down. Turns out the popular German pilot who was killed, Oberst Hoffman, was the station's commander. When the dust settled, Carlson was arrested by the very annoyed Germans, who had been listening to his play-by-play on their radio. One of his captors angrily said, "When you crash-landed your war was over, you had no business continuing the fight once you were on the ground."

For the first few minutes of his captivity, Captain Carlson was not exactly sure what the Luftwaffe personnel were going to do with him!

Meanwhile, the 334th's Blue Section, comprised of Thomas Bell, Carl Payne, Arthur Bowers, and Gordon Denson, destroyed seven enemy aircraft on the ground at Röhrensee and, later, Payne brought down an Me 262 in the air near Naumburg. While the four Mustangs were heading home, they were bounced by seven Fw 190s and Bf 109s. No one fired a shot as both formations were out of ammunition. The German leader looked over, waggled his wings and then something unbelievable happened – the two flights joined up! One of the Americans asked, "What the hell is this?" and another replied: "Beats me, ask the man who flies one." The 11 fighters flew on together for some 20 minutes until the Germans broke off and went their separate way. The four amazed Americans landed in France to refuel and returned to Debden at 1735hrs.

Carlson spent the last ten weeks of the European conflict as a PoW.

Swede elected to remain in the peacetime USAAF and was promoted to the rank of major on October 26, 1945. Carlson was released from active service on January 14, 1947, but rejoined the military later that year after he enlisted in the newly formed USAF.

In 1948–49, he flew F-82E Twin Mustangs with the 522nd FS at Bergstrom Air Force Base in Texas. During the summer and fall of 1950, Swede flew 46 combat missions against North Korean ground targets in F-51D Mustangs with the 12th Fighter Bomber Squadron (FBS) from Chinhae, South Korea.

He was promoted to lieutenant colonel on November 19, 1950.

On April 22, 1951, he ended his military flying when he received an honorable discharge from the USAF.

He is credited with destroying ten Luftwaffe aircraft – six air and four ground while flying with the 4th FG.

Kendall Eugene "Swede" Carlson died in his 58th year on January 25, 1977, at his residence in Tukwila, Washington.

Robert Coffey
Illinois Typhoon Pilot

When US citizen Robert Ellsworth "Bob" Coffey walked into the RCAF's No. 8 Recruiting Centre in downtown Windsor, Ontario, on Thursday, June 26, 1941, wishing to join the war effort, FL H. E. Fleming, the officer in charge, could have been forgiven for being a little bit skeptical after reviewing the applicant's impressive resume.

The more-than-qualified 26-year-old from Greenview, Illinois, had graduated from Purdue University the previous year with a Bachelor of Science degree in mechanical engineering. Robert Coffey was gainfully employed as an inspector/project engineer with the Allison Airplane Engine Company in Indianapolis, Indiana. There, he tested aircraft engines that powered, or would eventually power, military aircraft such as the A-36 Dive-Bomber, P-38 Lightning, P-39 Airacobra, P-40 Warhawk, P-63 King Cobra and P-51A Mustang. Bob was a licensed private pilot with 200 hours in his logbook. The aircraft that he personally flew was a 225hp Waco F-7 biplane. After a lengthy discussion, Fleming realized that this bright young man was indeed serious about enlisting and quickly processed his application. He swore Coffey in that day as an AC2 under Regimental No. R. 109592.

Bob Coffey was born in Greenview to Henry Jackson and Mary Fulton Coffey on March 30, 1915. There was one other sibling in the family, a younger sister, Jean. Coffey attended Greenview Grade School from 1921 to 1929, then Greenview High School from 1929 to 1933. After graduation, he worked for a couple of years diligently setting aside sufficient tuition money before enrolling at Purdue in 1936.

Coffey did not immediately begin flight training in the RCAF due to a large backlog of students who were waiting to get on a course. On June 28, it shipped him off to No. 4a MD at Saint-Hubert, Quebec. This temporary human holding area was slated to become No. 13 SFTS. The school was still under construction and did not open for its first intake of flying students until the following September.

On August 9, Coffey traveled to No. 3 ITS located at Victoriaville, Quebec. Assigned to Course No. 33, he graduated five weeks later on September 12, with an 88 percent average.

Promoted to LAC, Coffey's next stop was at No. 17 EFTS at Stanley, Nova Scotia, where he flew 81.55 hours on Fleet Finch biplanes. Easily passing out of this course with an 84 percent average on November 7, he was sent the next day to No. 8 at Moncton, New Brunswick.

On Course No. 42 at Moncton, Coffey flew 176.45 hours on Harvard Mk IIbs and was awarded his wings in a graduation ceremony on February 27, 1942. He so excelled at No. 8 that the air force promoted him to the rank of PO. Reflecting the change from the non-commissioned rank to officer status, his Service No. was changed from R. 109592 to J. 10256.

On March 29, Coffey began a flying instructor's course at the Central Flying School at Air Station Trenton, Ontario. There he flew additional hours on Ansons, Cranes, Yales, and Lockheed 12s. The course concluded on May 18.

Two weeks later, he began teaching others how to fly Harvards and Yales at No. 1 SFTS, Camp Borden, Ontario. Coffey instructed at Borden for the next 11 months, during which time he was promoted to FO.

Aiming to help relieve pressure on the OTUs in England, the RCAF established six of its own in Canada. The first was No. 1 located at Bagotville, Quebec, which principally operated, among other aircraft types, Hawker Hurricanes. Bob Coffey was posted to Bagotville on April 25, 1943, where he undertook Hurricane fighter conversion training for ten weeks until July 7.

During a 14-month period from June 3, 1942, to July 28, 1943, Japan retained a toehold on a tiny piece of North America when it invaded, garrisoned and occupied Kiska, Attu, and Agattu in the Aleutian Island chain. The Aleutians extend some 1,200 miles westward from the tip of the Alaskan Peninsula out into the northern Pacific Ocean.

With the incursion of Japanese military personnel on American soil, RCAF No. 118 FS was one of six RCAF units that responded to America's request for assistance. Dispatched from Dartmouth, Nova Scotia, in June 1942, 16 P-40s from No. 118 flew a record-breaking 4,000 miles across Canada to southern Alaska. That monumental transit effort took 15 days!

Coffey left Bagotville on July 10 and traveled to Canada's Western Air Command located at Vancouver, British Columbia. From there he was posted to No. 118, which was tasked with flying defensive patrols from Annette Island, Alaska. Annette, part of the Aleutian chain, is located 25 miles south of Ketchikan. This operating airfield was situated on a cold, inhospitable, wind-swept, boggy piece of land. Despite dawn to dusk patrols, the squadron saw no action as the enemy was safely operating well outside the range of their P-40Es at the other end of the island chain.

At the Canadian airmen's mess on Annette, a fellow could get a beer, and this was a real boon to the hundreds of Americans who were also stationed there. As their mess was dry, the Americans resorted to paying innumerable weekly courtesy calls to their guests' wet facility to see if there was anything more they could do or provide to their Canadian allies.

Robert Coffey: Illinois Typhoon Pilot

On July 28, 1943, after having been kicked off Attu and Agattu, the Japanese decided to cut their losses on Kiska and, in the middle of the night, under the cover of fog and darkness, withdrew their remaining 5,000-man force totally unobserved.

The six Canadian fighter and bomber reconnaissance squadrons that served in defense of the state of Alaska for just over one year had been under the command and control of the USAAF 11th Air Force.

With the Japanese threat to America's west coast removed, No. 118 was released from its Alaskan patrol duties with thanks from the US government.

Moving to Sea Island, British Columbia, the squadron was redesignated as No. 133 FS. From August 17 to October 7, it flew fighter affiliation training flights against Canadian B-24 Liberator and B-25 Mitchell bomber crews from the Boundary Bay and Abbotsford, British Columbia.

Leaving its P-40s in western Canada, the squadron's personnel traveled back across the country by train to "Y" Depot, Halifax, Nova Scotia. From there they left by ship on November 1, 1943, headed for Britain.

Arriving in the United Kingdom seven days later, the squadron was immediately sent to RAF Digby, Lincolnshire, where it equipped and began converting onto Hawker Hurricane Mk IVs.

Flying Officer Robert E. Coffey, DFC & Bar, sits on the tailplane of a Hawker Hurricane Mk IV at Ayr, Scotland, in January 1944. (Canadian National Defence Image Library)

A final renumbering was in the works for No. 133. On November 18, it became No. 438 FBS.

No. 143 Canadian Wing came into being at Ayr, Scotland, on January 10, 1944, as part of No. 83 Composite Group, 2nd Tactical Air Force (TAF). No. 143 was comprised of three Canadian fighter bomber units – 438 "City of Montreal Wildcat" Squadron (aircraft coded F3), 439 "Sabre-Toothed Tiger" Squadron (aircraft coded 5V) and 440 "City of Ottawa Red Bat" Squadron (aircraft coded 18).

Bob Coffey was promoted to FL on February 24, 1944. The wing personnel moved to Ayr and quickly converted from its trusted Hurricanes to another Hawker product, the Typhoon 1B. Declared operational on March 14, the wing relocated to Hurn, Dorset, England. Dashing across the Channel on daily low-level sorties, No. 143 destroyed, from March 26 to D-Day, German V-1 sites, radio installations, gun positions and bridges.

Typhoons formed the backbone of the 2nd TAF fielding on D-Day, with no fewer than 18 squadrons of the type. British, Canadian, Australian, and New Zealander air force pilots were convinced their aircraft, which were nicknamed "Tiffys," were the best all-round fighter bombers of World War II.

Designed by Sir Sydney Camm in 1937, only 15 token Typhoons were built at the main Hawker facility at Brooklands, England, before licensed production switched to Gloster Aircraft at Hucclecote, Gloucestershire, where the remaining 3,315 airframes were manufactured.

Heavily armed with four 20mm Hispano-Suiza Mk II cannons with 560 rounds of ammunition and eight 60lb 3in high-explosive underwing air-to-ground rockets or two 1,000lb bombs, Typhoons blasted everything the enemy tried to move in northern France and the Low Countries in the summer of 1944. Later Typhoon models had four bladed propellers, tear-drop canopies and were powered by a 2,260shp Napier Sabre IIC engine, which, at altitude, gave the aircraft a fighter-like top speed of 412mph.

During the Normandy invasion on June 6, 1944, the wing's aircraft, flying its sorties from Hurn, supported Canadian and British soldiers as they stormed ashore on Juno, Sword, and Gold beaches.

D-Day plus 16 saw 438 and 440 squadrons land in France at Advanced Landing Ground (ALG) B.6 Coulombs, while 439 headed for B.5 Fresne-Camilly, which was under enemy artillery fire as it arrived. Six days later, all three squadrons came together at B.9 Lantheuil located just south of Creully. The wing responded to the Army's request for close air support, attacking all types of enemy targets. In some cases, the bomb line was only five miles from its airfield.

Coffey and the other wing personnel lived in tents at these rough forward air strips; slit trenches dotted the area, offering the airmen limited protection from enemy air attacks and shell fire. For the first month and a half, the tired pilots and groundcrew slept through the thunderous barrages laid down by their own artillery firing, sometimes from positions just outside their base. While at B.9, the wing carried out 2,359 sorties against the enemy. As the Allied ground troops advanced, so did the wing. In August, it went to Amiens, France, then to Brussels, Belgium, in September, and finally to B.78 Eindhoven, Holland, on September 26.

In October, RAF Typhoon squadron No. 168 attached itself to No. 143, remaining with it until February 1945.

The surprise German attack on Eindhoven airfield on New Year's Day, January 1, 1945, began at 0920hrs and lasted a full 25 minutes. The German Air Force, in a coordinated effort, codenamed Operation *Bodenplatte*, utilized 1,035 aircraft to simultaneously strike 17 Allied airfields in France, Holland, and Belgium. Eindhoven, in addition to housing No. 143 Wing, was home to three Spitfire squadrons and four other Typhoon squadrons. Without warning, 60 Luftwaffe Fw 190A-8s and 190 D-9s from JG 3, raced in low over the snow-covered landscape strafing and bombing aircraft, equipment, personnel, and buildings. Fifteen personnel were killed and 40 were wounded. Fires started by the attackers exploded some of the Canadian bomb supply, which only added to the overall devastation.

A DFC was awarded to R. E. Coffey on January 13, 1945. The citation reads as follows:

> Flight Lieutenant Coffey has a fine record of successful operations. He has displayed excellent qualities as a leader. Prior to the invasion of Normandy he participated in numerous attacks on enemy installations in France, encountering heavy and accurate anti-aircraft fire. In July 1944, FL Coffey pressed home a successful attack on a bridge at Thury-Harcourt which was completely destroyed and during and after the battle in the Falaise Gap, he destroyed many locomotives, barges and an ammunition ship. He has led many successful sorties against railway targets in the battle area and has done effective work disrupting enemy communications and supply lines.

Coffey's time with 438 Squadron ended on March 14, 1945. The next day, he was promoted to SL and was given command of 440 Squadron.

Operating over the ever-moving frontline and, in most cases, flying directly over Germany, No. 143 carried out a total of 6,484 sorties from B.78.

April 13 found the wing on the move from Holland to Goch, Germany. Eight days later, it moved further into Germany to Celle. On May 4, it was taken off operations and the next day the German Army threw in the towel. May 8, 1945, was universally celebrated as VE-Day when Germany surrendered unconditionally.

Since D-Day, Bob Coffey and his fellow pilots at No. 143 had flown a grueling 10, 292 hours in support of army operations along 800 miles of brutal fighting in northwest Europe.

As part of the Allied Occupation Force, the wing moved on June 30 to Flensburg, Germany, which is situated in the northwest part of the country near the Danish border.

While traveling in Denmark on July 30, 1945, Bob Coffey suffered a fractured skull in a car crash. The next day he was admitted to the 50th Military Field Hospital in Germany where his condition was listed as critical. He never regained consciousness and died from his injuries at 0930hrs on August 1, 1945.

His parents were notified of his passing, as was his sister, 1st Lieutenant Jean Coffey, who was serving in the United States Army Nursing Corps (USANC) with the 104th General Field Hospital in England.

SL Robert Ellsworth Coffey, DFC, was buried on August 3 in Grave No. E 78 in the Graasten, Denmark Municipal Cemetery.

Coffey's grave is the sole military plot in that cemetery and is perpetually cared for by the CWGC.

On November 2, 1945, three months after his death, it was announced that Coffey had been posthumously awarded a Bar to his DFC effective September 3. The citation for this award reads as follows:

> This officer is now on his second tour of operational duty. In March 1945, he participated in an attack on the railway sidings at Winterswijk. Despite intense anti-aircraft fire, his squadron destroyed twenty-five trucks and damaged ten. On another occasion, this officer completely silenced heavy guns on a well defended enemy position. SL Coffey has at all times shown a high standard of devotion to duty. He has led attacks against a wide variety of targets displaying exceptional qualities of leadership and courage.

Bob Coffey's air force awards were forwarded by the Canadian government to his mother and father in Greenview on October 13, 1947.

Russell Curtis
Pennsylvania Bomber Pilot

On Monday, October 7, 1940, 19-year-old Russell Edward Curtis from Albion, Pennsylvania, crossed the Canada–United States border at Niagara Falls, Ontario, and voluntarily enlisted in the RCAF. Assigned Regimental Service No. R. 66257, Curtis began his air force career as an AC2 earning CAN$1.30 per day. He told FO O. W. Froom at the recruiting office that he had come to Canada to offer up his service in any capacity but hoped that he would be trained as a service pilot since he had 105 hours of civilian flight time recorded in his logbook. Froom's overall assessment of the applicant was positive: "Very bright – keen – pleasant – should turn out to be a first class pilot."

Curtis was born on May 20, 1921, in Springboro, Pennsylvania, to Frank M. Curtis and Lenora Whittaker. He grew up in the small rural Pennsylvania farming community of Albion and attended the local grammar school there from 1927 until 1935. This was followed by four years of secondary education at Albion High School. In September 1939, Curtis enrolled in a liberal arts course at Thiel College in Greenville, Pennsylvania. While in school, his various part-time jobs included working as a farm hand, assisting in a florist shop, and as a machine-gunner in the United States Army Reserve during summer camps held at Fort Meade, Maryland.

One month of basic training at No. 1 MD in Toronto, Ontario, was followed by two months of guard duty at RCAF No. 1 Bombing & Gunnery School at Jarvis, Ontario. On January 16, 1941, Curtis was sent to No. 1 ITS in Toronto from where he graduated five weeks later on February 21. Promoted to LAC, Russell, now earning $2.25 daily, was posted to No. 10 EFTS at Mount Hope, Ontario, where, over the next seven weeks, he amassed 73 hours flying de Havilland Tiger Moth biplanes. On May 3, Curtis arrived at No. 8 SFTS at Moncton, New Brunswick, where he completed his flight training flying twin-engined Avro Anson Mk II aircraft. He graduated and earned his RCAF wings as a SP on July 27, 1941.

The following Canadian aircraft manufacturers built a total of 2,882 Avro Anson Mk II and Mk V aircraft between 1939 and 1945: Canadian Car & Foundry in Fort William, Ontario; de Havilland Canada in Toronto, Ontario; Federal Aircraft in Montreal, Quebec; MacDonald Brothers in Winnipeg, Manitoba; National Steel Car in Malton, Ontario; and Ottawa Car & Aircraft in Ottawa, Ontario.

Ansons flew a staggering 4,976,431 hours in the British Commonwealth Air Training Plan during World War II.

Sergeant Curtis departed Canada by troop ship from No. 1 Port Transit Unit, "Y" Depot, Pier 21, Halifax, Nova Scotia, on August 19. He did not arrive in England until September 8 and was assigned to No. 3 Personnel Reception Centre at Bournemouth. Fifteen days later, on the 23rd, he began his advanced flight training at RAF No. 15 OTU at Mount Farm, Oxfordshire, flying Vickers-Armstrong Wellington Mk Ia "Wimpy" twin-engined medium bombers.

That November, No. 15 OTU merged with No. 21 OTU, resulting in the aircraft and crews having to relocate to a new airfield – RAF Moreton-in-Marsh. Russell completed the course on January 4, 1942, and was promoted to FS on the 27th of the month.

He shipped out to the Middle East where he joined RAF No. 104 Bomber Squadron at Kibrit, Egypt, on February 14, 1942. The squadron flew Wellington Mk IIs from this location and, in May, began operating from Landing Ground 106 in the desert. Curtis was promoted to WO2 on August 1. After completing 33 sorties involving 250 flying hours, the tour expired. Curtis returned to Canada on December 31, 1942, for a much-needed rest. He received a DFM, with the following citation:

> CURTIS, Sergeant Russell Edward (R. 66257) – Distinguished Flying Medal – No. 104 Squadron – Award effective 1 December 1942 as per London Gazette dated 4 December 1942 and AFRO 2069/42 dated 18 December 1942.
>
> Sergeant Curtis is a most determined pilot who, throughout his operational career, has always succeeded in his attacks which have sometimes been made in the face of severe ground opposition. Once, following an attack on the marshalling yards at Messina, his aircraft was hit and severely damaged. With great skill he flew it back to base, executing a masterly landing without injury to his crew. Three weeks later the engine of his aircraft failed when over the target area but by superb airmanship he managed to maintain height for two hours in bad weather conditions, before making a successful crash landing without injuring his crew. This airman's operational record is of the very highest standard and his technical ability is outstanding.

The Public Records Office Air 2/9606 has a recommendation dated November 3, 1942, which is rather more detailed than that published:

> This Non-Commissioned Officer has completed twenty-nine operational sorties and has always shown the greatest determination at bombing the target. Without exception on all trips that he has completed he has bombed in the target area, in many cases against severe ground opposition. On three of his trips he has saved

his crew through piloting of the highest order. Once after attacking Messina with a 4,000 pound bomb and hitting the marshalling yards, causing very large explosions and fires, his aircraft was hit and one of the fuel lines severed. This became evident shortly after leaving the target and one engine stopped. He managed to isolate the damaged system and returned to Malta where both engines cut out through lack of fuel. He was unable to make a landing on the aerodrome and successfully executed a perfect landing in the water just off shore without injury to the crew. Three weeks later while attacking Tmini aerodrome an engine failed over the target. He maintained height on one engine for two hours in conditions of low cloud and bad visibility found a flare path and made a successful landing without damage to the aircraft or injury to the crew. Yet again, returning from a raid, one engine caught fire over the Delta which he extinguished and as he was losing height fast, set course for the nearest aerodrome. He was unable to complete a circuit and had to land across the flare path. This landing he executed with great skill and brought the machine to rest again without damage or injury to his crew. This NCO's operational record so far is of the very highest standard and his ability to handle aircraft under adverse conditions gives an example of the ability he displays when under enemy fire.

WO2 Curtis was commissioned from the ranks on February 20, 1943. Along with his promotion to PO came new Regimental Service No. J. 24086. At the end of March, he posted to No. 1 Flying Instructor School at RCAF Air Station Trenton, Ontario, where he undertook a course from April 21 to May 24. Curtis did well at the school as evidenced by the following report filed by FO J. G. Stewart: "Throughout the course this man applied himself exceptionally well and has shown keen interest at all times. In my opinion he will prove to be an excellent instructor."

Four days before graduating, Curtis married Jean Rose Bourveau in Ottawa, Ontario, on May 20, 1943.

Curtis reported for duty on June 10 to No. 5 SFTS at Brantford, Ontario, where he was to instruct on Ansons. It turned out that teaching others how to fly was not really his cup of tea. FL A. T. Wilson filed the following report on August 12, 1943: "This officer has completed an operational tour of duty as a bomber pilot. A hard working pilot who has very little interest in instructing. It is suggested that he might be more suitably employed in some other capacity."

Promoted to FO eight days later, Curtis was posted to No. 12 Communications Squadron (CS) at RCAF Station Rockcliffe, Ontario, where he was employed as a ferry pilot. On December 8, he transferred to Western Air Command where he flew Lockheed Lodestars and Douglas Dakotas with RCAF No. 165 Transport Squadron from Sea Island, British Columbia.

Pushing all the while to get back overseas, Curtis was finally successful and embarked for England on April 24, 1944. He was posted on June 1 to No. 1666 Heavy

Flight Lieutenant Russell Curtis, DSO, DFM, flew many sorties on Avro Mk X Lancaster bombers similar to the one depicted. (Canada Department of National Defence)

Conversion Unit at RAF Wombleton in North Yorkshire where he underwent conversion training over the next 28 days onto the mighty four-engined Avro Lancaster Mk II bomber.

FO Curtis began his second operational tour on June 30, flying Lancasters with RCAF No. 428 "Ghost" Squadron from Air Station Middleton St. George, located in the county of Durham. He was promoted to FL on July 29.

At 1510hrs on September 12, 1944, Curtis and his crew of six took off in a Canadian-built Lancaster Mk X, coded KB793, on a rare daylight raid to Dortmund, Germany. It was his 55th sortie of the war. Near the target area, the aircraft was heavily hit by flak, which killed the rear gunner, FO J. J. Flood from Toronto, Ontario. Curtis was seriously wounded by the same antiaircraft fire, sustaining a compound skull fracture to the left side of his head. Although gravely injured, he insisted on completing the run-in to the target. After the bombs were successfully dropped, Russell lost his power of speech and then lapsed into a coma. Between them, the five remaining crew members collectively pooled their limited flying knowledge and managed to return the damaged bomber and their injured pilot to RAF Woodbridge in Suffolk. During the landing, the port tire burst, causing the aircraft to veer off the runway. This wild ride folded up the port landing gear, which in turn damaged the port mainplane and the propellers. All four motors were shock-loaded during the crash landing. When the dust settled, there were no additional injuries to the crew. FL Curtis was transported by ambulance to the Ipswich and East Suffolk General Hospital for an immediate operation. He regained his power of speech 12 hours after surgery.

FO Flood was buried on September 16 in the regional cemetery at Brookwood. The six surviving airmen all received medals of valor. Curtis and McGillivary were awarded the Distinguished Service Order (DSO). Smith, Wattie and Marshall received the DFC and Sergeant Rose was awarded a DFM.

On November 18, 1944, the Canadian Minister of National Defence for Air sent the following letter to Mr. and Mrs. F. M. Curtis who were residing at 8 Water Street in Albion.

> It is with a great feeling of pride that I once again extend to you and your family the heartiest congratulations on the additional honour and distinction which your son, Flight Lieutenant Russell Edward Curtis DSO, DFM has earned by the recent receipt of the award of the Distinguished Service Order. The citation accompanying this award reads as follows.
>
> "These Officers and Airmen have participated in a very large number of sorties and have displayed skill, courage and devotion to duty worthy of the highest praise. In August 1944, they were members of the crew of an aircraft detailed to attack Dortmund. Whilst on the bombing run the aircraft came under heavy anti-aircraft fire and was hit. Flight Lieutenant Curtis was wounded in the head. Despite the severity of his injury, this brave pilot remained at the controls and pressed home the attack. Not until the task was accomplished did he ask for assistance. He subsequently collapsed and was placed in a rest position. Flying Officer Dougal A. McGillivary, the Air Bomber, then took over the controls and set the aircraft on a course towards home. During the return flight his comrades, Flight Lieutenant Hugh F. Smith, Flying Officers Robert G. Marshall and Charles F. Wattie and Sergeant J. D. Rose set a fine example of coolness and co-operation and did everything within their power to assist in flying the aircraft home. Eventually an airfield was reached. Although he had never previously landed an aircraft, Flying Officer McGillivray succeeded in bringing it down, being greatly assisted by the advice and directors of Sergeant Rose, the Flight Engineer. These crew members displayed rare determination and great courage in perilous circumstances. Flight Lieutenant Curtis had sustained a compound fracture of the skull. Until the time he became incapable of further action, he had displayed the courage and tenacity of a fine leader. Again may I say that the personnel of the Air Force are indeed proud of your son's fine service record.

Russell Curtis was repatriated to Canada for medical reasons on December 28, 1944. Follow-up examinations revealed that a further operation was required to repair the damage to his skull. During a procedure on February 23, 1945, a metal plate was inserted in his skull. Curtis was honorably retired and released from the RCAF on April 23, 1945.

His DSO and DFM awards were formally presented to him by a Canadian government envoy in Chicago, Illinois, on November 28, 1947.

In 1949, he was associated with the Spartan School of Aeronautics in Tulsa, Oklahoma.

Russell E. Curtis passed away in January 1990, in his 69th year.

In addition to his DSO and DFM awards, Curtis was awarded the 1939–45 Star, Africa Star & Clasp, France & Germany Star, Defence Medal, Operational Wing & Bar, General Service Medal and the Canadian Volunteer Service Medal & Clasp.

His medals and logbook are on permanent display at the National Air Force Museum of Canada located at RCAF Air Station Trenton, Ontario, Canada.

James Dalglish
Pioneer Mustang Group Ace

Flying NAA P-51B and D Mustangs and Republic P-47D Thunderbolts in the ETO, the majority of Major James Buckingham "Jim" Dalglish's service time was spent with the 9th TAF, 354th and 363rd FGs.

The 9th TAF was formed as a joined-at-the-hip partner with the Allied 2nd TAF. Each existed for one reason only: to provide air supremacy and close air support to its respective ground forces during the invasion of Normandy. As the Allied armies advanced forward on French soil starting on D-Day, June 6, 1944, so too did the two TAFs, leapfrogging from one hastily prepared ALG to the next, living and operating as close as possible to the ever-moving frontlines.

The experience of the Allied forces in North Africa in 1942–43 had convinced the planners of Operation *Overlord* that two TAFs would be needed to successfully invade fortress Europe. One would support the US ground forces and the other the British and Canadian ground forces. Each would have its own fighters, fighter-bombers, medium bombers, night-fighters and reconnaissance aircraft.

The Normandy air war, which lasted from June 6 to August 28, 1944, saw 37 temporary ALGs built in France. Nineteen were American, prefixed by the letter "A," and 18 were British and Canadian, prefixed by the letter "B." The 9th utilized hundreds of Thunderbolts, Mustangs, Lightnings, Havocs, and Marauders in the prosecution of its campaign, while the 2nd used a similar number of Spitfires, Typhoons, Mustangs, Bostons, Mosquitos, and Mitchells. Once up and running, these 37 ALGs were sufficient to accommodate more than 1,900 combat aircraft.

Jim Dalglish was born in Rome, New York, on October 30, 1921. His father, George, was from nearby Elmira and his mother, Antoinette Halstead, came from Orange, New Jersey. James, his parents, and two older brothers lived at 604 North George Street. Jim's grade school years, from 1927 to 1936, were spent at the Fort Stanwix Elementary School. From 1936 to 1938, he attended Rome Free Academy High School and, from 1938 to 1941, Chapel Hill-Chauncy Hall, a private boarding school in Waltham, Massachusetts. Dalglish's athletic pursuits during his high school years included football, skiing, wrestling, swimming, and track. At 6ft 2in in height and weighing 190lb, he was a formidable sports competitor.

From July to October 1941, Jim worked in his hometown as a gas charger at the Revere Brass & Copper Company. Rome is very close to the Canadian border and the local newspaper carried many articles on Canada's massive effort to vastly expand its small air force. These reports also told of the RCAF's acute manpower shortage and how easy it was for American high school graduates, some as young as 17, to join up for pilot training. Dalglish knew that America would eventually be drawn into the war and his preference was to do his fighting in the air rather than from a muddy foxhole.

Not waiting to be drafted into the US Army, he headed to Ottawa, Ontario, where he voluntarily enlisted in the RCAF at No. 12 Recruiting Centre.

He entered Canada's air force on November 5, 1941, as an AC2 under Regimental Number R. 135902. Airman Dalglish left Ottawa that same day on a Canadian National Railway westbound passenger train. He arrived at his destination – RCAF No. 2 MD in Brandon, Manitoba – midday on November 7.

Completing his basic training, Jim traveled back east to RCAF Air Station Trenton, Ontario, on January 3, 1942. While waiting to get on a course, he performed guard duty there until February 28. Promoted to LAC, Dalglish began Course No. 48 at No. 5 ITS on March 2 at Belleville, Ontario. He graduated on April 24 with an 81 percent average, with the following written comment from the CO placed in his file: "Fine young airman with above average ability. Should make good aircrew material."

Posted on April 27 to No. 13 EFTS at St. Eugene, Ontario, Jim flew 77 hours on Fleet Finch II aircraft on Course No. 54 until July 3. LAC Dalglish graduated with a grade of 82.2 percent and the Chief Supervisory Officer had the following comment: "Above average type. Works very hard and is interested in all phases of his work."

Transferred to Course No. 59 at No. 2 SFTS at Uplands near Ottawa on July 6, Dalglish logged 183 hours on Harvard Mk IIs. He graduated with a mark of 78 percent on October 23, 1942, earning his wings and a commission as a PO. Jim stood eighth in his class at Uplands and the following comments from his superiors were noted in his records. From the CFI: "Ability as a pilot is above average in all respects. Appearance fair. Is eager, reliable and co-operative. Pleasing personality and a good sense of humour. A steady and dependable type." From the Uplands air station commander, the single comment: "I concur."

Jim's regimental number was changed from R. 135902 to J. 20140.

Months earlier, on May 11, Dalglish had traveled with several other American trainees to meet the joint Canadian–American military transfer train, which had stopped in Montreal, Quebec. One of Jim's brothers, Preston, was training to be a United States Marine Corps aviator. James tried to arrange a transfer to the Corps so that he could be with his brother. Major R. D. "Fish" Salmon, representing the Marines, turned him down as it was only interested in transferring graduate pilots

Major James B. Dalglish (second from the right) listens to fellow 354th FG pilots discuss fighter tactics. (US Department of Defense via Jack Cook)

at that point in the war. He advised James to stay where he was, continue with his training, and after he had earned his wings, then reapply to transfer.

PO Dalglish departed Halifax, Nova Scotia, by troop ship on November 20 and arrived in the United Kingdom on December 6. He was assigned to No. 3 Personnel Reception Centre at Bournemouth, where he remained until February 15, 1943.

With 276.25 flying hours recorded in his logbook, he began conversion training on Miles Masters and Hawker Hurricanes at No. 17 Pilot Advanced Flying Unit at RAF Calveley, Cheshire.

Completing this phase of his training on March 29, he was posted on the 31st to RAF No. 41 OTU at Hawarden in Flintshire.

No. 41's function was to train tactical reconnaissance (TR) pilots for the RAF Army Co-Operation Squadrons. While at this unit, Dalglish was promoted from PO to FO on April 23. Flying 39 hours on Mustang Mk Is and 14 hours on Harvards on Course No. 73, James graduated with a 75 percent average on May 25. WC A. D. Annand made the following comments: "Has done satisfactory work on this course. Is keen and enthusiastic. Should make sound fighter reconnaissance pilot. Above average in all respects."

On January 25, 1943, Jim's father received the following letter from W. C. McDougall, representing the CAS at RCAF Headquarters in Ottawa:

> Your son, Pilot Officer J. S. Dalglish (J. 20140) has requested that his officer's commission script be forwarded to you from this headquarters for safe keeping. The enclosed commission script represents the authority vested in PO Dalglish as well as the trust placed in him by His Majesty, The King. Would you be good enough to sign and return the enclosed receipt as evidence that the script has been received by you in good condition.

Given several days' leave, FO Dalglish was ordered to report on June 9, 1943, to RAF No. 613 "City of Manchester" Squadron. This unit was flying the Allison F3R-engined Mustang Mk I. James flew several dozen sorties with 613 from RAF Snailwell, Cambridgeshire, and damaged a Bf 109G in aerial combat on July 18 near Ljmuiden, Holland.

The squadron was earmarked to begin conversion from the Mustang to the de Havilland Mosquito in November 1943. This prompted Dalglish to request a transfer to the USAAF as he desired to continue to fly single-engine fighters.

613's Officer Commanding (OC), SL Charles Newman, wrote in a confidential report: "Dalglish, while with the squadron, showed keenness both on and off duty." He also said, "James carried out his duties efficiently and was an asset to the squadron generally." Jim officially left 613 on October 6 and was honorably discharged from the RCAF Special Reserve that same day. He joined the USAAF as a 1st lieutenant and was assigned Service No. 0-886127. An audit of his logbook revealed he had accumulated 446 hours of military flying time.

When the Mustang Mk I entered RAF service in April 1942, it had the best low-level performance of any existing British fighter. With a top speed of 382mph at 13,000ft, it was 28mph faster than the Spitfire Mk V. It was ideally suited for the army cooperation role and the RAF never found a more effective TR aircraft, using them up until VE-Day. Twenty-eight RAF and Commonwealth air force squadrons eventually employed a total of 618 Mk Is, Mk Ias and Mk IIs. The Mustang could acquit itself very well against any enemy aircraft that foolishly challenged it at its optimum operating level, which was from the ground to 13,000ft. It was the British who gave the Mustang its name and the type's first victory came on August 19, 1942, during the Dieppe raid.

On November 13, 1943, 1st Lieutenant Dalglish transferred to the 355th FS, 354th FG. Known as the "Pioneer Mustang Group," the personnel of the 354th, comprised of the 353rd "Fighting Cobras," 355th "Pugnacious Pups," and the 356th "Red Ass" FSs, arrived dockside at Liverpool, England, on November 1, 1943, onboard the troop ship HMS *Athlone Castle*.

The group had been formed a year earlier on November 15, 1942, at Hamilton Field, California, and had trained on the Bell P-39 Airacobra. Briefly based at Greenham Common in Berkshire, the group moved to Army Air Forces Station No. 150 Boxted, near Colchester, in mid-November and began to receive the Rolls-Royce-powered P-51B Mustangs.

It was the first FG to be equipped with the brand-new fighter and it would be the first to take it into combat. The Pioneer Mustang Group was a 9th Air Force asset but, for its first four months, it was loaned out operationally to the 8th Air Force so that its personnel could gain some combat experience. On December 1, the experienced 4th FG Executive Officer, Lieutenant Colonel Donald J. M. Blakeslee, who was seconded to the group for a few weeks, led the 354th on its first mission across the English Channel. He subsequently led it on missions over France and Belgium on December 2, 5, 11, 13, and 16.

The group's squadron codes were FT (353rd), GQ (355th), and AJ (356th).

Flying Mustang GQ-T on December 20, Dalglish claimed half credit of an Me 110. In GQ-T on January 30, 1944, he destroyed an Me 110, damaged another, and also damaged an Fw 190. Flying GQ-D on February 8, James claimed a 190 as damaged. In GQ-O on February 21, a Bf 109 was claimed as damaged. On March 6, again in GQ-O, he downed a Bf 109 and was given half credit in the destruction of another. Ten days later in GQ-A, he destroyed a Bf 109 and damaged another Messerschmitt in the same encounter.

With four aerial victories to his credit, Lt Dalglish transferred, at the end of March 1944, to the 381st FS, 363rd FG. This group, made up of the 380th, 381st and 382nd FSs, also operated Mustangs and flew its first mission from Rivenhall, Essex, on February 23, 1944. On April 8, James became an ace with the 363rd when he bagged a Bf 109 over Gifhorn, Germany. He was promoted to captain on April 23 and was the squadron's operations officer from that date until his tour expired in July 1944. Before leaving, he was able to down air-to-air three German V-1 buzz bombs – one on June 19 and two on June 25. He had been flying combat for more than a year and was sent home for a much deserved rest.

Returning to Europe on October 17, Captain Dalglish began a second tour when he rejoined the 354th FG while it was operating from Orconte, Normandy. He was assigned to the 353rd FS, serving as its operations officer. Promoted to major in November, he continued to add to his score – an Me 410 on December 17 and an Fw 190 on December 26, along with a Bf 109 claimed as damaged. The last two kills came while he was flying a P-47D Thunderbolt from Meurthe-et-Moselle, France. The month prior, 9th Air Force Headquarters, in its infinite wisdom, decided to replace the 354th's Mustangs with Thunderbolts. The thinking was that the P-47 was a more rugged ground-attack aircraft and was less likely to fall victim to accurate ground fire. To the relief of the personnel at the 354th, their beloved Mustangs were returned to them in February 1945.

At 1230hrs on April 16, Major Dalglish shot down two Fw 190s near Chemnitz, Germany. A month later, on May 31, 1945, he assumed command of the "Fighting Cobras."

His final aerial tally was nine aircraft destroyed, six and one half damaged and three V-1 rockets. Major Dalglish's US awards included a Silver Star, a DFC and twelve Air Medals.

After Germany surrendered, the 354th served for a while as part of the occupation force. Many of the group's personnel began using captured Luftwaffe equipment for their own enjoyment – including cars, motorcycles, and, in some cases, aircraft!

Jim Dalglish had his own personal Fw 190, which he often flew. Another 354th pilot, Captain Bruce Carr, decided to get one for himself and hitchhiked to Linz, Austria, where he found a flyable machine. He had prearranged for some of his 353rd buddies to meet him in the air in their P-51s and escort him back to the base at Ansbach, Germany. Unfortunately, Carr could not get the gear down and slid the 190 in on its belly. After that incident, the practice of flying German aircraft was banned.

When he returned to the States from overseas service in December 1945, Major Dalglish contacted the RCAF inquiring about any gratuity pay that might be owed him for his Canadian wartime service. It was determined that he was eligible for some and he received a check in the amount of CAN$357.66 from the Department of Veterans Affairs in January 1946.

Jim Dalglish died of cancer on October 21, 1969, in Phoenix, Arizona. He was 48 years old.

Paul Davoud
Dean of the Night Fighter Squadrons

GC Paul Yettvart Davoud's World War II military awards are indeed impressive – the Most Excellent Order of the British Empire (OBE), the DSO, the DFC, two separate Mention in Despatches (MiD), Chevalier of the Legion of Honour/Croix de Guerre with Palm (France) and Commander, Order of Orange-Nassau with Swords (Holland).

Paul Davoud was born on November 25, 1911, in Provo, Utah. His Turkish-born father, Vehram Yettvart Davoud, an electrical engineer, was a naturalized American citizen. The older Davoud died suddenly on August 26, 1926, when Paul was 14 years old. After his father's death, Paul's Canadian-born mother, Isabelle Constance Tandy, moved Paul, his brother, Gordon, and sister, Tandy, to her family home at 161 King Street in Kingston, Ontario.

While living in the United States, Paul attended boarding schools in Salt Lake City, Utah, and Montclair, New Jersey. After moving to Canada, he completed his high school education at Kingston's Collegiate Institute.

Davoud began his military career in 1928 when he was accepted at the Royal Military College (RMC) in Kingston. Studying engineering at Canada's military university, his hard work was rewarded when he received, on graduation day in 1932, the Victor van der Smissen-Ridout Memorial Award. This award was given to the graduating cadet deemed to stand highest morally, intellectually, and physically at RMC.

During the summers of 1929–31, Paul trained with the RCAF at Camp Borden, Ontario. He was awarded his pilot wings on August 19, 1931, and held the rank of PPO. At the completion of his training, he received the Sword of Honour as the best all-round cadet. Unfortunately, there were no pilot slots available to him, so the air force placed him on a reserve list for call up at a future date.

Never one to be idle, Paul enrolled at Queen's University in Kingston in September 1932 to study mechanical engineering. While attending both RMC and Queen's, he was a star athlete who played first string on their respective football teams.

In February 1933, he left Queen's to accept a permanent commission in the RAF. FO Davoud undertook a refresher flying training course on Atlas and Siskin aircraft at No. 5 Flying Training School in England. Posted to RAF No. 17 Squadron, he flew Bristol Bulldogs, Hawker Harts, and Furies until March 1935.

He resigned his RAF commission after receiving a tempting offer from Canadian Airways President James A. Richardson to be that company's chief pilot and superintendent. Davoud's responsibilities entailed managing the flight operations throughout the province of Manitoba. In 1938, the Hudson's Bay Company, which was also headquartered in Manitoba, lured Paul away from Canadian Airways to specifically set up an air transport service throughout Canada's north for its fur trade department.

In Winnipeg, Manitoba, on October 14, 1939, 27-year-old Paul Davoud married Kilby McAdam Harding, a native of Montreal.

Canada declared war on Germany on September 10, 1939, and the air force lost no time recalling Davoud and others from the reserve list. Paul was reprocessed into the RCAF under Regimental Service No. C. 325 at No. 6 Recruiting Centre in Winnipeg on May 29, 1940.

At that point in the war, married personnel were generally not sent overseas. Instead, they were retained in Canada as instructors or staff pilots at one of the many newly built British Commonwealth Air Training Plan schools. Because of his vast flying experience – 2,885 hours piloting 20 separate military and civilian aircraft types – Davoud was advanced to the rank of FL. He was posted to the Flying Instructor School at RCAF Air Station Trenton, Ontario, on June 15, where he took up the duties of assistant CFI. For the next year, he taught the newly graduated flying instructors the art of how to instruct their students.

In February 1941, David was promoted from FL to SL. He transferred in early June to RCAF Overseas Headquarters in London, England. Once there, he pushed to immediately go on operations. Posted to RAF No. 60 OTU at East Fortune, he trained on Bristol Blenheim and Boulton Paul Defiant Night-Fighters. While at the OTU, he was chosen to form RCAF No. 410 "Cougar" Night Fighter Squadron (NFS) flying Bristol Beaufighters. Cutting short his OTU training, it took him less than two months to stand the squadron up at Ayr, Scotland.

Paul Davoud commanded the Cougars until September 4, at which time he was promoted from SL to WC. On September 5, he was given command of another Canadian NFS – No. 409 "Nighthawk."

Davoud's only aerial victory in the war was also the first kill recorded for 409 Squadron. On Thursday, November 1, 1941, while flying a Beaufighter Mk II from RAF Coleby Grange in Lincolnshire, he and his RAF navigator, Sgt T. Carpenter, intercepted and shot down a Dornier Do 217 twin-engined bomber over the North Sea.

Paul Davoud: Dean of the Night Fighter Squadrons

Group Captain Paul Y. Davoud OBE, DSO, DFC, MiD (2), second row fourth from the left, is pictured with one of his Canadian Hawker Typhoon Fighter-Bomber Squadrons in 1944. (Canada Department of National Defence)

Davoud's combat report describes how they closed in and shot the German raider down:

> I received excellent co-operation from Orby Ground Control Intercept. They put us perfectly onto the trail of an unidentified aircraft. Soon a blip appeared on the screen in Carpenter's 'little black box' showing the bogey to be well to port and 500 feet below our position. I increased speed and turned to port and obtained a visual at 6,000 feet. The bogey was silhouetted against the clouds in bright moonlight. I throttled back and lost height until slightly above and 400 yards to the rear of enemy aircraft who dove for cloud cover. I closed to approximately 200 yards, identified the bandit as Dornier 217 and fired a short burst observing hits on starboard main plane. The enemy returned fire and having closed to about 100 yards, I fired two long bursts, seeing the second burst hit his starboard engine. Just before Do 217 entered cloud, a big explosion blew his right engine and wing completely off. I pulled up to avoid a collision and the Dornier fell burning, straight into the sea. I then returned to base, landing at 2255 hours.

The unfortunate Luftwaffe crew was from Kampfgeschwader 2 (KG-2) "Holzhamer" Wing.

While on patrol on the evening of July 29, 1942, Davoud claimed a Heinkel He 111 as probably destroyed and a Do 217 as damaged.

Davoud, WC Paul Yettvart (C. 325) – Mention in Despatches – No. 409 Squadron – Award effective 9 June 1942 as per London Gazette of that date and AFRO 1000-1001/42 dated 3 July 1942.

Davoud, WC Paul Yettvart (C. 325) – Distinguished Flying Cross – No. 409 Squadron – Award effective 11 January 1943 as per London Gazette dated 2 February 1943 and AFRO 272/43 dated 19 February 1943.

This officer has been engaged on night flying operations for more than a year. He is a skilful pilot whose fine example and inspiring leadership have been worthy of high praise. He has destroyed one and probably destroyed another enemy aircraft.

WC Davoud's last flight with 409 was on February 4, 1943. That evening, he crashed his Beaufighter on landing after an engine failed. Badly burnt on his face and hands, Davoud was taken off operations for the next three months.

In June, he had recovered to the point that he was given command of RCAF No. 418 "City of Edmonton" Squadron, which had just been issued with de Havilland Mosquitos to replace its Intruders.

He later would be awarded a DSO for his brilliant leadership during his time spent as 418's OC from June 1943 to January 8, 1944.

The following extracts from *The Canadian Press* newspaper at the time continue Davoud's story. From November 25, 1943:

The Station Commander at RAF Ford, WC Gerald C. Maxwell Military Cross, DFC, Air Force Cross, a WWI fighter ace, stands beside the runway in the inky darkness as the sleek de Havilland Mosquito Mk IIs of 418 Squadron roar off the ground. He comments to Allan Nickleson, the newspaper reporter; "There go the finest pilots and navigators in the world. They have the best form of discipline. They never have to be told to do a thing. In the air or on the ground, all personnel seem to have the knack of knowledge to sense what is expected of them and carry out their work with precision and dispatch. They take off in the darkness, just two men in a Mosquito. They are lone raiders who are entirely on their own. They know they are expected to destroy enemy aircraft, shoot up airfields, wreck trains, destroy railway junctions and generally play havoc with Jerry in the night. They work alone, coming up on their target through expert navigation then finding their way home to land on a field engulfed in darkness. Ghost raiders, call them what you will, I'm lost in my admiration of their incredible skill, determination and courage. I have never met a squadron with such keenness and determination. A great deal of credit is due to their Commanding Officer, WC Paul Davoud, DFC, MiD from Kingston, Ontario. They're a squadron of which the RCAF and Canada can be well and truly proud."

Paul Davoud: Dean of the Night Fighter Squadrons

DAVOUD, GC Paul Yettvart DFC, MiD, (C. 325) – Distinguished Service Order – No. 418 Squadron – Award effective 2 March 1944 as per London Gazette dated 17 March 1944 and AFRO 766/44 dated 6 April 1944.

"Since being awarded the Distinguished Flying Cross this officer has completed many sorties involving attacks on airfields and other heavily defended areas in Holland, Northern France, Belgium and Germany. He is a forceful and courageous leader whose personal example and exceptional ability have been reflected in the fine fighting qualities and efficiency of the squadron he commands. His loyal and devoted service has been worthy of the highest praise."

On January 9, 1944, WC Davoud was promoted to GC and took over command of No. 22 Sector of the Allied 2nd TAF. This sector was comprised of the following 9 RAF/RCAF Hawker Typhoon Squadrons:

174 Squadron Typhoon 1b Aircraft Code – XP
175 Squadron Typhoon 1b Aircraft Code – HH
245 Squadron Typhoon 1b Aircraft Code – MR
181 Squadron Typhoon 1b Aircraft Code – EL
182 Squadron Typhoon 1b Aircraft Code – XM
247 Squadron Typhoon 1b Aircraft Code – ZY
438 (Canadian) Squadron Typhoon 1b Aircraft Code – F3
439 (Canadian) Squadron Typhoon 1b Aircraft Code – 5V
440 (Canadian) Squadron Typhoon 1b Aircraft Code – 18

An article from June 15, 1944:

Rockets are accurate but bombs are far more spectacular from the pilot's point of view. That is the consensus of pilots of an all Empire Typhoon squadron based in Southern England in which there are many Canadians serving. The squadron made its first rocket attack October 25, 1943, destroying the power house at Caen, France. Only recently was the use of rockets by Allied aircraft taken off the secret list. Since this sector, commanded by GC Paul Davoud, DSO, DFC, MiD of Kingston, Ontario, includes rocket-carrying Typhoons and Typhoon bomber squadrons, practically all types of targets can be assigned to it.

The aircraft take off from the same base after attending the same briefing and, after the show, compare observations. Frequently these various squadrons act as flak busters for the one completing the high or low-level mission. They strafe anti-aircraft defences on the deck while rocket projectiles or bombing attacks are delivered from above. As may be expected, the devotees of Rocket Projectiles [RPs] and bombs seek to out do each other in complete destruction of targets so that a slightly damaged bridge or rail junction does not have to be finished off with the other's weapon. Both have reported exceptionally good results recently. Two squadrons of RCAF Typhoon fighter-bombers, escorted by two RAF flak busting squadrons, accurately bombed and destroyed an important railway bridge south of Rouen on May 28 and disrupted rail communications near by. Rocket pursuit Typhoons, as the pilots have nicknamed themselves from the RAF unit using the same airfield, neatly dispatched enemy wireless installations in an old fortress in the Channel Islands the day previously and destroyed the German barracks near Dieppe the same day. The stone building just crumpled at the corners when the rockets drilled in and exploded, reported PO N. E. U. Arrons of Suffolk, England. The squadron has among its personnel one pilot from Trinidad, four Australians, three Canadians, a resident of the Orkneys and the remainder are from England.

From July 7, 1944:

The Typhoon, as versatile an aircraft as the Hurricane and Spitfire of Battle of Britain fame, is a veritable warship of the air that, as a rocket-carrying plane, is given front-line troops closer support than they have ever enjoyed. Not only is the support extremely effective, but it cheers the ground troops tremendously to see the rocket-carrying Tiffies scream down over their heads to obliterate an obstinate strong point in the path of their advance. Hauling eight sixty pound three inch high explosive underwing air-to-ground rockets or two 1,000 pound general purpose bombs, the Typhoon, together with its main armament of four 20mm Hispano-Suiza Mk II cannons with 560 rounds of ammunition, is pulverizing the German Armoured Corps. The targets these aircraft tackle varies from sortie to sortie. In Normandy the objectives usually are enemy armour and large buildings used as strong points. Earlier this week Typhoons in a sector commanded by GC Paul Davoud, were called in to help the Canadians fighting on Carpiquet airfield where the Germans had dug in seventeen tanks which were giving the dominion troops trouble. Two Canadians who took part in the attack, FO's Lorin Metcalf, 25 of St. Thomas, Ontario and Bert Thrilwell, 25 of Victoria, British Columbia, told about the attack; "The Canadian ground troops held the hangars at one side of the airfield and the Germans held the other. The opposing forces were not more than 150 or 200 yards apart. The tanks were dug in in V shape with the apex pointing toward the Canadians. The Germans had dug big holes and backed the tanks in and covered them with earth up to the top of the tracks. Diving at a speed of more than 400 miles per hour through very heavy flak," Metcalf said, the Typhoons launched their rockets at the tanks." Neither Metcalf nor Thrilwell knew how many tanks the squadron had knocked out because as soon as they fire their rockets, they pull out of their dive to avoid hitting debris blown into the air. But they were pleased to learn that the troops who watched the rockets streak home have been high in their praise ever since because the attack resulted in the pressure on the Canadians being eased considerably. Thrilwell said; "You feel you are helping the boys out and I get a big kick out of being able to do that."

Paul Davoud: Dean of the Night Fighter Squadrons

On July 13, 1944, GC Davoud requested to be returned to a flying job. In late August, he was given command of RCAF No. 143 Typhoon Wing, a post he held until January 1, 1945.

An article from August 4, 1944, continued:

> RCAF GC Paul Davoud, said today that the Germans seem hopelessly lost without direction from Field Marshal Erwin Rommel and he said the RAF was busy checking plane by plane in an effort to place the credit for strafing Rommel's car and cracking open the marshal's head. On brief leave from the front, Davoud told a press group that Rommel obviously was no longer directing the German defences because the Nazis generally were conducting their campaign like school children. One of the chief factors in cracking the morale of Nazi troops Davoud said, "is the vicious-sounding rocket-carrying Typhoons which sweep low with a piercing scream before launching their deadly accurate missiles."
>
> Although he no longer leads rocket carrying aircraft, having transferred to Typhoon fighter-bombers which carry bombs, Davoud is one of the foremost Allied experts in the new type of assault. A fair example of the value of the rockets occurred on July 29 in the St. Lô area of Normandy. Davoud said; "American P-47 Thunderbolts destroyed a Sienne River bridge and about twenty-five German tanks were left wandering in circles. The Americans, realizing what a fine target they made for rocketeers, call the Typhoons in and they destroyed seventeen."

In another article from February 27, 1945, by Kenneth C. Cragg:

> GC Paul Davoud of Kingston, Ontario stated that when the Americans broke through in the Cherbourg Peninsula last summer; "Hitler, the genius, got on the telephone and personally ordered German armour scattered along the front, out into the open in close packed formation on the highway! One of our typhoons saw them. He yelled back on his radio for help and went after them himself. We got eighty-nine Panther and Tiger tanks that day for the loss of three Typhoons. They told us later, that day's work was the equivalent of what might have been done by two Armoured Divisions."
>
> Canadian airmen have a tendency toward enthusiasm and Paul Davoud has a special brand of it for his flying artillerymen. Working with the infantry, he sent his Typhoons into action before Caen where they sprayed rockets, cannon fire and bombs a bare 400 yards before our troops. We used them just like artillery, he said. "The plan of close support is absolutely workable. We have proved it." In his group, half of the pilots are Canadians, but he makes a point that in no arm of the services is the morale higher than in the tactical air formations. When you get a cocky air force like we have, with good equipment, they can do anything. In the Caen battle he described how the pilots, rising over their air strips, could see to the

north the bulk of battleships popping shells over into the German lines and could see the shells exploding. Their own run, out and back, was but a ten minute affair. Then after the peak at Falaise, things happened that every one prayed for – the Germans put their vehicles on the road without air cover. We went after them with rockets, bombs and cannon. In one day, north of Falaise, the Allied Tactical Air Groups destroyed 3,000 vehicles. From the morale angle, the Typhoons are great boosters for our own soldiers and great breeders of fear for the enemy. The sound effect alone is quite something – the normal thunder of a Typhoon engine, the horrifying 'swish' of the rockets and the noise of the cannon. As Davoud himself said; "If I were on a French road and saw a Typhoon coming? Well, I'd write myself off right then and there."

He is in Canada on a brief professional visit and is returning soon to his post with Operational Headquarters of Tactical Air Force Group. He was one of the planners of air support for ground troops on D-Day.

Assigned on January 2, 1945, as operations director at No. 83 Composite Group, 2nd TAF under Air Vice Marshal, Sir Harry Broadhurst, GC Davoud had, until war's end, 42 squadrons (750 combat aircraft) under his planning and operational control.

The Allied document covering Germany's unconditional surrender was signed by Generaloberst Alfred Jodl in a brick schoolhouse at Rheims, France, at 0241hrs on May 7, 1945. The agreement officially took effect at 2301hrs on Tuesday, May 8, 1945.

GC Davoud was rotated back to Canada on June 20, 1945, to No. 1 Repatriation Depot at Lachine, Quebec. Two days later, at No. 5 Release Centre at Winnipeg, Manitoba, he became a civilian. On July 26, 1945, he was retired from the RCAF and was transferred to Class "E" of the general section of the Reserve.

He had several awards to his name:

Davoud, GC Paul Yettvart, DSO, DFC, MiD (2) (C. 325) – Officer, Order of the British Empire – No. 83 Group Headquarters – Award effective 14 June 1945 as per London Gazette of that date and AFRO 1219 dated 27 July 1945.

Group Captain Davoud has served with this Group since January 1944. He was given the task of forming and commanding two new airfields from squadrons and personnel recently transferred from Canada. He showed himself to be a Commander of considerable resource and ability and completed his task with great enthusiasm and efficiency. He arrived on the continent a week after D-Day and shortly afterwards a reorganization of the group placed him in command of No. 143 Wing. He filled this post with energy and distinction until January 1945 when he was appointed Group Captain, Operations of Group Headquarters. Previous to joining

83 Group this officer gave outstanding service whilst commanding a Canadian Typhoon fighter bomber Wing.

Davoud, GC Paul Y., OBE, DSO, DFC, MiD (2) (C. 325) – Commander, Order of Orange-Nassau with Swords (Holland) – Award effective 6 February 1948 as per AFRO 81/48 of that date.

In command of No. 143 Wing, Royal Canadian Air Force, stationed at Eindhoven, from September until December 1944 and through his excellent work he has greatly contributed to the liberation of the Netherlands.

In 1945, Paul Davoud received an appointment as assistant to John Tudhope, the Operations Manager of Trans Canada Airlines. Next, he worked with the Canadian Breweries/Argus Corporation in 1948 to establish an air service for them. In 1951, Paul accepted a position as General Manager of Field and Kenting Aviation.

Davoud went on from there to hold positions as vice president, sales and service with Orenda Engines from 1954 to 1959, Chairman of the Air Transport Board from 1959 to 1963 and vice president of sales for de Havilland from 1963 to 1971.

His last employment was as director of aviation services with the Ministry of Transportation and Communications for the Province of Ontario. He retired from this position in 1978 after completing 50 years of service to Canadian aviation.

In 1971, Canadian Forces Base North Bay, Ontario, honored this great airman when it named the base's public school the Paul Davoud School. It retained the name until 1990 when the base downsized and the school was closed. A year later, this structure became the new home for the Air Weapons Control and Countermeasures School and was dedicated as the Paul Davoud Building.

Retired GC Davoud was elected to the Canadian Aviation Hall of Fame in 1985.

Paul Davoud died on March 24, 1987, at the family residence at Wolfe Island, Ontario. This large island, part of the famous Thousand Islands, is an archipelago of islands that straddle the Canada–US border in the middle of the Saint Lawrence River.

Richard Dose
California Spitfire Pilot

On Tuesday, September 16, 1941, Richard Herman "Dick" Dose arrived in Ottawa, Ontario, to join the RCAF. Dose, a third generation German–American citizen, had traveled 2,867 miles across the North American continent from Solana Beach, California, to the RCAF's No. 12 Recruiting Centre specifically for that purpose. The 22-year-old had served for a short time as a flying cadet in the USAAC. Entering that program in November 1940, Richard received 35 hours of flight instruction on Boeing PT-17 Stearman biplanes at Glendale, California, but washed out in March 1941 due to flying deficiencies.

Richard H. Dose was born to Ottilie Fuchs and George Dose on March 1, 1919, in St. Louis, Missouri. He was educated in that city's school system from 1924 until 1936, first at Sherman Public School, then Roosevelt High School. Dick attended Washington University in St. Louis from 1936 to 1940, earning a degree in Chemical Engineering.

From 1937 until 1939, he was employed with Anheuser-Busch Breweries in its traffic department.

Richard's older brother Robert, a United States Marine Corps instructor pilot, was, at the time, stationed at Naval Air Station (NAS) Pensacola, Florida. During the summer of 1941, Dick lived with Robert, who, in his off-duty hours, took his brother flying in an attempt to refine his flying skills.

That extra coaching involving 22 flight hours in a Piper J-3 Cub paid off after Richard was accepted by the RCAF as a pilot trainee.

The RCAF recruiter, PO C. O. Summers, was duly impressed by the sincerity of the 6ft 1in, 190lb applicant when he noted the following remarks in his file: "Very determined to become a pilot. Good command of the English language and is fairly fluent in German. College graduate. Sports interest – Football and Baseball. Excellent type but a bit independent which the RCAF will rectify."

Dose enlisted in the Canadian air force for the war's duration as an AC2 earning CAN$39.00 a month.

Like the thousands of other American volunteers, he was allowed to wear "USA" shoulder flashes on his Canadian uniform. There was one other variation of this patch, which read "CANADA/USA." Those patch-wearing Americans were routinely stopped on the street in the communities in which they were training and thanked by the civilian population for coming to Canada and helping out with the war effort. Almost all were invited, at one time or another, by complete strangers to join them in their family homes for Sunday dinner. For those young Americans who could not get home for Christmas due to the great distances involved, those invitations from Canadian families to stay with them and celebrate the festive holidays as an extended member of the family were greatly appreciated. The unbreakable bonds of friendship forged from those great acts of kindness in wartime were never to be forgotten.

Assigned Regimental Service No. R. 125892, Dick headed off to Toronto, Ontario, at the end of October for basic training at No. 1 MD. On December 21, 1941, after completing that phase, he laterally moved over to No. 6 ITS in that city. After the eight-week course, Richard graduated on February 28, 1942. He was promoted to the rank of LAC and was given a pay raise of 90 cents per day, which increased his monthly earnings to $67.50.

For the next ten weeks, Dick flew Fleet Finch II biplanes at No. 7 EFTS at Windsor, Ontario. Posted on May 10 to No. 14 SFTS at Aylmer, Ontario, he flew 170 hours on Yale and Harvard advanced trainers. He graduated from Course No. 57 and earned his wings on September 24, 1942, as an SP. The next day, he was commissioned from the ranks as a PO. His Service No. was changed from R. 125892 to J. 14403.

One of the aircraft types that Pilot Officer Richard H. Dose flew at Air Station Aylmer, Ontario, was the NAA Yale. (Parr Yonemoto)

Taking his two-week pre-embarkation leave, Richard reported to "Y" Depot Pier 21, Halifax, Nova Scotia, on October 27 for overseas deployment. He arrived at No. 3 Personnel Reception Centre at Bournemouth on November 6.

On December 9, Dose was posted to RAF No. 53 OTU at Llandow, South Wales, where he flew Miles Master Mk IIIs and Supermarine Spitfire Mk Is and IIs. The course concluded early in April 1943. While there, Richard was promoted from PO to FO.

Dose arrived at RAF Digby on April 13, where he was assigned to fly Spitfire Mk Vbs with RCAF No. 402 "City of Winnipeg Bear" FS. The squadron flew many cross-Channel sorties from Kenley and Redhill, mainly in the ground-attack role.

At 1950hrs on June 8, 1943, Dick and three other members of the squadron, FO D. R. Drummond, PO W. C. Lawrence, and FS L. A. Moore, took off from RAF Coltishall, Norfolk, where they had landed to top up their fuel tanks. The four fighters were heading to Holland on a Rhubarb sortie. However, only three aircraft returned – FO Dose, in a Castle Bromwich-built Spitfire Vb, coded EP394, was missing.

402's OC, SL Lloyd V. Chadburn, sent the following message on June 10 to the Under Secretary of State at the Air Ministry in London:

> On June 8th, 1943, a section (FO D. R. Drummond – Red 1; FO R. H. Dose – Red 2) took off from Coltishall to do Rhubarbs, the object being to attack barges and locomotives. They entered the enemy coast in the area north of Noordwijkerhout and proceeded along the Leiden Haarlem Railway, turning right just before reaching Haarlem and flew until reaching the canal from Haarlem to Leiden, then south and attacked barges at Hoofddorp. After attacking the barges, Red 2 started to climb in a northwesterly direction into cloud cover and was followed by Red 1. When in cloud cover, Red 1 called Red 2 and asked if he knew where he was going. Red 2 answered that he did not. That was the last message received from him. Red section while strafing the barges experienced a moderate amount of light flak. Red 2 at no time gave any indication over the Radio/Telephone that he or his aircraft had been hit by flak. Red 2 failed to answer repeated calls by Red 1 after the last message.

On the same day, Chadburn sent the following letter to Richard's parents in California:

> Before receiving this letter you will have had a telegram informing you that your son, Dick, has been reported missing as a result of air operations. It is with great regret that I write to you this date to convey to Dick's family the feelings of my entire squadron.
>
> On the afternoon of June 8th, 1943, Dick, along with three other members of the squadron, took off to attack enemy targets in Holland. The operation went according

to schedule. After attacking transportation in Holland, Dick started to climb up into cloud cover followed by Flying Officer Drummond as they were heading back out across the coast to England. Soon after this Drummond called Dick over the R/T to see if he knew where he was. Dick replied that he was unsure of his position, whereupon FO Drummond told him to keep on the same heading and that would bring him out over the North Sea. That was the last message he had from Dick. He kept calling him on the radio but to no avail. There is no indication that Dick had been shot down and we hope that he may be a Prisoner of War. Dick was a very keen pilot and went full out for all types of fighter operations. His ready smile and pleasing personality is greatly missed in the officers' mess. Although he had only been with the squadron for a short while, he had taken part in several sweeps and had proven his worth as a fighter pilot. He took a keen interest in the squadron's sporting activities and was a star member of the softball team. If he is a PoW, you will hear this directly through the Air Ministry who will receive the particulars from the International Red Cross Society. Your son's effects have been gathered together and forwarded to the Royal Air Force Central Depository, Colnbrook, where they will be held until better news is received or in any event, for a period of at least six months before being forwarded to you through the Administrator of Estates, Ottawa.

May I now express the great sympathy which all of us feel with you in your great anxiety, and I should like also to assure you how greatly his comrades in the air force admire the heroic sacrifice your son has made so far from home in the cause of freedom.

Information from German sources in December 1943 led the Red Cross to notify the Air Ministry that Dick was killed on June 8, 1943, when his Spitfire crashed at 2044hrs at Wassenaar, Holland. He was buried in the Westduin Cemetery.

The RCAF records officer officially registered the details of Richard's death with the Province of Ontario's Bureau of Statistics on January 27, 1944, after changing his status from that of MIA to KIA.

Dose's earned wartime medals, which included the 1939–45 Star, Aircrew European Star, General Service Medal, and the Canadian Volunteer Service Medal & Clasp, were forwarded to his parents in California on August 15, 1946.

On March 17, 1950, a Memorial Bar was sent to Mr. George Dose on behalf of the Canadian federal government. The Memorial Bar is a companion award to the Memorial Cross. It is presented to the deceased's father, whereas the Memorial Cross is given to the deceased's mother. The Bar signifies the sacrifice made by a member of the military who has laid down his or her life for their country.

George Dunaway
Arkansas Tactical Reconnaissance Pilot

Twenty-one-year-old George Mason Dunaway, Jr. from Fayetteville, Arkansas, had all the necessary qualifications to join the USAAC pilot training program in 1940. Britain and its Commonwealth allies had been at war with Germany since September 1939 and George, being an impetuous individual, decided he was not going to wait around for the US to enter the fray that would eventually be known as World War II. Travelling to Windsor, Ontario, on Tuesday, October 8, 1940, Dunaway voluntarily enlisted in the RCAF at No. 8 Recruiting Centre as an AC2 under Regimental Service No. R. 67830.

Dunaway was an excellent air force candidate. The university graduate had extensive military training throughout his high school and college years in the ROTC and in the Arkansas Army National Guard. He was a field artillery sergeant proficient on the 37mm, anti-tank gun, the 3in stokes mortar, and the 155mm howitzer. The recruiting officer, FO C. L. Arnold, rated George above average in all categories and noted the following in his file: "Leaves an exceptional favourable impression. Well educated and very keen to serve."

George was born to George M. Dunaway, Sr. and Dana Mary Jones on March 1, 1919, in Tulsa, Oklahoma. He grew up in the small community of Caney, Kansas, where his father worked as a petroleum engineer. Dunaway's primary education began in 1924 at Caney Public School and concluded at Caney High School in 1936. George attended Oklahoma State Teachers College and the University of Arkansas from 1936 until 1940. After George's father suffered a debilitating industrial accident, his parents moved to 228 North Locust Avenue in Fayetteville.

Because of his previous US Army training, Dunaway zipped through the standard five-week basic training course at No. 1 MD at Toronto, Ontario, in only 14 days. From October 23 to December 8, he was assigned to perform guard duty at RCAF Air Station Trenton, Ontario. On December 9, 1940, he was posted back to Toronto to No. 1 ITS where, on Course No. 13, he achieved a 93 percent average, finishing second in a class of 116 students. George graduated on January 14, 1941,

George Dunaway: Arkansas Tactical Reconnaissance Pilot

The elementary aircraft Pilot Officer George M. Dunaway learned to fly on was the Fleet Finch Mk II at Windsor, Ontario, in 1941. (Canada Department of National Defence)

and was promoted to LAC. The school's WC wrote the following in his file: "Very good pilot material. Mature, fast thinking and keen. Alert, bright and smart."

Returning to Windsor, Dunaway flew 56.15 hours on Fleet Finch Mk II aircraft from January 16 to March 5 at No. 7 EFTS. The CFI of Course No. 18 stated the following: "Very good air sense. Intelligent flyer. Learns quickly and is smooth on the controls." The CGI wrote the following: "Definitely suitable for a commission. Above average deportment. Very neat in appearance. High average intelligence. Hard worker. An excellent squad commander." George graduated with an 84.7 percent average and was first in a class of 27 students.

The final phase of Dunaway's training took him to No. 10 SFTS at Dauphin, Manitoba. There he flew 117.80 hours on Harvard aircraft. Forty-eight pilots graduated from Course No. 25 at Dauphin on June 21, 1941, with George finishing third in the class with an 84.1 percent average. The school's CGI commented: "Quiet, intelligent, superior type." From the CFI: "Above average ability. Aerobatics good. Most satisfactory progress."

LAC Dunaway was promoted to SP. The next day, the RCAF assigned him new Regimental Service No. J. 5796 – after commissioning him as a PO. George's pay had risen significantly over the short length of time he spent training in Canada's air force – from CAN$39.00 a month as an AC2 to $180.00 a month as a PO.

Having enjoyed the standard two-week pre-embarkation leave visiting family and friends, Dunaway departed Canada from "Y" Depot, Pier 21, Halifax, Nova Scotia, on July 9, 1941. The convoy arrived in Glasgow, Scotland, whereupon George, along with hundreds of other airmen, took a troop train to No. 3 Personnel Reception Centre at Bournemouth.

On August 18, PO Dunaway was posted on Course No. 36 to RAF No. 41 OTU at Hawarden in Flintshire. No. 41's function was to train TR pilots for the RAF Army Co-operation squadrons. George graduated on October 11, after having flown 69.50 hours on Westland Lysanders. The school's OC, GC N. C. Saward wrote the following in his file: "Above average. Has worked very hard. Is conscientious and has produced excellent results. Will make a very sound reconnaissance pilot."

Dunaway was posted to RCAF No. 414 Reconnaissance Fighter Squadron, which was flying Curtiss-Wright Tomahawk Mk Is and Lysanders from RAF Croydon, just outside London. The squadron had formed earlier that year, with the pilots carrying out intensive training that led to the unit becoming fully operational. Much of the training was devoted to innumerable exercises with the Army, during which the squadron practiced the technique of ground-air cooperation and tested both the efficiency of its equipment and the adequacy of its establishment in aircraft and personnel.

The Tomahawk Mk I was the equivalent of the USAAC P-40D Warhawk. It was during this prolonged period of training that one casualty was sustained when PO G. M. Dunaway was killed on November 21, 1941, while flying in bad weather over Dorset.

The RAF Accident Report dated November 23, 1941, stated:

> At 1130 hours on the morning of November 21, 1941, RCAF PO George Mason Dunaway was authorized by his Flight Commander, Flight Lieutenant H. C. Stewart, to carry out navigation training from Croydon to Barnstaple and return. He was instructed by FL Stewart that, in the event of weather deterioration, he was to return to the aerodrome immediately.
>
> At 1345 hours a message was received from the duty pilot at Croydon to the effect that PO Dunaway, in Tomahawk AH902, had crashed near the village of Charlton Marshall, North Dorset and that the pilot was dead.
>
> Squadron Leader (SL) Elms immediately departed by car to the accident scene. When he arrived he contacted the Dorset police, who showed him sworn statements which had been made by two soldiers who were eyewitnesses to the crash. From their statements, it was concluded the aircraft exited the cloud base 900ft to 1,000ft above ground and was spinning in a nose down attitude. With the engine roaring at full throttle, the aircraft continued to spin until it hit the ground. As the light was fading, SL Elms delayed the examination of the crash site until the following day.

The 22-year-old PO is buried at the Brookwood Military Cemetery, Surrey, England – Grave Reference 37 A.1.

George Mason Dunaway, Jr.'s decorations, which included the 1939–45 Star, Aircrew European Star, General Service Medal, and the Canadian Volunteer Service Medal & Clasp, were forwarded to his parents in Fayetteville, Arkansas, on January 17, 1950.

Clyde East
Virginia Mustang Ace

Clyde Bennett East was born at Cole's Hill plantation in the hamlet of Sheva in Pittsylvania County, Virginia, on July 19, 1921. He was the fifth of nine children of sharecroppers James and Mary East. Clyde was raised on a dirt-poor tobacco farm and, from the time he was first able to read, his favorite stories were those that centered around the aviators of World War I. In August 1925, when he was four, the family home was destroyed by fire. The Easts proceeded to construct a new house, but found themselves literally snuggling under blankets of snow on Christmas morning because the roof had not yet been built.

On Independence Day in 1937, during his third year of high school, East rode in an airplane for the first time. After that experience, his desire to become a pilot grew even stronger. Graduating from Chatham Virginia High School in 1938, Clyde was disappointed to learn that he would need a minimum of two years of college before he could apply to join the USAAC pilot training program.

In June 1941, with US$10 in his pocket, the 19-year-old Virginian thumbed his way to Niagara Falls, New York. There he crossed the United States–Canada border into Niagara Falls, Ontario. His destination was the RCAF Recruiting Office in Hamilton, Ontario, some 60 miles distance.

Just a few miles outside the Falls, East had the good fortune to hitch a ride with an instructor from No. 33 Air Navigation School at Mount Hope, Ontario. The officer not only drove Clyde to his destination, No. 10 Recruiting Centre, but briefed him during the trip on his future air force career.

Processed into the RCAF as an AC2, Clyde spent the next several weeks at No. 1 MD in Toronto, Ontario. It was there that he picked up the nickname "Stonewall." East had mentioned to someone that he and American Civil War Confederate General Thomas Jonathan "Stonewall" Jackson were born in the same rural area of Virginia.

East attended No. 1 ITS in Toronto and graduated at the beginning of October. One of Clyde's barracks' mates was from Hamilton, and one weekend when they were given leave, he took Clyde home to meet his family. Introduced to his friend's sister, East had no way of knowing that he had just met his future wife, Margaret Ann.

Promoted to LAC, Stonewall was posted to No. 4 EFTS at Windsor Mills, Quebec, where he flew yellow Fleet Finch biplane trainers. He was doing well on the course until an instructor caught him and another student indulging in a game of unauthorized aerial horseplay.

East failed a 50-hour check ride the instructor sprung on him, which effectively washed him out as a pilot trainee. For the next four months, Clyde languished at the Re-Selection Centre at RCAF Air Station Trenton, Ontario. This essentially was a recycling depot for washouts from every type and every stage of RCAF aircrew training. Clyde spent his time there telling anyone who would listen that he was not ready for the test and for that reason he should be given another chance. To his complete surprise, the ploy finally worked.

Clyde East was a very lucky young man as only one out of every 100 washed out students was ever sent back by the Re-Selection Board to resume flight training. In March 1942, Stonewall had to start from the beginning, but this time he was careful not to break any rules or regulations along the way.

Later in life, he candidly admitted that he probably made it because he was a volunteer from the United States; he doubts that the authorities would have gone to so much trouble for a Canadian in similar circumstances.

While all of this was going on, Clyde was dating and corresponding with Margaret Ann.

In November 1942, Clyde was awarded his RCAF wings flying single-engined Harvard and Yale trainers at No. 6 SFTS at Dunnville, Ontario. He graduated in the top 10 percent of his class and was commissioned as a PO.

He sailed in January 1943 from Pier 21, Halifax, Nova Scotia, on a troop ship headed for England. Assigned to No. 3 Personnel Reception Centre at Bournemouth, East had to wait two months before going to an OTU.

At the end of March, Clyde began conversion training on Mustang Mk Is at RAF No. 41 OTU, Hawarden in Flintshire. No. 41's function was to train TR pilots for the RAF Army Co-operation squadrons. Graduating

Flying Officer Clyde B. East in 1943. In the background, a Mustang Mk I belonging to RCAF No. 414 "Black Knight" FS. (Canadian National Defence Image Library)

at the end of April, Stonewall was posted to RCAF No. 414 "Black Knight" Squadron, which was flying the Allison F3R-engined Mustang Mk Is from RAF Dunsfold, Surrey.

In July, the squadron moved to Gatwick in southeastern England and, in August, to Ashford in Kent. In October, it operated from airfields at Woodchurch, Kent, and Redhill, Surrey. On November 3, it moved back to Gatwick and settled down in winter quarters for a long stay. Ranger operations over France and the Low Countries continued for a few days with considerable success. That month, East was promoted to FO.

After completing 26 Rhubarb sorties into France, Belgium, and Holland, where he attacked rail, motor, and barge traffic, Stonewall transferred from the RCAF to the USAAF on January 11, 1944, with the rank of 1st lieutenant. His total flight time with the RCAF amounted to 491 hours.

Assigned to the 15th Tactical Reconnaissance Squadron (TRS), 10th Photographic Group (PG), 9th Air Force, East logged some 200 flight hours in Supermarine Spitfire Vbs before the squadron took delivery of the Rolls-Royce Merlin-engined F-6C and F-6D Photo Reconnaissance Mustangs.

East commented on the Spitfire's low-level flying qualities: "We flew the clipped-wing version of the 'Five B' with derated engines, which meant it was much faster and had more power at lower altitudes. However, as you climbed, it would lose power to the point that at 13,000 feet that was about as high as you could effectively operate the type before performance began to seriously erode. It was however a great airplane for low altitudes and it was the best flying I ever had."

On D-Day, at 1900hrs, East and his wingman bounced four German Fw 190s that were in a landing pattern near Laval, France. Both F-6C pilots claimed a single victory. East later said: "We may have actually shot down a third airplane. We saw only two aircraft go down, but we left three fires burning on the ground."

On December 17, 1944, a few days before the Battle of the Bulge, Lieutenants Clyde East and Henry Lacey spotted, at 1435hrs, a Messerschmitt Bf 109 east of Giessen, Germany. The enemy aircraft, sporting a gaudy orange and white color scheme, was leisurely flying down the autobahn at 200ft. East pulled in behind and fired two short bursts from his four Colt-Browning M-2 .50 caliber heavy machine guns. The Luftwaffe pilot took no evasive action. The doomed aircraft rolled up on one wing, fell to earth and exploded on impact.

In a letter home, Clyde described the action: "He never knew what hit him. I made one pass, firing about seventy-five rounds and must have killed the pilot outright."

Noting that the Mustangs were originally painted Olive Drab, Clyde commented on their transition to bare metal: "One or two months into the P-51 operations in Europe someone directed us to 'take that damn paint off' because nobody cared if the enemy pilots saw you. It did, however, remove about one hundred pounds of weight."

Returning from a month's leave of rest and recuperation (R&R) at the end of December 1944, East transitioned into the newer F-6D. He fondly recalls that variant, "It was a great airplane. It had six .50-caliber machine guns instead of four like the earlier model. The bubble canopy gave you far more visibility than in the earlier Mustang, which was great for speed, but it hardly had any visibility to the rear because of the heavily metal-framed canopy."

At 1300hrs on March 15, 1945, newly promoted Captain East downed a Bf 109 in a Mustang F-6D, 15 miles west of Aschaffenburg.

Stonewall became an ace at 0945hrs on March 24, 1945, by bagging his fourth and fifth kills – both Bf 109s – while on a routine reconnaissance mission from Schweinfurt to Fulda.

On March 27, 1945, at 1630hrs, Clyde and his wingman, Lt Henry Lacey, literally stumbled onto a flight of six German Stukas that were dive-bombing a convoy of US 4th Armored Division vehicles as they attempted to cross a bridge deep within enemy territory. To make matters worse, a line of Junkers Ju 87 bombers could be seen in the distance preparing for additional attacks. Immediately engaging the Stukas, East opened fire and brought down two – one crashing after the crew bailed out and one crash-landed on a sand bar adjacent to the riverbank. Lacey claimed a third Stuka, but that kill was never confirmed.

Captain East claimed one half of a Ju 188 night fighter near Wittenburg at 0830hrs on April 4, 1945. One hour later, 15 miles south of Leipzig, he was victorious over an Fw 190.

Between 0800hrs and 0910hrs on April 8, 1945, five miles northwest of Dresden, Clyde brought down two Ju 87s, one half of a He 111 and a Siebel Fh 104 Hallore.

Commenting on the sudden turn of events with his enemy aerial encounters, Clyde said:

> We had never seen an enemy airplane before D-Day and the philosophy on air-to-air combat was generally that if we saw one we would attack it. Later on, there were many other encounters with pilots of the 15th Squadron and there really were no rules – nobody ever said anything about not shooting them down. By early April 1945, we were shooting down airplanes day after day. Up to that time I had eight or nine victories and one day my wingman and I went out and shot down six airplanes between us.
>
> The next day we received an edict from Major General Weyland, Commander of the 9th Tactical Air Force, saying, "No more attacking of enemy aircraft – you are to fire only in your own defense." What got the General so upset was that we'd shot down a transport and a small twin-engined wooden liaison aircraft. From that point on, we had to focus our activities on fighters only.

A Bf 109 fell to the guns of East's Mustang five miles south of Hof, Germany, at 1500hrs on April 13, 1945.

On May 8, 1945, Captain East's 14th and last victim was a Fieseler Fi 167 Torpedo-Bomber, which was brought down early in the morning of the last day of the European war.

Clyde Bennett East had flown more than 200 sorties, which translated into 350 combat flying hours. He had shot down 14 enemy aircraft, not too shabby for a TR pilot whose main purpose was to observe and take pictures and who was only supposed to shoot back in self-defense.

Captain East's last assigned aircraft, an F-6D Mustang serial number 44-14306 coded 5M-K, was named *Lil Margaret*.

After the war, Clyde remained in the service as a regular air force officer. Stationed at March Air Force Base in Riverside, California, he married Margaret Ann, and it was there where the first two of their six children were born. Assigned to the 12th TRS, East transitioned into the jet age, flying the Lockheed RF-80A Shooting Star.

By April 1949, East had logged more than 1,000 hours of jet time and was reassigned as the squadron operations officer with the 161st TRS at Langley Air Force Base (AFB), Virginia.

With the outbreak of the Korean War in June 1950, he was ordered to Itazuke, Japan, to join the 8th TRS and, by October 1950, he had flown more than 60 combat sorties over North Korea. East was appointed as the operations officer of the newly activated 45th TRS, a specially organized low-altitude unit flying brand new RF-51D Mustangs never before assigned to tactical units. Clyde recalled:

> We insisted on flying beyond the bomb line in pairs of RF-51s because we were taking heavy doses of light flak at low altitudes. On almost every flight we experienced the highest loss rate of any unit in Korea.
>
> In 1951, however, T-33s out of Taegu were also used for reconnaissance work because you could put someone in the backseat with binoculars and with that second pair of eyes, you'd get twice the visibility.

By the end of his Korean tour in September 1951, East had flown over 130 combat sorties in RF-51s, RF-80s and T-33s.

Further assignments saw the East family relocate to Shaw AFB in South Carolina, where two daughters were born.

In 1954, Clyde became an air advisor to the Italian Air Force (IAF). East explained: "I answered the call for a guy who was jet-qualified and who had photo reconnaissance experience to be an instructor for the IAF. My job was to help them transition from the Republic F-84G Thunderjet into the new RF-84F Thunderflash." He and his family lived in Rome and Verona, and he vividly recalled flying both Republic jets. "Next to the Spitfire, the F-84G was about the friendliest airplane anyone could ever fly. It was a great airplane."

In Italy, the East family added to their numbers with the birth of two more daughters. Later the girls relinquished their Italian birthright and became American citizens.

Returning to the US in July 1957, Major East attended the USAF Air Command and Staff College at Maxwell AFB in Alabama. He was then assigned to Shaw AFB as the squadron commander of the 18th TRS. At that time, the 18th was one of only three air force squadrons to receive the hot new supersonic McDonnell Douglas RF-101 Voodoo.

In May 1959, East led the "One-O-Wonders" on a mass non-stop deployment from South Carolina to de Laon-Couvron AFB in France, utilizing extensive inflight refueling on the trans-oceanic flight. While there, the squadron participated in numerous NATO combined air and ground exercises, perfecting its low-altitude navigation and reconnaissance operations.

In July 1962, East, now a lieutenant colonel, was the commander of the 20th TRS. That October, during the Cuban Missile Crisis, Clyde East was engaged in hazardous missions as dangerous as any that he had flown in combat. He personally flew some of the 100 photo missions over Cuba, as ordered by President John F. Kennedy and his staff. Some were as low as 400ft and at blistering speeds exceeding 726mph.

In February 1965, East was offered the position of military consultant at the Rand Corporation. As he put it, "the offer was too good to pass up." Retiring from the USAF that month, he worked at Rand until 1993.

East lived with his wife in Oak Park, California, just north of Los Angeles. There, he led a busy life, keeping up with six children and eight grandchildren.

During his remarkable 24-year air force career, this Go Fast Reconnaissance Pilot was awarded the following military medals: for World War II – Silver Star, DFC, 37 Air Medals (AMs); for Korea – 2 DFCs, 5 AMs; for the Cuban Missile Crisis – DFC.

Clyde B. East passed away in his 94th year on July 30, 2014.

David Fairbanks
New York Tempest Ace

Forty-two years before Tom Cruise famously flipped the bird to another pilot in the 1986 blockbuster movie *Top Gun*, a frustrated World War II Hawker Tempest pilot, out of ammunition, gave that same rude finger greeting to a Messerschmitt Bf 109 pilot over Germany in 1944.

From the December 17, 1944, combat report of FL David Charles "Foob" Fairbanks, RCAF:

> I was flying Blue One on a sweep to Rheine, Germany and had turned on to 270 degrees at 2,000 feet near Burgstein when I saw an aircraft about 1,000 feet below heading east. It passed under our formation and I immediately rolled on my back and gave chase. As I pulled out of the dive, I recognized the enemy as a Bf 109 and began to close in. The enemy aircraft pulled straight up and when I was about fine hundred yards behind, it was in a stalled position standing on its tail. The pilot baled out, the aircraft bunted and went straight into the deck and I saw the pilot land a short distance away in some trees.
>
> I claim one Bf 109 destroyed.
>
> I rejoined the formation and we continued on 270 degrees at 3,500 feet and were ten miles southeast of Emmerich, Germany when I sighted three Bf 109s at one o'clock to us flying in the opposite direction at the same level as ourselves. I broke into them and they broke in our direction. I saw something fall away from the leading enemy aircraft – it might have been the canopy or the pilot – I am not sure. I fired at this aircraft head-on from 800 yards. It put its nose down and passed beneath me. Then I broke round and picked out another Hun and got on its tail. I had quite a job staying behind it, but managed to get in a few quick bursts with no results. The enemy aircraft was taking good evasive action and I overshot him once and ended up directly above him. I got behind him again and finally, firing from one hundred and fifty yards, obtained strikes on his starboard radiator which immediately streamed glycol. His propeller started to windmill when we were down to 600 feet and a considerable amount of flak was coming up. The enemy aircraft circled in order to make a forced landing, but I pulled up and attacked once more from one hundred yards and saw strikes on the port side of the fuselage in

front of the cockpit. Then the enemy aircraft was at deck level and glided into some trees near Dingen, Holland and exploded.

I claim one Bf 109 destroyed.

I climbed again and with my section set course for Nijmegen. We passed near Emmerich and were just crossing the Rheine River when two Bf 109s passed my starboard side slightly below at 4,000 feet and flying in the opposite direction. One was being chased by another Tempest and I broke into the second one. The enemy aircraft continued straight and level just at the base of the cloud. I quickly closed the range from below to approximately 150 yards. I fired but only my port cannons worked. After a few bursts I saw strikes on the enemy's starboard wing. He did only a very slight turn to starboard and continued on. I rolled onto him again and fired until my ammunition ran out. I overhauled the enemy aircraft and came right up under his wing – the pilot was looking out the opposite side and didn't have a clue. After several seconds, he finally became aware of my presence! I rolled over top of him, held my aircraft steady, gave him the finger and came home.

I claim one Bf 109 damaged.

David was born to Frank and Helen Fairbanks in Ithaca, New York, on August 12, 1922. His father, a Cornell University professor, died unexpectedly when David was still in his teens. Graduating from Ithaca High School in June 1940, Fairbanks listed his sports interests as football, swimming, and skiing. During the summer harvest seasons, he often worked on local farms operating farm machinery.

Growing up, the young Mr. Fairbanks had an insatiable appetite for anything aeronautical. His heroes were all the aces of World War I and he read everything that he could lay his hands on that described, in great detail, their aerial adventures. He built and flew model aircraft, and, at the local airport, he was not above scrounging airplane rides whenever he could.

From the first day of the war in Europe, September 3, 1939, he followed the news reports with unbridled enthusiasm and interest. Too young to serve in the USAAC, David and two of his friends, hoping to join the RCAF, left home in January 1941 and made their way to the Peace Bridge, which spans the Niagara River between Buffalo, New York, and Fort Erie, Ontario. David's entry into Canada was barred by a Canadian customs officer as he only had 20 cents in his pocket! He reluctantly thumbed his way home, sleeping in barns along the way.

A month later, on February 18, the 18-year-old, with a sufficient sum of money and his mother's signed parental consent in hand, successfully crossed the border and voluntarily enlisted in the RCAF at No. 10 Recruiting Centre in Hamilton, Ontario. His pay was CAN$1.30 per day, his rank AC2 and his assigned Service No. was R. 66474.

He listed his home address as 424 East State Street in Ithaca.

Fairbanks spent his first six weeks in uniform at No. 1 MD in Toronto, Ontario. On April 9, he reported for guard duty to RCAF Air Station Dartmouth, Nova Scotia, where he remained until May 27. From there he was sent to No. 3 ITS at Victoriaville, Quebec. He graduated from this unit on July 2 and was promoted to LAC.

David returned to Canada's east coast to No. 21 EFTS at Chatham, New Brunswick. There he began his flight training on Fleet Finch biplanes, graduating on September 1 with a 73.78 percent average. The next day, Fairbanks was posted to No. 9 SFTS at Summerside, Prince Edward Island, where he completed his pilot training on Harvard Mk II aircraft. He proved to be an exemplary student – quiet, but very alert. One of his instructors recorded that he was amazing in his quickness to learn. Graduating near the top of his class on November 21 with a 78.13 percent average, LAC Fairbanks was promoted to SP. Later that day, the RCAF assigned him a new Service No. J. 9069, after commissioning him as a PO.

With 180 hours of flying time on Finches and Harvards in his logbook, this newly minted officer, now earning $6.00 daily, was posted to the Central Flying School at RCAF Air Station Trenton, Ontario, on November 23. There he undertook an advanced flying instructor's course, which he completed on February 28, 1942.

While at Trenton, PO Fairbanks earned a "C" Level Instructor's Certificate and logged an additional 150 flight hours piloting Cessna Cranes, de Havilland Tiger Moths, Fleet Fawns, Harvard Mk Is and Lockheed 12s.

After taking two weeks of personal leave, he reported to No. 13 SFTS at Saint-Hubert, Quebec, on March 14 to begin his instructor pilot duties.

Over the next year, Fairbanks became a thorn in the flesh of the Saint-Hubert station commander. Frustrated at being retained in Canada in a training role, he submitted numerous transfer requests, all of which were turned down. To ward off boredom, he indulged in various flying games with his fellow pilots. Night formation flying was not part of their training syllabus so, naturally, he and the other instructors practiced it. Another of his night games was to creep up on an unsuspecting Harvard and, when within feet of his quarry, flick on his landing and navigation lights, signifying a successful interception and kill.

Near the end of 1942, Fairbanks was a day late returning from a weekend pass. The vengeful station commander had him placed under open arrest, charged him with being AWL and insisted he be court martialed! The matter was referred to the Air Officer Commanding (AOC) of No. 3 Training Command Headquarters in Montreal, Quebec. After due deliberation, the AOC decided that being AWL was a trivial offence and was to be dealt with in the usual manner at station level. The court martial charge, however, was not to stand and was to be dismissed. This message was conveyed to Saint-Hubert by SL C. E. Bennett, who was replying on behalf of the AOC. David was given a sharp dressing down and had to pay a small fine.

January 21, 1943, saw his instructor rating upgraded from level "C" to "B."

A Hawker Tempest Mk V, the aircraft type flown by Squadron Leader David C. Fairbanks, DFC & Two Bars. (Canada Department of National Defence)

Fairbanks was promoted from PO to FO on February 12.

On March 27, his latest transfer request for a combat assignment was approved. He traveled to "Y" Depot, Pier 21, Halifax, Nova Scotia, where he gratefully awaited his departure from the training airfields of Canada.

Arriving in England by ship on April 8, he was sent to No. 3 Personnel Reception Centre at Bournemouth. Shortly thereafter, David reported to No. 17 Pilot Advanced Flying Unit, RAF Calveley, where he transitioned onto Miles Masters and Hawker Hurricanes.

Leaving No. 17 on August 3, he was sent to RAF No. 58 OTU, Grangemouth and Balado Bridge, Scotland, where he flew Master Is, IIIs and Supermarine Spitfires.

On October 5, he was transferred to RAF No. 57 OTU, Eshott and Boulder in Northumberland, where he flew the same aircraft types until December 30. Much to his chagrin, the RAF utilized him as a flight instructor at No. 57 from October to December.

David Fairbanks: New York Tempest Ace

Foob, now a FL, managed to finally secure a coveted combat slot on January 12, 1944, when he joined RAF No. 501 (County of Gloucester) Squadron, which was flying Spitfire Mk IXs from Friston, East Sussex.

His first aerial victory came at 0610hrs double daylight saving time on June 8, when he downed a Bf 109 and claimed another as damaged southwest of Le Havre, France.

Foob was transferred on August 11 to RAF No. 274 Squadron, which was flying the latest Hawker aircraft, the Tempest Mk V, from West Malling, Kent.

The Tempest design was an outgrowth of the Hawker Typhoon Fighter-Bomber. With a thinner wing, plus many other improvements, the Napier Sabre IIC-powered Mk V became, at low and medium altitude, the fastest Allied fighter of the war. Heavily armed with four 20mm Hispano-Suiza cannon and able to haul upwards of 2,000lb of bombs and rockets externally, Tempests pulverized all types of enemy targets as German troops retreated from France and Belgium in 1944.

The squadron moved to Manston, Nottinghamshire, on the 17th where it set up shop to intercept incoming Fi 103 V-1 flying bombs. On the 29th, David shot down a German buzz bomb and the resultant blast nearly took him and his Tempest with it. One moment he was blazing away at the fast, nimble target and the next instant he was flying through its exploding debris.

Of the 1,771 V-1 flying bombers the RAF and RCAF shot down between June and September 1944, Hawker Tempests accounted for 638 of this number. Tempests were also fast enough to engage Me 262 jet fighters, 20 of which they destroyed before VE-Day (May 8, 1945).

The squadron moved on September 20 to Coltishall, Essex. Nine days later, as part of the 2nd TAF, it moved yet again – this time to the continent where it set up operations in Belgium.

On November 19, while strafing a locomotive, Foob's Tempest, coded JJ-F, was hit by flak on the leading edge of the port wing. The enemy shells flipped his aircraft upside down, and for a moment, the ground was rushing up to meet him. Desperately, he kicked the controls and righted the Tempest mere feet above terra firma. One of his fuel tanks had been riddled and a fire was burning out of control in one wing. Resisting the temptation to bail out, Fairbanks set course back to his airfield at Volkel. The fire ate away a gaping portion of the wing, scorched most of the paint off the fuselage, and burned all the fabric off his rudder. When he reached his base, the fire had died out and he landed safely. That superb piece of flying won him the first of his three British DFC awards.

Fairbanks' two favorite service aircraft were the Supermarine Spitfire and the Hawker Tempest. He so liked the Tempest, he once wrote that it was, "The hottest kite this side of Ithaca."

Late in December 1944, David transferred to RAF No. 3 Squadron, which was also flying Tempests. At 1405hrs on January 4, 1945, he downed an Fw 190 eight miles northeast of Hengelo. Ten days later in the Paderborn and Gütersloh areas, he bested a Bf 109 and an Fw 190 in just five minutes. On the 23rd, he was given half of an aerial credit, sharing in the destruction of a Ju 52.

In a report dated January 8, 1945, SL A. H. Baird recorded the following:

> 274 squadron pilot FL D. C. Fairbanks total flight time is 1,462 hours. He is possessed of a very strong personality and as a result has considerable influence over his fellow men. He has always used this characteristic to the best advantage for the good of the squadron. An extremely keen and enthusiastic pilot and officer, he has shown himself to be aware of his responsibilities in both capacities and has always carried out his duties with dash and vigour.

In that same report, GC P. G. Jameson wrote, "A fine type of officer who has proved himself to be a daring and skillful pilot. He possesses a quiet but strong personality and is liked and respected by all those with whom he serves."

On February 9, David was promoted to SL and was sent back to No. 274 to take over as CO. The squadron diarist happily enthused "the 'Terror of The Rheine' is to return to us!"

Over a Rheine airfield on February 11, Foob stalked an enemy jet. The two played a game of hide-and-seek for several minutes, flying in and out of clouds. Finally, the German pilot settled into his landing approach, apparently satisfied he had lost the troublesome Tempest. Just as the jet's undercarriage slid down, Fairbanks swooped out of the clouds, jettisoned his drop tanks, and bore straight in to within 300 yards of his victim. The four 20mm Hispanos barked for less than two seconds but that was all that was needed. The German's starboard engine flamed, and the aircraft plummeted down to explode in the center of the airfield. David claimed this kill as a Messerschmitt Me 262, but it was not until after the war that the Luftwaffe verified it as an Arado Ar 234B Reconnaissance Bomber, the first aircraft of its type to be shot down by Allied forces.

Early on the morning of February 28, 1945, Fairbanks took off leading five other Tempests on an armed reconnaissance patrol over Osnabrück, Germany. They destroyed a locomotive and re-formed at 5,000ft between two cloud layers. Coming head-on toward them was a mixed force of Fw 190s and Bf 109s, numbering 40 aircraft. Fairbanks called out a head-on attack and ordered his pilots to drop long-range tanks. He said, "Time was so short it was difficult to select a suitable target and lay off deflection." He did not remember any return fire from the enemy aircraft. He thought they were just as surprised as he was and that they also did not have enough time to line up a burst. Fairbanks continues:

> As soon as we passed the last man, I called a left 180 degree break back toward the formation. As we turned there were few aircraft to be seen. They had scattered

in all directions. I started to chase one, but he went into a cloud and I lost him. Shortly after this, I pushed my aircraft down into cloud and came out underneath and saw a 190. By this time my No. 20 had lost me. I closed the range on this aircraft and before I was ready to fire, I noticed some tracers coming my way. I was near the ground and thought it was flak. A few more tracer rounds went by me as I was getting ready to fire at the enemy aircraft. I fired and hit the 190 which burst into flames. The next instant I was hit hard! It was not ground tracer I had seen, but shells from the aircraft behind that hit me. I can remember seeing wing ribs and torn skin on the left and right upper wing surfaces and I was having difficulty keeping the aircraft level. The engine was missing and puffs of glycol were shooting by. No doubt my rad had been punctured. I held the stick hard over right to keep level and applied right rudder. With the controls in this position, I knew I was not going home. I decided that it was time to bale out. Holding the controls with my right hand, I tried to jettison the canopy with my left, but it wouldn't budge. I tried several times, but didn't have enough strength in my left hand alone. I let go of the controls and pulled the jettison handle with both hands and away she went. I can only remember that the canopy was gone and that I leaned my head to the left into the slipstream. The next thing I remember I was on the ground.

The 20-year-old Luftwaffe pilot who shot David down at 0800hrs that morning was Unteroffizier Karl-Georg Genth from 12./JG 26. Flying from Plantleunne airfield, Genth was piloting an Fw 190D-9 long-nosed Dora fighter, coded Yellow 15. Interviewed in Germany through his son, Thomas Genth, he recalls the details of that aerial battle:

> I remember Fairbanks' Tempest shooting at and chasing an Fw 190, but I do not remember an explosion on that plane. I believe all our fighters returned safely to our airfield. Our three aircraft were turning hard and each time I fired, Fairbanks' aircraft would slip from my view. Tightening my turn even more, the Tempest reappeared just long enough for me to shoot and I observed my 20 and 30mm cannon shells striking his aircraft.

After he landed, JG 26's commander, Hauptmann Walter Krupinski, asked Genth for additional details as another German pilot, Oberleutnant Theobald Kraus, had claimed the same aircraft. A few days later, Krupinski awarded the victory to Genth as his description of the attack matched the shell holes found in the crashed Tempest wreckage.

Escaping from his doomed aircraft, Foob, still wearing his headset and oxygen mask, broke his nose when he bailed out. Upon landing, he was immediately surrounded by German home guard troops who herded him at rifle point into a nearby barn. His hands were tied, and he was led back outside where a crowd of angry civilians began to jostle him. One man swung a pistol in his direction. Fairbanks thought, "My God, I'm to be shot like an animal." At the top of his lungs, he began shouting the only German word he knew: "Kommandant, Kommandant."

"Are you hurt?" a friendly accented voice asked. Turning his head, Fairbanks discovered a flak battery officer beside him. He was taken away, his hands were untied, and he was given a cigarette. The German had been educated in England and spoke of the war in a sad objective way. He escorted Fairbanks to a local jail where David spent two nights discovering cuts, bruises, and aching muscles he never knew he had.

Foob guessed his parachute did not fully deploy before he landed, and it was a miracle that he was still alive. Twice more he came near to being shot by hostile civilians, but each time his captors failed to carry out their threats. After a week of this nerve-wracking treatment, he was sent to the safety of a regular PoW camp.

Fairbanks had flown one operational tour, totaling 160 sorties, which covered 250 combat flight hours.

Late in April 1945, advancing Allied troops freed Fairbanks and his fellow prisoners.

July 8 saw him repatriated to Canada.

On October 12, 1945, after serving 55 months in uniform (28 of these overseas), SL Fairbanks retired and was released from the RCAF.

In a Canadian Department of Veterans Affairs (DVA) letter, it was recommended that D. C. Fairbanks be given all possible financial assistance in the pursuit of the continuing of his education. Part of this document read: "A fine type of American youth with an exceptionally brilliant air force record."

With some financial backing provided by the Canadian federal government, David entered Cornell University in 1946 and graduated with a degree in mechanical engineering in 1950.

In Ithaca on September 14, 1948, he married Phyllis May Guterman.

Having more contacts in Canada than in the US, after graduation Fairbanks accepted an employment position with Dominion Bridge in Montreal, Quebec.

D. C. Fairbanks reentered the world of military flying on September 1, 1951, when he joined 401 RCAF Auxiliary FS at Saint-Hubert, flying Harvards and de Havilland Vampires.

He left Dominion Bridge later that year and went to work for Sperry Gyroscope where he remained for the next four years. Two of these he spent on an exchange posting with the RAF in England, flying Gloster Meteors with No. 504 Auxiliary Squadron.

David moved to Toronto in 1955 after landing a job with de Havilland Aircraft of Canada Limited as a test pilot. Initially, his job was to demonstrate the Beaver and Otter aircraft to prospective clients on four continents. Because of conflicting work schedules, he reluctantly retired from the RCAF on November 16, 1956, after flying Vampires and Lockheed T-33 Shooting Stars with 411 Reserve FS at RCAF Station Downsview, Ontario.

Later in his de Havilland career, he became manager of flight operations and shared in the delivery and demonstration of the company's products all over the world. He was actively engaged in the preparation and planning of the Dash 7 into the Short Take-off and Landing (STOL) market.

At age 52, he suffered a massive heart attack and died in Toronto on February 20, 1975.

On May 12, 1976, David Charles Fairbanks was posthumously honored with Canada's leading aviation award, the McKee Trophy, which was accompanied by the following citation:

> Mr. Fairbanks, a native of Ithaca, New York and an engineering graduate of Cornell University, was Manager of Flight Operations at the de Havilland Aircraft of Canada with complete responsibility for all test flying and all matters pertaining to the company's flight operations around the world. Squadron Leader Fairbanks joined de Havilland as a Test Pilot in 1955, following a brilliant career as a fighter pilot in the RCAF during World War II. His decorations included the Distinguished Flying Cross and Two Bars. During his twenty years in de Havilland flight operations, he demonstrated the Beaver, Twin Otter, Caribou and Buffalo aircraft in some eighty countries around the world with great skill and credit to the company and to the Canadian aircraft industry. Mr. Fairbank's expertise in the development of STOL aircraft was widely recognized by his flying colleagues and his advice and guidance was constantly sought by regulatory authorities in both Canada and the United States regarding the establishment of STOL operating procedures.

SL David Charles "Foob" Fairbanks was the sole American, and one of only four RCAF personnel in World War II, who was awarded a British DFC and Two Bars. He was the highest-scoring Tempest ace and that type's most decorated pilot. Officially, he is credited with 13.5 aerial victories and three aircraft damaged. An exceptionally brilliant air force record indeed!

Frank Gallion
The Long Journey Home

In February 1993, a dredging vessel operating in the area of Wieringer Vlaak-Ijsselmeer, Netherlands, struck an underwater object while widening a channel in the Zuiderzee. A diver sent over the side to investigate the obstruction found the wreckage of an American World War II P-47D Thunderbolt fighter resting in 12ft of water.

Two years later, the local Dutch authority was able to fund the salvage and recovery of this aircraft, which had been shot down during a large air battle on November 3, 1943. Inside the cockpit, still strapped in the seat, salvagers discovered the skeletal remains of 29-year-old USAAF pilot FO Frank Donavan Gallion.

Gallion was born to Niva Hattie Groff and John Franklin Gallion in the village of Killbuck, Ohio, on September 19, 1914. He was educated at Millersburg, Ohio Grammar and High School from 1922 until 1934. He worked on the family farm in the heart of Amish country for the next four years until his father passed away. From 1938 until 1941, he had several low paying occupations, which caused him to frequently change employments. Some of the jobs he held were machine operator, truck driver, part-time fireman, and special police constable.

When he learned that he could combine his love of aviation into a steady career with the RCAF, he traveled from the south shore of Lake Erie to No. 11 Recruiting Centre in Toronto, Ontario, on September 13, 1941. There, he voluntarily enlisted as an AC2 under Regimental Service No. R. 133609.

His four-week basic training took place at No. 1 MD, which was also located in Toronto. From October 11 until January 4, 1942, Gallion served on guard duty at No. 4 Bombing & Gunnery School at Fingal, Ontario, and at No. 1 SFTS at Camp Borden, Ontario.

On January 5, he was posted back to Toronto on Course No. 44 at No. 1 ITS. The course graduated on March 1, with Gallion finishing 60th out of a class of 78 students. The school's WC wrote in his file: "A better than average type. Cool and dependable. Has a fine service spirit. Second aircrew recommendation – Wireless Operator Air Gunner."

Promoted to LAC, Gallion was sent, on March 16, to No. 9 EFTS at St. Catharines, Ontario, where he flew 90.05 hours on Fleet Finch II and de Havilland Tiger Moth biplane trainers. Course No. 51 at St. Catharines concluded on May 22, 1942, with Frank achieving a 64.5 percent passing grade covering seven subjects. The CFI noted the following: "This student has shown an interest in his flying training and has applied himself very well. Has difficulty doing steep turns and tends to be rough in his use of the controls. Has had some difficulty in instrument flying and keeping the aircraft on a constant heading." From the CGI, the following comments: "Possesses ability to become a capable service pilot, but will have to work hard in all phases of his training. Conduct, deportment and attitude towards service life – satisfactory."

On May 25, Frank was back at No. 1 SFTS at Camp Borden where, over the next three and a half months, he flew a total of 176.60 hours on Course No. 56 on two NAA products – the Yale and the Harvard. Graduating on September 11, 1942, LAC Gallion became SP Gallion. His squadron commander noted the following: "This student is rough on the controls and is inclined to be over confident. Discipline is good. Possesses average flying ability."

Frank used his two-week pre-embarkation leave to return to the States where, in Galion, Ohio, on September 21, he married Miss Phyllis Zerman. At the end of a five-day honeymoon, he reported in at No. 1 Port Transit Unit, "Y" Depot, Pier 21, Halifax, Nova Scotia, for onward deployment to the United Kingdom. He arrived in England on November 5 and was sent to No. 3 Personnel Reception Centre at Bournemouth.

On December 1, he was assigned to RAF No. 17 Pilot Advanced Flying Unit at Calveley. There, until March 2, 1943, he flew the 825shp Pratt & Whitney Twin Wasp Junior radial-engined Miles Master Mk III advanced trainer.

Gallion was posted to RAF No. 56 OTU at Tealing, Angus, Scotland. On Course No. 57, he flew 73.15 hours on Hawker Hurricanes and Miles Masters until May 3. SL R. P. Davidson assessed Frank's piloting, formation flying, air combat maneuvering, and marksmanship as average.

While finishing up his training in Scotland, the easy-going Gallion received a request from the USAAF asking if he would consider transferring to its service. For a number of reasons, he decided to do it, chief among them was that he would immediately be commissioned as a FO. Also, the move would more than double his monthly rate of pay.

Frank Gallion appeared before a USAAF Medical Board in London, England, in early May and was accepted under Service No. T-190742. He was honorably discharged from the RCAF Special Reserve at RAF Tealing on May 26, 1943, after having served one year and 255 days.

He listed his home address as 104 West Clinton Street in Millersburg, Ohio. His service award card showed that he had earned the following Canadian medals: the Defence Medal, General Service Medal and the Canadian Volunteer Service Medal & Clasp. These were requested by his family and forwarded to them on May 3, 1996.

A Republic P-47D Thunderbolt was the aircraft type Flight Officer Frank D. Gallion went missing in over Holland on November 3, 1943. (US Department of Defense)

From June through to September, Frank was assigned to the CCRC at USAAF Station 342, Atcham. There, he converted to American flight procedures, flying Piper Cubs, Supermarine Spitfire Vbs, Miles Masters, and Republic P-47C and D Thunderbolts.

On October 10, 1943, Gallion joined the 334th FS, 4th FG, based at Station F-356 Debden, located two miles southeast of the village of Saffron Walden, Essex. The 29-year-old fighter pilot never had the chance to amass any amount of aerial combat experience because 24 days after joining the squadron, he was KIA.

On Wednesday, November 3, 1943, under Field Order No. 168, Lieutenant Colonel Don Blakeslee led a ramrod target support mission to Wilhelmshaven, Germany, from 1135 to 1350hrs. Using Halesworth, Suffolk, as a forward operating base, one 334th Thunderbolt crashed on take-off but the pilot was not injured. Crossing the Dutch coast, the remaining 11 P-47s were bounced over the province of Noord-Holland by ten Messerschmitt Bf 109G-6s belonging to JG 3.

While the 334th battled the Germans, Blakeslee went ahead with the rest of the group to rendezvous with the Boeing B-17 bombers over Hippolytushoef.

The Luftwaffe commander of JG 3 "Udet," based at Schiphol, Holland, was Major Kurt Hans Friedrich Brandle. Claiming his 179th and 180th victories of the war at 1230 and 1231hrs, respectively, Brandle quickly downed two inexperienced 334th P-47 pilots – FO Frank D. Gallion and 1st Lieutenant Ivan R. Moon. The German ace had flown more than 700 combat sorties on both the Eastern and Western Fronts.

The 31-year-old Brandle did not have time to savor his last two victories as he died later that afternoon after being shot down over the North Sea by a Spitfire Mk IXb pilot from RAF No. 132 (City of Bombay) Squadron. No. 132, based at RAF Detling, had been tasked that day to escort 18 USAAF Martin Marauder B-26 bombers to a target near Amsterdam.

Five JG 3 109s were lost in that aerial dog fight off the Dutch coast. Brandle's body washed ashore on December 30, 1943, at Zandvoort, Holland.

On the fateful day Gallion was shot down, he was flying Mike Sobanski's P-47D-1-RE Thunderbolt *Mike III*, serial no. 42-7924, coded QP-F.

On November 17, 1943, Frank's wife received a 17-word telegram stating that he was MIA. At the war's conclusion, Gallion's name was inscribed on the Wall of the Missing at the Netherlands American War Cemetery at Margareten.

In August 1945, his mother placed a memorial headstone in his honor in the local Millersburg, Ohio, cemetery. His wife, Phyllis, never remarried and worked much of her life as a hairdresser. She died in 1990.

Gallion's brother, Ottmar, said that for years the family wondered if Frank had been captured by the Germans and had possibly died in a PoW camp.

For 52 years, the crashed fighter remained undisturbed on the floor of the Zuiderzee until discovered by the Dutch dredging crew.

Gallion's dog tags and other personal items found in the cockpit confirmed they were in fact his remains. His family members attended a ceremony for him in the Netherlands, after which his remains were flown to the JPAC Central Identification Laboratory in Hawaii where they were positively identified.

On May 28, 1996, Frank Donovan Gallion was laid to rest in the Pleasant Grove Cemetery in Millersburg. His long journey home was over.

Edward Gimbel
Illinois Spitfire Ace

For Chicago, Illinois, native Edward Lester "Buddy" or "Eddie" Gimbel, the working years of 1937 to 1940 were full of a series of frustrating employments that ended shortly after each began. Gimbel grew up in the "Windy City" during the Great Depression, but never succeeded in finding meaningful work after graduating from Waller High School in June 1935. To survive, he took any job he could find. His family, like so many others of the time, did not have the financial wherewithal to send him to college. Buddy harbored a lifelong dream to fly and was terribly disappointed when, early in 1940, the USAAC rejected his application for flight training. He was unable to meet its educational requisite of having two years of higher learning.

Hearing the RCAF was accepting high school graduates for pilot training, Eddie purchased a one-way bus ticket from Chicago to Detroit, Michigan. Crossing the border from the United States into Canada at Windsor, Ontario, on Wednesday, October 9, 1940, the 23-year-old, 6ft tall Chicagoan enlisted in the RCAF at No. 8 Recruiting Centre on Quellette Avenue.

Assigned Regimental Service No. R. 67829, Gimbel's rank was that of an AC2. Gimbel did have some military training that he brought to his new career as he had spent a year as a private in his high school's ROTC program before the unit disbanded. Also, in 1934–36, he was a gunner in the Illinois Army National Guard with the rank of corporal.

Edward Lester Gimbel was born in London, England, on December 28, 1916, to Hilda Benson and Ralph Edward Gimbel. Eddie's father was born in Liverpool and his mother in Sweden, but both eventually became naturalized US citizens. Eddie attended Lincoln Grade School in Chicago from 1922 to 1931, then Waller High School from 1931 to 1935. He took night courses in mechanical engineering from 1936 to 1937 at Armor Institute of Technology.

His first job was at the National Die Casting Company where he worked as a machinist. His employment there lasted eight months, then he was laid off. Next, he was at the Commonwealth Edison Company as a salesman. He left there after four months as the pay was too small. His third job at the American Can Company as a machinist lasted almost a year. This factory also ran out of orders resulting in a general lay-off and shut down. When Buddy applied to the RCAF, he was working on commission basis as a repairman for the Hoover Vacuum Company. He listed his Chicago home address as 841 Belden Avenue.

Buddy's interview report, compiled by FL W. L. Scandrett, contained the following assessment: "Average American boy who has had difficulty obtaining regular employment. Is now employed as a door-to-door salesman. Intelligent, keen and sincere. Should do for air crew."

Eddie spent his first several weeks in uniform in Toronto, Ontario, at No 1 MD. He found it easier than most new enlistees to adapt to the structured air force way of life due to his previous military experiences. He left Toronto on December 9 and headed for No. 1A MD in Picton, Ontario, where he remained until March 29, 1941. Two days later, he was back in Toronto performing guard duty at No. 1 Equipment Depot.

On April 9, a space opened up for him in Toronto at No. 1 ITS. Promoted to LAC, Buddy graduated from this course on May 17, 1941. Sent the following day to No. 10 EFTS at Mount Hope, Ontario, Eddie flew 56.55 hours on Fleet Finch and Tiger Moth biplanes on Course No. 28 until July 3. Next, he was off to No. 14 SFTS at Aylmer, Ontario, to fly Harvard Mk IIs. After accumulating 97.35 flight hours on the yellow perils, LAC Gimbel earned his wings and graduated as an SP on September 25.

Taking his two-week pre-embarkation leave, he returned to Chicago to visit family and friends before heading off to the European war. Traveling by train from Chicago directly to Halifax, Nova Scotia, Sgt Gimbel shipped out from Pier 21 on a fast troop ship on October 10, arriving in the United Kingdom ten days later.

On November 17, Eddie began his fighter conversion training on Miles Masters and Supermarine Spitfire Is and IIs at No. 52 OTU at RAF Aston Down, Gloucestershire. He logged 48.10 hours on these types and graduated on March 12, 1942.

Assigned to RCAF 401 "Ram" FS, Buddy flew Spitfire Mk Vbs from Gravesend and Eastchurch. In July, he was promoted to FS. That same month, the squadron received new Spitfire Mk IXs. With this upgrade in equipment, 401's pilots were now on an equal footing with the latest Bf 109 and Fw 190 variants flown by their adversaries.

In September, FS Gimbel was promoted from the ranks to that of PO. To that point he had flown 180.85 hours on Spitfires. His operational sorties were comprised of 37 sweeps, 16 patrols, five scrambles and four air-sea rescues. He shot up some factories and trains and claimed one and one half Fw 190s as probably destroyed.

His service number was changed from R. 67829 to J. 15890 reflecting his officer status. Gimbel damaged an Fw 190 on September 6, shared in the destruction of another on October 9 and was awarded a half Fw 190 kill on November10.

Captain Edward L. Gimbel, DFC, MiD, is pictured with his P-51D Mustang *Hard Luck* at Debden, England, in March 1945. (US Department of Defense)

For the latter half of 1942, 401 Squadron mounted its operations from several British airfields, among them Kenley, Biggin Hill, and Martlesham Heath. Eddie's personal Spitfire carried the name *The Brat*.

On January 27, 1943, RCAF 403 "Wolf" FS relieved 401 at Kenley as the latter was due to stand down for a rest. Eddie, who wished to remain where the action was, managed to wrangle a transfer over to 403, just as the Wolves were receiving the latest Spitfire model, the Mk IXc. Buddy continued to add to his score, knocking down an Fw 190 over Goderville, France, on January 17 and another 15 miles northwest of Dunkirk at 1430hrs on February 27. Gimbel's victim, who was killed in this latest action in his Fw 190A-4 coded "Black 9," was Leutnant Karl Müller-Gobs from 5./JG 26.

On March 15, PO Gimbel was awarded a British DFC in a ceremony at Buckingham Palace. The citation for this award read as follows: "This officer has taken part in a very large number of sorties over enemy territory, including a number as escort to heavy bombers. Pilot Officer Gimbel, who is an excellent section leader, has destroyed three enemy aircraft. In addition, he has damaged or destroyed several locomotives. He has at all times displayed great keenness and devotion to duty."

At that point, Buddy had flown a total of 466 hours.

On April 4, 1943, the following telegram was sent from the squadron to RCAF Headquarters 11 Group: "Immediate from 403 Squadron. Spitfire IX BS110 missing over St. Valery, France at 1430 hours this day as a result of enemy air action. RCAF J. 15890 PO E. L. Gimbel, DFC, Missing. Kindly notify next of kin, Grandmother Mrs. Hattie Gimbel, 2845 North Burling Avenue, Chicago, Illinois, USA."

Three days later, on the 7th, the following after action report was submitted to the Air Ministry:

> No. 403 and 416 Squadrons, led by Wing Commander Johnson took off at 1345 hours as first withdrawal cover to Boeing B-17 Fortresses returning from a raid on Boulogne-Billancourt, France. The English coast was crossed at Beachy Head at 10,000 feet and the French coast at Quiberville at 24,000 feet at 1415 hours. Rendezvous was made east to northeast of Rouen at 1432 hours. At that time, Fw 190s in pairs and fours were making head-on and flank attacks on the first box of bombers. The Wing Leader gave permission for 403 Squadron to go after the enemy aircraft. Blue 1 (FL Magwood) broke to port to attack an Fw 190 which had come through the bomber stream. At this point Blue 3 (PO Gimbel) and Blue 4 (FO Cameron) turned to starboard and were not seen again by Blue 1. PO Gimbel went after a 190 about 2,000 feet below the bombers. He fired a burst and pieces fell off the enemy aircraft, after which it rolled over and went down. This was seen and confirmed by Blue 4. As Blue 3 and 4 broke from the attack, three 190s closed from behind in line astern from a distance of 200 yards. Blue 4 called "Watch out Ed" to Blue 3 as he broke sharply upwards to starboard. There was no reply from Blue 3. FO Cameron then saw a Spitfire, which he believed to be PO Gimbel going down in a gentle dive streaming smoke. This was the last seen or heard of Pilot Officer Gimbel.

The RCAF's casualties officer, on behalf of the CAS in Ottawa, Ontario, forwarded the following air mail letter to Mrs. Gimbel on April 8:

> It is my painful duty to confirm the telegram recently received by you which informed you that your grandson, Pilot Officer Edward Lester Gimbel, DFC, is reported missing on active service. Advice has been received that your grandson was the sole occupant of an aircraft which failed to return to its base due to enemy action near St. Valery, France on April 4th, 1943. I desire to point out that this does not necessarily mean that your grandson has been killed or wounded. It might be that he is a Prisoner of War and inquiries have been made through the International Red Cross Society and all other appropriate sources. Official announcement that your grandson has been reported missing will not be made through the press for at least five weeks and, until then, you are requested not to give out any information to the press or radio. It is possible that he has landed in

enemy territory and in that event publicity at this time might imperil his chance to escape. You may be assured that any further information received will be communicated to you immediately. May I join with you in the hope that better news will be forthcoming in the near future.

A day later, SL L. S. Ford, OC of No. 403 FS, sent the following letter to Hattie Gimbel:

Before you receive this letter, you will have had a telegram informing you that your grandson, Pilot Officer E. L. Gimbel, has been reported missing as the result of air operations. On the afternoon of April 4th, 1943, Ed, as he was known by his comrades, left with the squadron on an operational flight over enemy territory. Enemy aircraft were encountered and, after the ensuing flight, Ed's aircraft did not return. He is therefore listed as missing as a result of air operations. It is definitely confirmed by his comrades that he shot down one enemy aircraft on that operation. This is one of the greatest losses to our squadron as Ed was an excellent flier and extremely popular with everyone. The proof of his skill is evidenced in his being awarded the DFC with a record of three destroyed, one and one half probables and two and one half damaged. He was selected to represent the squadron to make public appearances and give his impressions of fighter squadrons on several occasions during the recent Wings for Victory campaign. Regulations require that his kit and possessions should be forwarded to the RAF Depository where they will be held until further news is received, or in any event for a period of at least six months, before being forwarded to you through the Administrator of Estates, Ottawa. May I express in closing how sorry I am to have to send you this distressing news and if any further information is desired, you may request same from RCAF Headquarters, London.

While listed as missing, Eddie was promoted on July 21, 1943, from PO to FO. Four days later, the Air Ministry in London received news from Headquarters, RAF Gibraltar, that Gimbel and four other Commonwealth Airmen had safely arrived from Spain the day before! A telegram from London to Ottawa on August 11 advised that Gimbel and two others, FS D. Nolan and FL J. Sale, were safely back in the UK.

On August 19, Air Commodore F. G. Wait, AOC of RCAF Overseas Headquarters, sent the following letter to the Department of National Defence for Air in Ottawa:

FO E. L. Gimbel, DFC, embarked for the United Kingdom on 10 October 1941 and after a period of training at No. 52 OTU, was posted to No. 401 RCAF squadron on 12 March 1942 on Spitfires. He served with this squadron until 27 January 1943 when he was posted to No. 403 RCAF squadron. Flying Officer

Gimbel was forced to abandon a very badly damaged aircraft over France on 4 April 1943. He landed safely and evaded the enemy, making his way through Spain where he was interned for thirty-six days. Making his way to Gibraltar, he was returned to the United Kingdom on 11 August 1943. This officer has a total flying time of 485 hours which includes 185 operational hours completed in some 81 sorties over enemy territory. In view of the foregoing this officer qualifies for a clear month's leave in Canada and arrangements have been made for his repatriation for this purpose. He is to be returned to the United Kingdom for further operational duty at the expiry of his leave.

Buddy arrived back in Canada on September 3 and spent an extended period of leave with his family and friends in Illinois until October 22. Arriving back in England on the 30th, he spent eight days at No. 3 Personnel Reception Centre in Bournemouth, whereupon he returned to duty with 403 Squadron on November 8.

Eddie flew operationally with 403 until Monday, December 20, 1943, when he was posted to RCAF 421 "Red Indian" FS. That posting date was a memorable one for Ed Gimbel, for not only was he promoted from FO to FL, but he shot down his fifth Luftwaffe aircraft and became an ace.

Patrolling in Spitfire EN398 near Merville-Douai, France, at 1115hrs, Buddy shot down and killed Leutnant Bernhard Torpisch in his Fw 190A-6, coded "Black 11," from 4./JG 26.

Gimbel's record of five kills, one-and-a-half aircraft probably destroyed and one damaged were all against the formidable Fw 190. In each engagement, Eddie was flying a slightly superior aircraft, the Mk IX Spitfire.

FL Gimbel was awarded a MiD on January 14, 1944. This was his second British decoration.

Eddie Gimbel was implicated in a serious matter on June 2, 1944. It involved the discharge of a firearm within the confines of RAF Tangmere. He was ordered to stand a general court martial at No. 127 Wing Headquarters. The primary charge against him was under Section 41 – negligently discharging a revolver causing grievous bodily injury – and a secondary charge under Section 40 – improperly discharging a revolver. The military court found him not guilty of either offence and he was acquitted.

Shortly after the incident, FL E. L. Gimbel DFC, MiD decided to transfer to the USAAF. He had been thinking of making that move for some time. Now that his spotless RCAF record was somewhat blemished, it was time to move on. At his request he was honorably released from the RCAF on June 13 after having served 44 months in uniform. In a report dated June 24, SL W. A. Conrad stated the following: "FL Gimbel was a Flight Commander in 421 Squadron under my command for a period of four months. His conduct on and off duty was always satisfactory and as a subordinate commander he proved himself a diligent, conscientious pilot and officer. His posting from this unit took place after he had been totally acquitted by Court Martial of implication in an unfortunate incident and this has no reflection on his character or ability."

Buddy joined the 336th FS, 4th FG as a captain on June 28, 1944. On March 1, 1945, he was wounded in action and crash-landed his P-51D Mustang (serial number 44-14029) *Hard Luck* near Brussels, Belgium. The aircraft was subsequently salvaged.

On April 16, 1945, Lt Col Sidney S. Woods led part of the 4th on a freelance strafing mission to Prague, Czechoslovakia, from 1200 to 1740hrs. As it swept into the Prague area at 1500, it found three airfields crammed with German aircraft. For what seemed like an eternity, the Mustangs made run after run in the midst of heavy flak, destroying 61 Luftwaffe aircraft. The intense airfield flak claimed eight pilots – two were killed and the rest captured. Among the PoWs was the mission leader, Lt Col Woods. Captain Gimbel went down in P-51D (serial number 44-72769). After being hit, he zoomed his Mustang to 3,000ft and bailed out. A couple of parachute shroud lines wrapped around his neck, choking him during the descent. This caused him to lose consciousness. A farmer found him and turned him over to the Gestapo.

He was held prisoner at the Böhmerwald Concentration Camp for 15 days until he and the other captives were freed on May 1, 1945, by the advancing US Army's 97th Infantry Division.

Germany unconditionally surrendered seven days later on May 8.

Eddie had flown with the 4th for ten months but was unable to add any additional claims to his tally.

Captain Gimbel returned to the US where he was honorably discharged from the USAAF on August 11, 1945. Later that month, he married his long-time sweetheart Marion Martins.

On October 21, 1948, RCAF Headquarters in Ottawa sent the retired FL the following medals and awards he had not previously received: 1939–45 Star, Aircrew Europe Star, Defence Medal, Canadian Volunteer Service Medal & Clasp, War Medal 1939–45, Operational Wings and Pilot's Flying Badge.

Edward Lester Gimbel passed away in Chicago on April 25, 1977, at the age of 61.

Frederick Glover
North Carolina Mustang Ace

When Frederick Wendall "Freddie" Glover voluntarily enlisted at No. 8 Recruiting Centre on October 17, 1941, in Windsor, Ontario, he was a few weeks shy of his 26th birthday. He was considered an old man by many of his contemporaries who, for the most part, were single and barely out of their teens. Freddie, however, had two factors working in his favor. He had several years of practical work experience under his belt and was a licensed private pilot with 133 flight hours recorded in his logbook.

By the end of the war, he would rise to the rank of major, flying P-51 Mustangs with the 336th FS, 4th FG, USAAF. In the 4th's individual scoring race, he is listed seventh overall with 22.80 Luftwaffe aircraft destroyed (10.30 air and 12.50 ground).

Glover was born to Brona and Alpha Glover in Asheville, North Carolina, on December 4, 1915. His boyhood was spent in Asheville, but when Freddie was just a teenager the family moved to Knoxville, Tennessee, where his father was employed with the Southern Railroad. Growing up, Freddie's interests were baseball, flying, and sports. After graduating from high school, he served four years in the USN. Glover worked several occupations – drug store clerk, railroad station clerk, and as a railroad station master. For three years, he played professional baseball as a third baseman in the St. Louis Cardinals farm system. In 1939, he was on the roster with the Hamilton, Ontario, Red Wings in the Pennsylvania–Ontario–New York (PONY) league. He would never talk that much about his baseball career, and one was left to conclude that his success in this field was modest.

Sometimes, when things were not going his way, he was rather touchy and could become very bellicose. In the summer of 1941, he and several of his friends traveled to Fort McPherson, Georgia, to enlist in the USAAC pilot training program. The army insisted successful applicants must have a minimum of two years of college education. Freddie figured that since he already was a pilot, the army would exempt him of that academic requirement. When told, "The army can't use you," he replied in a loud gravelly voice, "Well to hell with you, friend."

Hearing the RCAF's requirements were a little less stringent, Glover packed up and headed north to Canada. His assigned RCAF Service No. was R. 137139 and his rank at the time of enlistment was as an AC2.

From October 17, 1941, to March 28, 1942, he was at the following training facilities: No. 1 MD, Toronto, Ontario; Air Station Trenton, Ontario; and No. 5 ITS, Belleville, Ontario.

On March 13, he was promoted to LAC. Freddie was granted several days' leave, at which time he returned to North Carolina and married Miss Faye Cecil Cherry of Hayesville. This union did not survive, and the couple divorced in Sarasota, Florida, in 1945.

Freddie began his flight training on Fleet Finch II biplane trainers at No. 22 EFTS at L'Ancienne-Lorette, Quebec. Glover completed this phase successfully on June 6 and the next day reported to No. 2 SFTS at Uplands to complete his training on Harvard and Yale trainers. He was promoted to SP and received his wings in a graduation ceremony on September 25, 1942.

One of Glover's classmates at Uplands was Peter G. Lehman from New York City. Lehman's father officiated at the graduation when he pinned wings on his son's and Freddie's tunics. At the time, the older Lehman was the governor of the state of New York.

Major Frederick W. Glover's 4th FG P-51D Mustang is parked in a "Victory Display" under the Eiffel Tower at war's end in 1945. (US Department of Defense)

1st Lieutenant Peter G. Lehman served in the 4th FG from August 25, 1943, to the day of his death, March 31, 1944. While participating in a low level, mock dogfight near Duxford, Lehman's P-51B Mustang suddenly flicked over and spun in.

After taking the standard two-week pre-embarkation leave, Glover left Pier 21 "Y" Depot, Halifax, Nova Scotia, on October 10 on a troop ship bound for England. When he arrived in the United Kingdom on the 27th, he was seconded to the RAF training pool. From November 5 to 19, he was at No. 3 Personnel Reception Centre at Bournemouth on England's south coast.

From November 20, 1942, to April 1, 1943, he served at RAF Tatenhill, Staffordshire, with No. 15 Pilot Advanced Flying Unit, flying twin-engine Airspeed Oxfords. From there he went to RAF Llandwrog, Wales, where he stayed until May 24, flying twin-engine Avro Ansons and single-engine Westland Lysanders with No. 9 Observation Squadron.

In May 1942, every American citizen who was serving in the RCAF was notified they could apply for transfer now that the US was in the war. For a non-commissioned pilot like Freddie, this was a step up to officer status and it meant a significant increase in his monthly salary.

Glover wanted desperately to be where the action was and applied for his release from the RCAF so that he could join the USAAF. His request for severance was granted on May 26, 1943, in London, where he was honorably discharged after having served one year and 222 days. He gave the RCAF a home address of 18 Eola Avenue, Lucerne Park, Asheville. He joined the USAAF that same day as an FO with 539 flying hours recorded in his logbook.

His next stop was at USAAF No. 342 Atcham, where he converted to the Republic P-47 Thunderbolt with the 495th Flying Training Group (FTG).

Instead of securing a coveted combat assignment at the conclusion of his training, Freddie was posted to the 310th Ferry Squadron, flying P-38 Lightnings from Speke Air Depot, Liverpool, to operational squadrons. He fretted and he raged, telling anyone who would listen that his job was to fly fighters in combat and not chauffeur them from one point to another. Finally, to clearly make his case, he power-dove a twin-engine Oxford transport from three miles up. He did not kill himself, but his scheme worked. When he taxied the "broken Oxford" up to the control tower, trailing pieces of wire and canvas on the tarmac like a bridal train, they decided to get rid of him and sent him to the 4th!

He was assigned to the 336th FS on February 19, 1944. The first night he was at Debden he did not unpack his bags, as he was not sure he was still going to be a member of the group the next morning. Colonel Donald J. M. Blakeslee, the famous 4th commander, was in the Officers' Club with some others when Glover was brought in. Freddie, never having been in combat, was greeted by the Colonel with, "Hm, hot shot Lightning pilot huh." "Well I think I can fly a plane as good as anybody else I see standing around here," Glover snapped looking Blakeslee square in the eye. "Have a drink," Blakeslee snarled. It was an order – a sort of smile-when-you-say-that. The two later became great friends when the colonel discovered Freddie was one of the few who relished hunting and fighting the Germans just as much as he did.

Two months after Glover joined the 4th, Supreme Allied Commander General Dwight D. Eisenhower visited Debden on April 11 to personally present DSCs to Colonel Blakeslee and to Captain Dominic S. Gentile. In the general's entourage that day were the following: Brigadier General Jesse Auton, 65th Fighter Wing Commander; Major General William Kepner, 8th Air Force Fighter Commander; Lieutenant General James Doolittle, 8th Air Force Commander; and Lieutenant General Carl Spaatz, USAAF European Commander.

To demonstrate "the punch" of the Mustang to General Eisenhower, General Auton fired the guns of FO Freddie Glover's P-51B *Rebel Queen* into the gun butts at the 336th hangar.

Only weeks earlier, the 4th had converted to the P-51 and the outrageous but true story of how the "Debden Eagles" obtained the Mustang well ahead of many other 8th Air Force fighter groups is classic Don Blakeslee.

On March 10, 1943, the 4th's Supermarine Spitfire Vbs were replaced with the American-built P-47 Thunderbolt. Don Blakeslee never liked the ponderous Republic Aviation product and was constantly looking for ways to get rid of it.

In November 1943, the newly formed 354th FG arrived in England and was equipped with the Merlin-engined Mustang. The 354th, named "The Pioneer Mustang Group," needed someone with combat experience to lead it on its first few missions and Colonel Blakeslee was the natural choice. After each sortie, Blakeslee would fly his borrowed P-51 from Boxted back to Debden where he would hold court beside the aircraft and enthrall his pilots with enthusiastic accounts of the Mustang's combat and flying capabilities. "It's the ship," Blakeslee would say.

Blakeslee's boss at 8th Air Force Headquarters was Major General William "Bill" Kepner. After flying the Mustang on six missions, Blakeslee knew this was the aircraft he and the 4th just had to have. He went to see the general and implored him to re-equip his group with 51s so that he could take the air war into any part of Hitler's Germany. Kepner was sympathetic to Blakeslee's request but told him the 4th was well down the list for such a conversion. There were several other groups ahead of him and he could not spare the down time needed for 4th personnel to switch to another new aircraft. In desperation, Blakeslee said, "General if you give me those P-51s, my guys will convert in 24 hours!" Kepner asked, "Colonel, how is that possible?" Blakeslee replied, "The Merlin engine in the Mustang is the same as the one in the Spitfire and my maintenance people have been trained on that motor. Besides, the Mustang flies much like the Spitfire and all my pilots are Spitfire qualified."

General Kepner gave Don Blakeslee his P-51,s with the first three aircraft arriving at Debden – one designated as a familiarization aircraft for each squadron on February 14, 1944. Two days later, after the remaining 45 Mustangs were delivered and, at the conclusion of his briefing for the group's first pony mission, Blakeslee turned and said to his pilots as they headed out the door, "We'll learn to fly them on the way to the target." And that's exactly what they did!

Glover could never get enough combat. On the wall in his room was a map of the European continent, which he would spend endless hours studying until he knew every railroad crossing and Luftwaffe airdrome in Germany. He was a great natural pilot, and, in combat, he inspired the admiration of those in his squadron for the animal cunning and craft with which he stalked his opponents.

On April 30, 1944, Glover was shot down by airfield flak while strafing Lyon-Bron airdrome in France. He was picked up by the French Resistance and returned safely to Debden on May 28.

The narrative of Glover's combat report of August 8, 1944, is as follows:

> I was flying Green 4 in Becky Squadron at 18,000 feet near Gardelegen, Germany. At 1245 hours Captain Otey Glass reported a Bf 109 flying above us at 21,000 feet. I gave chase, climbing to 27,000 feet and caught him. He did two snap rolls and spiraled down to the left. At 10,000 feet, heading straight down, we were indicating 550 miles per hour. On the pull out I blacked out but was still behind him when I came to. On the deck at 350 miles per hour, I fired a thirty degree deflection shot and thanks to the K-14 computing gun sight, hit him in the right wing. I tried to hit his belly tank but could not. Two additional bursts of thirty degrees of deflection shooting hit him in the engine and cockpit area. From twenty feet above the ground, he turned on his side and went into the trees. I claim one Bf 109 destroyed.

On a mission to Merseburg, Germany, on November 2, 1944, the group encountered 15 Bf 109s and five Me 163 rocket-powered fighters. Two of the Me 163s fell to the Mustangs' guns – Freddie got one and his roommate and good friend, Major Louis Herman "Red Dog" Norley, the other.

Back at Merseburg 19 days later on the 21st, Glover called "bandits" at 1140hrs over Dummer Lake just as the 4th was rounding up scattered B-24s for the return trip home to England. Six Bf 109s went down in this engagement, with Freddie claiming three.

Glover was promoted to 2nd lieutenant on April 20, 1944, to 1st lieutenant on June 26, to captain on September 11, and to major on December 22. Four rapid promotions in only eight months – five, if you count his promotion to squadron commander. He was the 336th's CO from August 24, 1944, to June 2, 1945.

The last P-51D Mustang Freddie flew was 44-64153, coded VF-B, and was unnamed. It did, however, carry colorful artwork depicting an eagle wearing a US army infantry helmet, which was superimposed on a US flag. Twenty-four red/white/black kill flags were painted in a neat row along the base of the canopy frame.

Major Glover transferred to the peacetime air force on July 5, 1946, and served until September 29, 1949, when he was honorably discharged from the USAF.

Freddie operated a crop-dusting business and was tragically killed on July 7, 1956, 14 miles southeast of Hazlehurst, Georgia. He was flying to Hazlehurst on business and was not sure exactly where it was. He swooped down in his light plane to the nearest road where he hollered his question on directions to motorist Quitman Sears, who was driving a convertible. Just as Sears was pointing the way, one wing of Freddie's plane hit a tree and the aircraft crashed. Glover died in the wreckage before an ambulance arrived. He was 41 years old.

John Godfrey
Rhode Island Mustang Ace

Captain John Trevor Malcolm "Johnny" Godfrey was one half of the duo Winston Churchill referred to as the Damon and Pythias of the 20th century. The other half was Captain Dominic Salvatore "Gentle" Gentile, who was better known by his Americanized name Don Gentile.

Together these two fighter aces destroyed 58.4 Luftwaffe aircraft in the air and on the ground. Britain's top-scoring World War II ace, Group Captain J. E. "Johnnie" Johnson stated the Gentile–Godfrey team, "were the best pair ever to fight over Germany." They were even paid an offhanded compliment by the head of the Luftwaffe. Hermann Göring, in a Berlin radio speech, called Gentile and Godfrey the "Debden Gangsters" for their unorthodox fighting style. He said he would give two Luftwaffe fighter squadrons for their capture!

Johnny flew as Gentile's wingman and, on their first mission, Gentile experienced vertigo in thick cloud cover and spun out. Recovering at less than 1,000ft above the ground, Gentile looked over just as he broke through the cloud base and there was Johnny glued to his wing. Congratulated by Gentile on his superb flying ability, Godfrey simply shrugged and walked away.

At the height of their aerial exploits in 1944, they flew P-51B Mustangs with the 336th FS, 4th FG, USAAF.

Godfrey's P-51 (coded VF-P) was named *Reggie's Reply* in honor of his older brother, Reginald Godfrey, Jr. Reggie lost his life on October 15, 1941, when the Canadian ship he was sailing on to England, the motor vessel *Vancouver Island*, was torpedoed in the North Atlantic by the German submarine U-558. One hundred and five souls (passengers and crew) perished. There were no survivors.

Gentile's Mustang (coded VF-T) was named *Shangri-La*. Both pilots had a large red and white rectangular shaped checkerboard pattern painted on their aircraft just below the exhaust manifolds. This non-standard, eye-catching scheme enabled the pair to quickly rejoin in the event they were separated in combat.

John T. M. Godfrey was the youngest of four sons born to British parents, Ethel and Reginald Godfrey. John came into the world on March 28, 1922, in Montreal, Quebec. The family moved to the United States in 1923 and became, in time, naturalized American citizens. John was raised and educated in Rhode Island and graduated from

Woonsocket High School in 1940. As a typical teenager, he was somewhat rebellious and a little aimless as he was not sure what he wanted to do. His parents, who were considered prosperous for the time, opined that he should go to college. John knew that was really not for him, as he never enjoyed classroom instruction. After several family arguments on the subject, he ran away from home and tried to enlist in the Canadian Army. His father, Reginald Godfrey, Sr., an influential industrial plant manager, had agents dispatched from the Federal Bureau of Investigation (FBI) to retrieve his wayward offspring. Johnny was contravening the 1939 US Neutrality Act by offering to swear allegiance and serve in a foreign military service. Besides, he was only 18 and in the eyes of the law was considered a minor.

His father obtained employment for him at the Fram Corporation in Rumford, Rhode Island. John stayed there a while and next went to work as a truck driver for the Firestone Tire Company in Providence. After a few months, he decided to take off again, but his father, anticipating his movements, intercepted him just as he was boarding a train at the railroad station in Boston. His father found him another job – this time at the NAS Quonset Point as a material checker.

In early August 1941, his parents, fearing that he was about to bolt for the third time, made a covenant with him. He could go to Canada with their blessing where he would try to become a RCAF pilot. If he failed, he would promptly return home and would willingly go to college. John never did go back to school.

He traveled to Montreal, Quebec, and enlisted at the RCAF's No. 13 Recruiting Centre on August 12, 1941. His assigned Service No. was R. 120082. While waiting for his paperwork to be processed, he stayed at the YMCA on Drummond Street.

AC2 Godfrey was sent to No. 4 MD in Valcartier, Quebec, until September 11 and from there he went to No. 4 Repair Depot in Scoudouc, New Brunswick, where he performed guard duty until November 9. The next day, he reported to No. 3 ITS at Victoriaville, Quebec. When he arrived, he was summoned to the GC's office where he was given 14 days' special leave and was advised to return home as quickly as possible as there was a family emergency. It was at the train station in Rhode Island where his parents informed him of the circumstances of his older brother's death.

Returning to No. 3, Johnny, who was filled with resolve to avenge Reggie's death, settled into his studies and training with a newfound maturity. He completed the ITS course on January 17, 1942, and was promoted to LAC. By January 18, he was at No. 4 EFTS at Windsor Mills, Quebec, where he began his pilot training on ski-equipped de Havilland Tiger Moth biplane trainers. Successfully completing that phase, he next reported to No. 8 SFTS at Moncton, New Brunswick, where he flew Harvard Mk IIs on Course No. 11.

In a graduation ceremony on October 9, 1942, he received his RCAF pilot wings and was promoted from LAC to SP. Later that day, he was given new Service No. J. 21278 as he had been commissioned a PO.

He took his two-week pre-embarkation leave on October 10–23. Godfrey set sail on a troop ship for England from "Y" Depot, Pier 21, Halifax, Nova Scotia, on the 24th and arrived in England on November 5. He was at No. 3 Personnel Reception Centre until the 16th. He reported on the 17th to No. 5 Pilot Advanced Flying Unit, RAF Calveley, where he transitioned onto Miles Masters.

While at this unit, Johnny took two unauthorized days off on December 26 and 27, 1942. The RCAF considered him AWL. He was admonished on the 28th and forfeited two days' pay.

He completed his training at No. 5 on January 25, 1943. The next day he reported to No. 57 OTU, RAF Eshott and Boulmer in Northumberland, where he learned to fly the Supermarine Spitfire.

PO Godfrey requested severance from the RCAF in order to join the USAAF and this was honorably granted on April 26, 1943, when he resigned his Canadian commission in London. Within days, he joined the USAAF as a 2nd lieutenant.

He took his P-47 Thunderbolt training at USAAF Station No. 342 Atcham and joined the 336th FS on September 22, 1943. Godfrey flew with the 4th for 11 months before he was shot down, but that was all the time he needed to become one of the group's highest scoring pilots, with 30 enemy aircraft destroyed (16.33 air and 13.67 ground). He actually accomplished this feat in only eight months, as he was on leave in the States from May 5 to July 24, 1944, attending war bond rallies, factory tours, and parades.

His aerial victories are as follows:

December 1, 1943: Bf 109
December 22, 1943: Half of a Bf 109, shared with Captain Vasseure Wynn
March 6, 1944: Bf 109
March 8, 1944: Two Bf 109s and half of a Bf 109, shared with Captain Don Gentile
March 23, 1944: Two Bf 109s
March 29, 1944: Two Fw 190s
April 22, 1944: Three Bf 109s
April 24, 1944: Fw 190
May 1, 1944: Bf 109
August 5, 1944: Three Ju 52s
August 6, 1944: Me 410

Below is Godfrey's combat report of April 22, 1944, and his claim for three 109s:

> I was flying White 3 in Becky section. As we let down from 25,000 to 15,000 feet I reported fighters forming up below us. They were in a gaggle flying in threes, so we orbited and took the bounce. For a while we lost them but finally caught sight of them in a Lufbery. I split up from my No. 1 and orbited the outskirts of the circle.

I could not get inside the circle without getting a couple on my tail. One broke off and tried to break away. I closed to about 350 yards and gave him about a fifteen degree deflection shot. I got a lucky hit and he straightened up for me. I clobbered him really good and noticed strikes in the cockpit and engine. He pulled up and rolled over with flame and smoke pouring from him. This 109 went straight in.

On my second 109 I caught another one trying to sneak away. I fired at about 300 yards at this one with ten degrees deflection. I did quite a bit of shooting and noticed strikes in the cockpit and engine. The kite began to smoke and I overshot to starboard and pulled up preparing to make another attack. The Jerry was smoking and losing altitude, I guess he figured he didn't stand a chance for he bailed out at approximately 1,500 feet. Those two aircraft were confirmed by my wingman, Lieutenant La Jeunesse, who stuck behind me during the fight. He did a very good job.

On my third I saw a 109 turning on the deck. I dove down in a steep turn. I got very close to this one and started firing allowing quite a bit of deflection. He got lower and lower, above the trees. I had quite a job keeping on his tail as I would get in his slipstream and nearly flicked into the deck. Two of my guns jammed but I still kept firing. I saw a good strike in his cockpit and he lost speed. I overshot him sliding up to port. He seemed to flick and went straight into a bunch of trees. I wanted to get a picture of him burning so I made a port turn. I looked back and found out that I had a 109 on my tail instead of my wingman. My wingman called up to say that he had lost me but I did not hear him. I dropped flaps and made a tight turn. The 109 could not get deflection on my so I kept up the turn. Fortunately another Mustang came in and shot him off my tail. I was too shaken to get a picture of my last Jerry so I hot-footed it for altitude.

I claim three Bf 109s destroyed.
Ammunition Expended – 734 Rounds.
John T. Godfrey, 1st Lt., Air Corps.

In England, Godfrey was dating an army nurse, Lt Charlotte Frederick from Rochester, Pennsylvania. Charlotte worked as a surgical nurse at the Newport Field Hospital, which was just two miles from Debden. When outbound on a mission, Johnny would make a wide orbit and fly low over the hospital tents, so low in fact the tent tops rippled from his prop wash like wheat fields in the wind. Godfrey would give Charlotte their signal – "three sharp throttle blasts" – to let her know that he was on his way. Surgeons looked up from their operating tables, shaking their heads; night duty nurses were awakened, and everyone wished the guy in the red-nosed Mustang would carry on his courtship at another location. On his return, he would repeat the process and, on a couple of occasions when he had a particularly good day, he would dive on the hospital from 15,000ft, pulling out close to the ground where he would then perform victory rolls.

John Godfrey: Rhode Island Mustang Ace

When he was brought down on August 24, 1944, the Debden padre drove over to the hospital to tell Charlotte. A nurse found her and told her the padre wanted to see her. Charlotte knew exactly why he was there and passed out.

Godfrey and some fellow 336th pilots had been strafing a German airfield eight miles northeast of Nordhausen. Godfrey got four parked Ju 52s, Melvin Dickey got three and Pierce L. Wiggin one. Johnny was flying a new P-51D, coded VF-M, and as they worked the field over his kite was hit. He was forced to belly in after losing his engine coolant and spent all but the last few weeks of the conflict as a PoW in Stalag Luft III.

Godfrey thought that it was airfield flak that was responsible for shortening his war, but it was later determined that Melvin Dickey, his wingman, had shot Johnny down by accident.

When captured, Godfrey stood at attention before the German interrogator just as the little book said to do. The German had spent enough time in prewar America that he actually had a Brooklyn accent! "Now look," he said, "I'm Hans and you're Johnny. You're a captain in the American air force and I'm a captain in

Lieutenants Fred Haddad (foreground) and John T. Godfrey at Station No. 342 Atcham in the summer of 1943, before being assigned to FGs. Fred went to the 352nd FG and John to the 4th FG. (US Department of Defense)

the Luftwaffe. What we want to know is how do you Americans spot our airfields? Take the one over which you were shot down. We had twelve Ju 52s parked there. Recently some so-and-so came along and destroyed three of them. Then your group today got eight!" Godfrey didn't think it was wise to disclose that it happened to be his squadron that had done both jobs.

According to some, Johnny had the keenest eyes in the 4th. His vision was superb to start with and he sharpened it by training – as he practice flew around Debden, he would strain his eyes to sight distant objects. Vision was key to becoming a high-scoring ace. In a letter to the author, Colonel Steve "The Greek" Pisanos, who flew with the 4th from October 1942 to March 1944, said: "Godfrey and Gentile both had the eyes of hawks." They also had a very unique working arrangement in that whoever spotted the enemy first, that person planned and led the attack with the other flying wingman.

Godfrey stuck to his name, rank, and serial number in response to his captor's questions. The German strove to break him down by showing that he knew everything about him. "Now Johnny, the plane you were shot down in today was coded VF-M. Why weren't you flying your own Mustang VF-P?" His interrogator even quoted parts from conversations that had taken place between 4th pilots three nights earlier in the Officers' Club at Debden! It was then and there that Johnny fully understood the information gathered and contained in the Luftwaffe's dossier on each of the pilots at the 4th was far more exhaustive than anyone had imagined.

Shortly after the European conflict ended, a 4th FG P-51D Mustang was painted to represent Godfrey's famous Mustang VF-P. It was flown to Paris, France, and was displayed with other USAAF aircraft under the Eiffel Tower in a Victory Display.

John T. M. Godfrey was discharged as a major from the USAAF on January 27, 1946. He became a successful businessman in the lace industry and was elected as a Rhode Island State Senator in 1952, serving two years. In 1956, he was diagnosed as having Amyotrophic Lateral Sclerosis (ALS, more commonly known as Lou Gehrig's Disease) and died at his home in South Freeport, Maine, on June 12, 1958, at the age of 36. He was survived by his wife and two sons, aged 10 and 12.

Archibald Harrington
New Jersey Mosquito Ace

1st Lieutenant Archibald Allan "Ack-Ack" Harrington was probably the only member of the USAAF who earned a British DSO and DFC award while flying on detached service in World War II with the RCAF.

Later in his USAAF career, Harrington earned the following American awards: the DSC, a DFC, and an air medal with seven Oak-Leaf Clusters.

During the 18 months (June 29, 1943–December 28, 1944) Harrington was assigned to RCAF No. 410 "Cougar" Squadron, he flew 86 sorties, covering 217 operational hours on de Havilland Mosquito Mk XIII and Mk XXX night fighter aircraft.

Ack-Ack and his equally talented radar operator/navigator, RAF Sergeant Dennis G. Tongue from Birmingham, England, worked as a team and were credited with shooting down seven German warplanes. Tongue was commissioned from the ranks during his tour and finished the war as a flying officer, earning himself a DFC & Bar.

Their first two kills, a Ju 88G-1 and a Ju 88, were destroyed using the Mosquito Mk XIII. Their five remaining claims, a Ju 87, an Fw 190 and three Ju 88G-1s, were brought down using the improved Mk XXX.

Their first victory occurred on March 14, 1944, at 2316hrs near Wrotham, Kent, England. Harrington and Tongue were on their way back to their base at RAF Castle Camps, Cambridgeshire, in Mosquito HK521 after an uneventful patrol. In the distance, they spotted searchlight beams, bomb bursts, and burning incendiaries on the ground. Even though they were short on fuel, they decided to investigate and obtained a contact. Showers of window (bundles of aluminum strips meant to disrupt the radar signals of pursuing aircraft) and skillful evasive action taken by the enemy aircraft made it difficult to retain the radar contact, but Tongue held on until Ack-Ack sighted the target, Ju 88G-1 B3+CK from Kampfgeschwader (KG) 54. A short burst of only 35 rounds from the four belly-mounted Hispano-Suiza 20mm cannon had a spectacular effect on the target. Strikes flashed on the enemy cockpit and wing roots;

a red glow appeared in the cockpit and almost immediately both engines burst into flames. The fire grew until it enveloped the whole center section and a solid sheet of flame streamed back two or three times the length of the aircraft. Large pieces of debris flew off and explosions erupted through the flames as the Junkers went down through the clouds, its course marked by a bright glow. Suddenly, there was a brilliant flash below and then darkness closed in. As the bomber was going down, Harrington flew around it, noting the large black crosses on the fuselage and the swastika on the tail fin. The German pilot, Unteroffizier H. Heide, and his crew successfully bailed out and were immediately taken into custody as PoWs.

Their second kill came three months later at 0042hrs on June 19, near Vire, France. Aboard Mosquito MM571, Harrington and Tongue were patrolling in an east–west direction just south of the American lines when ground control intercept put them on to a target. Closing on the single radar contact, Harrington suddenly realized that it was two aircraft flying in very close formation. As soon as he visually spotted them, the two bogies broke in opposite directions. From their movements, Ack-Ack suspected both were fitted with rearward warning radar. He pursued one, closing to 400ft, where he identified it as a twin-engined Ju 88 bomber. Recognition was difficult at first as the enemy had two large bombs mounted on external racks between the engines and fuselage. Satisfied that it was German, Harrington moved in to 200ft, pulled his nose up and tripped his guns. No strikes were seen. In the next second, the enemy aircraft blew up! One wing and engine tore away and went hurtling past the Mosquito. Masses of smaller debris and burning oil splashed over the Mossie, puncturing holes in the leading edge of the wing and smearing the fabric on the wings and fuselage. Ten seconds after the wreckage disappeared into the dark void, there was a vivid explosion on the ground, which lit up Harrington's aircraft some 10,000ft above. Archie and Dennis returned victorious to their temporary operating station at RAF Zeals in Wiltshire.

Archibald Harrington was born in Zanesville, Ohio, on June 10, 1914. His father, Orval Flavell Harrington, was born in Michigan and his mother, Lillian Allan, came from Scotland. Harrington's father died when he was just a boy, and his mother married a man named Robbins. For some unknown reason, Archibald Allan Harrington became known as Frederick Allan Robbins and, although he was never formally adopted by his stepfather, he used that name all the way through grade and high school.

In 1921, the Robbins family moved from the United States to Canada. Archie was listed as being registered in September that year in the first grade at the Wellington Street Public School in Sarnia, Ontario. The family then relocated back to the States where Harrington next attended McCausland Avenue Public School in St. Louis, Missouri, for the school year 1922–23. A return to Zanesville saw Harrington enrolled in the local public school system there from 1923 to 1925. Yet a further move in the summer of 1925 took the Robbins family to Atlantic City,

New Jersey, where Archie finished his education in June 1933 after graduating from Atlantic City High School.

By 1933, Harrington's mother had divorced her second husband and was married to a gentleman named Frank Venino. Her name change prompted Archie to drop the Robbins surname and he reverted to using his given birth name.

Archibald was an extrovert and naturally gravitated toward sales jobs when he began his working career. His first employment in 1933 was as a driver for M. Wagenheim & Sons in Atlantic City. From 1934 to 1936, he was a sales manager with Rice & Rice, a barber supply company in Chillicothe, Ohio. He returned to work at Wagenheim & Sons as a driver-salesman in Atlantic City in 1936. Harrington next worked for Dugan Brothers Bakery in Newark, New Jersey, from 1938 to 1940 as a driver-salesman.

Growing up, Archie had a keen interest in aviation and one of his hobbies was collecting aircraft memorabilia. While working in Newark, he took up flying. He amassed more than 90 hours' flying time on Stinsons and Luscombes, but never actually got around to taking the test for his private pilot license.

Unable to meet the USAAC educational requirement for pilot training, the 6ft, 192lb Harrington traveled to the RCAF's No. 13 Recruiting Centre in Montreal, Quebec, and voluntarily enlisted in its service on March 3, 1941. Assigned Regimental No. R. 79208, AC2 Harrington spent the next two months at No. 1 and No. 4 MDs in Toronto, Ontario, and Quebec City, Quebec, respectively.

At the end of April, he was sent to No. 12 Equipment Depot in Montreal where he performed guard duty until May 27. His flight training began in earnest after he arrived at No. 3 ITS at Victoriaville, Quebec, on the 28th. Harrington did very well at No. 3, scoring 82 percent on his final examinations on Course No. 27, which concluded on July 3. Out of 238 students, he ranked 38th in his class. The following comments were noted in his file: "Very good background. Likes the service life. Self confident and mature. Alert and cheerful."

Passed to No. 12 EFTS at Goderich, Ontario, Harrington, who had been promoted to LAC, flew 55.05 hours on Fleet Finch aircraft on Course No. 33 until September 1, 1941. He also logged 11.30 hours on the Link Trainer. He finished the course with a 78.6 percent average, which placed him fifth in a graduating class of thirty-one students. As good a student as he was, Archie's instructors recorded that he needed to be watched, as he was overly confident of his flying abilities. From the CFI, H. A. MacPherson: "Respectful, but somewhat careless about dress. Likes flying but is inclined to be a little over confident. Tries to give one the impression his flying is better than it really is. Flying ability in general is average. Instrument flying needs constant checking. He learns and thinks fast." From the CGI, K. S. Hopkinson: "Inclined to be too sure of himself. He is a boisterous type. Has maintained an average progress but will bear watching both in flying and ground school. Conduct average but he is careless about his personal appearance."

The de Havilland Mosquito was the aircraft type 1st Lieutenant Archibald A. Harrington DSO, DFC, used to destroy several enemy aircraft while flying on detached service with RCAF No. 410 "Cougar" Squadron. (Canadian National Defence Image Library)

Harrington was posted to No. 1 SFTS at Camp Borden, Ontario, on September 13. Logging 94.30 hours on Yales and Harvards on Course No. 38, he was awarded his wings and commissioned as a PO on December 19, 1941.

Three weeks prior to graduating, he damaged the port wing of Harvard No. 2606 at Edenvale, Ontario. With FO W. L. Holmes on board, Archie was completing an exercise of eight circuits and landings. On his final landing attempt, he closed the throttle and pulled back on the stick while the aircraft was still 3ft off the ground. This caused the Harvard to stall and flick, slightly damaging the left wing. Neither occupant was injured.

Assigned new Regimental No. J. 9422, Harrington reported on February 2 to the Flying Instructor's School at RCAF Station Trenton, Ontario. There he logged an additional 97 hours flying Cranes, Harvards, Lockheed 10s, and Yales on Course No. 52. Graduating on March 26 with a Category "C" instructor's certificate, Harrington reported for duty on March 28 to No. 2 SFTS Uplands, located near Ottawa, Ontario.

There he flew 342.10 hours as a flying instructor up until November 15, 1942. The OC at Uplands, GC F. A. Sampson, had this to say about Harrington's time at No. 2:

> Would make a good operational pilot. His flying is above average and he likes action. This instructor puts in long flying hours conscientiously doing his job, but contributes nothing other than his work to the unit. He is argumentative and is

inclined to be conceited. He is an American citizen, but is a good RCAF officer. Should pay greater attention to orders and regulations in order that he as an instructor will set a good rather than a bad example to his trainees. One breach of air force flying regulations – a low flying charge logged on July 19.

While stationed at Uplands, Archie met, courted, and married Elda Miriam Lewis, the daughter of the mayor of the City of Ottawa. The two were wed in a civil ceremony on November 4, with the wedding and reception taking place at the bride's family home at 168 Cartier Street.

Harrington was granted 14 days' embarkation leave on November 16, as he had been posted overseas. While boarding the troop ship on December 12, at Pier 21, Halifax, Nova Scotia, he slipped and fell on the gangway fracturing his right fibula. The ship's hospital applied a plaster of Paris cast and, when the boat arrived in Glasgow, Scotland, Harrington was transferred to the Hairmyres Emergency Medical Service (EMS) Hospital at Kilbride.

On January 15, 1943, Archie was medically cleared to return to flying duty as his broken ankle had completely healed.

On February 11, Harrington, newly promoted to the rank of FO and earning CAN$7.50 daily, was posted from No. 3 Personnel Reception Centre at Bournemouth to No. 12 Pilot Advanced Flying Unit at RAF Grantham, Lincolnshire. There he flew Airspeed Oxfords on Course No. 2 until March 29. WC A. H. Abbott recorded the following observations in Archie's file: "An extremely competent pilot but has a strong tendency towards over confidence which needs watching. Above average in all respects. A good sense of leadership through previously being an instructor on service aircraft in Canada. Has worked hard at flying but has been a difficult pupil in regards to discipline."

Ack-Ack was transferred the next day to No. 54 OTU at RAF Winfield, Scottish Borders. On Course No. 31, he logged 84 flying hours on Beaufighters, Beauforts and Blenheims until June 15. The intelligence officer at No. 54 had Archie take a visual aircraft recognition test covering 30 separate types. Archie scored 99 percent on the examination.

FO Harrington, at the age of 28, was now fully qualified to go to war. He was posted directly to RCAF 410 Squadron, which was stationed, in the summer of 1943, at RAF Coleby Grange, Lincolnshire, flying Mosquito Mk XIIIs. The invitation to transfer to an American military service was sent out by the US government to all Americans who were then serving in the RCAF. Harrington's letter caught up with him just as he arrived at 410. After thinking it over, he decided to join the USAAF with the rank of 1st lieutenant. The incentive for him to transfer was compelling, first and foremost being able to fight under the US flag, better pay, and, as a newly married man, a $10,000 life insurance policy payable to his wife should he not survive the conflict.

At his request, Archie was honorably discharged from the RCAF on June 29, 1943, in London. At the time, the USAAF had precious little in the way of experience or equipment in the night-fighter community overseas. Therefore, the decision was made to return Archie, USAAF Service No. O-885992, to 410 Squadron so that he could gain some operational combat experience in the field for which he had recently trained.

With a full load of gas, de Havilland's "Wooden Wonder" had more than a six-hour endurance while cruising at 235mph. This gave the Mosquito crews the freedom to roam far and wide over most of occupied Europe. Powered by two 1,710shp Detroit-built Packard V-12 Rolls-Royce Merlin engines, the aircraft raced along at 385mph at sea level. Both the Mk XIII and Mk XXX models had their nose-mounted Browning .303 caliber machine guns removed in order to accommodate an Airborne Intercept radar unit. Even with the reduction in firepower, the four belly-mounted .79in cannons, containing 620 rounds of ammunition, were more than adequate to deal with any threat encountered.

Harrington's third victory, a Ju 87 Stuka dive-bomber, was downed on September 26, 12 miles north of Aachen, Germany. Archie and Dennis were operating that evening from a Forward Operating Location, B.48, at Amiens-Glisy, France, and were logged airborne at 1955hrs. Two hours into their patrol, the pair were advised of trade by Circular ground control operators. Descending to 1,500ft, Dennis acquired the target at a distance of three miles. Harrington quickly closed the gap, identified it as a Ju 87, and opened fire; "I believe the pilot was killed outright. We followed the aircraft around and delivered two additional bursts. The enemy aircraft then passed under my wing and exploded violently on the ground, where it could be seen to burn very nicely." The time was 2141hrs.

Victim number four, a Focke Wulf Fw 190, was destroyed a month later on October 29, at 1855hrs near Sint Anthonis, Holland. At this point the hunter/killer "Cougar" team of Harrington and Tongue were recommended for British DFCs.

Kills five, six and seven on the evening of November 25, 1944, over Muntz, Jackerath and Hunxe, Germany, took only 18 minutes. This rare triple feat using only 540 20mm cannon rounds not only made Ack-Ack an ace, but he also became 410's second highest-scoring pilot of the war.

Harrington and Tongue took off from B.51 at Lille-Vendeville, France, at 1740hrs aboard Mosquito MM767, coded RA-D. They did an uneventful patrol for well over an hour before being handed off from Greengrocer and Bricktile ground control operators to Rejoice control. The following is Ack-Ack's account of that sortie as told to the squadron's historian:

> I was finally handed over to Rejoice control and told of trade ahead between 10,000 and 15,000 feet. Then I was told of joy fifteen miles to port and to steer 100 degrees. Contact obtained crossing to starboard above, range four miles. Closed fairly rapidly to two miles. Then target commenced moderate evasive action. Visual

obtained at 4,500 feet, height 16,000 feet. Closed right in and finally identified a Ju 88G-1. Dropped back to approximately six hundred feet and opened fire. Strikes seen in cockpit, engines, and wing roots, followed by explosion and debris. Enemy aircraft, piloted by Hauptmann Erwin Strobel, dove steeply. I followed him on the airborne radar and visually. Victim from Nachtjagdgeschwader 4 was seen to strike the ground and burn. Our aircraft had been hit by debris as we fired, shaking the aircraft badly. Position given by Rejoice was at Muntz. Time 2008 hours.

Climbed back up and Rejoice gave us another chase on vector of 280 degrees, head-on, range eleven miles. At the same time observer obtained a head-on collision contact, above at range of three miles. Did hard port orbit, and no joy. Continued orbit, searching and regained contact, hard over to port, on an aircraft doing a hard port turn. Apparently the enemy pilot, Lieutenant Fensch, was trying to intercept us. Target commenced very violent evasive action and increased speed, climbing, diving and turning. Closed very slowly to 4,000 feet range and target did even more violent evasive, getting out to 6,000 feet range. This lasted for nine to ten minutes. Visual obtained finally between 4,000 and 3,500 feet. Closed in very slowly at 270 miles per hour at a height of 12,000 feet. Identified the target as another Ju 88G-1. Dropped back to five hundred feet, and opened fire. Strikes seen on cockpit, engines and wing roots, followed by explosions. Enemy did a half roll and went to port, then became straight and level, finally going into a loop. It stalled at the top of the loop and went into an inverted spin. Aircraft from NJG 4 was seen to hit the deck followed by a large explosion, illuminating the houses in the vicinity. Position given by Rejoice as near Jackerath. Time 2019 hours.

Climbed back up and obtained two contacts. One to port, range three miles and one to starboard, range four miles. Asked Rejoice which one was hostile; advised to take our pick as both were hostile. Intercepted the one to port through moderate evasive action. The furthermost aircraft came in head-on to starboard and above, appearing to intercept us. We continued interception, my observer constantly clearing our tail with night vision glasses in starboard turns as well as controlling the interception. Visual finally obtained at 4,500 feet. We closed in to about seventy-five feet and identified the enemy aircraft as a Ju 88G-1. The German pilot, Unteroffizier Goebel, who was still taking evasive action, suddenly throttled back and I narrowly escaped ramming him. Then I dropped back to about three hundred feet and opened fire. Strikes seen in cockpit, on engines and wing roots. Debris flew off. Aircraft then started burning in the port engine area, fire spreading to cockpit and starboard engine. The Junkers went down in spiral dive to starboard. I followed, taking pictures of him burning. The aircraft went into cloud and a few seconds later a very large explosion lit up the underside of the cloud and burned fiercely. Rejoice was unable to give me a definite fix as I was then off their tube, but approximate area was somewhere north around Hunxe. Time 2026 hours. I then took some violent evasive action myself, including hard orbits, as Rejoice seemed to think there might be someone on my tail. I claim three Ju 88G-1s destroyed.

All three aircraft from NJG 4 were Ju 88G-1 night fighters. These were identifiable by a blister under the nose and radar aerials projecting from the nose. Large black crosses could be seen under the wings and close to the engine nacelles. Harrington believed the enemy tactics were for two night fighters to fly in line astern, approximately two miles apart, the rear one covering the other. He and Tongue, therefore, concentrated on intercepting the Tail-end Charlie. Throughout the chases, they were held by the German ground radar and could hear the enemy controller over their radio telephone. No return fire was encountered in the combat, but the Mosquito was slightly damaged by flying debris.

The duo's successful combat on November 25 earned Lt Harrington a DSO award and FO Tongue a Bar to his DFC. Archie's two British gallantry awards were both dated January 18, 1945, but for some reason were never reported in the *London Gazette*.

Archie's tour with 410 ended on December 28, 1944, when he was sent home for a well-deserved rest. Before taking up his duties as a pilot instructor at Army Air Force Base, Hammer Field, Fresno, California, Archie was busy moving his wife from Canada to the States. Hammer Field, which came under the control of the 4th Air Force, opened in June 1944 for specialized night-fighter training. Archie was assigned to "A" Squadron, 450th Base Unit, flying Douglas P-70s and Northrop P-61 Black Widows.

On March 7, 1945, RCAF Overseas Headquarters in London queried RCAF HQ in Ottawa, asking if Harrington had been awarded a DSO and DFC. This prompted the following reply two days later from Air Vice Marshal J. A. Scully, who replied on behalf of the CAS:

> Reference Lieutenant A. A. Harrington, DSO, DFC, (O-885992) formerly FO A. A. Harrington, DSO, DFC, (J. 9422). The subject officer received the Distinguished Service Order and the Distinguished Flying Cross as an American Army officer serving with a Canadian squadron. Lieutenant Harrington has inquired concerning the investiture of his British decorations. It is presumed, since they were awarded to him as a member of the US Army Air Corps, and as he is now on active duty in the United States, that they will be forwarded by the United Kingdom authorities to the British Ambassador in Washington for presentation. May this be confirmed, please.

Air Commodore E. E. Middleton in England replied in writing on March 20 with the following information: "It is advised that Lt. A. A. Harrington's decorations will be forwarded by the Central Chancery of Knighthood to the British Ambassador in Washington, and the presentation will be made there."

On July 4, 1945, Archie wrote a letter to the Department of National Defence in Ottawa asking if he was entitled to any war service gratuity pay. Based on his

849 days of RCAF service, the Canadian federal government forwarded him a cheque in the amount of CAN$336.42 on August 20, 1945.

Lt Harrington attended a formal ceremony at the British Embassy in Washington D.C. on November 7, 1945, where he was presented with his two awards earned one year earlier.

In March 1946, Archie was stationed at McChord Field, Tacoma, Washington, where he was assigned to the 464th Base Unit. He was promoted to captain in October 1948, and in September 1949, served in the Headquarters section at Wright-Patterson Air Force Base in Dayton, Ohio. In January 1951, Captain Harrington transferred to the United States Air Force Reserve (USAFR).

On February 15, 1954, Lieutenant-Colonel Philip G. Cardin, the Air Attaché at the US Embassy in Ottawa, wrote a letter on behalf of Captain Harrington to SL Eric T. Sherlock at RCAF HQ, regarding additional Canadian medals that Archie believed he had earned, but had not yet received. SL Sherlock's reply on behalf of the CAS dated March 2, was as follows:

> Records indicate Captain Harrington qualified for the following awards prior to transferring to the USAAF – Defence Medal, Canadian Volunteer Service Medal and Clasp, War Medal 1939-45 and RCAF Operational Wings and Bar. Captain Harrington was awarded the British DSO and DFC subsequent to his transfer to the USAAF. It is understood that these awards were presented to him at the British Embassy in 1945. It is not possible to grant Captain Harrington the 1939-45 Aircrew Europe, France or Germany Stars since he had not qualified for these awards prior to his transfer to the US Forces. Although he was employed on operational duties with an RCAF squadron for some considerable time, he was in fact a member of the USAAF from June 30, 1943, consequently he would be qualifying for US awards from this date onwards and not British awards. The foregoing information is supplied to clear up any misunderstanding Captain Harrington may have concerning his entitlement to additional awards. It would be appreciated if the enclosed awards were forwarded to United States Air Force HQ for onward transmission to Captain Harrington.

Archie rose to the rank of lieutenant colonel and retired from the military in August 1963 after 20 years of service.

On February 15, 1988, at the age of 73, Archie Harrington died of cardiopulmonary arrest at his home in Vacaville, California. His death certificate, signed by Doctor M. Ellis, from the David Grant Medical Center at Travis AFB in California, indicated that he had been suffering from lung cancer for almost a year. Predeceased by his wife Elda, Lt Col Harrington was survived by a son, David, who was listed at the time as living in Old Chelsea, Quebec, Canada.

Ralph Hofer
673 Days in the RCAF

The life and times of World War II fighter ace 1st Lieutenant Ralph "Kidd" Hofer have been well chronicled over the past 79 years in numerous books, newspapers, and magazine articles.

Kidd Hofer's connection to Canada began on Monday, July 21, 1941. That is the day the 21-year-old Chicagoan wandered into the RCAF Recruiting Office in downtown Windsor, Ontario.

Hofer was in Detroit, Michigan, and crossed the US–Canada border into Windsor to have a look around, as he had never been to Canada. When he emerged from the tunnel under the Detroit River, a friendly Canadian customs officer mistook his intended visit and assumed that he was looking for the Recruiting Office located on Ouellette Avenue. What Hofer did not realize was that several thousand other US citizens, who were clamoring to get into the European war, had made the trek before him – "Came over to join up, I suppose. That building right over there is where you go."

Hofer's curiosity was aroused, and he entered No. 8 Recruiting Centre to find it full of Americans who enthusiastically told him what a great deal it was. Ralph was so caught up in the moment that he not only filled out but signed an enlistment form that an RCAF sergeant placed before him. He found himself in the air force as an AC2 with the assigned service number R. 109807.

Hofer was born Ralph Halbrook on June 19, 1920, in Salem, Missouri. His father, Clyde Halbrook, was an ironworker and his mother, Opal Robinson Halbrook, a housewife. When Ralph was three, his mother divorced his birth father and married Arthur J. Hofer. The Hofer family then moved from rural Dent County, Missouri, to the bustling city of Chicago where Ralph and his older sister, Mildred, were raised. Later in life, Ralph had his surname legally changed from Halbrook to Hofer.

Ralph graduated from Steinmetz High School, but never really excelled at his studies. This greatly frustrated his teachers, as they had him pegged as one of the smartest students in the school. Hofer loved sports of any kind – football, boxing, baseball, and skating. He was a superb athlete and excelled at all of them. The one sport that he relished above all others was boxing and he would often refer to it, with all its moves and counter moves, as physical chess.

Ralph Hofer: 673 Days in the RCAF

Between 1939 and 1941, Ralph fought under the ring name "Junior" Halbrook but was also known around the Cook County gymnasiums as Kidd Hofer.

In 1940, he entered the Chicago area Golden Gloves Boxing Competition and went all the way to the finals, winning the title in the novice light heavyweight division. Besides winning boxing purses, Ralph earned money playing football in a local semi-professional league.

On his RCAF entry papers, Ralph indicated that he had no given second name nor initial. He gave the recruiter a current home address of 4211 Ottawa Avenue in Chicago. He stated that he was single, age 21, and that his father, Clyde Halbrook, was deceased. He declared that he served one year in the ROTC in high school. He also declared he had flown 12 hours as a passenger in an aircraft and had three hours dual flight instruction time. One of the questions on the form asked about his work history or occupation. Ralph's initial written response was none, but as an afterthought he answered that he had boxed for the past two years. Hofer spent the next several days at Windsor's YMCA on the RCAF's tab waiting for his birth certificate and high school diploma to be forwarded from home. Ralph, however, was not as forthcoming with his personal information as he should have been. Clyde Halbrook, his father, was very much alive. Hofer was not single, but married to one Jean Pasquini, who was known as Jean Halbrook. She and Ralph's infant daughter, Carol Lee Halbrook, resided with her parents, Mr. and Mrs. Jack Pasquini, at 2846 No. 73rd Court, Elmwood Park 35 in Chicago. Jack Pasquini, Hofer's father-in-law, was a merchant and Ralph listed him as one of his references on the application. These discrepancies were not immediately caught by the RCAF and would not surface until a year later.

For some reason, Ralph's mother was unable to locate his birth certificate or his high school diploma. As these papers were crucial to the enlistment process, replacement documents were obtained and forwarded to the RCAF for its consideration.

In a deposition, Opal Hofer of Norwood Park Township, Cook County, Illinois, a housewife, swore before a local Chicago Justice of the Peace that she was the mother of one Ralph Hofer who was born on the 19th day of June 1920 at Salem, Missouri. She made her affidavit to remove any questions that may arise as to the nationality and date of birth of her son. She further swore that she was married to Arthur J. Hofer, and they resided together at 4211 Ottawa Avenue in Chicago. The odd thing about this document is that it was dated July 12, 1941, nine days before Ralph enlisted.

The second document relating to Ralph's education was dated even earlier, July 9, 1941. It was from Mr. Daniel F. O'Hearn, the principal of Steinmetz High School, 3000 North Narragansett Street, Chicago, Illinois.

In a "To Whom it May Concern" letter, Mr. O'Hearn certified that Ralph Hofer honorably completed a four-year course prescribed by the Board of Education for the high schools of the city of Chicago. He further elaborated that Hofer's graduation diploma was granted on June 27, 1939. Mr. O'Hearn went on to say that, as the Board of Education was closed for the summer, a duplicate diploma could not be issued. He closed his letter with the hope the information he was supplying would be sufficient for Ralph to enter into a fine and honorable service, such as the RCAF.

Hofer had his first regular monthly paycheck since leaving school and was earning the princely sum of CAN$39.00 monthly.

In late July and early August, Ralph attended No. 1 MD in Toronto, Ontario. The RCAF then sent him, from August 10 to October 27, to perform guard duty at No. 14 SFTS in Aylmer, Ontario. While there, Hofer experienced his first of nine run-ins with air force discipline when he seriously violated one of the King's regulations.

On September 22, he was sentenced to 72 hours of detention in the guard house plus four days confined to barracks with pack drill. The charge was Conduct to the Prejudice of Good Order and Air Force Discipline.

Later in his career, while flying P-47 Thunderbolts and P-51 Mustangs with the USAAF at Debden, England, Ralph learned that Air Station Aylmer was also the place from which several of his 4th FG contemporaries graduated and had earned their wings – aces such as Major Pierce Winningham "Mac" McKennon from Fort Smith, Arkansas; Captain Bernard "Big Mac" McGrattan from Utica, New York;

Two of the top-scoring 4th FG aces, 1st Lieutenant Ralph Hofer (left) and Major James Goodson (right) discuss their various victories. (US Department of Defense)

Captain Albert Lewis "Smiley" Schlegel from Cleveland, Ohio; Captain Vasseure Howe "Georgia" Wynn from Dalton, Georgia; Captain Edward Lester "Buddy" Gimbel from Chicago, Illinois; and Lieutenant Paul Sydney "Rip" Riley from York, Pennsylvania. They were all stationed together at RCAF Aylmer for 32 days in the fall of 1941. It is unknown if they knew each other at that time.

From October 28 to December 19, Ralph was on Course No. 39 at No. 5 ITS at Belleville, Ontario. He graduated with a 64 percent average and was ranked 114th out of a class of 127 students. Prior to beginning the course, he was promoted to LAC along with a pay raise of $6.00 per month. The OC No. 5 remarked that LAC Hofer was: "Quick tempered and immature but, overall is a good-hearted boy." He also said that, in his view, Ralph was unsuitable for a commission.

Posted to No. 22 EFTS at L'Ancienne Lorette, Quebec, on December 22, Hofer began flight instruction on ski-equipped Fleet Finch IIs on Course No. 45, which concluded on February 27, 1942. Ralph flew the little yellow biplanes for 66.20 hours (37 dual and 29.20 solo) and in the process managed to improve his grade averages by obtaining 73 percent on his instrument flying examination and 77 percent on his flight test. The CFI wrote the following in his file: "General flying fair. Needs more experience on instruments." The CGI made the following notations: "Immature. Not very obedient. Tries hard. Pleasant personality."

Hofer's next posting should have seen him sent to an SFTS, but instead he was shipped off to No. 5 MD at Lachine, Quebec. Lachine was known at the time as the place where some of the more difficult air force discipline cases were sent for correction.

On March 15, Hofer was found to be AWL from No. 5 for a period of three days, 11 hours and one minute. The penalty for Ralph's second infraction was confinement to barracks for five days and the forfeiture of four days' pay. Ten days later, on the 25th, he was facing his third charge: failing to get a haircut and failing to report for duty watch parade. As punishment, Ralph spent two additional days confined to barracks.

On March 28, Hofer was sent to No. 8 SFTS in Moncton, New Brunswick. There he was to finish his training flying Harvard Mk IIs on Course No. 52, which ran from March 30 to July 17. It did not take Kidd long to get into trouble again. For failing to attend Church Parade on April 12, Ralph spent another three days confined to barracks.

The fifth charge, on April 27, found Hofer locked up in the guardhouse for three days for neglecting to obey general orders, namely doing unauthorized aerobatics between 1845 and 2000hrs on April 27.

Ralph's sixth infraction occurred on July 3, when, after being ordered to show up on time for parade by his squadron commander, he was one hour and 15 minutes late. Kidd spent another three days in confinement.

Finally, on graduation day, July 17, 1942, LAC Ralph Hofer was awarded his wings after logging 157.15 hours on single-engined Harvard trainers. He was promoted to SP and was given a raise, which boosted his monthly pay to $111.00. SL H. Bryant, Ralph's squadron commander, recorded the following in his file: "Good average pilot. Displays ability and co-ordination. Weak on forced landings. This man knows he is good. Can do much better work."

From WC N. S. Anderson: "This pupil catches on quickly, but is inclined to be a smart aleck. Pupil's choice – Fighters." Anderson would not recommend Ralph Hofer for an officer's commission and the station commander, GC W. W. Brown, concurred.

Ralph was then given the standard two-week pre-embarkation leave and was directed to report by August 1 to "Y" Depot, Pier 21, Halifax, Nova Scotia.

Days before he graduated from Moncton, Hofer authorized a pay assignment of $20.00 to be forwarded each and every month to his wife, Jean Pasquini-Halbrook. It was at this point Ralph's air force records were amended to reflect that he was, in fact, a married man.

Before leaving Canada, all RCAF personnel were required to complete a form entitled Airman's Statement At Embarkation. Sergeant R. Hofer R. 109807 filled out and signed his on August 3, 1942. He admitted that he was married to Jean Pasquini-Halbrook and appointed her his legal next-of-kin. He stated that he had made a will and had completed the necessary documentation for dependent's allowance. The first person he wanted notified in the event of a casualty was his mother, Mrs. A. J. Hofer, at 2705 North Santa Fe Drive in Englewood, Colorado. The Hofer family had moved from Illinois to Colorado in 1942. The second or alternate person to be notified was his father, Mr. Clyde Halbrook, in Salem, Missouri.

Hofer was scheduled to leave on a troop ship for overseas deployment on September 15, 1942. The ship sailed, but Ralph was not on it! When he finally showed up three days, ten hours and 29 minutes late, the air force charged him with his seventh violation of the King's regulations. For being AWL, WC A. Woods reprimanded Hofer and fined him the equivalent of four days' pay.

The RCAF tried again on October 2 to send Kidd off to war, but he literally missed the boat, this time by 22 hours. Facing his eighth charge, Ralph was fined another day's pay and this time was severely reprimanded by WC Woods.

The third attempt to ship SP Hofer overseas was successful and the ship docked in the United Kingdom on November 5. The next day, Ralph was assigned to No. 3 Personnel Reception Centre at Bournemouth.

While waiting for a fighter training slot to open up, Hofer had his ninth and final run-in with his RCAF superiors. On November 24, they found him guilty of being AWL for two days, two hours and 20 minutes. SL Sutherland admonished Ralph and fined him three days' pay in the amount of $11.10.

On December 1, Kidd Hofer reported to No. 17 Pilot Advanced Flying Unit at RAF Calveley where he flew Miles Masters and Hawker Hurricanes until January 19, 1943.

From there, he was passed to No. 59 OTU at RAF Milfield, Northumberland, where he flew an additional 83.55 hours until March 29 on Hurricanes and Masters on Course No. 28. Ralph earned a 75.5 percent average on his ground examination test, a 66.75 on his flying test and only 60 percent on the RAF's assessment of his character and leadership skills. In his file, the following was recorded: "An average pilot whose formation and general flying are of average standard. He has completed his night-flying exercises without any trouble. He tends to be overconfident, however, and should be carefully watched. He is keen on his work, but has no self discipline."

On April 8, Ralph reported for duty at RAF No. 286 Army Co-operation Squadron, which was stationed at RAF Weston-super-Mare at north Somerset. Flying Hurricane Mk Is, IIcs and IVs, No. 286 was a second line utility squadron, which fulfilled the target-towing, radar-calibration and gun-laying training roles for anti- aircraft units based in southwest England. The squadron, in service since 1941, was scheduled to be inactivated at the end of June 1943. Rather than go through all the trouble of trying to relocate to a new unit, Hofer decided to take advantage of the repatriation agreement worked out between Canada and the United States in May 1942 governing the transfer of trained personnel.

He requested his service with the RCAF be severed and asked to be transferred to the USAAF. Sergeant Ralph Hofer's request was honorably granted on June 10, 1943, when the RCAF discharged him in London. Financially, it was to Ralph's advantage to go this route for, after transferring, the USAAF commissioned him as an FO at more than double his previous pay. Kidd had also been in uniform for 22 months and had yet to see any combat.

The improbable story that first surfaced in 1944, that FL George Frederick "Buzz" Beurling, Canada's leading World War II ace, was one of Hofer's gunnery instructors in England is untrue. While Hofer was undergoing conversion training at the CCRC on P-39 Airacobras and Spitfire Mk Vs at USAAF Station 342 Atcham from early July to the middle of September 1943, Beurling was instructing on Spitfires at Rednal, West Midlands.

Buzz was posted from Rednal on September 5, 1943, to RCAF 403 FS at RAF Kenley, while Kidd Hofer joined the 334th FS at Debden directly from Atcham on September 22. This interesting pairing was a great story, but the facts are Beurling's and Hofer's military paths never crossed. However, during the period Ralph did spend at Atcham, he was in very good company with the likes of future 4th aces 1st Lieutenant "Tom" Biel, Major "Freddie" Glover, and Captain "Big Mac" McGrattan, who were all there at the same time he was.

The likeable and legendary 1st Lieutenant Ralph "Kidd" Hofer died in action on Sunday, July 2, 1944. The body of the 24-year-old was found in the wreckage of a 335th FS P-51B Mustang coded QP-X at the German-occupied Mostar-Sud Airport in Yugoslavia. Hofer was buried by the Germans in a common grave, together with the remains of 21 other US airmen.

On January 21, 1948, Hofer's wife wrote a letter to the Canadian government seeking information on any insurance or paid up bonuses that might be available to survivors of RCAF personnel who were killed in the war. In follow-up letters from the Department of Veteran Affairs (DVA), dated February 4 and 25, and addressed to the Department of National Defence (DND), the DVA instructed the DND to consider Jean Halbrook's letter a formal application for entitlements and they requested that she be kept apprised of her claim.

On March 22, Jean Halbrook forwarded to the DND a Statement of Death from the War Department in Washington which read as follows: "The records of the Department of the Army show that First Lieutenant Ralph Hofer, 02045177, Air Corps, who gave his date of birth as 19 June 1921, was killed in action 2 July 1944 in the European area. This official statement was furnished 18 March 1948 to Mrs. Jean Halbrook, 2846 North 73rd Court, Elmwood Park 35, Illinois. By authority of the Secretary of the Army, signed Edward F. Witsell, Major General, The Adjutant General of the Army."

On April 22, Air Commodore J. Murray, acting on behalf of the CAS advised Mrs. Halbrook by letter that her application for payment of War Service Gratuities had been approved and had been passed to the payments section for processing. On May 1, 1948, Jean Halbrook received a check from Ottawa for the amount of CAN$266.62. She also received notice that Ralph's daughter, Carol Lee Halbrook, would receive $12.00 monthly until she reached the age of majority.

Kidd Hofer was reburied in the United States on April 26, 1950, in plot 790254-256 at the historic Jefferson Barracks National Cemetery located at 101 Memorial Drive in St. Louis, Missouri.

Adam Kline of Los Angeles, California, provided the following additional information on the life and escapades of Kidd Hofer. "My father, Glenn Kline (Class of 1941), was a personal friend of Ralph's at Steinmitz High School. Although Hofer was the older of the two boys, they boxed together at the same gym located on the corner of Sawyer and Naraganset Avenues in Chicago."

Glenn Kline told his son that the story about Ralph unintentionally joining the RCAF was poppycock. Kidd was fleeing from Jack Pasquini after Ralph impregnated his daughter, Jean. Jack threatened to kill Ralph and, as he had gangster connections, Ralph took the threat seriously! That explained Hofer's quick departure to Canada in 1941. Adam's mother and Jean Pasquini also knew each other and were school classmates. Glenn Kline confirmed that Ralph could at times be crazy and reckless.

Glen Holland
New York Mosquito Ace

In the early morning hours of April 21, 1944, RCAF de Havilland Mosquito pilot, FL Glen Allen "Happy" Holland, Jr. from Bronxville, New York, engaged and destroyed one Luftwaffe Ju 88G-1 night fighter belonging to NJG 7. According to German military authorities, Holland may well have been responsible for the destruction of up to three other Junkers from that squadron that same evening.

Flying with RAF No. 605 "County of Warwick" Squadron, Holland and his navigator, FO Roger Howard "Wilkie" Wilkinson, had taken off at 0011hrs from their home station of RAF Manston, North Ramsgate, Kent.

The pair were on a night intruder sortie in Mosquito NS928 to one of their favorite hunting grounds – the Münster-Handorf airfield in northeastern Germany. Happy and Wilkie were hoping to catch the Ju 88 crews unawares as they took off and landed at their base. With its heavy armament and high speed, the powerful and versatile twin-engined "Mossie" was the ideal aircraft to undertake the dangerous Intruder, Flower and Day Ranger missions in the ETO.

No. 605 flew the Mk VI fighter-bomber variant. In addition to the nose armament of four .303in Colt-Browning machine guns with 500 rounds per gun and four 20mm Hispano-Suiza cannon with 155 rounds per gun, the aircraft could also carry two 500lb bombs in its rear bomb bay and under each wing. With long-range fuel tanks installed in the forward bomb bay and two 100gal slipper tanks underwing, the standard radius of action was extended from 1,300 to 1,870 miles. Powered by two 1,460shp Rolls-Royce Merlin-21 or -25 engines, the aircraft's top speed at sea level was 385mph, some 89 miles an hour faster than the Douglas Mk III Bostons the type replaced.

Worldwide, Mosquito production totaled 7,781 airframes. Britain built 6,435, Canada 1,134 and Australia 212. The most numerous model produced was the Mk VI with 2,584 units being constructed.

After a transit flight covering 543 miles, Holland and Wilkinson arrived over the target area a little after 0130hrs and began the hunt for victims.

Glen Holland was born to Glen Allen Holland, Sr. and Dorothy Jane Rauen in Chicago, Illinois, on August 1, 1919. There were four younger children in the family –

a brother John, and sisters Bonnie, Dorothy, and Jo-Ann. Glen was educated from 1925 to 1933 at an unnamed Chicago public school. He attended Sullivan High School in Chicago for one year.

For the school year 1934–35, he was enrolled at Miami-Edison High School in Miami, Florida. His father's work as an industrial designer eventually took the family to New York where they set up residence at 83 White Plains Road in the affluent community of Bronxville in Westchester County. Holland graduated from Bronxville High School in June 1937.

He accepted a junior salesman's position with the Yale & Towne Manufacturing Company and worked there for the next two years out of the Chrysler Building located at 42nd Street and Lexington Avenue in midtown Manhattan.

He served in the New York National Guard from 1936 until 1941, first as a private, then as an officer cadet. He learned to fly in 1938 and earned a private pilot's license.

Wishing to further his education, Holland enrolled at Cornell University in Ithaca to study mechanical engineering in September 1939. He interrupted his education to join the war effort and decided he could best put his 220 hours of flight time to good use by joining an air force.

Realizing the United States was not going to become involved in the European conflict any time soon, Holland drove to Ottawa, Ontario, on January 21, 1941, and enlisted in the RCAF at No. 12 Recruiting Centre as an AC2. Assigned Regimental Service No. R. 82636, he was assessed by the recruiting officer to be an excellent pilot candidate who would be worthy of a commission. Noted in the file were the following comments: "Very fine type of an American. Wishes to be an active service pilot. Considerable flying time. Intelligent, good appearance, keen."

On March 6, Holland finished up his basic training at No. 1 MD at Toronto, Ontario. For the next several weeks he stood guard duty at the newly constructed No. 14 SFTS at Aylmer, Ontario. Air Station Aylmer officially opened with its first cadre of students for single-engine pilot training on July 3, 1941.

Returning to Toronto on May 3, Glen, along with 176 other students began Course No. 25 at No. 1 ITS. Scoring a 90 percent average covering six subjects, Holland stood 29th in the class when the course concluded on June 6. The school's OC made the following notations in the file: "Keen and dependable. Splendid initiative. Will make a fine leader. Highly recommended for a commission."

Promoted to LAC, Holland was passed to Course No. 30 at No. 6 EFTS at Prince Albert, Saskatchewan, on June 9. There he flew 95.05 hours on de Havilland Tiger Moth biplane trainers. He graduated on July 27 with an 85 percent average. The school's CFI made the following observations: "This pupil is keen and ambitious, but somewhat over confident. Needs to be watched until he has more experience. Should develop into a valuable service pilot." The school's commander had the following comments: "Flying ability is above average. This airman was found guilty of low flying and flying outside of the prescribed solo area. He received punishment for both occurrences. Tends to be over confident and bears watching in this regard."

The final phase of his training to wings standard took place from July 28 to October 7 at No. 4 SFTS at Saskatoon, Saskatchewan. There, on Course No. 34, Holland flew 147.70 hours on twin-engined Cessna Cranes. The Chief Ground Instructor made the following observations: "An above average student possessing a high degree of ability and industry. Aptitude and attitude toward service life quite good. Is keen and clever. Has leadership abilities. Excessively talkative. Will improve greatly with added responsibilities." The school's CFI stated the following: "A particularly good type of student. Very anxious and keen to learn. Has a preference for navigation. Shows the qualities of a leader."

Commissioned from the ranks as a PO, Glen was posted on October 10, 1941, to the Central Flying School at Trenton, Ontario. His Service No. was changed from R. 82636 to J. 7917. The instructor's course he undertook ran from November 24 through to February 12, 1942. After flying a variety of service aircraft for 87.10 hours, Holland reluctantly graduated. He clearly did not want to become an instructor and tried everything he could think of to get out of the course!

Flight Lieutenant Glen Holland is seated front row, left side. This picture was taken at No. 36 OTU Greenwood, Nova Scotia, in July 1943. His Navigator, Flying Officer Roger Wilkinson, is standing directly behind him. (Mark Cullen, cullenancestry.ca)

FO M. L. Giles noted the following: "This man is very irresponsible and displays no leadership qualities. He should be watched very closely."

For most of 1942, Glen served as a general duties pilot at a variety of RCAF Air Stations – Rockcliffe, Ontario; Lethbridge, Alberta; Winnipeg, Manitoba; Sydney, Nova Scotia; and Mossbank, Saskatchewan. It was while he was stationed at Rockcliffe that he met Miss Lucy Claire Mary Turner from Hurdman's Bridge, Ontario. The couple married on July 18, 1942, at Cyrville, Ontario.

Holland was promoted to FO on October 1, 1942.

Glen finally got his chance to get into the war when he was posted on July 5, 1943, to RAF No. 36 OTU at Greenwood, Nova Scotia. There, on Course No. 1, he flew 66.80 hours on de Havilland Mosquitoes. His training on the "Wooden Wonder" concluded on August 28. WC J. S. Hamilton noted the following: "Very keen. An above average pilot. Good sense of humour. Slightly slap-dash on airmanship. Should do well under a good flight commander."

This training facility formally changed hands from British to Canadian control on July 1, 1944. RAF No. 36 OTU became RCAF No. 8 OTU. Throughout, the mission remained the same, to train Mosquito pilots.

Holland and several thousand military personnel left New York harbor aboard the ocean-going liner RMS *Queen Elizabeth* on October 8. The high-speed ship, sailing without escort, docked in England eight days later on the 16th. Glen spent only nine days at No. 3 Personnel Reception Centre at Bournemouth before being assigned to RAF No. 60 OTU at High Ercall, Shrewsbury, on October 26.

His promotion to FL came through on October 10, during his passage across the north Atlantic Ocean. Holland completed his tactical Mosquito training on December 27. To this point, he had logged a total of 1493.40 flight hours as a military pilot.

Weeks before he finished up at the OTU, Glen made an application to transfer to the USAAF. In December 1943, the Americans had precious little in the way of experience or equipment in the night-fighting community in Europe. When the USAAF could not guarantee that he would remain in the trade for which he had trained, Holland requested the transfer be held in abeyance.

Remaining with the RCAF, Glen reported for duty with RAF No. 605 Squadron at Bradwell Bay, Essex, on December 28.

The Holland–Wilkinson team opened their scoring when they damaged an unidentified enemy aircraft on February 24/25, 1944. The next evening, they were successful in destroying a Messerschmitt Bf 109 fighter. On a sortie on March 19, the duo intercepted and destroyed a Junkers Ju 88 bomber. The pair shot down two hostile aircraft on March 23/24 – one was a Focke Wulf Fw 190 fighter and the other aircraft was unidentified.

On April 26, 1944, WC N. T. Starr, the OC No. 605 Squadron, sent the following confidential flying battle casualty signal to his headquarters:

The crew of Mosquito NS928, comprised of RCAF FL G. A. Holland (pilot) and RAF FO R. H. Wilkinson (navigator) took off from this station at 0011 hours on April 21, 1944 on a scramble to the Münster-Handorf airfield. Nothing has been heard from them since. They were a fully experienced crew having completed eighteen operational trips with this squadron. They were carefully briefed before take off. Owing to radio telephone silence being maintained, it is impossible to give an opinion as to their failure to return.

This was followed by a letter, dated May 5, 1944, sent by Starr to Holland's wife:

It is with the deepest regret that I have to confirm the telegram sent by the Air Ministry on April 22nd, informing you that your husband, Flight Lieutenant Glen Allen Holland failed to return from an operation against the enemy. Your husband was flying with his navigator, Flying Officer Howard Wilkinson, on an intruder sortie to Germany. They had done many similar sorties together and were an able and experienced crew.

On this occasion they were going to one of their favourite target areas and I am at a loss to know the cause of their failure to return. Your husband, "Happy" as we knew him, was without doubt the most enthusiastic pilot we had in the squadron. His great offensive spirit combined with his grand personality and happy outlook on all things made him one of the most popular pilots and with his navigator, who was of similar temperament, one of the best crews we had. His loss is greatly felt in the squadron. All his personal effects have been assembled and dispatched to the Committee of Adjustment, Central Depository, Colnbrook, Buckinghamshire, who will take charge of them and from whom you will hear in due course. Once more may I assure you how deeply I feel with you in this difficult period and if I can be of any further assistance to you, please do not hesitate to let me know. I will most certainly inform you if we hear any further news whether it be good or bad.

According to German military and civilian records, Happy and Wilkie's final combat took place at 0200hrs on April 21, 1944. The pair were stalking a Junkers Ju 88G-1 when suddenly a mid-air collision occurred between the two. The Luftwaffe crew managed to parachute to safety, while the Mosquito crashed two kilometers north of Everswinkel, Germany. The wreckage of NS928 landed on the Grosse-Beckmann farmhouse of Herr Joseph Spitthover. Holland and Wilkinson were killed instantly, along with the farmer and his wife Frau Anna Spitthover. The couple's son and Spitthover's mother survived. Both airmen were buried the next day in the town's Catholic cemetery under the supervision of Herr Bernhard Hartmeyer, the town's chief of police.

The following items were found at the crash site – a watch, four coins, and one identity disk. These items were turned over to the Luftwaffe personnel at the Münster-Handorf air base.

Holland's death was officially registered with the Ontario provincial government in 1944.

On May 18, 1946, a Royal Australian Air Force investigator, FL E. T. Haines, visited the graves of Holland and Wilkinson where he met with the local parish priest, Father Jagers, the town clerk, Herr Middendorf, and Spitthover's son. The officer had a white cross placed at the site with the following inscription from Rupert Brooke, "Some corner of a foreign field which is forever England."

Spitthover's son described the crash and his subsequent meeting with the German pilots. After the first attack, the German crew thought the Mossie had rammed them. Also, they were under the impression that Holland's aircraft was the only one operating in the area that evening and was responsible for bringing down three other Ju 88G-1s belonging to their unit. Haines, in his report, requested that a further investigation be undertaken with a view of a gallantry award being considered. The awards office later dismissed the information on the basis that the evidence came from enemy sources and was, therefore, unreliable.

Spitthover's son requested, from Haines, a photograph of Holland and Wilkinson, which he wished to incorporate on a tablet which would hang on a wall in the rebuilt farmhouse. The inscription will read as follows: "On the 21st of April 1944, an English Mosquito aircraft crashed into this house and in the flames died Herr Joseph Spitthover and Frau Anna Spitthover, along with two English airmen, G. A. Holland and R. H. Wilkinson."

The remains of the two airmen were exhumed in June 1947 and re-interned in the Reichswald Forest War Cemetery at Kleve, Germany. This military burial site is maintained to very high standards by the Commonwealth War Graves Commission.

Holland's earned wartime medals include the 1939–45 Star, the General Service Medal, the Canadian Volunteer Service Medal & Clasp, the Aircrew European Star, and Operational Wings.

It is a great tragedy that Holland and Wilkinson were never recognized for their achievement of downing between five and possibly eight enemy aircraft during World War II.

David Howe
Pennsylvania Mustang Ace

USAAF Captain David Wayne Howe, from East Hickory, Pennsylvania, was just one of the many 4th FG aces who won their wings in the RCAF in World War II. Howe flew two operational tours with the 334th FS, destroying 8.5 Luftwaffe aircraft (6 aerial and 2.5 ground) in the process.

Racking up 502.05 combat flying hours from September 22, 1943, until March 18, 1945, and covering 116 missions, Howe never had a single abort due to a technical or a mechanical issue. This was all due in part to the great care lavished on his aircraft by his crew chief, Staff Sergeant (S/Sgt) Raymond Larmouth.

Howe was born to George Morris Howe and Elizabeth Jane Douglas on February 6, 1919. He completed his schooling in 1938, having attended East Hickory Elementary School and then Hickory Township High School. From 1938 until 1940, he helped his father run the family farm. When he voluntarily enlisted in the RCAF on September 22, 1941, at the Toronto, Ontario, Recruiting Centre, he was gainfully employed at the General Electric Company in Erie, Pennsylvania. At the time, he was working towards obtaining his civilian private pilot's license and had flown a total of 20 hours (18 dual and 2 solo).

The air force assigned the 22-year-old Regimental Service No. R. 141131. Completing his basic training at No. 1 MD in Toronto on November 22, AC2 Howe was posted to No. 1 Bombing & Gunnery School at Jarvis, Ontario, where he performed guard duty until February 13, 1942. From there, he was off to No. 5 ITS at Belleville, Ontario, until April 11. Promoted to LAC, Howe reported in the next day to No. 20 EFTS at Oshawa, Ontario, where he began his flight training on the ubiquitous de Havilland Tiger Moth biplanes.

He graduated from Course No. 53 at Oshawa on June 19, after having flown 93.25 hours (48.50 dual and 44.35 solo). The chief supervisory officer recorded the following in his file: "This trainee is slow to learn and requires constant drilling, however, is making steady progress and retains what he is taught. Dependable and sincere. Average pilot."

From June 22 until to October 9, David flew a combined 150.50 hours on two NAA aircraft, the Harvard Mk II and the Yale, at No. 1 SFTS at Camp Borden, Ontario. Graduating from Course No. 58 as an SP, he stood 35th in a class of

Captain David W. Howe poses on the wing of his 4th FG P-51D Mustang at Debden, England, in 1944. (US Department of Defense)

62 students. He was graded satisfactory in all subjects and his conduct throughout his training was rated as good. While at Borden, David voluntarily took and passed a St. John Ambulance First Aid Course.

Sergeant Howe embarked for England on a fast troop ship from No. 1 Port Transit Unit "Y" Depot, Halifax, Nova Scotia, on October 27, 1942.

After a nine-day voyage, the ship disembarked its cargo of several hundred airmen at Greenock, Scotland. Howe's stay at No. 3 Personnel Reception Centre at Bournemouth was very brief, as he was posted on December 1 to the RAF No. 17 Pilot Advanced Flying Unit at Calveley. There, for the next several weeks he flew Miles Master Mk II advanced trainers.

On March 2, 1943, Sergeant Howe was assigned to Course No. 47 at RAF No. 55 OTU, where he flew Hawker Hurricanes and Masters from RAF Annan, Scotland. While there, Howe was promoted to FS. The course concluded on May 18, with the following comments recorded in his file: "An above average leader and a good average pilot. Will do well in a squadron after a little more experience."

On June 2, 1943, the 24-year-old Howe was granted an honorable discharge from the RCAF in London, in order to facilitate his joining the USAAF as an FO. He had served with distinction for one year and 208 days in Canada's air force.

From mid-June through to mid-September, FO Howe was at the USAAF CCRC Station 342, learning American flight procedures. His conversion flying there was on Supermarine Spitfire Vbs, Miles Masters, and Republic P-47C and D Thunderbolts.

He arrived at the 4th FG on September 22, and was assigned to the 334th FS. He flew his first combat mission on October 2. Below is one of his filed combat reports dated September 28, 1944. This detailed report covers one of the six Luftwaffe fighters he shot down in aerial combat.

While at the 4th, Howe received three promotions, attaining the rank of captain in November 1944. He flew P-47 Thunderbolts coded QP-C and QP-Z. Later, when the group was assigned the superlative NAA Mustang, he flew P-51s coded QP-C, QP-G, QP-L, and QP-S. He ended his second tour as the 334th's assistant operations and gunnery officer.

He left Debden without any fanfare on April 3, 1945, and rotated stateside. By August, he was out of the USAAF. Saddened by the loss of so many of his friends during the war, Howe did not fly for several years.

In 1951, he went to work as a test pilot at Bell Aircraft in Buffalo, New York. His first duty at Bell was as a copilot of a modified Boeing EB-50 Superfortress, which was used as a launch ship for the X-1 and X-2 series of rocket planes.

During a flight over Lake Ontario on May 12, 1953, X-2 pilot Sip Ziegler was running pressurization tests on the liquid oxygen fuel system. He was in the X-2 suspended beneath the belly of the EB-50. The volatile fuel exploded, destroying the rocket, and killing Ziegler instantly. Frank Wolko, an observer who was in or near the bomb bay, was blown clear by the explosion, but died when his parachute did not open. Howe, pilot William Leyshon, and the remaining crew then had to deal with fires on board the aircraft and the loss of an engine. They managed to land the damaged Boeing safely back at Bell's test facility.

In 1953, David graduated from the USAAF's Experimental Test Pilot School. Back at Bell, he was assigned to the Vertical Take Off and Landing Program. He made the first tethered flight on the Model 65 Air Test Vehicle in 1955.

David was selected as the chief test pilot for the company's follow-on program – the X-14. On May 24, 1958, Howe became the first pilot to transition from a hover to level flight. With further development, this new technology would eventually be used in aircraft such as the United States Marine Corps' AV-8 Harrier jet fighter series. He continued to work on other projects at Bell until his retirement.

In April 1963, he asked the RCAF in Ottawa to forward his earned wartime Canadian medals. These included the General Service Medal, the Defence Medal, and the Canadian Volunteer Service Medal & Clasp.

He gave a home address at that time of 310 Campus Drive in Snyder, New York.

In Erie, Pennsylvania, on May 22, 1995, David Wayne Howe died after suffering a massive stroke. He is buried in Section 4-B, Row 15, Site 4 at Arlington National Cemetery in Arlington County, Virginia. His wife, Ann M. Kennedy Howe, passed away in 2003.

Clarence Jasper
California Intruder Ace

Clarence Murl "Jas" Jasper was born in Ottawa, Kansas, on March 29, 1915. When he was eight, his family moved to Long Beach, California. When not in school, Clarence would ride his bicycle five miles from his home to the Long Beach Municipal Airport where he would while away the daylight hours watching the airport's flight activities. As the years went by, young Mr. Jasper would run errands, sweep out hangars, and wash planes in exchange for airplane rides and flight instruction.

One of the airport tenants, Earl S. Daugherty, taught him how to fly. After graduating from Long Beach Poly High School in 1933, Jasper enlisted in the USN. He was hoping to become a naval aviator as he held a private pilot's license. The navy, however, had other plans and Jas wound up serving four years as a gun pointer on a heavy cruiser.

In 1941, the 26-year-old was living and working in Spokane, Washington. He had never given up on his dream of becoming a military pilot and had seen RCAF recruiting posters at several airports he frequented. The general information circulating in the local civilian flying community was that the Canadians were training pilots as young as 17 and as old as 42 and it did not matter whether one was married or single. All that an applicant needed to enlist, educationally speaking, was a high school diploma.

Jas traveled 392 miles from Spokane to the RCAF's No. 1 Recruiting Centre in Vancouver, British Columbia, where he voluntarily enlisted on Monday, June 2, 1941. The air force welcomed him with open arms.

Jasper fit in perfectly with the RCAF and its regimented training syllabus. His entry rank was as an AC2. For the first two months of his career, he, like so many others, had to pull some guard duty.

Jasper was assigned in early August to No. 4 ITS in Edmonton, Alberta. He graduated from there on September 24, 1941. Promoted to LAC, Jas was posted to No. 5 EFTS at High River, Alberta. There he flew 50+ hours on de Havilland Tiger Moth biplanes until November 21, 1941. The next stage in his training took him to No. 12 SFTS at Brandon, Manitoba, where he flew 143 hours on twin-engined Cranes and Ansons.

C. M. Jasper was awarded his pilot wings in a graduation ceremony on March 13, 1942. Finishing in the top 5 percent of his class, he was commissioned as a PO under Regimental No. J. 10611.

Jasper was a rock steady pilot who excelled at all stages of his training, no doubt helped in part by his stint in the navy. Posted to the RCAF's Flying Instructor School at Air Station Trenton, Ontario, he undertook an instructor's course from March 30 to May 17, 1942.

For the next 13 months (May 19, 1942–June 22, 1943), he taught others how to fly Cessna Cranes, Avro Ansons, and NAA Harvards at No. 11 SFTS at Yorktown, Saskatchewan. His flight time to that point totaled 1,460 hours.

In June, he was promoted to FO and was offered the opportunity to fly the de Havilland Mosquito. Jasper jumped at the chance and, within days, was on his way to RAF No. 36 OTU at Greenwood, Nova Scotia. His training on the powerful and versatile Mossie concluded on September 12, 1943.

Embarking from New York City on October 8, Jasper arrived in England on October 16. From October 26 to December 27, he undertook additional training with the RAF at No. 60 OTU, Shropshire. He knew how to fly the Mosquito, now he had to learn how to use the "Timber Terror" in combat.

Jas was posted, on December 28, to RCAF No. 418 "City of Edmonton" Squadron, which was based at RAF Ford in West Sussex.

There he was paired with his navigator/observer, FL Oscar Archibald Joseph "Archie" Martin from Ottawa, Ontario. As a team, they flew Mosquito Mk VIs on Intruder, Flower and Day Ranger missions in the ETO. Their personal Mosquito, coded TH-K, was named *Earthquake McGoon*. All 418 Squadron aircraft were illustrated with Al Capps' *Li'l Abner* cartoon characters.

Hermann Göring, the Luftwaffe commander, caustically remarked about the "Wooden Wonder" in 1943:

> It makes me furious when I see the Mosquito. I turn green with envy. The British, who can afford aluminium better than we can, knock together a beautiful wooden aircraft that every piano factory over there is building and they gave it great speed which they have now increased yet again. What do you make of that? There is nothing the British do not have. They have the geniuses, and we have the nincompoops. After the war is over, I'm going to buy a British radio set – then at least I'll own something that works.

From the middle of July 1943, 418's operations were becoming more closely integrated with those of bomber command. Those bomber-support missions, codenamed Flower, were to appear regularly and often on the unit's work schedule throughout the next 15 months. The sorties entailed interdicting and destroying German bombers as they returned to their bases. It also included going after the

Luftwaffe's night-fighter force, the NJG, at its home airfields. While the German night-fighters combed the Allied bomber tracks hunting for victims, they, in turn, were being hunted by the Mosquitos. At the same time, the squadron was keeping the pressure up by intruding on Hitler's transportation systems strafing trains, truck convoys, troop concentrations, and railroad marshalling yards.

By November 1943, the squadron had introduced the Day Ranger mission. These deep penetration sorties into enemy territory on a freelance basis were far more dangerous than the more familiar Night Intruder operations. Day Rangers involved two Mosquitos attacking any worthwhile military target in broad daylight. Despite the added risk, this kind of operation proved very successful and, shortly after a sequence of high-scoring sorties in February 1944, Group Headquarters gave 418 the authority to conduct these at its own discretion. By the end of the war, it was found that more than 75 percent of 418's aerial kills had been made in daylight.

In February 1944, Jas was asked why he had not transferred to an American military service after the US joined the war effort on December 8, 1941. He replied, "There was no pressure and no reason to transfer. Some of the people I trained with, who did go back, were treated as stepchildren and were given lousy assignments. I decided to stay where I was and fly my Mossie."

This nose-on view shows the destructive firepower of the de Havilland Mosquito Mk VI flown by RCAF Flight Lieutenant Clarence M. Jasper, DFC. (Canadian National Defence Image Library)

Jasper's first claim was on March 12, 1944, when he damaged a Ju 86P on the ground at Clermont, France. On the night of April 12, 1944, Jasper planned an Intruder sortie into western Czechoslovakia. At 2259hrs, while en route to his target, he encountered and shot down an Fw 190, 12 miles southeast of Verdun.

On April 16, 1944, the squadron had its biggest single day since beginning operations. Early that evening, several enemy aircraft were nullified, and another temporarily put out of action. It all started at 1747hrs when the teams of Jasper–Martin and Harper–Rees intruded in late afternoon to the German-occupied airfield at Luxeuil, France, 35 miles from the Swiss border. Harper opened the scoring by blasting a Junkers W 34 liaison aircraft, which blossomed into a plume of flame then plummeted to earth. Meanwhile Jasper was making hay in the air-to-ground mode. Spotting a Caudron C.440 Goéland transport warming up on the drome, he gave it a two second squirt that left it blazing. Flying through the flames of this victim, he did likewise to a second Goéland parked nearby, which also went up in smoke. He then caught a Goéland in the act of taking off. It barely cleared the airfield boundary before going up. Next, Harper surprised another W 34, whose pilot had pushed the panic button and was desperately trying to land. Absorbing a three-second burst, the low-flying Junkers collided with a tree, lost its port wing, flipped onto its back and disintegrated. In this five-minute air-to-air and air-to-ground action, five enemy planes had been written off.

On May 14, 1944, at 1011hrs between Nancy and Croix de Metz, France, Jasper and Martin destroyed an He 111 bomber, which tried to evade them by flying in and out of a heavy downpour. On the ground at Azelot airfield, they strafed and blew up a Ju 87 Stuka dive-bomber.

At the end of May, Jasper was promoted to FL.

The pair downed the first of three V-1s in the air over the English Channel on June 19, 1944.

FL Jasper related the details of a Day Ranger sortie to Rostock, Germany, on June 27, 1944:

> I was leading a two plane element and my wingman was Squadron Leader Russell Bannock,[1] who was flying his first day sortie. We took off from RAF Coltishall at 1545 hours. We flew across the North Sea through broken clouds, showers and lightning. No contacts were made over Germany and at 1749 hours we recrossed the German coast at Graal-Muritz. Three minutes later, Archie spotted a Junkers Ju 88 bomber flying two miles out to sea at an altitude of 800 feet. We were at 300 feet when the sighting was made. I increased my speed to 290 miles per hour and began

---

1 SL, later WC, Russ Bannock DSO, DFC & Bar would go on to become the RCAF's highest-scoring Mosquito pilot with 11 aircraft shot down, four damaged, and 18 V-1 buzz bombs destroyed in the air.

to set up my attack from below and behind the Junkers. Before I got into a firing position, we were spotted by a large 10,000 ton ship that was further out to sea. The ship began firing off flares which alerted the enemy bomber crew to our presence.

For protection, the Junkers flew directly over the ship which was armed with 40mm Bofors cannons. I closed the throttle and began maneuvering in behind him. At one hundred and fifty yards, I pulled up into a twenty degree climb and, at seventy-five yards, fired a two second burst of cannon and machine guns. I saw strikes on both wing roots and the port engine burst into flames. A violent explosion followed, sending flaming pieces of the bomber into the sea. I pulled through to the right, but could not avoid flying through the flames and debris. I looked out and my left wing was burning like a yule log! I said to myself, "Jas, you stupid bastard, you really blew it this time." We were too low to bail out and the ice cold water of the Baltic Sea would kill a human in a matter of minutes. The fire died out but the rudder pedals were vibrating badly. I thought of heading to Malmo, Sweden which was only seventy miles away.

After checking the engine instruments and seeing that everything was working normally, I decided to head for home. It was a long trip back having to cross some three hundred miles of open water. We reached Holmsley South at 2113 hours. After getting out of the airplane I could see why I had problems. The fabric was burned completely off the rudder, as was a large strip on the port side of the fuselage and a smaller piece off the port wing.

In June 1944, while on a typical Flower sortie, a 418 crew saw a large rocket projectile heading northward. This was their first encounter with the new German V-1 flying bomb. Soon, the squadron was in the forefront of the defense of England against this new weapon and new tactics had to be developed. In order to close to within firing range, even the fast Mosquito had to be put into a sharp dive, giving the pilot very little time to line up a shot. From lift off in France to transmitting 22 miles across the narrowest part of the English Channel, to impacting British soil, the V-1's flight took just six minutes. Despite this, the squadron racked up an impressive score of 83 shot down and another 16 damaged.

On July 5, 1944, word came down from RAF Fighter Command's 11 Group that any V-1 shot down over the sea would count the same as an enemy aircraft destroyed in the air. One brought down over land would only count as half a victory.

The difference being that a buzz bomb, which contained 1,870lb of amatol-39 high explosive, that could be detonated over water was far less dangerous to life and property than one exploded on or over land. The military code name for the Fieseler Fi-103 V-1 Flying Bomb was "Diver."

It was a primitive example of a weapon that would come to be known years later as the Cruise Missile. Altogether, 9,521 V-1s were fired at England and 2,448 were launched against Belgium. The cost in lives was staggering – 22,448 casualties, most of whom were civilians.

Jasper and Martin's two other V-1s were brought down over the Channel on July 5 and 9.

Typical experiences of the V-1 hunters were described to the press by two 418 Squadron pilots. Stan Cotterill commented: "We used to stooge around just out from their launching area… Sometimes we could see the actual launchings, like a great half-moon of brilliant explosions. When the thing came up we dived on them vertically at full throttle. Several kites would line up on one bomb and, if the first one missed, another would go down for a try. Sometimes we were not always sure it was a buzz bomb. So we lined up the light with a star and, if it moved, in we went." Ross Gray told how, during attacks early in the anti-Diver battle, the flash of the exploding V-1's temporarily blinded the attacking pilots, who momentarily had to fly by the seat of their collective pants. He continued; "As the days went by, we developed a habit of closing one eye as we shot for a kill, so after the flash at least one eye would still be serviceable."

Tour expired after flying -39 sorties, Jas rotated back to Canada on August 12, 1944.

Three days later, he was awarded a British DFC, the text of which is as follows:

JASPER, FL Clarence Murl (J. 10611) – Distinguished Flying Cross – No. 418 Squadron – Award effective 15 August 1944 as per London Gazette of that date and AFRO 2052/44 dated 22 September 1944. American in the RCAF. Born in Ottawa, Kansas, 29 March 1915. Member, United States Navy, 1933-1937. Home in Spokane, Washington. Enlisted in Vancouver, 2 June 1941. Trained at No. 4 ITS (graduated 24 September 1941), No. 5 EFTS (graduated 21 November 1941) and No. 12 SFTS (graduated 13 March 1942). At Trenton, 30 March 1942 to 17 May 1942. Instructed at No. 11 SFTS, 18 May 1942 to 22 June 1943. To No. 36 OTU, Greenwood, 23 June to 12 September 1943. Embarked from New York, 8 October 1943; arrived UK 16 October 1943. Trained at No. 60 OTU, 26 October to 28 December 1943. No. 418 Squadron, 28 December 1943 to 30 July 1944. Returned to Canada and instructed at No. 8 OTU, Greenwood, 18 September 1944 to 30 July 1945. Released 14 September 1945. Victories as follows: 12 March 1944 – 1 unidentified enemy aircraft (probably a Ju 86P) damaged on ground; 12 April 1944 – 1 Fw 190 destroyed; 16 April 1944 – 1 unidentified enemy aircraft (possibly a Caudron) destroyed on ground and 2 other Caudrons destroyed; 14 May 1944 – 1 Ju 87B destroyed on ground and 1 He 111 probably destroyed in air; 27 June 1944 – 1 Ju 88 destroyed. Photo PL-25535.

This Officer is a most skilful and resolute pilot whose determination to engage the enemy has always been evident. He has completed many sorties and has destroyed three enemy aircraft in the air and others on the ground.

Public Record Office Air 2/9158 has a recommendation raised on 23 May 1944, which is much more detailed. He had flown 23 sorties (86 operational hours).

> This officer has completed 23 operational sorties over enemy and enemy occupied territory; of these 19 have been Intruder and Bomber Support sorties and 4 Day Rangers. Flying Officer Jasper has shown a marked determination to engage the enemy and has patrolled many of the most heavily defended enemy airfields. His unfailing keenness has rewarded him with the destruction of 6 enemy aircraft destroyed and the damaging of another. Much of the success enjoyed by this Squadron on recent daylight sorties has been due to the support and personal participation of this pilot. On March 12th, Flying Officer Jasper damaged a Junkers Ju 86P at Clermont. On April 16th this officer planned and led a very successful daylight sortie to Luxueil-les-Bains where he destroyed a Caudron Goeland in the air and 2 more on the ground. Again, on May 14th, Flying Officer Jasper planned and led a sortie in daylight to Haguenau. At Azelot, he destroyed a Junkers Ju 87 on the ground and at Nancy he shot down and destroyed a Heinkel He 111. Flying Officer Jasper has shown fine fighting qualities and has played an important part in the operations of this squadron. His usefulness to an operational squadron cannot be rated too highly and his personal example is most commendable.

Just before he left 418, the squadron moved its operations from RAF Ford to RAF Holmsley South, Hampshire.

FL Jasper requested to stay in the Mosquito community as an instructor.

He was posted on September 18 to RCAF No. 8 OTU at Greenwood, Nova Scotia. In June 1945, a month after VE-Day, the last graduating class of Mosquito pilots were congratulated by the Greenwood station commander. Led by FL Jasper and other instructors, the graduates then flew their 50–60 "Wooden Wonders" to an open-air storage facility for disposal and scrapping.

No. 8 OTU officially disbanded on August 1, 1945.

The shutdown of the flying schools of the BCATP was sadly well and truly underway.

C. M. Jasper was released from the RCAF on September 14, 1945.

He continued flying for the next 30 years and his last job was as a captain on Grumman Goose seaplanes, flying the route between Long Beach, California, and Santa Catalina Island for Golden West Airlines.

A heart attack finally grounded him in 1975. Jasper died in Long Beach in his 82nd year in 1997.

His record stands at seven destroyed in the air, three destroyed, and one damaged on the ground.

Paul Johnson
Connecticut Spitfire Ace

June 30, 1944, proved to be an excellent hunting day for RCAF FL Paul Gilbert Johnson, Jr. Piloting a 421 "Red Indian" FS Supermarine Spitfire Mk IXb, south of Bernay, France, at 0705hrs, Johnson destroyed a German Messerschmitt Bf 109G-6 flown by Oberfahnrich Rolf Jutting from 2./JG 53. Leading 421 on an armed reconnaissance patrol that cloudy Sunday morning, Johnson's encounter report reveals the details of his victory:

> We were flying approximately fifteen miles north of Bernay at 8,000 feet and in a southerly direction when fifteen Bf 109s were seen flying south at the same height. They turned to starboard and dove down through a hole in the cloud. I followed them down, lost them in the cloud but picked them up again at the cloud base which was about 1,000 feet above ground level. At this time we were southwest of Bernay. The remainder of the squadron had turned to port. My No. 2 and I engaged the enemy aircraft. I got on the tail of one and closing to two hundred yards, fired from dead astern. I gave him two short bursts and saw strikes on the starboard aileron, wing and fuselage. Black and white smoke poured from his plane. He went into a spin turning to port and crashed into the ground exploding. The enemy aircraft was carrying drop tanks which he failed to jettison.

In that same sortie, Johnson claimed a second "Gustav" as a probable.

While on patrol later that evening from the squadron's ALG B.2 located on the outskirts of the French village of Bazenville, Paul bagged two Bf 109G-6s from JG 27 east of Lisieux at 2030hrs. Those three victories that day, coupled with two previous ones, elevated Johnson to ace status. He was the second member of 421 to reach that lofty plateau, the first being SL Robert Wendell "Buck" McNair, who had commanded the unit a year earlier.

Paul Johnson, Jr. was born on March 5, 1920, in Bridgeport, Connecticut. His father, Paul Johnson, Sr., a contractor, came from the Norwalk area and his mother, Daisy, was from Bethel. Also residing in Bethel was Paul Jr.'s older married sister, Mrs. Evlyn Strobino.

From 1926 to 1934, Johnson attended Maplewood Junior High and, from 1934 to 1937, Bassick High School. Leaving his scholastic studies behind after completing eleventh grade, Johnson worked for a year as a screw mack operator and then as a foreman in a carpet factory. He attended night classes at Bridgeport Technical School from 1939 to 1940, studying engineering.

In the summer of 1940, Paul traveled to San Diego, California, where he secured steady employment as a carpenter with the Hays and Jackson Construction Company. One of his California acquaintances owned an aircraft and took him flying on several occasions. Johnson, who had a lifelong interest in aviation, was hooked. He flew five hours as a passenger with his buddy and was given three hours dual rudimentary stick time.

Growing impatient at the length of time it was taking the US to join the European war effort, Johnson made his way to Toronto, Ontario, where he visited RCAF No. 11 Recruiting Centre. There, he learned he had the necessary qualifications to enter the pilot training program in the BCATP.

He enlisted in Canada's air force on October 11, 1941, as an AC2 under Service No. R. 136048. On his attestation papers, he indicated that his mother was deceased and his father's whereabouts were unknown. Johnson gave the recruiter a temporary home address of 400 Wood Avenue in Bridgeport.

The interviewing officer, H. G. Raney, noted the following on Paul's application: "Average American type – rugged build, mature appearance who is keen to fly and fight. Alert and confident. Applicant has a quiet pleasant manner. Should respond well to RCAF training."

Johnson spent his first month in the service at No. 1 MD in Toronto. On November 11, he was sent to perform guard duty at No. 4 Bombing & Gunnery School at Fingal, Ontario. He remained there until January 4, 1942. Nearly every enlisted person was required to perform guard duty at some point in their RCAF career. Usually, these temporary postings were designed to alleviate the training pipeline from the backlog of bodies that, at times, completely overwhelmed the system. Acting as sentries at military installations all across Canada, these airmen were receiving their first taste of air force responsibility and discipline. In many cases, they patrolled empty hangars or unused runways carrying World War I bolt-action rifles, sometimes without any ammunition.

Back in Toronto on January 5, he resumed his training at No. 6 ITS. On Course No. 44 at this facility, Paul graduated on February 27, achieving a 70 percent average.

Promoted to LAC, Johnson began his flight training at No. 7 EFTS, Course No. 52, in Windsor, Ontario on March 29, 1942. Logging 96.25 hours on Fleet Finch biplanes, he graduated on June 6 with a grade of 72 percent, with the following comments from the CFI: "General flying very good. Tends to be slightly rough on the controls. Learns quickly and retains knowledge. Aerobatics good. Good average on instruments. Thinks and acts quickly. No outstanding faults."

On July 6, LAC Johnson reported to No. 14 SFTS at Aylmer, Ontario, where he completed his training to wings standard. Logging 20 hours on Yales and 130 hours on Harvard Mk IIbs, Johnson graduated from Course No. 59 with a grade average of 73 percent on October 23. Within hours, he was one of several SPs that were commissioned from the ranks as POs. His service number was changed from R. 136048 to J. 20050. Johnson's squadron commander at Aylmer noted the following in his file: "A well disciplined, intelligent, eager and conscientious pilot with above average ability."

The RCAF never intended to have NAA Yale trainers in its inventory. In 1939, with war looming in Europe, France ordered 230 export versions of the BT-9 (200 for its air force and 30 for its navy). It received 111 aircraft from its order before the country was overrun in 1940. Many of the remaining 119 airplanes were still at the factory at Inglewood, California, ready to be shipped overseas when news was received that France had capitulated. Britain took over the balance of the French order and transferred the aircraft to the National Steel Car Company at Malton, Ontario, where they were inspected and assembled.

The RCAF began operating the type designated as Yale Mk Is on August 23, 1940, at the following SFTS – No. 1 Borden, No. 2 Uplands, No. 6 Dunnville, and No. 14 Aylmer. These were used as intermediate pilot trainers through October 1943, but after a series of 24 accidents, many of which were fatal, the remainder were relegated to the wireless training role.

In 1946, the remaining airframes were sold as war surplus. As for the 111 aircraft received by the French, these were absorbed into the Luftwaffe. The Germans incorporated some of these into the unique "Zirkus Rosarius," which trained German pilots to fly and evaluate captured Allied aircraft. Of the 111 American-built trainers flown by the Germans, not a single example survived, although one is known to have been shot down by a pair of marauding RCAF P-51 Mustangs. In October 1943, 414 TRS pilots Lew May and R. C. Brown shared in this unique Luftwaffe kill. Yales were one of the few aircraft in the war that served in squadron strength on both sides.

Paul Johnson left Halifax, Nova Scotia, by troop ship on November 19, but did not arrive in England until December 6.

He began flying Miles Master IIs on Course No. 32 at RAF Calveley on February 11, 1943, with No. 17 Pilot Advanced Flying Unit. Graduating on March 21 with a 72 percent average, Johnson earned the following comments from the station's WC: "A very keen type whose flying is up to a high average standard."

From March 23 until June 1, Johnson flew Spitfires and Masters on Course No. 29 with No. 52 OTU at Aston Down. While there, Paul fired 5,200 machine gun and cannon rounds in air-to-air and air-to-ground exercises, with the overall assessment that his marksmanship was above average. After Johnson graduated

Flight Lieutenant Paul Johnson, DFC, is standing in the back row, fifth from the left in this RCAF No. 421 FS photo taken in 1944. (Canadian National Defence Image Library)

with a 73 percent average, the course commander made the following observation: "This officer is a good steady all round type. He will make a capable leader."

Paul Johnson received a promotion to FO on April 23, and was posted to RCAF 421 Squadron directly from the OTU. Johnson's final promotion to FL occurred on May 20, 1944.

All his overseas combat time was with 421, where he served his first tour from June 1 to December 3, 1943, and his second from January 9 to July 18, 1944.

Following the experience the Allied forces had in North Africa, the D-Day planners concluded that to successfully invade fortress Europe, two TAFs would be required. One would support the British and Canadian ground forces and the other would support the Americans. The British and Canadians numbered theirs as 2nd TAF and the US numbered its as 9th TAF.

To maximize the time over the rapidly moving frontline, the shorter-ranged fighter and fighter-bomber units were required to move into roughly prepared airfields in France as soon as the ground forces had advanced inland from the invasion beaches.

In the summer and fall of 1943, many dummy ALGs were built throughout southern England, which the various wings and groups used to practice moving. RCAF 421, 416 and 403 squadrons arrived at RAF Station Tangmere in Sussex on April 17, 1944. These three squadrons were immediately formed into No. 127 Canadian Wing. The wing's 54 Spitfire Mk IXs were coded as follows: 421 as AU, 416 as DN, and 403 as KH. Each 421 Spitfire carried, on the left side of the aircraft's fuselage, the then familiar Indian head emblem of the Frontenac Oil Company of Canada.

One of the company's well-known products was "Red Indian" aviation motor oil. The squadron's motto was "Bellicum Cecinere" ("They have sounded the war trumpet"). All 127 Wing sorties flown from D-Day until June 15 were from Tangmere. A fourth Canadian Spitfire squadron, No. 443, joined the wing at B.2 on July 16, boosting the wing's aircraft strength to 72 airplanes.

In North Africa, the first Servicing Commando Units (SCUs) were formed early in 1942. By the spring of 1943, six SCUs had been formed and their soldiers were trained to land on foreign soil with the assault troops. Proceeding to the proposed ALG locations, they brought their own trucks laden with tents, ammunition, fuel, and airfield defense weapons, including antiaircraft guns and machine guns. Each SCU comprised two officers and 148 men, including cooks and equipment for providing food to the aircrews. Every member of the SCU had to have combat training. They had to know how to drive and repair their vehicles, how to land from all kinds of landing craft, how to operate antiaircraft guns, and how to service a great variety of aircraft. The more skilled tradesmen were taught to become specialists on one type of aircraft.

These SCUs landed at Juno and Gold beaches in Normandy early on June 7, along with the British Royal Engineers' 12th, 23rd, 24th and 25th Airfield Construction Groups (ACGs). The task of an ACG was to construct an entire airfield, complete with runways, access roads, hangars, water system, communication system, and space provision for crews, ammunition dumps, and maintenance facilities. Each ACG was composed of a command company, two companies of sappers, two companies of pioneers, and one company of mechanical and electrical engineers for a total of 800 men. Each ACG brought its own equipment and materials – bulldozers, scrapers, rollers, and steel netting called Sommerfeld tracking. It leveled a field, laid the steel tracking, set up markers, and set up fundamentals such as the electrical system, latrines, and a communication system.

While the ACG unit was building the airfield, the SCU unit was defending the location and setting up antiaircraft guns, fuel dumps, ammunition dumps, facilities to re-arm and refuel aircraft, parts storage, and a maintenance depot. When the ALG was ready to receive aircraft, the ACG personnel moved on to another location, but the SCU stayed. The arriving aircraft were re-armed and refueled entirely by it.

Before No. 127 Wing moved from Tangmere to B.2, a wing advance party arrived to work alongside the SCU crew. On moving day, June 16, 1944, the wing's aircraft were ferried across the Channel and set up in their permanent dispersals. The wing's remaining pilots and ground crew were then flown over to B.2 by transport and the base was declared operational the same day. When the wing's full complement of personnel arrived from England, only then did the SCU move on to set up the next ALG.

In total, the Allies constructed 36 ALGs during the Normandy campaign – 19 British–Canadian prefixed by the letter B, and 17 American prefixed by the letter A. The American airfields were built by Engineer Aviation Battalions (EABs). These were a combination of engineers and servicing commandos. Though differently organized, both builders worked well with each other, and the amazing thing is that, in little more than a month after D-Day, 25 of the 36 ALGs in France were operational. Each British–Canadian ALG handled a wing of nearly 1,000 people, 54–72 aircraft, spares, fuel, food, a dozen antiaircraft guns, 200 vehicles, kitchens, messes, and a small village of tents.

So effective was Allied air superiority over Normandy, flown mostly by aircraft from the ALGs and to a lesser extent by squadrons based in England, that it prompted Field-Marshal Rommel to send a letter on June 12 to Field-Marshal Keitel, Commander-in-Chief of the German Army. It read:

> The enemy has complete command of the air over the battle zone and up to one hundred kilometres behind the front and cuts off by day almost all traffic on roads or by-ways or in open country. Manoeuvring by our troops on the field of battle in daylight is almost entirely prevented, while the enemy can operate freely. Neither our flak nor the Luftwaffe seem capable of putting a stop to this crippling and destructive operation of the enemy's aircraft.

While on patrol at 0806hrs on Tuesday July 18, 1944, Johnson spotted a German armored column moving along a main highway five miles east of Mézidon-Canon. The 24-year-old, who was the squadron's 'A' flight commander, immediately led his six Spitfires into a low-level attack. In his zeal to destroy these vehicles, Johnson failed to notice a large tree looming ever closer to his aircraft as he rapidly closed the distance to the target. Watching in total disbelief, the other pilots saw their leader's Spitfire crash through the tree-top at full throttle, tearing 3ft off the right wing! Johnson radioed that he could not gain altitude and that his mangled and twisted aircraft was almost impossible to control. He rejected the suggestion that he bail out or crash land, as he was more than 30 miles behind the enemy lines. Johnson pointed his barely flyable fighter, coded MK809, in the direction of B.2, which was some 40 miles away.

Relying on all his flying skills, he somehow managed to nurse his broken aircraft to within half a mile of Bazenville before it quit flying, forcing him to jump.

The wing medical officer recorded the following on Johnson's field medical casualty card: "Pilot baled out of a damaged aircraft at 0820 hours on 18 July 1944 – Parachute either did not open or opened too late to be effective – Instantaneous death from multiple fractures and lacerations after his body struck the ground."

Johnson's untimely death was witnessed by many of his fellow airmen at B.2, who silently prayed that he would make it back to the airfield.

FL Paul Gilbert Johnson is buried in Revieres Cemetery, Section XVIU, Row H, Grave 8 in Normandy, France. The cemetery is located half a mile down the road from where he crashed.

He was awarded a posthumous British DFC effective August 8, 1944. His medal was for gallantry in operational flying in conflict with the enemy. The citation reads as follows: "Flight Lieutenant Johnson has participated in many attacks on enemy airfields, communications and other targets on the ground and has proved himself to be a fearless and skillful pilot. He has displayed the greatest keenness to engage the enemy and has destroyed five hostile aircraft, three of them in one day."

At the time of the announcement of Paul's award, the RCAF in Ottawa received word that his father had died in Connecticut.

FL P. G. Johnson's final score was five confirmed, one probable and two damaged.

George Keefer
New York Spitfire Ace

WC George Clinton "Keefe" Keefer, Jr. shares the distinction of being one of the most highly decorated fighter pilots in the RCAF in World War II. Quite an honor when one considers he was an American citizen. Earning not one but two British DSO awards and two DFC awards, Keefer destroyed no fewer than 12 enemy aircraft in air-to-air combat. Some sources say his actual score lies somewhere between 14 and 17.

Flying Hawker Hurricanes and Supermarine Spitfires, Keefer flew a total of 455 combat sorties during the war covering three operational tours. He flew a fourth tour as an instructor pilot at an OTU in Egypt. Remarkably, in all that flying he never received so much as a scratch!

Keefer Jr. was born in New York City on July 11, 1921. He was the only child of George Clinton Keefer, Sr., an American from Albany, New York, and Sara Marshall Cook, a Canadian from Dorchester, New Brunswick. George's mother became an American citizen at the time of the marriage.

Keefer, Sr. was the comptroller of the Mutual Life Insurance Company of New York. The family, which was financially well off, was able to provide their son with the best education that money could buy. He was enrolled in two of the nation's top boarding schools. Keefe's grade school years in 1927–35 were spent attending the Fessenden School in West Newton, Massachusetts. His high school years, 1935–39, were spent at the preppy Phillips Exeter Academy located in Exeter, New Hampshire. George's parents tragically died when he was a young man. Keefer, when not attending school, lived with his mother's sister, Mrs. Grace Hughes in Charlottetown, Prince Edward Island. During the summer vacation months of 1939 and 1940, Keefe could be found working at Earle Baker's Imperial Esso service station in Charlottetown as an attendant. He enrolled at Yale University in September 1939 to study mechanical engineering.

A little over a year later on October 15, 1940, George, then 19, voluntarily enlisted as an AC2 in the RCAF at No. 15 Recruiting Centre in Moncton, New Brunswick. Assigned Service No. R. 72646, Keefer, who was used to the semi-regimented lifestyle of boarding school, fit in perfectly with the air force's structured training system.

Arriving at No. 1 MD in Toronto, Ontario, on October 18, George spent three weeks there until he was assigned to perform guard duty in that city at No. 1 Equipment Depot. Remaining in Toronto at No. 1 ITS, he was promoted to LAC.

Posted on December 10 to No. 11 EFTS at Cap-de-la-Madeleine, Quebec, Keefer completed the course flying Fleet Finch II biplanes on January 28, 1941. He concluded his training to wings standard on Yale and Harvard trainers at No. 2 SFTS Uplands, Ottawa, Ontario on April 10, 1941.

Graduating near the top of the class, Keefe was commissioned with the rank of PO. Reflecting his officer status, his Regimental No. was changed from R. 72646 to J. 5022.

Arriving in England on May 20 by troop ship from "Y" Depot Halifax, Nova Scotia, George spent a few weeks at No. 3 Personnel Reception Centre in Bournemouth awaiting his assignment.

For fighter conversion training, he attended No. 59 OTU, RAF Crosby-on-Eden in Cumbria flying Hawker Hurricane Mk Is from June 16 to July 28.

Assigned to the Middle East, Keefer left England for North Africa on a British aircraft carrier that was carrying additional aircrew and replacement Hurricane aircraft for the RAF desert squadrons.

In October he joined RAF No. 274 Squadron, which was operating from Gerawala, Egypt, flying Hurricane IIbs and IIcs.

Wing Commander George C. Keefer DSO & Bar, DFC & Bar, was one of the most highly decorated RCAF fighter pilots in World War II. (Canadian National Defence Image Library)

On June 4, 1942, Keefer, now an FO, was returning from a sortie when he noticed a flare fired by someone on the ground. Diving down to investigate, he found a lone figure stranded on the desert floor. Keefer landed his aircraft on the sand and rescued South African Air Force (SAAF) P-40 Kittyhawk pilot John Lane of No. 2 Squadron. Lane, who had been shot down by flak, sat in the pilot's seat and Keefer, at 5ft 9in tall squeezed in and sat in his lap. Between them they managed to fly the single-seat fighter and themselves to safety.

After having flown 179 sorties over a ten-month period, Keefer was relieved of operational flying and was awarded his first DFC. During his time with No. 274 Squadron, he shot down two Italian Macchi C. 202 fighters, a German Ju 88 and a Bf 109F. He also claimed a Bf 109E as a probable and five MC. 202s and one Bf 109E as damaged.

George spent six additional months in Egypt, from August 1942 to February 1943, teaching P-40 fighter tactics to newly arrived pilots at the Middle East Central Gunnery School located in the canal zone at El Ballah.

He returned to England on March 30.

Keefer was posted in early April to RCAF Staton Digby where he moved back and forth between two Canadian fighter squadrons – No. 412 and No. 416.

Newly promoted to FL on May 14, Keefer was permanently assigned to 412 "Falcon" FS, which flew Spitfire Vbs with RAF No. 10 Group from southeast England. On June 25, he assumed command of 412 and was promoted to SL. That October, 412 became part of No. 126 RCAF Wing at Biggin Hill and received, in November, upgraded equipment in the form of Spitfire Mk IXbs.

Keefe was promoted to WC of No. 126 on April 12, 1944, three months before his 23rd birthday.

W. Barry Needham of Wynyard, Saskatchewan, spent 26 months flying combat with 412, completing two tours of operation. Remembering George Keefer, he stated, "I thought he was one of the finest persons I ever met."

During his second operational tour, Keefe shot down a Ju 88, an Fw 190, a Bf 109G and an Me 110. He claimed an Fw 190 as probably destroyed and another as damaged.

George C. Keefer was awarded a Bar to his DFC effective April 1944 and the citation read as follows: "SL Keefer has always performed his duties with unfailing coolness and courage. On many occasions he has escorted large formations of bomber aircraft over enemy territory, achieving much success. Since the award of the Distinguished Flying Cross, he has continued to take part in operations with the greatest keenest and has engaged the enemy many times."

Keefe was sent back to Canada at the end of June 1944 for a much-needed rest. Bored with shuffling papers at RCAF Station Rockcliffe, Ontario, he managed to wrangle a third operations tour and returned to Britain on September 26, 1944.

In November, he went to work for GC James Edgar "Johnnie" Johnson as WC of RAF No. 125 Wing. Based at Eindhoven, Holland B.78, the wing flew the Rolls-Royce Griffon-powered Spitfire Mk XIVe.

Specifications for the Spitfire Mk XIVe:

Powerplant:	One supercharged Rolls-Royce Griffon 65 or 66 engine rated at 2,050shp
Wingspan:	36ft 8in
Fuselage Length:	32ft 7¾in
Maximum speed:	439mph
Armament:	Two Mk V Hispano-Suiza 20mm cannon with 120 rounds per gun and two Colt-Browning M-2 .50 caliber heavy machine guns with 250 rounds per gun. Provision for two 500lb bombs, one under each wing.

From September 1944 to VE-Day, May 8, 1945, most of the 20 Spitfire squadrons assigned to the 2nd TAF used the Griffon-engined Mk XIVe variant. Their main role was to seek out and destroy any and all targets behind German lines.

In his book *Wing Leader*, GC Johnson, Britain's highest-scoring World War II fighter ace, tells the story about "The bravest man I've ever known."

> We found a lot of Huns during the latter half of April 1945. We destroyed fighters, bombers, transports, dive-bombers, trains and a bunch of seaplanes we found floating on a lake. We could not catch the jets in the air, but we knew they were operating from Lubeck on the Baltic coast. We paid special attention to their airfields, shooting them down when they took off or came in to land. Some of the enemy leaders showed flashes of their old brilliance, but generally the rank and file were poor. On the evening of April 18, George Keefer led one of the squadrons on a sweep around the far side of the Elbe and I led a finger-four formation down sun from him. We swung toward the airfield at Parchim, Germany, which was neatly camouflaged in the midst of a woods. Heavy flak bracketed us and George led us into the cover of the low sun. On the airfield I saw a squadron of Messerschmitts about to take off. Five minutes later we returned in a fast dive from the sun. The 109s were still there. Hundreds of flak guns joined the heavy barrage against us. My heart sank. Probably we all thought the same thing – the war could only last a few more days. The pilots of the 109s below had probably left their cockpits for the engines had stopped. What were the chances of getting through the flak now that the gunners were roused? I reckoned that they were about 50-50.
>
> George said, 'Graycap Leader, I'm going in with my No. 2 [FO Trevorrow]. Cover us will you?' I wanted to say 'Is it worth it?', but only muttered, 'Okay George'. The two Spitfires became smaller and smaller as they went down in a fast dive.

Their grey-green camouflage merged into the spring greenery below and for a second or two I lost them. But the gunners on the ground saw them and the whole airfield seemed to sparkle with the flashes from the guns. We saw the Spitfires again when they streaked over the boundary of the airfield. We saw George's 20mm cannon shells bouncing on the concrete. I shouted into my microphone, 'Up a bit George, you're under deflecting!' Then his shells ripped into the first Messerschmitt in the line. It caught fire; its ammunition exploded and the cannon rounds slammed into the next 109. In a matter of seconds the whole lot were blazing and a great spiral of white smoke curled up from the airfield. 'You all right George?' 'Fine Graycap. Am climbing up.' 'Red 2?' 'I've been hit sir but she's flying' replied his wingman. 'Lead him home George and we'll cover you', I instructed. I twisted my neck for a final look at the airfield. All eleven Bf 109s were burning fiercely. It was the best and bravest strafing attack I had ever seen.

George C. Keefer and T. L. Trevorrow of RAF 130 "Punjab" Squadron both submitted combat reports for April 18, 1945.

Keefer reported:

I was leading twelve aircraft from No. 130 Squadron on an armed reconnaissance patrol. At 1930 hours while flying at 6,000ft I saw eleven Bf 109s parked at the end of the runway on Parchim airfield. I decided to attack followed by my No. 2. I levelled out at fifty feet and when 1,000 yards from the nearest enemy aircraft I opened up with all my ammunition. I saw strikes all over five of the aircraft which caught fire and explosions took place. The aircraft burned fiercely.

Trevorrow stated:

On April 18 I was flying No. 2 to WC Keefer in Red Section on a freelance sweep. At approximately 1935 hours we were passing close to Parchim airfield when from 7,000' I saw eleven enemy aircraft on the ground at the end of the runway apparently about to take off as the fans were turning. The WC and I went down while the others covered us from above. The WC went in first and I saw him start a fire in one of the aircraft and I fired into the middle of the bunch. I saw strikes immediately and there was a big flame and then an explosion. Debris flew up about 200' and as I flew through it my aircraft was hit. I claim six of the eleven planes destroyed and WC Keefer claims the other five.

Keefer's DSO was effective December 8, 1944, with the published citation reading as follows: "This officer has completed many sorties since being awarded a Bar to the Distinguished Flying Cross and his record is outstanding. Within the past few months, he has led large formations of aircraft on air operations during which

40 enemy aircraft have been destroyed. The successes obtained reflect the greatest credit on the skill, gallantry and resolution of Wing Commander Keefer. This officer has been personally responsible for the destruction of eight hostile aircraft."

George's third combat tour yielded him another four enemy aircraft destroyed – three Bf 109s, one Fw 190 and a claim for an Fw 190 as damaged.

A Bar to George's DSO was awarded on July 10, 1945, which read as follows:

> Since his appointment as Wing Commander of operations, Wing Commander Keefer has led and trained his wing to a high pitch of keenness and efficiency. Under his leadership, the wing has destroyed 191 enemy aircraft and damaged many more. In addition, a great variety of enemy ground targets have been successfully attacked. During this period Wing Commander Keefer has destroyed four enemy aircraft in the air, bringing his total victories to twelve aircraft destroyed. He has also destroyed at least sixty enemy transport vehicles. In April 1945, he completed a daring attack on 11 Messerschmitt 109s assembled on an airfield at Parchim. Despite intense and accurate anti-aircraft fire, the attack was pressed home and all the enemy aircraft were destroyed. This officer has completed three tours of operational duty and has proved himself to be a leader of the highest order and a cool and fearless pilot.

George Keefer returned to Canada via "R" Depot Warrington, England, on July 17, 1945. During his repatriation interview, it was revealed that his overseas flight time amounted to 1,383 hours (1,218 operational and 165 non-operational). Keefer had logged 648 hours on Spitfires and 570 hours on Hurricanes.

George Keefer decided to remain in the peacetime RCAF. For his exemplary service to Canada during the war, he received a plum posting for one year (September 1946 to September 1947) with the Canadian Joint Staff Mission in Washington, DC.

Returning from the States, he attended the RCAF Staff College in Toronto. Twenty-three weeks into the yearlong curriculum, Keefer decided to retire from active service and pursue other interests. At the end of February 1947, he left the college mid-way through his term, but not before the Chief Instructor GC C. L. Annis recommended that George be awarded the symbol "With Standing" (WS).

The following written recommendation was put forward to Air Commodore A. D. Ross, the college's commandant:

> Report on Student G. C. Keefer – J. 5022 – Retired
> 1. Written Work – This officer's written work was much above average. He is quick, thorough and neat. He has an active mind, the ability to think logically and independently and to express himself clearly.
> 2. Verbal Expression – Keefer took an active part in both formal and informal discussion. He speaks easily and well from a platform and is able to hold to his

convictions without appearing stubborn. He contributed many good ideas in class discussions.
3. Personality – He makes friends easily, is popular and is a good leader. Despite his outstanding operational record, he is modest in the extreme. He is ambitious and restless, but very taciturn about his own affairs. He has taken an active part in all college pursuits.
4. Future Employment – Though this officer has retired from the service, he did not leave the course until the twenty third week. He is considered highly qualified for the award of the symbol WS. It is recommended that he be awarded this symbol. WC Keefer should prove suitable in any type of staff employment. However, his interests lie predominantly in operational affairs and he would probably be best employed on such a staff.

C. L. Annis GC
21 February 1947

The commandant's response was short: "I concur. This officer's retirement is a distinct loss to the service. A. D. Ross AC."

On April 10, 1947, George joined the reserves flying de Havilland Vampires with 401 FS from RCAF Air Station, Saint-Hubert, Quebec.

G. C. Keefer DSO and Bar, DFC and Bar, received two postwar awards – the French Croix de Guerre with Gold Star on September 12, 1947, and a Netherlands Flying Cross on October 31, 1947. The citation accompanying his Netherlands Flying Cross read as follows:

> WC Keefer took over the duties of WC of No. 125 Wing in November 1944 while they were in winter quarters at Eindhoven, Holland. During this phase of active operations, under extremely adverse weather conditions, WC Keefer's indomitable courage and brilliant leadership maintained the morale of his wing at the highest level. This officer shows exceptional keenness to engage the enemy and his steadfast determination was worthy of the highest praise. In the subsequent battles through Holland to the German border, this officer's exceptional qualities remained well to the fore. He displayed outstanding devotion to duty.

George C. Keefer moved to Montreal, Quebec, where for 21 years he pursued a career in the Canadian aircraft industry working at Canadair.

In 1968, he resigned from his position there as vice president and purchased a plastics factory in Grandby, Quebec.

George Clinton Keefer, Jr., husband, father and business owner, died in his 64th year in Montreal in January 1985.

John Magee
The Poet Pilot

Descending in trail formation through a hole in the cloud cover, the No. 3 Spitfire of a flight of 11 suddenly collided with an oncoming RAF twin-engine Airspeed Oxford trainer. The violent mid-air collision just below the cloud base at 1130hrs on Thursday, December 11, 1941, over the village of Ruskington, Lincolnshire, was unavoidable.

The young American PO flying Supermarine Spitfire Vb AD291 coded VZ-H of 412 "Falcon" FS RCAF, was returning to his base at Wellingore. The 19-year-old fighter pilot was killed after he bailed out of his crippled aircraft at approximately 400ft – his parachute failing to fully deploy. The sole occupant of the Oxford, who also died, was on a solo flight from the Cranwell RAF College, SFTS. Eighteen-year-old RAF LAC Ernest Aubrey Griffin was flying a prescribed exercise in Oxford Mk II T.1052 at an altitude of 1,400ft.

Part of the official letter to the parents of the deceased PO read: "Your son's funeral took place at Scopwick Church Cemetery near the Digby aerodrome at 2:30 p.m. on Saturday, 13th December 1941, the service being conducted by Flight Lieutenant S. K. Belton, the Canadian Padre of this station. He was accorded full service honours, his oak coffin being carried by pilots of his squadron."

His white stone grave tablet, which has a chiseled RCAF crest and cross is inscribed as follows:

PILOT OFFICER
J. G. MAGEE
PILOT
ROYAL CANADIAN AIR FORCE
11TH DECEMBER 1941 – AGE 19

"Oh! I have slipped the surly bonds of earth,
Put out my hand, and touched the face of God."

The first and last lines of his immortal poem on his grave marker are the only clue that someone special lies in this small, but well maintained, English burial ground along with 54 other airmen from Australia, Belgium, Britain, Canada, New Zealand, and Germany.

John Gillespie Magee, Jr. was one of more than 8,864 Americans who joined and served in the RCAF in World War II.

John was born on June 9, 1922, in Shanghai, China, the eldest of four sons to missionaries John Gillespie Magee, Sr. and Faith Emmeline Backhouse. Magee, Sr. was from a very well-to-do Pittsburgh, Pennsylvania, family. Disregarding his family's wealth and influence, he chose to become an Episcopalian priest and was sent to China. There he met and married Faith, a Church of England missionary from Kent, England.

Magee, Jr. was educated in China, England, and the US from 1929 to 1940. Throughout his academic life, he was an excellent student possessed of exceptional intelligence. After three years of schooling in Nanking, China, he was sent to St. Clare Boarding School in Walmer, Kent, in 1931. Scholastically, he was far above average and started writing poetry at the age of 12. When he was 13, he moved to Rugby Public School and, at the age of 16, won its poetry prize for his poem *Brave New World*.

In 1939, John was joined in England by his mother and three brothers while his father remained in China. Against his wishes, he was persuaded to go to the US to finish his schooling in preparation to attend Yale University, his father's alma mater. He attended Avon's Old Farms School near Hartford, Connecticut, and published a collection of 17 of his poems, which were circulated among family members and personal friends. He found it difficult to make friends with boys his own age and they, in turn, found it hard to accept this English fellow who could quote Plato and Aristotle. John was homesick for England and wrote to his mother saying: "I shall never really be happy here – I am convinced that my place is in England and, if I ever get the opportunity, I am coming back."

In the spring of 1940, he became increasingly restless and one day he announced he was joining the RAF. Despite his best efforts, however, the US State Department refused to grant him an exit visa.

On his 18th birthday, his father, mother, and three brothers reunited with him in Connecticut for a joyous family reunion. Hearing the latest news that England was barely hanging on in the face of the seemingly unstoppable German war machine, his desire to join up became acute. Being the dutiful son that he was, John followed his parents' wishes and enrolled in Yale on a full scholarship in September 1940.

His focus, however, was not on his studies and, three weeks later, he traveled to Montreal, Quebec, where he unsuccessfully tried to join the RCAF. Standing 6ft 1in tall and weighing only 124lb, he was dismayed to learn that he was 16lb under their minimum weight requirement. The air force recruiter told him that, if he could get his weight up to 140lb, he was to come back and they would accept him.

Leading Aircraftman John Magee stands beside a NAA Harvard Mk IIb at Air Station Uplands, Ottawa, Ontario, in May 1941. (Canada Department of National Defence)

Packing on the pounds by overeating and avoiding any form of exercise, he returned to No. 13 Recruiting Centre in Montreal on October 10 and enlisted as an AC2 under Service No. R. 77134.

On his application, John listed his sports and hobbies as swimming, football, soccer, and model airplane building. He also stated he had ten hours' flight time as a passenger in a private aircraft – a Stinson SMA.

FO Louis Gelinas at the recruiting center wrote on Magee's form: "Above average, courteous and good appearance. Very good education. Intelligent and organized. Good pilot material. Recommended."

Magee spent 12 days at No. 1 MD in Toronto, Ontario, before being shipped off to RCAF Air Station Trenton, Ontario, where he performed guard duty from October 23 to December 22. Returning to Toronto, John began Course No. 14 at No. 1 ITS, which ran from December 23, 1940, to January 27, 1941. He passed all six subjects with a 77 percent grade average, but only managed to place 154th out of 186 students in the class.

Just prior to commencing flight training at No. 9 EFTS on Fleet Finch II biplanes at St. Catharines, Ontario, Magee was promoted to the rank of LAC. John soloed after only 6½ hours of flight instruction. His instructor, A. K. Patterson, considered him to be a natural pilot. Course No. 19 at St. Catharines ran from January 28 to March 17, with Magee graduating first in his class. He flew 92.95 hours in the yellow Fleets and had 11 hours of Link Trainer time. The CFI at No. 9, George Dunbar, recorded in Magee's file: "Above average in absorbing instruction. Good on instruments and aerobatics. Somewhat over confident."

He was awarded his RCAF pilot wings at No. 2 SFTS Uplands on June 16, 1941, and was commissioned at the rank of PO six days later – 13 days after celebrating his 19th birthday. The station commander at Uplands noted the following in John's file: "Shows plenty of initiative – smart appearance – however, lacks discipline and shows an unwillingness to obey orders."

When the air force commissioned Magee, it issued him new Regimental Service No. J. 5823, replacing his enlisted No. R. 77134.

He embarked for overseas service from "Y" Depot Halifax, Nova Scotia, by troop ship on July 5 after having enjoyed his two-week pre-embarkation leave with his family, who had recently moved to 2118 Bancroft Place in Washington, DC. John's father, who was close to retirement, was serving his last appointment as the assistant rector at St. John's Episcopal Church on Lafayette Square across from the White House. This place of worship is known as the President's church.

Magee was posted to RAF No. 53 OTU at Llandow in South Wales. On August 4, he began his fighter conversion training on Miles Master Is and IIs and Supermarine Spitfire Mk Is and IIs. It was with this unit, on September 3, when he wrote his immortal poem while on a high-altitude test flight in a newer model Spitfire Mk V.

Inspired by the ecstasy of this experience and back on the ground, he wrote a letter to his parents and told them he started composing the verse at 30,000ft and finished it soon after he had landed. He jotted down the words to *High Flight* on the back of his letter. His training concluded at Llandow on September 15.

Ivan M. L. Henson of Gloucestershire, England, managed to track down and interview Magee's roommate at 53 OTU. Retired RAF WC Roy Kingsford said John loved to read and write poetry, which he thought was rather odd for a budding fighter pilot. They played a lot of squash together and were very competitive both on the ground and in the air. They did not, however, always see eye-to-eye on some issues.

Magee was posted on September 23, 1941, to No. 412, which was, at the time, based at RAF Digby. The squadron moved from Digby to a satellite airfield at

Wellingore on October 20. Magee flew operationally with 412 for almost three months until that fatal mid-air collision.

W. Barry Needham said that he joined 412 the same day as Magee and quite possibly is the sole remaining pilot who flew operationally with him. Needham, then a SP, did not have a close relationship with John, but certainly knew him as they lounged around the dispersal hut while on readiness. Barry also said that on the morning of the accident, the entire squadron was up above the cloud layer, taking part in a wing formation flying practice.

Needham went on to say that one of Magee's close friends at 412 was Roderick Illingworth Alpine "Rod" Smith, who later in the war became a WC and a 14-kill ace. In a letter dated April 1987 addressed to David Magee, John's younger brother, Smith described rushing to John's crash site along with the squadron's intelligence officer, Hart Massey. They could not get close to the wreckage as the heat and flames were cooking and exploding 20mm cannon and .303in machine gun rounds.

Magee's aircraft engine was found 300 yards from the wrecked burning fuselage. The port wing was 500 yards from the airframe and the wing tip was a further 200 yards away. Nearby, they found a hole in the grounds with the imprint of Magee's body at least a foot into the soft soil. He had struck the ground with his back. There was nothing that either one could do.

The wing's medical officer, SL B. L. Hessen, said Magee died instantly. In his report he wrote, "Cause of death – Fractured cervical and lumbar vertebrae and multiple fractures of the ribs bilateral."

Following directly behind Magee in the No. 4 position and witnessing the tragic collision was SP Dwayne Linton, another American flying with 412. Linton was one of the principal witnesses at the Court of Inquiry, which was held at RAF Cranwell on December 19, 1941. The inquiry, which called ten other witnesses, was chaired by WC Simpson from RAF 21 Group. After hearing all the testimony, Simpson said that, in his opinion, the cause of the accident was due to the fast Spitfire formation suddenly appearing through a gap in the clouds and flying directly across the flight path of the Oxford. The inquiry did not have any corrective recommendations to make. The Air Vice Marshal commanding 21 Group, concurred with the findings of the inquiry when he wrote on January 18, 1942: "The accident scene is three miles equal distance between Cranwell and Digby. There is considerable air congestion in this district with no less than four flying units at Cranwell. I agree additional instructions would not obviate accidents of this nature as all fighter sectors have been informed to warn aircraft of the risk of collision when breaking clouds. It is probably less dangerous for fighter aircraft to descend slowly with caution in line astern than to break clouds and descend individually."

An audit of both pilots' flight logs showed Magee's total flight time was 286.45 hours while Griffin's was 89.45 hours.

John Magee: The Poet Pilot

The adventure and the thrill of aircraft flight was truly captured in all its glory by that young American when he penned those special words that have become identified as the sonnet of the air force.

> Oh! I have slipped the surly bonds of earth,
> And danced the skies on laughter-silvered wings.
> Sunward I've climbed and joined the tumbling mirth
> Of sun-split clouds – and done a hundred things
> You have not dreamed of – wheeled and soared and swung
> High in the sunlit silence.
> Hov'ring there, I've chased the shouting wing along
> and flung my eager craft through footless halls of air.
> Up, up the long delirious, burning blue
> I've topped the windswept heights with easy grace
> Where never lark, nor even eagle flew;
> And, while with silent, lifting mind I've trod
> The high untrespassed sanctity of space,
> Put out my hand, and touched the face of God.

Magee's *High Flight* was reprinted widely in American and British newspapers after Archibald MacLeish, Librarian of Congress, displayed it in an exhibition of poetry entitled "Faith and Freedom," which took place in Washington, DC in February 1942. MacLeish acclaimed Magee as the first poet of the war.

After his death, John's parents wrote a letter to the RCAF, which said, in part:

> We gave our consent and blessing to John as he left us to enter the RCAF. We felt as deeply as he did and we were proud of his determination and spirit. We knew that such news as did come might come. When his poem reached us, we felt then that it has a message for American youth, but we did not know how to get it before them. Now his death has emblazoned it across the entire country. We are thinking that this may have been a greater contribution than anything he may have done in the way of fighting. We will be forever proud of him.

John Gillespie Magee, Jr.'s poem has become a timeless classic of aviation literature reproduced the world over.

Magee's wartime RCAF squadron still exists today as part of the Canadian Armed Forces based at the Ottawa International Airport, flying Canadair Challenger jets worldwide in support of VIP and government officials. No. 412 has had an unbroken record of service since 1939.

To honor its poet pilot, the squadron's current workplace, in the Transport Canada hangar, is dedicated as The Pilot Officer John Gillespie Magee, Jr. Annex.

Joe McCarthy
The American Dambuster

In the early morning hours of Monday, May 17, 1943, 19 modified Avro Lancaster Mk III bombers from RAF No. 617 Squadron attacked the Möhne, Edersee and Sorpe hydroelectric dams in Germany's Ruhr industrial valley. The cost of the raid was exceedingly high, eight aircraft failed to return to RAF Scampton, Lincolnshire, and of the 133 aircrew who participated, 53 were killed and three others captured. The OC 617, WC Guy Penrose Gibson, had personally handpicked the crews from RAF Bomber Command's No. 5 Group two months earlier.

After that singular historic raid, also known as Operation *Chastise*, the airmen from Britain, Canada, Australia, New Zealand, and a sole American were immortalized as "The Dambusters."

The American, Joseph Charles "Big Joe" McCarthy, was a burly 225lb, 6ft 3in tall, 23-year-old from New York City.

Born in St. James, Long Island, New York, on August 31, 1919, Joe, who was fascinated by all things aeronautical, was raised in Brooklyn. His father was a New York City fireman and one of his grandfathers was a deputy sheriff. McCarthy's family had a summer home on Long Island where one of Joe's summer jobs was as a lifeguard at Coney Island. Money from this endeavor and other employments helped to pay for private flying lessons at nearby Roosevelt Field where, in 1927, Charles Lindbergh had taken off on his epic solo New York–Paris flight.

McCarthy made three separate attempts in 1940–41 to join the USAAC. Each time, they told him he would hear back from them, but he never did. The war was entering its second year and it bothered Big Joe that the United States was taking a neutral position in the conflict.

One of Joe's neighborhood, lifelong friends was fellow civilian pilot, Donald Joseph Curtin. It was Curtin who suggested that they should head north to Canada and join the RCAF. Because of the war, Don had been laid off from his job as a cruise director with the Holland America Steamship Company.

Speaking to a reporter, McCarthy recalled:

> Within two days, Don and I boarded a bus and headed for Ottawa, Ontario. We crossed the St. Lawrence river by ferry and the Canada Customs people helped us get a connecting bus to Ottawa.

We spent the night at the YMCA and the following morning, May 5, 1941, we proceeded to RCAF No. 12 Recruiting Centre. There we were told we would have to come back in six weeks. Don and I responded we didn't have the money to return again so if the air force wanted us they had better decide that day!

The WO in charge took a second look at the two American volunteers, changed his mind and had them sign enlistment papers. That was fine with both as all they wanted to do was fly.

Later that day, as AC2s, they, along with 13 other new recruits, were on a westbound train headed to No. 1 MD in Toronto, Ontario.

After basic training, both attended No. 1 ITS in that city, graduating on August 11.

Promoted to LACs, McCarthy and Curtin reported to No. 12 EFTS located at Sky Harbour Airport at Goderich, Ontario. There, they flew Fleet Finch biplanes, easily passing out of the course on September 26.

Next, the two friends were sent to No. 5 SFTS in Brantford, Ontario, where they learned to fly the twin-engined Avro Anson.

Once, during his training at No. 5, Big Joe, low on fuel and hopelessly lost, landed in a farmer's field to ask for directions after his navigation map flew out the open window of the cockpit. That slight blemish on his training record did not preclude him from earning his wings.

McCarthy and Curtin graduated near the top of their class on December 18, 1941, as SPs and, within hours, both were commissioned from the ranks as POs.

Their officer service numbers were only six digits apart – Curtin's was J. 9340 and McCarthy's was J. 9346. Taking their two-week pre-embarkation leave, they returned to the New York area where they spent time with their families over the Christmas and New Year holidays.

Don Curtin headed overseas before Joe and, after training at two OTUs, went on to fly Avro Manchesters and Lancasters with RAF No. 106 Squadron from Syerston in Nottinghamshire. Curtin was awarded a British DFC on his first sortie in July 1942 and a further award of a Bar to his DFC was approved in January 1943. During the eight-month period Curtin flew with No. 106, his boss was a 23-year-old WC named Guy P. Gibson.

Joe McCarthy left "Y" Depot, Halifax, Nova Scotia, on a banana boat that had been converted into a troop ship. Not long into the voyage, bad weather separated the ship from the rest of the convoy, and it had to proceed on its own all the way to England without a naval escort. Upon docking, it was surprised to learn it had arrived ahead of the rest of the ships.

April 1942 found Joe at No. 12 Pilot Advanced Flying Unit at RAF Grantham flying Airspeed Oxfords. The next month he was at No. 14 OTU, RAF Cottesmore, where he flew the Handley Page Hampden bomber. In August, he was posted to RAF Woodhall Spa, Lincolnshire, flying Manchesters and

Lancasters with No. 97 Conversion Flight. On September 21, Joe began his first operational tour with No. 97 Squadron, where he flew 29 Lancaster sorties up until March 11, 1943.

Curtin and McCarthy socially visited each other, and it was at Syerston where Joe first met Guy Gibson. McCarthy remembered Gibson as one of those men to whom leadership came as naturally as breathing; autocratic and impatient at times yet commanding instant respect.

McCarthy was a favorite of his fellow pilots and was known around the RAF bomber squadrons as "the big blonde American." Outwardly, he had a personality that matched his physique. His colorful American expletives were freely lavished on all who crossed his path. This was in marked contrast to the more austere profanity of the British pilots. Near the end of the war, he adapted to the British way, being seen with a pipe, a walking stick, and a dog on a leash. "If I'm going to be an officer and a gentleman," he said, "I'm going to have a crack at looking the part."

In March 1943, Joe received a telephone call from Gibson who told him, "I'm forming a new squadron. I can't tell you much about it except to say that we may be only doing one trip. I'd like you and your crew to join us." Joe was excited about the opportunity, but his crew was initially cool to the idea. They had just beaten the odds by completing their first tour. However, all but one of the crew of six eventually decided to follow their captain to the new unit originally designated "X" Squadron, then later changed to No. 617.

It is a foregone certainty that McCarthy's good friend, FL Donald J. Curtin, DFC & Bar, would have been a part of 617 if he and his entire crew had not been tragically lost in Lancaster W4886 in a collision over Nuremberg on February 25/26, 1943.

They are buried in the CWGC at Durnbach, Germany.

WC Gibson, who had survived 173 operational sorties, had been tasked by Sir Ralph Cochrane, AOC No. 5 Group, to set up the new squadron for a mysterious "special operation." Gibson, who at that stage knew nothing about the target, was given carte blanche by Cochrane to comb Bomber Command for its best aircrews.

McCarthy and his crew made their first flight with 617 on March 31, 1943. For the next several weeks, the squadron trained intensively for its dangerous mission using the Eyebrook and Derwent reservoirs. Days before the Dambusters Raid, McCarthy was notified he was to receive a DFC for the sterling work he had performed while at No. 97 Squadron. Within days of this notification, he was promoted to FL.

The Dambusters Raid and the ingenious bouncing bomb used were conceived in the brilliant mind of Dr. (later Sir) Barnes Neville Wallis. Wallis, a British engineer, also had a hand in designing the Vickers R-100 Airship, the Wellesley and Wellington bombers, and, later in the war, two earthquake bombs – the 12,030lb "Tallboy" in 1944 and the 22,000lb "Grand Slam" in 1945.

Wing Commander Joseph McCarthy DSO, DFC & Bar, is standing in the back row, second from right. This picture, featuring some of his fellow "Dambuster" flyers, was taken shortly after their historic raid on May 17, 1943. (UK Ministry of Defence)

When war broke out in 1939, Wallis searched for weaknesses in the enemy's industrial infrastructure. He finally settled on a plan to destroy Germany's great hydroelectric dams. The bouncing bomb, weighing 9,250lb, was packed with TNT, RDX, and other materials to enhance the efficiency of the explosion. Cylindrical in shape, it measured 5ft in length and 4ft in diameter. The Germans called Wallis's creation the "spinning depth charge." Each bomb was fitted with three pre-set hydrostatic pistols designed to detonate when the water pressure was equal to a depth of 30ft. As back-up, each bomb was fitted with a 90-second detonation fuse. The attacking Lancasters were to fly precisely 60ft above the water, releasing the bomb 450 yards from the target and at an exact airspeed of 223mph. Prior to release, an onboard hydraulic motor drive and belt system spun the bomb backwards to a speed of 500rpm. Skipping like a stone across a lake's surface, the backward spinning bomb struck the dam's wall, crawled down its concrete face and exploded at the prescribed depth.

On the clear moonlit evening of Sunday, May 16, 1943, McCarthy and his crew, anxious to go, climbed into their Lancaster "Q For Queenie," only to have the aircraft go unserviceable on the ramp. Undeterred, they rushed over to a spare aircraft, "T For Tom," only to find the navigation card giving them precise compass deviations vital for accurately flying the carefully charted route was not in the cockpit. The chances of flying the aircraft at low level, between 75ft and 120ft, through the myriad of flak emplacements and German NJG bases that lay between them and their target, were zero without it.

Big Joe climbed down from the cockpit for the second time that evening and with his "Irish temper" near boiling point, headed for the hangar where he ran into FS "Chiefy" Powell, 617's senior non-commissioned officer (SNCO). After a short, expletive-filled, one-sided conversation, Powell took off on the double to the squadron's instrument section where, unsure of what exactly it was he was looking for, managed somehow to locate the missing route card.

McCarthy finally got airborne in Lancaster ED825 – 30 minutes behind his section. He was the commander of the squadron's second wave assigned to attack the most difficult of the three dams – Sorpe.

Unlike Möhne and Edersee, Sorpe's concrete core was surrounded by an earthen wall. The planned bouncing bomb attack for the other two dams would be ineffectual against this target so a conventional bomb drop was briefed.

During the outbound leg, the crew reported seeing several enemy night fighters flying above them. Joe's front and rear gunners exchanged fire with some flak positions after their aircraft was coned several times by searchlights. At one point, Sgt Baston, the front gunner, asked for permission to open fire on a train only to discover it was an armored flak train. Return fire hit the aircraft in the port undercarriage nacelle and burst the tire.

McCarthy was the only member of his five-plane formation to reach the target. Of the others, one was shot down, another was so badly damaged by flak that the crew aborted, another crashed into an electrical pylon supporting power cables, and the fourth lost its bomb in the water when the plane bounced off the surface while flying too low.

Arriving over the valley, McCarthy initiated a diving attack as the dam was nestled at the bottom of two steep hills. Coming over the top of one hill, Joe, using full flaps to keep the speed of his 30-ton Lancaster under control, dove down the slope toward the 765-yard-long dam. To escape, he had to apply full power to his four American-built Packard Rolls-Royce Merlin engines and climb at a steep angle up the side of the second hill. If that was not difficult enough, a thick mist was filling the valley as he arrived. The blinding moonlight turned the mist into a writhing phosphorescent pall, which made it extremely difficult to judge the bomber's height above the undefended dam. On the third attempt to locate the target, Joe almost flew "T for Tom" into the water. It was not until the tenth run that bomb-aimer, Sergeant George "Johnny" Johnson, was satisfied and released the bomb from a height of just 60ft. It exploded squarely on top of the parapet, damaging and crumbling the crown of the earthen wall for more than 50 yards.

Shortly thereafter, a spare aircraft flown by Canadian Ken Brown dropped its bomb on the sixth attempt, causing further damage to the earthen wall with a second direct hit. The Germans, unsure of the dam's integrity, were forced to drain off more than 50 percent of the reservoir's capacity until the structure could be inspected and repaired.

The breaching of Möhne and Edersee, coupled with the damage done to Sorpe, was a tremendous propaganda victory for Britain and a colossal demoralizing blow for Germany.

Joe McCarthy received a DSO award for his part in the raids. He was presented with this medal along with his previously gazetted DFC by King George VI and Queen Elizabeth on June 22, 1943, at Buckingham Palace. Her Majesty chatted with several of the recipients, one of them being McCarthy. Big Joe, normally voluble, was reduced to shyness as The Queen took his massive hand in hers and asked him about his home life in Brooklyn. He could only mutter a few syllables in response to her questions.

After the Dambusters Raid, Joe continued to fly with 617 and one of Guy Gibson's successors, Leonard Cheshire, thought so highly of McCarthy's piloting abilities, he promoted him to SL.

On April 28, 1944, Joe was awarded a Bar to his DFC with the following citation: "Since being awarded the Distinguished Service Order, this officer has completed numerous sorties as captain of aircraft in which he has taken part in difficult and hazardous operations at low level. SL McCarthy has displayed exemplary skill and courage which, combined with his unfailing devotion to duty, have contributed much to the success achieved."

At 617, Joe was involved in testing a new high-altitude bomb sight. He flew a number of operations utilizing the new device against selected small targets in France, resulting in little or no collateral damage being done to nearby residential areas.

No. 617 also flew operations as pathfinders, dropping target indicators (TIs) at low-level. These marked the precise area the main bomber force was to bomb. On one occasion, Big Joe's reference point was a small building. Somehow, his TI went right inside the structure and, as no one could see it, he had to come around again to place another marker.

Joe McCarthy began his third operational tour with a raid to Toulouse, France, on April 5, 1944.

On the evening prior to D-Day, the entire squadron flew racetrack circuits at 800ft off Calais, dropping aluminum foil every three minutes. This tactic duped the German coastal radar operators into thinking a large surface fleet was approaching Pas de Calais when, in fact, the real force was approaching Normandy far to the west.

Joe was also involved in dropping the first 12,030lb Tallboy bomb on the Saumur railway tunnel. He released the weapon from 10,000ft and it struck less than 100 yards from the target, causing the tunnel to collapse. He dropped other Tallboys on submarine pens and V-1 factories.

His 67th and last bomber sortie took place on July 4, 1944, when he placed a Tallboy on a target near Criel, France.

McCarthy hated bureaucracy and had little patience and no time for ground staff who failed to appreciate the risks aircrew faced almost every night. On the occasion of the second desperate attempt by 617 to breach the Dortmund–Ems Canal – the first losing five Lancasters out of eight dispatched – Joe overheard a female officer remark: "My God, I hope they get there tonight. The trouble the AOC's gone to over this." McCarthy silenced her with a snarl, "The hell with you and all the AOCs. What about the seven lives in every kite!" and stormed out. Only three of the nine aircraft sent on the raid that evening returned.

Leaving 617, Joe spent a brief period as a staff officer with No. 6 Group Headquarters, then as commander of a fighter affiliation unit where he flew Hurricanes and Spitfires.

In November 1944, he was posted to the Royal Aircraft Establishment (RAE) at Farnborough.

When the European war ended, he remained at Farnborough where he served with the Foreign Aircraft Flight. This group had the task of locating and gathering a wide range of Luftwaffe aircraft for evaluation and flight testing. Some 75 German aircraft were flown directly to the RAE and another 50 were delivered by sea. SL McCarthy personally flew the Fw 200, Arado 232, Fw 190, He 219, and the Do 335. Joe also flew his first jet, the Meteor EE-360. By the time his duties at Farnborough came to an end in December 1945, he had flown more than 50 different aircraft types.

McCarthy returned to Canada early in 1946. He decided to remain in the RCAF and applied for Canadian citizenship, which was granted. Promoted to WC, Joe McCarthy had a varied and interesting postwar career from 1946 to 1968. He served at the following locations: Test and Development Establishment, Rockcliffe, Ontario; RCAF Staff College, Toronto, Ontario; No. 6 Repair Depot, Trenton, Ontario; RCAF Station, Chatham, New Brunswick; No. 2 RCAF Fighter Wing, France; RCAF Station, Trenton; No. 4 Flying Training School, Penhold, Alberta; 407 Maritime Patrol Squadron, Comox, British Columbia; Belgian Congo for the UN; and RCAF Staff Officer attached to the Commander's Office, US Naval Air Force Atlantic Fleet, Norfolk, Virginia.

McCarthy's last Canadian military flight was on April 9, 1968, as pilot in command of a Canadair CP-107 Argus maritime patrol aircraft.

Earlier that same year, the Canadian federal government destroyed the rich individual histories and traditions of Canada's Army, Navy and Air Force when it unified the three separate military branches into an all-encompassing "one size fits all" service.

Joe McCarthy, unwilling to participate in the tortuous demise of his beloved RCAF, retired after 27 years of faithful service.

For a few years, he sold real estate, and then, later in life, lectured at the USAF Air Warfare College at Maxwell AFB in Alabama.

Seventy-nine-year-old, retired WC Joseph Charles "Big Joe" McCarthy, DSO, DFC and Bar – the American Dambuster – died of emphysema at his home in Virginia Beach, Virginia, on September 6, 1998. He was survived by his wife Alice, two children, Joseph B. McCarthy and Karen Westergaard both of Virginia Beach, five grandchildren, and a brother, Frank, of Glendale, New York.

Charles McDonald
Louisiana Spitfire Pilot

Charles Edward McDonald was born to Rufus Eugene McDonald and Mary Alice Clements in Bossier City, Louisiana, on October 31, 1918. He was educated in that community from 1923 to 1934. Following high school, McDonald spent the next two years taking pre-med courses at Louisiana's Centenary College. From 1936 until 1939, he worked as an oil driller for the Telark Oil Corporation in Rodessa, Louisiana. On May 16, 1939, he married Genevieve Ethyl Rinehart. In the fall of 1939, he tried to join the peacetime USAAC, but as a married man, he was disqualified from entry into its pilot training program.

McDonald's marriage completely fell apart in the spring of 1940 and divorce proceedings commenced shortly thereafter.

Traveling 1,098 miles north to Canada, Charles arrived at the RCAF No. 8 Recruiting Centre located in downtown Windsor, Ontario, on Tuesday, September 10, 1940. The 5ft 7in tall, 180lb McDonald enlisted as an AC2 under Regimental Service No. R. 67749.

The RCAF interviewer, FO C. L. Arnold, was impressed with McDonald's confidence and sincerity and noted the following on his enlistment papers: "Well educated and very keen to serve. Good type American boy. Best suited for pilot."

Four days later, Charles was on a westbound Canadian Pacific Railway passenger train headed to No. 2 MD at Brandon, Manitoba. One month of basic training at this facility was followed by five weeks of guard duty at No. 2 Training Command Headquarters at Winnipeg, Manitoba. On November 17, McDonald was posted to No. 2 ITS at Regina, Saskatchewan. Graduating from there on December 21, he was sent to No. 6 EFTS at Prince Albert, Saskatchewan, where, over a two-month period, he flew 70 hours on de Havilland Tiger Moth biplanes.

At the beginning of his training at No. 6, he was promoted to LAC. On February 6, 1941, Charles was posted to No. 2 SFTS at RCAF Air Station Uplands, Ottawa, Ontario, to complete his training on Harvard and Yale trainers. He graduated from Course No. 21 on April 16 as an SP after having flown 110 hours on these types.

Sergeant McDonald headed overseas by troop ship in early May through "Y" Depot, Pier 21, Halifax, Nova Scotia.

After spending several days at No. 3 Personnel Reception Centre at Bournemouth, England, he was posted, on June 9, to RAF No. 53 OTU, which was operating from two airfields – Heston, Middlesex, and Llandow, South Wales. Over the next six weeks, he flew a total of 45 hours on Miles Masters and various early marks of Supermarine Spitfires.

On July 26, he was posted to RCAF No. 403 "Wolf" FS, which was operating Spitfire Mk IIas, Vbs and Vcs from RAF Ternhill, Shropshire. In August, the squadron moved its operations from Ternhill to Hornchurch, Essex. Over the next month, McDonald flew 15 sorties with No. 403, totaling some 40 flying hours.

On August 21, 1941, McDonald and his squadron mates were tasked to escort RAF Bristol Blenheim twin-engined bombers in an attack against the German-occupied airfield at Saint-Omer, France. Crossing the enemy coast at 1022hrs, the contingent was set upon by a large formation of Fw 190A-1s and Messerschmitt Bf 109F-2s fighters belonging to JG 26 and 2. Eight minutes into the battle, 20mm cannon and 13mm machine gun rounds from Leutnant Horst Sternberg's Fw 190 "Black 13" shredded Mcdonald's Spitfire, setting it afire over Wormhout, France. Charles, wounded in the legs by shell fragments and suffering burns on his hands and face, quickly exited his flaming aircraft.

One of the training aircraft Flying Officer Charles McDonald, MM, flew while on his way to earning his RCAF wings was the NAA Yale. (Canadian National Defence Image Library)

Sternberg would run his score to 23 victories before he was shot down and killed in combat by an American P-47 Thunderbolt pilot on February 22, 1944.

McDonald attempted to evade capture, but within an hour, he was taken into custody by ground troops. He was transported to a French hospital where his injuries were treated and dressed. His legs were x-rayed, but no surgical procedures were performed. He remained in the hospital under guard for the next 27 days.

McDonald was imprisoned in Stalag VIII-B at Lamsdorf in western Poland on September 24. He was not there very long before he was moved to Stalag Luft III at Sagan, Poland. He quickly surmised that an escape from this Luftwaffe-operated PoW camp was next to impossible. He managed to transfer back to Lamsdorf, where he voluntarily worked in the garden, growing vegetables that supplied the German messes. It took him a year to formulate an escape plan. Late in the evening of August 23, 1942, McDonald, along with two other airmen and an army soldier, climbed up into the attic of their hut through a hole they had made in the ceiling. Threading their way through the rafters, they reached a boiler room and unlocked a door from the inside using a homemade key. The camp perimeter fence was unlocked and, after evading a single guard, they scurried into the darkness.

Within days, the escapees established contact with the Polish underground. With the assistance of many brave people, Charles began a long journey to freedom through Poland, Germany, France, and Spain, eventually reaching Gibraltar. He arrived in Liverpool, England, on July 24, 1943, 23 months after he had been shot down. While in captivity, he had been promoted to FS. McDonald noted German troop locations and movements along his escape route as well as the effectiveness of the round-the-clock bombing campaign mounted by the Allies. Everything he saw and heard was passed on to Allied intelligence upon his return.

On August 4, he was promoted to PO. His Regimental Service No. was changed from R. 67749 to J. 18171, reflecting the new role.

In a letter dated August 14, the AOC RCAF Overseas United Kingdom, informed the Secretary of the DND for Air at Ottawa, Ontario, of the following: "As Flight Sergeant McDonald was imprisoned and escaped under conditions which make it impossible for him to operate again in this theatre of war according to the ruling of the Air Ministry Intelligence, steps have been taken to effect his repatriation for employment in Canada. This airman is very eager to return to operational flying and it is recommended that he be considered for such duties after a period of one month's clear leave if found to be fit."

Returning to Canada on September 7, McDonald was assigned to No. 1 Repatriation Pool at Rockcliffe, Ontario. GC T. G. MacFarlane, in a report dated November 2, stated that McDonald had been medically boarded since his return and was categorized as being fit for full flying duties. He did recommend that Charles take some refresher flying training at an SFTS as he had not flown an aircraft in more than two years.

In a document dated December 9, 1943, and stamped "SECRET," King George VI approved the award of a British Military Medal (MM) to PO C. E. McDonald in recognition of his distinguished service. It was clearly stated that the details of McDonald's award were never to be published under any circumstances. Until it was discontinued in 1993, the MM was a military decoration awarded to personnel of the British or Commonwealth militaries, below commissioned rank, for bravery in battle on land. McDonald was the only airman to receive this army award in World War II.

From November 10, 1943, until February 13, 1944, Charles was at No. 1 SFTS at Camp Borden, Ontario, undertaking refresher flying training on Harvard Mk IIbs. While at Borden, he was promoted to FO.

On February 22, he was posted to Western Air Command at Vancouver, British Columbia. From there, he was assigned to No. 163 FS, which was flying Curtiss-Wright P-40 Kittyhawk Mk Is and IIIs from Sea Island, British Columbia. This squadron disbanded on March 15, less than one month after Charles had arrived. McDonald and his fellow pilots were moved over to No. 133 FS at Patricia Bay, British Columbia. There they flew Hawker Hurricane Mk XIIs and P-40 Mk Is in defense of Canada's west coast.

Longing to get back into action, FO McDonald decided to seek his release from the RCAF. His request was honorably granted on July 28, 1944, when he transferred to the USAAF as a 1st lieutenant under Service No. AO-556772.

With the formation of the USAF looming on the horizon in 1947, McDonald and thousands of other airmen learned there were no positions available for them in the downsized peacetime air force.

Charles had always enjoyed the stability of military life so, on June 30, 1947, he resigned his commission in the USAAF. Later that same day, he enlisted in the USAF under Service No. 18316233 as a master sergeant.

Over the next three years, he managed to regain a commission and get back in the cockpit. He flew a tour on F-86E Sabre jets during the Korean War and rose to the rank of captain. While flying with the 60th Fighter Interceptor Squadron, the "Fighting Crows," an Air Defense Command unit, Captain McDonald was killed in the crash of F-86D-30 *Dog Sabre* at Westover Air Force Base at Chicopee, Massachusetts, on November 17, 1953.

His earned wartime medals include, in addition to the MM, the 1939–45 Star, General Service Medal, and the Canadian Volunteer Service Medal & Clasp.

Bernard McGrattan
Two Sets of Wings

Approaching Bernay, France, from the west, the 11 Fw 190A-8 fighters, under the command of Luftwaffe Hauptmann Herbert Huppertz, chanced upon four USAAF P-51B Mustangs flying just below the cloud deck. The American pilots from the 335th FS, 4th FG, were busily engaged strafing German troops in a truck convoy on the great road bridge over the Risle river.

The experienced German airmen were from JG 2 "Richthofen"– eight were attached to 3 Staffel based at Cormeilles-en-Vexin and the remainder were assigned to 1 Staffel based at Fontenay-le-Comte.

Satisfied that his flight had not been detected, Hauptmann Huppertz ordered his men to climb for altitude. Using the setting sun and evening mist as cover, he proceeded to set up the classic bounce. Unaware of the impending danger, the Americans were within seconds of being trapped low on the deck, leaving them little or no room to maneuver. The Germans had an almost three to one advantage, along with the element of height and surprise. The A-8 variant they were flying was equal in speed to the Mustang, but its armament heavily outgunned the P-51. These Fw 190s carried four 20mm wing-mounted cannon and two cowl-mounted 13mm machine guns. The Mustangs were armed with four Colt-Browning MG53-2 wing-mounted 12.7mm machine guns.

The four Mustang pilots were excited, and they were tired – excited as this was the "Big Show," Tuesday, June 6, 1944, the invasion of Normandy – and bone tired as they were flying their second mission of the day. It was approximately 2020hrs and most of the squadron's personnel had been up since 0130hrs that morning.

The American flight leader of the 335th's "Blue Section" was 24-year-old Captain Bernard "Big Mac" McGrattan from Utica, New York. Other pilots in his flight were FO Walter Smith from Birmingham, Alabama; 1st Lieutenant Harold L. Ross, Jr. from Greensboro, North Carolina; and 2nd Lieutenant Cecil E. Garbey from Tulsa, Oklahoma.

McGrattan was a nine-month combat veteran with the 4th, an ace who had eight and a half confirmed aerial kills. Ross had been with the 335th for two months, Smith and Garbey only one month each.

The German attack came out of the west, driving the Mustangs east deeper into France. The Germans had cut off the Americans' escape route back across the Channel to their base at Debden in Essex, England.

The P-51 pilots managed to flee and fight over a distance of 29 miles when, at 2035hrs, two miles northwest of Évreux, Hauptmann Huppertz from 3./JG 2 downed the first P-51 from a height of 1,500ft.

The three remaining P-51s, with their Rolls-Royce Packard Merlin engines roaring at full throttle, somehow managed to get turned around and back onto a westerly heading, but it was too late. The deadly trap was well and truly sprung.

The second Mustang fell at 2054hrs at Bernay from a height of 1,500ft and was claimed by Leutnant Christian Eickhoff from 1./JG 2. The third and fourth Mustangs went down two minutes later also at Bernay, both from a height of 1,800ft and were claimed by Leutnant Wolfgang Fishcher and Fähnrich Fritz Beer both from 1./JG 2.

Huppertz shot down a total of five Allied aircraft that day – the Mustang, three Hawker Typhoon fighter-bombers, and one Republic P-47D Thunderbolt.

The next day, he claimed another P-47, bringing his total to 70 aircraft. On June 8, at 1715hrs, this "Luftwaffe Experten" was shot down and killed in aerial combat near Cabourg, France, by Major Rockford Vance "Rocky" Gray, an American P-47 ace from the 371st FG. Five days earlier, Huppertz had celebrated his 25th birthday and, after his death, was posthumously promoted to the rank of major.

Big Mac was not scheduled to fly on June 6, as he had completed his first tour and had used up all of his allowable extensions. According to his crew chief, S/Sgt Sy Koenig, McGrattan's bags were packed, and he was awaiting transport back to the States when D-Day came along. He wanted to be part of history, so he begged the 4th Group commander, Colonel Donald J. M. "Horseback Leader" Blakeslee, to let him participate. Since the 4th was short on pilots and this was an all hands on deck effort, Blakeslee, a RCAF alumnus like McGrattan, allowed him to go.

Captain McGrattan was planning to marry his English fiancé who was serving in the Women's Royal Naval Service and who was three-and-a-half months pregnant with his child. Both had applied for military permission to get married on three separate occasions, but officials kept putting off their requests due to the imminence of the invasion.

Bernard McGrattan was born to Elizabeth Yogerst and Bernard Charles McGrattan at Buffalo, New York, on March 9, 1920. From 1926 until 1934, McGrattan attended St. Johns Evangelist Roman Catholic Grammar School. This was followed by three years of higher learning at South Park High School in Buffalo. During the years 1935–37, Bernard worked part-time repairing bicycles at the F. J. Eberhardt Company. He was also employed as a garageman at the Western Auto Supply Company.

McGrattan moved with his father to Chicago after the death of his mother in 1937. He completed his education at Seneca High School in that city in 1939. This

Bernard McGrattan: Two Sets of Wings

was followed by a one-year general arts course at Chicago's Wilson Junior College. Part time jobs in the Windy City included ushering at the Riviera Theater and as a lifeguard for the Chicago Parks District Commission.

By September 1941, Canada had been involved in the war for two years, but the United States, by adopting a position of neutrality, had managed to stay out of the European conflict. This would all change early on Sunday morning December 7, 1941, at the US naval base at Pearl Harbor, Hawaii.

The US declared war on Japan the next day, and on Germany and Italy shortly thereafter.

McGrattan wanted to become a fighter pilot but did not meet the prewar USAAC's mandatory requirement of having two years of college education to enter flight cadet training. Canada, however, was accepting high school graduates, provided they could pass a physical and a battery of tough entrance examinations and aptitude tests.

On Tuesday, September 23, 1941, the 21-year-old crossed the border at Buffalo and entered the province of Ontario at the town of Fort Erie. He traveled an additional 90 miles to the city of Hamilton where he voluntarily enlisted in the RCAF for the duration of the war at No. 10 Recruiting Centre. His assigned service number was R. 131218 and he started his air force career as an AC2. He told the recruiter, FO Lawrence, that his permanent residence was 18 Higby Road in Utica, New York. On his application, he listed his occupation as a salesman. He said his mother was deceased and that his father was living and working in Chicago, Illinois. FO Lawrence was impressed with the 6ft 3in tall, 187lb applicant and endorsed his application for pilot training.

Bernard was sent, on September 25, to No. 1 MD at Toronto, Ontario, for basic training. Graduating from there on October 27, he spent the next two months on guard duty at No. 1 Training Command Headquarters in Toronto.

Course No. 43 at No. 6 ITS in Toronto ran from December 22, 1941, until February 13, 1942. Of the 79 students in the class, McGrattan ranked 66th. He graduated with a 76 percent average and was promoted to LAC. The school's

4th FG Ace Captain Bernard McGrattan was shot down and killed along with his entire flight on D-Day, June 6, 1944. (US Department of Defense)

WC made the following notations: "Alert, cautious, cheerful type. Well balanced, co-operative and enthusiastic. Leadership material and shows a fair team spirit. Requires some work on his navigation."

Passed to No. 7 EFTS at Windsor, Ontario, Bernard began flight training on March 2 on Fleet Finch II biplanes on Course No. 50. There, he accumulated 60.35 flying hours on type. Of the 39 students in the class, he stood 24th. He was judged to be an average trainee whose instrument flying was rated as good.

Graduating on April 24, 1942, with a 69.1 percent average, McGrattan was posted on May 11 to No. 14 SFTS at Aylmer, Ontario. Flying 160.50 hours on NAA Yale and Harvard trainers on Course No. 55, Bernard completed his training on August 28.

He was awarded his RCAF wings along with a promotion to SP. McGrattan's instructors entered the following comments in his file: "Tends to be rough and a little erratic with the controls. Will need checking to improve his flying up to a good average standard. Link navigation training above average. Works hard but suffers from overconfidence. Conduct and appearance fair."

Bernard was given the standard two-week pre-embarkation leave, during which time he tidied up his affairs and said goodbye to family and friends. He reported to "Y" Depot Pier 21, Halifax, Nova Scotia, on September 12 for onward deployment to a war zone. He arrived in England on October 8. From October 9 to 26, Sergeant McGrattan was at No. 3 Personnel Reception Centre at Bournemouth.

On October 27, he was sent to RAF No. 5 Pilot Advanced Flying Unit at Calveley, located northeast of Shrewsbury. There he flew 41.40 hours on Miles Master Mk Is and IIIs on Course No. 33 until February 20, 1943. FL G. P. Hall wrote the following in his file: "Trained in Canada. Navigation satisfactory. An average pilot. Needs more practice at instrument flying. Night flying – has shown steady improvement and is now very sound. Fit to fly operational aircraft solo at night without further dual after day experience on type. A satisfactory non commissioned officer who is keen on his work."

Bernard was promoted to FS on the 28th. Two days later, he was posted to No. 55 OTU at RAF Annan, Scotland, where he flew Master Is and Canadian-built Hurricane Mk Xs.

Having requested severance from the RCAF in order to join the USAAF, McGrattan was honorably discharged in London on May 25, 1943, after having served one year and 245 days.

He earned the following Canadian decorations and medals: the Defence Medal, General Service Medal and the Canadian Volunteer Service Medal with Clasp.

At the time, the USAAF did not permit enlisted personnel to be pilots, so qualified, trained fighter pilots, like Bernard McGrattan, were immediately commissioned at the lowest possible officer rank, which was FO.

Bernard McGrattan: Two Sets of Wings

This specially created rank was used only in World War II as it enabled RCAF non-commissioned pilots to laterally move into the USAAF officer corps. McGrattan was assigned Service No. O-2044954.

After a period spent at USAAF Station No. 342 Atcham converting to the Republic P-47 Thunderbolt fighter, he joined the 335th FS 4th FG on September 18, 1943.

Throughout his brief RCAF career, McGrattan had always been known as "Mac." When he arrived at the 335th, another pilot had the same nickname. That was Major Pierce W. "Mac" McKennon who had joined the squadron several months earlier. The solution was simple – McKennon remained "Mac" and McGrattan became "Big Mac" for, at 6ft 3in tall, McGrattan was 3in taller than McKennon.

2nd Lieutenant McGrattan was promoted to 1st lieutenant in February 1944 and to captain on May 29.

List of aerial victories, all in 1944:

February 22:	Fw 190 at 1517hrs in the vicinity of Erkelenz, western Germany, while flying a P-47D Thunderbolt.
March 3:	Ju 88 at 1225hrs northeast of Magdeburg, Germany, while flying a P-51B Mustang.
March 18:	He 111 at 1350hrs northeast of Augsburg, Germany, while flying a P-51B Mustang.
April 8:	Bf 109 at 1400hrs in the vicinity of Wolfenbüttel, Germany, while flying a P-51B Mustang.
April 19:	Bf 109 and half of an Fw 190 (shared with Captain Nicholas "Cowboy" Megura) at 1030hrs, 20 miles southwest of Eschwege, Germany, while flying a P-51B Mustang.
April 24:	Fw 190 at 1415hrs in the vicinity of Knokke, Belgium, while flying a P-51B Mustang.
May 1:	Bf 109 at 1830hrs in the vicinity of Losheim am See, Germany, while flying a P-51B Mustang.
May 29:	Fw 190 at 1500hrs over Fehmarn Belt, Germany, while flying a P-51B Mustang.

On D-Day, McGrattan was flying a Mustang coded WD-D, with the serial number 42-106576, while Smith's P-51 43-7172 was coded WD-H. Harold Ross was in Mustang 42-106786, coded WD-K, and Cecil Garbey flew P-51 WD-E with serial number 43-6575.

Eyewitness statements indicate that Cecil Garbey was strafed in his parachute after successfully bailing out of his crippled warplane. Harold Ross died while trying to protect the defenseless Garbey. Ross is buried in the local cemetery at Quittebeuf and Garbey lies in the village cemetery at Bacquepuis. Walter Smith is believed to be buried in the cemetery at Graveron-Sémerville. Positive identification of his body was impossible as the post-crash fire had burned it beyond recognition.

McGrattan's Mustang came down in a field between Tournedos-Bois-Hubert and Quittebeuf. He is buried in the Tournedos-Bois-Hubert cemetery. In the burial plot right next to him lies a fellow American ace, who was also brought down on June 6, 1944. 2nd Lieutenant Evan Devon "Mac" McMinn from Pittsburgh, Pennsylvania, flew P-47 Thunderbolts with the 61st FS, 56th FG from Boxted, England.

Big Mac had flown an uneventful sortie early on the morning of June 6, attacking railroad yards and bridges at Fleury, France. When a fellow pilot was scratched due to sickness later that afternoon, he volunteered to replace him. Apparently, he was disappointed that his flight had not encountered any enemy aerial opposition earlier in the day.

Captain McGrattan's only child, Carol, was born on November 21, 1944, five-and-a-half months after his death on D-Day. In 1966, at the age of 22, she left England and headed to Australia, where she married and had three children.

For the better part of 64 years, or as she says, "a lifetime," she was unsuccessful in her attempts to locate her father's RCAF pilot training history in Canada. Several years ago, she found a second cousin via the internet living in California. He applied to Ottawa for McGrattan's war service record only to be told the building containing that information had burned down.

She had pretty much given up any hope of ever finding that material until she received an email from Big Mac's crew chief advising her the author had what she was looking for. Sy Koenig contacted the writer in 2008, after he had placed a message on the 4th FG Association web page offering to freely supply Captain McGrattan's RCAF training history to a surviving relative. Sy then contacted Carol, who, in turn, emailed the author and the information changed hands.

Sy Koenig made the USAF his career and retired in 1964 as a senior master sergeant (SMS). He said, "McGrattan was the only pilot I ever lost and, when he died, it was the blackest day of my military career." He also said, "Me and McGrattan worked well together in our respective jobs and, in fact, were very good friends." He never knew until recently that, like himself, McGrattan came up through the enlisted ranks.

The subtitle "Two Sets of Wings" comes from the little-known fact that those Americans who earned their pilot wings in Canada were entitled to wear them on their USAAF tunics. They wore their USAAF wings over their left breast pocket and their RCAF wings over their right breast pocket. Right up until the late 1970s there were several two- and three-star USAF generals spotted in the halls of the Pentagon proudly wearing two sets of wings.

Pierce McKennon
Arkansas Mustang Ace

I was flying Greenbelt Blue I and was instructed, when we met the bombers, to take the last box. We had been with them a short time when a bunch of Bf 109s came in at about 26,000 feet; we were at 23,000 feet. They started coming in on the bombers and from there on out it was a mad rat race. I saw two Bf 109s flying along line astern. They were in a diving port turn. I started after them but some yellow nose Mustangs cut me out on the last one so I went after the first 109. The fight started at about 19,000 feet and went down to 5,000 feet. Three of my bursts really tore him up; strikes all over the cockpit, engine and wing roots. I knocked a lot of stuff off him and my kite gives evidence of this. At 5,000 feet he was in a gradual dive which grew steeper till he hit the deck and blew up. He was very easy to follow going down because of the great quantity of smoke he was leaving.

Combat Report of P. W. McKennon – US Army Air Corps
Ammunition used – 465 Rounds
Date – March 29, 1944
Time – 1410 Hours
Position – Velpke, 15 miles northeast of Brunswick, Germany

There was no mistaking that Major Pierce Winningham "Mac" McKennon was a native of the state of Arkansas. He flew several fighters that carried distinctive names and artwork. His most famous and colorful mount was red-nosed P-51D Mustang 44-72308, which he named *Ridge Runner III*. Beneath the name, there was an illustration of a tusky Arkansas razorback hog chasing 20 German swastikas. These kill markings were painted black on a white square and were outlined in red. Also trimmed in red was his canopy frame, the aircraft's letters WD-A and two RAF Spitfire rear view mirrors, which were mounted side by side on top of the canopy windscreen frame.

Serving two tours over a 26-month period, Major McKennon amassed 560 combat flight hours in the ETO in World War II. He was shot down by flak on two occasions, evaded capture both times, and, after each evasion, managed to return to flight status.

Mac finished the war with 21.68 enemy aircraft destroyed (12 aerial and 9.68 ground) and became a squadron CO for the last eight months of the conflict. Not too bad for a young man who washed out of the flying training program with the USAAC. Certainly not too bad for a 21-year-old university student who came to Canada, won his wings in the RCAF, lost them in a court martial, and then, unbelievably, won them a second time!

McKennon flew with the 335th FS, 4th FG, USAAF. The 4th, known as the "Debden Eagles," flew from Station F-356 in Essex, and became the highest scoring USAAF FG in World War II, accounting for 1,016 enemy aircraft destroyed in the air and on the ground.

Pierce W. McKennon was born to Inez and Parma McKennon at Clarksville, Arkansas, on November 30, 1919. He was raised in a privileged environment and was educated in Fort Smith, where he excelled in music and sports. His mother wanted him to pursue a career as a classical concert pianist and gave him a baby grand piano on his 16th birthday. His father, a dentist, was hoping his son would join him some day in his dental practice. In his last year of high school, Pierce entered and won a tri-state music contest, which earned him a four-year music scholarship to the University of Arkansas.

The study of music, however, only lasted a month when McKennon suddenly switched his major to chemistry. He did not abandon his musical interests altogether. He just deserted Beethoven and Mozart for Goodman and Calloway as the campus swing band could not play the former.

McKennon was halfway through his fourth and final year of university when he suddenly enlisted in the air corps as a flight cadet on February 10, 1941. He was sent to Hicks Army Airfield in Fort Worth, Texas, for training, but was released from this program on April 11, after having flown a total of 29 hours (24 dual and 5 solo) on Boeing Stearman PT-17 biplane trainers. The reason given was that he suffered from severe motion sickness, which seriously impaired his ability to safely pilot an aircraft.

Undaunted by this medical setback, he traveled to No. 8 Recruiting Centre in Windsor, Ontario, where, on May 10, 1941, he enlisted in the RCAF. AC2 McKennon was assigned Service No. R. 98281. From May 10 to 23, he was at No. 1 MD in Toronto, Ontario.

As the pilot training pipeline was overflowing, McKennon was sent to perform guard duty at No. 5 Equipment Depot in Moncton, New Brunswick, on May 24. He remained there until July 1.

From July 2 to August 8, he was back in Toronto at No. 1 ITS. On his last day there he was promoted to LAC.

He began his primary flight training on Fleet Finch II biplanes on August 9 at No. 7 EFTS back in Windsor. His motion sickness problem now behind him, McKennon successfully graduated from this course on September 25. The next day he reported to No. 14 SFTS at Aylmer, Ontario, where he completed his flight training on Harvard Mk IIbs.

P. W. McKennon was promoted to SP on December 19 and was awarded his RCAF pilot wings in an indoor graduation ceremony. The average time it took to train an air force pilot, from intake to wings parade, was 10–12 months. Mac was a natural flyer and breezed through the entire training syllabus in just over five months.

During his time at Aylmer, McKennon ran afoul of RCAF discipline on three separate occasions when it was found that he had been AWL. For each infraction he was fined several days' pay.

From December 20, 1941, to January 4, 1942, SP McKennon was given the standard two-week pre-embarkation leave, which he used to visit his family and friends in Fort Smith.

On January 8, he set sail on a troop ship from "Y" Depot Halifax, Nova Scotia, and arrived in England on the 21st.

He was at No. 3 Personnel Reception Centre at Bournemouth until March 16. The next day, he reported to No. 5 Pilot Advanced Flying Unit at RAF Ternhill. There he began his fighter conversion training on Miles Master Is, IIIs and Hawker Hurricanes, finishing the course on April 20.

On the 21st, he reported to No. 61 OTU at RAF Rednal in Shropshire, where he learned to fly the Supermarine Spitfire. Exactly a month later, while on a local flight, Mac decided to pay a visit to Ternhill, where he proceeded to perform unauthorized low-level beat-ups and aerobatics. When he landed back at Rednal, he was immediately arrested and placed in the lock-up for the next three days.

An RCAF Court Martial convened at Rednal on June 23, 1942, resulting in P. W. McKennon being found guilty of the specified charge of Conduct To The Prejudice Of Good Order and Air Force Discipline. He was sentenced to be reduced to the rank of LAC and was stripped of his wings.

For reasons only known to the RCAF, it decided to give Mac a second chance. It kept him at Rednal and allowed him to re-muster as a general duties pilot where his flying was closely monitored for the next four months. On October 14, he was retested, won back his wings, and was promoted once again to SP.

In anticipation of joining the USAAF, Mac applied for and was granted an honorable discharge from the RCAF in London on November 23, 1942, after having served one year and 198 days.

The recommendations from No. 61 OTU on his discharge form stated the following:

> Conduct – Satisfactory;
> Character – Very Good;
> Qualifications – Pilot is above average. He is very keen to be operational and should make an excellent fighter pilot.

4th FG ace Major Pierce W. McKennon sits in his NAA P-51D Mustang while conversing with his crew chief, Staff Sergeant Joe Sills. (US Department of Defense)

P. W. McKennon joined the USAAF as a 2nd lieutenant two days later. He spent the next three months at F-342 Atcham in Shropshire where he flew Supermarine Spitfire VBs, Master IIIs and Republic P-47C and D Thunderbolts.

Pierce joined the 4th FG on February 22, 1943. After three attempts and almost two years of training he finally became the only thing he truly wanted to be – a fighter pilot!

Perhaps one of the reasons the RCAF reinstated McKennon's flight status was because of his exceptional piloting abilities, which were prevalent throughout his training and were later displayed with the 4th.

The following comments were recorded in the 4th operational diary:

> February 9, 1944 – Some local flying was done this afternoon involving a P-51 Mustang. Lieutenant McKennon has been delegated to fly it conducting certain experiments. McKennon handled the aircraft well and it was a pleasure to see him flit through the sky and beat up the field. Whenever the noise of the P-51 was heard, all the pilots would dash outside to see what was going on.

> February 10, 1944 – McKennon again flew the Mustang. It is learned that he is testing certain apparatus and instruments under the direction of the Medical Corps [MC]. It is a treat to see "Mac" tearing about in this P-51.

Pierce McKennon: Arkansas Mustang Ace

In an FG that was filled with larger-than-life personalities and characters, Pierce W. "Mac" McKennon stood out. He was a showman who had an acute sense of mimicry and a gift for slapstick. At the piano, he was the group's one-man morale section. The late Captain Robert H. "Bob" Wehrman of Old Greenwich, Connecticut, explained:

> Mac had the greatest method of dealing with pre-mission jitters not just for himself but for everybody. You could always tell who was set for a mission that day – they got fresh eggs and bacon. A lot of us would be so worried or scared we could not eat. Not Mac, he ate like a horse, and he would eat yours if you were going to leave it. When he was through, he would walk over to the piano in the corner of the mess, turn and look at each of us and say, "for those of you who are about to die," then he would sit down and play "The Old Rugged Cross" all the way through. When he was finished, he would launch into the most outrageous boogie-woogie version of that tune that you ever heard, and he never played it the same way twice! You could not sit there in a funk while this was going on. When he was through, everybody was raring to go. Mac loved boogie-woogie more than anything and I watched him countless times play "Tiger Rag" on the piano in the Officers' Club with a full pint of "bitters" clenched between his teeth. He would drain the glass, never spilling a drop and he never missed a note!

The first time Mac was shot down by flak was August 28, 1944, while strafing trains near Niederbronn-les-Bains, France, 20 miles behind the frontlines. He evaded the Germans, hooked up with the French Maquis, which hid him, and returned to Debden on September 24.

The second time was much more dramatic and occurred on March 18, 1945. Mac was leading 24 Mustangs on a penetration target withdrawal support mission to Berlin. Flying over Prenzlau airdrome they found it full of German aircraft, which had been pulled back from the front. Mac flew low to test for flak and several bursts smacked into his P-51. His oil pressure needle dropped to zero and he bailed out five miles west of the airdrome, landing in a small field. The orbiting Mustangs watched as German troops and trucks started to head toward their leader's landing site. Lieutenant George D. Green, from Whittier, California, flying a P-51D named *Suzon*, announced to the others that he was going to land and pick up Mac and they were to cover him. This was a no-no and went against standing orders. As Green touched down, McKennon took off running across the meadow to meet him. While taxiing, Green took the opportunity to shuck off and throw out all of his flying gear to make room in the single-seat fighter. McKennon, the taller of the two at 6ft, sat on the seat and Green sat on his lap. The Mustang's takeoff speed is normally 150mph and it usually used 800 to 900 yards to get airborne from Debden's concrete runways. McKennon and Green had a little more than 300 yards before they hit a tree line and this grassed makeshift runway was quite bumpy.

Committed to this daring rescue/escape and running out of room, they hauled the Mustang sluggishly off at 80mph. "Pull your wheels up," one of the pilots cried from above. The wheels came up and the wallowing P-51 ever so slowly started to climb. The pent-up jabber of the pilots who had watched the dramatic rescue in goose flesh suspense suddenly burst forth: "God damn, he made it." "Inky" Davis said, "I've sure as hell seen everything now." Green gasped, "God we're going to get home." The return trip of 600 miles took two hours and 35 minutes, with the pilots having to share the same oxygen mask part of the way as Mac had lost his when he bailed. At the debriefing back at Debden, Major McKennon calmly suggested to Colonel Trippet that Lieutenant Green be made a General at once. Green's rescue of McKennon was probably one of the shortest fighter pilot evades of World War II.

Less than a month later, a third encounter with flak nearly proved deadly. While strafing parked aircraft on April 16, 1945, at Gablingen airdrome in Germany, an airfield gunner put an explosive 13mm round through the top of McKennon's canopy. Despite being wounded on the right side of his head, face, and neck and bleeding profusely, Mac managed to land at a forward operating location where they picked the shrapnel from his wounds and bandaged him up. He was advised not to fly back to Debden, but he ignored the advice and flew home. That would be his last combat mission, as he was medically grounded until his wounds healed. Three weeks later, on May 8, 1945, Germany unconditionally surrendered, and the European war was over.

Major McKennon stayed with the 4th until the last of its personnel arrived stateside aboard the RMS *Queen Mary* in New York on November 9, 1945. The next day, the 4th was inactivated at Camp Kilmer, New Jersey. Major McKinnon applied for and was granted a permanent commission in the peacetime air force, retaining his wartime rank.

He was married on May 13, 1946, and became an instructor pilot at Randolph AFB, near San Antonio, Texas.

At 1150hrs on June 18, 1947, Pierce Winningham "Mac" McKennon was killed in the crash of an AT-6D Texan five miles northeast of Randolph Field. Also killed was his student, a navigator who was training to be a pilot. The accident investigation board concluded that, as part of the student's training, Mac had chopped the engine power simulating an inflight emergency. In the attempted recovery, the aircraft was badly mishandled resulting in the fatal accident. Twenty-seven-year-old Major McKennon left behind a 21-year-old widow, "Bootsie," who was two months pregnant.

His son, Pierce Junior, was born in January 1948.

If you ever read up or do any research on the 4th, you will find that Mac McKennon's name always surfaces and, if you happen to speak with a veteran who served with that famous FG, chances are that before the conversation is over they will have told you their favorite story of that "Boogie Woogie" piano-playing Mustang ace from Fort Smith, Arkansas.

Evan McMinn
Pennsylvania Thunderbolt Ace

Evan Devon McMinn was born to Winona Johnson and William Thomas McMinn in Akron, Ohio, on April 25, 1919. Evan's parents were originally from Kirkland, Texas, and relocated to Ohio in 1918 after his father, an unemployed rubber worker, secured steady employment at the Goodyear Tire & Rubber Company. When Evan was 12, the family moved to 200 South Fairmount Street in Pittsburgh, Pennsylvania.

McMinn was educated at Gladstone Junior Technical and Connelly Vocational high schools in Pittsburgh, graduating in 1938. He worked as a parts clerk for the next three years at local automobile dealerships. His hobbies were flying and model aircraft building. Another of his interests was the tearing down and rebuilding of internal combustion engines.

With 44 hours of flight time recorded in his logbook, the 22-year-old private pilot headed off to Canada on Tuesday, October 28, 1941, to join the RCAF. He voluntarily enlisted for the duration of the war at No. 10 Recruiting Centre in Hamilton, Ontario. McMinn began his career as an AC2 under Regimental Service No. R. 139067.

FO C. C. Conover, who interviewed him, recorded the following in his file: "A good type of US lad. Keen to fly and should do well in training. Nice appearance, clean cut. Best suited for pilot or observer."

AC2 McMinn was sent for basic training to No. 2 MD at Brandon, Manitoba. He was posted to No. 3 ITS at Victoriaville, Quebec, from March 16 until May 8, 1942. The school's commander said of him: "A straight forward, alert, aggressive, determined individual." Promoted on May 8 to LAC, McMinn soloed after only 6 hours and 55 minutes of dual flight instruction on Fleet Finch II biplanes on Course No. 56 at No. 11 EFTS at Cap-de-la-Madeleine, Quebec.

Leaving this school on August 1, after having accumulated 81 hours flying time on Finches, McMinn was sent to complete his training to wings standard on the 5,300lb, 550shp Harvard Mk IIbs at No. 13 SFTS at Saint-Hubert, Quebec.

There he flew 196.70 hours on the high-performance trainers, graduating as a SP on November 20, 1942. He traveled by rail on December 5 to No. 1 Port Transit Unit "Y" Depot, Halifax, Nova Scotia, in preparation for shipping overseas. McMinn left Canada from Pier 21 three days later and arrived in England on December 18.

56th FG ace 2nd Lieutenant Evan D. McMinn flew P-47 Thunderbolts similar to these factory fresh models pictured on this Republic Aviation production line. (US Department of Defense)

Bournemouth was used extensively in World War II as No. 3 Personnel Reception Centre. This is where all RCAF overseas airmen were processed. It was a great place for them to become acclimated to England and its customs before setting out to war. McMinn, unfortunately, endured a four-month long wait there before he was able to get on a course.

Assigned to No. 17 Pilot Advanced Flying Unit at RAF Calveley, Evan flew Miles Masters and Hawker Hurricanes from April 13 to May 24, 1943. While there, he was promoted to FS. On May 25, he reported to No. 61 OTU at RAF Rednal, where he flew Spitfires and Masters until August 12.

One year and 293 days after entering the RCAF, 24-year-old Evan D. McMinn honorably separated from that service on August 16, 1943, in London.

He joined the USAAF the next week as an FO under Service No. 0-886834. For the next three months, he was at the CCRC at Station F-342, Atcham. Located in Shropshire, five miles southeast of Shrewsbury, Atcham trained both 8th and 9th Air Force fighter pilots from June 15, 1942, to March 31, 1945. McMinn converted to American aircraft and flying procedures, flying Piper Cubs, Supermarine Spitfire Vbs, Miles Master IIIs, and Republic P-47C and D Thunderbolts. Later in the war, it was renamed the 495th Fighter Training Group.

Evan McMinn: Pennsylvania Thunderbolt Ace

McMinn was posted at the end of November 1943 to the 61st FS, 56th FG located at F-150 Boxted in Essex.

Led by the legendary Colonel Hubert A. "Hub" Zemke, the 56th was known far and wide as "Zemke's Wolfpack." An audit at the end of December 1943 revealed that Evan had accumulated, to that point, a total of 516.2 military flying hours.

McMinn was treated for minor injuries on January 1, 1944, after writing off P-47D Thunderbolt 42-8458 coded HV-F in a take-off accident.

Evan opened his aerial scoring at 1515hrs on February 21, 1944, when he downed a Bf 109 over the Zuiderzee. Herein is his combat report:

> I was flying as Halsted Blue 2 in B section on a withdrawal support mission on February 21, 1944 when we engaged three Messerschmitt 109s over the Zuiderzee at 23,000 feet. We climbed and turned with them until we reached 27,000 feet, at which time I saw two more 109s, one of which was on my tail firing at me. I tightened my turn and threw him wide. I came right on around to see him on Lieutenant Mussey's tail firing at him. I gave the enemy a short burst with about thirty degrees of deflection and saw strikes around the cockpit. He flicked over to the right and I followed, closing and firing the whole time. Smoking badly, he went spinning on down and I followed, firing continuously. He started to tumble end over end, so I broke off at 12,000 feet as I nearly collided with him. I could see flames around the cockpit and smoke pouring out. I climbed back up and saw two more 109s that joined the fight. As we were getting low on gas we decided to leave the area. I confirm one Bf 109 for Lieutenant Klibbe and claim one Bf 109 for myself. For confirmation of my claim see the reports of Lieutenants F. W. Klibbe and N. E. Brooks.

Evan's mount that day, a P-47D coded HV-D, used 375 rounds of .50 caliber Armor Piercing Incendiary (API) in the encounter.

The next day McMinn, in Thunderbolt HV-D, destroyed a Focke Wulf Fw 190 at 1310hrs over Lippstadt, Germany. He reported:

> I was a spare for Keyworth squadron and filled in when White 3 aborted. We met up with the bombers just as twelve Fw 190s were beginning their second attack. Red flight was fully engaged when we arrived. I saw two enemy aircraft positioning themselves for an attack on two P-47s, so I went after them. I fired on one using thirty degrees of deflection at a distance of two hundred and fifty yards. He peeled off and went straight down. I followed him from 25,000 to 9,000 feet, closed to fifty yards and fired whenever I got a good bead on him. We were going straight down, and as I hit him, pieces of his aircraft flew off hitting and shattering my windscreen, which in turn broke my sunglasses! My wingman, Captain Bowlin, saw the pilot bail out and I saw the ship hit the ground and blow up. I lost my

wingman when I pulled out of my dive. I came home alone. I claim one Fw 190 destroyed. Ammunition used 751 rounds of .50 caliber API.

On March 15 at 1050hrs, Evan, in HV-L, damaged a Bf 109 northeast of Dümmer Lake, Germany. The next day, at 1045hrs in P-47D HV-C, McMinn bested in combat Fw 190A-6 "Black 2" flown by Unteroffizier Albrecht von Fehr from 6./JG 26. Evan recounted:

> I was flying as Halstead White 2 north of Saint-Dizier, France when over thirty Fw 190s came into attack the bombers. I followed Lieutenant Colonel "Gabby" Gabreski down to 4,000 feet where he attacked two enemy fighters. One blew up in mid-air and the other caught fire after the pilot bailed out. We then dove through the overcast after some others. I had a difficult time staying with the Colonel as I could not release my belly tank. We were attacked by a 190 under the cloud deck and as I could not turn as tightly as the Colonel, I subsequently lost both of them. I pulled back up through the overcast and closed on a 190 pilot, firing at him from one hundred and fifty yards down to fifty yards. I saw hits all over the enemy aircraft and it burst into flames. I followed him back down through the overcast, and saw him crash and blow up. I did not see any parachute. Three 190s then started to chase me, so I pulled back up into the clouds, and set a course on instruments for home. They followed me for over sixty miles, shooting at me whenever I came out of the cloud cover. Short on fuel, they eventually gave up. I confirm two 190s destroyed by Colonel Gabreski and claim one for myself. Ammunition used 229 rounds of .50 caliber API.

Victories number four and five, which elevated McMinn to ace status, occurred at 1215hrs on May 22, 1944, near Rotenberg, Germany. In P-47D HV-Y, Evan shot down two Fw-190s and claimed a third as damaged. His combat report records:

> I was flying as Whippet Yellow Leader in Colonel Gabreski's squadron. At 22,000 feet over Rotenberg, the Colonel told me to take my flight down and shoot up a train that was moving west to east through the town. By the time I got down, it had passed through the community. I observed that it was only a locomotive with no cars attached. I opened fire and observed hits all over the target, which then stopped moving. Passing over the busted engine, I looked over to my left and saw fifteen Fw 190s taking off from Hopenhofer airfield. I pulled up and turned left in order to get on their tails, but there was so much flak coming up at me from the airfield defenses that I decided against it. I called the squadron and advised them to stay away from the airfield gunners. I lost sight of the fifteen that had taken off as they stayed low to the ground.
> Several additional 190s started rolling for take off, so I swung around the airdrome just outside the range of the flak guns. I then spotted the first group of fifteen forming

up southeast of the field at 3,500 feet. I called Colonel Gabreski and told him to come on down. I busted through the enemy formation damaging a 190 just as the Colonel arrived. I tried to get in behind one of the other Focke-Wulfs, but due to my excess speed, the German out turned me. I told my element leader, Lieutenant Neyland, to get him and he did! I then slid onto the tail of an Fw 190 that was firing at a P-47. I fired and he started to pour out a large volume of smoke. The pilot rolled his aircraft over and bailed out. I latched onto another 190 who was chasing a Thunderbolt. I opened fire, saw many strikes and the enemy aircraft burst into flames, going straight into the ground. I was looking for another target and spotted a 190 on my tail. I broke hard left, but not before he hit me with several 20mm cannon rounds which set my wing on fire. I was thinking of bailing out, but then decided I might be able to put out the flames. I broke away from the fight and climbed as fast as I could for altitude. I looked back and saw my wingman, 2nd Lieutenant J. J. Clark clobber a 190. Smoking badly the aircraft rolled over and the pilot bailed out. My wingman then joined up with me and, along with Flight Lieutenant Lanowski, we came out together. My wing was still smoking when we reached the Zuiderzee. Altogether, I saw at least ten fires burning on the ground in the Rotenberg area. I confirm one Fw 190 for Lieutenant Clark and claim two Fw 190s destroyed and one damaged for myself. Ammunition used 1354 rounds of .50 caliber API.

On June 1, Evan was promoted to 2nd lieutenant. Between February 21 and May 22, 1944, he had destroyed a total of seven German aircraft – five in the air and two on the ground.

In support of the Allied invasion of Normandy, on Tuesday June 6, 1944, the 56th flew a total of eight fighter-bomber roundtrip missions from England to France beginning at 0336hrs. Allied air losses for the day amounted to 132 aircraft – 55 fighters, 11 medium bombers, 41 troop carriers, and 25 heavy bombers. Included in the total number of fighters lost were five "Wolfpack" Thunderbolts that failed to return to Boxted. Of these five, all but one was downed by flak.

2nd Lieutenant E. D. McMinn went missing on the first mission of the day in P-47D-22 RE Thunderbolt 42-25963. It was later determined that he was shot down and killed some six miles northeast of Bernay, France, by intense ground fire while strafing a truck convoy.

On July 18, 1950, Major General Edward F. Witsell, the Adjutant General of the United States Army, forwarded to Mrs. Winona McMinn at 908 Lilac Street, Pittsburgh 17, Pennsylvania, an official statement of death relative to her missing son. The document stated that 2nd Lieutenant Evan D. McMinn, Service No. 0-886834, was killed in the line of duty in France on June 6, 1944.

Evan McMinn was awarded a Silver Star, three American DFCs and four Air Medals.

Michael McPharlin
Three Uniforms, One War

The Allied air forces flew a staggering 14,700 sorties on Tuesday, June 6, 1944, in support of the Normandy invasion. This impressive number of air movements encompassed all categories of aircraft. In some cases, patrols were flown upwards of 100 miles away from the five American, British, and Canadian beachheads, codenamed Omaha, Utah, Gold, Sword, and Juno. The German Luftwaffe, in the face of this overwhelming aerial onslaught, managed to fly only 319 sorties. Allied air losses on D-Day amounted to 132 aircraft (55 fighters, 11 medium bombers, 41 troop carriers and 25 heavy bombers). German losses were pegged at 22 (18 fighters and 4 medium bombers).

Of the 55 Allied fighters lost, 20 were P-51 Mustangs and, of this number, ten belonged to the USAAF 4th FG.

Operating from Station F-356 Debden, the 4th's three FSs – 334th, 335th, and 336th – flew a total of six missions to and from France that day, beginning at 0320hrs and ending at 2340hrs.

Seven of ten losses the group sustained occurred on the last sortie of the day. One of those 4th pilots killed was Major Michael George Hurschell "Wee Mac" McPharlin. Major McPharlin had obtained permission to tag along on the 4th's final D-Day mission with his ex-RCAF and RAF buddies. As a former RAF No. 71 Eagle Squadron member, Michael flew as often as he could with his old friends.

Wee Mac was the operations officer with the 339th FG based at Fowlmere, Cambridgeshire. Michael flew his 505th FS P-51B 42-106909 coded 6N-Z named *Wee Ginny* over to Debden late in the afternoon on June 6. McPharlin was assigned to fly as part of White section with the 334th under the command of Major "Mike" Sobanski. It was the 334th's 198th operational sortie of the war and its 67th using Mustangs.

Part way into the mission, a local controller overheard McPharlin tell Sobanski that he was aborting as his left engine magneto was out and his motor was running rough. He knew he could never make it back across the English Channel with a malfunctioning engine and was headed in the direction of the Allied lines where he would either crash land or bail out.

Michael McPharlin: Three Uniforms, One War

Nursing *Wee Ginny* along at 2,400ft on half engine power just below the cloud base, his luck ran out when he was intercepted by one of the "Abbeville Kids." Oberleutnant Franz Kunz, Staffel Kapitan of 2./JG 26, flying an Fw 190A-8, shot Wee Mac's Mustang out of the sky at 2055hrs northeast of Evreux.

Just hours earlier, JG 26 Geschwaderkommodore Josef "Pips" Priller had ordered Kunz to move his Staffel from Creil to Guyancourt.

Michael's crash site was confirmed the next day at 1100hrs on Wednesday, June 7, by the following written entry in the village of Reuilly communal register: "Major Michael McPharlin, US Army Air Corps, Service No. 0-885107, pilot, crashed at 8:55 P. M. on 6 June 1944, at the location called 'Les Champs Malades.' Recorded by Eloi Lebreton, town hall Secretary and Raoul Francois Vautier, Deputy Mayor."

One minute after McPharlin died, Captain Bernard L. "Big Mac" McGrattan, another ex-RCAF alumnus also flying with the 4th, was shot down and killed in the same area. The crash sites of both Mustangs lie within two miles of each other.

Michael McPharlin was born on June 16, 1913, in Blue Island, Illinois. His mother, Marie Mildred O'Neal, came from the Grand Rapids, Michigan, area and his father, George, a retired US Army captain, hailed from Hastings, Michigan. McPharlin was a small child and acquired the nickname "Wee Michael" early on. He attended Hastings High School from which he graduated in 1930. The years 1931–32 were spent at Bowdoin College in Brunswick, Maine, taking pre-med courses. In 1932–35, he studied organic chemistry at the University of Wisconsin in Madison. In 1935, he was awarded a one-year research scholarship studying histology at the University of Heidelberg in Heidelberg, Germany. Michael returned to Duke University as a medical student for the academic year 1936–37. It was at this point, and after having completed six years of an eight-year medical program, Michael had to leave school as he had run out of money. While pursuing his goal of acquiring a higher education, Wee Michael worked at a multitude of occupations – sailor, maritime quartermaster, gold miner, food chemist, surveyor, steeple jack rigger, and even as an extra in the 1931 movie *Cimarron*.

On August 31, 1937, Robinson C. Watters of Cambridge, Maryland, wrote the following letter of recommendation on Michael's behalf to the Adjutant General of the War Department in Washington:

> Mr. Michael G. H. McPharlin of Cambridge, Maryland who is anxious to enter the Aviation Cadet Corps, has asked me to recommend him for your consideration to which I do not hesitate to comply. This bright and ambitious young man is at present employed by the nationally known Philips Packing Company in a technical or scientific capacity and therefore is not one of the menial workers. Primarily he attended the famous Heidelberg University in Germany, but completed his education at Duke University at Durham, North Carolina. Regarding his character and personal habits, no adverse comments have been brought to my attention. As

one of his sponsors, may it be stated that I have retired from business activities in Baltimore and this letter is therefore written where I am well known in my old home town. I have the honor, Sir, to be Respectfully R. C. Watters.

This letter along with several others, including one from Mr. Stuart Rose, the associate editor of the *Saturday Evening Post*, was sufficient to get Michael a USAAC interview. He was turned down by the army for pilot training as he was one quarter inch shy of their minimum height requirement of 5ft 6in.

Michael determined the US Navy and Marines had similar height minimums so he did not bother to approach either service as their answer would have been the same.

In October 1939, while living at 486 West Stafford Street in Germantown, Pennsylvania, Wee Mac began corresponding with the RCAF in Ottawa, Ontario. To his delight and surprise, he was one of several candidates chosen for direct

Major Michael G. McPharlin stands beside his 339th FG NAA P-51B Mustang *Wee Ginny* at Fowlmere, England, in May 1944. (US Department of Defense)

entry into the Canadian Air Force's PPO training program. To facilitate the process, Michael moved to 10 Plymouth Street in Ottawa in November.

McPharlin's medical report completed by a captain in the Royal Canadian Army Medical Corps revealed the following information: "Age twenty-six, weight one hundred and twenty-two pounds, height five feet five and three quarter inches. Intelligent, well educated and co-operative, underweight thirteen pounds, but well built and firmly muscled with good athletic history and satisfactory responses."

His interview report, dated December 4, 1939, contained the following write-up and recommendation by FO W. S. Lighthall: "Officer calibre. Courteous, gentlemanly, ambitious and determined to succeed. This man has fought his way up against great obstacles and succeeded. Very well educated and experienced for his years. Would make an excellent pilot. Trained to study. Easy to teach. Strongly recommended as navigation officer."

Michael G. H. McPharlin was appointed and commissioned a PO in the RCAF Special Reserve effective January 2, 1940, under Service No. C. 1530.

Before the OC of Uplands Air Station in Ottawa on January 19, Wee Mac signed and swore an oath of allegiance to His Majesty King George the VI of England. It is assumed that Michael was unaware of the fact that by partaking in this swearing-in ceremony, he would cease to be a citizen of the United States.

Over the next five months, Michael trained at air stations at Ottawa, Trenton, and Borden. He also spent several weeks in Toronto, Ontario, at No. 1 ITS. It was in that city where he met his future wife, Miss Virginia Bertram, who lived at 232 Lomsmount Drive. Michael would always refer to her as "Wee Ginny."

McPharlin retired from the RCAF on July 17, 1940, after serving only 198 days. He had been the first American to be commissioned in its service in World War II.

GC A. T. N. Cowley, at Air Station Camp Borden, sent the following letter on June 28, 1940, to the AOC No. 1 Training Command Headquarters in Toronto.

> PO M. J. H. McPharlin who is undergoing intermediate training on Course 5, was reported to the OC Intermediate Training Squadron as having made slow progress prior to his first solo. He was tested by the Group Commander and, though not good, was considered safe and sent solo. His chief trouble at that time seemed to be lack of confidence. It was hoped that if he flew a heavier aircraft it would eliminate this fault.
>
> Shortly following his first solo he made a crash landing in Avro Anson No. 6005 at Gravenhurst, Ontario. His training has been continued since that time until a further report by his new instructor indicated that his flying progress was very slow and that he still lacked considerable confidence. He was then tested by his Flight Commander who agreed with his instructor that McPharlin's training should be discontinued.
>
> Finally he was again tested by the Group Commander and was found not only to lack confidence but that his general flying for the period of training he

has undergone was far too low a standard to justify any further consideration. It is therefore considered in the best interests of the service and the pilot himself that his flying training be discontinued and that he be returned to his home as he is unsuitable for further training due to a lack of flying aptitude. He does not wish to serve in any other capacity in the RCAF.

Michael had learned to speak German fairly well while attending Heidelberg University. When he washed out of flight school, the RCAF requested that he be examined by a German language expert with the view of possibly employing him in a counter-intelligence role. FL H. O. McDonald from No. 1 Training Command Headquarters tested McPharlin's oral capabilities in this regard with the following observations:

> In connection with an oral test and conversation, it was found PO McPharlin's ability was better than average. He is quite capable of understanding every day conversational German spoken at an ordinary conversational rate of speed and of phrasing reasonably fluent replies in the German language. It appeared to the writer that this officer had gained his knowledge of the German language by ear and this impression was subsequently confirmed by McPharlin. The deficiencies in grammar which are usually associated with this method of learning the language were apparent in the officer's conversation, but it is felt that a comparatively short period of study would be required to overcome most of this deficiency. It is the writer's opinion that PO McPharlin would be capable of carrying on a conversation in the German language and of subsequently rendering an accurate digest of it in English.

Wee Mac declined the RCAF's alternate offer of employment and returned to his Germantown residence.

His fighter pilot dream unfulfilled, the ever-persistent McPharlin next entered into correspondence with the RAF through the air attaché's office at the British Embassy in Ottawa. The first order of business, at least for the RAF, was to determine if McPharlin could fly, for he had told them that he could. In November 1940, he was sent to take an air test on a dual-controlled Fairey Battle trainer at No. 31 SFTS at Kingston, Ontario. No. 31, which had opened on October 7, was one of several RAF schools operating in Canada under the BCATP. Although staffed by RAF personnel, these air stations were wholly administered by the RCAF. In mid-1943, all remaining RAF training establishments were absorbed into the Canadian air force training system, resulting in the RAF staff being returned to England for reassignment. Michael passed his flight examination with flying colors.

He left Canada on December 10 as a newly commissioned PO, Service No. 89764, in the RAF Volunteer Reserve. His troop ship arrived dockside in

Glasgow, Scotland, on December 21. McPharlin undertook advanced training at RAF Sywell and Ternhill and was awarded his pilot's wings on May 9, 1941.

He joined RAF No. 71 Eagle Squadron in June, where he flew Hawker Hurricane Mk IIs, then Supermarine Spitfire Mk IIas and later the Vb variant. Wee Michael became fast friends with fellow American Oscar Hoffman Coen DFC from Walum, North Dakota. Oscar, a man of small stature like Michael, had been with the squadron since April 14, 1941. Before the war he had been a schoolteacher.

In October, Michael was seconded to RCAF No. 403 "Wolf" FS for six months, flying Spitfire Vbs. He returned to No. 71 in the spring of 1942.

On April 27 of that year, Michael teamed with Coen to destroy three Fw 190s over St. Omer, France, in just ten minutes.

According to his squadron mates, Michael, who was aggressive in combat, would utilize his fluency in German to taunt Luftwaffe pilots over their radio frequencies. He would fire off a steady flow of derogatory remarks, followed by an invitation to, "get off your fat asses and come up and fight."

McPharlin would go on to achieve ace status with five aerial and one ground kill. Flying air cover over the ill-fated Dieppe, France, raid on August 19, 1942, Michael went missing, but not before he had teamed up again with Coen to destroy a Ju 88 bomber.

Of the 6,086 infantrymen (most of which were Canadians) who made it ashore at Dieppe that day, 3,623 were either killed, wounded or captured. This military catastrophe strongly influenced Allied planning for the D-Day assault, which came almost two years later.

The Air Ministry's casualty branch in Whitehall sent a telegram on August 20 to the CAS's office in Ottawa advising that Michael McPharlin was missing on operations. The telegram requested that his mother, Mrs. Marie Miller in Hastings, Michigan, be notified along with his fiancée, Miss Virginia Bertram in Toronto. This was followed by another telegram two days later stating McPharlin had been located at Portsmouth, England, and was uninjured.

Just off the French coast, Wee Mac's Spitfire was attacked by a Fw 190 that shot up his plane, which rendered the aircraft's compass useless. Michael flew into a nearby cloud to lose his pursuer and when he emerged several minutes later, the enemy was gone. It took Michael a few minutes to figure out which way was home. He was halfway across the English Channel when he noticed his aircraft was desperately low on fuel. With the English coast in sight, he ran out of gas and bailed out. He inflated his life raft, climbed in and began paddling toward shore. Cold, wet, and exhausted, he eventually fell asleep. His raft was spotted by a lighthouse keeper who called out the air-sea rescue service. Hauled aboard the rescue launch, Michael's chills were chased away after they gave him a large water glass full of dark Navy rum!

When the three RAF Eagle squadrons, 71, 121 and 133, were incorporated into the USAAF at Debden on September 29, 1942, as the 4th FG, McPharlin and several other officers elected to return to the States as qualified combat instructors and advisers. Among them were Majors William James "Jim" Daley DFC, and Carroll Warren "Red" McColpin DFC.

Returning home in November, Michael married Virginia in December. The pair immediately set up housekeeping at DeRidder Army Air Base in DeRidder, Louisiana. They had one child, a daughter, who was born in 1943.

Captain McPharlin instructed on Army A-24B Banshee dive-bombers at DeRidder until July 1943, when the 339th Bomb Group converted to Bell P-39 Airacobras and became the 339th Fighter Bomber Group. The unit moved to England in March/April 1944 and were known as "The Lads From Fowlmere." Prior to flying its first operation on April 30, a further conversion to the P-51 Mustang occurred, resulting in the group being re-designated the 339th FG.

Major McPharlin was one week shy of his 31st birthday when he was killed. He is buried at Plot E, Row 1, Grave 43, in the Normandy American Cemetery at Colleville-sur-Mer, France. This hallowed 173-acre memorial, containing the remains of 9,387 American service personnel, is appropriately located atop a bluff overlooking Omaha Beach.

At the end of the war, Coen, then a full colonel, paid a courtesy call on Wee Ginny and her daughter out of respect for his very good friend. Virginia and Oscar's friendship blossomed over time, and they eventually married. Oscar formally adopted Wee Mac's daughter and raised her as his own child.

Michael McPharlin would have approved.

Nicholas Megura
Connecticut Mustang Ace

Another American-born, RCAF-trained fighter pilot who attained ace status while flying with the 4th FG, USAAF in 1943–44, was Captain Nicholas "Cowboy" Megura. Cowboy was one of Colonel Don Blakeslee's famous "Horsemen" who flew from Station F-356 Debden in Essex, England. Debden's airfield identifying letters were DB.

According to Blakeslee's rival, Colonel Hubert "Hub" Zemke, the commander of the 56th FG over at Boxted, the initials DB did not stand for Debden; they stood for Don Blakeslee.

Debden was a prewar-built RAF air station that opened on April 22, 1937. In 1940, its original grass landing fields were replaced with two concrete runways – 10/28 running east to west measuring 4,800ft x 150ft and 17/35 running north to south measuring 3,900ft x 150ft. The airfield was taken over by the 4th FG in September 1942 and was returned to RAF control in September 1945. Today, this historic airfield is a British Army barracks.

Nicholas Megura was born to Russian–American parents Alexander Megura and Anastasia Bashura in Ansonia, Connecticut, on July 28, 1920. The family lived at 108 Broad Street. Nicholas attended Grove Public School from 1925 to 1934, then Ansonia High School from 1934 to 1938. His sports interests were baseball and football. In 1939, he began taking night school courses at Central High School in Bridgeport, while, at the same time, holding down a full-time job as a machinist with the Remington Arms Company. From September 1940 to April 1941, Megura was employed as a sheet metal worker at the Vought-Sikorsky Aircraft plant in Stratford, Connecticut. From April to September 1941, he worked as a machinist at the Bullard Company in Bridgeport.

Megura's ambition was to join the war effort, but only as a pilot. This is not surprising seeing that he worked in the munitions and aircraft industry. However, he lacked the required two years of college necessary to enter any of the existing flight cadet programs of the US armed services.

He realized his one and only opportunity to become an air force pilot rested solely in Canada through the BCATP.

During World War II, the RCAF had recruiting offices spread across Canada in 17 major cities. On September 18, 1941, Megura traveled the short distance from Connecticut to Montreal, Quebec, where he voluntarily enlisted in Canada's air force at No. 13 Recruiting Centre as an AC2 under Regimental Service No. R. 132625. On his application, he gave a home address of 225 Helen Street in Bridgeport. While waiting for his paperwork to be processed, he was provided with a room in Montreal's St. Louis Hotel. One of the documents Nicholas signed was a declaration stating that he agreed to serve on active service anywhere in Canada and beyond Canada's borders. He agreed to stay in the RCAF for the duration of the war and possibly for a period of up to one year during demobilization should His Majesty King George VI, the King of England, require his services.

In 1941, there were three MDs in the BCATP – No. 1 Toronto, Ontario, No. 2 Brandon, Manitoba, and No. 3 Edmonton, Alberta. The next year, two more were added – No. 4 Quebec City, Quebec, and No. 5 Lachine, Quebec.

F. J. Hatch, in his excellent 1983 book *Aerodrome of Democracy*, describes life at a MD, where a new recruit spent a strenuous five to six weeks:

> When not being interviewed, tested or lectured to, the would be airman spent long hours drilling on the parade square. He learned how to march, how to salute and how to bring his eyeballs around with a click. He became the proud possessor of boots, tunic, fatigue pants, cap, shirts, underwear, socks and all the odds and ends which comprised the equipment of the airman in embryo. He learned that boots must be kept well shined, buttons polished, face clean shaven at peril of his liberty. He slept upper or lower bunk according to his liking. He received the princely salary of $1.30 a day. By the end of his recruit training, the young man was ready to move a step higher.

Megura was sent by train on September 20 to No. 1 MD, where he remained until October 27. The next day, he was standing guard duty at RCAF No. 4 Bombing & Gunnery School at Fingal, Ontario. With no training slot open to him, the air force sent Nicholas, on November 24, to No. 1 SFTS located at Camp Borden, Ontario, located near the city of Barrie. Once again, he pulled guard duty, this time until December 21, 1941. The next day he was back in Toronto at No. 1 ITS. There, he studied and was given pre-flight instruction in aerodynamics, engines, navigation, meteorology, mathematics, and science. Cowboy graduated from this course on February 28, 1942, and was promoted to LAC.

Remaining in the greater Toronto area, Megura reported on March 1 to No. 1 EFTS at Malton, which today is the site of Toronto International Airport. There, he flew de Havilland Tiger Moths until graduating on May 9. The Tiger Moth was the most numerous elementary trainer used in the BCATP, with some

Nicholas Megura: Connecticut Mustang Ace

High-scoring 4th FG ace Captain Nicholas Megura sits in the cockpit of his NAA P-51B Mustang for a publicity photo in May 1944. (US Department of Defense)

1,546 eventually being employed. Most were powered by the British Gipsy Major engine, but several dozen used the American-designed Menasco engine.

Nick began advanced training on May 10 on Harvard Mk IIs, Course No. 55 at No. 13 SFTS at Saint-Hubert, Quebec. He graduated as an SP on August 28 and was awarded his wings. Two fellow Americans in Megura's graduating class that day were Sergeants Neil "Dutch" Van Wyk from Paterson, New Jersey, and Robert Elbe from East Orange, New Jersey. Cowboy and Dutch would reconnect a year later, in 1943, when both flew with the 4th FG.

Sergeant Megura reported on August 29 to No. 1 OTU at Bagotville, Quebec, where he learned basic fighter tactics flying Hawker Hurricanes. This course concluded on November 14, 1942.

Seven days later, Nicholas left Canada from Pier 21, Halifax, Nova Scotia, on a troop ship headed for England. Arriving there on November 30, Cowboy remained at No. 3 Personnel Reception Centre at Bournemouth until December 27.

The next day, he reported to RAF No. 59 OTU at Milfield where he flew Miles Masters and Hurricanes until January 9, 1943. Megura was sent, on January 10, to RAF No. 55 OTU at Annan, Scotland. There he flew Master Is and Hurricane Mk Xs until March 23. On the same course with Nicholas was future 4th ace, Captain Bernard L. "Big Mac" McGrattan.

SP Megura transferred from the non-commissioned ranks of Canada's air force to the commissioned ranks of the USAAF as an FO on March 24, 1943. Nicholas Megura was honorably discharged that same day by RCAF Overseas Headquarters in London, after having served one year and 188 days.

The agreement for the immediate transfer of qualified personnel between the services had been agreed upon by the two federal governments in May 1942. SL Thompson, who signed Megura's discharge papers, said: "Megura's conduct and character while in the RCAF had been very good and his qualifications as a fighter pilot were satisfactory."

The 5ft 8in tall, 22-year-old was sent to USAAF Station F-342 Atcham in Shropshire where he flew Supermarine Spitfire VBs, Master IIIs and Republic P-47C and D Thunderbolts. There was another future 4th "Horseman" in his class at Atcham and that was 1st Lieutenant Hipolitus Thomas "Tom" Biel.

Cowboy joined the 334th FS on July 3, 1943. He flew dozens of missions over the next seven months in P-47s but had no claims.

In February 1944, Colonel Blakeslee managed to convince his superior, Major General William "Bill" Kepner, that if the 4th was allowed to convert from the P-47 (Blakeslee never really like the Thunderbolt anyway) to the P-51 Mustang, the group could do a much better job shooting down enemy planes.

The conversion quickly followed, after which Megura went on a scoring spree. In an 11-week period, March 4 to May 22, Nicholas shot down 11.83 German aircraft and destroyed 3.75 more on the ground. Additionally, he put in claims for five Luftwaffe aircraft damaged in aerial combat.

Most of his victories were in *ILL WIND*, P-51B-5NA 43-6636 coded QP-N. Cowboy rose quickly in the ranks receiving three promotions from FO to captain in just ten months.

Megura's combat report recorded:

> I was flying the Pectin Blue 3 position, southeast of Mannheim, Germany. Before the rendezvous, nine plus aircraft were reported at 3 o'clock below. Pectin Blue Flight went down to investigate and identified them as Bf 109s. We were overtaking them very rapidly although we still had our wing tanks on. Closed in on a 109 on the port side of their formation, meanwhile, an intrepid type, off to starboard, tried to position himself on us. I gave the chap I tacked onto, a squirt out of range, no strikes seen. Skidded over to the one on the right who was working his way behind us. Opened fire within range and closed fast, strikes were seen on his port wing and pieces were falling off. Made a slight change in my deflection, saw strikes all over the fuselage and engine. Flames were seen coming out below his engine. I had to skid aside for fear of collision. The enemy plane seemed to stagger, flipped over on its back and started down, gushing flame and black smoke. Just before he hit the cloud his belly tank exploded. I pushed everything to the firewall and climbed up

among upper squadron with my wing tanks still intact. Off to the side and 4,000ft below, I saw two 109s giving chase to a P-51. Broke down and positioned myself on a 109 and opened fire. I could not turn tight enough, so I dropped wing tanks to one side, but the Huns were diving for the clouds. With my wing tanks gone I could not continue on with the show. I went home with a few others who were in the same predicament. March 18, 1944, 334th FS, time 1335 hours, ammunition used 500 rounds, position southeast of Mannheim, Germany. Claim one Bf 109 destroyed.

This was confirmed by Biel: "After breaking off my engagement with a 109, I looked to my starboard and saw Pectin Blue 3 Lieutenant Megura clobbering the 109 who immediately broke into a mass of flames. This 109 fluttered down with flames and black smoke trailing it."

A second report described the following:

I was flying as Pectin Green 3. At the rendezvous the bombers were under attack. Upon seeing us, the Huns broke down to the deck. I picked out an Fw 190 and gave chase. I easily overtook him in a dive and he immediately went into a tight turn at tree-top level. A Bf 109 joined the scrap but could not draw deflection, so he broke off the attack and climbed to 1,000ft. The Fw 190 levelled out and I fired for a couple of seconds. Large pieces were observed coming off his aircraft. I must have killed the pilot outright, or shot away his controls, for he plunged right into the ground and exploded. This pilot kept his belly tank on throughout the whole engagement. The 109 came back down and I finally worked around in back of him. He went into a cloud and came out on top, as I was closing in. Two Fw 190s joined in the fight from above, so I let down into the cloud and flew on instruments for ten minutes. Broke through the cloud and climbed to 20,000 feet, joined up with another P-51 and set course for home. We came across a barrage balloon, near Wesel, flying at 18,000 feet. Fired two long bursts into it. When we left, it was starting to descend very slowly. March 23, 1944, 334th FS, time 1115 hours, ammunition used 510 rounds, position Münster, Germany. Claim one Fw 190 and one balloon destroyed.

Nick's Mustang *ILL WIND* was lost on May 9, 1944, 20 miles southwest of Saint-Dizier, France, while being flown by 1st Lieutenant Vernon Burroughs, who became a PoW.

Captain Megura was brought down 13 days later on May 22, in P-51B 43-7158 coded QP-F. While tangling with three Bf 109s north of Hamburg, Germany, Cowboy's Mustang was inadvertently hit in the glycol tank by friendly gunfire from an American Lockheed P-38L Lightning pilot.

Megura's section escorted him to Laaland Island, Denmark, and broke off as he headed for neutral Sweden. He crash-landed his damaged aircraft at Sweden's

Kalmar airfield where he was briefly interned for five weeks He was prohibited from re-entering combat in the ETO after his repatriation due to the rules of his internment with the Swedish authorities.

Nicholas returned to Debden on June 28 and was assigned to non-operational duties. His flying was restricted to within England's borders.

He returned to the United States on July 16, 1945.

Cowboy was awarded the DSC in 1944. The citation is as follows:

> Megura, Nicholas. The President of the United States takes pleasure in presenting the Distinguished Service Cross to Nicholas Megura 0-2044894 First Lieutenant US Army Air Forces for extraordinary heroism in connection with military operations against an armed enemy while serving as a pilot of a P-51 airplane in the 334th FS, 4th FG, Eighth Air Force, in aerial combat against enemy forces on 6 and 8 March 1944, in the ETO. On each of these dates First Lieutenant Megura shot down two enemy aircraft. First Lieutenant Megura's unquestionable valor in aerial combat is in keeping with the highest traditions of the military service and reflects great credit upon himself, the 8th Air Force, and the USAAF. Headquarters: US Strategic Forces in Europe, General Orders No. 25, 1944.

Additional awards Nick received were six DFCs, four Air Medals and a Purple Heart.

At war's end, Captain Megura joined the reserves. After serving a second stint in the military, he retired with the rank of lieutenant colonel. For years, he owned and operated Monroe Concrete in Bridgeport, Connecticut, and resided in that city at 85 Pinepoint Drive.

On Friday, November 4, 1988, triple ace Nicholas "Cowboy" Megura died in Bridgeport at St. Vincent's Medical Center. He was 68 years old.

George Mitchell
The Oldest Volunteer Pilot

George Eric Mitchell from Diamond Springs, California, held the distinction of being the oldest recruit accepted for pilot training in the RCAF in World War II. When he signed his attestation papers on October 21, 1940, at No. 12 Recruiting Centre in Ottawa, Ontario, he was closing in on his 40th birthday. In the majority of cases, he was twice the age of the average young male enlisting in Canada's air force. The recruiter, FO E. L. O'Leary, was so impressed with Mitchell's determination and keenness to go and fight the Nazis, he decided that, in spite of his age, he should be given the opportunity. O'Leary obviously looked favorably on the fact that George held a mechanical engineering degree from the University of California and was a licensed private pilot with 276 flight hours recorded in his logbook. O'Leary's assessment of Mitchell's potential was summed up thusly: "Good type, very keen to do something for the common cause. His civilian activities have been varied and are of a good nature. A flight test will indicate suitability as an instructor. Is suitable for a commission."

Mitchell indicated on his application that he was divorced from Edith Marion Landis, that his parents were deceased and that he had no children. His home address of 602 Alcatraz Avenue in Oakland was recorded in his file. His only living relative and next of kin was Stewart A. Doyle, an uncle living in Sydney, Australia. While waiting for his paperwork to be processed, Mitchell stayed at Ottawa's posh downtown Chateau Laurier Hotel.

George was born on May 29, 1901, in Paris, France. His father, Robert Mitchell, came from Yorkshire, England, while his mother, Elizabeth "Bessie" Doyle, hailed from Melbourne, Australia. George's father was an "English Gentleman," who held substantial gold-mining interests in the state of California. His mother, a world-renowned violinist, performed under the stage name Eileen O'Moore or Eileen Mitchell O'Moore.

Mitchell's education began in 1907 at the prestigious Mill Hill Boarding School in London, England. George and his mother moved to America after his father's death in 1914. He attended San Diego High School in his freshmen year and completed his secondary education at Berkeley High School in southern

California in 1918. From there, it was on to University of California, Berkeley, where he obtained his degree in 1921.

On July 1, 1926, George became a citizen of the United States after swearing an oath of allegiance at the El Dorado County Superior Court in Placerville, California.

During the first eight years of his working career, Mitchell owned and operated two California mines and was the general superintendent at a third. Closing out his mining operations in 1929, he opened the Laguna Garage on Dewey Boulevard in San Francisco. He ran this facility until 1936, when he accepted a position as the instructor in charge of the automotive division at North Point Engineering and Trade School. He remained there until the fall of 1940 when he suddenly packed his bags and traveled north to Canada to join the war effort.

George was assigned Regimental Service No. R. 74313 and was sent to RCAF Air Station Rockcliffe, Ontario, where he was to undertake a flight test at No. 12 Communications Squadron. FL D. J. McGlinn administered the air test and was disappointed with the results.

He felt Mitchell would need a lot of extra flying training – perhaps 20–30 hours. He did believe that George was worth the bother and eventually would be suitable as an elementary instructor.

AC2 Mitchell was sent to No. 1 ITS at Toronto, Ontario, where he completed the four-week basic training course in November. Promoted to LAC, George was posted directly to No. 1 SFTS at Camp Borden, Ontario, where he flew just over 52 hours on Harvard and Yale aircraft. On December 23, he washed out after failing a 50-hour check ride.

Borden's station commander, GC R. S. Grandy, posted George and two others back to No. 1 MD at Toronto noting that, "They had failed to display inherent flying ability." Mitchell maintained a positive attitude in spite of his personal setback and expressed the desire to stay in the RCAF in some other capacity. The GC did recommend that George be given special consideration in this regard when he appeared before the Re-Selection Board. The Board was where one tried to salvage one's air force career by re-mustering to another trade. Mitchell languished in Toronto until February 17, 1941, when a final determination on his future was made.

For years, one of George's many hobbies was collecting pistols, rifles, and shotguns. He was an expert marksman who had several shooting trophies to his credit. Someone at the Re-Selection Board delved into his background and decided that he would probably excel as an air gunner.

Mitchell was posted to No. 1 Bombing & Gunnery School at Jarvis, Ontario, where he graduated from Course No. 6 on March 15, 1941, and was promoted to the rank of sergeant. Three days later, he was at Pier 21, "Y" Depot, Halifax, Nova Scotia, awaiting onward deployment to a war zone.

He left Canada on April 5 and, after a 15-day ocean voyage, arrived at No. 3 Personnel Reception Centre at Bournemouth, England. A week later, he

Flying Officer George E. Mitchell DFM shot down three enemy aircraft while flying as a tail gunner on Short Stirling heavy bombers with RAF No. 7 Squadron. (UK Ministry of Defence)

was posted to No. 20 OTU at RAF Lossiemouth, Scotland. There he crewed up flying in Vickers Wellington twin-engined medium bombers. On June 12, after an intensive six-week training period, George and the new crew were posted to RAF No. 7 Squadron at Oakington, Cambridgeshire.

No. 7 was the first RAF squadron to employ the Short Stirling four-engined heavy bomber and the first to take it into combat. Mitchell manned the Stirling's rear gun turret position and flew his first sortie in aircraft N3663 on a raid to Kiel, Germany on June 26, 1941.

Mitchell was awarded a DFM, which was gazetted as follows on July 25, 1941:

> On June 29, 1941 this airman was the rear gunner of an aircraft which was detailed to attack Bremerhaven, Germany. On the return journey an attack was made by a Messerschmitt Me 110 Night-Fighter twenty miles northwest of Texel. Despite an intense concentration of cannon and machine gun fire from the attacker, Sergeant Mitchell withheld his fire until the enemy came within close range. He then fired a burst of 600 rounds from his four Browning .303 calibre machine guns. The enemy aircraft broke off the attack with its port engine aglow. It was subsequently confirmed that this aircraft was destroyed. Sergeant Mitchell displayed great courage and has set an excellent example.

George was commissioned from the ranks as a PO on October 14, 1941. He was issued new Regimental Service No. J. 15022, which reflected his change in rank.

On subsequent sorties, Mitchell's defensive gunnery skills continued to come to the fore. On November 24, while attacking shipping in the North Sea south of Borkum Island, Germany, two Luftwaffe Messerschmitt Bf 109s swooped in on the attack. One enemy aircraft went down in flames and the other was driven off in a damaged condition. During a daylight sortie on December 18 to bomb shipping in the harbor at Brest, France, Mitchell's aircraft was damaged by flak, then attacked by fighters. George destroyed one aircraft that was seen to crash.

He received his DFM in a presentation ceremony at Buckingham Palace on November 4, 1941. Of the 8,864 US citizens who served in the RCAF during World War II, George Mitchell was the first of 234 Americans to receive a British decoration for bravery and valor. He was also the first graduate of the BCATP to be so decorated.

FO George Eric Mitchell DFM was killed in action while flying with the Royal New Zealand Air Force (RNZAF). He had completed his first tour with RAF No. 7 Squadron, and, after a period of leave, he signed up for another with New Zealand's No. 75 Squadron. The Kiwis were flying Wellingtons from RAF Feltwell in East Anglia.

On April 6, 1942, George and his crew took off at 0114hrs on a night-bombing sortie to Cologne, Germany. They were never heard from again. The wreckage of their Wellington Mk III, X3489, was located in the vicinity of Cologne. There were no survivors. Mitchell and crew initially were buried in the Cologne South Cemetery and later were re-interned in the Rheinberg British War Cemetery at Nordrhein-Westfalen, Germany.

George's promotion from PO to FO came through five days after his death.

Mitchell's earned wartime medals included the 1939–45 Star, General Service Medal, Aircrew European Star, Operational Wings, and the Canadian Volunteer Service Medal & Clasp.

Gerald Montgomery
An Above Average Pilot

Almost all who hailed from the state of Texas and served in the RCAF in World War II were invariably known as "Tex." However, this was not the case for a 20-year-old college student from Star Route No. 2, Littlefield, Texas. Gerald Emerson Montgomery had the same last name as popular British Field Marshall Bernard Law Montgomery. Sharing that famous surname meant equally sharing the universally applied nickname "Monty." The young Texan wanted to join the war effort as a fighter pilot in June 1941, but was rejected by the USAAC as his eyesight was not perfect.

G. E. Montgomery was born at Miners Hospital in Raton, New Mexico, on July 10, 1922. His father, Chester Paul Montgomery, came from Cartersville, Georgia, and his mother, Wilma Dodson, was born in Jacksboro, Texas. Gerry graduated with honors from Spade High School in Spade, Texas, in 1939. From 1939–41, he attended North Texas Agricultural College in Arlington, where he studied aeronautical engineering, and then industrial aeronautical engineering. In college, he was an infantry captain in the ROTC.

Traveling 1,100 miles from his home to Canada, Montgomery voluntarily enlisted in the RCAF at No. 8 Recruiting Centre in Windsor, Ontario, on Friday, August 8, 1941. His rank was as an AC2, his assigned Regimental Service No. was R. 109984, and his starting pay was CAN$33 per month.

The RCAF interviewing officer, FO W. D. Stroud, noted in his report: "A good average type. Some advanced education. Courteous, straightforward and intelligent. Keen on soldiering and has two friends who are currently serving in the RCAF. With training he should become good pilot material."

Gerry had logged civilian flight time in Piper Cubs, totaling 70 hours as a passenger, eight hours dual instruction and one hour solo. The wiry, 5ft 11in tall, 155lb Montgomery listed his sports interests as swimming, tennis, and football.

Prior to enlisting, he had been employed as an inspector at the Willard Storage Battery Company in Dallas.

Three days into his air force career, Monty was on a westbound train heading to the RCAF's western induction center at No. 2 MD in Brandon, Manitoba. Assigned to Course No. 34 at No. 2 ITS at Regina, Saskatchewan, he graduated on

September 20 with a 75 percent average. It was recommended that he continue to be trained as a pilot and was considered suitable for a commission. In the remarks section of his file, the WC noted the following: "This airman from the United States is quiet and slow of speech. Somewhat nervous but very anxious to fly. Has worked hard on the course which at times he found difficult. He will need to continue to apply himself to become an above average pilot."

Monty was promoted to LAC and received a pay raise of $12 per month. He was posted, effective September 24, 1941, to No. 19 EFTS at Virden, Manitoba. There, on Course No. 39, Montgomery flew 66.30 hours on de Havilland Tiger Moth biplanes. Graduating on November 21 with a 79 percent grade average, the school's CFI wrote the following in his file: "Assimilates instruction easily, no bad flying habits, instrument flying to high average standard and deportment and punctuality good."

Passed to No. 2 SFTS Uplands, Ottawa, Ontario, on November 24, Monty flew 128 hours on Harvard Mk IIs on Course No. 43. The mild-mannered Montgomery had a slight brush with RCAF discipline while at this facility. On February 28, 1942, at 0145hrs on Sparks Street in downtown Ottawa, Gerry called Sergeant J. T. Murphy and Corporals M. A. Siddons and R. A. McRae, "a bunch of bastards."

WC W. R. MacBrien sentenced him to two days' detention on the charge of conduct to the prejudice of good order and air force discipline and three days for using insubordinate language to a superior. As the sentences ran concurrently, he spent only 72 hours of his 120-hour sentence in the lock-up.

Gerry received his wings in a graduation ceremony on March 13, 1942. His squadron commander noted the following: "Above average pilot. Very capable. Instrument flying smooth and accurate. Gave an above average test. Navigation above average." Promoted to SP, Monty received a pay raise of $66, which bumped his gross salary to $111 per month.

Sergeant Montgomery used his two-week pre-embarkation leave to return to Dallas where he married Martha Elizabeth "Liz" Ferguson on March 23, 1942. He was slated to leave Canada for overseas duty and was actually at Pier 21, Halifax, Nova Scotia, at the end of March preparing to board a ship when he suddenly was recalled to No. 2 SFTS.

He returned to Uplands for a short stint as a flight instructor. Monty brought his new bride to Canada and, for the next four months, until July 31, 1942, the couple lived off station at 17 Fifth Avenue in Ottawa.

One of Monty's students was fellow American Hipolitus Thomas "Tom" Biel. Later in the war, they became great friends while flying P-51 Mustangs out of Debden, with the 334th FS, 4th FG, USAAF.

On April 2, while flying Harvard No. 2665, Montgomery ran out of gas.

He force-landed the powerless 5,300lb trainer at RAF No. 31 SFTS Kingston, Ontario. This air station, situated 90 miles southwest of Ottawa, is located at the

4th FG pilot Major Gerald E. Montgomery (center) reads a newspaper in the 334th FS ready room. (US Department of Defense)

point where Lake Ontario empties into the Saint Lawrence River. W. C. MacBrien fined Monty $25 for his cockpit inattention and verbally reprimanded him. The fine was levied as this was the second time in three months Monty had run the tanks dry in a Harvard and had to force-land at Kingston. The previous occurrence was on January 28 at 1630hrs in Harvard No. 2987.

Returning to Halifax on August 6, Gerry, now with more than 300 hours of flight time recorded in his logbook, boarded a troop ship at "Y" Depot, along with hundreds of other army and air force personnel for a 12-day sea voyage to England. With her husband's departure from Canada, Liz moved back to the US and took up residence in Leonard, Texas.

Six days after arriving in Britain, Monty was assigned to RAF No. 5 Pilot Advanced Flying Unit at Ternhill and Calveley. There he flew 50-plus hours on Miles Master Is, IIIs and early model Hawker Hurricanes. Toward the end of the course, Montgomery was promoted to FS and was earning $5.25 per day, a sum that included flight pay.

On September 22, 1942, Gerry started flying Hurricanes and Miles Masters on Course No. 40 at No. 55 OTU, RAF Usworth, Sunderland. Logging 80.35 additional flight hours on Hurricanes, Gerry graduated on December 15. In air-to-air gunnery exercises, his hit ratio averaged 6.2 percent of 3,200 rounds fired. WC W. D. David, the unit OC, made the following observations in his file: "An average pilot who will improve with further experience. Discipline and punctuality very good."

FS Montgomery was posted, effective January 15, 1943, to RAF No. 245 "Northern Rhodesian" Squadron, where he flew Hawker Hurricane Mk Is on convoy patrols from RAF Peterhead, Aberdeenshire, Scotland.

A month later, Monty decided to take the American government up on its offer to transfer him into the USAAF as an officer. He was honorably released by the RCAF's Overseas Headquarters in London on February 22 after having served one year and 199 days in Canada's air force.

After transferring, Monty was able to send extra money home to his wife, as his monthly income had nearly doubled.

Monty spent the next three months at the USAAF CCRC at Station F-342. There he converted to American aircraft and flying procedures flying Piper Cubs, Supermarine Spitfire Vbs, Miles Master IIIs and Republic P-47C and D Thunderbolts.

He joined the 334th FS, 4th FG as a 2nd lieutenant on May 15, 1943.

Montgomery's three aerial victories were achieved while flying a P-47C Thunderbolt, which he named *Texas*. The massive Republic aviation product carried artwork and the squadron code QP-H.

On August 16, 1943, under USAAF flying orders No. 105, Lieutenant Colonel Donald J. M. Blakeslee led the 4th pilots on a ramrod close escort mission to the Paris–Le Bourget Airport from 0805 to 1055hrs. The group caught up with the B-17s at 0912hrs as they flew at 28,000ft.

Just then, more than 60 German Fw 190 "Dora" fighters from JG 2 "Richthofen" attacked the lead box of bombers head-on.

Blakeslee took the 4th up and over the forts with the 334th making the initial bounce. Soon, all sections from all three squadrons were involved in the fight, which lasted for the next 40 minutes. The Huns came in from all directions in gaggles of six and eight. Battles raged all around Paris, giving the Partisans quite a show as 18 JG 2 aircraft were brought down. The American losses amounted to four B-17s and one P- 47. The single Thunderbolt loss was 1st Lieutenant Joseph G. Matthews from Wallington, New Jersey. Matthews evaded his captors and managed to return to Debden in October. Several badly damaged Thunderbolts safely returned to England. 2nd Lieutenant G. E. Montgomery went on the 4th's score sheet that day claiming his first aerial victory.

Gerald Montgomery: An Above Average Pilot

On January 14, 1944, on USAAF flying orders No. 217, Lt Col Selden R. Edner led the 4th on a freelance mission to Magny-la-Fosse, France, from 1345 to 1630hrs. Arriving over the area at 1445hrs, the group flew south at 25,000ft, whereupon it spotted 15 Fw 190s flying below and east of its position. The 336th FS made the bounce, engaging the Germans from 18,000ft to the deck. The 4th then regrouped and was vectored to Soissons, France, where 12-plus Doras were observed flying at a lower altitude than the P-47s. The 334th led the attack, fighting the Huns all the way down to 2,000ft. The following is Monty's combat report claiming his second aerial victory:

> I was flying the White 3 position when Pectin squadron bounced twelve or more 190s flying at 8,000ft. Overshooting the box of Fws, I skidded to starboard and made my attack from the enemies 3 o'clock position. A 190 broke formation, diving and turning the same direction as I. Pulling one ring of deflection, I fired and observed only one strike. He straightened his dive and continued downward. I fired several more bursts from 800 to 1,000 yards observing no additional strikes. Enemy aircraft continued diving steeply until I was forced to pull out at five hundred feet to keep from going into the deck. The last thing I saw was a high column of smoke where the 190 had crashed. Indicated air speed 500 to 550 miles per hour. Ammunition used 717 rounds.

Gerry's victim was Major Wilhelm Gath, the II. Gruppe Kommandeur of JG 26. Flying his Fw 190A-6 "Green 1," Gath, a 14-kill ace, was wounded in the encounter, but managed to parachute sight unseen from his doomed aircraft before it crashed.

On February 10, 1944, Lt Col Edner led a penetration support mission to Nienburg, Germany, from 0939 to 1255hrs. Contact was made with the bombers at 1102hrs. The Huns had harassed the bombers from Holland to Hanover. In a combined effort, upwards of 30 Bf 109s and Fw 190s hit the bombers head on with a determined aggressiveness. Fights raged from 28,000ft to the deck. Separated from the group, Monty spun out after bouncing five Messerschmitts east of Zwolle. He joined up for mutual protection with four 78th FG P-47s and came home. The 4th overall had a good day – eight enemy aircraft destroyed with no losses.

Later that afternoon, the 334th pilots gathered at Debden for a ceremony to pay £30 (approximately US$120) to the pilot who got the 50th kill for the squadron. Prior to the mission, the squadron's score stood at 48. Since Gerry, Tom Biel and Vic France each claimed a Bf 109 destroyed, they agreed to split the pot three ways.

On February 14, 1944, the 4th began converting onto the NAA P-51 Mustang. Monty was eventually assigned three P-51D Mustangs, all were coded QP-H and all were named *Sizzling Liz*.

The first P-51 (serial number 44-14119) was lost on November 21, 1944, while being flown by Lt Carmen J. Delnero, who was KIA over Meerane, Germany.

The second (serial number 44-72382) was transferred to another squadron. The third Mustang (serial number 44-15326) was adorned with 15 German crosses, partly reflecting the 14½ aircraft Gerry destroyed while ground strafing.

In June 1944, Monty completed his first tour and returned to the US for a month's leave. During his second tour, he became the 334th's operations officer in November.

Major Montgomery's combined air and ground total of 17½ aircraft destroyed placed him tenth overall on the 4th FG scoring list.

On April 28, 1945, Monty made an application to the Canadian government for any war service gratuity that was due him based on his service time in the RCAF. His claim was investigated and approved on June 14. A check in the amount of CAN$229.79 was forwarded to the Montgomery household in Littlefield, Texas.

Gerri Montgomery Prescott, Monty's youngest daughter, relayed the following information regarding the tragic disappearance of her father over North Korea on March 3, 1952:

> My father was unable to remain in the USAAF after WWII as too many pilots were applying for too few slots in the greatly reduced peace time army air corps.
>
> In 1947, he was accepted into the Texas Air National Guard's 136th Fighter Bomber Group. His unit was mobilized when war erupted on the Korean Peninsula on June 25, 1950. In 1951, he held the rank of Lieutenant Colonel and was the Deputy WC at the 136th. Under 5th Air Force control, the 136th morphed into the 136th Fighter Bomber Wing and later into the 58th FBW.
>
> On that fateful March 3, 1952, bombing mission, mounted from Taegu, Korea [now Daegu], my father's Republic F-84E-15-RE Thunderjet was incapacitated by Russian Anti-Aircraft-Artillery ground fire. Successfully bailing out, he was last seen standing in the shallow Chongchon River waving to his squadron mates as they flew overhead. It took them just a few minutes to turn the flight around to come back for a second pass. When they did, there was nothing to be seen – no pilot, no parachute, not even enemy troops.

Gerri Prescott and her older sister have searched for years, longing to know their father's fate. Twelve months after he was classified as MIA, the USAF officially declared him dead on February 20, 1953.

In 1998, Gerri Prescott went to North Korea along with a delegation of US Department of Defense officials looking for answers, but nothing substantive was learned. She found a document on file in Hawaii suggesting Monty may have been a PoW. She was also told her father's name was given out in radio propaganda broadcasts originating from Pyongyang, North Korea, and Beijing, China. Each year, she and her sister attend defense department briefings in Washington, DC for the families of missing Korean war service personnel. Seventy-one years on, the family knows no more about Lt Col Montgomery's disappearance than they did on that cold March day in 1952. Their never-ending search continues.

As a tribute to Monty, David Marco has painted his restored, flyable P-51D Mustang as *Sizzling Liz*. Ironically, Marco's aircraft came from a batch of 150 Mustangs that Canada purchased at the end of World War II from surplus USAF stock. These P-51Ds served in RCAF reserve squadrons up until the mid-1950s.

Leslie Moore
Massachusetts Spitfire Ace

Leslie Albert "Les" Moore was born in Hamilton, Ontario, on February 5, 1921. His mother, Alice Myne Trigor, hailed from England and his father, John Thompson Moore, came from Belfast, Northern Ireland. Les was the youngest of seven children. By 1923, most of the family had moved to the United States where they became naturalized citizens.

Les grew up in Leonardsville, New York, and Mount Hermon, Massachusetts. He completed his education in 1940 at Northfield Mount Hermon preparatory school where he excelled in track, skiing, and basketball. After graduation, he worked for a while as a truck driver and later as a stockman at the S. S. Kresge Company. He wanted to join the USAAC to become a fighter pilot but was unable to meet its minimum requisite of having two years of college.

Hearing the RCAF was accepting applications from high school graduates for aircrew training, the 20-year-old Moore traveled, on August 26, 1941, from his residence at East Troy, New York, to RCAF No. 10 Recruiting Centre in Hamilton.

On that day, Moore voluntarily enlisted as an AC2 and was issued Regimental Service No. R. 122857. The air force interviewer, FO F. S. Mills, wrote in his file: "Good type of American lad. Should do well in training as a pilot."

Les was immediately posted for six weeks of basic training to No. 5A MD at Val Cartier, Quebec. On October 11, he was sent to No. 31 OTU in Debert, Nova Scotia, where he performed guard duty until November 22. At the time, No. 31 was instructing newly minted pilots on how to fly and operationally use the twin-engined Lockheed Hudson coastal patrol bomber. Airman Moore was posted on the 23rd to No. 3 ITS at Victoriaville, Quebec, for instruction in subjects such as navigation, aircraft recognition, armament, etc. Athletics were also high on the school's agenda, together with the never-ending cycle of marching and drilling.

Completing the course on February 14, 1942, Les was promoted to LAC. The next day, he transferred to No. 11 EFTS at Cap-de-la-Madeleine, Quebec, where he spent the next two months learning how to fly Fleet Finch II biplane trainers. Graduating from there on April 11, Moore was posted to No. 13 SFTS at Saint-Hubert, Quebec, Course No. 53, where he flew Harvard Mk IIbs. After logging 143 hours on the type, he graduated and earned his wings on July 31, 1942, with a 66.40 percent grade average.

Moore was promoted to SP and given the standard two-week pre-embarkation leave. He reported to "Y" Depot, Pier 21, Halifax, Nova Scotia, on August 15 for onward deployment to England.

He sailed from Canada six days later on a fast troop ship, which arrived at Glasgow, Scotland, on September 1. His stay at No. 3 Personnel Reception Centre in Bournemouth was unusually short, as he was immediately assigned to RAF No. 5 Pilot Advanced Flying Unit at Ternhill and Calveley on September 11. There, over a four-week period, he flew 50-plus hours on Miles Master Is, IIIs and early model Hawker Hurricanes. The final stage of his fighter training on the superlative Supermarine Spitfire took place from October 13, 1942, to January 25, 1943 at RAF No. 57 OTU at Eshott and Boulmer in Northumberland.

Sergeant Moore was posted to RCAF No. 402 "City of Winnipeg" FS effective January 26. The squadron began life flying Hurricane Mk Is in March 1941. Progressing through the Mk IIa and IIb variants, the unit commenced operations in November as the air force's first "Hurribomber" squadron.

In April and May 1942, the squadron resumed its pure fighter role when it relocated to RAF Colerne Wiltshire, and converted to Spitfire Mk Vbs. Cross-Channel sorties into France followed from RAF Kenley and Redhill, Surrey. In June 1942, a further upgrade in equipment saw the squadron convert to the Spitfire Mk IXc variant. This model was flown from RAF Digby until April 1943, when another conversion was undertaken, this time to the Mk Vc. These were flown until June 1944 from several stations, most notably RAF Horne, Surrey, and Merston, West Sussex. For July and August, it was back onto the IXcs. 402's final move was to RAF Hawkinge, Kent, in late August where the squadron undertook its final conversion, this time to the Rolls-Royce Griffon-powered Spitfire Mk XIVes, which it operated until the end of the war.

Les Moore was promoted to FS on January 31, 1943. On April 15, 1943, he received a further promotion after being commissioned from the enlisted ranks as a PO. His Regimental Service No. changed from R. 122857 to J. 17857.

Moore opened his scoring on June 13 in Spitfire AD462 when he claimed a Focke Wulf Fw 190 as a probable over the North Sea. In aircraft AA880 on September 4, he destroyed a German Fw 190. In that same encounter, he damaged another Fw 190. Flying AB524 early in the evening of September 27, Moore and another pilot badly damaged a Messerschmitt Bf 109G fighter near Fécamp. His last claim with 402 Squadron was in AA880 on October 8 when, 35 miles west–northwest of the Hague, Moore and three other pilots downed a Luftwaffe Dornier Do 24

Squadron Leader Leslie A. Moore DFC, AFC flew various marks of Supermarine Spitfires, including Mk IXs, similar to the one depicted here. (Parr Yonemoto)

three-engined reconnaissance flying boat. Each was given a one-quarter share of the kill.

Moore was promoted to FO on October 16.

On March 2, 1944, Moore's time with 402 Squadron ended when he was transferred to the newly arrived No. 441 "Silver Fox" FS as a flight commander. Nine days later, Les was promoted to FL.

Moore continued to add to his score. On March 28, in a Mk IXb Spitfire, he damaged a Heinkel He 111 bomber near Dreux, France. On that same sortie, he teamed up with two other squadron members to destroy a Messerschmitt Me 410 fighter-bomber. Each pilot was awarded one-third share of the kill. Teamwork paid off again on April 28 when Les and a fellow 441 pilot downed a Caudron C.440 Goéland twin-engined transport near Dreux. Each was given a half credit for the kill.

On July 2, three miles west of Lisieux, Moore's flight encountered eight Bf 109 fighters. Expertly deploying his four Spitfires, he and the other Canadians tore into the German force destroying five of the enemy without suffering any damage or losses. Moore personally accounted for two and a half of the total number of aircraft shot down.

When his tour expired on July 22, Moore was briefly assigned to the RAF's Headquarters, Air Defence of Great Britain. From there it was on to No. 53 OTU at Kirton in Lindsey in Lincolnshire where he served as an instructor. There he taught his students the art of combat tactics utilizing Miles Master IIs, Miles

Martinets and various marks of Spitfires. This non-operational tour lasted from August 4, 1944, until February 5, 1945.

Moore was awarded a British DFC on August 8, 1944, the text of which is as follows: "This officer has participated in a large number of sorties involving attacks on a wide range of targets. In July 1944 he took part in an engagement against eight enemy aircraft, five of which were shot down, two of them by FL Moore. In the fight, this officer led his small formation of aircraft with great skill, setting an inspiring example. He has destroyed six hostile aircraft."

Moore was promoted to SL on February 22, 1945, and assumed command of RCAF 402 Squadron shortly thereafter.

Just a month later, Moore was KIA.

In a letter sent to Moore's mother in Philadelphia, Pennsylvania, dated April 4, 1945, WC of RCAF No. 126 Wing, Geoffrey Wilson Northcott DSO, DFC & Bar, eloquently expressed his sorrow at the loss of her son and of his good friend:

> Before receiving this letter you will have received a telegram informing you that your son, SL L. A. Moore, has been listed missing, believed killed on air operations over Germany. It is with the deepest personal regret that I write you at this time to convey to you and Les' family the feelings of the entire wing.
>
> On March 25 at about 7:30 in the morning, Les led his squadron on an armed reconnaissance over German territory. About three-quarters of an hour later he sighted an enemy train and immediately led his squadron down to attack it. The attack was carried out very successfully, but Les' aircraft must have been hit by enemy flak, as he did not recover from the dive, but crashed immediately after passing over the train. It is presumed that he was killed instantly.
>
> I have known Les since he started operational flying. He joined 402 Squadron when I was commanding it. From the first, Les showed outstanding ability both in the air and on the ground. I had the pleasure of recommending him for his commission and later recommending him for the position of flight commander and the rank of FL in 441 Squadron.
>
> Les proved his ability as a fighter pilot and leader of men beyond question and it was not long before he was awarded an immediate DFC and nobody has more richly deserved this award than Les.
>
> After completing a non-operational tour in England, Les expressed a strong desire to get back on operations and was offered command of his old squadron. He accepted and in the month he was with the unit he was exceedingly popular with the pilots and especially the ground crew boys. They practically idolized him and considered it an extreme honour to work on his aircraft.
>
> Les' passing was a loss, both to the squadron and wing, that will be practically impossible to fill. While our loss cannot be compared to yours and your family, I do

want you to feel that Les was much more to us than just another pilot. He definitely was a leader of men and a gentleman and I also would like to ensure you how much we will all honour the gallant sacrifice your son has made for the cause for which all free men in the world are fighting.

I might mention that his personal effects have been gathered together and sent to the RAF Central Depository where they will be held for approximately six months and then forwarded to you.

His citation read:

MOORE, S/L Leslie Albert, DFC (J. 17857) – Air Force Cross (AFC) – No. 402 Squadron – Deceased. Award effective April 3, 1945 as per London Gazette of that date and AFRO 802/45 dated May 11, 1945. Public Records Office Air 2/9061 has citation, drafted when he had flown 795 non-operational hours, 183 instructional in the previous six months.

This officer was posted to No. 53 OTU as a flying instructor and Flight Commander in August 1944. He has carried out his duties with the greatest keenness and enthusiasm. He has maintained the highest standards in his work which is of a most exacting nature. He is largely responsible for the excellent morale and spirit of the Operational Training Unit.

The AFC was established by King George V on his birthday, June 3, 1918. It is awarded to an officer or WO for an act or acts of valor, courage or devotion to duty whilst flying, but not while in active operations against an enemy.

On June 21, 1947, RCAF WC W. A. Dicks, on behalf of the CAS in Ottawa, Ontario, requested of the CO of No. 4 Military Recovery and Exhumation Unit of the British Army of the Rhine that a casualty enquiry be instituted and carried out in the British Occupied Zone relative to the following:

1. Spitfire 14 reported missing 0730 hours on March 25, 1945 – Armed reconnaissance while attacking a train in the Münster area Germany.
2. The pilot was J. 18757 SL L. S. Moore.
3. The squadron left base at 0645 hours on the 25th of March 1945 to carry out an armed reconnaissance in the Münster area. SL Moore was seen to attack a locomotive at approximately 0735 hours. He carried out a dive out of the sun, opened fire at a range of eight hundred yards closing in to about fifty yards. The aircraft struck the ground and disintegrated. In view of the attack being carried out at such close quarters, it is presumed that his aircraft was hit by flying debris and damaged beyond control. The pilot was not seen to bail out.
4. May an investigation be instituted please?

In response to the Canadian request, RAF Flt Lt R. A. Topp was assigned as the investigating officer for enquiry No. G.1785. His investigation began in Westkirchen, Germany. The following is his report to Ottawa:

> Aircraft: Owing to the damage to the main railway line at the time, most of the trains carrying munitions and troops were diverted along the side line Neubeckum – Warendorf, which runs by Westkirchen. It was one of those trains that the aircraft in question was attacking at approximately 0700 hours on Palm Sunday in March 1945. There were seven other aircraft of the same type in the immediate area at the time.
>
> The attacked train had a defence of four heavy calibre flak guns mounted on the rear car and it was one of these that shot the aircraft down. The aircraft exploded in the air and disintegrated into very small pieces. Most of the wreckage that crashed near the train fell on land owned by Herr Horstmann. It was his and other people's opinion that the crashed aircraft in question was a Spitfire. Most of the wreckage had long since been removed when I attended the site, but I did find part of a five bladed wooden propeller bearing serial numbers 50559 and 340882.
>
> The train's flak gunners ran to the scene of the crash and recovered some of the pilot's papers which they took with them. According to Herr Horstmann and policeman, Herr Heine, a small Roman Catholic prayer book was found in the field a day later. From notations made inside, it was determined the dead pilot was a Canadian Major. Unfortunately his name and unit were not recorded in the book. Herr Heine stated the pilot's uniform was blue, very much like that of a RAF uniform. The unnamed pilot was buried that evening in Westkirchen Church Cemetery alongside seven RAF bomber aircrew members. Witnesses of the burial were Sister Loepping, Herr Mense and the Church Caretaker, Herr Woestmann.
>
> On June 26, 1947, the bodies of the bomber crew were exhumed and laid to rest elsewhere. The remains of the fighter pilot were left as no information regarding his identity had come to light.
>
> Exhumation & Re-Internment: There was no cross on the unidentified pilot's grave. Captain Butcher oversaw the exhumation on July 28, 1947. The process was witnessed by myself. As the body was possibly that of a Canadian, a tooth chart was taken. The clothing found in the coffin consisted of an officer's service dress trousers, black tie and shirt. An examination of the skull revealed a rifle calibre bullet had entered the forehead, passing completely through from front to back. This appeared peculiar as the evidence given stated the aircraft was shot down by flak likely 20mm calibre or larger. It is, therefore, probable that rifle fire from the troops on the train, who were under attack, might well have been the cause of this shoot down. The pilot was quite likely dead at the controls before the aircraft blew up. However, Captain Butcher

informed me that he will have the badly burnt remains examined by a Pathologist Major Manston, Rhine Army Headquarters and any forthcoming information will be communicated to this section. The body of the pilot has been re-interned in Plot 19, Row D, Grave 14 in the Reichswald Forest British Military Cemetery.

The pathology report later confirmed the remains were in fact that of 24-year-old SL L. A. Moore. His death was registered by the RCAF with the Province of Ontario Vital Statistics Branch on October 23, 1945.

On November 10, 1945, a Memorial Cross bearing the cypher of King George VI was sent by the Canadian federal government to Moore's mother at 223 West Front Street in Plainfield, New Jersey. This award, together with a Royal Message of Sympathy, was forwarded to her in recognition of the loss of her son, Leslie Albert Moore DFC, AFC, on active service on March 25, 1945.

John Morgan
Texas MoH Awardee

John Cary "Red" Morgan was born to Verna Johnson and Samuel A. L. Morgan on August 24, 1914, in Vernon, Texas. Morgan became fascinated with flight at an early age after a barnstormer's aircraft flew low over his house. The 6ft 2in tall, 210lb Texan graduated from the high school division of the New Mexico Military Institute at Roswell, New Mexico, on May 31, 1932.

Morgan, nicknamed "Red" for his flaming red hair, attended several colleges in succession, including Amarillo College, Schreiner Institute, West Texas State Teachers College, and the University of Texas at Austin.

Morgan's sister would often joke that John was a "distinguished alumni" of many schools as he kept getting kicked out. In his freshman year at Austin, John had all of 3½ hours of flight instruction when he soloed his first aircraft. His father, a corporate attorney for Texaco Oil, was not exactly thrilled with his son's newfound pastime of spending tuition monies on flying lessons. Morgan's dad, a frequent passenger in the very early days of commercial airline travel, believed that one had to be a superhuman genius to safely fly the wooden and wire contraptions called airliners. There was some question in his mind whether his son would ever be up for that task.

In 1935, John's father pulled him out of school and sent him to the Fiji Islands. For the next two years, Red enjoyed the exotic South Sea location, working as a supervisor on the A. C. McCown pineapple plantation. Morgan managed to become involved in Fiji's first automobile accident, even though there were only two registered cars on the island at the time!

John returned to America from the South Pacific in 1937 specifically to enlist as an aviation cadet in the USAAC. Because of his poor academic record, the Army turned him down. He then went to work at Texaco as a truck driver at its Oklahoma City terminal. Later, while working at one of its oil-drilling sites in Pampa, Texas, Morgan suffered a broken neck in an industrial accident. A full 55gal oil drum broke free and Morgan foolishly tried to arrest its momentum by grabbing it. It nearly killed him. Because of the seriousness of the injury, the Selective Service system later classified Morgan as 4-F – unfit for military service.

Early in the European war, the American public was evenly divided on whether or not the United States should go to the aid of Great Britain. Twenty-six-year-old J. C. Morgan had no such doubts about fighting Hitler and, on August 1, 1941, he traveled north to Windsor, Ontario, and voluntarily enlisted in the RCAF. Red was sworn into that service for the duration of the war at Windsor's No. 8 Recruiting Centre as an AC2 under Service No. R. 109911. He stated his home address was 2822 North Classen Boulevard in Oklahoma City, Oklahoma. He told the recruiter, FL H. E. Fleming, that he had a combined 3½ years of military training from two of the schools he had attended.

Getting into the Canadian air force was not all that difficult for the 4-F-classified Morgan. As Red later put it: "They didn't ask me if I'd ever broken my neck and I didn't tell them." Somehow, he managed to pass a physical examination and was declared medically fit for pilot training.

Morgan was posted on August 2 to No. 2 MD at Brandon, Manitoba, for six weeks of basic training. Finishing there on September 13, he was shipped off to perform guard duty at No. 10 SFTS at Dauphin, Manitoba. Remaining there until October 26, he then undertook seven weeks of intensive training at No. 2 ITS at Regina, Saskatchewan. Graduating on December 20, he was promoted to LAC. Morgan's primary flight training began on December 21, 1941, on de Havilland Tiger Moth biplanes at No. 19 EFTS, Course No. 45 at Virden, Manitoba. This phase of his training concluded on March 14, 1942.

For reasons unknown, Morgan was returned to No. 2 MD until March 28. Two days later, he reported in at No. 16 SFTS at Hagersville, Ontario, where he flew Avro Anson twin-engined trainers for the next several months. On October 23, Red Morgan was awarded his pilot wings in a graduation ceremony and was promoted to the rank of SP.

Red embarked for England on a troop ship departing from Pier 21, Halifax, Nova Scotia, on October 27. Arriving in the United Kingdom on November 5, 1942, he was sent to No. 3 Personnel Reception Centre in Bournemouth.

Twelve days later, he was assigned to No. 18 Pilot Advanced Flying Unit at RAF Church Lawford in Warwickshire where he began flying twin-engined Airspeed Oxfords. The course finished on March 16, 1943, and newly promoted FS Morgan moved over to the aircrew reception center in anticipation of a posting to a RAF operational bomber squadron.

On March 23, 1943, John Morgan formally transferred from the RCAF to the USAAF. His honorable discharge was signed by SL Thompson. Morgan had served one year and 235 days in Canada's air force.

John Morgan entered the USAAF as an FO. This rank was created and used only in World War II. It allowed those US citizens who were serving as non-commissioned pilots in the RCAF to smoothly transfer into the American air force as officers.

The repatriation agreement to transfer thousands of trained military personnel from Canada to the United States had been worked out at the highest levels of both federal governments in May 1942. However, there were some old school army officers who greatly resisted the spirit of the concept. Some of the returnees were openly greeted with hostility and were reminded that they had not gone to college, were considered to be an undisciplined lot, and were told: "The Army has agreed to take you, but we don't have to like it."

What was particularly irksome to a few was that the returnees were entitled to wear two sets of wings on their US uniforms. They wore their USAAF wings over their left breast pocket and their Canadian wings over their right breast pocket. At social functions and dances, women seemed to gravitate to those pilots whose uniforms sported double wings. They just assumed the wearers of them to be highly trained or superior airmen. The cagey pilots did nothing to dispel these erroneous assumptions and happily went along with whatever was mistakenly believed.

Morgan was assigned to fly Boeing B-17 Flying Fortresses with the 326th Bomb Squadron (BS), 92nd Bomb Group (BG), based at RAF Alconbury, Huntingdon.

On a mission to Germany on Monday, July 26, 1943, Morgan was the copilot of a B-17F named *Ruthie II*. The 92nd's target that day was the Continental Gummiwerke A. G. Wahrenwalderstrasse tire plant at Hanover, some 150 miles west of Berlin.

It was Morgan's fifth combat mission, and he was not scheduled to fly that day as he had been grounded for committing some minor air force infraction. He actually was on report and was supposed to be confined to his barracks. However, he snuck out of his quarters, attended the briefing, and bluffed his way on to the aircraft, telling his replacement the orders had been changed and that he would be flying the mission after all.

The crew members of *Ruthie II* were as follows: pilot, 1st Lieutenant Robert L. Campbell; copilot, FO John C. Morgan; navigator, 2nd Lieutenant Keith J. Koske; bombardier, 2nd Lieutenant Asa J. Irwin; top turret gunner, S/Sgt Tyre C. Weaver; radio operator, Technical Sergeant (T/Sgt) John A. McClure; ball turret gunner, Sgt James L. Ford; waist gunners, Sgts Eugene F. Ponte and Reece B. Walton; and tail gunner, S/Sgt John E. Foley.

Morgan piloted the aircraft during takeoff and *Ruthie II* climbed out over the North Sea with the rest of the bomb wing. A little over an hour later, just as the bomber stream reached the Dutch coast, it was attacked by more than 100 Luftwaffe Fw 190 and Messerschmidt Bf 109 fighters. Campbell had just taken over the controls when the first group of fighters swooped in. On their first firing pass, the Germans knocked out *Ruthie II*'s oxygen system to the radio, waist and tail gun positions. The second attack came a moment later, shattering the intercom system between Morgan, the tail, waist, and ball-turret positions. A 20mm cannon

Flight Officer John C. Morgan, MoH (left) is about to be interviewed for a radio broadcast in England in September 1943. (US Department of Defense)

round entered the flight deck shattering the copilot's window. Fragments from the .79in shell missed Morgan, striking Campbell and splitting open his skull.

Seriously wounded and in a semiconscious state, the 6ft, 185lb, muscularly built Campbell slumped forward, locking his arms around the control column. This motion sent the aircraft into a dive. Morgan seized the controls on his side and, by sheer strength, pulled the plane back into formation. Having no response to his calls for assistance over the inter-phone, Morgan concentrated as best he could to keep the dying pilot from disrupting the flight controls. Morgan reasoned that keeping within the protection of the formation gave the crew the best prospects for a return to base, besides there was good reason to believe the bombs could yet be delivered to the target. The same burst of cannon fire that critically wounded Campbell also struck top turret gunner S/Sgt Tyre Weaver, cleanly severing his left arm at the shoulder. Weaver slid down into the rear of the nose compartment and slumped on the floor behind the navigator, Lieutenant Keith Koske, who immediately went to his aid. Unsuccessful in giving a morphine injection because the needle was damaged, and also unable to apply a tourniquet because the arm was cut off too close at the shoulder, Koske realized that unless medical aid was forthcoming, Weaver would bleed to death. He made a quick decision. Adjusting

Weaver's parachute, he placed the ripcord ring in his right hand, opened the nose door and proceeded to push him out into space 25 miles due west of Hanover at 24,500ft. Unfortunately, Weaver, suffering from shock, immediately pulled the cord causing the chute to billow inside the plane. Koske managed to bundle it up, tuck it under Weaver's right arm and pushed him clear. The ball turret gunner later reported seeing the parachute open. Weeks later, word reached England that Weaver was alive and well in a German hospital. He was repatriated to the States late in 1944 after spending time as a PoW in Stalag Luft IV at Pomerania.

At an aircrew reunion in 1980, Weaver said, "I would always remember Koske's smile of encouragement as he pushed me out the aircraft."

The crazed pilot continued to try to wrest the controls away from Morgan and smashed at the copilot with his fists, knocking some of his teeth loose and blackening both his eyes. Unknown to Morgan, several of the crew members were unconscious from lack of oxygen and were threatened with death by anoxia. Red was thinking about subjecting Campbell to anoxia by cutting off his oxygen supply. In spite of the wild efforts by the mortally wounded pilot to seize the controls, Morgan chose to complete the mission and not cut off Campbell's oxygen.

For two hours, Red Morgan held his position in the formation – flying the bomber with one hand and fighting off the pilot with the other. Lieutenant Koske eventually decided to go up to the flight deck to check in with the pilot and have a look around. He found Campbell slumped in his seat, his head a mass of blood. Morgan told Koske to get Campbell out of his seat as the plane could not be landed from the co-pilot's position. Morgan and Koske then struggled for 30 minutes getting the fatally injured pilot out of his seat and down into the rear of the navigator's compartment, where Lieutenant Irwin held him from slipping out the open hatch. Koske later related that he had tried to use the inter-phone several times but received no answer. He remembered someone complaining shortly after the first attack about the lack of oxygen.

Ruthie II reached the target and successfully dropped its bomb load. Returning to England, Red headed for the first British air station he saw on the Norfolk coast. With the fuel gauges registering on empty, he quickly moved the battered B-17 into the busy traffic pattern at RAF Foulsham. S/Sgt John Foley, who had sustained injuries to both arms, cranked the wheels and flaps down by hand.

1st Lieutenant R. L. Campbell died from his injuries an hour and half after the aircraft landed. The surviving crew members suffered various degrees of frostbite. *Ruthie II* was declared damaged beyond economical repair.

Returning to Alconbury, Morgan did not bother to tell anyone the details of the mission. Once again, he was put on report and confined to barracks. There was even some discussion as to whether or not he should face a general Court Martial and be discharged from the air force. Then, the brass began hearing the stories through the grapevine of the crew's harrowing ordeal. After further investigation, they could not ignore Morgan's remarkable feat of airmanship and heroism. Morgan's bosses then had to adjust the mission date on paper from the 26th to the 28th so that the recommended award for valor would not reveal the fact that Morgan had disobeyed his superiors by skipping out on his grounding. Apparently, the 8th Air Force did not want anything to stand in the way of John C. Morgan receiving the Medal of Honor (MoH).

Lieutenant General Ira Clarence Eaker presented Morgan with the nation's highest award at a special ceremony at 8th Air Force Headquarters at Bushey Park on December 18, 1943. The presentation was broadcast live that evening on the BBC radio news.

The MoH citation reads:

> For conspicuous gallantry and intrepidity above and beyond the call of duty, while participating on a bombing mission over enemy occupied Continental Europe on July 28, 1943. Prior to reaching the German coast on the way to the target, the B-17 aircraft, in which FO Morgan was serving as co-pilot, was attacked by a large force of enemy fighters, during which the oxygen system to the tail, waist and radio gun positions was knocked out. An attack placed a 20mm cannon shell through the windshield, totally shattering it and the pilot's skull was split open leaving him in a crazed condition. The pilot fell over the steering wheel, tightly clamping his arms around it. FO Morgan at once grasped the controls from his side and, by sheer strength, pulled the aircraft back into formation despite the frantic struggles of the semiconscious pilot. The inter-phone had been destroyed, rendering it impossible to call for help. At this time the top turret gunner fell to the floor and down through the hatch with his arm shot off at the shoulder and a gaping wound in his side. The waist, tail and radio gunners had lost consciousness from lack of oxygen and, hearing no fire from their guns the co-pilot believed they had bailed out. The wounded pilot still offered desperate resistance in his crazed attempts to fly the aircraft. There remained the prospect of flying to and over the target and back to a friendly base wholly unassisted. In the face of this desperate situation, Morgan made his decision to continue the flight and protect any members of the crew who might still be in the ship and for two hours he flew in formation with one hand at the controls and the other holding off the struggling pilot before the navigator entered the steering compartment and relieved the situation. The miraculous and heroic performance of FO Morgan on this occasion resulted in the successful completion of a vital bombing mission and the safe return of his aircraft and crew.

Lieutenant General Eaker directed Morgan not to fly any additional combat missions, but Morgan decided that if the war was not over for the Allies, then it was not over for him. He was given the opportunity to be sent home after receiving the medal but chose to stay with his unit.

Morgan transferred to the 482nd BG in October 1943 to fly H2X radar-equipped B-17 aircraft. He was promoted to 2nd lieutenant that November.

On March 6, 1944, Morgan was the copilot in the lead B-17 that was carrying the 3rd Division commander, Brigadier General Russell Wilson, on the USAAF's first major attack against Berlin. The group going in had not encountered any serious fighter opposition, but over the outskirts of Berlin at 20,000ft, heavy flak rose up directly in the path of the command aircraft. After taking more than one direct hit, the aircraft continued on its bomb run, although one engine and a fuel tank were on fire. The bomber began to tumble out of control and the pilot, Major Fred A. Rabo, gave the order to abandon ship.

Seconds later, the B-17 exploded, killing eight of the 12 men aboard. One of the survivors was Morgan. Subsequently recalling his miraculous escape, he said:

> I was just conscious of something terrific happening and I had a faint idea of a lot of metal tearing at me and then I was falling. I don't think I ever lost consciousness. I had my parachute tucked under my arm when she blew. I kept trying to put it on when I was falling feet first but, the pressure kept pushing it up too high and when I was falling headfirst it kept pushing it past my chest. I guess I was on my back when I finally got it fastened on. You think clearly when you're so damned near dead.
>
> Three or four seconds after the chute popped open, I landed in the top of a tree. I then fell out of the chute, dropped thirty feet and landed on my feet. I felt I'd busted every bone in me, what a jolt.

Morgan was arrested by soldiers of a flak battery approximately "ten seconds" after landing in the middle of Hitler's Berlin. He was interned in Stalag Luft 1 at Barth, Germany, for the next 14 months, the only MoH recipient in the ETO to become a PoW.

When Morgan was released from the service at war's end, he returned to Texaco and worked as an aviation representative in its sales department in Chicago. While there, he met a young co-worker, Chris Ziegler, who became his wife in 1947. He worked his entire adult life at Texaco, finishing his career as division manager, Los Angeles, in the international aviation sales department. He held a commercial pilot's license for many years, but seldom used it. Whenever he needed to feed the urge to fly, one of his many pilot friends would take him up for a spin. When they got together, the talk usually focused on current developments in aviation.

In 1948, authors Sydney "Sy" Bartlett and Beirne Lay, Jr. published their novel *Twelve O'Clock High*. Both had served as officers in the 8th Air Force during the war – Bartlett as a major and Lay as a lieutenant colonel.

In the 1949 movie of the same name, John Morgan was used as the model for the movie's primary character, Lieutenant Jesse Bishop. The exact wording of Morgan's MoH citation was used as dialogue in the script to describe the actions of Bishop under similar circumstances and, like Morgan, Bishop's character was awarded the MoH and later became a PoW.

When questioned of his valor and heroism, Morgan replied:

> There's no such thing as a hero... I was pushed into circumstances where I was forced to act. You can never say how you're going to react to something until it happens, but I think most people would have done the same. I have great respect for others who have the medal, but I really don't think about it for myself. I'm very proud to have it and many good things have come to me because of it. I've met interesting and fine people and been privileged to work in aviation and for Texaco for most of my adult life. I don't dwell on the past. Frankly, I think it would be boring for people to hear about it.

Strategic Air Command General Curtis Emerson LeMay, in his autobiography *Mission With LeMay: My Story*, paid John Morgan the ultimate tribute: "He flew like a homing pigeon to the target in spite of the fact that he had every right and reason to turn back or bail out."

John Cary "Red" Morgan died of a heart attack on January 17, 1991, in Papillion, Nebraska. He is buried in Grave 59-351 at Arlington National Cemetery in Arlington County, Virginia.

Clifford Newton
Michigan Lancaster Pilot

Clifford Sinclair "Apple" Newton came into the world in Charlevoix, Michigan on April 14, 1922. He was the youngest of six children born to Archibald Place Newton and Lucinda Jane Smith. Newton's father was from Roseville, Michigan, while his Canadian-born mother hailed from Meaford, Ontario. Cliff's mother passed away when he was just two.

Newton attended Central Grade School in Petoskey, Michigan, from September 1928 until June 1935, then Petoskey High School from September 1935 until June 1940. He worked locally in that community as a truck driver for the Zipp Lumber Company.

In September 1941, the family moved to the greater Detroit area where Clifford was employed at Hudson's Department Store as a stock clerk. He left there for a better paying job as a metal polisher at the Allison Aircraft Division of General Motors. That employment only lasted a month.

World War II suddenly and violently exploded on the American scene early on Sunday morning, December 7, 1941, after Imperial Japanese Navy (IJN) forces bombed and strafed military facilities at Pearl Harbor, Hawaii, killing and wounding 3,684 US military personnel. That attack unleashed a tsunami of patriotism in every able-bodied American citizen.

Clifford had flown 22 hours recreationally in a friend's aircraft as a passenger and decided he wanted to fight the war from the air rather than on the ground. He rightly figured his best bet was to go to Canada as its educational requirements for pilot training were lower than in the States. On December 11, with his high school diploma and references in hand, Newton crossed the international border at Detroit, Michigan, into Windsor, Ontario, and headed to the RCAF No. 8 Recruiting Centre located on Ouellette Avenue. There he voluntarily enlisted for the duration of the war as an AC2 under regimental service number R. 145305.

Incidentally, the day he enlisted was the same day Germany and Italy declared war on the United States.

While waiting for his paperwork to be processed, Newton stayed at Windsor's YMCA on the RCAF's tab. He told the recruiter that his sport interests were football and basketball and that his permanent home address was 4260 Allendale Street in Detroit.

After five weeks of basic training at No. 1 MD in Toronto, Ontario, Newton spent the next five months pulling guard duty at RCAF Air Station Trenton, Ontario. This very long delay in his training was due to a backlog of recruits who were waiting to go on course.

On August 1, 1942, Clifford married 19-year-old Betty Margaret Howell in Detroit.

After a very brief honeymoon, he returned to the war effort whereupon he was posted to No. 5 ITS at Belleville, Ontario. He graduated from there on August 29, 1942. Promoted to LAC, Newton was sent to No. 13 EFTS at St. Eugene, Ontario, where he flew Fleet Finch II biplanes until October 23. He was then passed to No. 9 SFTS at Centralia, Ontario, where, up to and including March 12, 1943, he flew twin-engined Avro Ansons. Five days after Clifford earned his wings and graduated as an SP from Course No. 67, his son, Clifford James Newton, was born in the Motor City on St. Patrick's Day, March 17, 1943.

Newton was not recommended for an officer's commission by his Centralia instructors. They felt he was a natural pilot but, for whatever reasons, he did not or would not completely apply himself to the task at hand.

Sergeant Newton embarked by troop ship from Canada's "Y" Depot, Halifax, Nova Scotia, on April 8. After a 10-day sea voyage, he arrived at No. 3 Personnel Reception Centre in Bournemouth, England.

For a short period, he was stationed at RAF Bridgnorth at Stanmore, Shropshire. His next posting took him to RAF Kidlington, Oxford, where he flew twin-engined Airspeed Oxfords at No. 20 Pilot Advanced Flying Unit until September 7, 1943. Two days later, he was promoted to FS. Posted to No. 16 OTU at RAF Upper Heyford, Bicester, Apple flew Vickers Wellington bombers until graduating on April 26, 1944. During his time at No. 16, Newton was promoted to WO2. Clifford's training continued with an eight-week posting to No. 1654 Heavy Conversion Unit based at RAF Wigsley, Nottinghamshire, flying twin-engined Avro Manchester and four-engined Short Stirling heavy bombers. Before leaving Wigsley, he was promoted to the rank of PO. His regimental number was changed from R. 145305 to J. 87580 reflecting his officer status.

On August 9, Newton was posted to fly four-engined Avro Lancasters with RAF No. 9 Squadron at Bardney in Lincolnshire.

Over the next three months, he flew more than two dozen night-bombing sorties against a variety of German industrial targets.

The most memorable mission for Newton, his crew and the squadron, was known as Operation *Catechism*, and took place on November 12, 1944. That day, No. 9 and No. 617 Squadrons were detailed to attack and destroy the 42,900-ton German Kriegsmarine battleship *Tirpitz*. The leviathan, moored in a fjord south

RCAF Flying Officer Clifford S. Newton flew Avro Lancaster heavy bombers with RAF No. 9 Squadron. (UK Ministry of Defence)

of Håkøya Island three miles west of Tromsø, Norway, was the sister ship of the famous *Bismarck*.

Thirty-two modified Lancaster B Mk I special aircraft, each carrying a single Barnes Wallis-designed 12,030lb armor-piercing Tallboy bomb, took off at 0300hrs from RAF Lossiemouth, Scotland. Arriving in clear weather at 0941hrs over the target area, 29 Tallboys were dropped, scoring two direct hits on the port side of the battleship. Additionally, there were five near misses, with the massive bombs falling into the water within 30–100 yards of the enemy vessel. At 0952hrs, *Tirpitz*, listing more than 60 degrees to port, suffered a tremendous internal explosion. The ship then rolled over and buried its superstructure in the mud. Nine hundred and seventy-one of its crew perished.

On Boxing Day, December 26, Newton was promoted to FO.

A huge New Year's Eve bash was planned for December 31, 1944, at RAF Bardney. No sorties had been scheduled for the squadron that evening and everyone was looking forward to better times in the coming year. The war was entering its sixth year and rumors were rife that it might all be over in a few short months. However, later that day, orders from Bomber Command's No. 5 Group came down the pike, scheduling an early morning sortie involving 102 Lancasters and two de Havilland Mosquitoes. The target was the Dortmund–Ems Canal viaducts at Ladbergen, Germany. No. 9 Squadron's contribution to the effort was to be ten aircraft. Newton's crew was one of the ten selected and much to their chagrin, their partying that evening was abruptly curtailed.

Briefing for the raid began at 0600hrs. FO Newton was assigned Lancaster Mk I NG252 coded WS-R. With a crew of seven, a full fuel load, and carrying 14 1,000lb general purpose bombs, the aircraft's gross weight topped out at 68,000lb.

The crew list for NG252 on the morning of January 1, 1945, was as follows: pilot, FO C. S. Newton; navigator, FS P. Grant; flight engineer, Sgt C. Booth; bomb aimer, PO R. Flynn; wireless operator, Sgt L. G. Kelly; mid-upper gunner, FS E. H. Cooper; and rear gunner, PO R. S. Stevens.

At 0745hrs, NG252 lifted off from Bardney's 6,000ft main runway after a 3,600ft take off run. Rising just 50ft into the cold grey sky, the aircraft dangerously began to swing to port. Witnesses on the ground heard one or both of its port engines falter just as the Lancaster became airborne. The flying control officer on duty saw the airplane level out and make what appeared to be a slow climbing turn to port never gaining more than 250ft in height. The aircraft slowly descended earthward with the port wing tip hitting the ground. The bomber slid along the ground on its bomb bay doors until coming into contact with first one tree then a second. These obstacles were approximately 5ft in diameter at breast height. Upon impact the aircraft burst into flames.

This was immediately followed by three thunderous explosions as part of the bomb load detonated. Newton and five of his crew died instantly with the aircraft's wreckage being scattered over a wide area. The lone survivor, PO Flynn, who was blown clear of the inferno, was seriously injured.

On January 9, 1945, the OC RAF No. 9 Squadron wrote the following letter to Newton's wife in Michigan:

> Before you receive this letter you will have been informed by RCAF Headquarters in Ottawa, Ontario of the very sad loss of your husband, Clifford Sinclair Newton. Unfortunately it is not possible owing to the time taken to communicate under present conditions, to ascertain your wishes regarding the funeral, and therefore to arrange for his burial without reference to you. You will, I am sure, understand the necessity for this action, and I sincerely trust that the arrangements we were able to make were what you would have wished. Your husband's funeral took place at No. 3 RAF District Cemetery, Harrogate, North Yorkshire, England, on the 5th of January 1945 at 10:30 A.M., the service being conducted by an RCAF Chaplain in this station's chapel. Owing to war operations, it was not possible to accord him full service honours, but a firing party was provided and the coffin was covered with the Union Jack; the last post was sounded at the end. Wreaths were sent from the Commanding Officer, officers and airmen of RAF Station Bardney and from the officers mess. The grave site is number 16, Row D, Section H. You will wish to know that all war graves are taken care of by the Imperial War Graves Commission,

whose duty it is to arrange both for the temporary marking of the grave by a wooden cross and ultimately for the erection of a permanent headstone. I am instructed to explain also that the question of re-internment, if this were desired, could only be considered at the conclusion of hostilities. May I now express the great sympathy which all of us feel with you in the sad loss which you have sustained.

Your husband was the pilot in an aircraft engaged on an operational mission which crashed on taking off from this airfield on January 1, 1945. It may be some consolation to know that your husband's death must have been instantaneous. Your husband had been with this squadron for a number of months and proved himself to be a most successful pilot. His loss is a great blow to us all. I should like also to assure you that your husband's comrades in the RAF admire the unselfish sacrifice he made so far from his homeland in the cause of freedom and in service of his country and of the empire.

Your husband's personal effects have been carefully collected and forwarded to the RAF Central Depository. In due course you will receive a further communication concerning these items from the Administrator of Estate in Ottawa. If there is anything further I can do for you, please do not hesitate to write to me.

Eleven witnesses offered testimony at the Court of Inquiry, which convened at RAF Bardney on January 4. AC A. Hesketh, in his written report dated February 9, 1945, made the following observations: "Serious loss of power on the aircraft's port side appears to be the obvious primary cause of this accident. The reason for the loss of power cannot be ascertained, but some fault in the fuel supply to one or both engines would appear to be the most probable cause."

The RCAF records officer officially registered FO Newton's death with the Province of Ontario's Bureau of Statistics.

Twenty-two-year-old Newton was awarded the following air force medals: 1939–45 Star, France and Germany Star, Defence Medal, General Service Medal, and the Canadian Volunteer Service Medal & Clasp.

These were forwarded to his wife in October 1949. They were subsequently returned to Ottawa as unclaimed. Betty Newton had remarried, moved on and left no forwarding address. It is not known if any member of the Newton family subsequently claimed his earned World War II medals.

Leland Norton
California Havoc Pilot

On Saturday, May 27, 1944, USAAF Captain Leland Francis Norton from San Bernardino, California, was piloting the lead aircraft on a bombing mission against a German-controlled railroad marshalling yard at Amiens, France. On board the Douglas A-20J-5 twin-engined Havoc light bomber, belonging to the 409th BG, were three other crew members: bombardier, 2nd Lieutenant Robert Thomas Taugner; armorer/gunner, S/Sgt Paul Duran; and mechanic/gunner, AC2 Julian Herbert Tate. All were on their 16th combat mission of the war.

The A-20J-5 variant carried an additional crew member in an extended acrylic glass nose section. The variant's mission function was to lead the bombing formations while the standard A-20s dropped their loads when signaled by the leader.

Seconds before reaching the target area, an accurate flak burst incapacitated both Curtiss-Wright R-2600-23 Cyclone engines of Norton's aircraft. Fighting to steady the doomed plane, Norton gave the bail-out order. Taugner and Duran safely parachuted out but were immediately arrested by German soldiers upon landing. They spent the next year as PoWs. Norton and Tate also managed to exit the plunging A-20, but the wind blew their parachutes dangerously close to the burning wreckage on the ground as they descended. As the pair drifted several meters over the raging inferno, the internal 3,000lb bomb load suddenly detonated. Both died instantly from multiple fragmentation wounds.

Leland F. Norton was born on March 12, 1921, in San Bernardino to Thomas F. Norton and Vernice K. Hopkins. From 1926 until 1941, he was educated at the following local schools: Elliot Grammar School, Arrowview Junior High, San Bernardino Senior High, and San Bernardino Junior College. From 1936 until 1941, he was also employed in a variety of occupations – oil company salesman, shoe salesman, and bartender.

Eager to get into the war, the 20-year-old traveled, on August 29, 1941, north up the Pacific Coast Highway to the RCAF No.1 Recruiting Centre at Vancouver, British Columbia.

Leland Norton: California Havoc Pilot

Captain Leland F. Norton died over France on May 27, 1944, while piloting a Douglas A-20 Havoc, similar to the one depicted. (US Department of Defense)

He duly impressed his interviewer, FO McDonald, who recorded in his file that Norton was a desirable applicant who was keen, alert, of smart appearance, confident and mature.

Assigned Regimental Service No. R. 128674, AC2 Norton boarded an eastbound transcontinental train headed for No. 1 MD at Toronto, Ontario. He concluded his basic training at that facility on October 10. His next posting was to No. 1 Technical Training School at St. Thomas, Ontario, where he performed guard duty from October 11 to December 7. This was followed by eight weeks of further training at No. 6 ITS back in Toronto. On February 15, 1942, he began his flight training on de Havilland Tiger Moth biplanes on Course 49 at No. 20 EFTS at Oshawa, Ontario. The course finished up on April 10, with the following remarks recorded by the CFI: "A very eager pupil, anxious to fly even on his days off. Likes instrument flying. Early in the course was inclined to be a little rough on the controls, but has developed into an average pilot."

With 76.30 hours of elementary flying time recorded in his logbook, LAC Norton reported in on April 13 to No. 13 SFTS at Saint-Hubert, Quebec, on Course No. 53 for advanced training on NAA Harvard Mk IIbs.

Leland ceased training at Saint-Hubert on May 11, 1942, after accumulating only 37.05 flying hours. He had met with personnel assigned to the joint Canada–US military transfer train at Montreal that same month and decided to laterally transfer from the RCAF to the USAAF now that America was finally in the war.

There was no pressure to transfer as it was an individual's personal decision. Assigned US Service No. 0-792301, Norton completed his flying training on twin-engined Cessna AT-8 Bobcats and Beechcraft AT-10 Wichitas at Columbus, Mississippi, on September 6, 1942.

Upon graduation he was commissioned a 2nd lieutenant and served in the state of Maine and in Greenland during the remainder of 1942 and most of 1943 doing air-sea rescue work. During that period, he kept applying for combat duty and finally achieved his goal when he was sent to DeRidder Army Air Base at DeRidder, Louisiana, for training on the A-20. Leland was assigned to the 409th BG, which formed at DeRidder.

The 409th was assigned to the 9th Air Force, which then moved from Louisiana to USAAF Station No. 165 at Little Walden, Essex, England, in February–March 1944 to begin operations.

Captain Norton was awarded an American DFC for his actions on May 27, 1944, and was buried in a military cemetery in France. In 1952, his parents journeyed to that country and made arrangements to have his remains returned to the US. He now rests in the Mountain View Cemetery at San Bernardino, California.

San Bernardino Army Airfield opened in July 1942. In March 1950, it was renamed Norton AFB in honor of its local fallen son.

Norton AFB was a major west coast logistics depot and was one of six Military Airlift Command's strategic airlift bases. A portrait of Captain Norton hung in the Officer's Club until the base closed on April 1, 1994.

One further honor was bestowed on this young aviator when the city of San Bernardino dedicated a place of learning as the Captain Leland F. Norton Elementary School.

Richard Patterson
Virginia Spitfire Pilot

RCAF FO Richard Fuller Patterson, from Richmond, Virginia, was one of a minority of World War II servicemen who did not smoke. This was surprising considering his family's affiliation with the American tobacco industry.

Patterson, known among his friends and colleagues as "Fuller," was an heir to the family-founded Lucky Strike Tobacco Company. The brand was introduced by R. A. Patterson in Richmond in 1871 as a cut-plug chewing tobacco product. In time, it emerged as a cigarette. Lucky Strike became the top selling cigarette in the US in the 1930s, selling a record 40 billion in a single year!

Fuller was born to James Thomas Patterson and Mattie Allen Gregory in Richmond on September 21, 1915. The family, which included a younger brother and sister, resided at 4101 Grove Avenue. Patterson's father passed away in 1924 and a few years later his mother married a gentleman named H. B. Handy.

Fuller's elementary and high school years were spent at Richmond's St. Christopher's School (1921–31) and the Madison County Woodberry Forest School (1931–34). Woodberry was established by Captain Robert Stringfellow Walker in 1889 as a private, all-male boarding school. Walker had served as an officer in the 43rd Battalion, Virginia Cavalry "Mosby's Rangers" during the American Civil War.

From 1934 to 1938, Patterson attended Princeton University earning a BA degree in International Affairs. He spent one year at Harvard's Law School, then in the fall of 1939, just as war was erupting on the European continent, he decided he must go to the aid of those nations who were being invaded and overrun by the Nazi regime. Richard held a private pilot's license and had learned to fly under the government-sponsored Civilian Pilot Training Program.

When he voluntarily enlisted in the RCAF at No. 13 Recruiting Centre at Montreal, Quebec, on March 26, 1940, he had 150 flight hours recorded in his logbook. Assigned Regimental Service No. R. 54504, AC2 Patterson made quite an impression on the interviewing officer, G. M. Marshall. He noted the following observations in his report: "Good type, good intellect and a good education. Little

Flying Officer Richard F. Patterson leans on the rear fuselage of his RAF No. 121 Eagle Squadron Supermarine Spitfire Mk Vb in 1941. (Canada Department of National Defence)

work experience, but a great record in the field of sports. Reflects a good family background. Licensed pilot. Courteous. Highly recommended."

Patterson had actually applied to join Canada's air force back in December 1939, but as the infrastructure for the training program had yet to be laid out, the would-be aviator was advised to go home and wait for a call back.

The well-educated, 25-year-old Southerner explained to the recruiters that he had no practical work experience, as his summer months had been occupied with traveling abroad in Europe and Africa. A few of his summer vacations were spent as a councilor/coach at several boys' camps. Fuller's club memberships included Princeton Tower Club, Lincoln's Harvard Law Club, and the Country Club of Virginia. His hobbies were sports of any kind. He was All State Football 1934, All State/All Southern Basketball 1934, Pole Vault State Champion 1933 and 1934, and National Intercollegiate Pole Vault Champion 1938. Additionally, he raced boats, skied, shot skeet, played baseball, ran track, played tennis, and golfed.

Patterson's basic training took place from March 28 to April 28 at No. 1 MD at Toronto, Ontario. Remaining in that city, he began instruction at No. 1 ITS on Course No. 1. Promoted to LAC, Richard began his primary flight training on May 23 at the civilian-operated Vancouver Aero Club at Vancouver, British

Columbia. He passed out of the course with an 82.4 percent average on July 20, 1940. That same day, the training facility's name was changed from the Vancouver Aero Club to RCAF No. 8 EFTS.

On July 28, he reported to No. 1 SFTS at Camp Borden, Ontario, where he flew single-engined Harvard and Yale aircraft until September 17. Richard placed first out of a graduating class of 45 students. SL Kennedy at Borden noted the following: "Very reliable. Hard worker. Good leader and organizer. An athletic genius."

Patterson was commissioned from the ranks as a PO and was assigned replacement Regimental Service No. J. 2928.

The RCAF posted him to the Central Flying School at Trenton, Ontario, where he was to undergo a six-week flying instructor's course.

On October 10, 1940, Patterson wrote the following letter to the OC of "A" Flight at the school, outlining his objection and concerns of his current posting:

> When I enlisted at the Recruiting Centre in Montreal in March 1940, the Recruiting Officer verbally promised me that I would be sent overseas when my course was completed. I made it quite clear that my sole purpose in coming up from Virginia was to proceed overseas as soon as I possessed the necessary flying qualifications. I considered this opportunity guaranteed after my interview with the officer. In addition my name was among those leading the Norwegian Air Force list which was soon to be considered and I gave up that opportunity to serve with the RCAF on the strength of the interview. I was called up into the first training class of the British Commonwealth Air Training Plan. I have completed my training, taking all courses conscientiously with the end view that I would be sent overseas. I graduated first in my class at RCAF Borden and was first American to receive wings and a commission under the new scheme. I was then informed I was to become a flying instructor. I desire, above all, to serve the British Empire to the maximum of my ability and it is my firm conviction that I can best do so if employed on an operational fighter or bomber squadron overseas. Although I fully realize that my case is one of many, I feel that my disappointment at not being sent overseas will have an adverse reaction on the interest I show in my flying duties. This letter is respectfully submitted for your consideration and I am certain the facts outlined above have justified my application for active service overseas.

Richard did complete the instructor's course at Trenton on January 6, 1941. For the next two months, until March 10, he instructed at No. 6 SFTS at Dunnville, Ontario.

On March 27, he was sent overseas, embarking from Canada via RCAF Debert, Nova Scotia. To that point, he had flown in excess of 400 hours on ten separate military aircraft. He arrived at No. 3 Personnel Reception Centre at Bournemouth 13 days later.

On April 23, 1941, Fuller was assigned to RAF No. 56 OTU at Sutton Bridge, Lincolnshire, where he logged 55.60 hours flying Hawker Hurricane fighters. WC Maguire assessed him: "A good steady type of an American pilot who is a cool and calculating fighter."

Patterson managed to finally get into the war in early June when he was posted to RAF No. 121 Eagle Squadron. No. 121 was formed with Hawker Hurricane Mk Is on May 17, 1941, at Kirton in Lindsey in Lincolnshire. As part of Fighter Command's 12 Group, the squadron was declared operational on July 21 after delivery of newer Hurricane Mk IIbs. In October, the squadron received Supermarine Spitfire Mk IIas and, in November, changed over to the Spitfire Mk Vb variant.

Richard was promoted to FO on November 6, 1941. Encounters with enemy aircraft were rare and for the remainder of the year, the squadron primarily flew convoy patrol missions with the occasional sweep or escort duty into part of Western Europe. SL R. P. Powell, Fuller's boss at No. 121, stated the following: "A fine pilot and a good officer. It is strongly recommended that he be retained in the service."

On a ground-attack sortie to Knokke-Heist, Belgium, on December 7, 1941, R. F. Patterson went missing in Spitfire W3711 coded AV-H. He was initially listed as MIA, but that was changed on December 20 to KIA after notification of his death was received through the International Red Cross Society. Fuller was positively identified after the wreckage of his downed fighter was located in the vicinity of Blankenberge, Belgium. He was accorded a military funeral and buried in Grave 525, Row C at the Bredene Churchyard Cemetery.

In 1943, the date and place of his death was registered with the Vital Statistics Department of the Province of Quebec.

In 1946, a Memorial Cross bearing the cypher of King George VI was sent by the Canadian federal government to Patterson's mother. This award, together with a Royal Message of Sympathy, was forwarded to her in recognition of the loss of her son.

Patterson's decorations, which included the 1939–45 Star, Aircrew European Star, General Service Medal, Operational Wings, Canadian Volunteer Service Medal & Clasp, and the Defence Medal, were also forwarded to the family in Richmond.

Patterson was posthumously awarded the Belgian Croix de Guerre with Palm in July 1948.

Donald Pieri
Illinois Spitfire Ace

On January 1, 1945, pilots from RCAF No. 442 "Caribou" FS intercepted, at 0915hrs, a combined force of 40 German Fw 190D "Doras" and Fw 190A-8 "Shrikes" minutes before they were set to bomb and strafe elements of the Allied 2nd TAF located at B.88 Heesch, Holland.

Ironically, B.88 was also the destination of No. 442, which was returning to its temporary Dutch airfield after an uneventful early morning armed reconnaissance patrol. Heesch was home to four other Canadian Spitfire squadrons – 401, 402, 411, and 412. All were assigned to RCAF No. 126 Wing. Outnumbered more than three to one, the 12 Spitfire Mk IXes tore into the much larger force, completely foiling the planned attack.

Several enemy aircraft were shot down and a similar number were severely damaged. So successful and so one-sided was the rout that no damage was done to B.88 and no Canadian aircraft was lost. The Luftwaffe fighters were from JG 6 "Horst Wessel" and were part of Operation *Bodenplatte*.

One of the pilots who destroyed two 190s and badly damaged two others west of Venlo that New Year's morning was FL Donald Mathew Pieri, an American from Elmhurst, Illinois.

The day prior, Pieri had opened his scoring when he and fellow 442 pilot, FO M. A. Perkins, shared in the destruction of a Messerschmidt Bf 109G-1, 15 miles southeast of Münster. The pair harried the 109 pilot to the point that he slammed into the side of a small hill in a desperate attempt to evade his pursuers.

Operation *Bodenplatte*, launched early on New Year's Day, January 1, 1945, was an attempt by the Luftwaffe to cripple Allied air forces in the Low Countries. The Germans had husbanded their resources in the preceding months at the expense of the defense of the Reich units in what was a last-ditch effort to keep up the momentum of the German army during the stagnant stage of the Battle of the Bulge.

This operation proved to be a dismal failure for the Luftwaffe as its aircraft losses were irreplaceable. The losses suffered by the Allied air forces, on the other hand, were made up within weeks. The operation failed to achieve the desired victory, even temporarily, and the German army continued to be exposed to air attack. *Bodenplatte* was the final major Luftwaffe offensive during World War II.

Donald Mathew "Tex" Pieri, the son of Donald J. Pieri and Catherine V. Cash, was born in Pecos, Texas, on April 15, 1919. Pieri's father, a retired US Army lieutenant, relocated the family from Texas to 312 Addison Avenue in Elmhurst, Illinois, after securing a position with the Illinois State Employment Service.

Don Pieri graduated from Glenbard High School in Elmhurst in June 1938. He worked a part-time job all the way through high school as a service station attendant. From 1939 to early 1941, he studied mechanical engineering at Ohio State University. When the money for his schooling ran out, he left college and went to work for a short time as a punch press operator at the Columbus Bolt Works in Columbus, Ohio.

On April 18, 1941, the 22-year-old traveled to No. 8 Recruiting Centre at Windsor, Ontario, where he voluntarily enlisted in the RCAF. Pieri's attestation papers revealed that he had successfully completed three years of training as a cadet in the field artillery with the Civilian Military Training Corps.

Assigned Regimental Service No. R. 98120, Pieri's air force career began as an AC2.

The next day, he traveled 200 miles east by train to No. 1 MD at Toronto, Ontario, remaining there until May 4. From May 5 to June 21, Pieri performed guard duty at No. 6 SFTS at Dunnville, Ontario. Returning to Toronto, he undertook classroom instruction from June 22 to July 27 at No. 1 ITS. Promoted to LAC, Pieri flew Fleet Finch II trainers from July 28 to September 25 on Course No. 34 at No. 9 EFTS, St. Catharines, Ontario.

Sent to No. 2 SFTS Uplands, Ottawa, Ontario, Tex flew advanced single-engined trainers until December 19, 1941, where, in a graduation ceremony, he was awarded his wings and was commissioned from the ranks as a PO. His Regimental Service No. was changed from R. 98120 to J. 9430. Posted to the Flying Instructor School at Air Station Trenton, Ontario, on December 21, Pieri trained as an instructor, completing the course on March 31, 1942.

Don Pieri married a Canadian girl, Evelyn Armstrong Innes, in Toronto on June 27, 1942.

He instructed on Harvards and Yales at No. 14 SFTS in Aylmer, Ontario, from April 1, 1942, to January 22, 1943.

He was promoted to FO on October 1, 1942.

Aylmer, one of 29 SFTSs operated by the RCAF in Canada in World War II, began operations on July 3, 1941, on 500 acres of farmland purchased by the federal government. There were approximately 50 buildings at No. 14, all with red asphalt roofs and green-painted cedar shake siding. The dominant features of this air station were its five hangars measuring 112ft x 125ft and three double runways measuring 3,000ft x 160ft. At its training apex, the school employed upwards of 100 aircraft comprised mostly of single-engined NAA Harvards and a few dozen Yales.

On September 7, 1945, No. 14 SFTS disbanded after having graduated 4,144 pilots for the war effort. The school's success, however, was not without cost.

Flight Lieutenant Donald M. Pieri DFC achieved ace status flying Supermarine Spitfire Mk IXes, similar to the one depicted here. (Parr Yonemoto)

During the four years the station operated, 26 training accidents took the lives of 12 instructors and 26 students. By 1962, what was left of the vacated RCAF complex was turned over to the Ontario provincial government for conversion into the present-day Ontario Police College.

On January 25, 1943, Tex was earmarked to continue his instructor duties when he was posted to No. 1 OTU at Bagotville, Quebec. This Hawker Hurricane unit, part of Eastern Air Command, opened in July 1942 and conducted a total of 29 pilot training courses, from which 940 fighter pilots graduated. No. 1 OTU ceased operations on October 28, 1944. Forty-one pilots were killed during Hurricane conversion courses undertaken at Bagotville.

FO Pieri transferred on October 25, 1943, to RCAF No. 130 "Panther" Squadron, which was flying Hurricane Mk XIIs from Goose Bay, Labrador. The squadron disbanded on March 15, 1944, after flying 8,817 hours in the air defense and convoy escort roles.

Don Pieri was promoted to FL on November 1, 1943.

Eager for an overseas combat assignment and believing the war was passing him by, Pieri finally was able to embark from Canada on a troop ship headed to England on May 25, 1944.

He began his Supermarine Spitfire training at RAF No. 57 OTU Eshott, Northumberland, on August 7, 1944. For the next two months, Tex was assigned to No. 83 Group Support Unit at Westhampnett, West Sussex.

Three-and-a-half years after enlisting, an extremely frustrated Don Pieri finally made it to a frontline RCAF squadron when he was posted to 442 on November 3, 1944.

In early March 1945, No. 442 returned to England to re-equip with the P-51 Mustang Mk III. No. 126 WC Geoffrey Northcott privately spoke to some of his best pilots asking them to stay on Spitfire operations. Northcott implied they would see more action remaining where they were, and they would not have to go through another time-consuming aircraft conversion process. Tex Pieri, Robert Bruce "Bill" Barker, and Red Francis took him up on his offer. Pieri and Barker went over to 412 "Falcon" FS while Francis went to 401 "Ram" FS.

Flying Spitfire NH471 on March 25, Tex bested a Bf 109G-6 in aerial combat five miles south of Winterswijk, The Netherlands.

In the Hagenow area of Germany, on April 19, Pieri was given credit for the destruction of one and a half Fw 190s. Pieri's sixth and final victory occurred on April 30, 1945, when he downed a Luftwaffe Fw 190 15 miles east of Hamburg.

Interviewed by telephone at his home in Oakville, Ontario, on Wednesday, March 23, 2010, Pieri's former OC at 412, SL Maurice David "Dave" Boyd DFC, filled in some of the details of Tex's last flight on Thursday, May 3, 1945.

On that day, Boyd led 12 Spitfire Mk Ixes on a one hour 45-minute armed reconnaissance patrol in the area northwest of Hamburg, Germany. Pieri was not scheduled to fly as it was his day off. His best friend, Bill Barker, who was on the schedule, suddenly became ill. Tex drove Bill over to the hospital whereupon the medical officer grounded and then hospitalized him. Pieri volunteered to take Barker's place flying Spitfire MK827.

The following is Dave Boyd's Incident Report dated May 10, 1945:

> 412 Squadron took off from B.116, Wunstorf, Germany at 1050 hours on May 3, 1945 on an armed reconnaissance to an area northwest of Hamburg. FL Pieri was flying as Red 5. At approximately 1120 hours, Pieri and his No. 2 attacked some motorized enemy transport, five miles southeast of Elmshorn. Coming off the target, Pieri called up on the radio telephone stating that he thought he had been hit. His wingman told him that he was streaming smoke. His OC told him to return to base, but Pieri did not think it was serious and replied that he would remain with the formation which was flying in a northeasterly direction at 4,000 feet. A few minutes later, Pieri said he thought he had better return to base and Red 1 told him to steer a course of 210 degrees. Pieri turned onto this vector and started climbing. He was last seen by the pilots of Red section on that heading entering cloud at 8,000 feet. A couple of minutes later Pieri called to say; 'things were getting too hot and he would have to bail out'. Red 1 replied that he must be very close to the Elbe River and to keep going for as long as possible. There was no further radio contact with Red 5. The remainder of Red section orbited the position where they presumed Pieri had bailed out and had their position fixed by "Kenway" 483 Group Control Centre. There was a great deal of cloud in the area and it was assumed that Pieri was in cloud when he exited his aircraft. The cloud base started at 1,500 feet and topped out at 10,000 feet.

Donald Pieri: Illinois Spitfire Ace

When Don did not return, the squadron figured he was safely down somewhere and would eventually show up. By the time Pieri's wife, Evelyn, received the telegram at her residence at 1055 Davenport Road in Toronto reporting him Missing on Operations, the European war had been officially declared over. She was eagerly looking forward to her husband's return to Canada.

Dave Boyd's term as commander ended on May 30, 1945. On that date, SL Dominic Joseph "Dewey" Dewan assumed command of 412 Squadron. Dewey made the air force his career and returned to Germany in 1948 as part of the Allied Occupation Force. It was Dewey who found out the gruesome details from RCAF investigators of Don Pieri's sad demise three years earlier.

The not-so-lucky Pieri was brought down by ground fire northwest of Hamburg. He bailed out in cloud and landed safely. Don walked into a German farmhouse looking for assistance and was shot dead by a fanatical member of the Hitler Youth movement. The killer then ordered a 14-year-old boy to bury Pieri in an unmarked grave. The killer was never identified nor held accountable for his action. That individual could not accept the fact that Germany was a beaten nation and was within days of surrendering. The day before Pieri's death, it was announced on Hamburg radio that Hitler and Goebbels had committed suicide in the dying Berlin capital. It was also reported that massive numbers of German soldiers were unconditionally surrendering in northern Italy and western Austria.

The day after Don was killed, a message arrived at No. 126 Wing Headquarters. It read: "From 83 Group Headquarters to all units – all hostilities on the second front will cease at 0800 hours tomorrow – May 5th, 1945."

One of 412's best pilots, FL Donald Mathew Pieri became the squadron's last wartime casualty. His name is inscribed on Panel 278 at the Runnymede Air Forces Memorial at Surrey, England. This impressive memorial contains the names of 20,332 airmen who have no known graves.

Dave Boyd said Pieri was a good pilot, brave and very aggressive. He recalled an earlier incident:

> We were returning late one afternoon from a sortie, and I unknowingly overflew a German quad-mounted 20mm antiaircraft site. We should have been at 8,000 feet, but through my own stupidity, I was leading the formation at 4,000 feet! They opened up on us and blew a large hole in my port wing destroying the gun bay. Without a word, Don peeled off, dove down and wiped out the seven-person enemy gun crew.

D. M. Pieri's British DFC was presented to his widow and four-year-old daughter on November 7, 1949, at Government House in Ottawa, Ontario.

Clinton Pudney
New York Halifax Air Gunner

RCAF air gunner FS Clinton Landis Pudney from Buffalo, New York, was one of only 20 air force personnel who received the George Medal (GM) during World War II.

The award was instituted by King George VI on September 24, 1940. The medal was initially only to be given to civilians for acts of great individual bravery but, as the war dragged on, members of the military were included as recipients.

Clinton Pudney, the only son of Herbert E. Pudney and Catherine A. Bennett, was born in Oneonta, New York, on September 20, 1922. There were two older sisters in his family, Emily and Katherine.

Pudney was educated at Sidney Public School in Sidney, New York, from 1927 until 1936. This was followed by four years of higher learning at North High School in Binghamton, New York.

In March 1941, the 19-year-old began working as a production mechanic at the Curtiss-Wright Corporation's Kenmore Avenue plant in Buffalo. Clinton was satisfied with his career choice, but secretly yearned to pilot the P-40B and C model Warhawk fighters that he was helping to build.

Pudney's father died in 1933 and, as he was financially assisting his mother, there was no time nor money with which to attend college. Unable to meet the qualifications for pilot training in any of the prewar American military flying programs, Clinton crossed the border at Buffalo on Thursday, September 15, 1941, and entered the province of Ontario at the town of Fort Erie. He traveled an additional 90 miles to the city of Hamilton, Ontario, where he voluntarily enlisted in the RCAF at No. 10 Recruiting Centre. FO C. C. Conover interviewed Pudney and noted the following observations: "A clean cut US lad who is keen to serve. Should make a successful pilot with training."

Assigned Regimental Service No. R. 139022, AC2 C. L. Pudney shipped out to No. 2 MD at Brandon, Manitoba, for basic training. From January 3 until February 14, 1942, Clinton performed guard duty at No. 13 SFTS at Saint-Hubert, Quebec. Moving through the system, Pudney passed the course at No. 3 ITS at Victoriaville, Quebec, on April 25. Promoted to LAC, he began flight training the next day on Fleet Finch biplanes at No. 22 EFTS at L'Ancienne-Lorette, Quebec.

Clinton Pudney: New York Halifax Air Gunner

When the course concluded on June 15, Clinton was not among the graduating students. His instructors felt that he lacked the necessary self-confidence and airmanship to become a pilot, so they washed him out of the flying program.

Pudney transited to the Re-Selection Centre at Air Station Trenton, Ontario, where, after a series of tests and interviews, it was decided he would be retrained as an air gunner.

On August 2, he was posted to No. 4 Bombing and Gunnery School at Fingal, Ontario, situated nine miles southwest of the city of St. Thomas.

Fingal opened on November 25, 1940, and, up until the time the station closed on February 17, 1945, some 4,142 non-pilot aircrew members graduated either as navigator/air bombers, wireless air gunners, air gunners or flight engineers. Other Allied airmen who graduated from No. 4 included members of the RAF, RAAF, and RNZAF. The aircraft types that operated from this facility over a five-year period included Fairey Battles, Northrop Nomads, Westland Lysanders, Bristol Bolingbrokes and Avro Ansons.

On September 11, 1942, Pudney was awarded his air gunner badge and was promoted to the rank of sergeant. At Fingal, he excelled in his new trade, placing fourth in his class overall.

Within days he was posted to Pier 21 "Y" Depot, Halifax, Nova Scotia, for onward deployment to a war zone. Clinton departed Canada by troop ship on October 27 and arrived at No. 3 Personnel Reception Centre in Bournemouth, England, on November 6. He was assigned, on December 20, to No. 1659 Heavy Conversion Unit at RAF Leeming in Yorkshire. There, he crewed up and began operational training as a mid-upper gunner on Handley Page Halifax four-engined heavy bombers.

Flight Sergeant Clinton L. Pudney GM was killed in a training flight on June 16, 1943, when a Handley Page Halifax heavy bomber crashed after suffering a lightning strike. (UK Ministry of Defence)

The events leading up to Pudney being awarded the GM are as follows.

Returning from a routine sortie over the North Sea on January 28, 1943, Halifax Mk II, HR832, in which Sgt Pudney was flying, struck high ground, crashed and burst into flames six miles north of Thwaite in the Yorkshire Dales. Three members of the crew were killed and the others, with the exception of Pudney, were too severely injured to extricate themselves from the burning wreckage. Though suffering from severe facial lacerations, blood loss, and in a state of shock, Pudney entered the blazing aircraft several times and succeeded in bringing all his companions out. He then walked two miles over the rough moors to obtain help.

WC R. S. Turnbull, the OC No. 1659, sent a letter dated February 2, 1943, to Mrs. Catherine Pudney at 306 15th Avenue in Belmar, New Jersey, explaining the details of the accident:

> By now you will have been informed that your son, Sergeant Clinton Pudney, was in an aircraft which crashed on the afternoon of January 28, 1943. Your son, along with a full crew, took off on a local flight on the morning of January 28, 1943. Nobody actually saw what happened, but it is known that they ran into some very heavy cloud which obscured the surrounding country. It would appear that when they attempted to break cloud to check their position, the aircraft struck a hill, which itself was in cloud. Your son was only slightly injured. Your son was the only American in the aircraft, the others coming from parts of Canada and England. Complete details are not yet available, but from what I hear, your son conducted himself in a most gallant manner and it is thought that it was through him that some of the other members of the crew were taken to safety. Apparently your boy was able to get out of the aircraft immediately and, after looking after his companions, he walked over the Yorkshire Moors, a distance of about two miles, to try and get help. He finally reached a cottage where the people took him in and took care of him as best they could until help arrived a short time later.
>
> Clinton is now at the Catterick Military Hospital and is coming along splendidly. I do not think it will be long before he is up and about. This unit is in constant touch with the hospital and we are seeing to it that he is well supplied with comforts. I can assure you that he is receiving excellent medical attention and everything that can be done is being done. I hope by the time this letter reaches you, Clinton will be up and around. If there is anything that I can do for you at any time, please do not hesitate to get in touch with me.

Pudney was promoted to FS on March 11.

On April 8, 1943, Clinton was posted to RCAF No. 405 "City of Vancouver" Squadron, which was based at Gransden Lodge near Cambridge. The squadron was the first RCAF bomber squadron formed overseas, and was also the RCAF's only pathfinder unit.

Pudney completed four operational sorties over Germany before tragically losing his life in a non-operational plane crash on June 16. The details of the crash, taken directly from the accident investigation report dated June 18, 1943, reveal the following information: "Seven crew members from RCAF No. 405 Squadron were killed at 1900 hours on June 16, while flying in Halifax Mk II, MR832. The aircraft, on a routine cross country sortie, came apart in the air after being struck by lightning over RAF Sutton Bridge. The wreckage is scattered over a wide area. The intact fuselage fell at Clifton Farm in Norfolk and was quickly consumed in the post crash fire."

The OC No. 405, WC J. E. Fauqier, sent the following letter dated July 5, 1943, to Clinton's mother:

> It is with deep regret that I must confirm the information given in the Air Ministry's recent telegram that your son, FS C. Pudney, was killed in an air accident while engaged in a training flight on the 16th of June 1943, near RAF Air Station Sutton Bridge. It would appear from the evidence that the aircraft was struck by a very large discharge of lightning which caused the crash. Your son, although comparatively new to this squadron, was very popular and is greatly missed in the sergeant's mess. He and his crew were regarded as exceptionally able and his loss is keenly felt. Owing to the time taken to communicate under present conditions, it was not possible to ascertain your wishes regarding the funeral in the time available and I had to therefore arrange his funeral without reference to you. You will, I am sure, understand the necessity for this action, and I sincerely hope that the arrangements we were able to make were what you would have wished. Your son's funeral took place at the Sutton Bridge churchyard on Saturday, June 19, 1943. The coffin covered with a Union Jack Flag was carried by his fellow airmen. As the coffin was lowered, the last post [sic] was sounded. Wreaths were sent from the officers of this squadron, the senior non-commissioned officers and the airmen. You will wish to know that the graves are taken care of by the Imperial War Graves Commission, who will erect a temporary wooden cross, pending the provision of a permanent memorial. I am instructed to explain that the question of reinterment, if this was desired, can only be considered at the conclusion of hostilities. Your son's effects have been gathered together and sent to the RAF Central Depository at Colnbrook, from where they will be forwarded to the Administrator of Estates in Ottawa, Ontario, who will be writing to you in this regard in due course.
>
> In closing, may I say that my brother officers and myself, and all the rest of the squadron feel the deepest sympathy with you, in your sad loss. If there is anything I can do at all to help you, please do not hesitate to get in touch with me.

On August 7, 1943, the minister of National Defence for Air in Ottawa sent the following letter to Mrs. Pudney: "At this time of great sorrow it is felt that you and the members of your family will wish to know the circumstances surrounding the honour and distinction which have come to your son, FS Clinton Landis Pudney, GM, through the posthumous award of the George Medal for great gallantry in the performance of his duty while serving with the RCAF."

The minister then recited the details of the crash on January 28, 1943, in the Yorkshire Dales and closed his letter with the statement that the personnel of the air force was proud of Clinton's fine service record.

Twenty-one-year-old FS Pudney never knew of his rare award as it was not gazetted until July 13, 1943. The RCAF records officer registered Pudney's death details with the Province of Ontario's Bureau of Statistics.

On September 25, 1943, a Memorial Cross bearing the cypher of King George VI was sent by the Canadian federal government to Mrs. Pudney. This award, together with a Royal Message of Sympathy, was forwarded to her in recognition of the loss of her son while on active service.

Three years later on November 8, 1946, a still grieving Mrs. Pudney sent the following letter to RCAF Headquarters in Ottawa:

> I have been hearing rumours that my son, Clinton Landis Pudney, has been found alive. Do you know anything about it, or is someone trying to unloose my mind? You reported to me that Clinton was killed in action in England on June 16, 1943. Of course, I am on pins and needles since hearing this and will be glad to know the truth. Enclosed is a letter for him in case he is now in Canada. Please see that he gets it and if he is not in Canada, you may destroy the letter. Thanking you so much for a quick reply.

The following response was forwarded by the RCAF casualty officer on behalf of the CAS:

> In reply to your letter concerning your son, FS Clinton Landis Pudney, GM, I must inform you that the information previously passed to you that your son lost his life at 1900 hours on June 16, 1943 at Clifton Farm, Pullover Road, Clenchwarton, Norfolk County, England, is confirmed.
>
> His funeral took place at 1500 hours on Saturday June 19th, at Sutton Bridge, Spalding, Lincolnshire, as you were previously advised. There is no foundation to any of the rumours that he might possibly be alive. May I, at this time, offer my deepest sympathy in your sad loss of a very brave son.

Clinton Pudney's remains are buried in Grave 29, Section S, in the St Matthew Churchyard Cemetery at Sutton Bridge.

In addition to the GM, he was awarded the following medals: 1939–45 Star, Aircrew European Star, War Medal, and the Canadian Volunteer Service Medal & Clasp.

Robert Reed
Ohio Reconnaissance Pilot

On Good Friday, April 23, 1943, an overseas cablegram arrived at the residence of Mr. and Mrs. C. B. Reed, 116 Wood Street in Lowellville, Ohio. It was a casualty notification from the Air Ministry in London, England, advising the couple that their 24-year-old son, RCAF FO Robert Burns "Bobby" Reed, had died as a result of a flying accident the previous day. When the tragic news reached the small northeastern Ohio town, Reed's mother was on her way home from attending a mid-day religious service at Holy Rosary Catholic Church.

Robert was born in Lowellville on September 17, 1918, one of five children of Clinton Bernard Reed and Maizie Caldwell. Lowellville, located on the Mahoning River and nestled in the picturesque rolling foothills of the Allegheny Mountains, was a great place to grow up. Robert attended Lowellville Public School from 1924 to 1932 and graduated from Old Mill High School in 1936. He worked most of his summer vacations at the Lowellville Water and Electric Department, where his father was the superintendent. Reed was a senior in a liberal arts program at the University of Mississippi when, late in 1940, he suddenly decided to join the RCAF.

February 18, 1941, was the date he voluntarily signed his enlistment papers at the No. 8 Recruiting Centre on Ouellette Avenue in downtown Windsor, Ontario. Accepted into the air force as an AC2 under Regimental Service No. R. 83403, Reed told the interviewer, FO H. E. Fleming, that he had machine shop training and had spent two years in the ROTC while in college. He indicated his sport interests were baseball, boxing, football, and track. Fleming wrote in Reed's file: "Alert, intelligent and pleasant. Very good type. Should be good pilot training material."

From February 19 until April 2, Robert undertook his basic training at No. 1 MD at Toronto, Ontario. This facility was located on the 352-acre site formerly occupied by Canada's largest yearly fair – the Canadian National Exhibition. The recruits were housed on two floors of the huge livestock pavilion, which could accommodate, after modifications, upwards of 5,000 personnel at any given time. Reed's ROTC experiences gave him a leg up over the average enlistee who sometimes found the process of moving from the civilian world to a military lifestyle intimidating.

Waiting to get on a course, an obligatory stint of guard duty followed. For seven weeks – April 3 until May 27 – Reed and several others were at RCAF Air Station Yarmouth, Nova Scotia, where they guarded Bristol Bolingbroke Mk 1 aircraft belonging to No. 119 Bomber Reconnaissance Squadron. This unit, part of the HWE, was tasked to fly daily anti-submarine sorties over the St. Lawrence River and the Atlantic Ocean.

On May 28, Robert was posted to No. 3 ITS at Victoriaville, Quebec. He completed the course on July 14, 1941, and was promoted to LAC. From there he was off to No. 12 EFTS located at Sky Harbour Airport at Goderich, Ontario. There he flew Fleet Finch Mk I and II biplanes until graduating on September 13. To complete his training to wings standard, he reported to No. 1 SFTS at Camp Borden, Ontario, where he flew a total of 101.05 hours on single-engined Harvard and Yale aircraft. The course concluded with a graduation ceremony on December 19. Reed and his classmates were promoted to SPs.

At every SFTS graduation, the top four or five students were immediately recognized and awarded with an appointment to the rank of PO. Reed was one of those who received an officer's commission that day and this necessitated changing his Regimental Service No. R. 83403 to J. 9424. At the time of his appointment, he had a total of 157 flight hours in his logbook.

During the Christmas leave period of 1941, Reed brought four of his Uplands classmates home to Lowellville to celebrate the holiday season with his family. Three were RAAF pilots – Norman Clark, Kenneth Slatyer, and John Horgan. The fourth was a fellow American, Victor Nicholas "Vic" Cabas from New Castle, Pennsylvania.

On January 8, 1942, Robert reported in at "Y" Depot, Pier 21, Halifax, Nova Scotia, for onward deployment to England. He arrived at No. 3 Personnel Reception Centre at Bournemouth on January 21.

On February 12, he left the United Kingdom and headed for the RAF Middle East Command (MEC) in North Africa. As part of RAF No. 216 Group, Reed was seconded to as a pilot serving at Kasfareet, Suez, then at Almaza, Egypt.

His tour over, he returned to Great Britain on September 24 for a period of leave. On October 1, 1942, he was promoted to FO. Robert let his family know that he was back in England and was looking forward to joining an operational squadron.

He was posted on January 19, 1943, to RAF No. 41 OTU at Old Sarum, Wiltshire, where he trained as a TR pilot until April 11.

RCAF No. 430 (City of Sudbury) Reconnaissance Fighter Squadron stood up on January 1, 1943, at Hartfordbridge Flats, Hampshire. Assigned to RAF Army Co-Operation Command, 430's first aerial mount was the Buffalo-built Curtiss-Wright Kittyhawk Mk I and II aircraft. These were flown from RCAF Dunsfold,

Robert Reed: Ohio Reconnaissance Pilot

An NAA Mustang Mk I is being inspected at the RAF air depot at Burtonwood, Cheshire, by RAF and USAAF personnel. Flying Officer Robert B. Reed lost his life flying this type of aircraft on April 22, 1943. (UK Ministry of Defence)

Surrey, for a short period in January and February 1943. Twelve days after receiving its Kittyhawks, the squadron began re-equipping with the Allison F3R-engined P-51 Mustang Mk I.

The fair-haired, young American officer, known to the Dunsfold village residents simply as Bobby Reed, joined No. 430 Squadron on April 12, 1943. In less than a fortnight, he was dead.

Flying accidents with this squadron during the first few weeks of training resulted in the death of three officers with one other being seriously injured. FO R. B. Reed was unfortunately one of the recorded fatalities.

On April 22, 1943, FL Clarke, OC "B" Flight of No. 430 Squadron filed the following accident report:

At 0945 hours on the morning of April 22, 1943, I authorized FO Reed to fly Mustang 1 AM255 to carry out a pin-point navigation exercise in the vicinity of Dunsfold. Thirty minutes later while I was up flying, the weather began to close in and I instructed flying control to recall all our aircraft. All aircraft were contacted and reported to the effect that they understood the message 'to return to base'. FO

Reed was contacted again a few minutes later and was asked if he knew where he was. He answered, 'Yes, I am about eight miles from base'. Flying control then asked him if he required a homing signal to which no reply was received.

Repeated calls to FO Reed went unanswered.

The wreckage of Reed's Mustang was found in the hilly region of Hindhead, Surrey. The aircraft had apparently impacted on high ground while flying in poor visibility.

FO Reed was given a full military funeral and was laid to rest in the Brookland Military Cemetery at Woking, Surrey.

Bobby Reed earned the following medals while serving in the RCAF: 1939-45 Star, Aircrew European Star, General Service Medal, Defence Medal, Africa Star, and the Canadian Volunteer Service Medal & Clasp.

In 1949, a Memorial Cross bearing the cypher of King George VI was sent by the Canadian federal government to Reed's mother. This award, together with a Royal Message of Sympathy, was forwarded to her in recognition of the loss of her son. The Memorial Cross is often referred to as the Silver Cross for Mothers.

Besides his parents, Bobby left the following family members to mourn his loss – sisters Mrs. Margaret Kerwin of Kent, Mrs. Katherine Hammer of Cleveland, Mrs. Betty Brooks of Columbus and a brother, Mr. Arthur Reed, a teacher at Lowellville High School.

Albert Schlegel
Down Over France

On August 28, 1944, Captain Albert Lewis "Smiley" Schlegel, the newly appointed operations officer of the 335th FS, 4th FG, took off on a mission from USAAF Station F-356, Debden, Essex, and never returned. No trace of the high-scoring ace nor of the new P-51D Mustang he was flying were ever found.

Decades after his disappearance, his fate and resting place have finally been revealed.

The following is taken from the 335th's operational diaries, dated August 28, 1944:

> An exciting show takes place today. The task is to strafe transportation in the Strasbourg, France area. Briefing was called at 0600 hours and Colonel Blakeslee briefed for a takeoff at 0648 hours. Under Field Order No. 538 and equipped with full ammunition and petrol, our squadron took off at 0655 hours and crossed in at Dunkirk at 0738 hours at 15,000 feet. Reaching the Sarrebourg area, they let down to 4,000 feet where weather prevented them from going any further. In strafing that area, our pilots made the following claims – two locomotives destroyed, thirteen locomotives damaged and thirty-eight goods wagons damaged. Lt. Russell damaged a railroad crane as well. Pilots reported railroad traffic running west from Strasbourg. When they returned at 1400 hours, three of our pilots were not in the group.
>
> Captain McKennon bailed out near Niederbronn-les-Bains as his kite was hit by flak. He was seen to land in some trees, so we are almost certain that he is alive. However, Major Thomson and Captain Schlegel were also missing and none of the pilots can account for them. So no comment is possible as to their whereabouts, but they may have bailed out as well; they are classed as Not Yet Returned.

Pierce W. "Mac" McKennon successfully evaded capture and, with the assistance of the French underground, made a safe return to Debden the next month. Major Archibald M. Thomson eluded the Germans for a short while until being captured and interned as a PoW.

No information relating to Captain Schlegel was ever forthcoming.

Schlegel had returned from leave in the States ten days earlier on August 18 and was to begin his second combat tour. At the time of his death, his victory total stood at 15 – ten aerial and five ground.

The new P-51D, coded WD-O, he was lost in was assigned to Smiley on August 24, just four days before he died. Most of his victories between March 8 and April 24, 1944, were in a P-51B-10NA Mustang.

Albert L. Schlegel, Jr. was the only son of Albert Lewis Schlegel, Sr. and Lillian Olive Honsberg. Albert, Jr. was born on August 20, 1919, in Glenville Hospital in Cleveland, Ohio. The family, which also included three daughters, resided at 12905 Thornhurst Avenue in Garfield Heights, Ohio.

In 1931, Albert's father, an attorney, died after suffering a massive cerebral hemorrhage. Albert attended Miles Jr. High School from 1925 to 1935 and completed his academic studies at John Adams High School, graduating in 1938 with a B average. Money was tight in the Schlegel household so any thought of Albert going to college was out of the question.

From early 1939 to 1941, Schlegel worked as a mechanic at the Breuning Auto Glass Company on East 21st Street. He hoped one day to join the military and, to that end, had completed four 30-day army summer civilian training camp sessions. He also had a keen interest in airplanes, no doubt generated in part by his proximity to the annual Cleveland National Air Races.

Schlegel took some aviation ground school courses sponsored by the Cleveland Woman's Chapter of the National Aeronautics Association. This is where he first learned of the recruitment program underway in the United States for the RCAF. This not-so-secret operation, known as the Clayton Knight Committee, openly set up information/screening offices for interested applicants in luxurious hotels in New York, Cleveland, Atlanta, Memphis, Kansas City, Dallas, San Antonio, Los Angeles, San Francisco, and Spokane.

Assured by the representatives of that organization that he would not lose his American citizenship or be in violation of the American Neutrality Act by serving in a foreign air force, the 21-year-old Schlegel traveled on February 25, 1941, from the south shore of Lake Erie to the RCAF's No. 11 Recruiting Centre in Toronto, Ontario. Seeking additional information, he learned that to begin pilot training, the air force needed his high school diploma, his birth certificate and, after he had passed a thorough medical examination, he would be placed in the training pipeline.

Sworn into the RCAF under Regimental Service No. R. 97118 as an AC2 on March 3, Albert avoided having to swear an oath of allegiance to England's King George VI. As an American volunteer, he had to agree to obey his superiors and abide by all air force regulations.

His starting pay was CAN$1.30 per day.

Albert Schlegel: Down Over France

He listed his hobbies as model airplane building and stamp collecting. Albert boxed, wrestled, and played baseball and football throughout high school. In his senior year, his nose was badly fractured in a boxing match. FO J. B. Richardson interviewed Schlegel and recorded these comments: "Good clean cut American lad. Keen and has taken US courses with the idea of getting a US commission. Will develop into good aircrew material. Pleasant and good appearance."

When Albert enlisted, he brought with him a recommendation letter from R. H. Ring, mayor of the city of Garfield Heights in Cuyahoga County. The letter read as follows: "I am glad to have the opportunity of recommending Albert Schlegel to the RCAF. I have known his family for the past sixteen years and have watched his progress through school with a lot of satisfaction. He has a fine reputation in this community and can be trusted at all times. I can highly recommend him as to character, integrity and ability."

Albert was at No. 1 MD in Toronto until March 24. From March 25 to May 16, he was stationed at No. 6 SFTS at Dunnville, Ontario, on guard duty. He was assigned, on May 17, to No. 1 ITS in Toronto, Course No. 26, which concluded on June 20, 1941. Schlegel ranked 46th out of the 169 students in his class and achieved a final mark of 88 percent. The CO at the ITS recorded the following in his file: "Dependable, hard working trainee with the right service spirit. Good common sense for his age. Second aircrew recommendation, Air Observer."

Promoted to LAC and given a pay raise of 20 cents extra per day, Schlegel was passed to No. 12 EFTS at Goderich, Ontario on June 21. This airfield, located on a bluff overlooking the picturesque sandy beaches of Lake Huron, was an unforgettable location for any young man to be at in the golden summer months of 1941. With the competing distraction of girls, swimming, boating, dancing, and fishing, it is a wonder any actual flight training was accomplished in that ideal setting.

Albert flew 55.20 hours on Course No. 31 at Goderich on Fleet Finch IIs, graduating on August 8. The school's CFI recommended that Schlegel's advanced training be on single-engine aircraft. He had this to say regarding Albert's time at No. 12: "Interested, anxious to learn, seldom makes the same error twice. Instrument flying is reasonably good, aerobatics good, general flying somewhat above average. Is quick to detect and correct small errors."

LAC Schlegel was posted, on August 9, to No. 14 SFTS at Aylmer, Ontario, located in the rural farming community of Elgin County. Albert flew Harvard Mk IIbs on Course No. 35 and received his wings when his class graduated on October 23, 1941. Schlegel was appointed an SP and, after receiving a boost in pay, was earning $111 monthly.

He was granted his pre-embarkation leave and was directed to report to "Y" Depot, Halifax, Nova Scotia, by November 11.

On November 10, a Canadian National telegram from Jersey City, New Jersey, arrived at the "Y" Depot office in Halifax containing the following message:

"From: Sgt. Pilot Gray R. 79093, Sgt. Pilot Farrell R. 79164 and Sgt. Pilot Schlegel R. 97118. Just arrived in New York from west coast will be in Halifax Sunday." The three were traveling together and no disciplinary action was taken when they arrived in Halifax a few days late.

That November, Albert authorized that the sum of $24 be deducted from his wages each and every month and sent home to his mother.

Leaving Canada on a troop ship, Albert arrived in the United Kingdom on November 23 and was sent to No. 3 Personnel Reception Centre in Bournemouth.

Sergeant Schlegel was charged on November 26 with disorderly conduct after speaking in an insolent manner to FS Dann while in his barrack room at Bletchley Hall. WC Kempsted verbally reprimanded him for his outburst.

Schlegel was posted on December 9 to No. 59 OTU, RAF Crosby-on-Eden, Carlisle. Flying Hurricanes on Course No. 12, Albert's training was to conclude on February 17, 1942.

Schlegel was within nine days of graduating when a motor vehicle accident on February 8 put him in the Carlisle City General Hospital. His more serious injuries were a broken right leg and foot. He also suffered facial injuries, a concussion, and was in severe shock. The next day, a dental surgeon removed four of his upper incisors, which were broken off at the gum line. Schlegel, who was a passenger in the car's rear seat, was catapulted face-first into the dashboard by the force of the collision. On March 4, he was transferred to the RAF hospital at Weeton, North Yorkshire, and on June 9, was admitted to the RAF Rehabilitation Centre at Hoylake in Merseyside. He remained there until he was medically cleared to return to flight status.

Not having graduated from the OTU and not having flown an airplane in seven months, Schlegel was required, in September, to retake the training at No. 59. Promoted to FS, he resumed training on October 7, 1942, on Hurricanes and Miles Masters, this time on Course No. 24 at

4th FG ace Captain Albert L. Schlegel proudly sports two sets of wings, Canadian and American, on his USAAF uniform. (US Department of Defense)

Albert Schlegel: Down Over France

RAF Milfield, Northumberland. SL W. Vale, the CFI, noted the following when the course ended on December 29: "An average pilot. Formation flying quite good generally but still requires more practice. Good airmanship and navigation. Keen on night flying and completed his exercises very satisfactorily. As a Non Commissioned Officer, he is a sound and capable leader."

Schlegel decided to transfer from the RCAF to the USAAF as the latter would immediately commission him an FO and this would double his monthly rate of pay. This would allow him to send additional money each month to his mother and three sisters.

With 249.30 flying hours recorded in his logbook, FS Albert L. Schlegel appeared before a USAAF medical board in London in early January and was accepted into that service. He was honorably discharged from the RCAF Special Reserve at RAF Abbey Lodge, London, on January 25, 1943, after having served 694 days.

Albert was sent to Station No. 342 Atcham for his USAAF conversion training in February. FO Schlegel started out flying Spitfires and P-39s but, halfway through the course, switched over to the Republic P-47 Thunderbolt after that type was introduced into the training syllabus.

He officially joined the 335th FS on July 3, 1943. Smiley flew P-47s until the 4th converted to the P-51 Mustang on February 14, 1944. On March 5, he was appointed the 335th's "B" Flight commander. 1st Lieutenant A. L. Schlegel was promoted to captain on April 14.

It was in the P-51 where Schlegel and so many other 4th pilots suddenly began to shine. The transition to this superlative new mount is evident in Albert's combat reports of April 8 and April 22, 1944, respectively.

From April 8:

> I was flying Green 1 in Greenbelt Squadron. We were on course and on time when the bombers called for help. We headed south and joined them, finding them quite happy. Shortly after two large gaggles of enemy aircraft were sighted, so we attacked them. During the attack I saw two white-nosed P-51s with two Fw 190s on their tails, so I took my section down to help them. Green 3 went after one; I got a few deflection shots at another then he broke for the deck. Before I could close on him, another P-51, piloted by Lt. Monroe got behind him so I continued on down giving him cover. After a long chase Monroe got strikes all over the 190, the coupe top came off and the 190 crashed in some trees, burning. A little after that I spotted an airfield with a Me 210 sitting on it. As I came over the trees, on the edge, there were two Fw 190s taxiing across – one made the trees, the other seeing he couldn't make it turned his nose into my attack. I closed very close and saw many strikes. Just as I was about to make another attack on that airfield, Lt. Monroe called me and said that he was chasing an Fw 190 but as he was out of ammunition, he'd keep him busy till I came up. After a short chase I got quite a few strikes on the fuselage

of the 190 and set the droppable belly tank on fire. Then large pieces started coming off and he crashed into the deck and burst into flames. Just as we set course for home, I sighted a Bf 109 and we gave chase. He must have had everything forward because continuous black smoke came from the exhaust. After quite a long chase, we were just getting into range of him when an Fw 190 came in from above. Both Lt. Monroe and myself turned into him. As soon as we did this the Bf 109 pilot turned and crash-landed in a small ploughed field. I did not see the pilot come away from the 109. The Fw 190 pilot started to turn in a tight circle above a forest. I fell in line astern, firing with a large deflection at about 250 yards. Meanwhile Lt. Monroe kept making attacks trying to straighten him out. I don't recall seeing any strikes and after about the fourth or fifth circuit with twenty degrees of flap and one hundred and ten miles per hour airspeed indicated, I was still drawing deflection, but was on the verge of flicking into the trees. So I broke off and Lt. Monroe saw the smoke from the results. Later I shot up the locomotive of a train.

Aircraft used: P-51B-10NA No. 42-1076464. Ammunition used: 1035 Rounds .50 Calibre Armoured Piercing Incendiary [API] & Tracer [T]. One Fw 190 destroyed; One Fw 190 destroyed (shared); One Bf 109 destroyed (shared); One Fw 190 damaged (ground); One train damaged. Time 1415 to 1500 hours. Location Brunswick, Germany. April 8, 1944.

From April 22:

I was flying Red 1 in Caboose Squadron; both my No. 2 and No. 4 had aborted. We let down to 10,000 feet in the Kassel area and someone reported twenty plus Bf 109s forming up. The other two squadrons bounced these. Just about then two Bf 109s came into attack White Section from above. Red 3 and myself turned into them and they broke down. Red 3 chased one and I chased the other but lost him against the trees when my windscreen steamed up. I climbed back up and joined some other P-51s in an attack on a larger gaggle of enemy aircraft, the fight ending up on the deck. I attacked a 109 from about eighty degrees allowing a little over two rings, opened fire under two hundred yards and saw strikes on the area just above the wing root; it started smoking immediately. Someone called "Damned good shooting" over the radio telephone. I had to straighten out and climb to avoid another P-51, which I later learned was piloted by Lt. Carlson who saw my 109 crash and burn. I returned to the fight and saw two enemy aircraft burning on a field. Just about then I saw a 109 who looked as if he were about to crash-land. The P-51 that was chasing him overshot and the 109 pulled up behind him and attacked. I started after him firing at deflection of between thirty to forty degrees at a long range and observed no strikes. The attacker finally broke and turned, climbing into me. I opened fire at about one hundred and fifty yards at about seventy to eighty degrees allowing two rings. I could only see the spinner of the 109, the rest being hidden under my wing. But it's very possible that I was hitting him. He slid under me and when I did a tight turn back onto him, I found that he had straightened out and was heading for the ground. Remembering his former tactics I slowed up and followed him down getting strikes; when he was just a few feet off the ground I clobbered him. His right wing hit and tore off and the rest of him I lost in the dust and smoke.

Aircraft used: P-51B-10NA No. 42-106464. Ammunition used: 340 Rounds .50 Calibre API & T. Two Bf 109Gs destroyed. Time 1750 hours. Location South of Kassel, Germany. April 22, 1944.

The 4th's intended mission on August 28, 1944, was to strafe ground targets in the Strasbourg, France, area. Unable to reach its primary objective because of bad weather, the group let down through the cloud cover over Sarrebourg, France, some 49 miles west of its goal. It was a very costly ground attack for when it was over, three Mustangs had been lost to accurate German ground fire.

Major General Edward F. Witsell, the Adjutant General of the Army in Washington, DC sent the following letter, dated February 14, 1950, to Captain Schlegel's mother in Cleveland:

> I am writing you relative to the previous letter from this office in which you were regretfully informed that a Finding of Death had been made in the case of your son, Captain Albert L. Schlegel, 02044921, Air Corps and that the presumptive date of his death had been established as 29 August 1945. Under the revised provisions of the Missing Persons Act, the Department of the Army is empowered to establish an actual date of death and issue an official report of death in any case where the circumstances under which that person became missing in action lead to no other logical conclusion. As you were previously informed, your son, as the pilot of a P-51 aircraft, departed 28 August 1944, on a ground strafing mission to Strasbourg, France. While over the target area he called by radio that his plane had been hit and that he might have to bail out. An extensive investigation conducted in the area concerned reveals beyond a doubt that an American fighter's plane exploded and crashed into the Saar River at the time your son's distress call was heard. Due to the swift current of the river and recurrent floods, no trace of the aircraft could be found. He was never reported as a Prisoner of War, an internee nor as having returned to duty. In view of the above, plus the fact that more than five years have since elapsed without any report having been received indicating his survival, it is logical to conclude that your son met death by drowning or was killed when his plane exploded and crashed.
>
> The records of the Department of the Army, therefore, are being amended to show that Captain Schlegel was Killed in Action on 28 August 1944, when his plane exploded and crashed into the Saar River at Sarrebourg, France. Pursuant to the

provisions of Public Law 490, 77th Congress, 7 March 1942, as amended, official reports will not be issued by the Department of the Army which will indicate the actual date of his death as that shown above. The issuance of this official Report of Death will not effect any payment or settlement of accounts which has been made on the basis of the Finding of Death. My continued sympathy is with you in the great loss you have sustained.

In 1951, Lillian Schlegel Eaton, who had remarried on November 1, 1947, applied to the Canadian government for any gratuity that might be due her as a result of her son's air force service. The Department of Veterans Affairs in Ottawa, Ontario, investigated her claim and determined that at the time FS Schlegel transferred to the USAAF on January 25, 1943, she was in fact partly dependent on his income. A check in the amount of CAN$370.31 was approved and forwarded to her.

On December 8, 1958, the Canadian government sent the Schlegel family the following medals Albert had earned while serving in the RCAF – Defence Medal, Canadian Volunteer Service Medal & Clasp, and the War Medal 1939–45.

Captain Albert Lewis Schlegel's name was recorded on the tablets of the MIA at the Lorraine American Cemetery at Saint-Avold, France.

In 2017, Schlegel's nephew, Perry Nuhn, a retired USAF colonel, discovered updated information on the fate of his uncle. Perry found that Schlegel did not crash in his flak-damaged Mustang as everyone had surmised, but bailed out in the vicinity of Valmy, France. On that day, August 28, 1944, villagers reported seeing an Allied airman being brought to the local train station escorted by German soldiers. A few minutes later, they heard two gun shots. A body was later discovered not far from the station. The remains, identified only as X-73, were then transferred to the American cemetery at Champigneulles. In 2016, investigators had the skeletal remains sent to a laboratory in Nebraska where it was positively determined they belonged to Captain Schlegel. After 72 years, the mystery of his disappearance was finally revealed. This triple USAAF World War II ace was buried with full military honors in the Beaufort National Cemetery. Hundreds of people gathered on the road leading to this young flyer's final resting place. A flyover by current members of his old squadron, the 335th FS, flying F-15E Strike Eagles from Seymour Johnson Air Force Base, completed the final gravesite tribute.

William Smith
West Virginia Fighter Pilot

One of the lesser-known combat pilots who flew with the USAAF's famed 4th FG in 1943–44 was Captain William Ballard Smith. Assigned to the 334th FS, Smith flew three aerial mounts during his time with the 4th.

The first was a Republic Aviation P-47C-5 Thunderbolt named *Little Butch*. This was followed by two NAA Mustangs, a P-51B-7 and a P-51D-10. The latter two aircraft were unnamed. All three ships carried the fuselage code QP-Y. Smith is credited with destroying five-and-a-half German aircraft, three aerial and two-and-a-half ground.

William B. Smith was born to Hatty Anderson and Eustace Byron Smith on July 20, 1914, in Bluefield, West Virginia. From 1921 until 1933, he was educated at Graham Grade and Graham High School. Both of these learning facilities were located just across the state line in Bluefield, Virginia.

For the next eight years, Smith was steadily employed as a furniture salesman with the Chicago House Furniture Company in Bluefield.

In the summer of 1941, Smith, like millions of other Americans, knew that war was on the horizon for the United States. He had never been in an airplane, but somehow, he knew that flying was the only platform from which he wanted to go and fight Nazi tyranny. At age 27, he was automatically disqualified from entering any of the American flight cadet programs, as he was considered too old. Additionally, he could not meet their hard and fast requisite of having two years college education.

To become a military pilot, William's only option was to go to Canada and voluntarily enlist in the RCAF. The Canadians were taking applications for flight training from people aged 17 to 42, and all that was needed for an interview was a birth certificate and a high school diploma.

Early on Wednesday morning, August 6, 1941, Smith walked through the doors of No. 11 Recruiting Centre in downtown Toronto, Ontario, to begin his aviation journey. He had arrived in Toronto from Virginia after enduring a 14-hour long, 607-mile road trip.

Assigned Regimental Service No. R. 123267, AC2 W. B. Smith was sent to No. 5A MD at Valcartier, Quebec, for four weeks of basic training.

On September 2, he reported for guard duty at No. 13 SFTS Saint-Hubert, Quebec. He was then posted to No. 3 ITS at Victoriaville, Quebec, on October 27. William graduated from Course No. 39 at this facility on December 19, 1941, with a 76 percent grade average. He finished 41st out of 88 students in his class. The unit's CO stated: "Fair education and is dependable. Ambitious and energetic."

Promoted to LAC, Smith's next stop was at No. 4 EFTS at Windsor Mills, Quebec. There, on Course No. 45, he flew 71.30 hours on Fleet Finch Mk II biplanes. He graduated with a 68 percent average on February 27, 1942. The CFI commented: "This student has made steady progress and should become a good service pilot."

Smith was posted, on March 19, to RCAF No. 9 SFTS at Air Station Summerside, Prince Edward Island. There, on Course No. 51, he flew 152.55 hours on Harvards. The course concluded on June 19, with William earning his wings as an SP. The Chief Instructor (CI), SL J. W. Gledhill, noted the following: "This man's training and ability is that of an average student. He required a lot of patience and work, but

4th FG pilot Captain William B. Smith was killed in action on September 13, 1944, while strafing a Luftwaffe airdrome. (US Department of Defense)

his response was most satisfactory. Now quite competent as a pilot in all respects. Hard worker and is reliable."

Sergeant Smith was sent, on August 11, 1942, to No. 1 OTU at Bagotville, Quebec. This Hawker Hurricane unit, part of Eastern Air Command, had just opened for business and William and his fellow classmates were the first cadre of some 29 pilot training courses undertaken at this facility. By October 9, he had logged 67.45 flying hours on the type on Course No. 1. The school's CI made the following comments: "Exceptional pilot. Outstanding in all characteristics. Should make a good officer."

A total of 940 fighter pilots graduated from No. 1 OTU before it ceased operations on October 28, 1944.

Smith reported in on October 24 at No. 1 Port Transit Unit, "Y" Depot, Pier 21, Halifax, Nova Scotia, for deployment to the United Kingdom. His fast troop ship crossed the North Atlantic Ocean and arrived at Glasgow, Scotland, on November 4. This was followed by an overnight troop train ride, which finally deposited the tired airmen at their destination – No. 3 Personnel Reception Centre, at Bournemouth.

Three weeks later, on November 24, William was posted to No. 56 OTU at RAF Tealing near Dundee, Scotland. There he flew 42 hours on Miles Masters and Hurricanes on Course No. 52. He graduated on January 12, 1943, with a 71.3 percent average and the following comments from WC J. M. Littler: "A very competent pilot. Has dash, initiative and a sense of responsibility. Very keen on his work and is reliable. Formation flying very good. Discipline very good. Will make a good squadron pilot."

Several months earlier, Smith had been contacted by the American government, offering to transfer him into the USAAF as a pilot and officer upon completion of his RCAF training. The advantages for him to do so were many. Now that his country was at war, he could fly and fight under the US flag. His monthly pay would double over what he had been earning in the employ of the Canadians, and he would move from the non-commissioned ranks to the commissioned ranks.

William would also have the benefit of a US$10,000 life insurance policy, which was not available to any Canadian or British service personnel.

Many Americans were torn in their loyalties when it came time to make the decision to transfer. Just over half of the 8,864 serving in the RCAF were quite content to legally stay where they were for the duration of the war. Many felt they owed Canada a big debt as it, as a country, had spent a considerable amount of time and money on their training. But patriotism is and always will be a very powerful lure.

In that regard, between May 1942 and May 1945, some 3,797 American citizens who were serving in the RCAF laterally transferred to an American military service of their choosing.

W. B. Smith was one of that number who did exercise the transfer option. His move over to the USAAF as an FO took effect on February 24, 1943. He had served one year and 202 days in Canada's air force.

After he was processed into the USAAF, Smith was sent to Station No. 342 Atcham in March for three months of conversion training.

Smith arrived at Station F-356 in Essex on May 23, 1943, and was immediately assigned to the 334th FS. He flew his Thunderbolt on numerous missions until the end of 1943 but did not claim any German aircraft destroyed.

Promotions were as follows: November 15, 1943, promoted to 2nd lieutenant; December 21, 1943, promoted to 1st lieutenant; March 28, 1944, designated flight commander of "C" Flight; April 15, 1944, designated flight commander of "B" Flight; and May 1, 1944, promoted to captain.

On February 28, 1944, Major James Clark led the 4th's first Mustang mission against Noball targets in the vicinity of Boulogne-la-Grasse, France, from 1310hrs to 1620hrs. Both the 334th and 336th FSs got 12 aircraft up, while the 335th put up 11 planes. There were, however, several aborts due to mechanical problems. The group reached the Initial Point (IP) at 1411hrs, but despite much vectoring from Jensen ground radar controller, no enemy aircraft were located.

Northeast of Paris, a section of P-51s dropped down to beat up the German-occupied airfield at Soissons. William Smith, Cowboy Megura, Duane Beeson, and Vermont Garrison ganged up on a single Junkers Ju 88 twin-engined bomber that was about to take off. They blew it to pieces. Each pilot was awarded a one quarter share of the kill.

On March 27, 1944, Major James Clark, now the newly appointed group operations officer, led a target support/freelance mission to the Luftwaffe-occupied Pau-Point-Long aerodrome in France. Rendezvous was made with the Boeing B-17 bombers at 1407hrs at 23,000ft over the Bay of Biscay. The Fortresses already had a P-38 Lightning escort, so Clark took two squadrons and went to join some other B-17 and Consolidated B-24 Liberator bombers flying at 12,000ft. The 335th FS continued on the planned route, while the 334th and 336th provided escort to the airfield at Cazaux, France.

After the field was bombed, the two FSs dropped down and, from 1445hrs to 1500hrs, literally tore the place apart, destroying 23 aircraft on the ground and one in the air. Later, 1st Lieutenant Smith was given credit for the aerial destruction of a Bf 109G Messerschmitt fighter, as well as one strafed on the ground.

On April 8, 1944, Major George Carpenter led a freelance/general support mission to the Hamburg region from 1135hrs to 1620hrs. Southwest of Bremen, Germany, the group heard bombers calling for help. The Mustangs turned south and rendezvoused at 1300hrs near Nienburg with four combat wings of B-24s flying at 24,000ft. Another group of P-51s arrived, so Carpenter broke escort by pulling ahead of the bomber formations.

At 1320hrs near Celle, Germany, an estimated 100 Fw 190s and Bf 109s were spotted heading for the bombers from the northeast in gaggles of threes and fours. The fight ranged over a 30-mile area, from 23,000ft right down to the deck. The 4th claimed 33 enemy aircraft destroyed and nine damaged. Six B-24s went down, with chutes being seen everywhere. Smith was credited with the aerial destruction of an Fw 190. The 4th lost four Mustangs in the melee, two pilots were killed and two became PoWs.

On April 22, 1944, Colonel Don Blakeslee led a fighter sweep from 1620hrs to 2030hrs to the region of Kassel, Germany. Several aborts occurred as a result of the new "paper babies" hung on the wings. Though these external fuel tanks would later become standard equipment, they caused many headaches at first. As the group passed Kassel at 18,000ft, 20-plus 109s were forming up 12,000ft below. Losing altitude by orbiting, the 4th bounced the Germans and fought them to Warburg, then chased them southwest to the Edersee reservoir area. Several Messerschmitts attempted to shake off the P-51s by performing aerobatics right on the deck, but the Mustang pilots picked them off, destroying one after another. Seventeen Luftwaffe fighters went down for the loss of one Mustang. William Smith was given one half credit for the aerial destruction of a Bf 109.

His tour completed, Captain Smith was on leave in the States during June–July. He returned to Debden to begin a second tour on August 17, 1944.

On September 13, 1944, Lieutenant Colonel C. Kinnard led a penetration target withdrawal support mission to Ulm, Germany, from 0836hrs to 1345hrs. The group's assigned bombers had aborted so they picked up several combat wings of B-17s over the Rhine river. Blue Section of the 334th FS then dropped down to strafe the Schwäbisch Hall-Hessental airfield. Smith's gunfire destroyed an unknown fighter on the ground and, as he pulled off the target, his P-51D Mustang was struck in the engine and cockpit area by 20mm cannon rounds fired by the airfield gunners.

His aircraft flew on for about a mile, climbed to 400ft, rolled inverted and exploded on impact when it hit the ground.

On February 21, 1946, Brigadier General Leon W. Johnson, Chief of the USAAF Personnel Services Division in Washington, wrote the following letter to Captain Smith's father in Bluefield:

> I am writing to you in reference to your son who gave his life in the service of his country during the European conflict. In an effort to furnish the next of kin with all available details concerning casualties among our personnel, the Army Air Forces recently completed the translation of several volumes of captured German records. In regard to Captain William B. Smith, these records indicate that he was killed on September 13, 1944 when his P-51 Mustang was damaged by enemy ground fire while strafing a German airdrome. His plane crashed a mile and a

quarter east of the field at Schwäbisch Hall-Hessental, which is approximately ten miles south of Ulm, Germany. Neither time nor place of burial was given. The Quartermaster General in his capacity as Chief, American Graves Registration Services, is charged with the responsibility of notifying the legal next of kin concerning grave locations of members of the military forces who are killed or die outside the continental limits of the United States. If the report of your son's burial has not been confirmed and you have not been notified by the Quartermaster General, that official will furnish you definite information immediately upon receipt of the official report of interment from the Commanding General of the Theatre concerned. May the knowledge of your son's valuable contribution to our cause sustain you in your bereavement.

As he has no known grave, Captain Smith's name is inscribed on the tablets of the missing at the American Cemetery and Memorial at Épinal, France.

Michael Sobanski
The Bounced Around Ace

Late in the day on Tuesday, June 6, 1944, while strafing a German supply train in western France, Major Mike Sobanski inadvertently flew P-51B Mustang *The Deacon* through some telegraph wires.

Suspecting damage, he asked his wingman, 2nd Lieutenant Edward J. Steppe, flying P-51B *Turnip Termite*, to visually check his aircraft. Steppe advised the damage did not appear to be serious. Sobanski acknowledged the transmission and said he was attacking a second train.

Minutes later Steppe was heard to radio a warning to Sobanski, "Watch those behind you White Leader."

Both pilots were assigned to the 334th FS, 4th FG, USAAF. Flying from Station F-356 in Debden, England, they were on their third mission of the day in support of the Normandy invasion.

Born on July 29, 1919, in New York City, Mike's full Christian name was Wacław Władysław Michael Sobanski. Somewhere along the way, he just became known to his friends as "Winslow" or "Mike."

World War II started on Friday, September 1, 1939, at 0440hrs when Germany bombed the unprotected town of Wieluń, Poland. At the time, Mike was a 20-year-old student at the University of Warsaw. He immediately tried to join the Polish air force but was told there was no time for training. Feeling that he had to do something, he enlisted in the Polish army as an infantryman.

On September 9, he was headed for the Vistula front when German Stuka Ju 87 dive-bombers overtook his troop train, destroying it. The wounded Sobanski was pulled from the wreckage and placed on another train. Lying on straw, he rode for five days before arriving at a hospital but had to wait two additional days before he received medical treatment.

The German army was rapidly advancing, so Mike and the other wounded were moved yet again. Near Brest-Litovsk [now Belarus], they were captured.

The Germans did not think that Mike could walk so they did not bother to guard him. In the middle of the night, on September 22, he limped out of the infirmary unchallenged. Sobanski managed to make his way to his father's bombed out home at 11 Karlowicza Street in Warsaw and salvaged, from the rubble, enough civilian clothing so that he could change out of his army uniform. Eluding the Gestapo, he was able to obtain a US visa at the American embassy, which allowed him to leave Poland safely.

Early in the summer of 1940, he reached members of his US family who were living at 400 East 57th Street in New York City. Mike's foster father was Harry Bruno, a World War I fighter pilot and a renowned author. Harry had flown with, and was a good friend of, William Avery "Billy" Bishop, Canada's high-scoring World War I ace and hero.

Desperate to pay the Germans back for invading and destroying his country and, in particular, his father's home, Mike traveled on August 23, 1940, from New York to No. 12 Recruiting Centre in Ottawa, Ontario, where he enlisted in the RCAF. His rank was as an AC2 and his Regimental Service No. was R. 54384. He told the recruiter, FO E. L. O'Leary, that his mother had died of natural causes in 1938 and that his birth father, Winslow F. Sobanski, a retired Polish Army colonel, was living in Warsaw.

Herein are O'Leary's observations of Sobanski: "Applicant does not speak English very well but will likely learn it quickly. Tall swarthy chap who is well educated. Intelligent and mature for his years. Calm, self-possessed and has a determined quiet manner. Rather reserved, but this is undoubtedly due to his upbringing. Will

4th FG ace Major W. Michael Sobanski was shot down and killed in action on D-Day, June 6, 1944. (US Department of Defense)

probably become more affable when he associates with others of his own age. Will be a valuable asset to any aircrew."

From August 24 until the end of September, Michael took his basic training at No. 1 MD in Toronto, Ontario. From there he was sent to No. 2 SFTS, Uplands, Ottawa, Ontario, where he pulled guard duty until the first week in November.

From November 11 to December 9, he was back in Toronto on Course No. 10 at No. 1 ITS. He did well there, placing 82nd out of class of 198 students. Written in his file was the following comment: "Hard working, alert and has plenty of courage."

On December 10, Sobanski was promoted to LAC. He began his pilot training on Fleet Finch Mk I and II biplane trainers, Course No. 15 at No. 12 EFTS at Goderich, Ontario. The course ran from December 11, 1940, until January 28, 1941. Mike was having difficulties comprehending the English language and when he fell so far behind his fellow classmates, the air force washed him out of training. He only had ten hours of dual instruction but was not given the opportunity to go solo as the RCAF judged his piloting abilities as poor. Following are the CFI's comments: "This airman is very studious. Has worked hard and is a good student. However, very much handicapped by his lack of knowledge of the English language. He is unable to fly straight on takeoffs and once in the air has difficulty with depth perception. Unsafe and lacks judgment."

Mike was returned to No. 1 MD on January 14, 1941, for additional language instruction. At the end of February, he was sent to the Re-Selection Centre located at RCAF Air Station Trenton, Ontario. This was the recycling depot for washouts from every type and every stage of RCAF aircrew training. Mike was furious at the way he had been treated and called Harry Bruno in New York asking him what he should do.

Harry called his old friend Billy Bishop, who had the rank of Honourary Air Marshal in the RCAF. Bishop fixed it so that Sobanski would be given a second chance. One can only imagine the consternation Bishop's telephone call must have caused the brass in Trenton and Ottawa as they tried to figure out the connection between the lowly ranked American LAC and the AM.

On April 29, Sobanski resumed his flight training, this time on de Havilland Tiger Moths at No. 6 EFTS, Course No. 26 at Prince Albert, Saskatchewan. After 67.55 hours in the air and 10.50 hours in the link trainer, Mike graduated with a 68 percent average on June 9, 1941. His instructor, Sergeant L. Waite, made the following comments: "This pupil needs very careful coaching as it appears that he suffers from an inferiority complex. Timid, but very keen and conscientious. Will show satisfactory progress with patient instruction. It is strongly recommended that he receives an experienced instructor at the SFTS. His conduct while at this school was more than satisfactory."

Mike reported on June 10 to No. 4 SFTS, Saskatoon, Saskatchewan, where, on Course No. 30, he flew twin-engined Avro Ansons and Cessna Cranes. On July 1, after receiving only 12.05 hours of dual instruction, his training was curtailed for the following reasons: "This student is average in the air, but has difficulty landing twin-engined aircraft. Not a natural pilot but tries very hard. Trainee is bright and is a willing worker. He is from Poland and is very eager to get overseas and into action. Strongly recommended that he be placed on single engine aircraft."

July 27 found Sobanski at No. 1 SFTS, Camp Borden, Ontario, where he resumed flight training, this time on single-engined NAA Harvard and Yale aircraft. On October 7, he graduated with his classmates from Course No. 34 and received, in the process, the RCAF pilot wings he so coveted. From his squadron commander came the following observations: "Progress was very slow. Requires a lot of instruction. Judgment of height and speed is not too good. Will need a lot of flying experience to make up for a lack of natural flying ability." From the CGI: "Put forth an excellent effort. Considerably handicapped by the language issue. Conduct exemplary." The last thoughts came from the CFI: "Ability is limited. Very keen and conscientious. Discipline and attitude excellent. Sobanski has succeeded only by his exceptional desire to go overseas."

The day prior to graduation Mike was promoted to SP. He took his two-week pre-embarkation leave from October 8–23.

His long training ordeal over, Sobanski departed Pier 21 "Y" Depot, Halifax, Nova Scotia, by troop ship on November 3 and arrived 11 days later in England. He was at No. 3 Personnel Reception Centre in Bournemouth until January 5, 1942, waiting to go on a course.

Mike was posted to RAF No. 57 OTU, Hawarden, Wales, where, on Course No. 31, he flew 63.3 hours on Miles Masters and Supermarine Spitfires from January 6 to April 7. He also logged 12.3 hours in the Link Trainer.

The OTU WC wrote the following in Sobanski's file: "This non-commissioned officer's saving grace is his cheerful disposition. He is below average as a pilot and is frequently addicted to day-dreaming. It is, nevertheless, felt that he possesses the ability as a fighter pilot, albeit of a dormant variety. With firm handling and constant supervision, he might become an average member of a squadron. He is not recommended for a commission."

On April 7, 1942, Mike reported to RAF No. 132 Squadron at Peterhead, Aberdeenshire, where he flew Spitfire Mk IIbs until April 26. The next day, he moved over to RAF No. 164 Squadron, which was also based at Peterhead. This squadron was flying the improved Spitfire Mk Vb variant.

On May 19, he was assigned to RCAF No. 416 (City of Oshawa) FS, which was also flying the Spitfire Vb model from Peterhead. Sobanski flew operationally with 416 until moving over on September 1 to fly the latest Spitfire model, the Mk IX, with RCAF No. 402 (Winnipeg Bear) FS at RAF Kenley, Greater London. That month he was promoted to the rank of FS.

Sobanski had not shot down any Germans to this point and thought he might have better success if he joined the USAAF. There were several advantages for

Mike to consider transferring. The most important was that, as an American citizen, he would fly and fight under the Stars and Stripes.

The saying that a person "bought the farm," meaning they had died, originated in World War II. When a US service personnel was killed, the US$10,000 insurance policy in most cases was more than sufficient to pay off the mortgage owing on the family farm. This insurance policy was usually a factor in the decision to transfer to the USAAF.

After serving two years and 31 days in the RCAF, Sobanski's requested severance from Canada's air force was honorably granted in London on September 22, 1942.

Within days, the 23-year-old joined the USAAF as an FO. On October 9, he was assigned to the 336th FS at the 4th FG.

For the next 21 months, until the day of his death, he flew all three aircraft types operated by the 4th – Spitfires, P-47 Thunderbolts, and P-51 Mustangs.

On May 25, 1943, Sobanski transferred within the group from the 336th FS over to the 334th FS.

Sobanski flew operationally with the 4th for just over one year but did not get his first aerial victory until January 31, 1944. From that date until his last kill, he claimed six and one third enemy aircraft destroyed – five air and one and one third ground.

List of victories, all in 1944: January 31, Messerschmitt Bf 109 over Gilze en Rijen, Holland, while flying a P-47D Thunderbolt; March 4, Ju 52/3M while flying a P-51B Mustang; April 13, Fw 190 in the area of Ludwigshafen, Germany, while flying a P-51B Mustang; April 19, Bf 109 in the vicinity of Kassel-Eschwege, Germany, while flying a P-51B Mustang; May 28, Bf 109 in the area of Wittenberg-Magdeburg, Germany, while flying a P-51B Mustang.

Mike's last kill, which made him an ace, was unique in that none of his P-51's four Colt Browning .50 caliber MG53-2 heavy machine gun rounds actually struck his victim's aircraft. The following is his written combat report describing that mission:

> I was leading Cobweb squadron on an escort mission to Germany. Some fifteen to twenty Bf 109s were sighted coming in high from the southeast head-on heading towards the middle bunch of bombers where 336 squadron was positioned. I expected the enemy aircraft to swing around and hit the bombers from the rear, but instead they swept in the opposite direction from the box we were with, and continued until they got to the end box, making a starboard turn. Our squadron used its superior height, 32,000 feet, and followed them in the turn in a shallow dive. As soon as they made their turn we dropped our tanks and went down fast. I spotted a few P-51s trying to climb from below and sort of following the tail end of the 109 formation – without closing though. This more or less upset my plan of attack as I couldn't very well tell where the P-51s ended and the 109s began in the gaggle below. I missed out on a couple of chances when P-51s either cut me off or made passes at me. We

managed though to split up the enemy formation and I found a single bluish-grey Bf 109 flying a perfect line abreast formation with a P-51 at some one hundred and fifty yards distance. Both pilots didn't seem to realize their mistake and only caught on when I attacked the 109. He dove straight down and I momentarily lost him in the haze, finding him again when he started pulling back up. I fired a few short half second bursts closing in, and was just going to position myself better on him, as I saw no strikes. Much to my surprise he jettisoned his canopy and bailed out. I watched his aircraft half roll and crash, then I took a picture of him in the parachute. I claim a Bf 109 destroyed and one scared Hun. Ammunition used – 89 rounds.

Mike's promotions to 2nd lieutenant and to 1st lieutenant are not documented. He was promoted to captain on May 13, 1944, and, 19 days later, to the rank of major on June 1. From April 15, 1944, until the day he was shot down, he was the 334th's Commanding Officer.

After Lt Steppe's warning on June 6, 1944, heard by other 4th pilots over their radios, nothing more was heard from either one.

For the past 79 years, it was generally believed and recorded that both went down in the region of Dreux, France.

A search of Luftwaffe combat reports reveals that both Americans were killed in aerial combat in a different area by the following JG 2 "Richthofen" pilots: Fähnrich Hans-Joachim Voormann from 12 Staffel claimed a P-51B Mustang six miles northwest of Evreux, France, at 2103hrs from a height of between 3,600ft and 4,500ft; and Unteroffizier Karl Biehlolawek, from the same unit, claimed the second Mustang nine miles northwest of Evreux at 2104hrs from a height of between 2,400ft and 3,000ft. The German victors were flying up-gunned Focke Wulf Fw 190A-8s.

Two aviation researchers, Mr. Malcolm Bates in England and Mr. Benoit Cottereau in France, have, through diligent detective work, pinpointed the exact location of Major Sobanski's crashed Mustang (coded QP-J). The aircraft came down north of Evreux in Normanville near the hamlet of Caer.

The day after the crash, June 7, French farmer Florent Bulo filed a report at 1000hrs at the Normanville town hall. His declaration included the time of the crash, Major Sobanski's name and his USAAF serial number. This information was recorded in the Etat-Civil of Normanville.

In 1946, Major Sobanski's remains were re-interned in Plot C, Row 33, Grave 1 in the 90-acre Ardennes American Cemetery at Neupré, Belgium.

"The Pole," as Mike was called by his fellow pilots at Debden, was only 25 when he died. Despite the number of obstacles and frustrating delays that he experienced in his military flying career, he did manage to fulfill his dream of becoming a fighter pilot and an ace.

His Canadian awards included the Defence Medal, War Medal, and the Volunteer Service Medal & Clasp.

William Sprinkle
Instructor Pilot

Flying Officer (FO) William Arthur "Bill" Sprinkle from Seattle, Washington, flew a multitude of aircraft types during the four-and-a-half years he honorably served in the RCAF in World War II.

He racked up hundreds of flying hours on de Havilland Tiger Moths, Avro Ansons, Fleet Finches, Cessna Cranes, NAA Harvards, Fairey Battles, Douglas Dakotas, Lockheed Hudsons and Venturas, Westland Lysanders, Handley Page Hampdens, Airspeed Oxfords, Bristol Blenheims and Bolingbrokes.

William was born to John Martin Sprinkle and Ruth Farnsworth in Boise, Idaho, on September 12, 1917. He attended Whittier Elementary School in that city from 1924 to 1928. The family then moved to Seattle where he finished his grade school education in 1932 at John Hay Elementary. Four years later, Sprinkle graduated from Seattle's Queen Anne High School.

For the next five years he was employed locally as a painter with the Colotyle Corporation.

Lacking the two years of college required by the USAAC for pilot training, Sprinkle traveled from Seattle to Vancouver, British Columbia, where he voluntarily enlisted in Canada's air force on April 22, 1941. He was sworn in at the RCAF's No. 1 Recruiting Centre as an AC2 under Regimental Service No. R. 101088. The interviewing officer wrote the following in his file: "Candidate has a good appearance. Keen to serve. Mannerism good, appears to be a good aircrew material. Recommended for Pilot or Observer training."

As No. 2 MD at Brandon, Manitoba, was full to capacity with new recruits, William and some others took their basic training at No. 2A MD at Penhold, Alberta.

On July 2, he was posted to No. 2 ITS at Regina, Saskatchewan. Graduating from there on August 5, Sprinkle was sent to No. 1 EFTS at Malton, Ontario, where, over the next several weeks on Course No. 35, he flew 68 hours on de Havilland Tiger Moth and Fleet Finch biplane trainers.

Having been promoted to LAC, Sprinkle graduated from Malton on September 25, finishing tenth in a class of 32 students.

He completed his training to wings standard flying twin-engined Avro Ansons on Course No. 39 on December 19, 1941, at No. 5 SFTS at Brantford, Ontario.

Flying Officer William A. Sprinkle piloted many aircraft types while instructing in the RCAF including Fairchild-built Bristol Bolingbrokes like the one depicted. (Canadian National Defence Image Library)

Again, he did very well, finishing 14th out of a class of 52. The majority of his classmates graduated as SPs, but several top students, including Sprinkle, were commissioned as POs. His Regimental Service No. was then changed from R. 101088 to J. 9343 reflecting his officer status.

Due to his maturity and temperament, the RCAF decided Bill would make a good instructor pilot and, in that regard, he reported on December 21 to the Central Flying School at Air Station Trenton, Ontario, for additional training. He graduated on March 30, 1942, with an A2 instructor's certificate.

The city of Belleville abuts the town of Trenton and it was during his time in the area that William met and courted Miss Catherine Anita O'Connor. Her brother, John, worked at the air station and one weekend he brought Sprinkle home for Sunday dinner to meet his family. This was a common courtesy extended between airmen during the war, particularly when one of them was stationed so far away from their loved ones. In William's case, it was a 2,700-mile one way journey from Trenton to his home in Seattle.

From March 31 until September 8, William served as a staff pilot at RCAF Rockcliffe, Ontario, and at No. 4 Bombing & Gunnery School at Fingal, Ontario.

On September 10, he reported for duty as a test pilot to No. 6 Repair Depot back at Trenton. On September 19, he and Catherine were married in Belleville. He was promoted from PO to FO on July 1, 1942.

William Sprinkle: Instructor Pilot

Sprinkle embarked from Canada for overseas duty by troop ship on December 29. After a slow sea voyage of some 16 days, the convoy's supply of personnel and equipment disembarked in the United Kingdom on January 14, 1943.

Bill arrived at RCAF No. 3 Personnel Reception Centre in Bournemouth the next day. Five weeks later, he was posted to RAF No. 12 Pilot Advanced Flying Unit, Grantham/Spitalgate in Lincolnshire for operational training on twin-engined Oxfords and Blenheims.

At 0015hrs on April 14, 1943, Sprinkle sustained serious leg injuries when he crash-landed Blenheim L1508 at Harlaxton airfield while on a solo night-flying training exercise. In a report dated April 15, GC C. W. MacKay, the OC No. 12, outlined the details of the crash, which was not attributable to enemy action:

> Officer in charge of night flying states that at 0005 hours on April 14th, a message was received from FO Sprinkle indicating that the starboard engine of his early model blunt-nosed Mk I Blenheim had failed while he was on a precision night flying exercise. He was immediately given permission to land, made an approach, but overshot the six hundred and fifty yard long runway by three hundred feet. The aircraft was observed to go around again maintaining an altitude of three to four hundred feet on one engine. Turning into the wind, L1508 suddenly lost height, struck the ground and burst into flames upon impact. The aircraft wreckage came to rest on the main east coast railway line. The starboard Bristol Mercury Mk XV engine is to be examined by the manufacturer. Recommend that no action be taken with regard to the pilot.

On April 15, FL W. R. Gunn, the RCAF casualties officer in Ottawa, Ontario, wrote the following letter to Sprinkle's wife, who was residing at 1621 Queen Anne Avenue in Seattle:

> Confirming my telegram of recent date, the RCAF Casualties Officer, Overseas, has advised me that your husband, FO W. A. Sprinkle, was dangerously injured on active service as a result of flying operations near Harlaxton, Lincolnshire, England at 1215 hours on April 14th, 1943. He sustained a compound fracture of the left ankle, a lacerated scalp and burns. He is also suffering from shock and was admitted to the Grantham Emergency Medical Services hospital at Lincolnshire. I hasten to relieve your anxiety in regard to his care and you may rest assured that he will receive the best of medical attention. Please be assured that any further information received at these Headquarters will be communicated to you immediately.

After many months in the British hospital, Bill was repatriated to Canada on October 24, 1943. He was medically boarded as unfit for combat flying due to the severity of his leg and ankle injuries. However, he continued to serve in the RCAF in a training capacity.

On September 12, 1944, he was cleared to return to limited flight duties when he was posted to No. 3 OTU with Western Air Command at Patricia Bay, British Columbia.

On March 22, 1945, Sprinkle moved over to No. 122 Squadron, co-located at Patricia Bay and Port Hardy, British Columbia. With the defeat of Germany and Japan in May and August 1945, respectively, Sprinkle was honorably discharged from the RCAF on October 23, 1945, at No. 8 Release Centre at Vancouver.

Returning to the States, he joined Commercial Credit Corporation, where he began a career in banking and finance. In 1949, he went to work at the Union National Bank in Minot, North Dakota. There, he rose to the position of vice president. At the age of 43, Bill died in Great Falls, Montana. His early death on December 15, 1960, was a direct result of complications from his wartime injuries.

William's service awards included the Defence Medal, General Service Medal, Pilots Flying Badge, and Canadian Volunteer Service Medal & Clasp.

Sprinkle's daughter, Liz Loynes, was told her father was in a lower body cast and a wheelchair for several months after the crash. She remembers her mother saying, "he never walked another day without suffering extreme pain." After his military demobilization, he never flew an airplane again.

In 2011, the Sprinkle family was contacted by an RAF No. 51 Squadron researcher in Edinburgh, Scotland, named Neil Smith. He connected with them on behalf of the family of Sergeant Alexander Barrie, a Handley Page Halifax gunner who flew with No. 51 Squadron. It was Sergeant Barrie who rushed into Sprinkle's burning Blenheim that evening to save their father.

Barrie tragically went missing in action with his entire crew a week later over the North Sea. He was posthumously awarded a bravery medal for his heroic effort in saving Bill Sprinkle from certain death.

In May 2012, several members of the Sprinkle family traveled to Scotland where they met Neil Smith and members of the Barrie clan.

In a small Scottish pub, the group spent an enjoyable evening trading histories and getting to know one another. It was also a golden opportunity for the Sprinkle family to personally thank the descendants of Sergeant Barrie, not only for his wartime service, but for their very existence.

Claybourne Waldrop
The Extended Three-Day Pass

At the conclusion of World War II, RCAF FL Claybourne "Alabama" Waldrop returned to Canada to be demobilized along with thousands of other military personnel.

Waldrop, an American citizen, had completed two tours of operations, flying 67 sorties comprised of anti-submarine, convoy, air-sea rescue, and coastal patrols on Consolidated B-24 Liberators.

In appreciation for their wartime service, the Canadian government, through the Department of Veterans Affairs, offered to financially assist those ex-military personnel who wished to further their education at college level. Waldrop thought this was a great idea and took advantage of the offer when he enrolled at the University of British Columbia studying civil engineering from September 1945 to May 1946.

Claybourne, however, had some serious unfinished business back home that needed to be dealt with. To clear his conscience and his good name, he returned to Birmingham, Alabama, to face the consequences of an impetuous decision he had made several years earlier. The 26-year-old pilot, who had earned a MiD award for gallantry while flying with the RAF, was, in fact, a wanted man back in the United States.

Claybourne Waldrop was facing a charge of being AWOL from the United States Army for a period of five years and three months.

Waldrop was born in Adger, Alabama, on October 30, 1919. He was raised and educated in Birmingham and graduated from West End High School in that city in May 1938. He worked a year as a clerk for J. Blach and Sons, then secured a position with the Tennessee Coal, Iron and Railroad Company as a crane operator. In October 1940, he read in the local newspaper that plans were afoot to federalize the Alabama Army National Guard. This meant, at least to him, that the US would soon be in the thick of the fighting in Europe.

Flight Lieutenant Claybourne Waldrop, MiD, flew two tours on Consolidated B-24 Coastal Command Liberators. His service while in the RCAF was exemplary. (Canadian National Defence Image Library)

Waldrop, who was just itching to go fight the Nazis, joined the 31st "Dixie" Division as a private on November 6. True to the news reports, the Guard was mobilized as a federal unit just 18 days later. The US Army, however, had no foreseeable plans to do any fighting anywhere, let alone in Europe. Bored with marching in circles around Florida for seven months, Waldrop – serial number 1948276 – decided to take matters into his own hands and join another military service.

When the Army gave him a three-day weekend pass on Saturday, June 7, 1941, Corporal Waldrop used the time to travel directly from his Army post at Camp Blanding, Florida, to the RCAF's No. 13 Recruiting Centre in Montreal, Quebec.

The 21-year-old was officially sworn into the RCAF on Thursday, June 19, 1941, as an AC2. Assigned Regimental Service No. R. 108293, Waldrop was sent the next day for recruit training to No. 1 MD in Toronto, Ontario.

Claybourne was posted on August 3 to No. 1 Bombing & Gunnery School at Jarvis, Ontario, where he performed guard duty until September 12. The next day he was back in Toronto at No. 1 ITS where he satisfactorily completed the curriculum on November 7.

Promoted to LAC, Waldrop was in western Canada two days later learning to fly de Havilland Tiger Moths at No. 15 EFTS at Regina, Saskatchewan. After accumulating 67 hours and 25 minutes' flight time on the yellow two-winged biplanes, Waldrop graduated on December 28, 1941.

On January 18, 1942, he reported to No. 7 SFTS at Fort MacLeod, Alberta. There, he flew 127 hours and 10 minutes on twin-engined Avro Ansons on Course No. 47 with No. 2 Squadron.

On May 8, Claybourne was awarded his pilot wings in a graduation ceremony and was commissioned as a PO. His Regimental Service No. was changed from R. 108293 to J. 11581.

He requested, and was approved for, an overseas posting, but at the last minute, it was canceled. For the next six months, May 22 to November 10, Waldrop served as a staff pilot flying Anson Mk 1s at No. 1 Central Navigation School at Rivers, Manitoba. There he logged an additional 347 hours and 15 minutes of flight time.

From November 14, 1942, to January 29, 1943, Alabama flew Anson Mk IIIs on a Navigation Reconnaissance Course at No. 1 General Reconnaissance School at Summerside, Prince Edward Island. In addition to being a pilot, Claybourne Waldrop was now a qualified navigator.

On November 21, 1942, Waldrop married his life-long sweetheart, Avis Margaret Middleton on Prince Edward Island. The two, who had known each other all their lives, decided on a Canadian ceremony as Claybourne was not sure he could re-enter the US without being arrested. The bride traveled the long distance from Birmingham to Canada's east coast for the nuptials.

PO Waldrop arrived at RAF No. 111 OTU at Nassau, Bahamas, on Sunday, February 21, 1943. No. 111 was formed on August 20, 1942, to train General Reconnaissance Coastal Command crews on US-built B-24 Liberators and B-25 Mitchells. While on training sorties, No. 111's aircraft were usually armed as their aircrews were always on the lookout for German U-boats, which occasionally operated in their training area.

Claybourne graduated from co-pilot's Course No. 3 on May 31, flying twin-engine B-25s with "B" squadron, then four-engined B-24s with "C" squadron. His flying time to that point amounted to 668 hours and 50 minutes.

Waldrop, dressed in his RCAF officer's uniform, successfully transited from Nassau through Miami, Florida, on June 2 on his way back to Canada. After leaving Canada, he arrived at No. 3 Personnel Reception Centre at Bournemouth in the United Kingdom on Thursday July 8, 1943.

He further trained at No. 1 Conversion OTU at Thornaby-on-Tees, North Yorkshire, until August 20.

Finally, after being in the RCAF pipeline for 26 months, Alabama was posted, on August 21, to his first operational squadron, RAF No. 59 at Aldergrove, Northern Ireland. He flew his first patrol as a copilot on a General Reconnaissance Liberator Mk V four days later.

In September, he was promoted to FO.

In the latter part of November, Claybourne spent two weeks receiving extra instruction flying Airspeed Oxfords with No. 1509 Beam Approach Training Flight at Dyce, Scotland. He returned to flying operations with No. 59 on December 7, the squadron having relocated from Aldergrove to Ballykelly, Northern Ireland.

On Tuesday, February 15, 1944, Waldrop was back in Nassau with No. 111 to take his B-24 captain's course. This time he had to transit to the Bahamas through the ports of New York and Miami. Claybourne graduated on March 17 with an above average rating from the instructors.

Returning overseas, Alabama was posted on May 2 to RAF No. 53 Squadron at St Eval, flying Mk V, VI and VIII Liberators.

Waldrop and his crew flew together for the next year until May 25, 1945, which was the date of his 67th and final sortie of the war.

His promotion to FL came in September 1944.

Not all of the squadron's sorties were flown directly from St Eval. Some were from Reykjavik and Geck, Iceland, while others were from St Davids, Wales, and Squire's Gate, Lancashire.

Claybourne's long return journey to Canada began at Bircham Newton on June 19, 1945. Passing through RCAF "R" Depot at Torquay, England, his next stop was at No. 1 Repatriation Depot, Lachine, Quebec. He arrived on September 15, 1945, at No. 8 Release Centre at Vancouver, British Columbia.

On Thursday, October 4, 1945, he officially retired from the RCAF with 1,724 hours and 40 minutes of flight time recorded in his logbook.

After the year of schooling at UBC, Waldrop returned on July 1, 1946, to the family residence in Birmingham. He immediately advised the Adjutant General of the Army in Washington of his whereabouts. A month passed and when no response to his letter was forthcoming, he mailed a second one on August 1 complete with a copy of the first.

He was visiting with his in-laws on Wednesday, September 4, when his mother called telling him there were two Military Policemen (MP) on her doorstep. They were looking for him to execute an arrest warrant charging him with desertion in time of war. He was also facing a lesser charge of being AWOL for 1,914 days.

Claybourne recalled his response to the first charge: "The US was not at war when I left on June 7, 1941, and was at peace when I returned on July 1, 1946."

Arriving at his mother's residence, Claybourne was arrested, handcuffed, and was referred to as Army Private Waldrop, even though he had attained the rank of corporal prior to leaving for Canada. One of the MPs, who was sympathetic to his plight, suggested the news media might be interested in his story. Waldrop could go one better than that.

His father-in-law, Robert Middleton, just happened to work as a typesetter at the *Birmingham News*. Middleton arranged to have an *Associated Press* reporter available when his son-in-law was locked up 30 minutes later in the Alabama Jefferson County jail. Two days later, Claybourne was moved a distance of 60 miles to the stockade at Fort McClellan in Anniston, Alabama.

Waldrop's true story, which some say could have only come from the fertile mind of a Hollywood screenwriter, was picked up and carried worldwide by the international press. This was evidenced by the numerous newspaper clippings he received from many of his former RCAF and RAF buddies who were now living on several continents.

The US Army was not too pleased with all the publicity the Waldrop case was generating and it was certainly not used to being placed under the microscope of public opinion.

Claybourne Waldrop: The Extended Three-Day Pass

Meanwhile, Claybourne was not resting solely on his notoriety. Shortly after his arrest, he wrote a very detailed letter to the Canadian Minister of National Defence for Air in Ottawa, explaining his predicament. He respectfully asked the Canadian government for its help. In closing, Claybourne explained his actions: "I acted as I did only because I felt the United States and all other free countries were being attacked indirectly and would presently be attacked directly by the same forces who were so grievously besetting Britain at that time."

Within hours of receiving the letter, GC W. A. Dicks, the RCAF records officer, was on the telephone with his American counterparts in both Washington and Fort McClellan offering the Canadian government's assistance to FL Waldrop in whatever manner possible.

GC Dicks followed up the telephone calls with two letters dated September 19 and 27, 1946, respectively. These were addressed to Major C. W. Armstrong, c/o the Post Judge Advocate's Office, Headquarters Fort McClellan, Fort McClellan, Alabama, USA.

The letter on September 19 stated:

> In reply to your letter September 14, it is advised that the fingerprints of your Claybourne Waldrop are identical with the fingerprints of one Claybourne Waldrop who served with the Royal Canadian Air Force during World War II. Waldrop made application for enlistment at the RCAF Recruiting Centre, Montreal, Quebec on 8 June 1941 and was taken on strength 19 June 1941 as standard aircrew – Regimental No. R. 108293. He underwent aircrew training, graduated as a pilot and was subsequently commissioned as a Pilot Officer, General List No. J11581.
>
> During his service with the RCAF, Waldrop carried out two tours of operation overseas and attained the rank of Flight Lieutenant. He was honourably retired from the RCAF 4 October 1945 on being transferred to the Reserve, General Section, Class E. It is also noted that Waldrop, on enlisting, gave his permanent address as 1233-16th Place Southwest, Birmingham, Alabama, USA. and on being retired, he states that his intended place of residence was 3831 West 50th Avenue, Vancouver, British Columbia, Canada. A copy of your letter, together with the fingerprint card submitted are being returned herewith.

The follow-up on September 27:

> Further to our letter of 19 September 1946, enclosed are photostatic copies of the Attestation Paper, Records of Service and Discharge Certificate of Flight Lieutenant Waldrop, an ex-Officer of the RCAF. These documents are proof of his actual enlistment, a history of his service and his final release. A review of various reports submitted during his training and subsequent employment on operations show him as above average in general deportment, conduct and ability in flying duties.

During his service, he was granted the following honours and awards; 1939–45 Star, Atlantic Star, Canadian Volunteer Service Medal and Clasp, War Medal 1939–45, Operational Wings and Pilot's Flying Badge. The Operational Wings were awarded for successfully completing tours of operation against the enemy, involving sixty-seven sorties and seven hundred and twenty-eight combat flying hours. In addition, he was Mentioned in Despatches for gallant services during operations against the enemy. This additional information is forwarded in the event it may be of some assistance in arriving at a finding in the case pending against Waldrop.

In a letter to a friend dated September 16, 1983, Waldrop reflected on his time spent in the stockade:

> Myself and the other non-homosexual "Criminals" were kept in a large cage, a la bear cage at zoos, so that we could be seen by the guards at all times. The homosexuals were locked up in individual cell-rooms – I wonder why? Ward No. 35 was a mental ward and I was there for questioning by "Shrinks," so that I couldn't later thwart the prosecutor at my "General Court Martial" by pleading insanity. I was charged with Desertion in Time of War, which is punishable by death.
>
> The crazy Lieutenant who was going to defend me recommended that I plead innocent, his thought being that after all of those years the Army had probably lost the roll-call reports and wouldn't be able to prove that I wasn't there all of that time – which of course was only 1,914 days!

He went on to say that during his horrible six weeks of incarceration he was assigned to kitchen police duties from Monday to Saturday. Sundays were set aside for cleaning pots and pans.

One Sunday, one of his brothers, not realizing that prisoners do not have any days off, drove 120 miles round trip from Birmingham to see him. Claybourne was not allowed to have any visitors and was not even told by the guards that his brother was there to visit him.

The newspapers kept Alabama's story on their front pages the whole time that he was jailed. It was not too long before the Army realized it could not win a war against an outraged public, who were clearly on Claybourne's side. After all, the war was over, and he had openly apologized to America for his actions. To conclude the matter to everyone's satisfaction, the Army decided to offer Waldrop a compromise.

Claybourne continues the narrative:

> One day in late October two armed MPs escorted me to the office of the Fort McClellan Adjutant General. The officer was working on some papers at his desk when my guards announced they were escorting Private Waldrop to see him. He

looked up and immediately asked, 'What do you want to do?' I responded that I was a prisoner and made no such decisions. He then announced the federal government would give me an Honorable Discharge and drop all charges if I agreed the 1,914 days I was away was considered as leave without pay. I dramatically announced that I would accept the offer. He then asked if I wished to go home while the paperwork was being processed. I replied that things would move faster if I remained where I was. They gave me a nice room and fed me three magnificent meals a day.

Then I discovered there was a nice hotel on the base and I could live there for a dollar a day. Avis joined me and we spent several days of easy living strolling around the beautiful grounds of the base. I used to wave and throw kisses to my former jail mates who were simply amazed at the incredible turn of events my case had taken.

I was honourably discharged from the United States Army on November 8, 1946. Ironically, my discharge was signed by Captain Sherbert B. Jones who was my Company Sergeant at Camp Blanding, Florida when I departed on my rather extended three-day pass on June 7, 1941!

For the next five years, Claybourne Waldrop worked at a wide variety of occupations – millwright, farmer, draftsman, foreman, blacksmith, inspector, and surveyor.

In 1951, he secured a position with the Federal Aviation Administration (FAA) as an air traffic controller. He retired from the FAA in 1976 as a supervisor.

In retirement, he traveled the world – all 50 States, all Canadian Provinces, and 31 other countries.

Claybourne never forgot his wartime buddies and, if he was not visiting or corresponding with many of them, he was trying to locate the few who had dropped off the radar screen over the years. He was a meticulous record keeper and carefully preserved virtually everything relating to his World War II military service.

On Monday, March 17, 2003, Retired RCAF Flight Lieutenant Claybourne Waldrop, MiD, passed away in his 84th year.

Claude Weaver
The Youngest Allied Ace

On Friday, January 28, 1944, three Supermarine Spitfire Mk IXcs from No. 403 "Wolf" FS, RCAF provocatively overflew Luftwaffe-occupied fighter airfields at Valenciennes, Douai, Vitry-sur-Seine, and Épinoy. The German personnel at these former French bases watched in awe as the Canadian trio flew a perfect line abreast formation just below the 3,000ft cloud deck.

Just after 1445hrs, 32-year-old Oberstleutnant Heinz-Gerhard Vogt from 7th Staffel/JG 26 (7./JG 26) scrambled his fighters from Grévillers in an attempt to intercept the cheeky enemy raiders.

Fighting in western France since 1940, JG 26, flying its yellow-nosed Focke Wulf Fw 190A-6s, was more commonly known as "The Abbeville Kids."

Knowing his enemy's altitude and direction, Vogt's Staffel took off on a northeasterly heading. The German pilots climbed just far enough into the overcast so that they would be able to spot the Canadian aircraft as they flew on a reciprocal course beneath them. However, both flights managed to pass each other sight unseen. Reversing his course, the experienced oberstleutnant located and engaged the Canadians at 1537hrs, just as they overflew his airfield.

In the ensuing dog fight, two of the Spitfires, flown by FL Thornton and FO Foster, were badly damaged. Using all their flying skills, the pair managed to make good their escape back across the English Channel to RAF Kenley. The third aircraft, coded MA642 and flown by the section leader, was chased and shot down by Vogt as it raced for the protection of nearby clouds.

Gerhard Vogt had just scored his 18th kill. He watched his opponent open his canopy as he prepared to bail out of his crippled warplane. His victim was a 20-year-old American flying in the service of the RCAF. PO Claude "Weavy" Weaver III was also an ace and had 12½ aerial victories to his credit.

As Weaver exited his fighter, he pulled his ripcord prematurely causing his parachute to billow too close to the falling plane. His body passed safely under the aircraft's tail, but some of the inflated parachute panels passed over the top of the tailplane. Vogt watched in horror as the unthinkable happened – several parachute shroud lines caught, then became entangled, anchoring the pilot to the fighter's tail. Pilot and aircraft fell together as one to the frozen earth below. Amazingly, the violent impact did not immediately end the young American's life. Weaver was rushed, barely alive, to a local hospital by French authorities, but mercifully died three hours later from massive injuries.

The horrific image of Weaver's last moments stayed with Vogt until he himself was shot down and killed in aerial combat on January 14, 1945.

Claude Weaver III was born in Oklahoma City, Oklahoma, on August 18, 1923. His father, Claude II, was Oklahoma's Assistant State Attorney General. His grandfather, Claude I, was a Federal Court judge, who previously had served as a US congressman.

There were two other children in the Weaver family, a younger brother, David, and an older sister, Virginia. The family lived in a large two-story house at 1201 Northwest 38th Street and were considered, for the time, to be financially well off.

Claude Weaver dropped out of Classen High School midway through his 11th grade studies so that he could join the RCAF. He was only 17 years old when he interrupted his formal education to begin his great adventure. Perhaps he was inspired after watching newsreel clips at his local movie theater of those intrepid RAF Spitfire and Hurricane pilots who had so valiantly defended England during the Battle of Britain.

Maybe it was British Prime Minister Winston Churchill's stirring speech of August 20, 1940, when he said, "The gratitude of every home in our island, in our empire and indeed throughout the world, except in the abodes of the guilty, goes out to the British airmen who, undaunted by odds, unwearied in their constant challenge and mortal danger, are turning the tide of the World War by their prowess and by their devotion. Never in the field of human conflict was so much owed by so many to so few."

Retired USAF Captain W. M. "Mac" Palmer from Austin, Texas, provided the true story behind Claude's motivation to join up. He was a close friend of Weaver's and went through grade and high school with him in Oklahoma City. Mac says, "Claude was a fantastic athlete who swam, boxed and played tennis. When he was fifteen, Weaver broke his neck in a diving accident and had to wear an upper body cast for almost a year. He was very smart and could obtain good grades when he applied himself. Claude, however, was constantly in trouble with school officials for acting out or talking too much in class. He was also a school yard bully who was quick to pick a fight, particularly with students from the other city high schools, over matters as trivial as the loss of a high school football game."

One too many of his after-school serious altercations finally landed him in court. He did, however, have the very good fortune to appear before a judge who just happened to be a friend of his grandfather. The judge decided Mr. Weaver needed some discipline in his young life and offered him a choice – join a military service or face a term of incarceration in juvenile reform school.

Claude, who always wanted to be a pilot, had only one option and that was to go to Canada. His parents reluctantly bought him a bus ticket to Detroit, Michigan, whereupon he crossed the United States–Canada border at Windsor, Ontario, and enlisted in the RCAF at No. 8 Recruiting Centre on February 13, 1941.

The air force assigned him Regimental Service No. R. 83374 and his rank was that of an AC2. He spent the early part of his RCAF experience at two makeshift training facilities, as a large influx of applicants had temporarily overwhelmed the system. From February 14 to March 20, Claude and others were at 1A MD, Picton, Ontario, while it was still under construction. It officially opened on April 28, 1941, as No. 31 Bombing & Gunnery School. From March 22 to May 3, he served guard duty at RCAF Air Station, Sydney, Nova Scotia.

On May 4, Weaver reported to No. 3 ITS at Victoriaville, Quebec. He passed out of this course with a 75 percent average on June 7 and was promoted to LAC.

Days later, he began his flight training on Fleet Finch II biplane trainers at No. 17 EFTS at Stanley, Nova Scotia. Weaver graduated from No. 17 on July 26, 1941, with a 70.6 percent grade average.

At this point, he had 56.6 flying hours recorded in his logbook plus eight hours of Link Trainer time. In his file from No. 17 was the following notation: "Learns quickly and has above average intelligence, but is inclined to be cocky and a smart aleck."

Weaver was posted on July 27 to No. 8 SFTS at Moncton, New Brunswick.

His dream was to fly fighters so one can only imagine how disappointed he was when he learned that he would finish his training flying twin-engine Avro Ansons. He suddenly realized the RCAF was streaming him to fly multi-engine aircraft, bombers or perhaps even transports. His grades and his attitude plummeted. He crash-landed an Anson off station and the cause of the accident was attributed to pilot carelessness. Disciplinary action was taken and, as punishment, he was confined to barracks for seven days.

In a graduation ceremony on October 10, Weaver was awarded his RCAF pilot wings and was promoted to the rank of SP. However, he had not applied himself to the final stage of his flight training and almost did not make it through. He barely obtained a passing grade and ranked 39th last in his graduating class.

On his final assessment his squadron commander noted the following: "Discipline Poor. Has too much to say. Is a wise guy." The station's CO WC W. W. Brown, knowingly or unknowingly steered Weaver happily back into his realm when he recommended fighters were the only type of service aircraft he should fly.

The station's CFI, SL Keith Louis Bate Hodson from London, Ontario, had the final say as to whether or not Weaver would graduate with his classmates. He tempered his "yes" decision with the following remark: "Very young. Has a schoolboy complex. But lots of courage."

Keith Hodson stayed in the RCAF after the war and rose to the rank of Air Vice Marshal. Sixteen years after Weaver's tragic death, Hodson was killed in an eerily similar bail-out accident. On July 5, 1960, Hodson jumped out of a crippled T-33 jet trainer near Colorado Springs, Colorado. His parachute momentarily caught on the plane's tail, and, after several agonizing seconds, he managed to free himself. But in his wild struggle to survive, several parachute shroud lines wrapped around his neck. When Hodson reached the ground, he was dead from strangulation. At the time, Hodson was the Deputy Chief of Staff at North American Aerospace Defense Command Headquarters.

Claude Weaver happily left Moncton with 144.95 flight hours on Ansons recorded in his logbook. Taking the standard two-week pre-embarkation leave, he returned home to visit with family, friends and, in particular, his high school sweetheart, Ramona Yergler.

Returning to Canada, Claude left "Y" Depot, Halifax, Nova Scotia, on November 2 on a troop ship bound for England. Arriving on the 14th, he was sent to No. 3 Personnel Reception Centre in Bournemouth.

From December 6, 1941, to January 5, 1942, he flew Miles Master trainers with an Advanced Flying Unit at RAF Cranwell. From February 10 to April 15, Claude flew Miles Masters and Hawker Hurricanes at No. 56 OTU, first from Sutton Bridge, Lincolnshire, and later from Tealing, Dundee, Scotland.

After graduating, Weaver was posted on April 16 to RCAF No. 412 "Falcon" FS, which was flying Spitfire Vbs initially from Wellingore and later from Martlesham Heath in Suffolk.

FL W. Barry Needham of Wynyard, Saskatchewan, spent 26 months flying combat with 412, completing two tours of operation. "I remember Claude extremely well," Needham recalls. He had led Weaver on a Rhubarb mission, a strafing sweep at low level by a few aircraft, to the Ostend, Belgium, area on May 21, 1942. He said the weather that day was lousy, low cloud, which they flew in and out of while just a few feet above the water. Eventually, they were separated and that is when they should have turned around and aborted their mission. However, they did not. Barry shot up some barges and a flak position. When Claude returned, he reported flying out of the soup into brilliant sunshine right over the middle of Ostend harbor. The Germans put up the most horrendous flak barrage but missed.

Volunteering to go to Malta, Weaver left 412 in the middle of June.

Along with 30 other Spitfire replacement pilots, he reached the island on July 15, 1942, via the British aircraft carrier HMS *Eagle* to participate in Operation *Pinpoint*. Claude then joined RAF No. 185 "Malta Squadron" at Qrendi Airfield where he flew a mixture of Spitfire Vbs and Vcs.

In his first contact with the enemy on July 17, Weaver shot down a Messerschmitt Bf 109. Over the next six days, he added four more 109s to his score, a double on the 22nd and two more on the 23rd, achieving the coveted title of ace.

Pilot Officer Claude Weaver III DFC, DFM, MiD is home on RCAF leave prior to departing for overseas service. His father, Claude II (middle), looks on admiringly. An unidentified US congressman on the left completes the picture. (Weaver family collection via W. M. Palmer)

The squadron's diarist recorded the following, "Shorty Reid with Sergeant Weaver, one of the new boys, each accounted for a 109F type. The boys also escorted the RAF high-speed rescue launch that went out of its way to pick up the downed Jerries." Weaver was successful again five days later, as the diarist continued: "Weaver maintained his good work, this time shooting down two nasty Bf 109Fs." The following day, Weaver saw yet more action: "A flight went to town on a radar plot of fifteen+, with Sergeant Weaver scoring another double – two Bf 109s again – a really excellent record."

At the age of 18, Claude Weaver became the youngest Allied fighter ace of World War II. WC Brown's assessment of the type of service aircraft Weaver should only fly was absolutely correct.

Before he turned 19, Claude added half of a Ju 88 on July 24, a Bf 109 probable on August 2 and two additional Bf 109 kills on August 17.

Days after celebrating his birthday, Weaver claimed another Bf 109 probable on the 25th and, two days later, he accounted for a Ju 88, a Bf 109 and a Ju 88 probable. His score to that point stood at nine-and-a-half confirmed and three probables.

Weaver's string of kills almost ended at 1458hrs on July 31 when he was bested in combat by Oberstleutnant Gerhard Michalski of 4./JG 53, who was flying a Bf 109G-2.

After becoming Michalski's 41st victim, Weaver crash-landed Spitfire EP343 on Malta.

Gerhard Michalski survived the war, flying a total of 652 combat missions. His final aerial tally was 73 victories.

For destroying five-and-a-half German aircraft in only eight days, Weaver learned on September 4 that he was being awarded a DFM. Part of his published award read as follows: "This non-commissioned officer has shown great zeal and initiative in combat. Though relatively inexperienced he has, by his dash and personal courage, been an inspiration to the other fighter pilots of his unit."

Flying Spitfire Vc XBR112 on a fighter sweep to Comiso airdrome in Sicily on September 9, Weaver shot down an Italian Macchi MC.202 Folgore fighter. To achieve this victory, he had to chase and catch the 352 Squadriglia aircraft in a near vertical dive. Weaver's engine was then shot out by his victim's wingman, Paolo Damiani, who had worked his way unnoticed in behind Claude's aircraft. Claude's element leader suggested that he put his Spitfire down in the shallow surf parallel to the beach at Scoglitti. Weaver replied, "No thanks," and announced he was landing directly on the beach. He also said, "I'll get a boat and I'll be back."

Sergeant Weaver pulled off a beautiful wheels up landing with the result that there was no noticeable damage to his aircraft other than a bent propellor. For a few minutes, he eluded his captors in the sand dunes, but he was eventually discovered hiding in some tall grass a short distance away.

On September 22, Claude's mother, Retha Dellinger Weaver, received a letter from No. 185's CO, SL C. F. O. Swales, who stated the following:

> By now you have heard from official sources that your son is missing. I have every reason to believe that he is a Prisoner of War as he was seen to make a forced landing in enemy territory. The Italian wireless broadcast that an enemy plane had been forced down and the pilot, an American, was a PoW in their hands. Your son was a very good pilot and an excellent shot. His loss is very much felt in the squadron as his efforts had most certainly added to the score of enemy planes shot down.

Claude spent the next year in Camp P.W. 21 at Chieti, Italy.

Barry Needham returned to Canada late in 1943 on a month's leave before heading back to begin his second tour. During the trip home, he met FL Dennis "Dogass" Newman from Buffalo, New York. Newman, an RCAF Wellington bomber pilot, had been in the same camp as Weaver. He told Barry that when Italy surrendered the Italian camp, guards slowly drifted away. The camp's British Senior Officer (BSO) told everyone to stay put as the Allies were on their way.

He warned them that if anyone left, he would personally see to it that each would be court-martialed.

Newman, Weaver and several others, including Lieutenant Harold "Mouse" Rideout, a 26-year-old P-40 Warhawk pilot from Ashburnham, Massachusetts, said to hell with that and took off. Weaver teamed up with Rideout in the bid for freedom. The pair were always packed and ready to go on a moment's notice. They had a good supply of energy bars on hand made from sugar and chocolate they had melted together from their Red Cross packages. Those weekly packages, routed through Switzerland by the boxcar load, literally saved the prisoners' lives. Each week an 11lb package, plus 100 cigarettes was evenly divided between two men. As neither Weaver nor Rideout smoked, their weekly tobacco allotment greatly enhanced their trading and buying power for other essentials.

It is a good thing they did not listen to the camp BSO, as several days later the empty guard towers were staffed by well-armed German paratroopers. Weeks later, P.W. 21 closed. The remaining prisoners were moved several times, eventually winding up at Stalag Luft III located near the village of Sagan, Germany.

Newspaperman, novelist and Hollywood screen writer, David "Westey" Westheimer, the author of *Von Ryan's Express* and *My Sweet Charlie*, knew Weaver while both were interned in P.W. 21.

Westheimer, a USAAF B-24 navigator, was shot down on December 11, 1942, during a bombing raid to Naples harbor. In his 1992 book, *Sitting It Out*, David described Claude's life as a PoW:

> A powerfully built RCAF fighter pilot from Oklahoma City, Weaver, a double ace at only nineteen, would stride around the compound, his blonde head arrogantly held high. When our Red Cross parcels arrived, Claude, who was a super trader, would roam the camp like a timber wolf looking for victims. He had no shame! The more lopsided the bargain, the better he liked it. He traded a British Army Colonel two tins of British sugar – four ounces for a tin of English biscuits. Weaver then went off and within an hour returned with two bags of Canadian sugar – eight ounces that he had traded for the biscuits. And he gloated. Weaver was so good at the barter game, he once traded soap, coffee and tea for a guard's rifle!! The BSO made him return it.
>
> Claude was wild and reckless and always got into trouble with his captors. On cold sleety nights he would go to the window and call out to the freezing guards walking the wire outside our bungalow, 'Dormi Bene Sentinello' – 'Sleep well, Sentry'. Weaver had the most solitary confinement time of any American in the camp. Late one evening, in one of his many escape attempts, he tangled himself in the wire and was discovered as he tried to break free. The guards knew Weaver by sight and hated him because of his constant taunts. Several proceeded to beat him with their rifle butts. He was saved from certain death when an Italian Red Cross officer stopped them. The officer convinced the guards that Weaver's escape

attempt was just a youthful prank. He took Claude aside and told him there had been too many attempts and the camp commandant was pressuring the guards to clamp down. He also told Weaver that if he tried it again, he more than likely would be shot.

The most difficult part of Claude and Harold's journey was that they had to navigate their way through 300 miles of German-occupied territory. Rideout picked up the story in his report to military intelligence:

> Once outside, we wondered how the Italian farmers would receive us. We both had long handle-bar moustaches, Claude was in his RCAF uniform and I wore khaki. At first many Italians thought we were German. But when they realized we were American, everything was fine. You know they all had a cousin or a friend in New York City. Two days out in a tiny village in hill country, they discovered we were American PoWs. They treated us like kings. They fed us, called the mayor and had a great celebration. They offered us guns which we refused. Two young Italian fellows who wanted to join General Badoglio's army in the south and fight for the Allies, offered to act as our guides. We set out on the mountain trails. The country was beautiful and we enjoyed the warm days and cool September nights. We finally decided we had to get out of our uniforms, when we began seeing prints of German hobnail boots on the trail. We discarded our uniforms and obtained some tattered clothing from our guides. Once we came upon a German convoy, so we sat down on a hillside with a shepherd, shared some of our cigarettes and watched the trucks and tanks roll by. We left our guides behind as they were traveling much slower than we were. We could see our pilots bombing Foggia on the east coast. In one village we entered, the people began calling to one another up and down the street "Americanos, Americanos." The Germans in the village came after us so we took off. We were racing down a steep slope and that's when Claude took a mean fall and injured his ankle. But we kept going for another mile or two. His ankle swelled up like a balloon. Then we came across an armed soldier wearing shorts. We thought he was British as they often wore shorts. When we got closer we saw the swastikas on his uniform. Claude said he'd take him if he had to. We said "Buon Giorno" and walked right past him. He gave us a dirty look and said "Nichts." Our ragged clothes had fooled him.
>
> By this time Claude's ankle was giving him fits. We came upon a deserted farm and I made a bed for him in the hayloft. I set out to find help, some food and discovered a British convoy roaring down a road. I tried to flag them down, but they weren't about to stop for an excited looking Italian. Finally some sappers directed me to a bridge which was under repair. After I convinced the Canadian Captain in charge of who I was he loaned me a vehicle to bring Weaver in. We got back to the trail to the farm and there was this man with a donkey. With the last

of the cigarettes and some soap, I convinced the man to loan me the donkey for Claude to ride.

Later in a radio interview in London, Weaver completed the rest of the story: "Rideout put me to bed and said he was going across to the British lines for help. I thought I'd never see him again. But that night, as I hobbled around the farmyard on a crude crutch I had made, I saw a man in an old floppy hat coming up the trail on a donkey. It turned out to be Lieutenant Rideout. He'd found the British lines and came back for me."

Newspapers reported the pair reached Allied lines a year to the day after Claude had been imprisoned. Rideout reportedly was leading the donkey with Weaver perched on its back. Claude was wearing a jaunty alpine hat, carrying a shepherd's crook and running a temperature. They had walked for nine days and nights to reach safety.

RCAF Overseas Headquarters in London received a message on October 8, 1943, advising that Weaver had arrived safely at Malta. He returned to England on the 18th and was pleased to learn that eight days earlier he had been promoted to WO2.

The next day, he was commissioned from the ranks as a PO and was assigned new Regimental Service No. J. 18784. Anxious to return to flying combat, Weaver joined RCAF No. 127 Wing on October 27, initially flying with 421, then 403 squadrons.

On November 30, he was invested with his DFM Award at Buckingham Palace, where he briefly met King George VI during the ceremony.

In his book, *Lucky 13*, WC Hugh Constant "Hughie" Godefroy, recalls meeting Claude Weaver late in 1943. Godefroy was the commander of RCAF No. 127 Wing:

> I received a rather unusual replacement, PO Claude Weaver, DFM. He had been shot down on a strafing expedition over Sicily while stationed at Malta. He had been interned in an Italian PoW camp. The Italians treated their prisoners without the slightest respect for the Geneva Convention. Disregarding the fact that it is the duty of a captured combatant to try to escape, the Italians brutally beat Claude after his first two attempts to gain his freedom. At last he escaped and made contact with the advancing Allied troops in Italy. Claude was an American who trained in Canada and who wanted to stay in the RCAF after the war. Having heard of the treatment he had endured at the hands of the Italians, I fully expected to meet a very subdued character.
>
> When he presented himself at my office, I found myself faced with a tall, blonde, keen-looking fellow who had just turned twenty. He had a neatly trimmed moustache, bright eyes and his uniform, buttons and shoes were in impeccable order. The only sign of past military experience was the DFM ribbon below his

wings. It was evident in talking to him that he wanted to get back on operations as quickly as possible. I delegated him to 421 Squadron and told him to get checked out on a Spitfire Mk IX and fly around and get familiar with the country.

On the day he did his first solo, the wing was grounded by bad weather. Just after tea, I got a phone call from Alex Hamilton, our Wing Engineering Officer.

'Hughie, have we had anybody flying operational today'?

'No, Alex, there's just been the odd fellow doing some local flying. Why?'

'One of the aircraft in 421 Squadron came back with the spinner missing from its prop. It's obviously been blown off by a cannon shell. Who is this guy Weaver?'

'He's a new second tour replacement; was he flying the aircraft?'

'He was!'

'Have them send him up to my office immediately!'

Twenty minutes later, Claude Weaver came into my office looking a little sheepish.

'Weaver, I told you to go out and do some local flying. Where did you go?'

'It didn't take me long to get familiar with the area, sir, so seeing that I was up, I went over to France and did a little strafing.'

'If that's the kind of thing you're going to do, Weaver, you might as well pack up your bags and go back to Air Force Headquarters.'

For a moment, I thought he was going to cry. He pleaded with me to let him stay.

'Okay, Weaver, I'll give you one more chance. From now on I will decide if, and when, you will venture over enemy territory. Do you understand?'

'Yes, sir, I promise – I promise!'

This was not the last time I would have to deal with Claude Weaver. Inwardly I was delighted with his keenness and with his reaction to the threat of being turfed, I was sure that he wouldn't play that trick again.

In December, Claude was asked in a radio interview why he had not transferred from the RCAF to the USAAF. He replied, "Well, it would take me a few months to train on the P-47 Thunderbolt. Anyway, when the invasion comes, I want to be flying a Spitfire."

On December 30, Weaver was flying in a four-plane section, which was being led by Canada's top-scoring fighter ace FL George "Buzz" Beurling. The other two pilots were Hart Finlay and William Bliss.

Southeast of Paris, they came upon an American heavy bomber group, which was being harassed by a mixed force of 109s and 190s. Breaking up the German fighter attack, Beurling and Bliss each destroyed an Fw 190, while Weaver and Findlay each downed a Bf 109.

Claude's last victory, which brought his tally to 12½, occurred on January 21, 1944, when he shot down an Fw 190 west of Lens, France.

The last written entry in Weaver's RCAF records, which are held in The National Archives in Ottawa, Ontario, simply states: "January 28, 1944 – Missing from 403 Squadron – Presumed dead."

The squadron's diarist made the following entry that fateful day:

> The weather today was unfit for a sweep. Readiness was done by the squadron. In the afternoon a ranger sortie was organized by Claude Weaver. The section then flew to RAF Manston to board additional fuel. Only three of the four aircraft got airborne from there. When they got in around Douce they were bounced by twelve+ Fw 190s. They were all hit. Unfortunately, Claude Weaver has not returned. This is a great shame as we shall miss his exceptional eyesight and the very fine spirit which he displayed at all times. We all sincerely hope that he will be back in a month or so.

403's OC, in a report to Headquarters, described it this way:

> Three aircraft of this squadron took off from Manston on this operation and swept Lille/Amiens. They entered the French coast at Nieuport and swept the Lille area and then turned southwest toward Amiens, the section was flying line abreast at 3,000 feet and below the cloud layer. All aircraft were heavily engaged, FL Thornton and FO Foster's aircraft were both hit. When last seen PO Weaver was breaking up into cloud with two enemy aircraft on his tail. Sample 42 [the fourth aircraft] did not take off from Manston due to engine trouble.

On March 2, 1944, the Oklahoma City native who proved he could fly and fight with the best either side had to offer, was posthumously awarded a British DFC. His medal was presented on May 5, 1945, to his next of kin. The citation read as follows:

> Within recent months this officer had taken part in numerous low level attacks against a variety of targets, such as airfield and gun emplacements and throughout has displayed great determination in air fighting. He has destroyed a further seven enemy aircraft bringing his victories to twelve. His successes are an excellent tribute to his great skill, courage and resolution.

On June 8, 1944, Claude Weaver was MiD. However, there was no citation recorded for this award.

A second tragedy befell the Weaver family on March 5, 1945, when Claude's brother, David, was killed in action on the island of Iwo Jima while serving with the United States Marine Corps (USMC).

The youngest Allied ace of World War II peacefully rests far from Oklahoma in Grave No. 9 in the Meharicourt Communal Cemetery in Somme, France. The CWGC meticulously maintains the graves of 40 other Allied airmen at Meharicourt – 21 British, 12 Canadian, six Australian, and two New Zealanders.

Claude Weaver is counted as a Canadian. In this quiet country setting, these 41 decorated airmen are grouped together in one section of the cemetery known as the British Plot.

In 1994, Barry Needham visited several cemeteries in France while attending 50th anniversary D-Day celebrations. He accidentally stumbled upon Claude's grave at Meharicourt and was shocked when he saw that he was only 20 years old when he died. He could hardly believe that fact. Needham knew Weaver was young, he just never realized how young. The subject of age never came up in their conversations. Barry wonders how it was possible that Claude could join up and go through pilot training at the age of 17. He said, "Regardless, he was a hell of a pilot."

Mac Palmer purchased two copies of David Westheimer's PoW memoir, *Sitting It Out*, and sent one to Weaver's sister. Westheimer graciously signed her copy with the following personal inscription: "For Virginia Weaver Higbee, in memory of your brave brother Claude, from his barracks mate, friend and admirer."

Vasseure Wynn
Georgia Fighter Ace

World War II fighter pilot Vasseure Howe "Georgia" Wynn, Jr. was born in Kiefer Creek, Oklahoma, on October 11, 1917. His father, Vasseure Howe Wynn, Sr., was a native of Rome, Georgia, while his mother, Willie Lou Hannah, hailed from Dalton, Georgia. Wynn, Jr. was just a few months old when the family returned to its home state and settled in the small community of Dalton. In 1920, a daughter, Frances, was born into the household. Wynn, Sr. died in the early 1930s when his son was a teenager.

Vasseure attended Font Hill Public School from 1922 to 1930, then Dalton High School from 1930 to 1934. Growing up in the foothills of the Blue Ridge Mountains, he was active in swimming, hunting, tennis, and golf.

From January 1935 to July 1936, Wynn was employed as a page in the United States House of Representatives in Washington, DC. He then spent the next two years working as a junior clerk at the Justice Department in the offices of the FBI. From July 1938 to January 1941, he clerked at the United States Department of Agriculture. Along the way, Georgia furthered his education by taking correspondence courses at Columbus Junior College. He had a great interest in aviation and obtained a private pilot license, No. 18643-40, in September 1940.

From July 1940 until January 1941, he served in the US military as a private in the District of Columbia's Army National Guard.

In spite of his better than average government connections, Wynn was unable to qualify for pilot training in the USAAC. He was one year shy of its minimum requisite of having two years of college. The local civilian flying community, however, was abuzz with information on how easy it was for an American to join the RCAF. To quickly build up its air force, Canadian recruiters began taking applications from would-be pilots from all across North America. The RCAF quickly got its message out by putting up recruiting posters at every civilian flying club and airport in Canada and in all 48 states.

Wynn preferred to fight the war from an airplane, so he was not going to wait around to be conscripted into the US Army.

Armed with his birth certificate, high school diploma and logbook, which showed 99 hours of recorded flight time, the 23-year-old headed north at the end of February 1941 to the RCAF's No. 12 Recruiting Centre in Ottawa, Ontario.

There on March 4, he was sworn in as an AC2 under Regimental Service No. R. 95640. Wynn agreed to stay in the RCAF for the duration of the war and possibly for a period of up to one year during demobilization should His Majesty require his services.

The interviewer, FO T. G. Holley, recommended that Wynn be accepted for aircrew training either as a pilot or as an observer. At the bottom of the report, he wrote: "Good appearance and manners. Dependable steady type. Good flying experience with private pilot's license. Keen to fly as a pilot. Excellent material for aircrew."

For the next 18 days, Georgia was at No. 1 MD in Toronto, Ontario, for basic training. From March 23 until May 28, he was assigned to perform guard duty at No. 4 Bombing & Gunnery School at Fingal, Ontario.

Wynn returned to Toronto on May 29 where he began the first phase of his military flying career at No. 1 ITS. The school was located on the grounds of the former Eglinton Hunt Club. Graduating from there on July 3, Vasseure was promoted to LAC. Along with the promotion came a CAN$0.95 a day raise, which bumped his earnings up to CAN$2.25 daily.

Georgia was posted on July 4 to No. 9 EFTS at St. Catharines, Ontario, where, on Course No. 32, he flew the de Havilland Tiger Moth biplane for approximately 65 hours. He passed out of the course on August 30, 1941, achieving a grade of 62 percent.

On September 2, Wynn was posted to Course No. 37 at No. 14 SFTS at Aylmer, Ontario. There he flew 160 hours on Harvard Mk IIs until graduating and earning his wings as an SP on November 21, 1941. He passed out of the course with a grade of 69 percent. With the promotion came another raise in pay, from $67.50 to $111 monthly.

Later in his career, while flying P-47 Thunderbolts and P-51 Mustangs with the USAAF 4th FG at Debden, England, Wynn learned that RCAF Air Station Aylmer was also the place from where

4th FG ace Vasseure H. Wynn shot down German aircraft over the island of Malta and in the ETO. (US Department of Defense)

several of his 4th FG contemporaries had been stationed or graduated – aces such as Major Pierce Winningham "Mac" McKennon, Captain Bernard L. "Big Mac" McGrattan, Captain Albert Lewis "Smiley" Schlegel, Captain Edward Lester "Buddy" Gimbel, 1st Lieutenant Ralph "Kidd" Hofer and Lieutenant Paul Sydney "Rip" Riley. For 32 days in the fall of 1941, McKennon, Schlegel, Gimbel, Hofer and Wynn were all stationed together at Aylmer, but it is unknown if they knew each other at that time.

Georgia, who was slated to be posted overseas to a war zone, was granted 14 days pre-embarkation leave on November 22. He left Canada through "Y" Depot, Pier 21, Halifax, Nova Scotia, on December 13. The slow transatlantic passage took 11 days with the ship finally docking in Glasgow, Scotland, on Christmas Eve. This ocean voyage was followed by an overnight troop train ride that covered the entire length of Britain – some 900 miles. Wynn and several hundred airmen arrived mid-day on the 25th at No. 3 Personnel Reception Centre at Bournemouth. This staging area is where the newly arrived Canadian aircrews received their assignments, had a few days to acclimate themselves to the British money system and generally learn how to effectively navigate around the country.

On February 20, 1942, Wynn was sent to RAF No. 56 OTU at Sutton Bridge, Lincolnshire, for five weeks of fighter training on Hawker Hurricanes.

Halfway through the course, the entire OTU was moved from Sutton Bridge over to RAF Tealing at Angus, Scotland. The course concluded on March 27.

Georgia was posted to RAF No. 504 (County of Nottingham) Squadron, which was based at RAF Ballyhalbert, Northern Ireland. There he flew Spitfire Mk Vbs on convoy patrols and bomber escort missions.

The lack of aerial action in and around the Belfast area caused Vasseure and a few others to volunteer to go to Malta. Wynn arrived on the strategic Mediterranean Island on July 15, 1942, as part of Operation *Pinpoint*. He and 30 other fighter pilots air-delivered Spitfires to Malta after taking off from the deck of the Royal Navy aircraft carrier HMS *Eagle*.

Their launch point from the boat was approximately 60 miles off the coast of North Africa. Each aircraft was fitted with a 90-imperial gallon long-range belly tank for the 650-mile one-way journey. Landing on the tiny island, Georgia was immediately assigned to RAF No. 249 "Gold Coast" Squadron, which was flying the Spitfire Mk Vb and Vc variants from Ta' Qali Airfield.

At 1130hrs on July 28, while flying Spitfire BP869, Wynn claimed a German Messerschmitt Bf 109F as damaged.

On August 13, during a mid-afternoon patrol, Vasseure and two of his squadron mates downed a Ju 88 twin-engined reconnaissance aircraft. The trio of Wynn, PO Ripley Ogden "Rip" Jones and PO George Frederick "Buzz" Beurling caught up with the Ju 88 15 miles west of Linosa flying at 14,000ft. The German aircraft, coded F6+KK, was flown by Unteroffizier H. Schmiedgen. Jones attacked first followed by Wynn. Both pilots scored cannon and machine gun hits on the enemy's fuselage, but it was up to Beurling to administer the coup de grace at close range. Each pilot was given a one-third credit for the kill.

Southeast of Zonkor, Malta, in BR373 on October 14, Georgia claimed a Bf 109F as probably destroyed.

The next day in BR373, Wynn downed a Messerschmitt 109F and damaged another. A day later, in Spitfire EP177, he claimed a Ju 88 as a probable.

Georgia was promoted from PO on October 5, 1942. His Regimental Service No. was changed from R. 95640 to J. 16127. This was done to reflect his officer status.

With the air battle for Malta having been won and his operational tour over, Wynn returned to England at the end of November. Some 976 RAF, German and Italian aircraft were lost in the June 1940 to October 1942 deadly siege of that tiny 17-mile long by 8-mile wide Mediterranean island.

After a period of leave, Vasseure was posted to the Air Fighting Development Unit at RAF Marham in Norfolk. His job there was to fly fighter aircraft in the bomber affiliation role. On a routine flight on January 25, 1943, Georgia crash-landed Spitfire Mk IIa P8047 at 0945hrs when the plane's landing gear collapsed on touch down. The following is a written report of the incident:

> Aircraft touched down before the undercarriage was in the locked down position. Pilot complained that the warning horn did not blow. Tests for the functioning of the undercarriage revealed that it was working correctly. Lights were working properly, but the horn did not blow. This accident occurred during a normal landing. The undercarriage lights did not show green and although the horn did not blow, the pilot failed to check that the wing pegs were fully out and that the undercarriage was locked by the simple method of side-slipping the aeroplane. This pilot has evidently become careless in his cockpit drill.

An audit of Wynn's logbook revealed that he had flown a total of 430 hours on military aircraft.

Georgia's invitation from the US government to transfer from the RCAF to the USAAF caught up to him in England. After considering all the pros and cons, he decided to do it. Before leaving the Canadian air force, he was promoted on May 5 from PO to FO. His honorable discharge from the RCAF took effect from June 29, 1943. Wynn was sworn into the USAAF the next day as a 1st lieutenant.

For the next three months, he was assigned to the USAAF CCRC at Station F-342 Atcham. While there, he converted to American aircraft and flying procedures piloting Piper Cubs, Supermarine Spitfire Vbs, Miles Master IIIs, and Republic Aviation P-47C and D Thunderbolts.

Georgia joined the 334th FS, 4th FG at Station F-356 on September 17, 1943.

On December 22, 1943, Wynn was credited with destroying one Bf 109G-6 in aerial combat and was awarded a half share in the destruction of another. The following is his combat report:

> Time 1405 hours. Place Enschede, Holland. Ammunition used 266 rounds of API. I was flying as Red 4 in my squadron in support of a bomber mission to Münster, Germany. Just after the bombers turned back from the target, I followed Red 3 down on a bounce and saw two Bf 109's flying at right angles to him. I broke off to engage. I closed to a range of 250 to 200 yards and fired on the No 2 enemy aircraft. I observed flashes all over the cockpit area. I pulled up over top of him and stall turned in time to see another Thunderbolt pilot attacking the same aircraft I had just fired on. I thought it was my Leader Red 1, but later learned it was Lieutenant "Johnny" Godfrey of the 336th FS. The enemy aircraft fell off to the right and went down in flames. I closed on the other 109 pilot who was climbing slightly off to my left. I gave him a two second burst and he blew up, his starboard wing coming right off. I was then engaged by another Bf 109 who was coming in fast on my six o'clock position. I dove into a cloud, lost him and came home alone. I claim one Bf 109 destroyed and one Bf 109 destroyed which is shared with Lieutenant Godfrey.

At 1155hrs on March 2, 1944, over Sankt Goar, Germany, Georgia shot down a Bf 109G-6 while flying his assigned P-51B Mustang QP-X.

On April 9, Wynn was promoted to captain.

A little over five weeks later, on April 13, Vasseure was shot down by a Focke Wulf Fw 190A-7 pilot south of Aschaffenburg, Germany. The Fw 190 was then promptly dispatched by 334th pilot, Captain Nicholas "Cowboy" Megura. Cowboy zoomed in behind the unsuspecting German and shot him down.

Another of Wynn's close friends at the 334th was 1st Lieutenant Hipolitus Thomas "Tom" Biel. Like Wynn and Megura, Tom Biel had transferred over to the USAAF from the RCAF in 1943. Later, while sitting out the remainder of the war in a German PoW camp, Wynn was shocked to learn that Biel had been killed in aerial action over Worms, Germany, on April 24, 1944.

Georgia is credited with destroying a total of 5.83 German aircraft, ground and air, during World War II.

During the Korean War, Wynn flew Republic F-84E Thunderjet fighter-bombers with the USAF 27th Fighter Bomber Wing (FBW). At 1015hrs on January 21, 1951, near Suncheon, South Korea, he damaged a Mikoyan-Gurevich MiG-15 swept wing fighter in a dog fight.

Vasseure was promoted to the rank of major on December 15, 1951, and retired from the air force in October 1962.

Vasseure Howe Wynn died on May 8, 1987, in his 69th year in Orange Park, Florida. He was predeceased by his first wife, Suzanne Sherman, in 1967, and was survived by his second wife, Zeffie McCormick.

Henry Zary
New York Spitfire Ace

On Tuesday, February 25, 1941, graduate student Henry Paul Michael "Hank" Zary requested and received an extended leave of absence from his teaching position at New York University (NYU) located in Washington Square, in New York City. Henry was instructing there while working toward completing a Master's degree in biology.

The next day he traveled to No. 12 Recruiting Centre in Ottawa, Ontario, where he voluntarily enlisted in the RCAF. Like so many other fine young men of his time, the 22-year-old put his life and future plans on hold to go and fight for world freedom. The recruiter who interviewed Zary, FO T. G. Holley, wrote the following observations in his file: "Ambitious energetic type. Clean cut with a fine education. All round athletic and good student. Excellent recommendations. Should be an outstanding student."

Henry had logically concluded the quickest way to a war zone was through Canada and the RCAF.

After the war, he planned on resuming his studies as he wanted to be a medical doctor. The air force considered him to be of high learning ability and undoubtedly the Canadian federal government would have financially assisted him in this regard.

Born to Polish-American parents, Doma Stacek and David Zarytkiewicz, in New York on November 23, 1918, Henry was educated in the New York public school system. He attended Public Schools No. 33, 70 and 91. He graduated from the prestigious Manhattan Stuyvesant High School, which taught advanced curriculums in mathematics and science.

He obtained his Bachelor of Science degree from NYU. There were two older children in the Zarytkiewicz household at 2357 Davidson Avenue in the Bronx, a brother, Edward, and a sister, Marie. Edward tragically died in 1926 at age 17 and Henry's father died in 1937 at the age of 54.

With their father gone, the financial responsibility to support their mother fell to Henry and his sister.

Hank legally shortened his surname from Zarytkiewicz to Zary on November 4, 1938.

The RCAF assigned AC2 Zary Regimental Service No. R. 95580. Sent initially to No. 1 MD in Toronto, Ontario, Henry remained at that facility until March 24. Due to an overflow of personnel at Toronto, he and several hundred other airmen were sent, on March 25, to No. 1A MD at Picton, Ontario, to complete their basic training.

On May 16, Hank was assigned to Course No. 26 at No. 3 ITS at Victoriaville, Quebec. Graduating from there on June 21 with an 84 percent average, he was promoted to LAC. Zary placed 13th out of a class of 175 students.

The WC at No. 3 had this to say about him in a written report: "Very good educational background. Neat, keen and alert. Splendid type of American youth. Commission material."

Henry was passed to No. 11 EFTS at Cap-de-la-Madeleine, Quebec, where he amassed 85 hours flying Fleet Finch II biplanes until August 20. Next, he was posted on Course No. 37 at No. 9 SFTS at Summerside, Prince Edward Island, where he flew 161 hours on Harvard Mk IIbs from September 1 to November 21, 1941.

He completed his training to wings standard and graduated fourth out of a class of 52 students. FL Webster, his squadron commander, commented: "A good sound pilot with no outstanding faults." From the CGI: "Above average student. Hard worker. Conduct and deportment good," and from E. M. Mitchell, the CFI: "Very quick to learn. Exceptional spirit. Eager to fly. An above average pilot."

Henry was immediately commissioned a PO and was issued new Regimental Service No. J. 9261.

As an officer, Hank's net monthly income was CAN$187.50. The differential in pay from that of a lowly LAC at $45 a month, to that of a PO was substantial and the increase enabled Zary to send additional money home each month to help his mother and sister.

He left Canada on a troop ship from Pier 21, Halifax, Nova Scotia, two days after graduating and arrived in Britain on December 10. Assigned for less than a month to No. 3 Personnel Reception Centre in Bournemouth, he volunteered for duty in North Africa.

At that point in the war there were nearly 3,000 RCAF airmen waiting in hotels in and around Bournemouth's summer resort community patiently waiting to go on course. There were only 11 OTUs in all of England in late 1941 and each course was six weeks in duration with a maximum intake of only 90 students per class. The wait to get into action for some aircrew was frustratingly long.

On January 8, 1942, Zary sailed from the United Kingdom on a British warship, which was heading to Egypt. Upon arrival, Henry was assigned to MEC Headquarters where he worked in a staff position. On May 16, he managed to get himself posted to an RAF Hurricane fighter-bomber squadron, but before he could get in any amount of flying time, he fell ill with pleurisy. He had contracted the nasty bacterial infection locally. Normal breathing for Henry was difficult and painful. He was immediately taken off flight operations and hospitalized, where he was treated with large doses of sulfa drugs. The RCAF decided Hank's condition warranted that he be returned to England for advanced treatment, and this was done on October 24. While recuperating, he was promoted to FO.

Although he was improving, the air force was considering returning him to Canada to serve in a non-flying role, and it came close on several occasions to permanently deeming him medically unfit to fly.

Over the winter of 1942/43, Zary's health improved significantly to the point that he was cleared to resume flight operations. Not having flown an aircraft in more than a year, he was posted, on January 14, 1943, to RAF No. 5 Pilot Advanced Flying Unit at Calveley in Shropshire. Hank flew Miles Masters and Avro Ansons on Course No. 41 until February 21, whereupon he earned the following high praise from the school's commandant: "Trained in Canada. A good average pupil. Navigation good. Night flying good. Is a keen pilot full of dash and initiative. Confident in handling his aircraft."

Passed to No. 53 OTU, RAF Llandow in South Wales, Henry flew Miles Masters and Supermarine Spitfires on Course No. 30 until graduating on April 27, 1943. The school's WC noted in Hank's file: "He is a very good pilot."

On April 28, Zary was posted to RCAF No. 421 "Red Indian" FS, which was flying Spitfire Mk Vbs from RAF Kenley. The following month, the squadron was issued 18 brand new Spitfire Mk IXcs.

In August that year, No. 421 became part of No. 127 Canadian Wing assigned to the newly formed Allied 2nd TAF. The two other Canadian FSs that made up the remainder of the wing were No. 403 "Wolf" and No. 416 "Lynx."

Hank Zary flew many sorties with 421, damaging a Bf 109 on July 10 over Elbeuf, France, and another on September 19 near Poix. Henry was promoted to FL on November 21, 1943. The wing moved on April 17, 1944, to RAF Tangmere in Sussex in preparation for the D-Day assault.

On May 8, Hank teamed up with fellow American 421 pilot Paul Gilbert Johnson, Jr. from Bethel, Connecticut, to shoot down a twin-engined Messerschmitt Me 110 fighter bomber. The pair then went on to destroy a Ju 88 bomber on the ground. Joining up with two other pilots from their squadron, the four proceeded to ventilate two additional Ju 88s on the ground.

No. 127 moved its aircraft and personnel to France on June 16, 1944, setting up at ALG B.2 at Bazenville.

Hank Zary destroyed a single-engined fighter at 1800hrs on June 28 when he bagged a reconnaissance Bf 109 near Caen – one of 26 enemy aircraft the RCAF shot down between dawn and dusk over the Normandy front. Zary's victim was Leutnant Heinrich Weimer from 1./NAG 13. Weimer and his wingman were trying to photograph British positions from a height of 6,000ft.

Hank took over as No. 421 "B" Flight commander on July 1.

A 4th Canadian Spitfire FS, No. 443 "Hornet," joined No. 127 at B.2 on July 15, boosting the wing's aircraft total to 72. This addition increased the wing's manpower strength to 1,093, which was made up of 104 pilots, 100 ground officers and 889 ground personnel of various trades and ranks.

On Tuesday, July 25, the wing's intelligence officer briefed the squadrons that the US 1st Army was planning a break-out at Saint-Lô. The 2nd TAF's job that day was to attack any German columns trying to reinforce the battle area from the east. The US 9th Air Force would provide the same coverage to the western end of the lodgment area.

SL Wally Conrad led 12 "Red Indian" Spitfires off at 1030hrs from B.2 on an armed reconnaissance patrol covering Pont-l'Eveque and the Seine river.

Thirty minutes later and ten miles southeast of Rouen, the squadron spotted more than 40 Bf 109Gs headed straight toward it at 13,000ft.

The combined force of Messerschmitts from III./JG 1, led by Gruppekommandeur Hauptmann Erich Woitke, and I./JG 5, led by Gruppekommandeur Hauptmann

Squadron Leader Henry P. Zary DFC stands beside his No. 421 "Red Indian" FS Supermarine Spitfire Mk IXc at RAF Kenley in 1943. (Canadian National Defence Image Library)

Theodor Weissenberger, managed to shoot down only one Spitfire in the melee despite the fact they outnumbered the Canadians more than three to one.

421's score for the sortie was five Bf 109G-6s destroyed with Henry Zary accounting for three. Herein is his combat report:

> I was flying east, leading "B" flight in the Les Andelys area at 10,000 feet when forty+ Bf 109s were sighted at 10,000 to 15,000 feet on a reciprocal course. I broke to the right as the enemy aircraft opened fire. After an orbit to starboard, I followed two who pulled up climbing, one of them turning to port and diving. I fired at the latter and saw strikes on starboard wing tip then, the enemy aircraft straightened out and dove gently. The pilot then jettisoned his coupe-top and baled out. His chute did not open. Two 109s came towards me, line astern, 50 degrees to starboard. I fired a four second burst of machine gun and cannon at the second enemy aircraft and saw a huge explosion in his cockpit. Enemy aircraft disintegrated and fell down. I climbed to rejoin the circling Spitfires 7,000 feet above me. Four enemy aircraft came down flying in an easterly direction, apparently homeward bound. I fired at the last aircraft who dove to the deck and I followed. My guns were empty, but I remained above and behind him reporting his position and my lack of ammunition to my SL. I dove on the enemy aircraft anyway. The enemy pilot turned sharply to starboard to evade – hit a tree – then stalled into the ground. Smoke from this burning aircraft was confirmed by FO Neil who replied to my request for confirmation.

On August 11, it was announced Henry Zary had been awarded a British DFC. The citation for his award, effective September 19, 1944, read as follows: "This officer is a most distinguished fighter whose keenness to engage the enemy has always been apparent. In July 1944, he took part in an engagement against a superior force of enemy fighters, three of which he shot down. This officer has completed a large number of sorties and has destroyed six enemy aircraft."

Tour expired, Henry Zary returned to Canada in mid-September for an extended period of personal leave and rest.

He was sent back to England to begin a second combat tour on December 5, 1944. Henry resumed flight operations with No. 127 Wing, which had moved the previous month from Bazenville, France, to Kleine-Brogel, Belgium. The wing had more sophisticated equipment now as well and were flying Spitfire Mk XVIs.

This variant, powered by a Detroit-built 1,750shp Rolls-Royce Packard Merlin 266 engine, gave the aircraft a top speed of 434mph at altitude. Of the 23,159 Spitfire and Seafire models that poured from British factories, 1,054 were Mk XVIs and these were built at the Castle Bromwich, West Midlands, facility. Improvements to this model included a gyro-computing gunsight, increased internal fuel tankage and a universal "E" wing featuring armament of two 20mm Hispano cannon and two .50 caliber Colt Browning M-2 heavy machine guns.

For a brief period, Hank was assigned to RCAF No. 416 FS.

On February 16, 1945, Hank Zary was promoted to SL and assumed command of RCAF No. 403 "Wolf" FS, which was then located at Evere, Belgium. Two months later, the squadron moved to Goch, then to B.114 Diepholz, Germany.

On April 21, Zary, flying Spitfire XVI TB752 coded KH-Z and sporting a red, white and blue propeller spinner, blasted a Bf 109G from the sky near Schnackenburg, Germany. His combat report reads as follows:

> I was "Kapok" leader on an armed reconnaissance in the area of Parchim. When returning, I sighted two Bf 109s attacking ground targets. They were climbing when we gave chase. They climbed to 7,000 feet and I closed on the starboard aircraft, telling FO Leslie to take the port one. Closing to 600 yards, line astern, I opened fire with a four second burst to 400 yards, strikes cutting a third of the starboard wing, fin and rudder off. Strikes were also observed on the cockpit and the aircraft crashed out of control.

Hank Zary became the final American Spitfire ace of World War II. His last claim was made on April 25 when he damaged a Messerschmitt Me 262 and a Ju 88 on the ground while strafing the German airfield at Schwerin.

Two weeks later, on May 8, 1945, Germany surrendered unconditionally, and the European war was over.

Henry's health took a serious downturn late in May when his pleurisy flared up without warning. He arrived back in Canada aboard the hospital ship *Letitia* on July 16, 1945, and was medically discharged from the RCAF on October 11 of that year.

Retired SL Henry Paul Michael Zary DFC, age 27, succumbed to the insidious lung disease on Monday, February 11, 1946, at the Royal Edward Laurentian Hospital in Montreal, Quebec.

His four-and-a-half years of service in the RCAF can only be described as exemplary.

Zary's last aerial mount, Supermarine Spitfire XVI TB752, survived the war and is currently displayed in the Spitfire Memorial Museum at Manston, Kent, England.

In 1947, the Canadian government forwarded the following medals, commendations, and awards to Henry's mother and sister in New York: DFC, 1939–45 Star, Aircrew Europe Star with Clasp, Africa Star, France and Germany Star, Defence Medal, War Medal, Canadian Volunteer Service Medal & Clasp, and RCAF Operational Wings.

MEDITERRANEAN THEATER OF OPERATIONS

John Avise
Iowa Hurricane Pilot

On Saturday, October 17, 1942, 30-year-old RCAF FO John Ellsworth "Bucko" Avise from Mason City, Iowa, took off at 1120hrs from RAF Aboukir, Egypt, in Hawker Hurricane Mk II HL842.
In what was to have been a routine 30-minute delivery flight at less than a 100-mile distance to Landing Ground 44 at RAF Wadi El Natrun, both pilot and aircraft vanished along the route into the vast North African Sahara Desert. No trace of the Hurricane nor the likeable officer, assigned to RAF No. 103 Maintenance Unit (MU), were ever found.

J. E. Avise was born on October 3, 1912, in Mason City to Dennis E. Avise and Edna M. Thraves. The family, which included an older brother, resided at 10 Seventh Street Northwest. John's father owned and operated a barber shop.

From 1917 until 1930, Avise was educated at the local public and high school. He spent one year attending Mason City Junior College. His scholastic achievements won him an appointment to the United States Naval Academy at Annapolis, Maryland. He graduated from this prestigious military school on May 31, 1934, with a Bachelor's degree in engineering.

John's desire was to become a naval aviator, but the Navy decided he would be best suited to a non-flying career in ordnance and gunnery. Shortly after graduating, he resigned his midshipman commission and enlisted in the USMC Reserve. He began pilot training in Boston, Massachusetts, but this only lasted two months and ended abruptly in August 1934 when his unit was placed on the inactive list. He served in the Marine Reserve until 1938, but in a non-flying capacity.

On November 23, 1935, John married Louise Cornelia Leach in Oakland, California. She was a Mason City girl and the pair had been dating for some time. Avise established himself in California where he pursued a career as an accountant/auditor. He got into this line of work through Price Waterhouse and finished up with McLaren, Goode & Company in San Francisco. John and his wife lived in the Golden State for five years and resided at 3475 16th Street in San Francisco.

While vacationing in British Columbia with his wife in the summer of 1940, John took the opportunity to visit the RCAF's No. 1 Recruiting Centre in downtown

Vancouver. He had never lost interest in becoming a pilot but, at age 28, he was considered too old to join any US military flying service and the fact that he was married also disqualified him from entering its ranks.

Canada's air force was quite happy to have Avise sign enlistment papers on August 20, 1940, as it viewed him an ideal candidate for aircrew training.

When Avise voluntarily enlisted, his wife moved from their California home to 212 4th Street Northwest in Mason City to be closer to her relatives.

The following letter of reference, signed by D. J. W. Patrick, one of the partners at McLaren, Goode & Company, highly recommended John's services to the RCAF:

> Mr. John Avise has informed me of his desire to enlist with the RCAF and of the requirement pertaining to a letter of recommendation. In view of this requirement and with an intimate knowledge of the character and capabilities of Mr. Avise, I am exercising the privilege of recommending his application for whatever duties he should be deemed best fitted. Mr. Avise has been on the staff of our firm for several years and his work has been consistently excellent. His contacts with clients and members of the firm and staff have reflected his excellent scholastic and character training. I am making this recommendation as a former soldier of Canada, having served overseas in World War I with the 47th Battalion, 4th Division of the Canadian Expeditionary Force. It is my belief that Mr. Avise will conduct any duties to which he may be assigned in a manner befitting the personnel of the RCAF.

Assigned Regimental Service No. R. 585516, AC2 Avise traveled 2,085 miles east by train to No. 1 MD in Toronto, Ontario. He spent the next four weeks at this basic training facility before being assigned, in September, for guard duty at No. 1 Equipment Depot located at the Queens Quay in that city. On November 29, he began aircrew training on Course No. 12 at Toronto's No. 1 ITS. He graduated at the top of his class with a 95 percent average on January 3, 1941.

The school's WC made the following notations in his file: "Will make an excellent pilot. American citizen. Recommended for a commission. Topped his class. Graduate of Annapolis. Steady and reliable and would fill an Observers position equally as well as a pilot."

Promoted to LAC, Avise saw his pay increase from CAN$1.30 to $2.25 per day.

Passed to No. 10 EFTS at Mount Hope Airport in Hamilton, Ontario, John began flying Fleet Finch IIs on Course No. 17 on January 4. After accumulating 74.75 hours on type dual, solo and instrument, he graduated on February 21.

The CFI made the following comments: "Exceptionally good trainee. Would make a good instructor." The OC wrote: "Keen to fly. A steady hard working reliable individual." Avise, with a grade average of 85 percent, placed third in the class of 28 students.

At the start of the war, the BCATP EFTS courses were seven weeks in duration. Early in 1941, the course length was increased to ten weeks. Most students required 60–75 hours of elementary flight time before advancing up the chain.

Fleet Aircraft of Canada at Fort Erie, Ontario, built a total of 431 primary biplane trainers for the RCAF designated Finch Is and IIs. The Finch I, Model 16R, was powered by a 160shp five-cylinder Kinner radial engine, while the Model 16B Finch II was powered by a 130shp five-cylinder Kinner radial engine. Early in the war, these fully aerobatic, easy-to-fly, wood, fabric and metal trainers equipped 12 of the 32 EFTSs in Canada. The remaining schools used another docile biplane trainer – the ubiquitous de Havilland Tiger Moth.

From March 5 to May 17, 1941, John, on Course No. 22 at No. 6 SFTS, Dunnville, Ontario, flew a total of 115 hours on Harvard and Yale aircraft.

He was awarded his wings and was commissioned a PO two days prior to the class graduation ceremony. His Regimental Service No. was changed from R. 58516 to J. 5472. Avise stood fifth out of a class of 47 students and maintained an 80 percent grade average.

His squadron commander stated the following: "Progress good. Navigation good. A high average pilot." From the CGI: "Very satisfactory. A good effort shown throughout," and from the CFI: "Keen and reliable. Has a good sense of duty."

Returning from the standard two-week pre-embarkation leave, John departed Canada from "Y" Depot, Pier 21, Halifax, Nova Scotia, on June 19, 1941. The convoy arrived in Glasgow, Scotland, in early July, whereupon Avise, along with hundreds of other airmen, took a troop train to No. 3 Personnel Reception Centre.

After further training on Hawker Hurricanes and Miles Masters at an undocumented OTU, Mike was posted, on December 10, 1941, to the Almaza Transit Camp near Cairo, Egypt.

Midshipman John E. Avise's graduation picture was taken at the US Naval Academy at Annapolis, Maryland, in May 1934. (US Department of Defense)

On January 7, 1942, he was assigned a flying billet with RAF No. 261 Squadron, which operated Hurricane Mk Is from Haifa. In mid-February, Avise, who was suffering from pneumonia, was grounded and sent to air force headquarters at Levant, Iraq, where he rested.

On April 27, he resumed his operational piloting duties with RAF No. 213 "Ceylon" Squadron, which was flying Hurricane Mk IIas and IIcs in the desert in support of a major ground offensive spear-headed by the British 8th Army.

Avise was promoted to FO on May 17, 1942.

John flew with No. 213 until September 26, when he was posted to No. 103 MU, which operated as part of RAF No. 206 Maintenance Group.

RAF GC W. J. Loughhead, the OC Aboukir, sent the following to John's wife on November 4, 1942:

> I have delayed writing to you regarding the sad news of your husband's disappearance as we have been hoping to hear some definite news. May I offer you my very sincere sympathy in this very trying time. You must be anxious for any details and I hope this letter will tell you all you want to know about the circumstances.
>
> 'Mike' as he was known among his fellow pilots at this station, took off at 1120 hours on the morning of October 17, 1942 from this aerodrome to deliver an aircraft to a unit not very far from here. This unit was well within our lines, but he did not arrive and we have had no news whatsoever since he left here. All units in the Middle East Command were signalled for any news, but no information was available. The aircraft that left shortly after his and which was going to return him to this station, landed safely at the destination. The crew waited two hours, but Mike did not turn up. They took off and backtracked on the route to see if he had force-landed somewhere, but without results. A very exhaustive air search was then made by the pilots from this station, but they failed to locate any trace of your husband or of his aircraft.
>
> Although no part of his route was over the sea, we deemed it advisable for the Sea Rescue Service to carry out a search in the event your husband had lost his direction. You will see that every possible means was explored to try and find him. I am at a complete loss to put forth any theory as to his disappearance. The distance he had to cover was not more than one hundred miles over the desert. Part of the way is on a regular air route. All we know at the moment is that he is missing and, if any further news comes to hand, a cable will be sent to the Air Ministry who in turn will transmit the news to RCAF Headquarters in Ottawa, Ontario and you will learn of it in the shortest possible time. Your husband had not been with this unit for very long, being posted in here on September 26, 1942. He had completed a successful spell of operational flying with RAF No. 213 squadron. He was a quiet efficient officer who was doing very useful work at this station. If there

is any further information you require or any advice we can give you, please do not hesitate to write me.

Due to the variable weather conditions over the desert that day, two other pilots on similar delivery flights as Avise were forced to return to Aboukir.

FL W. R. Gunn, the RCAF casualties officer in Ottawa, sent the following letter, dated May 21, 1943, to the Avise family. It was from the CAS and it read as follows:

> It is with deep regret that, in view of the lapse of time and the absence of any further information regarding your husband, FO John Ellsworth Avise, since he was reported missing, the Air Ministry Overseas now proposes to take action to presume his death for official purposes. I wish you would be good enough to confirm by letter that you have not received any further information or news concerning him. The presumption of death will be completed shortly after hearing from you and you will receive official notification by telegram at that time. May I extend to you my earnest sympathy in this time of great anxiety.

In a casualty notification on June 23, 1943, the air force advised John's family that it was officially declaring him as presumed dead.

Being the good accountant and planner that he was, Avise had the financial foresight to provide for his wife, Louise, should he not survive the war. Naming her sole beneficiary on the two whole life insurance policies, the death benefits paid out to her totaled US$11,000. This is roughly the equivalent of $189,000 in today's money.

FO J. E. Avise earned the following wartime medals: the 1939–45 Star, Aircrew European Star, General Service Medal, Africa Star, Defence Medal, and the Canadian Volunteer Service Medal & Clasp.

On October 11, 1949, a Memorial Cross bearing the cypher of King George VI was sent by the Canadian federal government to Louise (Avise) Parks in Mason City, Iowa. This award, together with a Royal Message of Sympathy, was forwarded to her in recognition of the loss of her husband, J. E. Avise, on active service in North Africa on October 17, 1942.

As he has no known grave, John's name is inscribed on Column 263 of the Alamein Commonwealth War Graves Cemetery at El-Alamein, Egypt.

An empty grave lying next to his mother and father in the old Altoona Cemetery in Altoona, Iowa, awaits the eventual discovery and return of the remains of J. E. Avise.

The circumstances surrounding his death and disappearance remain an unsolved mystery to this very day.

Leroy Clary
Wisconsin Beaufighter Pilot

Early on the morning of November 13, 1943, an anti-shipping strike force consisting of four Bristol Beaufighter TF Xs from RAF No. 47 Squadron, five Beaufighter Mk XIs from RAF No. 603 Squadron, and two NAA B-25G Mitchell medium bombers from the USAAF 310th BG, launched from their North African desert base at RAF El Adem, Libya. Their mission was to locate and destroy German surface vessels that were landing personnel and equipment on the Greek island of Leros.

Piloting Beaufighter TF X LZ127 was 23-year-old RCAF FO Edgar Leroy Clary, Jr. from Milwaukee, Wisconsin. The other crewman in the torpedo-carrying aircraft was his RAF navigator, FS Walter E. Finbow.

Leaving the Tobruk area, the 11 twin-engined aircraft flew more than 380 miles across the Mediterranean Sea to reach their destination. Finding no worthwhile seaborne targets to engage, the small force strafed some enemy gun posts on Leros.

Suddenly, the formation was set upon by six Luftwaffe Messerschmitt Bf 109G-6 fighters. The British and American aircraft swept around the northeast end of the island and a running 15-mile gunfight ensued.

Initially, the German attacks were concentrated on the rearmost B-25s, but the American gunners managed to beat them off. At 1003hrs, the JG 27 fighters from Kastelli, Crete, focused their attention on Clary's aircraft, which, for some reason, was lagging behind the others. Hit repeatedly by cannon and heavy machine-gun fire, the out-of-control Beaufighter, with one engine on fire, crashed into the Aegean Sea five miles southeast of Leros.

Clary Jr., the only son of Norma L. Lyons and Edgar L. Clary, Sr., was born on September 8, 1921, in Coal Grove, Ohio. The family, which included a younger sister, moved to Wisconsin when Edgar's father accepted a position as a foreman with the Simplex Shoe Company.

Clary was educated from 1927 to 1935 at Central Primary School and from 1935 to 1939 at North Division High School. From September 1939 until September 1940, he worked as a general office aide at Midwest Airways in Milwaukee. He attended the University of Wisconsin at Madison for one year, studying civil engineering. While at college, he learned how to fly and obtained a private pilot's license, No. 27889-40.

On September 4, 1941, Clary traveled from the family home located at 3003 North 2nd Street in Milwaukee to the RCAF's No. 8 Recruiting Centre in Windsor, Ontario. There he enlisted in Canada's Air Force under Regimental Service No. R. 126796 as an AC2.

In his declaration, Edgar stated he had 47 hours of civilian flight time recorded in his logbook. He also indicated that he played tennis extensively, football moderately, and swimming and hockey occasionally.

Five weeks of basic training at No. 1 MD in Toronto, Ontario, was followed by two months of guard duty at No. 1 Bombing & Gunnery School at Jarvis, Ontario.

On November 24, Clary reported to No. 3 ITS at Victoriaville, Quebec, where, on Course No. 41, he scored a phenomenal 96 percent. The school's WC said: "Good background. Alert, serious and straightforward. Has character and leadership qualities and is recommended for a commission."

Promoted to LAC, Clary was posted on February 2, 1942, to No. 22 EFTS at L'Ancienne-Lorette, Quebec. There, on Course No. 48, he flew 64.05 hours on Fleet Finch II biplanes.

Graduating on March 27 with an 84 percent overall average, Edgar received the following written comments from the CFI: "Flying progress steady and good. Instrument flying good. Uses good judgment." From the Chief Supervisory Officer, the following: "Above average type. Good personality. Responsible and dependable, an excellent student."

Passed to No. 2 SFTS Uplands, Ottawa, Ontario, Clary completed his training to wings standard after flying 221.75 hours on Harvard Mk IIs.

He graduated from Course No. 53 on July 31 and achieved the second-best set of marks out of 51 students in his class. He was awarded his pilot wings, promoted to the rank of SP and later that day was commissioned as a PO.

He was issued new Regimental Service No. J. 13088.

FL Stovel, Clary's squadron commander, wrote the following in his file: "An above average pilot. Keen but cautious in the air. Excellent airmanship. Cool steady type. Flies with confidence." CGI SL Wilson commented: "A very clever student. Led the course with top marks. Very conscientious and thorough in his work. Keen on a Reconnaissance course and would do very well at it." From the Chief Instructor: "An above average student. Pleasant personality. Popular with his fellow students. Very level-headed, reliable and mentally alert. Clean cut appearance. Pupil's preference – Bomber or Fighter Reconnaissance."

RCAF No. 1 General Reconnaissance School stood up at Summerside, Prince Edward Island, in July 1942. Clary spent three months at that air station honing his reconnaissance and long-range navigation skills flying twin-engined Avro Anson Mk III aircraft.

A TF X Bristol Beaufighter's four belly-mounted Hispano-Suiza 20mm cannon are reloaded by a servicing ground crew in 1943. (UK Ministry of Defence)

Clary departed Canada from Pier 21 "Y" Depot, Halifax, Nova Scotia on November 8, 1942.

He arrived at No. 3 Personnel Reception Centre in Bournemouth, England, on the 22nd. On December 16, he began flying twin-engined Airspeed Oxfords at No. 19 Pilot Advanced Flying Unit from RAF Dalcross, Scotland. The course concluded on February 3, 1943, where Edgar added an additional 63.60 hours flying time to his total. He received the following written comments from WC Sayers the unit's OC: "An above average pilot. Has made excellent progress on the course. He is very sound in all respects and should become a very reliable pilot."

Clary was promoted from PO to FO while at Dalcross. He was posted directly to RAF No. 132 Coastal OTU at Catfoss, East Yorkshire.

Utilizing Bristol Blenheims and Beaufighters, No. 132 trained coastal command strike crews in the art of torpedo-dropping and dive-bombing.

Once trained, the majority of those crews were deployed, in 1943, to Far East and Middle East squadrons.

Clary joined No. 47 Squadron at El Adem, Libya, on November 8, 1943. Five days later, his aircraft was tragically shot down and he and his navigator were listed as missing and both were presumed to have perished. It is entirely possible that Clary was flying his first combat sortie of the war.

The Beaufighter aircraft Clary flew was one of 4,199 manufactured. The TF X variant was powered by two 1,735shp Bristol Hercules Mk XVIII radial engines. At an all-up gross weight of 25,400lb, the aircraft's top speed, at low-level, was 330mph. Heavily armed with a combination of bombs, cannon, machine guns, rockets or a single torpedo, the aircraft, known as "Whispering Death," became the scourge of the Axis forces in most theaters of operations in World War II.

Eighty-four Allied pilots became aces flying Beaufighters. Thirty-nine others achieved part of their total score on the type. Four USAAF squadrons, in a lend-lease scenario, flew Beaufighters from February 1943 until May 1945, in the night-fighter role. The Beaufighter continued to soldier on in several different roles long after the war had ended.

The last flight of a Bristol Beaufighter occurred on May 12, 1960, at RAF Seletar, Singapore.

The OC of No. 47 Squadron filed the following circumstantial report relative to the loss of Beaufighter LZ127:

> At 0727 hours on November 13, 1943 four Beaufighters of No. 47 squadron, five Beaufighters of No. 603 Squadron and two B-25s of No. 310 BG took off from El Adem on an offensive sweep in the Leros area. Flying Officer Clary flew in aircraft "A."
>
> The formation passed through Kaso and Karpathos at 0907 hours and set course for Leros. At 0945 hours the formation reached Leros and were fired at by enemy land based flak posts. No hits were scored and the formation then flew at very low level up the west coast of the island. At 0950 hours, when northeast of Leros, six Bf 109s dove on the formation from 2,000 feet astern after they had jettisoned their external fuel tanks.
>
> A running fight ensued with the B-25s at the rear. Nine additional German aircraft were seen flying at 4,000 feet on a westerly course slightly to the north. There was no action from these aircraft. The sea was extremely rough and the spray on the aircrafts' windscreens in some cases completely obstructed the view forward. Aircraft "A" was seen to lag behind the others and four 109s carried out individual attacks. The port engine caught fire and aircraft "A" turned toward Leros as though intending to crash-land on the Island. Before landfall was reached, the Beaufighter suddenly dove into the sea followed by a big splash. Nothing further was observed of the ditched aircraft or of its crew.
>
> At 1020 hours the formation was west of Stampalia and the Messerschmitts broke off the attack. Only five 109s were observed at the break. The remainder

of the formation returned to base and landed at 1227 hours. Beaufighter "A" was placed in Category "3" status and the crew reported missing.

Five days later, on November 18, FL Smith wrote the following letter on behalf of the squadron to Clary's parents in Milwaukee:

> As you have just heard, your son, FO Clary, is missing from this squadron's operations. I am afraid I must tell you that there is little hope that he is alive. He was shot down on a highly important offensive operation near Leros. His aircraft was attacked by four Bf 109s, then crashed into the sea. I knew him personally when training in England and was so very pleased to meet him again in this squadron. You will understand his death is a great personal blow to me as well as to other members of the squadron. There is no doubt that the operation had to be carried out and your son died fighting in the course of it. His kit has been gathered together by friends and forwarded to the Standing Committee of Adjustments who will communicate with you shortly. I am really so very sorry for your loss and if there is anything further I can tell you please let me know.

FO Clary and FS Finbow have no known graves. Their names are commemorated on Column 271 at the Alamein Commonwealth War Memorial in Egypt.

At the end of the global conflict, Clary's earned wartime medals, the 1939–45 Star, Italy Star, Defence Medal, General Service Medal, and the Canadian Volunteer Service Medal & Clasp, were forwarded to his parents in Chippewa Falls, Wisconsin.

The RCAF officially closed its MIA file on FO Clary on February 12, 1947. It concluded that the crew of Beaufighter LZ127 perished at sea while on active service on November 13, 1943.

On October 18, 1949, a Memorial Cross bearing the cypher of King George VI was sent by the Canadian federal government to Clary's mother. This award, together with a Royal Message of Sympathy, was forwarded to her in recognition of the loss of her son.

Arthur Cleaveland
Ohio Warhawk Ace

The 65 German Junkers Ju 52/3m transports were flying 150ft above the wave tops of the Mediterranean Sea. The formation, in three large migratory bird-like vees, was bound for Sicily, where it was to load up with additional supplies for Rommel's beleaguered Afrika Korps. Riding shotgun with the transports were 15 Bf 109s, two Me 110s and three Me 210s. The 85-plane Luftwaffe armada was near the Cape Bon peninsula, which is northeast of the Tunisian coast. The time was just after 1800hrs on Palm Sunday, April 18, 1943.

Tipped off by Allied codebreakers that a large German air resupply operation would take place on this date, elements of the Western Desert Air Force (WDAF) had scoured the area between Tunis and Sicily all day without success. The first sweep was flown by the Americans, the second by the British, and the third by the South Africans.

The fourth and final patrol of the day was conducted by 65 American and British fighters. There were 46 P-40F-1 Warhawks from the 57th FG, 12 P-47D Thunderbolts from the 324th FG, USAAF and seven Spitfire Mk VIIIs from RAF No. 92 Squadron.

The Allied formation was flying in staggered layers like steps on a staircase. Captain James G. Curl, from Columbus, Ohio, commanding the 66th FS, was patrolling at 10,000ft. Hazy conditions made it difficult to see anything, so he decided to drop down to 4,000ft for a better look. After descending, he immediately spotted four Bf 109s that were flying at a higher altitude than he was, and he wondered if they were perhaps a fighter screen for something that was below his flight level. Curl looked down and around to see what else he could see and spotted the Ju 52 formations flying so low and so close together he could barely see the water beneath them. He had never seen so many targets at one time. The 66th FS, part of the 57th FG and named "The Terminators," struck first, but in a matter of minutes a huge "free for all" developed, involving 150 aircraft and all were maneuvering and firing in a very crowded sky.

Flying P-40F Warhawk #77 from the 66th was another Ohioan, 25-year-old 2nd Lieutenant Arthur Bernard "Barney" Cleaveland from Springfield. Barney had only been flying in the USAAF for four months, having transferred from the RCAF the previous December. He was, however, an experienced combat pilot.

Within seconds, the RCAF training that he received in Canada and his operational experience with the RAF over Europe and Malta kicked in.

Taking just 16 minutes, his fighter's six Colt Browning .50 caliber MG53-2 heavy machine guns downed five Ju 52s in rapid succession – four crashed in flames and one exploded. His was the largest score of the day and he used up almost all of the 1,686 rounds of ammunition his aircraft carried.

Low on fuel, the Allies broke off the attack.

Sixty German aircraft were destroyed – 59 Ju 52s and one Bf 109 against the loss of six P-40s. Twenty-four of the three-engined transports went into the Mediterranean and 35 crash-landed on the coast of Cape Bon. The six remaining Ju 52s managed to escape, but all had some degree of damage.

The WDAF had accomplished its mission and this lopsided victory went into the history books as "The Palm Sunday Massacre."

The Allies had seriously damaged General Rommel's air supply line and, after that devastating loss of equipment and personnel, the Germans abandoned daylight supply flights to North Africa.

For its actions on April 18, 1943, the 57th was awarded a Distinguished Unit Citation and 2nd Lieutenant Arthur Bernard Cleaveland was awarded a Silver Star.

In 1943, the principal Luftwaffe fighter in the MTO was the Bf 109F "Friedrich." To match the German fighter's higher operating altitude and speed, the Curtiss-Wright Corporation test flew a P-40 airframe mated to the superlative Detroit-built Packard Rolls-Royce Merlin V-12 engine on November 25, 1941.

Replacing the standard Warhawk's Allison inline V-1710-81 motor with the Merlin enabled the P-40's maximum speed at 18,000ft to increase to 373mph, which gave it a slight edge over its German nemesis.

Curtiss-Wright built, in total, 13,378 P-40s from 1938 to 1944. Of this number, 1,131 were the Merlin-engined P-40F & L variants and all were built in 1942.

Arthur B. Cleaveland was born in Springfield, Ohio, on April 24, 1918.

He, his mother, Pearl, his father, Orion, and his sister, Dorothy, lived at 700 North Belmont Street. His father had a good paying, steady job as a locomotive engineer with the New York Central Railroad. Barney's mother died suddenly in 1936. Graduating from Springfield High School in June 1939, Barney attended, until August 1940, Wittenberg College and Ohio State University.

Wanting to be a fighter pilot, but one year shy of the prewar USAAC requirement of two years of college, Barney traveled the short distance from his home to No. 8 Recruiting Centre in Windsor, Ontario, where he voluntarily enlisted in the RCAF on September 30, 1940. His rank was that of an AC2 and his assigned Regimental Service No. was R. 67804.

Arthur Cleaveland: Ohio Warhawk Ace

USAAF 2nd Lieutenant Arthur B. Cleaveland, Silver Star, poses in the cockpit of his Curtiss-Wright P-40F Warhawk at El Djem, Tunisia, in 1943. (US Department of Defense)

From October 1 to December 21, Cleaveland was at the following training facilities: No. 1 MD, Toronto, Ontario; No. 4 EFTS, Windsor Mills, Quebec; and No. 1 ITS, Toronto.

Barney graduated from the ITS with a 76 percent average and the following notations in his file: "Keen, alert and plenty on the ball. Excellent pilot material."

On December 22, he was promoted to LAC and began his pilot training on Fleet Finch biplanes at No. 7 EFTS in Windsor. He graduated from this school on March 17, 1941, after having flown 87 hours and 45 minutes on the yellow, docile, two wing trainers.

He spent a few days back at No. 1 MD and, on April 7, he reported to No. 2 SFTS, Uplands Ottawa, Ontario, where he began his advanced flying training on Yale and Harvard aircraft.

Barney flew a total of 5.75 hours on the difficult-to-land Yales before switching to the Harvard Mk IIb.

In his class at Uplands were several Americans. One was a very bright 18-year-old who would later go on to achieve immortality when he composed the poem *High Flight* on September 3, 1941, in England. The author of that inspirational piece was, of course, PO John Gillespie Magee, Jr.

Barney and his classmates graduated from Uplands on June 22, 1941, and were awarded their RCAF wings. A day prior to the ceremony, Cleaveland was promoted to SP and had accumulated, to that point, a total of 172 hours and 20 minutes of military flight time.

From June 23 to July 4, he was at "Y" Depot, Pier 21, Halifax, Nova Scotia, awaiting transportation overseas. On July 5, his troop ship set sail for England but did not arrive until the 29th – some 24 days sailing time. His ship, for some unknown reason, spent several days docked in Iceland before resuming the voyage.

Days after arriving in the United Kingdom, Sergeant Cleaveland was flying Miles Master II trainers from RAF No. 53 OTU at Llandow, South Wales.

On August 10, he flew his first fighter – an early model Spitfire Mk 1. Ten days later, while flying Spitfire R6602, he undershot his landing and tore the engine, two wings and undercarriage from the plane. He was not hurt and the cause of this Category 1 accident – aircraft written off – was attributed to inexperience.

Graduating on September 13 from the OTU, he reported on the 23rd to No. 411 RCAF "Grizzley Bear" FS, which was flying Spitfire Mk IIs and Mk Vs from Digby, Lincolnshire.

Barney participated in his first aerial action on October 31 when he chased a bogey "damned near to Holland," but was unable to catch it.

November 4 saw 411 involved in a terrific fight, with Barney recording later in his logbook that "he did not have a clue as to what was going on!"

While on a Rhubarb on November 9, he shot up two trains near Dunkirk and he and his element leader surprised and strafed 300-plus German troops that were training in an enclosed area. Between the two pilots, they estimated they killed and wounded in excess of 150 enemy personnel.

Cleveland's time with 411 ended when, on November 14, 1941, he was posted to RAF No. 601 "County of London" Squadron, which was flying Bell P-39D Airacobras from Duxford, Cambridgeshire.

As an interceptor, the P-39 was "less than ideal," resulting in most of the squadron's flight time being spent on low-level training in the local area.

No. 601 began converting to Spitfire Vbs on March 12, 1942, and on the 25th, it was posted from Duxford to Digby. RAF 601 and 603 Squadrons were then ordered to deliver 47 tropicalized Vokes filter-engined Spitfire Vcs to the besieged forces in Malta.

On April 13, pilots and aircraft assembled at the King George V Dock in Glasgow, Scotland, where all were loaded aboard the US aircraft carrier *Wasp* (CV-7).[1] Departing the Clyde Estuary on the 14th as part of Force "W" of the Home Fleet, the group included the British battlecruiser HMS *Renown* and two antiaircraft cruisers, HMS *Cairo* and *Charybdis*. Two US destroyers, *Madison* and *Lang*, served as part of Force "W's" destroyer screen.

Barney recorded in his logbook that he ate in the chief petty officers' mess and overall had a swell time during the six-day voyage. On the morning of the 20th, *Wasp* launched its deck cargo of Spitfires, each fitted with a long-range belly tank at 0400hrs off the coast of Algiers.

Barney's was the second aircraft off and he was the first American to fly a Spitfire from the deck of a US aircraft carrier.

Another notation in his logbook says: "Landed at Luqa airfield on Malta after a four hour and ten minute flight with only two gallons of petrol remaining! Shaky Do!" Apparently, they were a little bit off course.

The German and Italian air forces, however, had their arrival time pinpointed and as they landed to refuel, accurate high-level bombing decimated the reinforcements. Cleaveland later said that after two days of fierce fighting, just 17 aircraft remained serviceable of the original 47.

Barney flew eight missions from Malta from April 26 to May 24. As "Red 4," he damaged a Bf 109F over Sicily on May 10.

In a story printed in his hometown newspaper, he told a reporter that service life on Malta was very hard, as the island was bombed four to five times daily. He said that, contrary to reports circulated in the US, the Italians were very accurate bombers, especially from higher altitudes.

In a letter to his family, he told how a close friend was shot down in flames 50 yards from his position. He said, "I could see him struggling to get out but he could not!" Watching his friend die steeled his resolve to give no quarter to the enemy whenever they were in his gunsight.

He left Malta on June 14 as a passenger in an RAF Wellington bomber heading for Egypt. There, he joined RAF No. 80 Squadron, which flew Hawker Hurricane IIbs and cs.

On June 21, he was promoted to WO2. Then, on July 1, he received another promotion to WO1.

No. 80 Squadron flew many types of missions from several different airfields in Egypt and British Palestine from July 18 to October 9. One mission, on August 31,

---

1 USS *Wasp* (CV-7), a 14,700-ton aircraft carrier built by the Bethlehem Steel Company in Quincy, Massachusetts, was commissioned into United States Naval Service on April 25, 1940. It was sunk with 193 of its crew when struck by two of four torpedoes fired from Japanese Submarine I-19 on September 15, 1942, 150 miles southeast of San Cristobal Island.

saw the squadron scramble to intercept 32 Ju 87 Stuka dive-bombers escorted by 20 Bf 109s. Barney was credited with one half of a Bf 109, the destruction of which was confirmed by FL Foskett. He had solidly hit the enemy fighter with shells from his four 20mm cannon and was watching it come down when another pilot from his squadron zoomed in behind and exploded Barney's victim with his gunfire.

In mid-October 1942, Barney formally requested the RCAF release him from its service in order to facilitate his joining the USAAF. With 405.25 flying hours recorded in his logbook, the USAAF was looking to repatriate experienced fighter pilots like Barney into its service. He received an honorable discharge on December 12, 1942.

For the next 14 days, he was at 9th Air Force Headquarters in Egypt, where he was processed and commissioned a 2nd lieutenant.

His P-40 flight training with the 79th FG began on December 27 and concluded on January 19, 1943.

2nd Lt Cleaveland joined the 57th FG on January 22nd. The 57th was comprised of the following squadrons: 64th "Black Scorpions" FS with aircraft numbered 10 to 39; 65th "Fighting Cocks" FS with aircraft 40 to 69; and 66th "The Terminators" FS with aircraft 70 to 99.

For the next three months, Barney, assigned to the 66th, flew numerous convoy patrols, fighter sweeps, escort, fighter-bomber and dive-bombing missions.

Leaving the Cape Bon battle area at 1820hrs on April 18, 1943, the jubilant American and British flyers returned to their base at El Djem, Tunisia. Barney's success that day was not without incident, as return gunfire from his five victims and their escorts had put holes in his aircraft in 70 places. Within sight of his landing field, his P-40 ran out of gas.

As he was gliding in for a dead stick landing, he spotted another Warhawk stranded halfway down the runway – also out of gas. On his landing rollout, he tried to swerve around this obstacle, but ground looped his fighter, resulting in the plane going up onto its nose then crashing over onto its back. In the final moments of the accident, Barney threw his arm up to protect his face and head from injuries and fractured his arm when his body slammed into the gunsight. He was pinned in the wreckage for 20 anxious minutes before ground personnel could dig him out.

Barney's war was over.

He had proudly worn the uniforms of two air forces, flown with three, served on three continents, been away from home for nearly three years, and had piloted nine separate types of aircraft.

His broken arm required advanced treatment, so he was shipped home to a US Army hospital in Miami, Florida, which, before the war, had been the Biltmore-Miami Hotel. There he met his future wife, Martha, an Army nurse from Chicago.

In a June 1943 interview with Ohio's *Springfield Daily News,* he said, "Flying is a great game and I hope I can stay with it even though I know my combat flying days are over." He also said he "was looking forward to finishing out the war perhaps as a stateside flying instructor."

Three weeks prior to this interview, on May 24, 1943, he was promoted to 1st lieutenant.

Barney was released from active service on July 28, 1945, and remained in the Springfield area until August 24, 1946, when he re-entered the service of the USAF.

After serving a stint in Panama, he was promoted to captain on December 13, 1949.

He, his wife and two children, Sandra Ann and Arthur Bernard, took up residence in Arlington, Virginia, when Barney was assigned to the Pentagon, working with the State Air National Guard flying units.

In early 1950, he learned that a mole on his arm, which his parachute strap had rubbed and irritated, was malignant. Captain A. B. Cleaveland fought his melanoma for more than a year but lost his battle and died at the age of 32 on Sunday, April 15, 1951, in the Walter Reed Army Hospital in Washington, DC. Five days later, he was buried in Ferncliff Cemetery in Springfield, Ohio.

John Curry
Texas Spitfire Ace

John Harvey "Crash" Curry was born in Dallas, Texas, on August 12, 1915. As a young man, he was interested in aviation and obtained his private pilot's license in 1932. When paid flying jobs were at a premium, he resorted to barnstorming to earn a living. In the spring of 1940, the 24-year-old, who was looking for steady work, volunteered to go to Canada and join the BCATP as a flight instructor. With several hundred hours of flight time in his logbook, Curry was accepted as a direct entry officer candidate into the RCAF.

After an accelerated training program at Air Station Trenton, Ontario, Curry was commissioned as a PO on August 27, under Regimental Service No. C. 2645. His first posting took him to the newly opened No. 1 Bombing & Gunnery School at Jarvis, Ontario. For the next eight months, he flew Fairey Battle and Westland Lysander target tow aircraft for the training of student gunners.

Curry was posted in June 1941 to RCAF No. 118 FS, which was flying obsolete Grumman Goblin Is from Air Station Dartmouth, Nova Scotia. The squadron was tasked with the air defense of Halifax harbor together with a secondary mission of protecting Canada's east coast from an air invasion. The lumbering Goblin biplane fighters were replaced with Curtiss-Wright P-40 Kittyhawk Mk Is in November 1941.

Right around the time of the squadron's conversion, Curry, who had been promoted to FO, left Canada for England on November 20, 1941. Spending several leisurely weeks at No. 3 Personnel Reception Centre in Bournemouth, John was posted, in January 1942, to RAF No. 58 OTU at Grangemouth and Balado Bridge, Scotland. There he undertook fighter conversion training flying Miles Master Is, IIIs and Supermarine Spitfires.

Curry's first assignment was in March with RAF No. 137 Squadron in Norfolk. No. 137 had formed at Charmy Down on Westland Whirlwind fighter-bombers on September 20, 1941, and flew its first sortie a month later.

The sleek-looking, but under-powered, Whirlwinds were principally used for coastal patrols and low-level offensive operations across the Channel into northern France. A total of 116 aircraft were built and equipped only two RAF squadrons.

On February 12, 1942, while on a routine sortie, No. 137 ran headlong into 20 German Bf 109s ten miles off the coast of Belgium. The British pilots had stumbled upon the fighter screen that was providing air cover for the German Kriegsmarine battlecruisers, *Scharnhorst* and *Gneisenau*, as they made their famous Channel dash.

The Whirlwinds were overwhelmed and lost four aircraft and pilots in the skirmish.

Hawker Hurricane Mk IVs replaced the less-than-stellar Westland product in RAF service in June 1943.

Curry left No. 137 in April 1942 and reported to RAF No. 610 "County of Chester" FS, which flew Spitfire Vbs from East Yorkshire.

Not seeing any action, Curry volunteered to go to Malta.

He was promoted to FL on June 1, 1942.

Flying to Gibraltar on June 3, he and 30 other Spitfire pilots boarded the Royal Navy's aircraft carrier HMS *Eagle*. The *Eagle*'s mission, codenamed Operation *Style*, was to deliver 31 Spitfire Vcs by air to the beleaguered forces on Malta.

Launched from the carrier 580 air miles out from the Mediterranean island, Curry's group was the only Spitfire flight to be intercepted by the Luftwaffe. Nearing the mainland, they were jumped by 12 Bf 109s from II./JG 53, resulting in four of the British fighters being shot down – two in the area west of Pantelleria and two near Gozo.

Landing safely at Ta' Qali, Curry was immediately absorbed into RAF No. 601 "County of London" FS.

Between March 7 and October 24, 1942, British and American aircraft carriers reinforced Malta's three airfields – Ta' Qali, Luqa, and Hal Far – with a total of 367 Spitfires. The carriers utilized were HMS *Eagle* (eight trips), HMS *Furious* (three trips), and USS *Wasp* (two trips).

While on that small strategic island, Curry quickly made his mark being described by 601's flight commander Denis Barnham as "slightly built, suntanned and moustached. He was having the time of his life, although he complained incessantly that it was time the squadron got some pilots who wouldn't desert him every time he led them in a dogfight."

Curry's stay at Malta was very brief – only 20 days. He scored his first victory above the island when he downed an Italian Macchi MC.202 Folgore fighter.

RAF WC Percy Belgrave "Laddie" Lucas remembered the American pilots on Malta as, "A damn good lot – there's no doubt that they really were an absolutely super bunch. With those guys, it was always the 'art of the possible.' They were so positive that I admired them tremendously."

601 Squadron moved from Malta to Mersa Matruh, Egypt, on June 23, 1942. The direct four-and-a-half hour flight was accomplished by refitting a specially designed 90 imperial gallon external fuel tank to the belly of each Spitfire.

RCAF Squadron Leader John H. Curry OBE, DFC achieved all his victories flying the four-gun 20mm cannon-armed Supermarine Spitfire Mk Vc. (UK Ministry of Defence)

During two separate sorties over Burj Al Arab on September 1, John Curry destroyed two Bf 109s. On the 7th, he downed Bf 109F-4 "Red 4" from 2./JG 27. This aircraft was flown by Knight's Cross-holder Oberleutnant Hans-Arnold "Fiffi" Stahlschmidt, who died in the encounter. The 21-year-old German Staffelkapitan had flown more than 400 combat missions in North Africa and at the time of his death was credited with shooting down 59 Allied aircraft.

On September 11, Curry damaged an MC.202 and claimed a Bf 109F as a probable. On the 29th, he and two others shared in the destruction of a Ju 52/3m transport. In the intense fighting during the battle of El Alamein in October, Curry made six more claims, including three destroyed, to take his victory total to 7.333. All of his claims were in the four-gun 20mm cannon-armed Spitfire Mk Vc.

At the end of November, Curry was rested, being posted to the air staff at Middle East Headquarters in Cairo.

In June 1943, he took command of RAF No. 80 Squadron, flying his second tour on Spitfire Mk IXs from Kabrit, Egypt. Curry was promoted to SL on December 2, 1943. Flying mostly coastal patrols, 80 Squadron then moved to Italy in January 1944 in support of the British 8th Army.

During his RCAF service, John Harvey Curry was recommended for three awards, but only two were actioned. The following are his citations and gazetted British awards.

> CURRY, FL John Harvey (C. 2645) – Distinguished Flying Cross – No. 601 squadron – Award effective 1 February 1943 as per London Gazette dated 5 February 1943 and AFRO 373/43 dated 5 March 1943. American in the RCAF. Born on August 12, 1915 at Dallas, Texas; home there. Trained at Trenton and No. 1 BGS. Commissioned directly as a PO 27 August 1940; to FL, 1 June 1942; to SL 2 December 1943. Posted overseas 20 November 1941; repatriated 26 July 1944; posted to No. 1 OTU, 9 September 1944; released 25 September 1945. DFC presented at Buckingham Palace, 9 May 1944; OBE presented 16 January 1948.
>
> Flight Lieutenant Curry is an outstanding pilot who displays the greatest determination to engage the enemy regardless of the opposition encountered. He has destroyed at least seven enemy aircraft and is a source of inspiration to his fellow pilots.

Public Record Office Air 2/8933 has the earlier text of the recommendation for a non-immediate award, sent on December 21, 1942, from Headquarters, Royal Air Force, Middle East to Air Ministry: "This pilot is an excellent shot and is keen to come to grips with the enemy regardless of the numbers opposing him. The ease with which he gains superiority over his opponent and invariably shoots him down is an example which inspires the less experienced pilots in the squadron. He has now destroyed seven enemy aircraft confirmed, with two credited as probably destroyed in the space of three months."

His DFC citation was as follows: "CURRY, SL John Harvey, DFC (C. 2645) – Officer, Order of the British Empire – No. 80 squadron – Award effective 1 September 1944 as per London Gazette of that date and AFRO 2231/44 dated 13 October 1944." There is no citation in Canadian sources. Public Records Office Air 2/9221 has a recommendation (plus extensive supporting data). The first draft was compiled on March 30, 1944, noting he "had flown about 130 sorties; shot down 2 March 1944 and returned 18 March 1944." On April 1, 1944, Air Commodore Pike recommended a Military Cross, which was approved by HQ Mediterranean Allied Air Forces and by General Harold C. Alexander. It was in London that this was changed to an Officer, Order of the British Empire (OBE). The original narrative is quite detailed; the following is the draft completed before the final submission:

> On 2nd March 1944, Curry was engaged in a low flying operation near Rieti, Italy and while attacking three enemy tanks, return ground fire shot out his aircraft's engine. He made a forced landing in the snow-covered mountains near Rocca di Mezzo and, after

destroying certain equipment in his aircraft, made his way to a hut a short distance away. An hour later he returned to his aircraft and cut off pieces of his parachute which later were to serve for camouflaging himself against the snow. While by the aircraft, Curry saw 2 men approaching, so he made off in the deep snow in a southerly direction. One of the men, being on skis, soon overtook him and said that he was a Yugoslav resident who had come to help as an enemy search party was in the vicinity. The man offered Curry his skis but he could not fit them to his boots, and when twenty men were seen approaching down in the pass some two miles distant, Curry instructed the Yugoslav to ski back to the aircraft, obliterating his tracks from it. Curry then crawled through deep snow into the bush on the mountainside, continuing until he was exhausted. Later he continued his journey eastward until he reached a large plain near a slope on Monte Sirente where he found a wooden hut. He made a fire from the floorboards and rested while wolves howled in the vicinity. At daylight on 3rd March he continued his journey and was given some food in the village of Secinaro before making his way toward the hills. In Gagliano, Curry was given some clothes and food and managed to get some sleep in a stable where three Italians provided him with some straw for his bed. Next morning he left the stable and soon met two South Africans who had escaped and they took him to a Casetta where they met five officers from an Italian prison camp who were waiting for a guide to lead a party through the lines. Next morning, Curry, with others, was led to a cave where the party remained for seven days. At the end of this time, as no other guide had appeared, Curry and another officer set off south on March 12 through rough terrain to reach allied lines somewhere near Popoli. They were up to their knees in snow. Soon afterwards they started to ascend Montagne del Morrone and were forced to plough through snow which came up to their hips. After many vicissitudes they reached the top of the mountain and continued to the Morrone range, afterwards proceeding through the pass between the Morrone and Melilla ranges. In the valley an armed enemy patrol was seen but was evaded. Hungry and cold, they decided to climb Mont Melilla – 10,000 feet and achieved this feat after grueling experiences. Finally a gorge was reached and, while descending, the Sangro River came into view. They came out of the gorge and eventually reached safety on the 18th when they met up with soldiers from the Indian Army's 6th Lancers.

In July 1944, Curry returned to Canada where he took up duties as chief test pilot at the Air Test & Development Unit at RCAF Rockcliffe, Ontario.

At war's end, he returned to Texas where he worked in the aviation and aerospace industry building fighters for the US Navy and space rockets for NASA.

Curry later moved to Florida, where he worked until 1970 on the Apollo program at the Space Center. In retirement, he spent much of his time sailing his ocean-going 40ft sloop.

John Harvey "Crash" Curry OBE, DFC died on March 18, 2008, at the age of 92 at Oak Hill, Florida.

Richard De Bourke
The Almost Ace

On Wednesday, March 10, 1943, 29 Messerschmitt Bf 109G-6s, belonging to JG 77, were providing close escort to a Luftwaffe strike force of 16 Ju 87 Stuka dive-bombers. Their target – the British forces occupying Landing Ground (LG) Foum Tataouine, Tunisia.

At 1630hrs, several flights of RAF Curtiss-Wright Kittyhawk Mk IIIs appeared in the azure blue sky then swooped in to attack the enemy raiders. The fight, lasting only 17 minutes, was terribly lopsided.

The German fighter pilots, under the command of Major Joachim "Munch" Muncheberg, claimed numerous P-40s shot down for the loss of a single Bf 109. Muncheberg personally downed two Kittyhawks, one at 1633hrs and the other at 1648hrs. The German ace was killed in action 13 days later in a fight with American Spitfire pilots from the USAAF 52nd FG. Muncheberg's final tally amounted to 135 victories.

Officially, six Kittyhawks were brought down in that skirmish over the North African desert, and all belonged to RAF No. 112 Squadron. Pilots missing and presumed dead were FO David A. Bruce in aircraft FR295, FO George W. Wiley in a P-40 coded GA-D, PO Randolf C. Smith in FR131, FS John H. Oliver in FR361, and FS Richard P. "Dick" De Bourke in FR275. Their crash sites and remains were never located and their names are commemorated on columns at the Alamein War Memorial in Egypt.

The sixth pilot who was initially believed to have been killed was FL Robert R. Smith DFC, flying FR325. He was captured two days after the aerial battle and was subsequently listed as a PoW.

The 12 British fighters had taken off from the LG at 1545hrs and were tasked to fly top cover for RAF No. 250 Squadron, which was on a sortie to seek out and destroy German armored columns in the forward area.

The P-40K and M aircraft flown by No. 112 were powered by a V-1710-81 Allison, V-12 liquid-cooled, inline engine rated at 1,200shp. In 1942, the Curtiss-Wright Corporation of Buffalo, New York, constructed a total of 616 of these two models.

These variants were then supplied to several Commonwealth air forces, and all were designated in service as Kittyhawk Mk IIIs. No. 112 was the first Allied unit to

RCAF No. 14 SFTS at Aylmer, Ontario, is where WO2 Richard P. De Bourke earned his wings flying NAA Harvard Mk IIs in October 1941. (Canadian National Defence Image Library)

paint the "shark mouth" motif on its aircraft, securing it the nickname "The Shark Squadron." The fearsome artwork first appeared on its P-40s in mid-1941. The idea was actually borrowed from the Luftwaffe after a 112 Squadron pilot had seen a picture in a popular weekly magazine of a twin-engined Me 110 painted in a similar scheme.

Richard Patrick "Dick" De Bourke from Newton, Massachusetts, voluntarily enlisted in the RCAF at No. 13 Recruiting Centre in Montreal, Quebec, on December 26, 1940. Sworn into Canada's air force as an AC2, De Bourke was assigned Regimental Service No. R. 79049.

The 21-year-old was born in Dorchester, Massachusetts, on September 18, 1919, to Patrick Joseph De Bourke, a transplanted Canadian from St. John's Newfoundland, and Agatha M. Clair. The family, which included three other sons and two daughters, lived at 36 Floral Street in Newton. Richard attended Sacred Heart Elementary School in that community from 1925 to 1932, then Sacred Heart High School from 1932 to 1936. His first job was as a locker room attendant at the Charles River Country Club. Next, he worked locally as a clerk and truck driver for McMullin Hardware.

Richard De Bourke: The Almost Ace

De Bourke held a private pilot's license and had accumulated a total of 43 hours of flight time at the time of his application to the RCAF. He told his interviewer, FO Louis Gelinas, that he wanted to be a military pilot. Gelinas noted in the file: "No military training, but has some flying experience. Above average type. Good education. Neat appearance. Should be very good pilot material. Recommended."

Earning CAN$1.30 per day, De Bourke was sent, on January 11, 1941, to No. 1 MD in Toronto, Ontario, for several weeks of basic training. As this facility was filled to capacity, Richard and a few hundred other new recruits were sent east by passenger train on February 20 to No. 1A MD at Picton, Ontario.

On March 19, he returned to Toronto and, five days later, he was on his way to perform guard duty at No. 6 SFTS at Dunnville, Ontario. On May 17, he returned to Toronto to begin the first phase of his flying career at No. 1 ITS.

De Bourke was promoted to LAC on June 21, and was given a $0.95 a day pay raise. Posted to No. 7 EFTS at Windsor, Ontario, on Course No. 31, Richard flew yellow Fleet Finch biplanes until graduating with a 74.5 percent average on August 8. De Bourke's flight instructor said that he had progressed well in his training and was on the way to becoming a good service type, whereas his ground instructor stated that he had to be watched as his cockiness could have an effect on his fellow classmates.

On August 9, Dick began flying Yale and Harvard trainers on Course No. 35 at No. 14 SFTS at Aylmer, Ontario. Graduating with a 68.17 percent average, De Bourke was promoted to the rank of SP on October 24, 1941.

Richard's monthly pay rose substantially from $67.50 to $111 monthly.

With his RCAF pilot wings sewn on his tunic, this newly minted military aviator reported, on November 11, to Pier No. 21, Halifax, Nova Scotia, for onward deployment to England. He arrived by fast troop ship in the United Kingdom 12 days later on the 23rd. He and the other air force personnel took a troop train to No. 3 Personnel Reception Centre situated at Bournemouth on England's south coast. Richard did not have long to wait for a training slot to open up as he was posted on December 9 to No. 55 OTU at RAF Usworth in Durham. He spent the next three months learning to fly and how to tactically use Hawker Hurricane Mk Xs.

De Bourke arrived at Padgate in Warrington, Lancashire, on March 3, 1942. He transited by ship to the African continent, arriving there 24 days later on the 27th. From there, it was off for further training at the Middle East Central Gunnery School where he remained until May 15. While there, Dick was promoted to FS. He then spent the next eight weeks waiting for an assignment to an operational unit. De Bourke was finally posted to RAF No. 112 on July 18, 1942, while the squadron was operating from LG 175 at El Amiriya.

On November 1, 1942, while flying Kittyhawk FR264, De Bourke shot down two German Ju 87 Stukas and claimed another as a probable. During the encounter, return fire from one of the enemy gunners shot up his aircraft, wounding him in the shoulder. In a great deal of pain from the bullet wound, Richard managed to return to his LG, where he pulled off a perfect landing. It took 23 days of healing before he was medically cleared to return to flight operations.

On December 11, in FR213, Dick destroyed a Luftwaffe Bf 109F. Two days later, on the 13th in FR213, he blew another Bf 109 out of the clear blue desert sky.

On March 17, 1943, SL G. W. Garton DFC, OC No. 112 Squadron, sent the following letter to the De Bourke homestead on Floral Street in Newton:

> I regret having to inform you that your son, No. R. 79049 F/S, De Bourke, R. was missing from operations on 10 March 1943. In this, my squadron and I wish to offer you our deep sympathy. The actual details of the operation are briefly as follows. Your son, better known to us all as "Dick", was flying in a formation of twelve of this squadron's aircraft which took off from one of our advanced grounds at 1545 hours on March 10 to attack enemy transport and armoured vehicles in the forward area. Over the target, a formation of enemy bombers escorted by fighters was encountered and in the subsequent engagement our aircraft became somewhat scattered. Your son, and I regret to say five more of my pilots, failed to return. What happened to them is unknown. Other than this, there is nothing further I can say now, but I sincerely hope that news will soon be forthcoming which will dispel all our worst fears for your son's safety. During the eight months your son has been with my squadron, he always displayed exceptional keenness and a fine sense of duty which brought him some measure of success. With this, his cheerful disposition made him exceedingly popular with all pilots and ground crew. We all miss him immensely. Lastly, my squadron and I wish to convey to you our great appreciation of your son's work.

Richard De Bourke was credited with the destruction of four enemy aircraft and one aircraft as probably destroyed. All were in a six-week period in the latter part of 1942. After his death, it was learned that he had been promoted from FS to WO2 on October 24, 1942. For whatever reason, that information never made it through the official RCAF and RAF chains of command.

The Estates Branch of the Canadian Department of National Defence officially changed De Bourke's status on November 4, 1943, from that of missing to presumed dead. His overseas demise, at the age of 23, was then registered by the RCAF Records Officer with the Province of Quebec's Bureau of Statistics.

Richard P. De Bourke's decorations, which included the 1939–45 Star, Africa Star & Clasp, Defence Medal, War Medal, Operational Wing, and the Canadian Volunteer Service Medal & Clasp, were forwarded to his parents in January 1945.

James Gray
Third Time is the Charm

When World War II ended, the majority of military fighter pilots breathed a collective sigh of relief. Most had had their fill of fighting and, for those who had been overseas for several years, well, they just could not wait to go home and piece together their interrupted prewar lives. There were a few pilots, however, who did not want the conflict to end. With an end came the sudden realization they were out of a job. They would no longer have a wartime sortie to fly, nor a defined enemy to fight. In just an instant, those jousting aerial warriors were relegated to the footnotes of history and were referred to as "Yesterday's Man." Some of those unsettled souls found it difficult to transition into and live in a world that was finally at peace.

One of those individuals was RCAF FL James Osbourn "Tex" Gray, an American from Chillicothe, Ohio. The carefree, fun-loving, red-headed, 6ft 3in tall Gray served six years in the RCAF, flying and fighting in Africa, Italy, and Europe.

James O. Gray, son of Clyde Egbert Gray and Miriam Osbourn, was born on May 11, 1912, in Wilmington, Delaware. Attending several primary schools in Maryland, he graduated from Elk Ridge High School in that state in June 1930.

From June 16, 1932, until September 14, 1934, he was a midshipman at the United States Naval Academy at Annapolis, Maryland. The reason he gave for leaving before graduating was that he was deficient in the subject of mathematics.

That October he enlisted as a private in the USAAC and was assigned to the 96th BS at Langley Field, Virginia. He was appointed a flying cadet, but washed out of primary flight training on May 12, 1935, at Randolph Field in San Antonio, Texas.

Gray married Elsie A. Sharp on September 21, 1935, in South Mills, North Carolina. The union produced no children and the couple divorced on March 18, 1943.

From June 1935 until August 1937, Tex was employed as a marine steam engineer at the Newport News & Shipbuilding Company in Newport News, Virginia. While there, he, along with thousands of other shipyard workers, helped build USS *Yorktown* (CV-5) for the USN. That aircraft carrier was subsequently sunk by the IJN on June 7, 1942, during the Battle of Midway.

From September 1937 until December 1940, Gray was employed as a Spanish translator in the Field Services Division of the United States Department of Justice, Bureau of Prisons, at Chillicothe.

On Wednesday, December 3, 1940, the 28-year-old entered the RCAF's No. 8 Recruiting Centre on Ouellette Avenue in downtown Windsor, Ontario, and voluntarily enlisted in the RCAF. Tex told his interviewer, FO Fleming, that he had 42 hours of flight time at Randolph, but had not completed the course. He also indicated that he had always wanted to be a military pilot and the RCAF was probably his last best hope. Fleming believed Gray was a desirable candidate, had the potential to be an officer, and had gained enough experience in the USN and USAAC to justify being accepted into Canada's air force. It was noted in the file that Gray's wife resided at 155 West Water Street in Chillicothe, Ohio, and that his mother and father lived in Beltsville, Maryland. Tex owed US$550 on a new car, which he said he would sell if the air force accepted his application.

Later that afternoon, Tex was sworn in as an AC2 under Service No. R. 83075. While waiting for his documents to arrive from home, he stayed at Windsor's YMCA on the RCAF's tab.

Eight days later, he and dozens of other new recruits boarded an eastbound Canadian National Railway passenger train for the 200-mile trip to No. 1 MD at Toronto, Ontario. There, and later at No. 1A MD in Picton, Ontario, he undertook the four-week basic training course, finishing on January 11, 1941.

For the next three months, AC2 Gray performed guard duty on Canada's east coast at RCAF Air Station Dartmouth, Nova Scotia. On April 10, Tex was posted to No. 3 ITS at Victoriaville, Quebec.

This school was a former Catholic convent that had been taken over by the air force for the duration of the war. The classroom was actually the church itself, with the students sitting in the pews and the instructors lecturing from the pulpit.

Gray completed this phase of his training on May 14 and was promoted to LAC. From there, it was on to Course No. 28 at No. 17 EFTS at Stanley, Nova Scotia, where Tex excelled at flying de Havilland Tiger Moth biplanes. On July 3, he was posted on Course No. 32 flying Harvard Mk IIb aircraft at No. 8 SFTS at Moncton, New Brunswick. In a graduation ceremony on September 14, 1941, Gray was awarded his wings and was promoted to the rank of SP.

Returning from the standard two-week pre-embarkation leave, Gray sailed in a convoy on October 2 from Pier 21, Halifax, Nova Scotia, headed for the United Kingdom. He arrived in Glasgow, Scotland, on the 18th and, along with hundreds of other airmen, took a troop train to No. 3 Personnel Reception Centre at Bournemouth.

On November 3, Gray was posted to No. 2 SFTS at RAF Brize Norton, Oxfordshire, where he flew Harvards until December 1. The next day he transferred to No. 9 SFTS at RAF Hullavington, Wiltshire, for advanced training on Miles Master Mk Is and Hawker Hurricane Mk Is.

While piloting Hurricane L2102 on January 10, 1942, Tex collided with a Miles Master that was in the landing pattern in front of his aircraft. An incident report was filed with the Air Ministry, the content of which is as follows:

> Pilot's Report: I was ordered by my instructor to practice landings. I saw a Master four hundred yards in front and to the left of me while I was on the approach. I saw him land in front of me and then lost sight of him as the nose of my aircraft rose during the approach. After landing, I saw a Master land in front of me and thought this was the one I had seen previously. I, therefore, edged over to the right. Watching this aircraft I suddenly saw the Master I had followed in. It was stopped on the runway across wind directly in front of me. On my landing rollout, I applied the brakes and full left rudder, but could not turn in time to avoid a collision.
> Damage: Starboard main-plane, starboard centre section leading edge, starboard fairing, propellor and engine shock loaded. No technical or structural failure.
> Primary cause of the accident: Pilot of aircraft Hurricane L2102 failed to see Master in his path during the landing run.
>
> Secondary cause of the accident: The two aircraft collided.
> Hours flown solo on type: 1.20
> Hours flown solo on all types: 109.50
> General Remarks: Although there is no evidence of culpable negligence, the blame for this accident squarely rests with the Hurricane pilot who was responsible to avoid the aircraft landing in front of him.
>
> Signed – P. H. Cummings, Group Captain, Officer Commanding No. 9 SFTS, January 15, 1942.

Tex continued his training at No. 9, which early in 1942 became No. 9 Advanced Flying Unit. He completed the course on March 9 and, seven days later, was at Blackpool awaiting transport by air to the Middle East.

Gray was posted to RAF No. 267 Transport Squadron at Heliopolis, Egypt, on March 16. From that date until July 13, 1942, he flew Lockheed Hudson and Lodestar twin-engine aircraft on resupply missions to outlying LGs, carrying passengers, mail, and freight. While with No. 267, he was promoted on July 1 to FS.

Also based at Heliopolis was RAF No. 173, which undertook the same role as No 267, utilizing Lodestar Mk IIs. Gray flew with that unit from July 14 until October 4. A further promotion came his way on September 13 to WO2.

Tex spent the next seven days at Almaza, Egypt, before checking in at No. 1 Middle East Central Gunnery School for a two-week refresher course flying fighters.

He was posted on September 18 to RAF No. 94 Squadron at El Gamil, where he flew the 20mm cannon-armed Hawker Hurricane Mk IIc in the ground attack role. On December 11, 1942, Gray was promoted from the enlisted ranks to that of PO. He was given new Regimental Service No. J. 16543. A further promotion to FO followed on June 11, 1943.

Gray's time with No. 94 Squadron came to an end on July 15, 1943, when he was transferred to RAF No. 249 "Gold Coast" Squadron, which flew Spitfire Mk IXs from Qrendi Airfield on the island of Malta.

At this point in the war, the air battle for Malta had been won, so the RAF took the fight to Sicily, bombing and strafing any and all legitimate ground targets.

On September 18, Tex was posted to RAF No. 112 Squadron, which was operating Curtiss-Wright Kittyhawk Mk IIIs in the fighter-bomber role at Brindisi on the Italian mainland. During his time with No. 112, Gray was shot down by ground

Flight Lieutenant James O. "Tex" Gray has his locks trimmed by Corporal Honor "Nipper" Benson in this April 1945 picture. (Canadian National Defence Image Library)

fire on two occasions. The first was on December 2, 1943, in Kittyhawk FR439 (coded GA-K). His aircraft force-landed at LG Canne due to combat damage. The second was on February 29, 1944, in Kittyhawk FL886 (coded GA-B). He force-landed near the Anzio beachhead following flak damage and was slightly injured.

After flying hundreds of combat sorties with three RAF squadrons in three separate fighters, FO Gray became tour expired on July 31, 1944. From that date until December 30, he served as a staff officer at RAF Middle East Headquarters. Just days before he left, he was promoted to FL.

He arrived back in England on January 7, 1945. Tex elected to remain in Britain, and it did not take him long to secure another flying assignment.

On January 22, he moved over to No. 83 Squadron, where he test flew and delivered new Spitfires from RAF Dunsfold to operational units.

Gray began his second combat tour as a Hawker Typhoon IB pilot on February 26, 1945, with RCAF 439 "Sabre-Toothed Tiger" FBS. Operating over the ever-moving frontline in support of the army, the squadron moved on April 13 from Holland to Goch, Germany. Eight days later, it moved further into Germany from Goch to Celle. On May 4, it was taken off operations, and, the next day, the German army surrendered.

May 8, 1945, was universally celebrated as VE-Day, when Germany surrendered unconditionally.

Gray's time with 439 Squadron ended on June 30, 1945. He was credited with 193 operational sorties amounting to 202 operational hours.

With the end of the European war, Tex was given the option of returning home, staying in Europe with the British Air Forces of Occupation (BAFO) or going to the Pacific as part of the RCAF's "Tiger Force." He opted for the latter, but his plans were foiled when the US dropped two atomic bombs on Hiroshima and Nagasaki in August 1945.

Not yet ready to give up, Gray took the BAFO option and was posted to RCAF No. 416 (City of Oshawa) FS in September 1945. That month, the unit re-equipped with the Spitfire Mk XIV, but, on March 19, 1946, it disbanded at Uetersen, Germany.

Gray's long war was over and with little or nothing militarily left to do, he began the process to return to Canada. He left England on April 17, 1946, after being processed through the RCAF Repatriation Depot (RD) at Torquay, Devonshire. The majority of returning RCAF personnel came home via RD at Warrington, but this exit facility was closed in late May 1945. After an eight-day ocean passage to Halifax and a one-day train ride, Tex arrived at No. 1 RD Lachine, Quebec, on April 26.

Thirty-four-year-old FL J. O. Gray was honorably released and retired from the RCAF on June 3, 1946.

He had earned and was awarded the following medals and decorations for his six years of wartime service to Canada: 1939–45 Star, Africa Star & Clasp, Italy Star, France & Germany Star, Defence Medal, Operational Wing & Bar, and the Canadian Volunteer Service Medal & Clasp.

He indicated that he was returning to the US as he wanted to pursue a career in commercial aviation. Gray left the RCAF a forward mailing address in the care of a relative, William B. Gray in Abilene, Texas. On October 4, 1950, he supplied the RCAF with a new mailing address, care of General Delivery, Fort Hancock, Texas.

He disappeared sometime in 1956 and was never heard from again.

The following information is from his nephew, James Osbourn Gray Collins:

> I began, in 1978, to investigate the disappearance of my uncle. After the war it seems Tex had a flying circus and crop dusting operation in Loudoun County, Virginia. Some time later, Arthur Godfrey, the radio and television personality bought the airstrip and Jim's crop dusting venture moved to the site of the old Hondo Army Air Force Base just outside of San Antonio, Texas. The "crop dusting" and "flying circus" outfits that Tex had in Loudoun County were probably covers. The Central Intelligence Agency in Langley, not far away, was experimenting with low-level defoliant spraying. They recruited combat flyers who were adept at dogfights and escape and evasion to begin a campaign of anti-guerrilla warfare in the Caribbean and Central America. An important element in this campaign would have been defoliant spraying to remove the concealing cover of the jungle canopy. It is probable that Tex's stint at Loudoun County was a training period for this anti-guerrilla campaign, a campaign for which he would have readily volunteered because of his ironclad anti-communist views and his combat experience. After his training, the agency may have planted him at the Hondo site. That facility would have been more secluded (for continuing training) and made him more quickly available to the agency's areas of concern than the District of Columbia region. The family has come to believe that Tex was shot down or crashed in the jungle in Guatemala in 1956 during one mission of this anti-guerrilla campaign, a mission designed to overthrow an unfriendly pro-communist regime there.

Herold Marting
Indiana Fighter Pilot

Herold Fesler "Bud" Marting was born on March 1, 1911, in the village of Eckerty in Crawford County, Indiana. He was the only son of second-generation Pennsylvania Dutch parents, Uriah Marting and Lillian Fesler. Herold attended Danville Grade School in Danville, Indiana, from 1916 to 1924. He completed his secondary education at Danville High School in 1928. Following graduation, he enlisted in the USMC serving as a rifleman in the Continental United States, Haiti, and the Virgin Islands. Completing four years of general service duty, he was honorably discharged as a corporal in 1931.

Marting enrolled at Central Normal College in Danville, remaining there until 1933. From 1934 until 1937, he was employed by the US government accounting office as a junior accountant.

For the next three years, he worked as a personal assistant to Atlanta, Georgia, businessman C. C. Barnes. It was through this employment that Herold developed a keen interest in flying. He and his boss frequently flew to and from business meetings in the company aircraft.

Barnes, however, did not hold an instructor's rating, so the 245 flying hours Bud accumulated – dual, solo and as a passenger – could not be officially logged. C. C. Barnes unexpectedly passed away in 1940, leaving Herold without a job.

The resourceful Marting quickly found another position, clear across the country in Seattle, Washington, as an inspector with the Stetson-Ross Machine Company.

Later that year, with the war in Europe in full bloom, Bud, now 29, was looking to somehow get involved. He was well past the maximum age for acceptance into any of the American military flying programs, so, on Thursday, October 10, 1940, he traveled 119 miles north from Seattle to Vancouver, British Columbia, where he voluntarily enlisted in the RCAF at No. 1 Recruiting Centre.

The recruiting officer made the following entry in his file:

> An American citizen. Discharged USMC Corporal who earned a Good Conduct Medal. Has two years college and quite good civilian work experience. Considerable passenger flying experience and some solo – enough to have established an aptitude for flying. Is a good type, direct, straight forward and gentlemanly. Fully matured –

manly and confident. Courteous and accustomed to discipline. He is an above average amateur golfer. He is keen to serve as a pilot and I judge him to be a man who will do well.

Herold stated on his application that he was single. He was divorced and had a five-year-old daughter who lived with her mother in Indianapolis, Indiana.

Assigned Regimental Service No. R. 74733, AC2 Marting was sent to No. 2 MD at Brandon, Manitoba, for three weeks of basic training. This was followed by an additional month of instruction at No. 2 ITS in Regina, Saskatchewan.

On November 29, Herold was promoted to LAC. Moving quickly through the system, he furthered his flight training flying wooden and fabric-covered Fleet Finch II biplanes at No. 7 EFTS at Windsor, Ontario.

Graduating first in his class on January 16, 1941, with a mark of 88 percent, Marting was immediately posted to No. 6 SFTS at Air Station Dunnville, Ontario. There he flew Harvard and Yale trainers on Course No. 18. He graduated and earned his wings as an SP on March 30.

He faired very well on the course, finishing third in a class of 45 students. Later that day, he was commissioned from the ranks as a PO. His service number was changed from R. 74733 to J. 4919.

Marting was disappointed when he was posted, on April 6, to the Central Flying School at RCAF Air Station Trenton, Ontario, where he was scheduled to begin a five-week flying instructor's course. He begrudgingly completed the curriculum on May 10, but in the interim, managed to convince his superiors that he would be much happier serving in a combat role as opposed to remaining in Canada as an instructor. After all, that was why he came north – to fly and fight!

His persistence on this point paid off when he was posted on May 29, to No. 1 Port Transit Unit, "Y" Depot, Pier 21, Halifax, Nova Scotia, for deployment to England.

Herold remarried his former wife Frances in a ceremony in Indianapolis on May 14, 1941, during his two-week pre-embarkation leave. The troop ship carrying him and hundreds of others across the North Atlantic arrived at Glasgow, Scotland, on June 28. En route, the boat had to divert into Iceland for minor repairs. A day-long train ride, which ran the entire length of Great Britain from north to south, deposited the tired airmen at their final destination, No. 3 Personnel Reception Centre at Bournemouth.

On July 7, 1941, Herold began flying Miles Master Is and Hawker Hurricanes Mk Is at RAF No. 59 OTU, Crosby-on-Eden. Completing the course on August 26, Herold was posted to RAF No. 71 Eagle Squadron at Martlesham Heath.

The squadron was flying defensive patrols utilizing Supermarine Spitfire Vbs over southern England with the occasional offensive sortie over northern Europe.

There has been some suggestion that Marting was later assigned to RAF No. 121 Eagle Squadron, but that has not been substantiated by any official documentation.

When the United States came into the war on December 8, 1941, many of the Eagle Squadron members pushed for transfers to a more active combat zone, Marting among them.

While still in the RCAF, however, he was promoted to FO and shipped out on March 30, 1942, to RAF MEC. From April to July, he was assigned to No. 21 Personnel Transit Centre at Kasfareet airfield in Egypt.

On July 31, he was posted to RAAF No. 450 Squadron, which was flying Curtiss-Wright Kittyhawk P-40Es, P-40K/Ms, and P-40Ns in the fighter-bomber role during the North African campaign. When he arrived, the squadron was operating from LG 91 El Amiriya South and called itself "The Desert Harassers."

The pilots and groundcrew led a miserable nomadic lifestyle, living in tents, existing on rationed water, eating terrible food, and, on top of all that, were constantly moving back and forth to airfields in Egypt and Libya in support of the British 8th Army.

It did not take Bud long to run up a score. On September 15, 1942, he destroyed a German Messerschmitt Bf 109 fighter and damaged another at El Alamein while flying Kittyhawk Mk Ia coded EV160. On October 20, 1942, he destroyed an Italian Macchi C.202 fighter at Fuka while flying Kittyhawk Mk III coded FR251. On October 23, 1942, he destroyed a German Bf 109 fighter at El Alamein while flying Kittyhawk Mk III coded FR309.

On October 24, Marting took off with other members of his squadron from LG 175 El Sallum in support of an early morning bombing raid of the enemy airfield at El Daba, Egypt. While closing on an enemy aircraft that got airborne during the chaos, Herold's Kittyhawk Mk IV was struck by antiaircraft fire and crashed in the middle of a newly laid minefield. Landing safely by parachute, Bud was surrounded by soldiers from the 62nd Italian Infantry Battalion who promptly arrested him. One of them stole his watch. He was taken to their commander where he was fed breakfast and later was given some schnapps to drink. An hour later, he rode on a motorcycle, under escort, to the battalion's headquarters for questioning.

As a PoW, he refused to answer all questions put to him with the exception of his name, rank and unit. Sent by car to the unit's Divisional HQ, he was questioned for an hour by an intelligence officer but told him nothing of Allied operational matters. An Italian general and his subordinate staff at this location treated Bud courteously and gave him some coffee.

Put into a car with a driver and two guards, Marting was transported to another HQ site, where he was further interrogated, this time by a skillful Italian officer who spoke very good English. When the answers to the questions put to him were

Curtiss-Wright P-40N Warhawks on the Cheektowaga, New York, assembly line. Note the Curtiss license-built Republic P-47G Thunderbolts on the left line. Herold F. Marting MC was killed on September 22, 1943, while ferrying a Warhawk to a stateside training unit. (US Department of Defense)

not forthcoming, a frustrated Italian colonel burst into the room and demanded to know why America had declared war on Italy. His anger mounted when he began to shout that America and England had no business being in Africa.

At sunset, Marting was sent by car to the El Daba railroad station where he was turned over to two German officers who gave him bread, soup and water. Herold was moved to Luftwaffe HQ where one of their more experienced intelligence officers interrogated him. The German treated him with respect but questioned him thoroughly. He seemed to be very well informed and asked Bud, "How is your new squadron leader doing?" The SL had only been promoted two days previously. The German told Bud that the British forces had a total of 1,900 aircraft in Africa, including those in maintenance shops and asked when the British push would begin. Marting laughed the question off and asked when the Germans would start their own offensive.

Bud was able to ascertain that the following Allied PoWs were being detained nearby – Sergeants Ewing, Evans, Holloway, and Lindsay from No. 450 Squadron, PO Hogg from No. 112 Squadron, and Lieutenant MacKay, a SAAF pilot.

That evening, Herold was placed in a tent with four American PoWs. Each was given a blanket and made to sleep on the sand. Their guards took their boots to prevent them from escaping.

The following morning, they were awakened at 0600hrs. They were given a French Army overcoat, three days of food rations, and, along with seven guards, boarded a stake truck for the trip to Tobruk. They stopped at Gambut for the evening and arrived at their destination on the morning of the 26th. Their names were recorded on a manifest list for passage by air to Greece aboard a Junkers Ju 52/3M transport.

The first part of the journey was a one-hour flight to the island of Crete, where the plane refueled. From there it was a four-hour flight to Elefsina airfield near Athens. The prisoners were sequestered on the third floor of the Rex Hotel and were advised that they would be moved to Germany on October 30.

Herold devised an escape plan, which the others declined to participate in, deeming it too risky. They did, however, promise to cover up his departure for as long as possible. On the 29th, Marting stole a cap and a pair of trousers from the duffle bag of one of his guards who was taking an afternoon nap in an adjacent room. The other guard was in another room listening intently to a British Broadcasting Corporation radio broadcast. Herold quietly exited the building via the hotel's fire escape.

From the courtyard, he scaled a 12ft wall, walked several blocks, and, luckily, fell into the hands of members of the Greek resistance.

Herold was hidden from the Germans at various safe houses until December 12. Over a five-day period, he was moved across land and water, finally reaching the safety of Turkey on the 17th.

He arrived back in Cairo on New Year's Eve, 1942, and casually walked into the officers' mess to greet fellow American pilots Edward Miluck and Charles Tribken. Miluck later wrote, "What a New Year's Eve. Marting suddenly shows up and acted as if he had just stepped out for a drink."

The following message dated 9 February 1943 was sent from RCAF Overseas HQ in London to the Department of National Defence for Air in Ottawa, Ontario:

> A signal was received on 15 January 1943 from MEC HQ stating that FO H. F. Marting, J. 4919, had been shot down and taken prisoner on 23 October 1942. He was removed to Greece, where he managed to escape, reporting back to HQ Middle East on 31 December 1942. FO Marting has completed 140 operational sorties with a record of three aircraft confirmed and one damaged. He is an American citizen, formerly with RAF No. 71 ES and does not wish to be transferred to the USAAF. He is reported to have a good record and in view of his harrowing experience and the unusual circumstances in which he escaped from the enemy, his repatriation to Canada to carry on with the RCAF is

recommended. The circumstances of his case were reviewed at this HQ and as MEC HQ has agreed to release him, his repatriation is approved. Advice has now been received that FO Marting has proceeded by air, via the United States, in a USAAF aircraft departing on 6 February 1943.

Marting came down with scurvy while on the run from his captors in Greece. The disease left him feeling exhausted. Parts of his body would swell up and his gums and teeth bled. Consequently, he was not in the best of health when he returned to Canada on February 15. He was removed from flight status, hospitalized, treated with vitamin C and B complex and given extensive dental treatment. His condition improved, but he tired easily and periodically suffered from inflammation of the gums. He looked into transferring to the USAAF, but that was not possible as he was not medically fit to fly. Herold tried to persuade his wife to move to Canada, as it was a financial strain trying to maintain two households. She refused, stating she did not want their child uprooted halfway through the school year. She then gave him an ultimatum, return home or she would divorce him again. Bud, under a great deal of stress, took his situation to the air force and asked it to release him from its service on compassionate grounds.

A medical board comprised of seven RCAF officers convened in Ottawa on May 27, 1943, to consider FO H. F. Marting's case. Below is its findings and recommendations:

> This officer, aged thirty-two years, is an American citizen. His civilian experience included three years of general flying and maintenance training, four years' service in the ranks of the USMC and employment as an accountant with the United States General Accounting Office in Washington. He is married, having married, divorced and remarried the same woman and has one child.
>
> He was awarded the pilot's flying badge and appointed to a commission in March 1941, on graduation from No. 6 SFTS. He stood third in a class of forty-five and it was reported that he was an above average pilot, cool and steady, with no outstanding faults. He was at first posted to the CFS at Trenton, but in view of his strong desire for more active combat duties, he was posted overseas a short time later.
>
> After eight months of operations in the United Kingdom with No. 71 ES, the subject officer was posted to the Middle East. He was on operations in the Middle East for six months and his operational flying time there amounted to one hundred and forty hours.
>
> FO Marting was reported missing while on operations during the El Alamein attack on 24 October 1942. It was reported that his aircraft was one of a formation which set out on that day to escort bombers over a target and after bombing the target, one Kittyhawk was seen to engage the enemy at low level. It was not until the

remainder of the squadron arrived back at their base that it was determined that FO Marting's aircraft was missing.

It was later ascertained that, on being shot down, he was taken prisoner by the enemy. He was taken to Greece and, while awaiting transfer to a prison camp in Germany, he escaped. After a period of two months as a fugitive, he arrived back in Egypt. During this time he was on starvation rations and he noticed that his gums were painful and that he was very weak.

Upon reaching safety in Egypt, he reported sick. Scurvy was diagnosed and he was treated with Vitamin C.

FO Marting was reported to have a good service record and, in view of his harrowing experience and the unusual circumstances in which he escaped from the enemy, his repatriation to Canada to carry on his duties with the RCAF had been recommended and that he had departed directly from the Middle East by air on 6 February 1943.

A letter received from this officer, dated 23 March 1943, while he was on repatriation leave, indicated he was making enquiries with regard to the possibility of his transfer to the armed forces of the United States. The Officer Commanding, the Repatriation Pool, RCAF Station Rockcliffe, to which this officer was about to report, was instructed to advise him that such a transfer could not be effected.

On April 16, 1943, the subject officer requested that he be permitted to resign from the RCAF. He gave the following personal reasons for resignation. His wife was suing him for divorce as he was unable to return to the United States, that he found it very difficult to maintain his wife and daughter separately on his pay and allowances and that he had been offered positions by several airplane manufacturers in the United States, in which positions he felt he would be making an important contribution to the war effort. His chief reason for returning to the United States is to restore a normal relationship with his family.

In support of his resignation, a letter was submitted from his wife's attorney certifying that divorce proceedings were instituted against him on March 15, 1943. A letter from the Curtiss-Wright Corporation, headquartered in Buffalo, New York was also presented, stating that if FO Marting was released from the RCAF, he would be employed by them as a test pilot.

On May 4, 1943, a Medical Board categorized this officer as A4HBH and diagnosed him to be suffering from scurvy and operational fatigue. He is presently on strength at Air Station Rockcliffe. A proposed posting of this officer as an instructor to No. 1 OUT, Bagotville, Quebec, has been held in abeyance until such time that he is categorized as being medically fit for a return to flight duties. It was recommended that his case be reviewed in three months' time.

It is the Board's opinion and recommendation, that in view of this officer's excellent operational service record, his present physical condition and the unfortunate circumstances of his family life, an exception should be made in the application of the established policy governing the release of American officers from the RCAF by accepting the subject officer's resignation.

FO Marting was honorably discharged from the RCAF on June 6, 1943, when the Minister of National Defence for Air and the CAS signed off on the medical board's recommendation.

Bud returned to the United States and joined his wife and child who were residing in the small community of Farmland, Indiana.

On July 13, 1943, Herold was awarded a British MC in recognition of his distinguished service.

The MC, created on December 31, 1914, was a third level military decoration earmarked for commissioned Army officers of the substantive rank of captain or below. It formally recognized "an act or acts of exemplary gallantry during active operations against the enemy on land."

In 1931, the award was extended to those holding the rank of major and also to members of the RAF for actions on the ground.

At 1400hrs, on Wednesday, September 22, 1943, while on a regular aircraft delivery flight, 32-year-old Herold Fesler Marting, died in the crash of a P-40N Warhawk at Bishopville, South Carolina.

Reade Tilley
Florida Spitfire Ace

Reade Franklin Tilley was born on March 15, 1918, in Clearwater, Florida. He graduated from St. Petersburg's College in Tampa after which he enrolled in pre-med courses at the University of Texas at Austin. Growing up with a love for competition in the fast lane, the adventurous Tilley wanted to drive race cars, but when that proved impractical, he set his sights on flying fighters. He held a private pilot's license and had learned to fly through the US government-sponsored Civilian Pilot Training Program. His family could well afford to keep him in college, but a life of academia did not provide Reade with the stimulus he was seeking.

The 6ft 4in tall Tilley left university and tried to join the USAAC, but it turned him down, stating he was too tall to fly fighters.

With the European war raging, Reade flew commercially to Canada on June 10, 1940, and voluntarily enlisted in the RCAF at No. 10 Recruiting Centre in Hamilton, Ontario.

As an AC2, he spent the first five weeks of his career at No. 1 MD in Toronto, Ontario. Tilley was then posted on a six-week course to No. 1 ITS, which was also located in Toronto. He scored poorly on a mathematics test, resulting in the RCAF wanting to reclassify him from pilot trainee to air gunner.

He talked the air force into giving him a second chance, hired a tutor, studied hard, and, a week later, passed the examination. Promoted to LAC, Tilley was sent to No. 2 EFTS at Fort William, Ontario, on September 16 where he flew 52 hours on de Havilland Tiger Moth biplanes until November 17, 1940. The final stage of his training took him to No. 2 SFTS Uplands near Ottawa, Ontario. There, he flew 120 hours on Yale and Harvard aircraft, graduating as an SP on January 25, 1941.

Tilley left Canada from "Y" Depot, Pier 21, Halifax, Nova Scotia, and arrived in the United Kingdom in February. For fighter conversion training, he attended No. 55 OTU, RAF Annan, Scotland, where he flew Miles Master Is and Hurricane Mk Xs.

He was seconded to fly with RAF No. 121 Squadron in May.

Tilley was commissioned from the ranks as a PO in August and was assigned new Regimental Service No. J. 15011.

No. 121 (Eagle) Squadron was formed with Hawker Hurricane Mk Is on May 14, 1941, at Kirton in Lindsey in Lincolnshire. As part of Fighter Command's 12 Group, the squadron was declared operational on July 21 after taking delivery of newer Hurricane Mk IIbs.

In October, the squadron received Supermarine Spitfire Mk IIas and, in November, changed over to the Spitfire Mk Vb variant. Encounters with enemy aircraft were rare and for the remainder of 1941, the squadron flew primarily convoy patrol sorties with the occasional sweep or escort duty into western France.

Reade Tilley described the procedure for landing at Kirton in Lindsey:

> You get right down on the deck over the water and fly a course until you reach the railroad track. Crossing the track, turn ninety degrees to the right and follow the rail line. When you come to tracks that split off to the west, turn left. Climb to three hundred feet and maintain speed at one hundred and sixty miles per hour for exactly four minutes, watching for three smoke stacks on your left. Turn at the stacks, let down the gear and flaps, start to descend and there is Kirton in Lindsey.

The pilots of No. 121 Squadron had many wild social occasions to remember and most of these took place in their officers' mess. PO John I. Brown from Chicago, Illinois, describes one such party in 1941:

> The ante room in our mess was a large one, measuring one hundred and fifty feet long by fifty feet wide. There was a fireplace at one end, with two sets of double doors on the sides. It was furnished with large, overstuffed leather chairs, sofas and a piano. RAF No. 616 Squadron were leaving, and this was reason enough to have a party. We decided to have a tank battle in the mess. You turn all the furniture upside down, one squadron gets on one side and one on the other and you push the pieces trying to get one to the opponent's side of the room. The losing side pays for the drinks. In the course of these battles, clothes get ripped off and torn up. At this party Jimmie Daly was standing by the fireplace doing a fan dance using a shovel and brush from the fireplace. The members of the Women's Auxiliary Air Force thought that his routine was just great!
>
> James Edgar "Johnnie" Johnson and Reade Tilley ended up in the center of the room battling like crazy. Johnson had Tilley's head in a scissor hold to the extent that Reade could neither speak or breathe. In desperation, Tilley bit Johnson's leg and the party quickly ended.
>
> Everyone then staggered off leaving the clean up to their batmen. Our conduct in these affairs was completely honorable and in keeping with long-standing British traditions.

On December 16, 1941, No. 121 transferred to RAF North Weald as part of No. 11 Group.

Tilley got himself into a lot of trouble at North Weald after he tore down a wooden picket fence at the air station and burned the broken pieces as fuel. He later explained to his superiors that "his Nissen hut was too cold."

Bad weather in early 1942 hampered flight operations, but No. 121 did take part in the action of February 12 against the German battlecruisers *Gneisenau* and *Scharnhorst* and the heavy cruiser *Prinz Eugen*.

It was not until March 23 that No. 121 Squadron recorded its first kill when American SP Jack Mooney destroyed a Focke Wulf Fw 190 near Calais. That same day, Reade Tilley, in Spitfire AD463, was credited with the probable destruction of an Fw 190 off Cap Gris-Nez, France.

Tilley volunteered at the end of March to go to Malta, as he wanted to be in the thick of the fighting. He later explained:

> I volunteered because I didn't like the way we were flying over France. We were using the old line astern formations and were under orders not to follow the Germans even when they dove down through our flights because that was what they wanted. With that formation you spent so much time making sure you didn't run into the guy ahead of you that you didn't have time to look out for the Germans! That was not my idea of aerial warfare. I had read in the newspaper about all the action that was taking place in Malta and thought, what the hell am I doing here?

Reade was posted to RAF No. 601 Squadron, which was in the process of converting from Bell P-39D Airacobras to Spitfire Vbs at Digby.

In March 1942, British Prime Minister Winston Churchill asked US President Franklin Delano Roosevelt if the USN's 14,700-ton aircraft carrier USS *Wasp* (CV-7) could be used to supply Malta with badly needed Supermarine Spitfires.

The small eight-mile wide by 17-mile-long strategic British protectorate lying just 58 miles off the coast of Sicily was a huge thorn in the side of Axis plans to dominate the Mediterranean Sea. Whoever controlled Malta, controlled the Mediterranean and the vital shipping routes to and from North Africa.

At the time of the prime minister's request, Malta was within range of approximately 650 German and Italian combat aircraft and was in danger of being overrun or pounded into dust. An aircraft resupply mission by sea was urgently required as the island's defenders could only muster a handful of fighters to oppose the enemy on any given day.

With HMS *Eagle* laid up for a month undergoing temporary repairs to its steering gear and HMS *Argus* and *Victorious* not large enough to handle the desired aircraft numbers, Churchill specifically asked for America's assistance.

He sent the following signal to Roosevelt: "Would you be willing to allow your carrier *Wasp* to do one of these trips, provided details are satisfactorily worked out between the Naval Staffs? With her broad lifts, capacity and length we estimate that *Wasp* could take fifty or more Spitfires." Roosevelt signaled back, "Admiral King will advise Admiral Poland that *Wasp* is at your disposal as you requested."

With Roosevelt's approval, the mission, codenamed Operation *Calendar*, was on. It was determined two RAF Spitfire squadrons, No. 601 "County of London" and No. 603 "City of Edinburgh," would make the journey.

On April 13, pilots and aircraft, 47 topicalized Vokes filter-engined Spitfire Vcs, assembled at the King George V Dock in Glasgow, Scotland, where all were craned aboard *Wasp*.

On the morning of the 20th at 0400hrs, *Wasp* launched its precious cargo of British fighters some 60 miles off the coast of Algiers. To save weight in the already overloaded aircraft, two of the four 20mm cannon were left unloaded and just 60 rounds were loaded in each of the other two. Each Spitfire was fitted with a 90-imperial gallon, long-range belly tank for the 580-mile one-way journey. The German and Italian Air Forces, however, were ready for them and decimated the reinforcements. After two days of fierce fighting, only 17 aircraft remained serviceable.

Three weeks later, another request came from Churchill asking to borrow the large American carrier for yet another run. This time, under the codename Operation *Bowery*, *Wasp* once again off-loaded its dive- and torpedo-bombers at

USAAF Colonel Reade F. Tilley is in the back row second from the left. These former Eagle Squadron pilots elected to return to the States as advisers and instructors in 1942–43 after a tour of duty. (US Department of Defense)

the King George V Dock to make room for 47 Spitfire Mk Vcs. The only additional aircraft *Wasp* carried for self-protection were 12 Grumman F4F-3 Wildcat fighters from VF-71.

Leaving Scotland on May 3, 1942, *Wasp* and its British and American naval escorts sailed for the Mediterranean, arriving at the designated launch point just off the coast of Algiers. On the way, the warships passed close to Gibraltar in the middle of the night and were joined by the now repaired HMS *Eagle* with a cargo of 17 Spitfires, also destined for delivery to the island.

On Saturday, May 9, beginning at 0643hrs, the two carriers, in line astern and 1,000 yards apart, began launching their combined cargo of 64 Spitfires for the long flight to Malta.

One casualty occurred below deck in the crowded hangar. An RAF groundcrew member turned the wrong way and walked into a whirling propeller. He died instantly.

Another occurred above deck when the 23rd Spitfire attempted to take off. Flown by RCAF pilot R. D. Sherrington, the aircraft failed to gain sufficient flying speed due to the pilot inadvertently setting his propeller to coarse pitch. The aircraft dropped off the edge of the flight deck, splashed into the water and was run over by the carrier.

On a happier note, an aircraft piloted by RCAF pilot Jerrold Alpine "Jerry" Smith had the belly fuel tank pump on his aircraft malfunction just after take-off. Unable to complete the mission, Smith stooged around until the others had become airborne, after which he recovered back aboard the boat under the direction of Lieutenant Commander David S. McCampbell, *Wasp*'s senior landing signal officer. Smith successfully landed Spitfire BR123 after the deck had been cleared and *Wasp*'s skipper, Captain J. W. Reeves, Jr., had steamed the carrier into the wind at maximum speed.

On his first landing attempt, Smith was too high and McCampbell waved him off. Jerry came around again, and although his approach was a little fast, McCampbell gave him the signal to cut his engine. As soon as his wheels touched the deck, Smith stood on the brakes and came to a full stop just 15ft from the edge of the flight deck.

Wasp's crew went absolutely wild and gave him a great ovation.

That evening in the officers' wardroom, a great to-do was made over Jerry's incredible feat of airmanship, landing a Spitfire aboard a carrier without the use of an arrester hook or gear. The very impressed officers of VF-71 presented Smith with a cake, pinned Navy Wings of Gold on his Canadian uniform, and made him an honorary lieutenant (jg) in the USN.

Although Smith's fuel tank was repaired, he was not allowed to attempt to fly to Malta on his own and was offloaded from *Wasp* at Gibraltar on the carrier's return voyage.

Hosting the evening's festivities and loving every minute of it, was Lieutenant (jg) Douglas Fairbanks, Jr., the Hollywood movie star.

On May 11, 1942, *Wasp*'s captain and ship's company received the following witty signal from Winston Churchill: "Many thanks to you all for the timely help. Who said a *Wasp* couldn't sting twice?"

The Spitfire pilots flying from *Wasp* in operations *Calendar* and *Bowery* were mostly British with several Canadians, Americans, and Australians rounding out the numbers. Known RCAF-trained American pilots who launched from the carrier were Reade Franklin Tilley, Arthur Bernard "Barney" Cleaveland, and Leroy J. "Joe" Morsheimer.

On a per acre basis, Malta was one of the most bombed targets of World War II. More than 976 RAF, German and Italian aircraft were lost during the battle, which ran from June 1940 until October 1942. The majority of these disappeared beneath the waves of the Mediterranean, some crashed in Sicily, and approximately 184 were brought down on or close to the Maltese islands.

Arriving safely on Malta, Tilley flew several sorties with 601 Squadron until he was transferred, at his own request, to RAF No. 126 Squadron, which was based at Luqa airfield. Several of his American buddies with whom he had trained in Canada were already serving with this squadron.

On all his sorties, Reade flew with the canopy of his Spitfire locked in the open position, both for relief from the oppressive heat and to hasten his exit time in the event he had to bail out.

Tilley made an immediate impression on RAF WC Percy Belgrave "Laddie" Lucas. Reade was well thought of by his fellow pilots and Laddie described him as, "A warm gregarious soft spoken southerner. A highly skilled and dedicated man, you couldn't help but like him."

Eight days into his Malta tour in Spitfire Vb BR195, Reade damaged a Luftwaffe Bf 109. On May 8, he destroyed two Bf 109s. The next day, he damaged an Italian Air Force Macchi C.202 Folgore fighter. The day after that, he claimed one German Bf 109 probably destroyed and another as damaged.

May 14 was another good day for Tilley – two Bf 109s destroyed plus one Messerschmitt damaged. On May 23, he bested, in aerial combat, a Regia Aeronautica Re.2001 Ariete fighter.

On June 9, 1942, Tilley and several other pilots were flown to Gibraltar to lead another flight of replacement Spitfires to the island, this time from the deck of HMS *Eagle*.

Back into the fight on July 9, Tilley scored another double when he brought down a Junkers Ju 88 bomber and a Bf 109 fighter. He damaged an Italian Re.2001 on July 12 and claimed a Bf 109 as a probable two days later. His final claim was a Macchi C.202 on July 23. His total was seven destroyed, three probables, and six damaged.

Tilley and fellow pilot James E. "Jimmie" Peck were the first two Americans to be awarded a British DFC for their valor over the battered island. Tilley personally received his DFC in June 1942 from the island's governor, Lord Gort. The citation for his award is as follows: "This officer is a most determined pilot who has destroyed at least four enemy aircraft. On three occasions, by making feint attacks after having expended all his ammunition, he has successfully driven off enemy fighters which attempted to machine gun our aircraft as they landed. He has displayed great gallantry."

Tilley was once asked, "What makes an ace?"

He replied:

> Not everyone was gung-ho, nor was fighting that important to everyone. Some, Like Colonel Don Blakeslee of the 4th Fighter Group lived to fight. If he was not fighting the enemy, he was fighting his friends. Shooting down enemy planes was a combination of motivation, vision, flying ability, marksmanship and aggressiveness. Everyone had these things to varying degrees. Guys like Blakeslee and "Red" McColpin were great aviators who combined all these qualities. I knew a couple of pilots who were lousy aviators, but they could shoot real good and they shot down a lot of enemy airplanes, but I sure didn't ever want to ride with them. Those who were successful were not better shots but better hunters, able to stalk their prey and anticipate his next move. Fighting another airplane is a matter of seconds or tenths of seconds. To be effective, you fire in one second bursts. We only had from nine to thirteen seconds of ammunition in the Spitfire.

Reade greatly admired the courage of the groundcrews on Malta. On numerous occasions he observed them refueling and rearming aircraft in the midst of bombs falling all around. Some continued to work even as German aircraft made strafing attacks. A few would lay down their tools, pick up a rifle and fire off a few rounds in the direction of the pesky intruders.

Tilley was promoted to FO in August. His tour complete, he rotated off the island on August 16, 1942. He asked to be released from the RCAF and received an honorable discharge from that service in London on October 12. The next day, he joined the USAAF with the rank of captain under Service No. 0-885392. Tilley was assigned to 8th Air Force Fighter Command, where his first task was to carry orders for the invasion of northwest Africa to participating USAAF FGs.

He returned to the States where he headed up the fighter office at the USAAF Tactical Center. His job was to teach air combat tactics to officers who were destined to become squadron and group commanders in new units being formed stateside. On January 31, 1944, he was promoted to the rank of major.

Reade Tilley remained with the newly formed USAF following the war, serving initially in Europe where he went to work for General Curtis Emerson LeMay as director of public information on the Berlin Airlift.

Major Tilley was promoted to lieutenant colonel on February 20, 1951. Tilley was promoted to full colonel on April 19, 1955, and served under LeMay as his special assistant at Strategic Air Command (SAC) Headquarters at Offutt AFB in Omaha, Nebraska.

In 1951, the National Sports Car Championship race series was formed from existing marquee events around the nation, which included Watkins Glen, Pebble Beach, and Elkhart Lake. Many early races were held on air force bases, organized with the help of General LeMay, a renowned enthusiast of sports car racing. LeMay loaned out the facilities of his bases to the Sports Car Club of America after a tragic accident at Watkins Glen, New York, nearly ended sports car racing in America.

A small child was killed, and 12 others injured after a race car brushed against the crowds who were lining the course on the narrow village streets. The era of racing on public streets and highways with little or no crowd control came to an abrupt end. The pioneers of American road racing had to seek new venues and General LeMay saved the day, temporarily ensuring the survival of the sport until 1954, after which permanent sites were built around the nation.

During this period, Reade Tilley was able to hone his race car driving skills as a member of the SAC racing team. Driving an Allard, he competed against some of the top professional drivers of the era in a series of road race competitions throughout the country.

Colonel Tilley later served as director of information for the Pacific Air Forces during the Vietnam War.

After a remarkable air force career, Reade Tilley settled in Colorado Springs, Colorado, where he operated a public relations consulting business.

He passed away in 2001 in his 83rd year.

Frederick Vance
Virginia Fighter Pilot

Frederick Renshaw Vance, the only child of Deane H. Vance and Harriette A. Vance, was born in Durango, Colorado, on January 19, 1918. Fred's father was a USN flight surgeon in the Naval Medical Corps. Vance attended Annapolis High School in Maryland but left in 1934 after completing tenth grade.

For the next four years, he served in the United States Merchant Marine. There, his career flourished as he progressed in rank from able seaman to petty officer. From 1938 to 1940, he was a yacht captain in the employ of J. C. Addington, a wealthy businessman in Norfolk, Virginia.

Over the winter months of 1938, 1939 and 1940, Fred completed several correspondence courses in an attempt to round out his lack of formal education.

In October 1940, Vance borrowed US$50 from an acquaintance in order to finance a 676-mile road trip from his residence in Norfolk to Toronto, Ontario.

On October 31, the single 22-year-old voluntarily enlisted in the RCAF at No. 11 Recruiting Centre for the duration of the war. He was processed into Canada's air force as an AC2 under Regimental Service No. R. 80721.

The air force recruiter, FO J. O. Plummer, made the following observations: "Clean cut, good appearance, pleasant personality. Intelligence above average. Accustomed to handling boats, engines, etc. Very keen. Good type for aircrew."

Fred indicated that his parents were divorced. His remarried mother was residing in San Francisco, California, while his father was living in Denver, Colorado.

From November 4 until December 7, Fred took his basic training at No. 1 MD at Toronto. With no openings available at any of the ITSs, he was sent to perform guard duty at No. 8 SFTS at Moncton, New Brunswick.

On April 10, 1941, he was back in Toronto to begin Course No. 23 with 161 other students at No. 1 ITS. Vance graduated with an 83 percent average on May 16, earning the following comments from the school's CO: "Cheerful, keen, alert type of airman with plenty of fighting spirit. Deportment and conduct good. Applied himself quite well. Second recommendation – Air Observer."

Promoted to LAC, Fred was posted immediately to No. 10 EFTS at Mount Hope just outside Hamilton, Ontario. There, on Course No. 28, he flew 55.6 hours on the wooden and fabric-constructed Fleet Finch II biplane. He graduated with a

75 percent average on July 3 and earned the following praise from his instructors: "Progress has been average during the flying course. Needs more instrument and aerobatic practice. Works hard and is well disciplined. Examinations indicate a good student and a hard worker."

Vance's next stop on the training syllabus was to No. 14 SFTS at Aylmer, Ontario. There he flew the 5,300lb, 550shp Harvard Mk IIb.

Course No. 32, comprised of 40 students, ran from July 4 until September 25. Although Fred did graduate and received his wings as an SP, he found the last phase of the RCAF pilot training difficult to master. He flew a total 122 hours on the robust NAA trainer. These air movements consisted of instrument, dual, and solo flights.

RCAF Aylmer had two assigned landing sites that it utilized for offsite training – No. 1 Relief Landing Field (RLF) was a paved facility located ten miles west of the air station at Yarmouth Centre, Ontario, while No. 2 RLF was a grass facility located 17 miles to the east at Tillsonburg, Ontario. Anyone who trained at No. 14 SFTS would have flown from these sites as Aylmer had upwards of 100 operational Harvards at any given time. Vance would have most likely trained at all three sites.

Fred reported to "Y" Depot, Pier 21, Halifax, Nova Scotia, on September 27 for onward deployment to the United Kingdom. The ocean-going convoy, carrying hundreds of BCATP graduates, together with munitions and supplies, arrived in Scotland on October 30. Vance and the other air force personnel then traveled overnight by rail to No. 3 Personnel Reception Centre at Bournemouth.

Two weeks later, Fred was posted to RAF No. 58 OTU, Grangemouth, located at Stirlingshire, Scotland. There he trained as a day fighter pilot on Miles Masters and early model Spitfire Mk Is and IIs.

Graduating on March 1, 1942, Vance was assigned to RAF No. 121 Eagle Squadron, which was flying Spitfire Vbs from RAF North Weald, Essex. On March 25, Vance was promoted to FS.

At 1220hrs on May 20, 1942, Fred was attempting to land Spitfire Vb R6890 back at North Weald after a local training flight when he crashed. He was not injured in the crash landing. The details of the investigation are as follows:

> The pilot states that he was approaching to land on the completion of a practice flight. He made a normal circuit from the northeast to the southwest, completed his cockpit check and positively states his undercarriage was in the correct down position. The indicator light showed green and the visual indicators showed that the wheels were down. The horn did not sound on throttling back and the landing appeared quite normal. On touchdown, the left wheel buckled under the aircraft which caused a violent ground loop damaging the propellor, mainplane, radiator, undercarriage, etc. The port oleo leg had struck the runway near its edge which, with the adjoining area, formed a "dip" in the ground. Accompanying forces burst

the tire and may or may not have sheared the pintle bracket bolts at this stage. The aircraft ballooned, struck the ground a second time twenty yards beyond the runway, completely collapsing both oleo legs. Undercarriage is wrecked. Both mainplanes excessively damaged. Radiator and oil cooler wrecked. Propellor damaged and engine shock-loaded.

The principal cause of the accident is the uneven surface of the aerodrome as there is a considerable dip in the surface which runs from the runway right out to the perimeter track. The Station Commander has concluded that it would not be feasible to fill in this low area. The only real solution to the problem is to build a third runway. The RAF cannot justify the costs of constructing a third runway as the accident in question is rather unusual and is not likely to happen on a frequent basis. Although the pilot was held blameless, he did land too fast which aggravated the circumstances.

One week later, Fred was part of a shipping reconnaissance strike the squadron undertook to Vlissingen (Flushing), Holland. Led by FL Hugh Charles Kennard, the six Spitfires flew 197 nautical miles across the North Sea to reach the target area.

Spotting a Kriegsmarine 2,800-ton Narvik Class destroyer and two 787-ton M1940 type minesweepers, Kennard and his wingman, FS Bill Kelly, dove down in a screaming attack on one of the minesweepers. PO James Daley and FS Vance were ordered to go after the second sweeper. FL Barry Mahon and PO Gene

WO1 Frederick R. Vance, earned his wings flying NAA Harvard Mk IIs at No. 14 SFTS Aylmer, Ontario. (Canadian National Defence Image Library)

Fetrow then followed Kennard's example and attacked the first vessel. Both ships were badly shot about. Daley and Vance's target sent up a huge column of smoke after they witnessed a large explosion. As they were pulling up, Daley spotted eight Luftwaffe Bf 109G-2 fighters above and immediately attacked one, which Vance saw dive into the water. Vance put some lead into another, which staggered away smoking. Mahon also scored a damaged on a third 109. Low on fuel and ammunition, the pilots high-tailed it back to England at low level.

On May 31, Kennard and company returned to their previous successful hunting area off the Dutch coast. Northeast of Walcheren Island, they found two more German Naval minesweepers and immediately launched an attack. The first pair in was Fred Vance and his flight leader, FL Tommy Allen from South Carolina. Whether Allen was hit or merely misjudged his height on his second strafing run, no one will ever know. Vance saw Allen's Spitfire hit the water on the far side of one of the targets and bounce back into the air. Allen's voice came up on the radio saying his machine was coming apart and that he was going to ditch.

Going more than 100mph, he failed to get a good angle on his ditching attempt and struck the water in a nose down attitude. His fighter sank immediately. Barry Mahon thought that he had seen glycol streaming from Allen's plane before it bounced off the surface of the North Sea. The squadron searched for several minutes, but there was no sign of Allen. They returned home leaving one minesweeper badly damaged and the other one sinking.

In late August 1942, Fred requested a transfer to Malta. It was common knowledge amongst the ranks that the three American Eagle FSs were to be disbanded the following month and transferred, lock, stock and barrel, to the USAAF. These three squadrons would come together as the 4th FG under the umbrella of the mighty 8th Air Force, specifically 8th Air Force Fighter Command.

Vance, along with a few other Americans, declined the invitation to transfer as they were well established and happy with their training and combat experiences in the RCAF and RAF and decided to stay where they were.

On September 25, Fred was promoted to WO2. He spent the next several months flying Spitfires with RAF No. 185 Squadron on the island of Malta and with No. 22 Personnel Transit Centre at RAF Almaza near Cairo, Egypt.

On March 25, 1943, Vance was promoted to WO1. He was posted on April 24 to RAF No. 112 "Shark" Squadron, which, as part of No 239 Wing, was operating Kittyhawk Mk IIIs from Tunisia.

The P-40K and M aircraft flown by "The Sharks" were powered by a V-1710-81 Allison, V-12 liquid-cooled, inline engine rated at 1,200shp.

On July 13, 1943, three days after the invasion of Sicily began, Fred Vance, in Kittyhawk P-40M-5-CU coded FR478, was KIA while his squadron was dive-bombing and strafing enemy motor transport on the road between Carlentini and Lentini, Sicily.

After releasing his three bombs from an altitude of only 700ft, small arms and antiaircraft ground fire struck the underside of his aircraft causing it to erupt in flames. No radio communication from Fred was received and he made no attempt to take to his parachute. It is quite likely that he was dead at the controls or seriously wounded and in an unconscious state. His aircraft crashed three miles southwest of Lentini. His remains were recovered and buried in the Catania War Cemetery in Sicily in Section IV Grave L. 29.

In 1944, the date and place of his death was registered with the Vital Statistics Department of the Province of Ontario.

The 25-year-old from Norfolk, Virginia, was awarded the following air force medals: 1939–45 Star, Aircrew European Star, African Star & Clasp, Italy Star, War Medal, and the Canadian Volunteer Service Medal & Clasp.

On September 22, 1944, a Memorial Cross bearing the cypher of King George VI was forwarded by the Canadian federal government to Fred's mother, Harriette Carley, in San Francisco. This award, together with a Royal Message of Sympathy, was forwarded to her in recognition of the loss of her son, RCAF WO F. R. Vance, on active service in the MTO on July 13, 1943.

Around the same time, a Memorial Bar was sent by the Canadian government to Captain D. H. Vance, who was assigned to the Navy's pre-flight school at Chapel Hill, North Carolina. The Memorial Bar is a companion award to the Memorial Cross. It is presented to the deceased's father, whereas the Memorial Cross is given to the deceased's mother. The Bar signifies the sacrifice made by a member of the military who has laid down his or her life for their country.

Thomas White
Oregon Lightning Ace

Thomas Ace White lived up to his given middle name in World War II when, after becoming a fighter pilot, he shot down six Luftwaffe aircraft in the MTO. He rose to ace status early in 1943, flying P-38F and G model Lockheed Lightnings with the USAAF 97th FS, 82nd FG.

The P-38 Lightning did not fair very well after it was put into service in the bomber escort role in the ETO.

Introduced into combat before the type's testing was complete, the aircraft suffered several technical problems, chief among them being its turbo-charged Allison engines, which did not perform as advertised in the cold European environment. Later in the war and after its teething problems were solved, the Lightning became a real thoroughbred when it operated in the warm climes of North Africa and the Pacific.

Tom White was born to Walter E. White and Rita J. Gabriel in Hillsboro, Oregon, on March 24, 1921. His mother's family came from the Portland area, while his father, a druggist, was from McMinnville. The family resided at 407 North Downing Street in the popular ocean resort community of Seaside, Oregon. White attended Juneau Grade School from 1927 to 1935, then Grant High School in Portland from 1935 to 1939.

White began his working aviation career early in 1940 as an apprentice aircraft mechanic at the Cal-Aero Academy Flight School in Chino, California. While employed there, he started taking flying lessons. In March 1941, he switched employers and began working as a mechanic/crew chief on Boeing Stearman biplanes at the Rankin Aeronautical Academy in Tulare, California. He continued with his flight lessons and earned a private pilot's license. His ultimate goal was to become a USAAC flyer. However, try as he might, he could not get into any of the prewar US military services for he lacked one of the steadfast requirements – having two years college education.

Tom was confident that he would be accepted for pilot training in the RCAF. Some of his acquaintances, who were not as qualified as he, had already made the trek to Canada and had begun training.

The 20-year-old White traveled 922 miles north up the Pacific Coast Highway to Vancouver, British Columbia, where, on July 30, 1941, he voluntarily enlisted in the RCAF at No. 1 Recruiting Centre. Tom came prepared for the interview, bringing with him his birth certificate and his high school diploma. He also produced, for inspection, his civilian pilot logbook, showing 120 hours of dual and solo flight time.

The air force swore him in for the duration of the war as an AC2 under Service No. R. 118415. The FO who conducted the interview made the following notations: "Intelligent young man with considerable practical mechanical experience. Good appearance and personality. Flying experience one hundred hours solo. Is recommended to train as a pilot." White signed up for the duration of the war.

While waiting for a slot to open up in the training system, Tom was at No. 2A MD at RCAF Air Station Penhold, Alberta, from August 2 to the 22. Along with several dozen other new recruits, he was moved on the 23rd over to No. 3 MD at Edmonton, Alberta, where he completed his basic training on September 13.

The next day he reported for guard duty at No. 7 SFTS located at Fort Macleod, Alberta. On October 27, he began classes at No. 4 ITS back in Edmonton. White graduated from No. 4 on December 20 and was promoted to LAC. With this advancement in rank, Tom was now earning CAN$2.25 daily.

His next stop was at No. 5 EFTS at High River, Alberta. There, he and the other students on Course No. 48 flew the next ten weeks on fabric-covered de Havilland Tiger Moth biplanes.

Before the course began, the student body was split in half. One half of the group spent its mornings in the classroom taking ground school subjects while the other half was flying. In the afternoon, they reversed roles. For flight training, four student pilots were assigned to one flying instructor. Each student flew an average of 90 minutes daily, practicing eight to ten takeoffs, circuits, and landings.

Overall, there were 32 EFTS schools operating in Canada during the war. The most numerous trainer used at the elementary level was the prolific Tiger Moth, where, over the course of the war, the type logged a staggering 1,778,348 flying hours. Tom's training at No. 5 concluded on April 11, 1942.

White began the final phase of his flight training on twin-engined Avro Ansons on April 13 back at No. 7 SFTS at Fort Macleod.

One month after the Japanese attack at Pearl Harbor, Hawaii, negotiations between Canada and the United States were under way to voluntarily repatriate those American citizens who were serving in the RCAF.

Working together with great dispatch in May and June 1942, Canadian and American military officers from RCAF, USAAF, USN, and USMC traveled for 26 days by train 3,000 miles across the width of Canada, effecting the immediate release of 1,759 American members of the RCAF. As each was honorably discharged from the Canadian air force, they were simultaneously processed into an American military service of their choosing. They entered one end of the train as Canadian service personnel and exited the other as American service personnel. It was that efficient. No one was allowed to slip through the cracks.

When the "transfer train," as it was sometimes referred to, stopped in Edmonton on May 30, 1942, White decided to join the USAAF after having served 305 days in the RCAF. His honorable discharge form noted that his conduct and character while in the Canadian air force were very good. He received written assurances from representatives of the USAAF that he would be allowed to continue his military pilot training stateside, otherwise, he indicated to them that he planned on staying where he was.

He must have been doing exceptionally well in his training as it was quite uncommon for a LAC to transfer without first having completed the entire SFTS

Major Thomas A. White stands beside his P-38J Lockheed Lightning, which he flew with the 55th FG. (US Department of Defense via Jack Cook)

syllabus. In several similar circumstances, applicants were advised to stay in the Canadian training pipeline until they had earned their wings. After graduation they could reapply for transfer.

Tom White completed his Army Air Corps pilot training on September 29, 1942, flying AT-6 Texans at Luke Army Airfield near Phoenix, Arizona. He was commissioned as a 2nd lieutenant under Service No. 0-730690. His P-38 fighter training was undertaken at a stateside Lightning Replacement Training Unit in October–November. He was posted to the 97th FS, 82nd FG, on December 8, 1942.

White arrived overseas just prior to the group's move in January 1943 from Northern Ireland to Telergma, Algeria.

Once in North Africa, the 82nd immediately commenced an aerial campaign designed to disrupt and destroy the enemy's ability to resupply its desert forces by air and sea. The 82nd also flew dive-bombing and strafing missions against ground targets in support of the invasion of Italy, escorted medium bombers on shipping strikes in the Mediterranean Sea, and flew many close escort missions to Allied bombers raiding Naples and Rome.

At 1445hrs on January 8, 1943, Lieutenant White opened his scoring when he destroyed a Focke Wulf Fw 190A-4 "Wurger" five miles northwest of Kairouan, Tunisia. His next victory came 13 days later when he brought down, at 0955hrs west of Pantelleria, Sicily, a Bf 109F. A third swastika kill marking was painted on the nose of his personal P-38F-5-LO Lightning on January 31 after he destroyed, at 1250hrs, a Bf 109F, 60 miles west of Gabes, Tunisia. Hunting in that same area three days later, Ace was given credit for a Bf 109F that was officially listed as probably destroyed. Over Kairouan on February 15 at 1450hrs while flying a new P-38G-10, Tom downed an Fw 190A-4. His fifth victory, a Bf 109F, which officially made White an ace, occurred mid-day on February 28 in the sky over La Hencha Safaqis, Tunisia. His sixth and final aerial victory came on March 11, 1943, over Sicily against a Hungarian-built Me 210C "Hornisse" twin-engined fighter-bomber.

The 82nd moved on March 28, 1943, from Telergma to Berteaux, Algeria.

White's tour as a fighter pilot ended on April 12, when he was rotated back to America for a well-deserved rest.

He volunteered for a second combat tour on P-38s and was assigned to the 55th FG, which had just completed its conversion to the big Lockheed twin-boomed fighter. The group, earmarked to become part of 8th Air Force Fighter Command, arrived with its aircraft at USAAF Station No. 131 Nuthampstead in Hertfordshire in late August and early September 1943.

Tom, now a major, flew a P-38H with the 338th FS. His personal aircraft, coded CL-Y, was named *Janet*. In December, he was assigned a new P-38J model, coded CL-V, which carried the same name.

The public relations people at the 55th made a big deal out of Tom's given middle name and for a while, at least, it produced some great copy for the English news media.

White's second combat tour did not produce any additional claims. He returned stateside in the spring of 1944 just prior to the group's move to Wormingford in Essex.

Right up until the time he retired from flying, Tom piloted historic World War II aircraft on hundreds of air tanker/air spray missions throughout the Pacific northwest. He was type rated on Consolidated PBY Catalinas, NAA B-25 Mitchells, General Motors TBM Avengers, Lockheed PV-2 Harpoons, and Douglas A-26 Invaders.

He flew those classic relics from such places as Moses Lake, Washington, Missoula, Montana, Troutdale and Redmond, Oregon.

Thomas A. White died in his 53rd year at Portland, Oregon, on September 24, 1974.

PACIFIC THEATER OF OPERATIONS

Donald Aldrich
Illinois Corsair Ace

Threading its way west along the southern Lake Michigan shoreline, the dark blue Vought Sikorsky F4U-4 Corsair, bureau number 97148 coded EA-25, was only minutes away from landing at NAS Glenview, Illinois. The aircraft, belonging to USMC Air Engineering Squadron 12, was based at Marine Corps Base Quantico, Virginia.

At the controls was a decorated 28-year-old World War II fighter ace. Captain Donald Nathan Aldrich, an Illinois native, was coming home to visit his wife, Marjorie, and his 27-month-old son, Frederick. The child had been hospitalized for 23 days with a serious ear and throat infection.

Permanently assigned to Marine Corps Air Station (MCAS) Cherry Point in North Carolina, Aldrich was on temporary detached duty at Quantico where he was instructing.

Captain Aldrich had wanted some company during his three-hour cross-country flight home that Saturday, May 3, 1947, and had asked his friend and fellow Marine instructor pilot Rhinehart Leu to go with him. Leu, however, had made plans to play a round of golf with the base commanding general and did not think that it would be wise to cancel.

Aldrich, flying alone, made a wide sweeping left turn to the southwest before beginning his south to north landing approach into Glenview. As he bled off air speed and altitude, the normally dependable Pratt & Whitney R-2800-18W radial engine began to run rough... then suddenly quit. Glenview was now unreachable and, as he was over the populated south of Chicago, he had no choice but to try to find a safe place to set the seven-ton powerless aircraft down.

Captain Aldrich knew this area very well because, as a teenager, he had obtained his private pilot's license flying from the old Ashburn municipal airfield, which was just two miles south of Chicago's Midway airport.

Out of options and altitude, Aldrich trimmed up his aircraft and pointed it toward Ashburn, which was now in sight. Ashburn, located at 8400 South Cicero Avenue, was a very small landing site and had only two cinder runways, the longest being 1,600ft. Unknown to Aldrich, this field had been closed as an operating airport as it was slated to be redeveloped into a 70-acre housing estate.

Witnesses stated the Corsair glided silently down at 1255hrs at approximately 60mph. Several people tried to wave the fighter off as the runways were marked with large "Xs" at either end, signifying to all airmen that no landings nor takeoffs were to be attempted. The gull-winged fighter, committed to the landing, touched down, stayed on the runway for a few hundred feet then abruptly rolled off onto the soggy rain-soaked grass. Tragically, the main landing gear of the heavy fighter dug in, twisting, flipping, then breaking the airframe into two major pieces. The main part of the wreckage, containing Aldrich, came to rest upside down after sliding some distance in the mud.

A Navy medical doctor, Lieutenant E. B. Reilly, was quickly summoned from Glenview and pronounced Captain Aldrich dead at 1400hrs. His opinion was that Aldrich's chest was crushed in the attempted emergency landing.

In a terrible twist of fate, this young husband, father, and war hero died at the very airport where he first learned to fly.

Donald N. Aldrich was born to Lyell Aldrich and Mary Blievernight on October 24, 1917, in Moline, Illinois. Don's father, a mechanical engineer, owned and flew a Waco biplane. By the time Don was 12, he had logged more than 100 hours as a passenger. The airplane was sold in 1933 after his dad suddenly passed away. Through a variety of part-time jobs, Don managed to keep flying to pay for his flight lessons.

During his high school years, 1931 to 1935, Aldrich was a 2nd lieutenant in ROTC serving as a line officer and marksmanship instructor.

It was at Fenger High School where he met and dated his future wife, Majorie Blanche Adams. He attended university for one year and also took courses in mechanics and public speaking. From 1936 to 1938, he was employed at the Standard Forgings Company in Indiana and, from 1938 to 1941, at the Visking Corporation in Chicago.

Early in 1941, Don attempted to join the USAAC but was rejected because he had married Marjorie on June 22, 1940, in Joliet, Illinois. At the time, the US military flying services were not accepting married men. Later in the war this restriction was removed.

Like so many men his age, Aldrich's only desire was to become a fighter pilot. He knew it was only a matter of time before the US would be drawn into the European conflict and when that happened, he wanted to be at the vanguard of the fighting.

Hearing the RCAF would be more accommodating, particularly to a licensed private pilot, he traveled to No. 8 Recruiting Centre in Windsor, Ontario, on April 3, 1941, where he voluntarily enlisted as an AC2. Don listed his civilian occupation as a shipping clerk and gave a home address of 1445 East 67th Street in Chicago. He wrote the following on his Attestation Paper: "I am certain in my own mind, and with no thoughts of being cocky, that I would make an excellent pilot and officer and would be an invaluable aid to his Majesty."

Donald Aldrich: Illinois Corsair Ace

Assigned Regimental Service No. R. 98074, Aldrich was sent for basic training on April 13 to No. 2 MD in Brandon, Manitoba, where he remained until May 26. The next day, he reported to No. 2 ITS in Regina, Saskatchewan. Aldrich graduated from Course No. 27 on June 27 with a 79 percent average. He placed 69th out of 130 students in the class. The OC at Regina wrote the following in his file: "Excellent type, plenty of dash, above average intelligence."

Promoted to LAC, Aldrich commenced pilot training on July 15 at No. 19 EFTS at Virden, Manitoba. There he flew 79 hours on de Havilland Tiger Moth biplanes. Graduating from Course No. 33 with a 77 percent average on September 1, the notations in his file by his superiors were all positive: "Very good student, has a quiet effective personality and is prominent among his fellows. Has previous flying experience. Cautious, quick to learn. No bad habits. Is dependable. Discipline and punctuality good."

Don Aldrich's combined pilot time to that point totaled 116.15 hours – 79.15 military and 37 civilian.

He next reported to No. 12 SFTS at Brandon, where, on September 2, he began flying twin-engined Cessna Cranes on Course No. 37. He graduated third in his class with an 84 percent average on November 21, after having amassed 106 flying hours on type. His squadron commander noted: "After a slow start has shown remarkable progress. Is now an exceptional pilot. Recommended for reconnaissance work". From the CGI: "Above average. Capable willing worker. Conduct and deportment exemplary."

USMC Captain Donald N. Aldrich, Navy Cross, was the fifth highest-scoring Marine pilot of World War II. He stands fourth from the left in the line in front of the Chance Vought F4U-1A Corsair. Aldrich and others are participating in a VMF-215 Squadron medal ceremony on Torokina Island in February 1944. (US Department of Defense)

In a graduation ceremony, Don was presented with his RCAF pilot wings, along with a promotion to SP.

Approximately 10 percent of the students in all graduating classes in the BCATP were commissioned as officers.

From Course No. 37, there were 53 graduates and Don Aldrich was one of five who were commissioned that day as POs. As an officer, his Regimental Service No. was changed from R. 98074 to J. 8963.

He was such a good pilot, the RCAF tagged him to become a flying instructor. He reported, on December 24, to the Central Flying School at Trenton, Ontario, where he was checked out on Tiger Moths, Fleet Finch, Avro Ansons and Harvards.

Don Aldrich graduated on February 26, 1942, with a "C" category instructor's certificate. Don's ground instructor, FO T. Burke, wrote the following in his file: "Has been a very willing worker and has a good personality. With experience, he should make a very good instructor." Air examining officer, FL G. P. Silke, wrote, "Above average, no outstanding faults. Instrument and aerobatics very good. Will rate a higher category with more experience."

From March 2 to May 14, Aldrich instructed at No. 2 SFTS Uplands located just outside Ottawa, Ontario.

Don Aldrich secured an honorable discharge from the RCAF on May 14, 1942, when the transfer train stopped in Ottawa. He decided to join the Marines after discussing his career opportunities with the representatives of the other US military services at the railway station.

He spent a few months at Officer Candidate School and took some refresher flying courses mainly to acclimate himself to American aircraft and flying procedures. Don Aldrich was commissioned a 2nd lieutenant in the USMCR in October 1942.

Anxious to get into combat, he shipped out to the south central Pacific in April 1943, where he joined Marine Fighter Squadron Two One Five (VMF-215) on the island of Midway.

He was promoted to the rank of captain on June 15.

VMF-215, known as the "Fighting Corsairs," moved to the Solomon Islands in the Bismarck Archipelago on July 25, 1943. From there, it flew three combat tours principally using the F4U-1 Chance Vought Corsair.

Over a six-month period, from August 12, 1943, to February 9, 1944, Captain D. N. Aldrich became the fifth highest-scoring Marine ace of World War II after shooting down 20 Japanese fighter aircraft and claiming a further six enemy aircraft as probably destroyed.

VMF-215's first combat tour was flown from Henderson Field on Guadalcanal. It ended in early August with Aldrich claiming no kills.

Flying from Vella Lavella and covering Bougainville, the second tour concluded in November 1943 on the island of Munda, during which Don downed six enemy aircraft. The third tour began on January 27, 1944, from Torokina and concentrated on the Rabaul area. This tour was very productive, as Captain Aldrich shot down 14 Japanese combatants.

Don Aldrich was wounded in action twice – August 21, 1943, and January 28, 1944. On the latter occasion, his F4U-1A Corsair BuNo 17883, was so badly damaged, it was deemed unrepairable and was scrapped on the spot for parts.

Captain Aldrich opened his scoring on August 12, when he shot down a Mitsubishi A6M Zero-Sen "Zeke" and claimed another as probable near Balalae. On the 25th, 30 miles east of Kahili, another Zeke and a probable were claimed. The next day, a solitary Zeke fell to his guns between Kahili and Balalae. At 1600hrs on September 2 near Balalae, he destroyed two Zekes. Two more Zekes were blasted from the sky over Tobera on January 12, 1944. Two days later, over Rabaul at 1300hrs, Aldrich flamed another Zeke and added two probables to his score. Two additional Zekes on the 20th near Tobera went down, followed by a single Zeke 20 miles southeast of Cape St. George on the 22nd. A Kawasaki Ki-61 Hien "Tony" was downed on the 26th, along with a Zeke, and a claim was made for a Zeke probable.

At 0900hrs on January 28 south of Tobera, Captain Aldrich had his biggest day and the fight of his life when he succeeded in downing four Zekes. This was one of the encounters he was wounded in and, for the second time, his aircraft was so badly damaged he barely made it back to Torokina. Back in action on February 7 over Tobera, two more Zekes were blasted from the sky along with a claim for a Zeke probable. His last and 20th kill occurred on February 9 when he bested, at 1245hrs south of Tobera, a Nakajima Ki-44 Shoki "Tojo."

Marine Corps aces with scores higher than Don Aldrich were Joe Foss, VMF-121, with 26; Bob Hanson, VMF-214 and VMF-215, with 25; Greg Boyington, AVG and VMF-214, with 24; and Ken Walsh, VMF-124 and VMF-222, with 21.

When Captain Aldrich achieved his 20th kill on February 9, 1944, two of the above four aces, Boyington and Hanson, had been shot down. Boyington went down on January 3, 1944, and was captured. Hanson was shot down and killed in action exactly one month later on February 3.

The Marine Corps needed its remaining high-scoring aces alive and well and back in the US. Just that quickly, Captain Aldrich was barred from flying any more combat missions.

Don Aldrich returned to Chicago in March 1944 to a huge city welcome complete with speeches, parades and plaque presentations. Wherever he went, he was very uncomfortable with all the attention he received.

Aldrich was a very private person who did not enjoy being in the limelight. Any reference to him being a hero was quickly dismissed, as he felt the real "heroes" were the ones who were never coming home. Nevertheless, he did his duty participating in bond drives, factory tours, and any other public relations venues that supported the home-front war effort.

In October 1944, VMF-215 returned from its Pacific deployment to El Toro, California, where it served as a replacement squadron for the remainder of the war.

When Don Aldrich died, he had 2,395 flying hours recorded in his logbook. Rhinehart Leu had the unpleasant task of investigating his friend's death and returning his personal effects to his widow, Marjorie, who was residing at 1408 East Marquette Road in Chicago.

Several months after the accident, the Commandant of the Marine Corps, General A. A. "Archie" Vandegrift, sent Mrs. Aldrich her husband's previously awarded Navy Cross and Citation, which read as follows:

ALDRICH, DONALD N.
Captain, US Marine Corps Reserve Marine Fighting Squadron 215 (VMF-215), 1st Marine Air Wing Date of Action: January 5–February 15, 1944

Citation: The Navy Cross is presented to Donald N. Aldrich, Captain, US Marine Corps Reserve, for extraordinary heroism as Division Leader of Marine Fighting Squadron Two Hundred Fifteen (VMF-215), in action against enemy Japanese forces in the Solomon Islands and Bismarck Archipelago areas, from 5 January to 15 February 1944. Intercepted by vastly superior numbers of enemy aircraft while flying escort for our bombers during strikes over the strongly defended Vunakanau and Lakunai airfields on 20 and 26 January, Captain Aldrich fought gallantly against tremendous odds, immediately plunging to the attack and destroying four of the hostile planes. Returning from an escort mission deep in enemy territory, he and his wingman observed five Zeros attacking one of the pilots of his formation parachuting from a damaged plane and hurling themselves at the enemy with a fury that balanced the unequal odds, drove the Zeros away, enabling the pilot to make a safe landing. Disregarding severe personal wounds and damage inflicted on his plane during an escort mission over Tobera Airfield on 28 January, he continued the fierce engagement despite overwhelming aerial opposition and shot four hostile craft from the sky. Destroying a total of fourteen Japanese aircraft during this period of intense aerial operations, he contributed essentially to the protection afforded our bombers and his bold tactics and brilliant combat record reflects the highest credit upon Captain Aldrich and the United States Naval Service.

SPOT AWARD, ComSoPac: Serial 001635 July 20, 1944
Home Town: Chicago, Illinois.

George Carr
Florida Hellcat Ace

When USN Grumman F4F Wildcat fighter pilot Lieutenant Commander Edward Henry "Butch" O'Hare traveled to the White House on April 21, 1942, to receive the Medal of Honor, President Franklin D. Roosevelt asked him, "Butch, what kind of plane do you need to beat the Japs?" O'Hare replied, "Something that will go upstairs faster."

Prior to Japan's early morning attack at Pearl Harbor, Hawaii, on Sunday, December 7, 1941, Grumman's management team was already hard at work on a new design to replace the company's outdated Wildcat fighters. The replacement aircraft, named Hellcat, would be larger and much stronger; it would offer better performance and it would carry more fuel and ammunition.

Hellcats, like the company's Avengers and newer model Wildcats, featured the famous Grumman "Sto-Wing" in which the wings folded backward to lay alongside the fuselage. This design was a great space saver on a crowded aircraft carrier. The concept was the brainchild of Leroy Grumman, the company founder, who visualized it one day while fiddling at his desk with a draughtsman's soap eraser and two partly unfolded paper clips.

Needing to focus exclusively on building Hellcats, Grumman freed up plant space in its manufacturing facility by transferring the remaining F4F Wildcat and TBF Avenger production over to the General Motors Automobile Company.

General Motors had five idle car plants on the east coast – Tarrytown, Linden, Bloomfield, Baltimore, and Trenton. These were quickly organized into a team called the Eastern Aircraft Division of General Motors. Eastern Aircraft went on to build 5,928 Wildcats, designated as FM-1s and FM-2s, and 7,546 Avengers, designated as TBMs.

The XF6F prototype flew for the first time on June 26, 1942. In total, 12,275 Hellcat airframes eventually poured from Leroy Grumman's Bethpage, Long Island, factory in the unheard-of time frame of just over two years from January 1943 to November 1945.

The Hellcat turned out to be the single most important American carrier fighter in the Pacific Theater of Operation (PTO). Its complete superiority over the Japanese had, by late 1944, become so absolute that it enabled the Navy to maintain a continuous presence day or night over any combat zone or Japanese airfield in what became known as "The Big Blue Blanket." It was the F6F that principally destroyed the myth of invincibility, which, up until late 1943, had cloaked the Japanese Army and Naval air force pilots. Grumman's "stronger than a bridge" Hellcats would enjoy, by war's end, a kill to loss ratio over its opponents that exceeded 19 to 1.

Navy and Marine Hellcat pilots alone shot down 5,156 Japanese aircraft. Three hundred and six US Naval/Marine aviators achieved ace status while flying Hellcats in combat.

One of those Navy fighter pilots was Lieutenant George Raines Carr, who served with Fighter Squadron One Five (VF-15). Known as "Satan's Playmates" or the "Fighting Aces," VF-15 operated from US carrier *Essex* (CV-9) and emerged as the Navy's highest scoring Hellcat squadron.

G. R. Carr was born to Joel A. Carr and Fannie C. Patterson in Hopkins, Florida, on November 16, 1917. Unable to meet the requirements for pilot training as established by the prewar US military services, Carr did what thousands of his fellow countrymen did; he journeyed north to Canada and offered up his service to the RCAF.

On Saturday, February 8, 1941, Carr, then 23 years of age, crossed the border at Buffalo, New York, and entered the province of Ontario at the town of Fort Erie. He traveled an additional 90 miles to the city of Hamilton where he voluntarily enlisted in the RCAF at No. 10 Recruiting Centre for the duration of the war. He gave the recruiter a home address of 3410 2nd Avenue South in Saint Petersburg, Florida.

His records indicated that he graduated from Bogalusa High School in Bogalusa, Louisiana, in 1935 and, for several years, worked at a variety of jobs – hotel night manager, clerk, and bookkeeper. He told the recruiter that he had flown in a small plane as a passenger more than two dozen times and had undertaken seven hours of dual flight instruction.

As No. 1 MD in Toronto, Ontario, was full to capacity, Carr and hundreds of other new recruits were sent to No. 1A MD in Picton, Ontario, which served as a temporary personnel holding area. Picton was still under construction and would not open as a fully functioning Air Station until April 28.

One other notable American who was at Picton at the same time as Carr was Oklahoma City native Claude "Weavy" Weaver III. Weaver won his RCAF wings at the age of 18 and became the youngest Allied fighter ace of World War II while flying Supermarine Spitfires over the island of Malta.

AC2 George R. Carr, Regimental Service No. R. 66447, left Picton on March 15, and was sent to No. 1 Technical Training School in St. Thomas, Ontario, where he performed guard duty until May 2. Carr and dozens of other rifle-toting airmen were tasked to make sure several hundred Canadian air force ground trade school students remained in quarantine after a diphtheria outbreak at that facility.

With the recruit backlog finally cleared away, Carr began his pre-flight training on May 3 at No. 1 ITS in Toronto. George was on Course No. 25 and graduated on June 6 with an 86 percent average. The following notations were recorded in his file: "Smart, keen service pilot material. Recommended for a commission."

Promoted to LAC, he reported on June 6 to No. 19 EFTS at Virden, Manitoba. There he flew a total of 89 hours and 30 minutes on de Havilland Tiger Moth biplanes.

George graduated from Course No. 30 on August 8, 1941, with the following written comments from the CFI: "Keen, alert, aggressive, natural leader. Flying is above average. Gentlemanly mannered. No flying faults and improving rapidly." The CGI wrote: "Flight Senior awarded the prize of most promising pilot in his class. Splendid personality, correct deportment."

Carr was passed to No. 2 SFTS, Uplands, Ottawa, Ontario, on August 9 to complete his pilot training on Harvard Mk II aircraft. Graduating on October 24 from Course No. 35, Carr was awarded his RCAF pilot wings and was promoted to SP. His squadron commander noted: "High average pilot on both clear hood and instrument flying". From the Ground Instructor (GI): "Good student, neat but talks too much." The CI recorded: "Punctual, conscientious, very willing and well disciplined."

Sailing on a troop ship from Pier 21, Halifax, Nova Scotia, on October 26, Carr arrived in England on November 10. He was assigned to No. 3 Personnel Reception Centre in Bournemouth where he remained until December 5. The next day he reported to RAF No. 2 Glider Training School at Kidlington. On January 1, 1942, No. 2 became No. 101 Glider OTU.

While there, George flew obsolete Hawker Hector and Hart biplanes as a glider tow pilot.

He was posted on April 15 to RAF No. 296 Glider Towing Squadron located at Netheravon, Wiltshire. The next month, No. 296 began to receive twin-engined Armstrong Whitworth Whitleys. In July 1942, the squadron was split into two units – 296A flying Harts and Whitleys from Hurn, Dorset, and 296B flying Hectors and Whitleys from Netheravon. Sergeant Carr moved with 296A to Hurn where he flew both types of aircraft in support of numerous British Army training exercises.

G. R. Carr was commissioned from the RCAF ranks as a PO on August 15, 1942, and received, in the process, new Regimental Service No. J. 15913.

In October, 296A moved, yet again, this time to Andover, Hampshire.

Wanting something more challenging to do than towing General Aircraft Hotspur gliders around the United Kingdom, George Carr honorably resigned his Canadian commission on November 8, 1942, at RCAF Overseas Headquarters in London. The next day he was commissioned an ensign in the USN. His quick repatriation to the US forces came about as the result of an agreement worked out between Canada and the United States in May 1942, governing the transfer of trained military personnel.

George returned to the US where he spent several months in the naval air training system. Ensign Carr was assigned to VF-15 when the squadron was commissioned into service on September 1, 1943, at NAS Atlantic City, New Jersey.

He was promoted to lieutenant (jg) on January 1, 1944, and to lieutenant in June. The squadron served on the *Essex* from April to November 1944. It flew F6F-3/5 and F6F-3N/5N Hellcats and, at its apex, was a large 54-plane squadron.

"Satan's Playmates" flew only one tour, but what a deployment it was, shooting down 310 enemy aircraft – a naval record which has never been equaled!

The squadron started combat with 47 pilots and reached a peak of 61 early in November. It counted 26 aces among its ranks and its carrier air group commander was none other than Commander David S. McCampbell, the Navy's top scoring World War II ace and Medal of Honor winner. He was personally credited with 34 of the squadron's total of 310 victories.

Another luminary in the squadron was Lieutenant Bert Dewayne "Wayne" Morris, the Hollywood film actor. Morris was one of the first movie stars to enlist and was commissioned in the Navy Reserve. After training, he flew a year as an instructor but was unable to get into combat as the navy said he was physically too big to fly fighters. Wayne approached McCampbell, his brother-in-law, and

USN Lieutenant George R. Carr, Navy Cross, poses with fellow VF-15 squadron pilots aboard USS *Essex* in June 1944. Carr is kneeling at the right side of this picture. (US Department of Defense)

McCampbell arranged for him to be assigned to VF-15. Morris finished the war with seven kills.

Lieutenant George Raines Carr opened his scoring at 1025hrs on June 19, 1944, when he shot down, in just 17 minutes, five IJN Yokosuka D4Y1 Suisei "Judy" dive-bombers.

On that mission, Carr became a select member of the "Ace-in-a-Day" club and, for his actions, was awarded a Navy Cross. Returning to the carrier, George noted numerous oil slicks from downed enemy planes, then gave up counting as there were just too many.

The citation for Carr's Navy Cross award is as follows:

> The President of the United States takes pleasure in presenting the Navy Cross to George Raines Carr, Lieutenant US Navy for extraordinary heroism in operations against the enemy while serving as pilot of a carrier-based navy fighter plane in Fighting Squadron Fifteen VF-15 embarked from the USS Essex CV-9, in action against major units of the Japanese fleet during the first battle of the Philippine Sea on 19 June 1944. During repeated attacks upon numerous enemy air groups, Lieutenant Carr pressed home vigorous counterattacks against the outnumbering enemy forces and, despite constant fighter opposition, shot down five of the enemy dive-bombers and damaged many others thereby assisting materially in the total destruction by his squadron of sixty-seven enemy aircraft. By his superb airmanship and gallant fighting spirit he contributed to the defenses of our forces in the area and upheld the highest tradition of the United States Naval Service. Commander, Fast Carrier Task Force, Pacific – 3 August 1944.

On the 23rd, ten miles west of Orote, George downed a Mitsubishi A6M Zero-Sen "Zeke." At 0730hrs on the morning of September 10, Carr surprised and destroyed a twin-engine Nakajima Jini "Irving" night fighter north of Mindanao. Two days later, over Cebu and Opon aerodromes, a Nakajima Ki-44 Shoki "Tojo," a Zeke and one half of a Nakajima Ki-43 Hayabusa "Oscar" fell to his aircraft's guns.

A month later, on October 12, George blasted a Tojo to pieces and was given credit for one half of another Tojo, which he shared with a fellow Hellcat pilot. Carr's last victory, which brought his tally to 11½, came on November 13, 1944, at 1400hrs when he teamed up with another squadron member to down a Nakajima B6N Tenzen "Jill" torpedo bomber.

Around the time VF-15's tour was ending, the *Essex* came perilously close to being seriously damaged when struck by a suicide attacker piloting a Yokosuka D4Y3 "Judy" dive-bomber.

At 1256hrs on Saturday, November 25, 1944, Lieutenant Yoshinori Yamaguchi's aircraft penetrated the outer and inner defenses of the American task force, striking the *Essex* on the edge of the port side of the flight deck forward of the number two elevator. Punching a hole through the deck, the remaining wreckage of the flaming Judy caromed like a pinball along the 20mm gun mounts, killing 16 and wounding 44 US naval personnel.

George Carr flew 52 combat missions with VF-15 during its singular cruise and returned to the US when the squadron rotated home.

In addition to the previously awarded Navy Cross, Carr received two DFC awards, two Air Medals, two Strike/Flight DFCs and seven Strike/Flight Air Medals.

On June 12, 1946, he contacted RCAF Headquarters in Ottawa and gave them his current mailing address of c/o The Municipal Auditorium in Atlanta, Georgia.

After the war, George Carr returned to civilian life but greatly missed the aspect of flying military aircraft. He was accepted into the Louisiana Air National Guard with the rank of major, but, after only six months, he knew that guard flying was not for him.

He applied to return to the Navy and was reinstated at his wartime rank. George was assigned as an instructor at NAS Corpus Christi, Texas.

On December 4, 1952, after completing a routine flying assignment, Carr's Hellcat fighter suddenly stalled 200ft above the runway while he was attempting to land. The aircraft fell to earth, shattered into many pieces, and burst into flames.

Lieutenant Carr's remains were sent to his mother's home located at 613 Avenue D in Bogalusa. It arrived there in a flag-draped coffin on the old Gulf Mobile and Ohio Railroad.

As the American Legion conducted full military graveside rites in the Ponemah Cemetery, a squadron of Navy planes from Callender Field flew low across the cemetery in close formation in a final salute to one of their own.

Today, the local airport in Bogalusa is dedicated and known as the George R. Carr Memorial Airfield.

Hollis Hills
California Hellcat Ace

On August 19, 1942, FO Hollis Henry "Holly" Hills, an American serving in the RCAF with No. 414 "Black Knight" Army Co-operation Squadron, took off from Croydon, England, in the predawn darkness as wingman to FL F. E. "Freddy" Clarke.

Flying a reconnaissance sortie at wave-top height, the pair in their NAA Mustang Mk Is dodged search lights and antiaircraft fire over Dieppe, France, in support of Operation *Jubilee*. Over the target area, they were separated, but both safely returned to their English base.

The squadron had received its Mustangs only two months earlier and this was its first foray with them into combat.

Originally scheduled for only one sortie that day, Clarke and Hills accepted responsibility for another around mid-morning. The two observed strict radio silence as they flew across the 21-mile width of the English Channel at its narrowest point, but neither had any way of knowing that Clarke's radio had failed just after takeoff.

As they neared the coast west of Dieppe, Hills spotted a flight of four Fw 190s to his right at 1,500ft on a course that would take the enemy directly overhead of the two P-51s as they crossed the beach.

Hills broke radio silence and called his leader twice, but to no avail.

Clarke then turned left toward the Amiens road. This change of direction took them directly under the German fighters, which presented the enemy with the ideal bounce. Realizing that Clarke's radio was out, Hills swung his Mustang, coded AG470, wide to his leader's left.

Hills later recalled his thoughts and actions of that sortie:

> This put me right over the town dusting the chimney tops. I believe the 190s had lost sight of me as I had stayed under them. My plan was to cut off the lead Focke Wulf before he could open fire on Freddy. My timing all went to pot when a crashing Spitfire forced me into a sharp left turn to avoid a collision. That gave the 190 pilot time to get into firing position and he hit Freddy's Mustang with his first burst... Glycol was streaming from the radiator but there was no fire. I was able to

get a long shot at the leader but had to break hard right as his No. 2 was having a go at me. He missed and made a big mistake sliding by on my left side. It was an easy deflection shot and I hit him hard… I knew that he was a goner.

Clarke shared his memories as well:

> I was totally oblivious to the action that was unfolding above my head until the first cannon shells slammed into the oil cooler of my aircraft's Allison engine. The next thing I know is there is all hell and corruption going on. I'd been hit. The radiator was shot up, my instruments on either side of me were gone. The armour plating however saved my life. So I jettisoned the hood hoping that it hadn't been jammed by the shots and it wasn't. And I thought, they're right, it's nice in here – it's not windy at all. Instinctively I twisted my aircraft into a hard climbing right hand turn. I got it up to about 800 feet and that's all she'd give me. Without a radiator I knew that it was only a matter of time before the engine seized completely. Although we pilots had been offered the town's inland race track as a potential crash-landing site, I had no intentions of risking capture and preferred instead to take my chances in the Channel. I would never have made it had it not been for the timely return of Hills to the scene of my obvious distress. The 190 was tailing me and he was probably hoping to capture an intact Mustang. Holly saw him begin to slide behind me for the kill, which would stop me short of the Channel.

Hills continued, "I had to try to stop him, so I fired a short high deflection burst in his direction. I was hoping to get his attention and it worked. He broke hard left into my attack."

As Hills attempted to mix it with the German, proving that the P-51A could at least out-turn the 190 at low level, Clarke continued in his struggle to reach the water. It was a perilous moment, considering that no one had been known to "ditch" a Mustang and survive, principally because the large air scoop under the belly would act as a rather unfortunate rudder, directing the nose of the aircraft immediately toward the bottom. This did not happen in Clarke's case. Unfortunately, it is still unknown as to exactly what did happen in the last seconds of the crash landing. Clarke's memory recalls being only 10ft above the water, an airspeed indicator reading 90 knots, and the moment when he woke up in the bottom of a landing craft:

> I limped out to the water. Just as I crossed the coast the propeller seized as solid as a… there I am down wind, across the trough… everything's against ya. Using my trim to keep my tail down, the last thing I remember is about ninety miles an hour on the clock, trying to get that tail down. I wanted the tail to hit first to kill the speed before she flopped in, because it would just dive in if you hit the water with

the air scoop. The next thing I remember I came to in a landing craft...I hit the gun site I think. They say a young army guy dove into the water and got me out of the aircraft. I would give anything to have known who he was.

The wounded Clarke was transferred to the British destroyer HMS *Calpe*, which itself was under heavy attack for most of the late morning and into the early afternoon. After being treated for the wound to his head, Freddy returned to England where he and Holly were billeted in a requisitioned house.

Hills recalled: "About five the next morning, my door burst open. I was grabbed in a bear hug by what smelled like a huge clump of seaweed. It was Freddy Clarke, rescued by the amphibious forces. His head sported a huge bandage covering the severe cuts he had received in the ditching. We had all been warned that ditching a Mustang could be hazardous to your health."

Chris Clarke, Freddy's son, revealed the full extent of his father's head injuries suffered on August 19, 1942:

> The orbital bone above my dad's right eye was broken and pushed in. After the swelling went down it left an indentation in his forehead. He continued to fly over the next eight months, but was suffering from migraine headaches and periodic blackouts. He did not raise these symptoms with the wing Medical Officer or his superiors, but was "found out" when he later flew some sorties with his Squadron Commander. He was put on sick leave for two weeks and then returned to duty, only to be permanently grounded two months later in July 1943.

Clarke witnessed and officially confirmed Hollis' victory over the Fw 190. This was the first enemy aircraft shot down by a pilot flying a Mustang. And the unfortunate Freddy Clarke, well, he had the dubious distinction of being the first Mustang pilot to be shot down in World War II. FO Hills was awarded a MiD for his effort in the raid:

> Hills, FO Hollis Henry J. 5803 – Mention in Despatches – No. 414 Squadron – Award effective 1 January 1943 as per London Gazette of that date and AFRO 232/43 dated 12 February 1943. Home in South Pasadena, California. Enlisted in Toronto, 5 September 1940. Trained at No. 1 ITS (graduated 24 January 1941), No 7 EFTS (graduated 4 March 1941) and No. 10 SFTS (graduated 21 June 1941). Shot down a Fw 190 at Dieppe, 19 August 1942. NOTE: Unit identified in AFRO as No. 400 Squadron. Later transferred to US Navy with which he won an American DFC which is now in the Canadian War Museum AN 19890038-001. The same museum has a model of a Mustang in the colours of one flown by him. No published citation to award. Directorate of History and Heritage files have recommendation for MiD compiled by WC R. F. Begg, Commanding Officer, No. 414 Squadron on 23 August 1942.

During the battle of Dieppe on 19 August 1942, this officer accompanied his flight commander on two low reconnaissances over the approaches to the battle area. During the second of these, they were attacked by three Fw 190s. When FO Hills found he could not warn his flight commander, owing to a radio failure, he engaged the three enemy aircraft, shooting down one and driving off the other two, until the flight commander became aware of the situation.

Hollis Hills was born to Zelma Strother and Fred Hills in Baxter, Iowa, on March 25, 1915. The family moved to Pasadena, California, in 1927 when Hollis was 11 years old. At age 25, Hills voluntarily enlisted as an AC2 in the RCAF on June 5, 1940. It was in the air force where he picked up the nickname "Holly."

As the BCATP was still in its infancy, Hills and several hundred other aspiring trainees were required to perform guard duty at various military installations until classroom spaces became available for instruction.

Designed to be difficult, the ITS's curriculum was used as an introduction to air training and recruits that were not capable of serving to RCAF standards were quickly eliminated. In order to ensure each enlistee was placed in the position best suited to their capabilities and properly trained as such, the plan required that recruits pass through multiple levels of testing and schooling before they were posted. Trainees were immersed in a six-week basic training class that covered air force law, navigation, meteorology, aircraft recognition, the theory of flight, mechanics, and, of course, discipline.

Nine out of every ten men wanted to be trained as pilots, but often it was a Link Trainer that was the definitive moment in that decision.

The backlog of personnel waiting to get on course was so great that it was not until mid-December that Hills was finally able to begin his training program at No. 1 ITS in Toronto, Ontario. He graduated from there on January 24, 1941.

USN Commander Hollis H. Hills, Silver Star, became an ace flying Grumman F3F-5 Hellcats with USN VF-32 Squadron. (Canadian National Defence Image Library)

This school was formerly the Eglinton Hunt Club and received its first cadre of 221 pupils on April 29, 1940.

AC2s, incidentally, were at the bottom of the rank and pay structure earning CAN$1.30 a day plus free room and board.

Clearing the hurdle for pilot training, Hollis was promoted to LAC and was posted, on January 17, 1941, to No. 7 EFTS at Windsor, Ontario. There, he accumulated 60-plus hours of flight time on Fleet Finch biplanes and graduated on March 4.

Posted in early April to No. 10 SFTS at Dauphin, Manitoba, Hollis flew 150-plus hours on Harvard Mk IIs. His class was the second to graduate from that air station as the facility had opened earlier in the year.

Hills was awarded his wings and was designated an SP on June 21, 1941. Later that day, he was commissioned from the ranks as a PO and was given new Regimental Service No. J. 5803.

The recent Dauphin graduates were fully expecting to be sent overseas and were naturally disappointed to learn they would be retained in the BCATP as flying instructors and/or as staff pilots. Hills reported to the Flying Instructors School at Air Station Trenton, Ontario, where he undertook two months of additional training learning how to become an instructor.

Somehow, Hollis was able to swap orders with another pilot who wanted to stay in Canada and had no desire to be posted overseas.

Leaving Pier 21, Halifax, Nova Scotia, by ship, Holly arrived in England in August 1941. Spending four weeks at No. 3 Personnel Reception Centre in Bournemouth, Hills was sent to RAF No. 41 OTU at Old Sarum in Wiltshire.

There, he flew Westland Lysanders and Curtiss-Wright P-40 Tomahawks. Completing the OTU syllabus, Hollis was posted, on October 12, 1941, to RCAF No. 414 Squadron, which was operating from RAF Croydon located just outside of London.

The squadron flew Tomahawk Mk IIs and also operated some Lysanders in the tactical reconnaissance role. Much of the training was devoted to innumerable exercises with the army on which it practiced the technique of ground-to-air co-ordination. The squadron also practiced its dogfighting skills against Spitfires and Hurricanes from operational squadrons at Biggin Hill, Kenley, and Redhill.

During this prolonged period of training, one fatality occurred when American PO G. M. Dunaway crashed in Dorset on November 21 in Tomahawk AH902.

At the end of July 1942, Holly's total flight time was hovering near the 500-hour mark. While at No. 414, he was promoted to FO.

When 414 Squadron celebrated its first birthday in August 1942, it had logged about 3,000 hours of flying time of which only nine hours were on actual operations.

After a year of nothing but flying training, the pilots were beginning to "bind" about their operational inactivity, but they did not have much longer to wait. In the combined attack upon Dieppe on August 19, 414's pilots finally had an opportunity to carry out the role for which they had trained so long.

That day, the "Black Knights" were one of four army co-operation mustang squadrons detailed to reconnoiter the roads leading to the French coastal town. Between 0445hrs and 1130hrs, the pilots flew 18 sorties on this task and, although they found no enemy activity or troop movements on the roads, they did encounter intense flak and had several brushes with hostile fighters.

Having had a taste of combat, Hills now yearned for more. He was aware that many Americans were laterally transferring to the USAAF and some of his fighter pilot buddies were heading over to the 4th FG at Debden.

He had plans to join the 4th and fly Spitfires but was told he was needed at a P-38 unit. He then talked to the United States Navy Reserve (USNR) and, after weighing his options, he opted to transfer to that service.

Hills requested and received an honorable discharge from RCAF Overseas Headquarters in London on November 4, 1942. Four days later he was commissioned in the USNR with the rank of lieutenant (jg).

Holly returned to the US in December on the ocean liner *Queen Mary*. He was sent to NAS Jacksonville, Florida, for indoctrination. Next, it was over to NAS Miami, Florida, for gunnery training. After his first hop as a student at Miami, the roles were quickly reversed. Hills spent the next three months instructing the instructors on F2A-1, -2 and -3 Brewster Buffaloes and F4F Grumman Wildcats. Turns out, Hollis was the only pilot at Miami with any combat experience.

Hills was ordered to report on May 28, 1943, to Navy Fighter Squadron Three Two (VF-32). At the time, the squadron was forming at NAS Atlantic City, New Jersey.

VF-32 was assigned to the aircraft carrier USS *Langley* (CVL-27) and started out life with a mixed bag of General Motors FM-1 Wildcats and Grumman F6F-3 Hellcats. By the end of August 1943, it was an all-Hellcat squadron. The *Langley* departed the Philadelphia navy yard in December 1943 and headed for the Pacific where it joined Task Force (TF) 58.

The mission for TF-58 was to seek out, engage and destroy the Japanese fleet and naval air forces in the Philippine Sea and Leyte Gulf areas. TF-58 provided defensive cover and air support for the amphibious forces that captured the Gilbert, Marshall, New Guinea, Mariana, Palau, and Philippine islands and protected the forces that neutralized the Truk Atoll.

In 1945, it supported the amphibious landings at Iwo Jima and Okinawa, fought off Japanese kamikaze air attacks and struck airfields and strategic targets in Formosa and Japan.

Hills was promoted to lieutenant on January 1, 1944. His flight time at that point amounted to 880 hours and he had completed 45 carrier landings.

At 0750hrs on April 29, 1944, all of Hills' training came to the fore when he shot down, over Truk, three Mitsubishi A6M Zero-Sen "Zekes" and claimed a fourth as a probable. Then on September 13, he strafed and destroyed two Zekes on the ground at Dumaguete airfield in the Philippines. The aerial victory that elevated him to ace status occurred on September 21, when he blew another Zeke out of the sky over Manila Bay. That same day he destroyed a Mitsubishi Ki-21 "Sally" medium bomber on the ground.

Lieutenant Hills was shot down in F6F-3 Hellcat, BuNo 42904, by Japanese antiaircraft fire on September 22, 1944, over Subic Bay. He was rescued by the submarine USS *Haddo* SS-255.

VF-32 left the war zone in late October and returned to the west coast for reforming. Hills served on the *Langley* from October 1943 to September 1944. He transferred to VF-150, then on to VF-97. Neither squadron entered combat.

Postwar, Holly flew Grumman F8F-2 Bearcats with VF-62, Lockheed P2V-3 Neptunes and NAA AJ-1 Savages with VC-5, and, later as CO of VF-62, McDonnell F2H-2 Banshees and Grumman F9F-8 Cougars. He also served as operations officer at the Naval Air Test Center at Patuxent River, Maryland. There, while engaged in armament test flying, Holly piloted Grumman F11F-1 Tigers, NAA FJ Furies, Douglas F-4D Skyrays, and Vought F-8 Crusaders.

Hills was promoted to the rank of commander on July 1, 1954, and retired from the Navy ten years later. He ended his career with staff assignments in the Far East and England. Hollis then spent 16 years living in the United Kingdom and Spain before returning to the US in 1980. His favorite two aircraft were the F8F-2 Bearcat and the F11F-1 Tiger.

His USN awards include the Silver Star, two Air Medals, a Strike Flight DFC, and five Strike Flight Air Medals for 30 combat missions.

He said on several occasions: "The thing that I am most proud of is that in my 25 years as a military pilot, I brought back everyone I took out, wartime or peacetime."

Retired Navy Commander Hollis Henry Hills passed away on Saturday, October 31, 2009, at the William Childs Hospice House at Palm Bay, Florida. He was 94 years old.

His good friend Flight Lieutenant F. E. Clarke passed away four years earlier in 2005.

Christopher Magee
Blackest of the "Black Sheep"

As a member of the famed USMC "Black Sheep" FS in World War II, Captain Christopher Lyman "Maggie" or "Wildman" Magee was VMF-214's second highest-scoring ace with nine confirmed kills. Magee's record was eclipsed by the squadron's aggressive hard-drinking and hell-raising CO, Major Gregory "Gramps" or "Pappy" Boyington, who finished the war with a total of 24 victories.

If the Magee surname is familiar to the reader, it is because Wildman's first cousin was none other than John Gillespie Magee, Jr., the author of the famous aviation poem *High Flight*.

Christopher Lyman Magee was born to Fred and Marie Magee on June 12, 1917, in Omaha, Nebraska. The Magees were originally from the Pittsburgh area, where Fred was the editor-in-chief of the *Pittsburgh Times*. Over time, failing eyesight caused him to give up his position at the newspaper.

Fred moved his new bride to Omaha in 1916 where he worked for the commodities exchange. When Chris was a year old, the family moved to Chicago where his father accepted a position at the grain market exchange. Chris's younger sister, Zona, arrived in 1919, and a baby brother, Fred Jr., was born into the family in 1921.

C. L. Magee attended Chicago's St. Ambrose Elementary, then Mount Carmel High School, from which he graduated in 1935. Chris was a keen athlete throughout his academic years participating in almost every organized activity offered. He had a voracious appetite for knowledge and read every book he could lay his hands on, most of which came from the Chicago Public Library. Chris loved reading stories about the aviation heroes of World War I, and these were among his favorite subjects. He would often compare American ace Captain Eddie Rickenbacker and Germany's Manfred von Richthofen as the modern-day equivalents of Sir Lancelot and Galahad from the Arthurian Knights of the Round Table era.

However, Magee was rather delinquent when it came time to return his reading choices, as some books never made it back until years later. He could not be bothered to wait in line to check out his library selections, so he would quietly slip out a seldom used side door when no one was looking. This unorthodox check-out method allowed him to keep the material much longer and no one at the library was the wiser.

Christopher Magee: Blackest of the "Black Sheep"

Work was scarce in the mid-1930s, and although his parents were better off than most, there was not enough money in the family budget to send their oldest son to college. Chris worked for a few years and one of his better paying jobs was delivering electric light bills for US$15 weekly. He did manage to squeeze in one year of higher learning at the University of Chicago in 1938. The physically fit and athletically inclined Chicagoan boxed, ran track, and played end on the school's football team in his freshman year.

When Chris heard the news on September 1, 1939, that German forces had bombed and invaded Poland, he was ready and willing to go and join the fray. However, to become a pilot in the USAAC, Navy or Marines, he required one more year of schooling. Chris was not prepared to wait that long and began plotting the quickest way to a war zone.

In January 1940, he and two friends hitch-hiked to New Orleans, where they hoped to get hired as deck hands on an ocean-going freighter. Their goal was to work their way over to England, then join the RAF. During one interview, a ship's captain questioned the urgency of the trio getting to Europe. When they told him the truth, he flatly turned them down muttering something about how they would all be arrested, jailed and/or fined for violating the recently amended US Neutrality Act.

He sent them on their way and word quickly spread around the Louisiana docks to stay clear of the three young guys from Chicago.

Chris returned to Illinois and, a month later in March, headed to Windsor, Ontario, Canada, this time to join the RCAF. He was unsuccessful, and for the second time in just 60 days, his efforts to get into the war had been thwarted.

The BCATP had just gotten under way and, as it was still in its infancy, the Canadian air force was in a position to cherry pick its inductees from the thousands of applications it was receiving. For the first several months of the plan's existence, only licensed pilots and/or university students with a minimum of two years of higher learning were accepted. Over the next year, as the plan matured and demand for aircrew grew, the RCAF lowered its entry requirements for pilot training to include those who had graduated high school.

Other than returning to school, the 23-year-old Magee had only one other available option and that was to take and pass a USAAC equivalency test.

For the next four months, Chris studied advanced algebra, geometry, physics, chemistry, and trigonometry. He passed the Air Corps written examination and learned that he would begin cadet pilot training on March 22, 1941, at the Spartan School of Aeronautics in Tulsa, Oklahoma.

While there, the always impatient Magee learned the RCAF would take another look at his application, provided he had flown a military aircraft for a minimum of 35 hours. By then, Chris had convinced himself the United States was not going to get embroiled in the European war anytime soon, so he began to plan his exit from the Air Corps. Desperate to get into combat, he intentionally washed himself out of the Tulsa flight school through a series of planned careless landings. The Army tried to talk him into re-mustering as either a navigator or bombardier, but he politely turned it down. Magee left Oklahoma on May 20, 1941, after having flown 35 hours on Fairchild PT-19 trainers.

Wildman returned to Chicago to put his affairs in order before heading off once again to Canada. One of the things he did was to return all the library books he had accumulated over the years. To save his future reading privileges and not be assessed any large fines, he telephoned the main library and came up with the story that a tenant had moved out of his building and that person wanted to donate several dozen boxes of books to the good people of Chicago. The library sent a truck for the pick-up and Magee and one of his friends brazenly helped the driver load the vehicle.

C. L. Magee enlisted in the RCAF at No. 11 Recruiting Centre in Toronto, Ontario, on July 8, 1941, as an AC2. He breezed through his basic training at No. 1 MD in that city and was sent to No. 3 ITS at Victoriaville, Quebec.

Promoted to LAC, he was posted on December 20 to No. 21 EFTS at Chatham, New Brunswick. There he flew ski-equipped Fleet Finch biplane trainers. Chris, who was a natural pilot, was sent on March 27, to fly Harvard Mk IIs, on Course No. 53, at No. 9 SFTS at Summerside, Prince Edward Island.

The joint Canadian–American transfer train staffed with military officers from Canada and the United States stopped at Summerside in early May 1942. Its mission was to interview and repatriate any US citizen who wished to laterally transfer from the RCAF to a US military service. It was all strictly voluntary, and no pressure was used to switch military allegiances, as Canada and the United States, which share a 3,000-mile-long undefended border, were fighting the same enemy for the exact same reasons.

With 135 hours of RCAF flight time recorded in his logbook, Chris talked with representatives of the Army, Navy, and Marines. Looking to make the best deal he could, he laid out three conditions they would have to meet before he would consider transferring. He would only fly fighters; he would not become an instructor, and he would immediately be sent to a combat zone.

Only the Marines would agree to his terms. Chris, who was within a few scant weeks of receiving his RCAF wings, approached the OC at No. 9 to see if the Canadians could match the offer. They could not.

Chris Magee was honorably discharged from the RCAF on May 9 after having served a total of 309 days.

After several months of training on SNJ-3s at NAS Atlanta, Georgia, Magee earned his Naval Wings of Gold and was commissioned a Marine Reserve 2nd lieutenant on November 16, 1942.

He began flying Grumman F4F-3 and -4 fighters from Cecil Field at NAS Jacksonville, Florida, on January 23, 1943. Near the end of March, Magee was sent to NAS Glenview, near Chicago, for additional training.

Christopher Magee: Blackest of the "Black Sheep"

Chicago was where the Navy's inland training aircraft carrier USS *Wolverine* (IX-64) was based. The American Ship Building Company in Buffalo, New York, had converted the Great Lakes cruise liner SS *Seeandbee* into the mini-flattop over a six-month period. *Wolverine*'s crew began training the Navy's future sea-going pilots in the art of taking off and landing from a moving ship on August 12, 1942.

Operating exclusively in Lake Michigan, IX-64 sailed north from Chicago's Navy Pier out into the lake 50 or more miles every day, where, free from any interruptions, it conducted flight operations. A second training carrier, USS *Sable* (IX-81), joined *Wolverine* at Glenview on May 8, 1943. *Sable* had previously been registered before

A publicity photo taken in March 1945 of USMC Captain Christopher L. Magee, Navy Cross, when he was assigned to VMF-911. (US Department of Defense)

its conversion as SS *Greater Buffalo*. Both ships were coal-burning, side-wheel paddle steamers.

By war's end, the two vessels had completed 116,000 air movements, qualifying 17,820 Naval and Marine aviators.

Chris Magee spent five days on the *Wolverine* completing eight mandatory takeoffs and landings.

The Navy used various aircraft types for training on these two vessels and, from the ship's logs and accident reports, it is known that a total of 142 aircraft were lost from 1942 through to 1945, costing the lives of eight pilots.

The number and types of planes that sank to the bottom of Lake Michigan are as follows: 41 Grumman/General Motors TBF/TBM Avengers, one Vought F4U Corsair, 38 Douglas Dauntless Dive-Bombers, four Grumman F6F Hellcats, one Vought SB2U Vindicator, 37 Grumman/General Motors F4F/FM Wildcats, 17 NAA SNJs and three TDN experimental drones. Many of the types were older aircraft that had served in the North African and Pacific campaigns. The USN managed to salvage six of the crashed airframes from shallow water before the end of the war.

The remaining 136 aircraft sat in a semi-preserved state for decades in a deep, freshwater repository measuring 307 miles long by 118 miles wide. The lake's average depth is 279ft. Within the past several years, approximately 40 airframes have been recovered by salvagers for the Navy. Most were found to be in good condition with tires inflated, parachutes preserved, leather seats maintained and engine crankcases full of oil.

A sizeable portion of Lake Michigan's lost fleet of historic aircraft remains to be located and retrieved. However, the USN still exercises control and ownership of these aircraft, as they are considered to be, even after all these years, US government property.

Chris reported for duty to NAS Miramar on April 30 and a month later was promoted to 1st lieutenant. He left San Diego on USS *Rochambeau* on June 5 and, after a lengthy voyage, the converted troop ship docked in New Caledonia on the 23rd.

Magee was introduced to the Corsair on Espiritu Santo in the New Hebrides on July 2, 1943, and, as he said, "It was love at first sight." On July 25, he was assigned to VMF-124. Over the next two months, Chris read and familiarized himself with all aspects of the F4U. Through flight training and gunnery practice he accumulated 68 hours flying time on the inverted gull-wing fighter. He was very confident in this new aircraft and was just itching to take on the Japanese.

In early September, VMF-124 disbanded and this left Maggie and others like him in limbo assigned to a pilots' pool. This pool is where Major Boyington found the majority of 214's personnel.

Besides Chris Magee, four other Black Sheep squadron pilots were RCAF trained and these included Fred V. "Lighthorse" Avey from Portland, Oregon,

Christopher Magee: Blackest of the "Black Sheep"

Donald J. "Deejay" Moore from Amarillo, Texas, William D. "Junior" Heier from Kansas City, Missouri, and Henry Stuckert "Notebook" Miller from Jenkintown, Pennsylvania.

The Black Sheep's first combat tour ran from September 12 through to October 24, 1943. On September 11, the squadron flew 20 Corsairs from Espiritu Santo to the Russell Islands via Guadalcanal. When it arrived, it borrowed four planes to bring the squadron up to combat strength. On September 16, 1st Lieutenant C. L. Magee claimed a probable when he set a Mitsubishi A6M Zero-Sen "Zeke" on fire in a large melee over the island of Balalae. This was his first time in combat, and he was too busy to determine the fate of his adversary. The squadron moved to Munda airstrip on the island of New Georgia on September 17. The following day, Magee and the other Black Sheep pilots were up at 0400hrs planning a mission to provide air cover for a Navy task force, which was bringing men and supplies to the Marines' beachhead at Barakoma, Vella Lavella.

Chris took off with the others, but returned to the strip's coral runway when he noticed his plane had developed a severe oil leak. He found a replacement aircraft and quickly got airborne to catch up with his mates.

Frank Emulous Walton, 214's intelligence officer, relates Magee's encounter with the enemy that day in his book, *Once They Were Eagles*:

> I was finishing up a report with Bill Case when a plane called the control tower at 1330 hours requesting clearance for an emergency landing. It was Wildman Magee. Chris nursed his crippled Corsair onto the airstrip and as he flashed by us, we could see that one tire was flat, and jagged holes from battle damage were showing in his tail, fuselage and wings. The actual count was thirty hits from both cannon and machine gun rounds. Chris in his report stated, "Arriving late over Vella Lavella I could not find my flight so I joined up with three other F4Us.
>
> We spotted thirty Japanese Aichi D3A2 Val dive-bombers heading towards Bougainville. We nosed over, gained speed and came up under them in a low stern pass. One pulled off to the side. I followed and gave him three medium bursts of gunfire. His plane caught fire in the middle and he went down burning. By then I had lost the other Corsairs. Coming around a cloud I spotted fifteen Val's heading for our ships off Barakoma. Our gun batteries were throwing plenty of stuff at them but I knew they couldn't get them all, so, I pushed over and went after them." "All by yourself?" I asked. "Well, yes, there were no other friendlies around. I caught them about one hundred feet off the water and made a high side pass at the formation. One broke loose and my gunfire chopped off his tail. He nosed over and crashed in the water. The remainder jettisoned their bombs and headed home, so I picked out a straggler and started a high side pass at him. I passed over him before I could get in an effective burst, so I circled and made another high side run at him. He turned in to me and we came head-on. I gave him a long burst and saw pieces of

his cowling and fuselage flying off. Then he nosed under me. I was going to circle to finish him off when I heard a typewriter clacking sound, and holes began to appear in my right wing.

Looking back four Zeke's were on my tail. I dove into our ship's anti-aircraft fire trying to scrape them off my back. As I went down, I was kicking left and right rudder alternately to throw them off their aim. They wisely did not follow me! I climbed back up to my station, and resumed patrol over the landing area." "You climbed back on station when you knew your plane had been shot up?" I asked him. "There were no other planes in sight, so I thought I had better stay. In about fifteen minutes a division of P-40 Warhawks showed up, and I came on in."

"You ought to get a Navy Cross for that performance Maggie! I'm going to write up the recommendation." "Hell I don't want any medals," he said. "Just killing the little yellow bastards is enough fun for me."

Frank E. Walton, a traffic sergeant in the Los Angeles City Police Department (LAPD) before the war, did in fact write up the recommendation for Magee's Navy Cross award and Boyington enthusiastically signed it. Walton returned to the LAPD after the war, retiring as deputy chief in 1959.

A few days later, Magee's image as a "wildman" was solidified by his actions on a routine patrol. Chris had acquired a hand grenade from Marine ground troops and, against regulations, took it with him on the flight. On their way back to Munda, Chris and Gramps flew low over Choiseul Island looking for any targets on which to use up their remaining ammunition. The pair came across a 70ft barge full of Japanese soldiers and supplies that was crossing a small channel. Despite several strafing runs, neither Corsair was able to stop the vessel nor set it on fire. Chris, who was out of ammunition, took out the unauthorized grenade and, just like in the movies, tried to pull the pin with his teeth, with the result that he almost broke two of them in the process. Never one to give up, he came around again and this time he cradled the stick between his knees so that he could use both hands to free the rusted stubborn pin. Flying through small arms fire, he dropped the grenade from an altitude of just 50ft. It exploded directly on the moving target starting several small fires. When the pair left the area, the remaining Japanese were in the water as the barge was fully engulfed in flames.

On October 17, Chris led four F4U-1s as bait on a low-level sweep east of Balalae. Pappy, meanwhile, perched high and unseen in the clouds with ten other Black Sheep Corsairs, patiently waited to spring the trap. The Japanese, figuring Chris's four-plane division would be easy meat, launched 55 Zekes. During the 40-minute pitched battle, which began at 0915hrs, VMF-214 shot down 12 enemy aircraft and claimed several as probables. Boynton got three, Chris, Junior, Heier, and Burney Tucker each had two, with singles going to Bolt, Matheson and Olander. All Black Sheep aircraft safely returned to the base.

Christopher Magee: Blackest of the "Black Sheep"

At 1650hrs on October 18 over Kahili aerodrome on the island of Bougainville, Chris bagged three Zekes in just three minutes. Eleven Black Sheep members, together with eight pilots from VMF-211 and all under Boyington's command, tangled with more than 40 Zero-Sen fighters.

The sons of Nippon rose from their airfield to do battle after being challenged and insulted by Major Boyington over the radio. Magee's first kill of the day was on his initial pass as he flew inverted across the climbing Japanese formation. Turning for a second run, he spotted a Zeke diving away from a tangle of warplanes. Closing on his opponent, he blew it apart just as the enemy pilot started to climb back up into the fight. Chris zoomed his Corsair up into the swirling melee and found himself on the tail of a third victim, who apparently had no idea he was there. Three seconds of gunfire from the big Vought fighter at close range sent the Zeke spinning and burning into the water below.

On October 19, Boyington, Magee, Bob McClurg and George Ashmun volunteered to strafe Kara and Kahili airfields, where Allied intelligence believed enemy bombers were massing for a strike. The four Corsairs took off from Munda at 0450hrs and immediately ran into a tropical storm. Maintaining radio silence, they flew on through the high winds and rain trying to stay in formation. Ashmun lost the others in the darkness and diverted to the Japanese airfield on Balalae, which he shot up before returning home. The remaining three made it undetected to Bougainville where Boyington, with a wave of his wings, proceeded alone up the foggy coast to Kahili. With McClurg glued to his wing, Chris flew inland and managed to find Kara below a murky 800ft ceiling.

In the early morning light, the two F4Us with 12 guns blazing, made one pass across the Japanese strip just 40ft off the deck. Aerial reconnaissance photos taken later in the day revealed five burnt-out Mitsubishi G4M "Betty" twin-engined bombers at Kara. Boyington was also successful at Kahili, torching three bombers parked at the end of that airfield. Pappy was quite late returning home as he took a side trip to Vella Lavella to pick up a bottle of whiskey someone owed him.

Chris Magee was awarded a Navy Cross on September 29, 1944, and the citation read as follows:

> Magee, Christopher L. First Lieutenant, US Marine Corps (Reserve), Marine Fighting Squadron 214 (VMF-214), Marine Air Group (MAG) 11, 1st Marine Air Wing. Date of action: September 12 – October 24, 1943. The Navy Cross is presented to Christopher L. Magee, First Lieutenant, US Marine Corps (Reserve), for extraordinary heroism as a pilot of a fighter plane attached to Marine Fighting Squadron Two Hundred Fourteen (VMF-214), operating against Japanese forces in the Solomon Islands area from September 12 to October 24, 1943. Displaying superb flying ability and fearless intrepidity, First Lieutenant Magee participated in numerous strike escorts, task force covers, fighter sweeps, strafing missions and

patrols. As a member of a division of four planes acting as task force cover on September 18, he daringly maneuvered his craft against thirty enemy dive bombers with fighter escorts and, pressing home his attack with skill and determination, destroyed two dive-bombers and probably a third. During two subsequent fighter sweeps over Kahili Airdrome on October 17–18, he valiantly engaged superior numbers of Japanese fighters which attempted to intercept our forces and succeeded in shooting down five Zeros.

The following day, volunteering to strafe Kara airfield on Bougainville Island, he dived with one other plane through intense antiaircraft fire to a forty foot level in a strafing run, leaving five enemy aircraft blazing. First Lieutenant Magee's brilliant airmanship and indomitable fighting spirit contributed to the success of many vital missions and were in keeping with the highest traditions of the United States Naval Service. Spot Award, Serial 00164, Born at Omaha, Nebraska, Home Town Chicago, Illinois.

Its first six-week tour over, the Black Sheep flew its Corsairs back to the Russell Islands on October 24. Two days later, it hitched a ride on Army C-47s to Espiritu Santo. The next stop was Sydney, Australia, for seven days of R&R. The 1,700-mile, 12-hour flight to Australia, with a refueling stop in New Caledonia, was made aboard two packed Navy R4D transports.

According to Frank Walton, everything the squadron had heard about the amazing land down under was absolutely true. The food was fresh and varied, the liquor excellent and plentiful, and the women beautiful and friendly. All too soon its leave ended, and the squadron was back in the war zone.

Flying an upgraded Corsair variant, the F4U-1A, 214's second tour from the island of Vella Lavella ran from November 27, 1943, through to January 8, 1944. For the first three weeks, the Black Sheep did not encounter any enemy aerial activity, despite the squadron flying daily dawn–dusk patrols, strafing missions, and task force cover patrols.

On December 23, covering Army B-24 Liberators on a mission to Rabaul harbor, Chris added a single Zeke to his tally when he sent one crashing into Saint George's channel between the islands of New Ireland and New Britain.

Magee's ninth and final victory occurred on December 28 over Rabaul when he chased and shot down an IJAAF inline-powered Kawasaki Ki-61 Hien fighter.

Boyington told his boys in 1943, "If you ever see me go down, I promise I'll meet you in a San Diego bar six months after the war." Shot down on January 3, 1944, Pappy did keep his prophetic promise to his men, albeit in a different California city. On September 12, 1945, 22 former Black Sheep members, including Chris Magee, assembled at the St. Francis Hotel in San Francisco for a rowdy homecoming party for their skipper.

Christopher Magee: Blackest of the "Black Sheep"

Pappy had been found alive in the Japanese PoW Omori Base Camp near Tokyo. When last seen near Rabaul 20 months earlier, Boyington and his wingman, Captain George M. Ashmun from Far Hills, New Jersey, were hotly pursuing more than a dozen Zekes. Ashmun died in that engagement trying to protect his leader.

With Gramps gone, it was a sad group of fighter pilots who ended their second tour on January 8. Returning from their seven-day R&R trip to Australia, Chris and his fellow pilots managed to stay together for a month on Espiritu Santo, doing mundane chores such as ferrying planes from one island to another.

In March 1944, Magee and 14 other Black Sheep pilots were assigned to VMF-211. Their new squadron, known as the "Wake Island Avengers," was stationed on Green Island, which unfortunately was located in what was considered an inactive area. Over the next six weeks, VMF-211 flew numerous missions supporting Marine ground forces, however, it did not see nor did it have an opportunity to engage the enemy in aerial action. That same month, Chris received a promotion to captain.

Completing three tours, Wildman returned to America in May 1944. He wanted another crack at the Japanese, so he began thinking of ways he could get back into combat. After an extended visit with family and friends, Chris moved on to his next assignment with VMFT-911 at MCAS Cherry Point in North Carolina.

Nine Eleven was a replacement training squadron and for the next five months most of Magee's flying time was in SNJ trainers with occasional hops in Ohio-built Goodyear FG-1D Corsairs.

At Cherry Point, Chris met and married Molly Cleary, a Navy nurse from New York City.

The squadron's role changed from that of trainer to fighter in February 1945, and with the change came a new aircraft, the large twin-engined Grumman F7F Tigercat. This was Magee's ticket back into combat. He began to read everything he could about his new mount. VMF-911 was the only Marine unit scheduled to receive the Tigercat and was to employ them in the day-fighter role.

Problems with the plane's Oldsmobile 20mm cannon delayed deployment to the western Pacific in the spring of 1945. The squadron temporarily set up shop at El Centro, California, to test and rectify the overheating gun problem. The difficulty finally corrected, VMF-911 was declared fully operational in late July. The squadron flew its planes to NAS Miramar for onward deployment to Okinawa by aircraft carrier. Its F7Fs were craned aboard the boat, but the ship never left the dock. The atomic bombs dropped on Hiroshima and Nagasaki on Monday August 6 and Thursday August 9, 1945, respectively, convinced the Japanese government that its continued prosecution of an unwinnable war was hopeless.

C. L. Magee retired from the Marine Corps Reserve on October 6, 1945, as he was not interested in serving in the peacetime military. Several commercial airlines contacted Chris in Chicago offering him a job, but he said he was not the kind of person who would exploit his war record just to earn a paycheck.

The sudden transition from warrior to civilian was not easy for the free-spirited Magee. For a while, he was a deckhand on a liberty ship, bringing war brides to the states from Europe. He then hooked up with an old Chicago buddy and they ran a bootlegging business, supplying liquor to northern Michigan resorts and hotels that were located in dry counties.

Chris moved the illegal operation to Kansas, where he was eventually arrested. His souped up 1945 Lincoln Zephyr was confiscated, and he had to pay US$3,000 in fines just to stay out of jail. Magee was also employed as a courier for a shadowy group of American businessmen in Central America, who worked to overthrow Latin American dictators then replace them with pro-American democratic governments.

In the summer of 1947, Chris was hired as a crewman on an ore carrier sailing the Great Lakes.

In May 1948, he read in a newspaper article that the newly formed nation of Israel was looking for pilots. Chris and other like-minded volunteers joined the Haganah – Israel Defense Force – which was led by David Ben-Gurion, later that country's first prime minister. The hired guns were clandestinely flown to Tel Aviv on KLM Royal Dutch Airlines via Amsterdam, Geneva, Zurich, and Prague. In Israel, Chris flew with 101 FS, which was known as the "Angels of Death." The aircraft it flew were clapped out Avia S-199 fighters – a Czechoslovakian-built version of the Messerschmitt Bf 109G. That October, Chris was told he would have to sign up for one year if he wanted to stay in the country.

His six-month stay had unfortunately been right in the middle of several ceasefire agreements. Disappointed with the lack of action, and not having seen an enemy aircraft, he decided to leave.

Landing in New York, he learned from his in-laws that Molly had divorced him. She had taken their two small children and moved away. She made it clear that Chris was not to try to locate or contact them. He never did. Many years later he explained to a newspaper reporter that he alone was completely responsible for the failure of his marriage as he was never home.

When war broke out in Korea, Chris contacted the Corps and told them he was interested in putting on the uniform and getting back into the cockpit. The Corps said he would hear back, but he never did. Magee, at age 33, was too old for the fighter community.

He returned to work on the ore boats, then signed on as part of a construction crew that was building the Distant Early Warning radar sites across the top of the northern hemisphere. He spent six lonely months in Greenland and although the money was great, he was very happy to return to his hometown when his contract had run its term.

Magee never explained to anyone why it was that he robbed two banks in the mid-1950s. The first hold up occurred in Cicero, Illinois, at the branch of the

Christopher Magee: Blackest of the "Black Sheep"

Reserve Savings and Loan Company in 1955. His take was $3,000. The second one, on January 15, 1957, proved to be extremely lucrative – some $46,000. This amount was liberated from the Lincoln Way West Branch of the National Bank and Trust Company in South Bend, Indiana. In both robberies, Magee used a .45 caliber semi-automatic handgun, which was not loaded. The money from both heists was never recovered.

Chris was arrested in downtown Chicago in October 1957. He was convicted of armed robbery on April 29, 1958, and sentenced to 25 years in the federal penitentiary in Atlanta, Georgia. Due to legal errors made in his trial, Chris was granted a new trial in 1959. The outcome, however, was the same – guilty as charged. However, the judge did reduce the original sentence from 25 to 15 years.

Chris spent the next seven-and-a-half years in the Leavenworth, Kansas, penal system before being paroled. He was a model prisoner who worked in the prison library. He wrote short stories and poetry and joined the staff of the prison newspaper, eventually becoming its editor.

Taking correspondence courses, Magee earned an English degree from Highland College and the University of Kansas.

Released from prison at age 49, Chris returned to Chicago where he edited community newspapers for the next ten years. He lived his remaining years quietly and anonymously in an old rent-controlled apartment on the city's south side.

In his 77th year, on December 27th, 1995, the man who some say had the heart of a warrior and the soul of a poet, died during a cancer operation in an Illinois Veterans Affairs' hospital.

Christopher Lyman Magee was, without question, the quintessential member of the Black Sheep FS.

His ashes were interned in Arlington National Cemetery in 1996.

Donald Moore
Texas Corsair Pilot

USMC 1st Lieutenant Donald Jay "Deejay" Moore, from Amarillo, Texas, was one of five "Black Sheep" FS pilots who undertook pilot training in the RCAF in World War II. The others were: Christopher Lyman "Maggie" Magee, Fred V. "Lighthorse" Avey, William D. "Junior" Heier, and Henry Stuckert "Notebook" Miller.

Serving two tours in the Bismarck Archipelago and flying 1,776 missions on Chance Vought F4U-1 and -1A Corsairs, the Black Sheep, in just 84 days of combat, destroyed 94 Japanese aircraft and claimed another 30 as probably destroyed. From a total of 49 pilots who served with this famous squadron, nine became aces and 11 were KIA.

Shortly after Marine Fighter Squadron Two One Four's (VMF-214's) formation at Turtle Bay fighter strip on the Island of Espiritu Santo in the New Hebrides, on Tuesday, September 7, 1943, the pilots held an informal meeting and chose "Boyington's Bastards" as their squadron name.

When that moniker was presented for approval to Marine Air Group 11 Headquarters, Captain Jack DeChant, the wing public information officer, turned it down saying, "That name will never fly with the press and the good folks back home." A less offensive and sanitized title, the Black Sheep, was proffered by DeChant for the squadron's consideration. Meaning the same thing, the altered name was acceptable to 214's personnel. Even though they had to drop their first choice, the irreverent pilots made sure to incorporate the black bar of bastardy in the design of their squadron patch.

Don Moore was born to Earl D. Moore and Nellie A. Hall on November 20, 1922, in Crosswell, Michigan. The family relocated from Michigan to Texas where they took up residence at 901 North Grant Street in Amarillo. Don's father was a police officer. Deejay attended, in succession, Buchanan Street Public School, then Amarillo High School.

Finishing his formal schooling in June 1940, he took a one-year mechanical engineering correspondence course while holding down a full-time position as a mechanic at the Douglas Aircraft manufacturing facility at Santa Monica,

California. Yearning to become a pilot, Moore was unable to meet the rigid entry requirements for pilot training in the prewar USAAC.

On July 29, 1941, the 19-year-old traveled north to Montreal, Quebec, and enlisted in the RCAF at its No. 13 Recruiting Centre.

Assigned Regimental Service No. R. 117709, AC2 D. J. Moore was sent for basic training to No. 1 MD at Toronto, Ontario. On August 21, he was assigned to Air Station Trenton, Ontario, where he performed guard duty. The next phase in his training returned him to Toronto, where he attended No. 1 ITS until November 22.

Promoted to LAC, he traveled east to London, Ontario, to begin flight training on Fleet Finch biplanes at No. 3 EFTS. Graduating from Pilot Course No. 43 with a 78 percent average on January 30, 1942, Moore returned to Toronto to perform general duties at the MD until the end of February. Apparently, there were no openings at any of the SFTSs.

On March 1, with the backlog of personnel in the training pipeline cleared away, he began flying NAA Harvard and Yale aircraft on Course No. 50 at No. 1 SFTS at Camp Borden, Ontario.

After serving 295 days in the RCAF, Moore decided to laterally transfer from the Canadian Air Force to the US Marines now that his country was in the war. His honorable discharge was signed at Ottawa, Ontario, on May 19, 1942. His conduct and character while in the RCAF was rated as very good, while his piloting skills were rated as superior.

Moore entered the US Navy's aviation flying community where he finished his flight training on Grumman F4F-3 and -4 Wildcat fighters at Cecil Field at Jacksonville, Florida. He was awarded his wings and commissioned in the Marine Corps Reserve on January 12, 1943, under Regimental Service No. O-17036.

One of his classmates at Jacksonville, and who later became a good friend at VMF-214, was Captain Christopher L. Magee. Moore, Magee, and other military personnel shipped out from San Diego on the USS *Rochambeau* on June 5 and, after a three-week sea voyage, the converted troop ship docked in New Caledonia, which is located in the southwest region of the Pacific Ocean.

In September, the Black Sheep came together after Major Gregory "Gramps" Boyington formed the squadron from a group of unassigned pilots languishing in a pilot's replacement pool. He interviewed each one and had them fly on his wing so that he could assess their piloting skills before making his selection.

Don Moore was one of the more popular members of the squadron. He was a happy individual who was always smiling. At nighttime singalongs, he would lend his rich baritone voice to the many song fests. He purchased a silver trombone in Sydney, Australia, during the squadron's first seven-day R&R visit to the land down under. When not on duty, he carried it with him everywhere.

Donald J. Moore is in the third row second from the left in this VMF-214 "Black Sheep" Squadron picture taken in October 1943. (US Department of Defense)

He was an original member of the squadron and flew two combat tours, achieving three aerial confirmed kills in the process.

On a fighter sweep to the Rabaul/Simpson Harbour area on December 17, 1943, Moore downed two Mitsubishi A6M Zero-Sen Zekes. Bruce Gamble, in his excellent book *The Black Sheep*, described the encounter:

> As 214 approached the Rabaul area, Moore spotted a column of seven Zekes flying a few thousand feet below. Boyington, missing Moore's wing waggle signal, continued to lead the squadron towards the enemy airfield at Lakunai. Moore, on his own, descended and crept up unnoticed behind the tail end Zeke. When he squeezed the trigger, nothing happened! He pulled off the target, reefed the Corsair around and again charged his guns. Rolling wings level, he crept up behind a second Zeke, pressed the trigger and was met with complete silence from his six Colt Browning .50 caliber MG53-2 heavy machine guns. He chandelled up and away, rolled out behind another Zeke and charged his guns one more time!! This time they blazed forth knocking a wing off the doomed enemy aircraft which crashed in an unburned state. Moore, all alone proceeded to head home. Circling south, he headed out of the harbor climbing for altitude. Spotting a single Zeke heading back to a base at Rabaul, Don dropped down in a high stern run and fired a long burst at a range of three hundred yards. He followed his target through a slow roll and watched it

crash into the water opposite Vunakanau airdrome. On the way back to Torokina airfield, Moore encountered heavy weather and, due to a faulty compass, flew right past his intended landing site on Bougainville. Critically low on fuel he spotted two small islands through the overcast – Mono and Stirling – part of the Treasury Island Chain. His good fortune continued to hold as the "Seabees" of the USN's 87th Naval Construction Battalion were in the process of building an airstrip on Stirling! He zoomed the field once, circled and fired his guns to warn the workers he was coming in for a landing. The big fighter was rolling to a stop when Moore's luck finally ran out. A collision with a boulder protruding from the unfinished coral strip caused the F4U to flip over on its back. Don was knocked unconscious and suffered a lacerated left arm. The Seabees pulled him from the wreckage then liberated his helmet and goggles, the Corsair's clock and a few other items before he came to. Three days later, a Navy Consolidated PBY-5A Catalina returned him to the squadron at Vella Lavella. The squadron's Medical Officer grounded Don for another four days making sure his injuries were properly healing.

1st Lieutenant D. J. Moore was killed on Tuesday December 28, 1943. That day, three Black Sheep pilots, Moore, Captain J. Cameron Dustin, and 1st Lieutenant Harry R. Bartl, failed to return from a large fighter sweep to the Japanese airfields located on Rabaul.

At 0600hrs that morning, Major Boyington and 11 other VMF-214 pilots launched to join up with a much larger all marine force. Unfortunately, he did not have tactical command of the mission. Instead, the CO of VMF-216, in his first sweep as a tactical commander, led the combined formation of 46 Corsairs.

The pilots of 214 were very critical of the way he directed them into Rabaul.

He led them in a wide circling sweep out over the St George Channel, losing precious altitude in the process. The enemy aircraft, numbering between 50–60 Zekes and Hamps from Lakunai airfield, had plenty of time to takeoff and climb well above the Marines.

With a substantial height advantage, they dove out of the sun, swarming the Americans with an aggression not previously seen. When last seen, Moore's aircraft was lagging behind the others.

The highly popular, ever capable young Texan simply vanished. No trace of the three Black Sheep pilots or of their aircraft were ever found.

It was a somber group of Moore's buddies who packed his prized trombone and sent it to his family in Amarillo.

On January 14, 1946, the USMC officially changed Moore's status from that of MIA to KIA.

William Senger
North Dakota B-29 Pilot

On Saturday, April 16, 1941, 25-year-old meat-packing salesman, William John "Buck" Senger from Williston, North Dakota, voluntarily enlisted in the RCAF. Several of his extended family members, who lived in Holland and France, were trapped in their homelands and were unable to flee from their Nazi occupiers. This did not sit well with Buck, so in an effort to strike at the heart of tyranny, he signed up at No. 5 Recruiting Centre at Regina, Saskatchewan, as an AC2 under Regimental Service No. R. 94962.

He told the recruiter, FO E. J. Christie, that his leisure interests centered around golf, hunting, and fishing. He also mentioned he had 26 hours of dual civilian flight instruction to his credit but had not flown solo.

Senger had tried to join the USAAC, but as he was rapidly closing in on his 26th birthday, the army considered him too old for pilot training.

Buck was born in Harvey, North Dakota, on May 13, 1915. His father, John R. Senger, came from Amsterdam, Holland, and his mother, Mary Gesroh, was born in France. Senger attended Harvey Grade School from 1921 to 1929, then Harvey High School until 1932.

For the next nine years, he worked as a meat cutter/salesman at three major meat-packing companies in Fargo, Minot, and Grand Forks, North Dakota. During this period, his father died of natural causes and his mother married a man named Kraus. She and her new husband then relocated to St. John, North Dakota.

Senger's basic training began on April 22 in a converted sports arena at No. 2 MD in Brandon, Manitoba. From May 28 until July 15, he was back in Regina at No. 2 ITS. Promoted to LAC, he moved over to No. 19 EFTS at Virden, Manitoba, where he flew de Havilland Tiger Moth biplanes until August 31.

Buck completed his pilot training to wings standard on twin-engined Avro Ansons and Cessna Cranes back in Brandon at No. 12 SFTS on November 22, 1941.

Graduating as an SP, he was granted the standard two-week pre-embarkation leave. He used this time to visit family and friends prior to heading overseas from "Y" Depot, at Halifax, Nova Scotia.

After a 13-day sea voyage, Buck arrived in England on December 26 and was posted to No. 3 Personnel Reception Centre situated at Bournemouth.

From January 19 until March 14, 1942, Senger reluctantly undertook an RAF navigation instructor's course. He had no interest in serving as an instructor, so he removed himself from the equation by intentionally failing the curriculum. Buck was not the first, nor would he be the last American, to balk and then change in mid-stream a career path chosen by his RCAF planners. He had come to Britain to fight for freedom and that is all he intended to do.

From March 26 until June 30, Senger flew Airspeed Oxford Mk IIs from RAF Little Rissington, Gloucestershire, with No. 6 Pilot Advanced Flying Unit.

Next, he continued his training at No. 12 OTU at RAF Chipping Warden, Northamptonshire, where he flew twin-engined Vickers Wellington Mk III medium bombers.

In August, while at this unit, Buck and his crew were nearly shot out of the sky by "friendly fire." Herein is the incident report:

> While on a routine operational training exercise at 1330 hours on August 12, 1942, Sergeant Senger sighted a convoy over the North Sea. He fired off the colours of the day and flashed the recognition letter of the day on the aircraft's Aldiss lamp. He then altered course away from the ships. A Royal Navy destroyer, shepherding the convoy, commenced firing. The Wellington was hit and holed in several places with one of the more serious strikes severing fuel lines inside the plane. The pilot ordered the port fuel tanks to be turned off so as to stop the gasoline from leaking into the fuselage. The port engine subsequently failed.

USAAF Captain William J. Senger DSO, DFC flew the Boeing B-29A Superfortress from North Field, Guam, in the Mariana Island chain. (US Department of Defense)

Sergeant Senger feathered the propellor on the left engine and proceeded to the first airfield he saw after crossing the coast. During the landing phase at RAF Bissett, the aircraft's landing gear collapsed on touchdown, killing the Bomb Aimer and injuring the aircraft's Wireless Operator.

RAF WC W. M. Morris, from Training Group No. 91, attached no blame in the encounter to either Sergeant Senger or to any of his crew. A joint RAF–Royal Navy investigation into the friendly fire incident was then launched.

Buck was posted on September 21 to No. 1657 Heavy Conversion Unit at RAF Stradishall, Suffolk, where he flew four-engined Short Stirling Mk I, III and IV heavy bombers. Graduating on December 19, Senger was assigned to fly Stirlings with RAF No. 7 Squadron at Oakington. No. 7 was known far and wide as the elite Pathfinder Force (PFF) of Bomber Command.

Senger was promoted to FS on January 1, 1943. Four days later, he received another promotion to WO2.

On February 15, he was commissioned from the ranks as a PO. Reflecting his change in status, his Regimental Service No. was changed from R. 94962 to J. 17203. Buck was awarded the coveted Pathfinder Badge on April 15 and was immediately advanced two ranks to that of FL.

On June 3, Senger was awarded a British DFC. The citation read as follows: "A most able operational captain of aircraft, Senger has many successful sorties to his credit. With cool courage he has taken part in attacks against targets in Germany and Italy, resolutely pressing home his attacks despite the heaviest opposition. At all times showing a fine fighting spirit, this airman has, by his untiring efforts and conscientious attention to detail, raised the efficiency of his crew to a very high level."

On October 19, 1943, Buck was awarded the DSO. The DSO is the second highest British award for gallantry and valor. The citation read as follows: "This officer has completed a very large number of sorties involving attacks on a wide variety of enemy targets. He has displayed skill of a high order while his unfailing determination to inflict loss on the enemy has been a noteworthy feature of his work. FL Senger is a model of efficiency and his gallant example has proven to be a great source of encouragement."

After completing 46 combat sorties flying Short Stirlings and Avro Lancasters with No. 7 Squadron, Buck Senger decided to seek his release from the RCAF so that he could join the USAAF. His honorable discharge from the RCAF was signed on October 7, 1943, in London. Days later, he was accepted into the USAAF as a captain under Service No. O-886125. In November, he rotated stateside where he served as a flight instructor at Selman Army Airfield at Monroe, Louisiana, then later at Lockbourne Army Airfield at Lockbourne, Ohio.

The 39th BG, Very Heavy was activated at Smoky Hill Army Airfield at Salina, Kansas, on April 12, 1944. The group, consisting of three bomb squadrons – the 60th, 61st and 62nd – trained for months on the new long-range Boeing B-29A Superfortress bomber.

The B-29 was the world's first fully pressurized strategic bomber. Initially, it operated at altitudes that put it beyond the reach of intercepting Japanese fighters. It was massive in size. Its wingspan was 141ft 3in, the fuselage was 99ft long and it stood 27ft 9in high. With a 20,000lb payload, it could fly along at 357mph at 36,000ft.

A total of 3,960 were constructed by the following aircraft manufacturers: Boeing Airplane Company at Seattle and Renton, Washington, and at Wichita, Kansas; Glenn L. Martin Company at Omaha, Nebraska; and Bell Aircraft Company at Marietta, Georgia. No other aircraft ever combined as many technological advances in one design as did the B-29.

It was the Superfortress that ended the war in the Pacific after the type dropped two atomic bombs on the Japanese mainland in August 1945.

The first attack was a 20-kiloton weapon named "Little Boy," which flattened Hiroshima on August 6, causing 75,000 casualties. The United States then warned Japan that a second strike was imminent and that they should consider unconditional surrender. Unfortunately, the Japanese military high command refused to believe that the Americans had more than one of these weapons.

When no response was forthcoming, the US was compelled, on August 9, to drop a second 20-kiloton bomb. The target this time was the city of Nagasaki, the bomb was named "Fat Man" and 35,000 people unnecessarily died. By using these weapons, the Allies wished to avoid a direct invasion of the Japanese Home Islands at all costs. The country had been husbanding its military resources for a final all-out battle. Some planners estimated this would have caused more than one million Allied casualties. Japan surrendered five days later on August 14.

On January 5, 1945, Buck shipped out as part of the 39th to the PTO. The group, belonging to the 20th Air Force, arrived at North Field, Guam, and began flying combat operations on its B-29s against the Japanese mainland on February 18. Guam is part of the Mariana Island chain and is located 3,700 miles southwest of Honolulu, Hawaii.

Buck and his 11-man crew, known as "Crew 21," flew Superfortress 44-69773 *Two Passes and Crap*. The crew's first bombing missions were fairly routine and uneventful.

Mission No. 18 on May 15, 1945, was to the Mitsubishi engine plant at Nagoya, Japan. Over the target area, *Two Passes and Crap* took a direct flak hit in the number one engine. With the engine disabled, Buck feathered the propellor and set course for Guam on three good motors.

For a while, everything was fine until the flight engineer had to transfer fuel to engine number two, which was consuming more gas than normal. It was not long before the fuel transfer pump burned out and shortly thereafter that motor ran out of gas. Senger knew that a B-29 with two engines out on the same side could not stay in the air so he ordered the crew to fire off all the ammunition and toss anything overboard that would lighten the aircraft's weight. He opened the bomb bay doors to jettison the heavy long-range fuel tanks, but was unable to close them as there was insufficient power available. The plane, with most of its systems failing, was rapidly losing altitude. This was due to the excessive drag created by the open bomb bay doors and two dead engines.

Sixty-five miles north of Guam, Captain Senger ordered the crew to prepare for ditching. The radio operator began broadcasting Mayday distress calls alternately on emergency frequencies 7415 and 4475.

Visibility on the ocean's surface was clear with the wind velocity running at 20mph. The height of the waves ranged from 10–12ft. Flying into the wind at 100mph, the crippled aircraft struck the water with a loud impact, landing across the tops of the waves. Abrupt contact with the water at 1800hrs separated the nose section and the tail section from the main fuselage.

The eleven crew members and one passenger were seen to exit 44-69773 from various emergency escape hatches. Some of the crew was in one man seat-pack life rafts, while the others successfully managed to inflate two eight-man life rafts stored aboard the plane. By the time they lashed all the rafts together, 1st Lieutenant Howard Kolbert and S/Sgt Marvin Stanton, who were seen leaving the aircraft, were missing.

The remaining survivors spent a cold, wet evening bobbing up and down in the 15–20ft swells. By morning, the beat-up crew was so seasick they could hardly move. One member had sustained serious injuries and was in need of immediate medical attention.

That afternoon, and to the crew's great relief, a Consolidated PBY Catalina air-sea rescue aircraft found them. The plane circled overhead until a USN 1,430-ton Evarts Class destroyer hove into view. As the airmen were taken on board USS *Doherty* (DE-14), the destroyer's crew cheered wildly. *Doherty* had served on rescue duty during the Aleutian Campaign 1942–43 and Senger's crew were the first airmen they had picked up alive – hence their excitement. The rescuees were treated like royalty and were given the best the warship had to offer.

Meanwhile, the center fuselage section of *Two Passes and Crap* was still afloat. The ship's captain decided it should be sunk as it posed a navigational hazard to maritime safety.

Doherty moved to within 200 yards of the B-29 wreckage and commenced firing with its 3in main armament, together with its secondary weaponry of nine 20mm

Oerlikons and a quad-mounted 28mm cannon known as the "Chicago Piano." Enduring multiple hits, 44-69773 slowly slipped beneath the waves.

After flying a total of 64 combat missions with two air forces in World War II, and after having survived two airplane crashes, it was time for Buck Senger to go home. He had done more than his fair share of fighting.

On June 2, 1949, Senger wrote and asked the Department of Veterans Affairs in Ottawa, Ontario, to forward his military awards and medals to 15521 Ashland Way in Sacramento, California. These included the 1939–45 Star, Defence Medal, Pilot's Flying Badge, General Service Medal, Operational Wings, Canadian Volunteer Service Medal & Clasp, Aircrew European Star, and his previously mentioned DSO and DFC.

After the war, Buck continued to fly and operated his own crop-dusting business. He was tragically killed in a plane crash on June 21, 1954, while spraying crops at Yolo, California.

John Stickell
Illinois Bomber Pilot

John Harlan Stickell was a strapping American farm boy who piloted multi-engined heavy bombers in the ETO and the PTO in World War II. Flying Short Stirlings over Germany as a member of the RCAF, he earned three British gallantry awards – the DSO, the DFC and a MiD.

Transferring to the USNR, Stickell flew Consolidated PB4Y-1 Liberators in the central and western Pacific. There he won an Air Medal, an American DFC and, after his death from combat wounds in December 1943, a posthumous Navy Cross.

Months later, this highly regarded but little-known naval aviator, was duly honored by his country when, in a move usually reserved for presidents, admirals, senators and the like, the USN named a warship after this decorated airman from Gilson, Illinois. On October 31, 1945, 3,460-ton Gearing Class destroyer DD-888 was proudly commissioned into US Naval Service as USS *Stickell*. Gearings were the largest American destroyers constructed during World War II.

John was born to Harley Charles Stickell and Daisy Grace Lawrence on July 31, 1914, in Orange Township, Knox County, Illinois. There were four older children in his family – a brother, Lawrence, and three sisters, Madeline, Susan, and Helen. John attended Clark Chapel Grade School from 1918 to 1926, then Haw Creek Township High School from 1926 to 1930. For two years, 1931 and 1932, he studied mechanical engineering at the Bradley Technical School in Peoria. Stickell returned to Bradley as a part-time student in 1934 and again in 1937 to take diesel engine mechanic and welding courses.

He worked for the Caterpillar Tractor Company for several years, then part time as a mechanic and salesman at Strode's Ford dealership in Maquon. When not at the garage, he could be found helping his father on the farm. John's hobby was souping up racecars and motorcycles.

On January 29, 1941, the athletically built, 6ft 1in tall, 174lb Stickell traveled to No. 8 Recruiting Centre in Windsor, Ontario, where he enlisted in the RCAF.

He was interviewed by FL G. M. Marshall, who recorded the following in his interview report: "Serious, courteous and pleasant. Good intellect and is mechanically inclined. Has thought it over and is keen to enter the RCAF."

John Stickell: Illinois Bomber Pilot

Assigned Regimental Service No. R. 83279, AC2 Stickell spent his first few weeks alternating back and forth between two MDs at Toronto and Picton, Ontario. This was followed by a stint of guard duty at No. 1 Bombing & Gunnery School at Jarvis, Ontario.

Returning to Toronto on May 17, Stickell reported to No. 1 ITS where he was assigned to Course No. 26, which concluded on June 20. With 169 students in the class, John finished in the top half, earning an 85 percent grade average. The school's WC noted the following: "A solid aggressive type of trainee who applied himself well at this school. May be a bit slow, but is thorough and methodical and should be quite cool in tight spots."

Promoted to LAC, Stickell was posted on June 21 to No. 1 EFTS at Malton, Ontario. There, on Course No. 31, he flew 54.05 hours on de Havilland Tiger Moth biplanes, graduating on August 8. From the chief supervisory officer came the following comments: "Attitude good. Intelligent and can make use of his abilities. Industrious. Should make a good leader. Dress and discipline excellent. Tries hard and gets what he goes after."

Stickell was assigned to No. 5 SFTS at Brantford, Ontario, on August 8, 1941. Because the RCAF's food was both plentiful and good, John's weight rose to 188lb. The air force had decided he would be better off flying bombers than fighters.

Assigned to Course No. 35, John logged 108.35 hours on twin-engined Avro Ansons. Placing in the top third of his graduating class, Stickell was one of several at the wings parade on October 17 who were commissioned directly from the ranks as POs.

From John's squadron commander came the following comments: "General flying, high average. Instrument flying, average. Reliable pilot who should fit in well at an operational unit." And from the CFI: "Ability-average, conduct-good. A reliable type of lad who possesses initiative, perseverance and a good sense of responsibility. He is neat and tidy and well liked by class-mates. Good officer material. Recommended for a commission." Brantford's station commander, a GC, concurred.

While at No. 5, Stickell asked the RCAF to notify US Draft Board No. 2 in Galesburg, Illinois, as to his whereabouts. The air force complied and mailed to them his Canadian service particulars.

PO Stickell's service number was changed from R. 83279 to J. 8429. As an officer, he was given a significant pay increase rising from the lowly airmen's daily rate of CAN$1.50 to a heady sum of $6.25.

John Stickell left Halifax, Nova Scotia, on a troop ship bound for England on November 12, 1941. Arriving on the 22nd, he was sent to No. 3 Personnel Reception Centre located in Bournemouth.

For a while, at least, before heading off to prosecute the war, they lived in the lap of luxury in the town's finest hotels such as the Highcliffe, the Bath, the Regent, the White Hermitage and the Empress.

Stickell was sent, on December 6, to No. 1 SFTS at the RAF College at Cranwell where he remained until January 4, 1942.

The next day, he was posted to No. 1515 Beam Approach Training Flight Course No. 9, which concluded on the 12th. Stickell flew 11.55 hours over the shortened seven-day course and received a passing grade.

Assigned to No. 22 OTU at Wellesbourne Mountford on the 20th, John flew twin-engine Vickers Wellingtons until May 26.

The next day he reported to RAF No. 214 Squadron, which was stationed at Stradishall in Suffolk. While flying a four-engined Shorts Stirling Mk I bomber on July 12, 1942, Stickell damaged an aircraft at 0346hrs after a wheels-up landing in foggy conditions. The July 21 findings of the accident investigator are as follows:

> On the night of 11/12th July 1942, Stirling aircraft N3767 returned from operational flight in conditions of poor visibility. The captain was given permission to land and carried out a normal circuit, when he reached the funnel lights he could not see the flare-path. He continued his approach losing height and when he was very low saw the first flare straight ahead of him. He started to climb at once but the starboard wheel struck an object on the ground which broke the undercarriage lock. The captain continued to circle trying to get the undercarriage to lock but with no result. When he was given permission to land, it was decided to unlock the port undercarriage to make an even belly landing. This was done and a good belly landing carried out. None of the crew were injured. Duration of flight was six hours and ten minutes. It is considered that the accident was due to an error of judgement on the part of the pilot who undershot in conditions of bad visibility and hit a concrete mixer which was on the new extension of the runway. This obstruction was well back from the flare path in use. I attribute this accident to the captain's inexperience in flying heavy aircraft at night in conditions of bad visibility and I, therefore, recommend that disciplinary action should not be taken against him.

John flew with No. 214 until August 25, 1942, when he was transferred to RAF No. 7 Squadron based at Oakington, Cambridgeshire. He was promoted to FO on September 29, 1942. Within a couple days came another promotion to FL on October 1.

After having served two years and 67 days, FL John Harlan Stickell DSO, DFC, MiD formally requested that he be released from Canada's air force in order to facilitate his joining the American forces.

He was honorably discharged and retired by the RCAF in London on March 29, 1943. In a confidential report dated April 9, GC O. R. Donaldson of No. 7 Squadron noted that at the time of the transfer John Stickell had 790 flight hours recorded in his logbook. Donaldson's written opinion of FL Stickell was as follows: "A very steady and conscientious officer who sets a high standard both in conduct and general operational efficiency."

John Stickell: Illinois Bomber Pilot

The Stirling bombers Stickell flew with RAF No. 214 and 7 squadrons were built in two factories in Rochester, England, and Belfast, Northern Ireland. Designed by the Short Brothers Aircraft Company, Stirlings were the first four-engined monoplane bombers to enter RAF service and the first to be used operationally in World War II. As the war progressed, they were soon replaced by the Handley Page Halifax and the Avro Lancaster. Stirlings had a major design flaw in that they could barely reach their operational altitude of 16,500ft when fully loaded due to a poorly designed wing. Additionally, they could not be modified to carry the newer larger bombs, in excess of 4,000lb, which were being developed. From 1943 on, Stirlings were used as conversion trainers, transports, and glider tugs. In total, 2,383 were constructed – 712 Mk Is, 1,061 Mk IIIs, 450 Mk IVs and 160 Mk Vs. Postwar RAF figures reveal Short Stirlings flew 18,440 combat sorties. Total losses from all causes amounted to 791 aircraft.

The Canadian Minister of National Defence for Air wrote the following letter to John's parents on April 2, 1943: "I am writing to say how much all ranks of the RCAF join with me in warmly congratulating you and the members of your family on the honour and distinction which have come to your son Pilot Officer

USN Lieutenant John H. Stickell DSO, DFC, MiD, Navy Cross, in the foreground, fills out his enlistment papers at the Windsor, Ontario, RCAF Recruiting Office on January 29, 1941. (Canadian National Defence Image Library)

John Harlan Stickell DFC, through the award of the Distinguished Flying Cross for great gallantry in performance of his duty while serving with No. 7 Squadron of the RAF."

The citation on which this award was made reads as follows.

> Pilot Officer Stickell has taken part in attacks on Essen, Hamburg, Bremen and other heavily defended targets. Throughout, his captaincy and determination have been of the highest order. His personal example has been an inspiration to all. Pilot Officer Stickell has done twenty-five major operational sorties, twenty-three of which have been as captain on Stirling aircraft. Pilot Officer Stickell has recently joined the Pathfinder Force and has carried out seven attacks as a marker and the fact that he has on many occasions brought back photographs of the target has enabled him to qualify as a marker.

To this, Air Commodore Donald C. Bennett added: "This officer was the first member of Bomber Command to be awarded the PFF Badge on the conclusive evidence of his results and after an exacting test. His determination in attack and his skill are proved by the results he obtains. I recommend him most strongly for the non-immediate award of the Distinguished Flying Cross. The personnel of the air force are proud of your son's fine service record."

The motto of the PFF was "We Guide To Strike." In July 1942, RAF Bomber Command's Air Chief Marshal Sir Arthur Harris had tasked Australian Don Bennett with the job of setting up an elite Pathfinder Force. Formed one month later in August as part of 8 Group, the three-week training program under Bennett's tutelage began at RAF Warboys. Graduates wore the coveted PFF badge beneath their decorations, which in turn was worn under their pilot wings.

Each graduate was immediately advanced one rank commensurate with an increase in pay. PFF crews were required to fly 45 sorties as opposed to the standard 30. The Pathfinder's job was to lead the bomber stream to the target and mark it with colored flares for the main force to bomb. PO Stickell was awarded his PFF badge on September 11, 1942. Donald Bennett would go on to become, at the age of 33, the youngest air vice-marshal in the history of the RAF.

FL Stickell personally received his DFC award from King George VI at Buckingham Palace on February 15, 1943.

A further letter from the minister's office in Ottawa dated July 7, 1943, arrived at the Stickell residence in Gilson: "It is with a feeling of great pride that I once again extend to you and your family the heartiest congratulations on the additional honour and distinction which your son, Flight Lieutenant John Harlan Stickell DSO, DFC, has earned by the receipt of the award of the Distinguished Service Order, while serving with No. 7 Squadron of the Royal Air Force prior to his having been transferred to the United States forces."

The citation accompanying this award read as follows:

> During a most successful tour of operational duty in heavy bomber aircraft, this officer has proved himself to be a most valuable member of his squadron. He is an outstanding operational captain and has invariably made the utmost efforts to complete his duties, regardless of opposition and other difficulties. His courage, determination and devotion to duty have been most outstanding over a long period. Since the award of the Distinguished Flying Cross, Flight Lieutenant Stickell has completed numerous sorties all of them against heavily defended targets in enemy territory. Again may I say the personnel of the air force are indeed proud of your son's splendid service record.

Returning stateside, John was sent to NAS Corpus Christi, Texas, where he familiarized himself with naval aircraft and procedures until August 5.

On August 19, 1943, Lt Stickell joined bombing Squadron One Hundred and Eight (VB-108) while the squadron worked up to operational readiness at Naval Auxiliary Air Station Camp Kearney, California.

Established seven weeks earlier on July 1, at NAS San Diego, VB-108 was equipped with 15 PB4Y-1s. There, its 57 officers and 148 enlisted personnel were organized into 18 flight crews. Training hard to perfect low-level skip-bombing and strafing techniques, the squadron's aircraft left the mainland on October 2 and arrived safely at NAS Kaneohe Bay, Hawaii, the following day. Training continued in Hawaii and routine patrols began immediately. It was there the aircrew adopted the squadron name "Hawaiian Warriors."

On October 23, nine of the squadron's aircraft were flown to Canton Island in the Phoenix Island chain where it began its first tour with Fleet Air Wing 2.

On November 11, VB-108 moved from Canton Island to Motulalo airfield on Nukufetau in the Ellice Islands. The squadron's primary mission was the reconnaissance of enemy-held territories with the authorization to attack any targets of opportunity.

The Liberators VB-108 flew were modified Army-built glass-nosed B-24Ds. VB-108's aircraft were the first B-24s retrofitted at Litchfield Park, Arizona, with the new Erco 250 SH-1 powered nose-turret housing twin Colt-Browning .50 caliber machine guns. The navy eventually acquired 977 Liberators, which operated in both the Atlantic and Pacific theatrers.

VB-108's preferred method of attack was to approach the target at no more than 25ft above the wave-tops, then "pop-up" to 150ft for the precise dropping of bombs, all the while blasting their unfortunate victims with hundreds of rounds of heavy caliber machine gun fire.

In a surprise attack on December 6, 1943, VB-108 strafed and bombed Jaluit Atoll in the Marshall Islands where it sank a landing barge full of Japanese sailors, two cargo ships and severely damaged two other surface vessels. Jaluit, located 908 miles one way from the squadron's airfield, was a major enemy facility. The atoll's primary feature was a deep protected lagoon that could accommodate ships up to the size of an aircraft carrier. Jaluit's land mass was too narrow to build conventional runways for use by land-based aircraft, however, the IJN did operate a seaplane base, flying Kawanishi H6K5 "Mavis" flying boats belonging to the 24th Air Flotilla.

Jaluit was a well defended piece of real estate that fielded more than 60 antiaircraft guns of various caliber: 13.2mm, 20mm, 25mm and 75mm. Additionally, a dozen 6in naval coastal guns guarded the approaches to the lagoon and all this firepower was backed up by some 2,500 troops who were stationed there.

On Sunday December 12, Lt Stickell volunteered to lead a hazardous two-plane bombing strike against the underground oil storage tanks on Jaluit. Thundering in at tree-top level, the two PB4Y-1 crews were hoping to catch the Japanese gunners napping just as they had on a previous raid six days earlier. But not this time. No, this time the enemy was alert and ready and it seemed that the whole atoll erupted in deadly gunfire as the pair came into view. Every weapon that could be brought to bear was and they threw up a tremendous wall of flak trying to knock the American bombers out of the sky. Just as he was about to release his bomb load, Stickell's aircraft was raked by 13.2mm machine gun fire. One of those large .52 caliber rounds struck John in the torso gravely wounding him. In great pain and bleeding profusely, Stickell continued on the bomb run scoring a direct hit on the target. Lt Stickell safely flew his aircraft out of harm's way and relinquished the controls to his copilot. Only then did he allow the members of his crew to give him a shot of morphine and dress his wound.

Stickell's crew, realizing that he would never survive the long flight back to Motulalo, decided to head to Tarawa for medical help, which was 383 miles away. Approaching Tarawa, Stickell regained consciousness long enough to direct them to bypass the island as he did not want them endangering their lives by trying to land a damaged bomber on a short fighter strip. Heeding their skipper's request, they flew on to a joint Navy/7th Air Force bomber airfield at Nanumea, which was two 297 miles southwest of Tarawa.

By the time they landed, J. H. Stickell had lost a large volume of blood and was barely alive. The 29-year-old heroic Navy lieutenant lingered at death's door for seven days, finally succumbing to his wound on Sunday, December 19, 1943.

Jaluit was heavily bombed and shelled by the Americans in 1943 and 1944 with the result that it was effectively isolated from ever being re-supplied. Existing on a diet of vegetables and fish, 67 percent of the original Japanese garrison managed to survive until they surrendered to USS *McConnell* (DE-163) on September 5, 1945. The atoll had not seen a re-supply ship or a submarine in more than a year.

Susan Stickell, one of John's sisters, represented the family at the launching of DD-888 on June 16, 1945.

Lt John Harlan Stickell was accorded one additional honor by the US government. A 6,800ft long x 400ft wide bomber and fighter strip built on Eniwetok Atoll in the Marshall Islands in February 1944 was dedicated as Stickell Field. Principally developed as a Navy/Marine base, this facility housed, at one point, more than 300 combat aircraft.

Remnants of this unused forgotten airfield still exist today.

Specifications for the Gearing Class destroyer USS *Stickell* DD-888

Full Displacement:	3,460 tons
Dimensions:	Length 390ft 6in; Width 40ft 10in; Draught 14ft 4in
Crew:	336
Engines:	General Electric Twin-Screw Geared Turbines Generating 60,000shp
Max Speed:	36.8 knots
Max Range:	4,500 nautical miles
Armament:	6 5in guns; 12 40mm Bofor cannon; 11 20mm Oerlikon cannon; and 10 21in torpedo tubes
Builder:	Consolidated Steel, Orange, Texas
Ship Launched:	June 16, 1945
Ship Commissioned:	October 31, 1945

Decommissioned and struck from navy records: July 1, 1972.

Bibliography

Institutions/Places
The 39th Bomb Group
410 Squadron Historian
Air Historical Branch
Air Historical Section
Association of the 4th FG
The Commissioner's Office, Leonardtown, Maryland
Headquarters and History Office of the Air Force Flight Test Center
Library and Archives Canada
Mayor's Office, Ansonia, Connecticut
Mike Williams Archive
The Nanton Lancaster Society
Wade Meyers Studios
Washington Parish, Louisiana

Book Publications
Asher, Gerald, *Jets! The 412th Fighter Group and Project Comet*, Fox 3 Studios
Bishop, Arthur, *True Canadian Heroes in the Air*, Prospero Books (2004)
Caine, Philip D., *Eagles of the RAF: The World War II Eagle Squadrons*, University Press of the Pacific (2002)
Caldwell, Donald, *The JG 26 War Diary*, Grub Street (1996)
Clark, David, *Angels Eight: Normandy Air War Diary*, 1st Book Library (2003)
Dunmore, Spencer, *Wings for Victory: The Remarkable Story of the British Commonwealth Air Training Plan in Canada*, McClelland and Stewart Inc. (1995)
Freeman, Roger A., *The Mighty Eighth: A History of the US 8th Army Air Force*, The Book Service Limited (1970)
Fry, Garry L. and Jeffrey L. Ethell, *Escort to Berlin: The 4th Fighter Group in World War II*, Arco Publishing (1980)
Fydenchuk, W. Peter, *Immigrants of War*, WPF Publications (2005)
Gamble, Bruce, *The Black Sheep: The Definitive Account of Marine Fighting Squadron 214 in World War II*, Presidio Press (1998)
Godfrey, John T., *The Look of Eagles*, Ballantine Books Publishing Company (1973)

Bibliography

Hall, Jr., Grover C., *1000 Destroyed: The Life & Times of the 4th Fighter Group*, Putnam (1962)

Halliday, Hugh A., Tempest Tiger: SL David C. Fairbanks, DFC and 2 bars

Hammel, Eric M., *Aces at War: The American Aces Speak, Vol. 4*, Pacifica Press (1997)

Hatch, F. J., *Aerodrome of Democracy: Canada and the British Commonwealth Air Training Plan 1939-1945*, Department of National Defence (1983)

Hatch, FL F. J., *The History of No. 409 Squadron*

Heathcote, SL A. P., *Intruder: A History of No. 418 Squadron*, Air Historical Branch, RCAF (1977)

Hill, David Lee "Tex" and Reagan Schaupp, *Tex Hill: Flying Tiger*, Honoribus Press (2003)

Hitchins, WC F. H., *The War History of No. 414 RCAF Squadron*

Milberry, Larry, *Canada's Air Force: At War and Peace, Volume 2*, Canav Books (2000)

Nesbit, Roy Conyers, *The Armed Rovers: Beauforts and Beaufighters Over the Mediterranean*, Airlife Publishing (1995)

Olynyk, Frank, *Stars and Bars: A Tribute to the American Fighter Ace 1920-1973*, Grub Street (1995)

Ralph, Wayne, *Aces, Warriors & Wingmen: The Firsthand Accounts of Canada's Fighter Pilots in the Second World War*, John Wiley & Sons (2005)

RCAF 402 Squadron operational diaries

Reed, Robert T., *Lost Black Sheep: The Search for WWII Ace Chris Magee*, Hellgate Press (2001)

Shores, Christopher and Clive Williams, *Aces High*, Grub Street (1994)

Thomas, Andrew, *American Spitfire Aces of World War 2*, Osprey Publishing (2007)

Walton, Frank E., *Once They Were Eagles: The Men of the Black Sheep Squadron*, The University Press of Kentucky (1996)

White, Troy, *Kidd Hofer: The Last of the Screwball Aces*, Stardust Studios (2003)

Newspapers, Magazines, Websites

"Beaufighter," *FlyPast* Special, Key Publishing Ltd

The Canadian Press

The *Daily News*, Washington Parish, Louisiana

The *Eagle Eye*, Feb 2015 issue

Flight Journal magazine, article on Oscar Boesch written by James Busha

New York Times article by Michael Winerip

"No. 410 Cougar Squadron," *The Air Historian*

Oklahoman Newspaper, article by M. Hutchinson, Jay Marks

Star-Tribune newspaper – articles by Herman E. Melton (May 2002) and Amanda Winstead (Sept 2008) on Clyde East

The *Sunday Times* newspaper, UK

People

Carol and Neil Addicott
Malcolm Bates
Biel and Fibuch families
Dave Boyd
Chris Clarke
James Osbourn Gray Collins
Jack Cook
Chip Corley
Benoit Cottereau
Mark Cullen
Ann Dodds
Mike Furline
Karl-Georg Genth
Thomas Genth
Hugh Godefroy
Hugh A. Halliday
Ivan M. L. Henson
Adam Kline
Sy Koenig
A. H. Lankester
Liz Loynes
Rob Mears
W. Barry Needham
Colonel Perry Nuhn, Retired
W. M. Palmer
Colonel Steve "The Greek" Pisano, Retired
Gerri Montgomery Prescott
Harold Rideout
Dennis Russell
R. I. A. Smith
Maria Tuchscherer
Ann L. Waldrop-Trick
David Westheimer
Steve Wilke